versity of Ulster

International Management

Managing the Global Corporation

Dedication

To my mother,
Manju Som

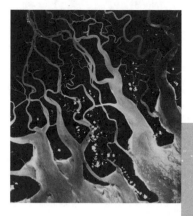

International Management

Managing the Global Corporation

Ashok Som

McGraw-Hill
Higher Education

London Boston Burr Ridge, IL Dubuque, IA Madison, WI New York San Francisco
St. Louis Bangkok Bogotá Caracas Kuala Lumpur Lisbon Madrid Mexico City
Milan Montreal New Delhi Santiago Seoul Singapore Sydney Taipei Toronto

International Management: Managing the Global Corporation
Ashok Som
ISBN-13 978-0-07-711737-5
ISBN-10 0-07-711737-9

**McGraw-Hill
Higher Education**

Published by McGraw-Hill Education
Shoppenhangers Road
Maidenhead
Berkshire
SL6 2QL
Telephone: 44 (0) 1628 502 500
Fax: 44 (0) 1628 770 224
Website: www.mcgraw-hill.co.uk

British Library Cataloguing in Publication Data
A catalogue record for this book is available from the British Library

Library of Congress Cataloguing in Publication Data
The Library of Congress data for this book has been applied for from the Library of Congress

Senior Commissioning Editor: Rachel Gear
Development Editor: Hannah Cooper/Karen Harlow
Senior Marketing Manager: Alice Duijser
Production Editor: Alison Holt

Text design by Hardlines
Cover design by Ego-Creative
Printed and bound in the UK by Bell and Bain Ltd, Glasgow

The McGraw-Hill Companies

Mixed Sources
Product group from well-managed
forests and other controlled sources
www.fsc.org Cert no. TT-COC-002769
© 1996 Forest Stewardship Council
FSC

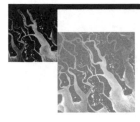

Table of Contents

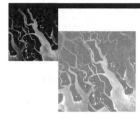

Preface

> ❝ The old order changeth
> Yielding place to new
> And God fulfils Himself in many ways
> Lest one good custom should corrupt the world
> *– Alfred Lord Tennyson, from* Morte d'Arthur *(Passing away of Arthur)* ❞

The world of the modern corporation is being transformed; the old order has started to change. The world is becoming 'borderless', as corporations compete to be more and more global. Globalization has become the name of the game. Consolidation through mergers and acquisitions is happening in most industries.

A study of the strategy of global firms encompasses any problem or opportunity in the international business arena. This textbook draws from both the external and the internal environment, the macro and micro economies of the firm. The uniqueness of this book is its **European** ethos. The advantage of this book is that it discusses and interlinks international management theory with European cases spanning the sectors of banking, building construction, heavy engineering, glass, pharmaceuticals, mobile telecommunications, media, retail and luxury brands. Most of the cases are of companies that are *in the top three in their sectors in the world*. To my knowledge, no other textbook highlights, as I do, the European multinationals.

Some of the simplest international strategy questions that can be discussed within the scope of this book are those listed below.

1 What is the emerging international corporate scenario? What are the worldwide developments? What are the trends concerning globalization? What are the expansion options for global companies?

2 How does one define global companies? What international strategies do they follow? How do the global companies manage themselves? How do they formulate their strategies? What strategic capabilities do they need to succeed?

3 What do 'organizational structures' mean for international companies? What are the advantages and disadvantages of using those structures in today's hyper-competitive international arena?

4 How does one conduct business in different geographic locations? How do companies deal with cross-cultural differences in the countries in which they are operating?

5 What are the rationales of consolidation? How are mega-mergers being managed?

6 How does one 'manage change' in this globalization regime? What is the role of corporate restructuring/re-engineering/redesigning in today's ever changing global landscape?

7 What are the strategies to manage emerging markets? What are the new imperatives?

8 What is the role of ethics and corporate social responsibility in international business?

9 How do we prepare for the future?

The approach taken to deal with these questions is to discuss them from a managerial point of view. The chapters herein discuss the extant theories, while the case studies try to probe the contextual familiarity, analytical abilities and debating skills. From a managerial perspective, this is a *unique* value proposition as it deals with immediate issues concerning global organizations in a multi-dimensional context, while focusing on examples of European multinationals that are world leaders in their respective industries. The methodology that is used in this book attempts to maximize the immediate learning experience.

> The important thing is not to stop questioning.
> Curiosity has its own reason for existing.
> One cannot help but be in awe when he contemplates
> the mysteries of eternity, of life, of the marvelous structure of reality.
> It is enough if one tries merely to comprehend a little of this mystery every day.
> Never lose a holy curiosity.
>
> – *Albert Einstein*

The book is divided into four parts (as represented graphically in Figure 1). The first three consist of two chapters each, while the fourth consists of three chapters.

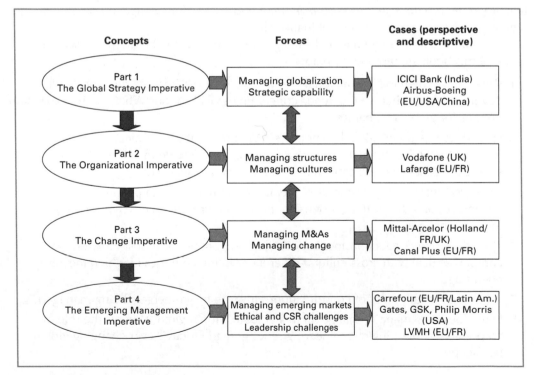

Figure 1 An outline of the book's structure

Part 1 examines the growth, profitability and globalization imperative of global companies, and examines their development of strategies. Chapter 1 focuses on the motivation that drives companies across boundaries, and raises issues on their growth imperatives. This chapter tries to understand globalization and international growth as a process, and how companies are deliberating on using their scarce resources to explore expansion options. For this reason the chapter examines the political, environmental, social and technological forces that shape growth opportunities for global companies. It also raises issues of country analysis and foreign direct investment. Chapter 2 identifies the strategic capabilities necessary to become a global company, and briefly dwells on definitional issues of MNCs. Within this framework it tries to understand the evolution of MNCs, their strengths and weaknesses, their biases, their tensions and how they can develop multi-level competencies and interrelated capabilities. It tries to link how national corporations have evolved and how they have gained competitive advantage. It pays special attention to the role of the state and the creation of national champions in this process.

Part 2 draws on the preceding discussion in Part 1 to further develop how global companies organize themselves. Chapter 3 revisits the evolution and development of different organizational structures, their strengths and weaknesses and how global companies are managing their organizational structures in tandem with their growth objectives. Chapter 4 discusses the challenges of managing across cultures. As global companies become bigger and bigger, managing effectively different subsidiaries becomes a challenge. It is more so due to the strong national heritages of companies that, though they have become global in their operations today, might still operate from a nationalistic mindset.

Part 3 draws on the change process that most global organizations face today in their complex and dynamic environment. Chapter 5 discusses the role of mergers and acquisitions, strategic alliances, and their pros and cons in the expansion process of the global company. The chapter explores the logic of M&As and touches upon the challenges of the post-merger integration process. Chapter 6 focuses on the organizational restructuring of global companies that is necessitated by any major external or environmental adjustments. The chapter discusses concepts to manage the renewal and change processes effectively, and how global companies might want to re-examine and integrate their change process with the overall design of the organization.

Part 4 focuses on the emerging management imperatives of operating and managing a successful global company. Chapter 7 focuses on emerging markets and the strategies adopted by successful and not so successful global companies. It discusses first entrants vs late movers in emerging markets, and draws upon the specificities of emerging markets and the resultant strategies that might be favourable under these circumstances. The role of ethics and corporate social responsibility in global business is discussed in Chapter 8. This chapter focuses on corporate social responsibility, dealing with issues such as corporate philanthropy, piracy, counterfeiting, governance and the social obligations of global companies. Finally, Chapter 9 discusses future leadership challenges and focuses on the roles, responsibilities and people skills that are required to catapult global companies to their next objective. Rather than be predictive at this stage, this concluding chapter acts as a point of departure for proactive discussions on the tortuous future evolution of the global company.

Custom Publishing Solutions

Let us help make our **content** your **solution**

At McGraw-Hill Education our aim is to help lecturers to find the most suitable content for their needs delivered to their students in the most appropriate way. Our **custom publishing solutions** offer the ideal combination of content delivered in the way that best suits lecturer and students.

Our custom publishing programme offers lecturers the opportunity to select just the chapters or sections of material they wish to deliver to their students from a database called Primis at www.primisonline.com

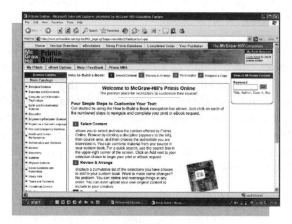

Primis contains over two million pages of content from:

- textbooks
- professional books
- case books – Harvard Articles, Insead, Ivey, Darden, Thunderbird and BusinessWeek
- Taking Sides – debate materials.

Across the following imprints:

- McGraw-Hill Education
- Open University Press
- Harvard Business School Press
- US and European material.

There is also the option to include additional material authored by lecturers in the custom product – this does not necessarily have to be in English.

We will take care of everything from start to finish in the process of developing and delivering a custom product to ensure that lecturers and students receive exactly the material needed in the most suitable way.

With a custom publishing solution, students enjoy the best selection of material deemed to be the most suitable for learning everything they need for their courses – something of real value to support their learning. Teachers are able to use exactly the material they want, in the way they want, to support their teaching on the course.

Please contact your local McGraw-Hill representative with any questions, or alternatively contact Warren Eels **e**: warren_eels@mcgraw-hill.com.

Make the grade!

30% off any Study Skills book!

Our Study Skills books are packed with practical advice and tips that are easy to put into practice and will really improve the way you study. Topics include:

- techniques to help you pass exams
- advice to improve your essay writing
- help in putting together the perfect seminar presentation
- tips on how to balance studying and your personal life.

www.openup.co.uk/studyskills

Visit our website to read helpful hints about essays, exams, dissertations and much more.

Special offer! As a valued customer, buy online and receive 30% off any of our Study Skills books by entering the promo code **getahead**

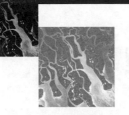

Acknowledgements

I revived the course called *Managing the Global Corporation* in the ESSEC-Mannheim Executive MBA programme, and this book originates from that course module. I started teaching the module in 2004. I am grateful to the participants in this programme for their insights and feedback. My work environment in a French *grande ecole* provided and sustained my interest in French and European corporations.

I acknowledge all my colleagues at ESSEC Business School, Paris-Singapore; the Graduate School of Business, Keio University, Japan; Tamkang University, Taiwan, and IIM Ahmedabad, India, during the last six years, who have helped to make this book a reality. My special thanks goes to my colleagues at the International Management Division, Academy of Management and Academy of International Business, from where I gathered inspiration and ideas to help me think in a global context.

I unhesitatingly acknowledge the support and encouragement fo Pierre Tapie, Françoise Rey, Maryse Dubouloy, Anne Vancaelemont, Sophie Magnanou, Eric Choley and my students (including Boris Gbahoué, Guillaume Poutrel, Emeline Nicolas, Boris Tyspin, Johannes Banzhaf, Saoussane Tayaa, Maria Roshni Mathew, Pelin Atamer, Frédéric Vaulpré, Iana Torres, Lilly Liu, and Deepak Yachamaneni) who supported me in writing, cases and developing course materials for this book. My most sincere appreciation goes to Lina Prevost for administration and logistics, and to my editor Tracy Donhardt, who helped me shape the manuscript.

I am grateful to the researchers and colleagues who have contributed their articles to the book. Despite the best efforts of the contributiors I remain responsible for any shortcomings. Finally, I would like to acknowledge my wife, Lalita, whose emotional and literary support made this project possible. I believe the arrival of our daughter, Mekhala-Zoya, brought the necessary providence to finally see the book in print.

Ashok Som

The publisher would like to thank the following reviewers for their comments at various stages in the text's development:

Sola Adesola, Oxford Brookes University
Thomas Amling at Leipzig University, Germany
Louis Brennan, Trinity College, Dublin
Philip Bryans, Napier University
Pawan Budhwar, Aston University
Paul Davis, Dublin City University
Joyce Falkenberg, University of Agder, Norway
Olivier Furrer, Radboud University Nijmegen
Paul Ryan, National University of Ireland, Galway

Every effort has been made to trace and acknowledge ownership of copyright and to clear permission for material reproduced in this book. The publishers will be pleased to make suitable arrangements to clear permission with any copyright holders whom it has not been possible to contact.

PART 1
The Global Strategy Imperative

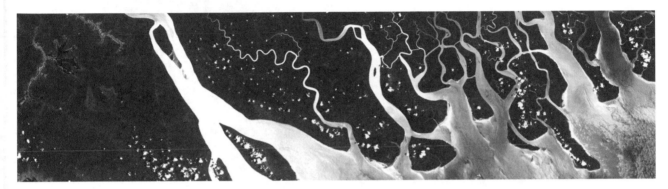

CHAPTER 1

Globalization and expansion imperatives

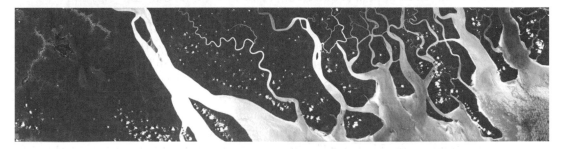

The 1980s and 1990s saw an upheaval in economic thinking and brought about major societal changes such as the collapse of the USSR and its system in eastern Europe, and the liberalization and globalization of most economies. During these two decades, firms conducted their business in a dynamic world of international business with the globalization of world markets marked by the emergence of new international businesses and the economic liberalization of developed and emerging economies. The dramatic surge in market reforms throughout the developing world created more than 75 emerging and post-socialist economies with a combined population of more than three billion people aimed at integrating themselves into the global market system. Dozens of these economies in Asia, Latin America and central Europe have succeeded in attracting large flows of capital and, most strikingly, more than 30 countries have established stock markets capable of attracting international portfolio investments. These changes have had profound implications for the world economy and are leading to a reallocation of global savings and investment. These changes have also propelled the most dynamic of the reforming countries into unprecedented levels of sustained economic growth, and reshaped global capital markets by introducing new opportunities for both portfolio and direct foreign investment.

Growth opportunities arose as countries such as the USA, and the industrialized nations of Europe such as the UK, France, Germany, Spain, the Netherlands, Portugal and others started developing their interests within their empires. These expansions began as trade. The opening of the sea route to India by Vasco da Gama in 1499 established the colonial power of Portugal in the Indian Ocean. The initial motivation was the spice trade, which was quickly followed by other commodities, such as textiles, raw silk, coffee and tea, indigo and precious stones. Stories of such trade appeared within the plots of William Shakespeare when he spoke about Antonio in *The Merchant of Venice*. The entire plot of *The Merchant of Venice* revolves around the wealthy merchant Antonio, whose ships are at sail for trading, while he has to lend a considerable sum of money to his friend

Bassanio, who plans to spend the money on wooing his beloved, Portia. The plot thickens when Antonio's ships do not return on time and he is supposed to give a 'pound of flesh' from any part of his body to Shylock, the moneylender. Traders like Antonio and, later on, companies that started with trading (like the British East India Company) have been the dominant vehicles of internationalization.

This discussion does not focus on trading corporations, however, but rather on corporations that have substantial foreign direct investment in other countries and are actively engaged in the management of their assets. In an age of globalization, it is prudent to begin the discussion with terminology and definitions. *Global corporations* are companies that have a pervasive influence in the global economy. The smaller global corporations have about 250 employees and operate in more than one country. The largest ones have about 250,000 employees and have operations in about 100 countries. Of these companies, the 500 largest account for about 2.5 per cent of world product, nearly half of world trade, 40 per cent of the world's manufacturing output, and 80 per cent of technological and royalty fees. In addition, they have influence with more than 85 per cent of the automobile sector, 75 per cent of the computer software and hardware industry, and 65 per cent of the soft drinks market. More than 80 per cent of these 500 corporations are based in the five richest nations around the world: the USA, UK, France, Germany and Japan. Over the last decade, there has been an increase in the number of emerging country global corporations, and some of the cases and articles in this book discuss them in detail. A detailed analysis and summary of existing issues for these corporations is presented in Chapter 2.

Globalization and growth imperatives

Authors have defined globalization in many ways. One simple definition states that 'globalization can be defined as the process of social, political, economic, cultural and technological integration among countries of the world'.[1] Evidence abounds that globalization results in increased levels of flow of capital, flow of goods and flow of skilled manpower. Another interesting definition of globalization comes from Narayan Murthy, Chairman and Chief Mentor of Infosys, the second-largest software company in India: 'I define globalization as raising capital where it is cheapest, produce where it is most cost effective and sell services where it is most profitable.' Still, there exists debate on the positives and negatives regarding globalization.

On the positive side, increased global trade and foreign direct investments brings technology, jobs, skills, R&D and wealth to regions around the world. With these transfers from developed nations, underdeveloped and developing nations have gained better infrastructure, more advanced educational opportunities and other improvements, which allow them to catch up with their developed counterparts. Though this pace of growth is likely to have some shortcomings in the immediate future, sustained industrialization will add value and create wealth in these regions. With the accumulation of wealth and

---

[1] As defined in Hodgetts, Richard M., Luthans, Fred. and Doh, Jonathan, P. (2006) *International Management: Culture, Strategy and Behavior*. McGraw-Hill Irwin.

advances in technology, industries are able to utilize cutting-edge technological innovations that are environmentally friendly.

On the negative side, increased globalization creates the inverted-U hypothesis, which states that there are limits to achieving superior performance, and global companies need to be aware of and be more responsive to the individual socio-cultural and economic needs. Critics cry foul when jobs are offshored to low-wage countries. Also they postulate that lower wages might be economically profitable to the global companies but do not necessarily mean better job conditions; nor do they translate to boosting the workforce up the social ladder. This issue of ethical and corporate social responsibility is discussed in Chapter 8. Also on the negative side are concerns related to environmental and social impacts. Activists and NGOs are vociferous in pointing out the shortcomings of globalization.

Pankaj Ghemawat argues 'why the world isn't flat' in a 2007 article published in *Foreign Policy*,[2] in which he criticizes *New York Times* columnist Thomas L. Friedman's bestselling book *The World is Flat*, one of the most recent proponents of globalization. Friedman argues that ten forces – most of which enable connectivity and collaboration at a distance – are 'flattening' the Earth and levelling the playing field of global competitiveness beyond anything the world has ever seen. Ghemawat argues: 'The total amount of the world's capital formation ... generated from foreign direct investment (FDIs) has been less than 10 per cent for the last three years (2003–5).' That is to say, '90 per cent of the fixed investment around the world is still domestic ... The levels of internationalization associated with cross-border migration, telephone calls, management research and education, private charitable giving, patenting, stock investment, and trade, as a function of gross domestic product (GDP), all stand much closer to 10 per cent.'

Globalization is here to stay. Stakeholders of globalization must be responsive and sensitive to the different perspectives, and incorporate the economical underpinnings of growth and profitability that proponents of globalization highlight. On the other hand, stakeholders also have to incorporate in their global strategies the cost of globalization and bridge the differences in the various regions of the world. In order to do this, they need to understand the **p**olitical, **e**conomic, **s**ocio-cultural, **t**echnological, **e**nvironmental and **l**egal (PESTEL) context in which they operate.

PESTEL analysis is an important tool that provides a non-exhaustive list of potential influences of the environment in which a corporation operates. It relates to the strategy–context–performance paradigm, which seeks to understand and organize information on markets and countries.[3] The strategy is the market's or the nation's explicit policies, designed to achieve its goals. The contextual components are the resources available to the stakeholders, and include how the stakeholders allocate these resources for optimal performance. Performance thus is assessing the market's or country's economic, social, political and international indicators. These macro-environmental factors help corporations, especially global corporations, understand the specificities of the diverse challenges of the external environment – their opportunities and threats – and aid them in building a better vision for the business landscape in the multiple markets in which they operate.

[2] Ghemawat, Pankaj (2007) 'Why the world isn't flat', *Foreign Policy*, 54–60.

[3] Dyck, Alexander, I.J. (1997) 'Country analysis: a framework to identify and evaluate the national business environment', HBS Note: 9-797-092.

The *political* environment can have a significant influence on global corporations. With changes in government policies, global corporations have to align their strategies immediately in multiple markets or they will quickly go out of business. The stability of the political environment is also a key concern for global companies when entering new markets. Policies related to regulation, taxation, cross-market cash flows, trade treaties, deregulation and liberalization of industries have a strong bearing on managing a global corporation. For example, regulations related to information and internet search data change every year in China, and corporations like Google, MSN and Yahoo! have to stay on top of them in order to understand and implement those regulations.

In India, the retail sector will soon be deregulated and liberalized, which has created tremendous interest on the part of Wal-Mart, Carrefour, Tesco and Auchan in entering this market. To do this, these corporations have to understand macro-*economic* factors such as inflation rates, interest rates, tariffs, exchange rate regime, among others, before entering this market.

In addition, the likes of Wal-Mart and Carrefour must understand the *socio-cultural* tastes and preferences of customers, which not only vary from country to country, but also within individual states in a country as large as India. Factors such as local languages, dialects, buying habits, religious beliefs, ethnicity, leisure time, spending power, cultural underpinnings, and so on, are critical for achieving success and growth in these markets.

In terms of *technology*, key issues are related to research funding by the government, level of interest in technology transfer vis-à-vis indigenous technology creation, maturity, status of intellectual property rights (IPRs) and acceptance of disruptive technologies by the local market. In 2007, German and Japanese companies were reported to shift substantial FDIs to India from China due to better IPR laws and protection rules.

Environmental factors are a growing concern in the globalization debate as they define not only the securing of key supplies and raw materials, but also waste disposal, pollution, carbon emissions (greenhouse effect, ozone layer depletion, global climate change), waste water management, etc.

Lastly, the *legal* and regulatory framework has an impact on the formulation and implementation of global business operations. This is more challenging as the framework usually differs across countries, and sometimes between the regions of a country. More often than not, global corporations have to pay special attention to regulations related to monopolies and private property, IPRs, consumer laws, labour laws, employment laws, and health and safety laws. Most of these factors are not mutually exclusive and global corporations have to be knowledgeable about these in order to manage their subsidiaries successfully. If doing business globally is so difficult, why do companies want to be global in the first place?

Rationale for being a global corporation: the economic imperative

Using a hypothetical scenario is one way to understand why companies want to go global if doing so is so difficult.

A group of young entrepreneurs living in a Paris suburb hits on an innovative idea. With some investment in R&D they have an innovative product. Clearly, the group would want to exploit their invention economically. To do so, they will need to understand the demand for their product in the local market. Since the product is an innovative one, market research would probably suggest that there would be high demand. The young entrepreneurs would need to secure capital and start manufacturing their product locally because that is where their main customer base is, and also to maintain close ties with and control over their production site and their R&D investments. As the product becomes successful in the Parisian market, and subsequently in the French market, demand will increase in neighbouring countries where consumer needs and markets are similar to that of France, such as Spain, Italy, Germany, the UK and Switzerland. These requirements would normally be catered to by increased production at their production site in Paris, thereby generating exports for France.

As the product matures and the production process becomes standardized, the entrepreneurs begin to see higher and higher margins. They also invest more and more in R&D to bring in the next generation of product. By the law of economics, super normal profits cannot be sustained for long. Competitors will try to enter the same market with similar products or a different version of the same product. But, by this time, revenue from exports might have become substantial and competitors are also eager to exploit this lucrative export market. To compete and neutralize such threats, the innovative company sets up production facilities in the countries where the demand and revenue are highest, thereby making the transition from exporter to a company that has foreign direct investment in foreign countries and is engaged in active management of those assets.

With time, the product becomes highly standardized and many competitors enter the business. As competition intensifies in the home country, the innovative company competes either on price or cost, or both. Competing on price might generate a *price war*. To compete on cost, the innovative firm decides to source its raw materials from less expensive outlets, and shift its production to the low-wage countries of eastern Europe (or China), such as Poland, Hungary, Romania and Bulgaria. The low-wage countries eventually become exporters, while France and the other developed nations become importers.

This discussion of hypothetical entrepreneurs demonstrates that this small company, which started in a suburb in Paris, has to expand to become a global corporation. This theory of becoming a global company was put forward by Professor Raymond Vernon[4] of Harvard Business School in 1966, in his well-known 'product life cycle' theory.

In summary, the rationale for becoming a global corporation was not inherent in the entrepreneurial corporation at the outset. But, traditionally, to compete and to exist, it had to *secure its key raw materials* from low-cost regions, venture into *new markets* and shift its production to *low-cost countries*. From an economic rationale, it boosted production in the homeland and achieved *economies of scale and scope*, it reduced its *factor costs* and its *R&D expenditure* by taking the same product to new markets (while it continued with its R&D for developed markets) and *extended the life cycle* of its products by introducing them in developing markets.

---

[4] Vernon, Raymond (1966) 'International investment and international trade in the product cycle', *Quarterly Journal of Economics*, May, 190–207.

Although product life cycle theory helped understanding of the pull theory of internationalization and how a corporation becomes global in its operations, during the late 1980s its predictive power became limited, as researchers like Christopher Bartlett and Sumantra Ghoshal[5] pointed out. With the global business environment becoming turbulent and hyper-competitive, researchers and corporations, in their search for greater explanatory power, developed an emerging strategic rationale for their global expansions.

Why be a global corporation? The strategic imperative

Apart from the economic imperatives, there are emerging strategic imperatives to becoming a global corporation. During the initial stages, as discussed earlier, global expansion was more opportunistic and related to a strategic survival of competitive forces. Subsequently, however, the corporation prioritized its options, and what were once survival mechanisms, which arose from competition, become secondary and three distinct sets of strategic imperatives emerge that are in tune with their global strategies.

First, foreign investments tend to occur more frequently among corporations that compete in an oligopoly in the home country.[6] Corporations in highly consolidated industries such as cement, oil, chemicals, automobiles, banking and semiconductors have been observed to follow each other to foreign destinations as soon as one of them starts its global expansion. A global chess game ensues, with moves and counter-moves. This is because an oligopolistic reaction is driven by fear that if the foreign expansion undertaken by one 'sister' is not matched by another 'sister', the loss of competitive advantage could result. The underlying assumption for this reaction is that the 'sisters' are *rational competitors* that operate by the same rules across a wide range of markets and with similar targets for return on capital. Examples of oligopolistic reaction have been shown by 'six sisters' in the cement industry, 'seven sisters' in the oil industry, the 'big three' in the automobile industry, the 'twins' of the cola industry, the 'three sisters' of the German chemical industry, and 'sister' banks in the Netherlands, Switzerland and Spain.

Second, corporations try to gain an advantage by *integrating the global knowledge* throughout their subsidiaries that has been accrued from their scanning and learning capabilities. Here they try to leverage the knowledge from their network of subsidiaries to gain an advantage from both local and foreign competitors. The geographical diversification smoothes out the volatility of the earnings cycle within individual markets.

Third, strategic imperative is the important advantage that a corporation brings due to its *strategic posture* and its competitive positioning in the market. Recent literature abounds focusing on global corporations entering markets by rapid, opportunistic or phased-in entry, depending on the corporation's perception of its strategic importance in the market and its ability to exploit that market. Here, cross-subsidization of markets has been an important strategic imperative for global expansion.

---

[5] Barlett, Christopher and Ghoshal, Sumantra (1989) *Managing Across Borders: The Transnational Solution*. Boston, Mass.: Harvard Business School Press.

[6] Guillén, Mauro, F. (2005) *The Rise of the Spanish Multinationals*. Cambridge, UK: Cambridge University Press.

An example from the cement industry clarifies the above three imperatives. For simplicity, cement Company A and cement Company B are operating in a closed market (Figure 1.1). Cement is very simple to make.[7] It is produced using limestone, which is abundant in most regions of the world, so it can be produced locally. Its production requires huge captive investment, which is written off after several decades. Fixed costs in the industry are particularly high and significant relative to variable costs, and generally account for more than 50 per cent of the overall production costs. These fixed costs are usually sunk costs, meaning that, once built, a cement plant can serve no other purpose. Since fixed costs are high relative to variable costs, the break-even point is high. With automation, labour costs have decreased, but energy consumption is the most significant variable cost. Thus, profits in the industry are sensitive to the level of utilization of the production capacity. Significant cash flow is generated only when production increases beyond the break-even point, which depends on the efficiency of the plant.

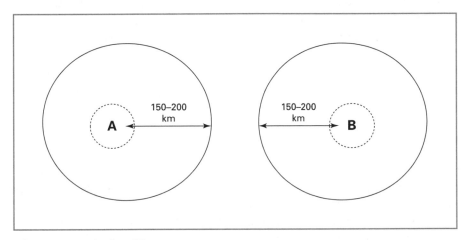

FIGURE 1.1 Cement companies A and B.

Another important feature that affects supply is transportation costs. In the USA, average transportation and distribution costs account for almost 25 per cent of the cement price. As a result, the sphere of sales is within 150–200 km from the production site. The cost of transportation is highest when it is by road, followed by rail, and is cheapest by sea.

When a buyer chooses between two cement producers, his/her decision is primarily based on price, with innovation accounting for little in the competitive process.

[7] It is manufactured by proportioning limestone and clay and then pulverizing that material. The pulverized material is supplemented by other raw materials, such as sand, mill scale and bauxite, to achieve the right quantities of calcium, silica, aluminium and iron (depending on the type of cement being produced). This mix is then ground further in a raw feed mill (dry process or wet process) before being 'cooked'. The raw feed then undergoes a burning process through the kiln. In the kiln, the raw materials are calcinated (heated to 1450°C) to produce clinker. The fuel required to heat the kiln accounts for almost 50 per cent of the operating costs. This is the reason why cement manufacturers are using waste materials as fuel. A small amount (5–10 per cent) of gypsum (which improves the setting time for the concrete mix) is then added to the cooled clinker and ground into a fine 'cement' powder.

However, differentiation between producers exists in a number of areas: (a) homogeneity of quality – the quality and colour of cement should remain constant throughout the entire construction period; (b) delivery delays; (c) technical assistance – to choose cement suited to specific construction purposes; and (d) deliveries with greater flexibility. Service quality is the only way to influence buyers when price differences are minimal.

In the example, Company A and Company B have their quarries in the centre of their respective markets. These are their 'natural markets'. This is because the cost of cement is directly related to its production costs (which fall steeply as the size of the plant and its rate of utilization increase) and transportation costs (which increase with distance). A cement producer is secure from competition within its natural market as the price it will normally quote, given the combination of production and transportation costs, is lower that that quoted by distant competitors. A producer is a *price leader* in the natural market of its cement plant, and distant competitors are *price takers*.

Company A, which was operating at 75 per cent capacity, decides to increase its capacity to 90 per cent. Due to the nature of the product, cement cannot be stored. Excess capacity in its own region will translate into a reduction in price if demand does not increase substantially. Company A, to compete and fully utilize capacity, is thus ready to supply distant buyers. The natural markets of both Company A and B depend on the strategic options taken by A and B regarding pricing policy. Cement buyers in the vicinity of a producing plant are in this sense captive. (If they have to buy from a distant producer, they will pay higher transportation costs, and therefore a higher delivered price.)

Thus, cement producers are driven to discriminate on price. Company A will charge 'phantom freight' to the nearest buyers (a higher price than if the real transportation cost had been charged) and will practise 'freight absorption' when selling to distant buyers (a lower price is charged than if the real transportation cost had been charged) in the vicinity of B's natural market. A price discrimination strategy, therefore, enables a producer to modify the boundaries of the natural market of its plant.

At this point, Company B, which was operating at 80 per cent efficiency, suddenly finds competition from A in its home territory. Its initial instinct would be to do exactly like A: increase capacity and attack A's market. Thus, competition in the cement industry initially occurs at the local level due to high transportation costs. Competition cannot be based on price as price cuts are easily spotted due to the nature of the product, which is undifferentiated. Competition is hence based on head-to-head market confrontation focused on price rebates and sales volume in order to expand market share. Any substantial price cut by a competitor results in a price war. Rivalry also occurs when firms want to enhance their respective competitive advantages on the basis of improved product quality or reduced production costs.

Due to high barriers of entry and increased consolidation in the industry, competition occurs at multi-point and multi-market level. Historically, cement firms entered different local markets as a business expansion strategy, to take advantage of growing markets and to hedge against local economic fluctuations. At the regional and national level, this has led to greater concentration and head-to-head confrontation between a reduced number of large multi-plant firms, which competed rationally. These 'sisters' enter markets dominated by their competitors, intending to create retaliatory threats. Once reciprocal multi-market competitive threats have been created, each competitor is generally left with a 'sphere of influence'. The building up of spheres of influence increases the chance of competitive stabilization. Under a multi-point competitive regime, each producer has possession of 'hostage' local plants owned by its competitors. Producers have strengths and weaknesses in various locations. They can retaliate against a competitive attack that occurs in one market by attacking in a different market where the competitor is weak. This interplay gives credibility to non-aggressive agreements, as well as to the threat of retaliation for transgressing rules. Larger producers buying smaller independent ones can help reinforce the multi-market competition game.

The six 'sisters' of cement – Lafarge (French), Holcim (Swiss), Cemex (Mexican), Italcementi (Italy), Taiheiyo (Japan) and Heidelbeger (German) – dominate the globe. Each of the six sisters still has clearly identifiable national origins and controls a significant share of its home market. The six sisters follow each other around the globe to enter new markets, grow by acquisition, and play the multi-point, multi-market chess game.

Being global: the growth imperative

An important question to ask in international business is, 'Why is growth imperative?' Bertrand Collomb, Chairman of Lafarge, the global leader in building construction materials industry states:

> First we are in the business where either you eat others or you are eaten. It is fight for survival and fight for the fittest and the option of being a small company in our business is not a good option because at some point you will be swallowed by somebody else. Now the option of being a very large business, which is not good, is not an option either because size will not protect you. We know very well that we are in a world where even very large companies, if they are not performing will not survive. So the only answer if you want to be a successful company is both growth and performance. And it's not an addition, it's a multiplication, so if you have no growth, nobody will be interested in you and if you have no performance, it's the same. So really the value creation and the leadership formula is a very simple one but very difficult to implement, which is to combine growth and performance.

Other rationales also exist, such as: opportunities for expansion; to leverage scale and scope economies; to compete globally with competitors; the whims of CEOs; the policies of nation states. For example, the growth of the *keiretsus* and *chaebols* after the Second World War was a testimony to the Japanese and Korean model of internationalizing businesses. *Keiretsus*, such as Mitsubishi and Matsui, are companies created with the support of the Japanese government. These companies expanded under the guidelines of the Ministry of International Trade and Industry (MITI), which laid down long-term plans and the groups' strategic planning for international expansion. They were all held by cross-stock ownership, were managed with a stakeholder orientation and evoked collective leadership. Their structures were either horizontally diversified or vertically integrated, with a bank at the centre of the structure. Their internal goals were dictated by financial institutions and the government supported them with research subsidies. Similarly, *chaebols* such as Samsung and Daewoo, were family-owned, family-orientated conglomerates with strong autocratic leadership. They were usually unrelated, vertically integrated, and their expansion options were based on the family's moods and government policies. They did not own banks but their internal goals were dictated by the government's agenda with cross-debt-payment guaranteed loans. The government enforced industrial policies through direct grants and subsidies. Their foreign direct investment (FDI) and global expansion was more of a concerted expansion strategy to compete with the US and European majors.

In the 1990s, more than 85 per cent of all FDI took place among the triad: the USA, Europe and Japan. From 2000 to 2007, the favoured destinations for FDI were in the emerging markets of Asia, Latin America and eastern Europe. And the emerging companies of these areas are themselves increasing their presence in developed nations. For example, the acquisition of Tetley by Tata Tea, Corus by Tata Iron & Steel Company, IBM's computer business by Lenovo, and others, bears testimony to this notion. According to the earlier discussion, corporations expanded abroad when they had exhausted the domestic market; they were mature and had deep pockets. This is no longer the trend, as corporations much earlier in their life cycle, much smaller in terms of revenues and assets, are identifying and pursuing global expansion. This has been more so due to the liberalization, privatization and deregulation of emerging markets, the advent of economic integration (EU, NAFTA, etc.), technological change and convergence.

Corporations expanding abroad are experiencing a new regime that has changed substantially over the past decade. Most of the previous global expansion occurred by means of a step-by-step, sequential approach over several decades, as propounded by Raymond Vernon. That is how many of the best-known global companies built their markets. Growth was usually pursued organically, moving slowly from exports to greenfield investments. Foreign subsidiaries replicated the home-country business model and sent expatriates to manage these FDIs. Expatriates developed the local talent and, with incremental expansions, moved to successive locations where expertise was required. The sequential approach entailed gaining experience, limiting risk, developing local talent, attaining profitability and, with cross-market cash flows, funding other expansions. That was the way companies like IKEA, Wal-Mart, Colgate-Palmolive, Lafarge and Vodafone expanded.

Today there is a different scenario. With cross-border mergers and acquisitions, corporations are quickly expanding their bases across the globe. The slow, incremental and sequential approach might be dangerous to global companies today, as the business landscape is changing rapidly. The competitive landscape is changing faster each day, keeping pace with the changes in the turbulent and hyper-competitive environment. For example, in 2006, Vodafone exited its Japanese business while, in 2007, its $11.1 billion acquisition of Hutchinson Essar in India changed the telecom business landscape in these two countries.

Thus, rather than choose adjacent or similar markets, corporations today are searching for the best opportunity both for immediate market access and costs. Corporations are scanning different business environments and analysing the threats and opportunities that different markets provide. As a rule of thumb, corporations consider the relative size of the markets, ease of operation, availability and cost of resources, perceived relative risk and uncertainty.

The next chapter discusses the strategic capabilities required for managing such investments, and dwells on definitional issues relating to multinational companies (MNCs). Within the definitional framework the chapter tries to understand the evolution of MNCs, their strengths and weaknesses, their biases, their tensions, and how they can develop multi-level competencies and interrelated capabilities.

Case introduction: ICICI Bank: path to globalization

The case of ICICI Bank examines the growth of India's premier bank. It focuses on the bank's evolution from a state-owned, project-financing institution to an efficient, customer-driven, global banking corporation. The strategy of domestic competition and international expansion is discussed.

This case appears after the readings for this chapter.

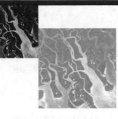

READING 1
Broadening the debate: the pros and cons of globalization*

Joyce S. Osland, San Jose State University

Globalization has become an increasingly controversial topic, and the growing number of protests around the world has focused more attention on the basic assumptions of globalization and its effects. The purpose of this literature review is to broaden the boundaries of the debate on globalization and increase our understanding of its influence beyond the economic sphere. The winners and losers resulting from globalization are identified along with empirical evidence of its impact on key areas: equality, labor, government, culture and community, and the environment. The literature indicates that globalization is an uneven process that has had both positive and negative effects. The article presents some of the arguments of various stakeholders in the globalization controversy.

The roots of globalization began to take hold in the 15th century with voyages by intrepid explorers who were funded by European monarchs seeking new trade routes. It continued throughout the years of the imperial expansion of Europe and the colonization of other lands primarily for the purpose of trade. In the mercantilist era, trading companies (such as the Hudson Bay Company and the East India Tea Company) served as surrogate colonial governments, merging trade and government. Later, trading companies were privatized, and intercontinental railways and transoceanic steamships made it possible to open previously protected markets. The global markets present in the early 20th century were disrupted by both world wars. After World War II, the World Bank and the International Monetary Fund (IMF) were founded to aid development in war-ravaged countries and lesser developed countries (LDCs). The English term *globalization* first made its appearance around 1960 (Waters, 1995). In 1995, the World Trade Organization (WTO) was created as a successor to the General Agreement on Tariffs and Trade (GATT) 'to help trade flow smoothly, freely, fairly and predictably'

AUTHOR'S NOTE: This article is largely an excerpt from part of a longer chapter coauthored with Kathy Dhanda and Kristi Yuthas, 'Globalization and Environmental Sustainability: An Analysis of the Impact of Globalization Using the Natural Step Framework', in Sanjay Sharma & Mark Starik (eds) *Research in Corporate Sustainability: The Evolving Theory and Practice of Organizations in the Natural Environment* (Cheltenham, UK: Edward Elgar, 2002, pp. 31–60).

Journal of Management Inquiry, Vol. 12, No. 2, June 2003, 137–154

DOI: 10.1177/1056492603252535

(World, 2003, p. 3).[1] In recent years, many nations have liberalized their trade policies – removing trade barriers and focusing on exports – which further stimulated globalization.

The level of global trade increased 14-fold in the period from 1950 to 1997 (World, 2003, p. 2). In addition to increased volume, beginning in the 1970s and 1980s, a shift to foreign direct investment and technology characterized globalization. Recent growth in globalization has been facilitated and driven by rapid improvements in international transportation, technology, and telecommunications (Wood, 1995). The Internet opened up service markets that were previously protected by geographical distance (Valaskakis, 1998). Today, cross-border capital flows are more important than trade flows, and some multinational enterprises (MNEs) now have budgets larger than the economies of many countries. Kobrin (1997), however, argued that foreign trade and investment are less important drivers of globalization than are increasing technological scale, interfirm alliances, and information flows.

Many businesspeople and, judging by the international business literature, many business scholars accept globalization as a fait accompli whose presence and benefits are largely unquestioned. In other circles, however, globalization has become a controversial topic, as first evidenced by labor protests in Korea and France, student riots in Indonesia, and the anti-World Trade Organization demonstrations in Seattle. A small but growing number of respected economists, sociologists, and political scientists criticize globalization and warn that protesters must be taken seriously to avoid dire consequences (Press, 2002, p. 12). Antiglobalization protests have become a familiar part of the social landscape, and there is little reason to suppose they will simply disappear. Furthermore, the issue is still fairly polarized with fervent free traders on one end of the continuum and radical protesters on the other. Polarization that prohibits room for dialogue seldom leads to lasting solutions, particularly in the case of complex issues. Therefore, this article is an attempt to help business practitioners, scholars, and students better understand the complexity of the issue and to challenge readers to think about win-win solutions benefiting more stakeholders.

The globalization debate continuum is anchored by these views: Proponents generally view globalization as an opportunity for economic growth and prosperity, whereas opponents perceive it as a threat to prosperity, political sovereignty, cultural integrity, and the environment. In developed countries, the primary concerns are the potential job loss for workers and the risk to contracting industries; developing countries worry about political sovereignty and losing control of their economies (Champlin & Olson, 1999). The burgeoning literature on globalization includes so many impassioned ideological arguments for or against it that a reader's first concern is to ascertain the potential bias of the author.[2] Many of these arguments lack empirical support. To complicate matters further, some of the existing economic research findings are highly contradictory. Much of the academic literature seems to fall primarily into pro and con categories. A recent review of the social science literature on globalization categorized it in terms of Hirschman's (1982) metaphor as either civilizing (positive), destructive (negative), or feeble (having no significant impact) and concluded that the feeble category was the least compelling (Guillén, 2001).

Disagreement over the definition of globalization impedes the debate. As Champlin and Olson (1999) noted, the debate cannot be resolved, not because we lack the definitive econometric analysis but because the debate is defined or framed in different ways. Is it simply an argument about the virtues of free markets and supply and demand, or does it include the broader sociocultural and environmental impact? Robert Reich described globalization as one of those concepts 'that has passed from obscurity to meaninglessness without ever having an intervening period of coherence' (Duin, 2000, p. B-1). This meaninglessness can be traced to its usage as an 'all-purpose catchword in public and scholarly debate' (Lechner & Boli, 2000, p. 1) with different connotations for different parties who support or oppose globalization.

Some definitions of globalization focus solely on cross-border trade – for example, globalization as the absence of borders and barriers to trade between nations (Ohmae, 1995). The International Monetary Fund describes globalization as 'the growing economic interdependence of countries worldwide through the increasing volume and variety of cross-border transactions in goods and services and of international capital flows, and also through the more rapid and widespread diffusion of technology' (International, 1999, p. 45). Although these definitions convey a sense of dynamic change and boundarylessness, they portray the outcomes of globalization too narrowly. Brown (1992) and Renesch (1992) defined globalization as the interconnections between the overlapping interests of business and society, a definition that acknowledges the broader context in which globalization takes place. To ensure a systems view, globalization is defined here as a process leading to greater economic interdependence and networks and the economic, political, social, cultural, and environmental results of that process. There is plentiful, if sometimes contradictory, research on the financial and economic aspects of globalization; the broader impact of these phenomena, however, has received less attention by business scholars.

This article intends to make three contributions to the existing debate and literature: (a) expand the boundaries of the debate by examining the impact of globalization on other areas in the broader system; (b) provide a balanced, objective analysis of the benefits and liabilities of globalization based on scientific research rather than on rhetoric; and (c) offer a description of the more common stakeholder perspectives in the debate. The empirical data on the impact of globalization indicate that it is an uneven process yielding mixed results. Therefore, most of the findings in this article are presented in terms of tradeoffs, highlighting both the positive and negative effects of globalization in the areas most affected: equality, labor, government, culture and community, and the environment.

The impact of globalization on equality

On the positive side of the ledger, globalization has resulted in increased access to more goods for consumers in many countries (Evenett, 1999), reduced prices due to competition with local monopolies, and increased food supply due to industrial agricultural in some countries (Mander & Goldsmith, 1996). Poor people in some countries have been able to buy cheaper imported goods rather than shoddy goods produced by local monopolies (Graham & Krugman, 1991). A recent study by the London-based Center for Economic Policy Research reports that globalization increased economic growth and improved the incomes of both rich and poor people.

The researchers claim that the number of people living in poverty today would be even greater without globalization (Gaunt, 2002).

A look at the statistics on equality indicates that globalization has resulted in both winners and losers, which is supported by Lee's (1996) economic analysis of income levels. According to one expert estimate,[3] 30–40% of the world population has benefited from globalization, whereas the rest has not (Valaskakis, 1998). Globalization is blamed for increasing the chasm between new groups of haves and have-nots – between the well educated and the poorly educated, between the technologically skilled and the unskilled, and between those living in countries that compete successfully in the global economy and those who do not (Frank & Cook, 1995; Pritchett, 1997; United Nations Development, 1999). Globalization has resulted in more jobs in developing countries, creating another group of winners depending on the level of wages they receive. There have been examples of spectacular development, like the Asian Tigers (Singapore, Taiwan, Hong Kong, and South Korea), as well as examples of countries that are marginalized from the global economy, such as sub-Saharan Africa. Some developing countries have suffered job losses in local industries that could not compete with foreign multinationals once formerly protected markets were opened (Lee, 1996). Some critics believe that the structure of the global economy favors developed countries over lesser developed countries.

Amidst the occasionally contradictory economic findings, one piece of incontrovertible evidence stands out. There is more inequality among and within countries today than in the past. Between 1870 and 1990, the gap in per capita income between rich and developing countries has grown fivefold (Temple, 1999). The gap between the richest and poorest 20% of the world population has widened significantly since 1960, when the income ratio of the richest to the poorest was 30 : 1, to 82 : 1 in 1995 (United Nations Development, 1996). There are 1.2 billion people living on less than $1 a day (United Nations Development, 2001), a figure that is increasing rather than diminishing. The richest 20% of the world's population receives 86% of the world's GDP, 82% of the export trade, and 68% of foreign direct investment; the lowest 20% receives only 1% of each (United Nations Development, 1999). A total of 358 people own as much wealth as 2.5 billion people own together – nearly half the world's population (United Nations Development, 1996). The global income of the poorest 20% of the world dropped from 2.3% to 1.4% of world GDP between 1989 and 1998 (Giddens, 2000). In virtually all developed countries, the gaps between skilled and unskilled workers in wages and/or unemployment rates have widened (Gottschalk & Smeeding, 1997; Murphy & Topel, 1997; Organization, 1997).

The notable exceptions – countries or commonwealths that have significantly reduced the gap since 1960 – include South Korea, Taiwan, Singapore, Ireland, and Puerto Rico. In the East Asian economies, trade liberalization contributed to reduced wage inequality accompanied by rapid economic growth (Lee, 1996). In Latin America, however, wage inequality increased following liberalization, meaning that skilled workers benefited disproportionately (Berry, 1996; Robbins, 1995; see also United Nations Conference, 1997; Wood, 1997).

Given its egalitarian roots and the historic propensity of most U.S. citizens to consider themselves middle class, it is surprising to discover that nowhere is the inequality between the rich and the poor as great as in the United States (Longworth, 1999). The worth of the average hourly wage is 12% lower than it was in 1973 (Longworth, 1999), whereas the average pay for a U.S. CEO is 200 times higher, $7.4 million in 2002 (almost half the 2000 average) (Lavelle, Jespersen, Ante, & Kerstetter, 2003). The after-tax income of the richest 1% of U.S. households increased 72% from 1977 to 1994, whereas that of the poorest 20% of U.S. households decreased by 16% (Scott, Lee, & Schmidt, 1997). As in other countries, some parts of the United States have prospered from globalization, whereas other regions struggle to keep up.

The Silicon Valley, for example, benefited from globalization until the recent economic downturn; since 2001, employment has decreased 20% (Joint Venture, 2003). Previously, developed countries were concerned about losing blue-collar jobs, but the next wave of globalization is shifting white-collar jobs – highly trained knowledge workers and service jobs – offshore to less expensive labor markets in Asia, Latin America, and Eastern Europe (Engardio, Bernstein, & Kripalani, 2003).

Researchers agree that the gap between rich and poor has widened; they disagree, however, on whether globalization has caused the gap by influencing wages. Although U.S. wages rose only 5.5% between 1979 and 1993, some economists claim that this is not the fault of globalization because international trade and investment have had little impact (Lawrence, 1995; Sachs & Schatz, 1994). Estimated shifts in product market demand, including the impact of imports, account for less than 10% of the increase in wage differential (Slaughter & Swagel, 2000). Other economists attribute labor inequalities to technological changes (Lawrence & Slaughter, 1993; Organization, 1997) rather than to globalization. Another contingent of scholars, however, points to globalization as the cause of inequality (Leamer, 1998; Rodrik, 1997; Wood, 1994). More recent research by Wood (1998) indicated a causal relationship between globalization and the increased demand for skilled rather than unskilled workers in developed countries. Furthermore, Zhao's research (1998) found that foreign direct investments adversely affect union wages and employment. Baldwin and Martin (1999) summarized the empirical literature, writing that virtually all studies found some effect of trade on the labor market in both the United States and Europe; the findings ranged, however, from almost 0% to 100% with a consensus range of perhaps 10–20% (p. 21).

Although globalization may not be the only factor involved in growing social inequality, it does seem safe to conclude that it has produced winners and losers on both the individual and country levels. The increasing gap between the haves and the have-nots raises the question of fairness. Intense debates over the fairness of the competitive advantages held by various countries are fought out at World Trade Organization meetings and trade negotiations. Increasingly, there are expressions of concern about the threat to political stability, because historically large, apparently insurmountable gaps between rich and poor have been a factor in revolutions (Marquand, 1998). In the opinion of Anthony Giddens (2000), sociologist and director of the London School of Economics, 'Along with ecological risk, expanding inequality is the most serious problem facing world society' (p. 34).

The positive and negative effects that globalization has on equality and wages appear in Table 1.

Positive effects	Negative effects
Income increased globally for both rich and poor, decreasing poverty	Greater chasm between haves and have-nots on individual and country levels
Increased wages for the well educated	Some downward pressure on wages for the poorly educated
Increased wages for technologically skilled	Some downward pressure on wages for technologically unskilled
Improved economic conditions in countries and regions that successfully compete in the global economy	Worsened economic conditions in countries marginalized from the global economy and in certain regions of developed countries
Rich have become richer	Poor have become poorer
Increased access to more goods	
Reduced prices due to competition with local monopolies	
Increased food supply in some countries	

Table 1 The impact of globalization on equality

The impact of globalization on labor conditions

Closely related to equality and wages, labor conditions is another area influenced by globalization. On the positive side, some workers in lesser developed countries have received more education and training from multinational companies due to globalization. Furthermore, there is some evidence that increased competition has resulted in upgrading educational systems to produce a more highly qualified workforce (Mander & Goldsmith, 1996; Schmidheiny, 1992).

The threat of job displacement is one of the most tangible concerns that critics have regarding globalization. Workers have more employment opportunities in some countries, but they have less in others where certain industries and firms (e.g., the import sector and small farmers) have been put out of business by global competition (Mander & Goldsmith, 1996). Daly (1996) noted that some people have less choice about how they make their living as a result of globalization. Increasing imports from low-wage countries are perceived by some as a threat to manufacturing jobs in industrialized countries, particularly in labor-intensive sectors (Wood, 1994).

The labor movement and human rights advocates argue that globalization has had a negative effect on labor standards and that it threatens hard-won improvements in labor conditions. They warn about the race to the bottom, which assumes that competition will drive labor standards (and also environmental standards) to the lowest common denominator. Rodrik (1997) found evidence of negative impact on labor conditions, but Drezner (2000) insisted that the race to the bottom is merely a myth used as a scare tactic by both multinational enterprises and activists. For example, Drezner (2000) cited a 1996 Organization for Economic Cooperation and Development (OECD) study that found a positive correlation between 'successfully sustained trade reforms' and improved core labor standards because multinationals tend to pay higher than average wages to attract better workers in developing countries (p. 65). Furthermore, the majority of global foreign direct investment (FDI) went to developed countries, which generally boast higher labor standards, during the 1990s (68.9% in 1992, 63.4% in 1995, and 71.5% in 1998), according to the United Nations Conference on Trade and Development (UNCTAD) (1992, 1995, 1998). There is no evidence that multinational enterprises choose to locate in countries where labor and environmental standards are absent or less stringent; other factors like stability, infrastructure, and the size of potential markets play stronger roles in strategic decisions.

Globalization critics, however, worry about the dynamics that occur when firms in developed nations with high wages transfer their manufacturing or processing operations to low-cost, lesser developed countries. Such transfers can be advantageous for the lesser developed countries, the recipients of new jobs, and the firms. When LDCs compete against one another to attract foreign employers to free trade zones or export processing zones (EPZs), however, critics fear this will degrade labor conditions.[4] Multinational enterprises are wooed with the lure of tax-free status for a set number of years, with facilities and infrastructure, and, in some countries, with exemptions from adhering to the national labor code. Five of the 11 nations examined in a U.S. Department of Labor study restricted their citizens' labor rights in export processing zones by allowing foreign firms to ignore national labor laws that were enforced elsewhere in the country (Charnovitz, 1992), which supports the race to the bottom argument. According to some sources, export processing zone workers are often temporary workers who are fired and rehired as needed to avoid having to provide them with benefits or career paths. When zone workers complain about working conditions, they may be fired (Klein, 2000).

The exploitative practices most commonly cited in export processing zones and outsourced factories are child labor, hazardous and unhealthy working conditions, absence of collective bargaining, repression of labor unions (Lawrence, Rodrik, & Whalley, 1996), and forced overtime (Klein, 2000). Labor union advocates and others fear that 'exploitative practices in low-wage exporting countries artificially depress labor costs, leading to unfair competitive advantage in world markets and a downward pressure on labor standards in rich countries' (Lawrence et al., 1996, p. 12). There is some evidence that globalization has caused downward pressure on wages (Lawrence, 1995) as well as on pensions and benefits (Krishnan, 1996; Sutherland, 1998) and has diminished the power of unions (Levi, 2000). Other economists argue that globalization has had very little negative impact on labor conditions and wages (Krugman, 1994).

The form of ownership and the transitory nature of many overseas factories have resulted in a different form of social contract between employer and employee. The reliance of some multinational enterprises on local subcontractors who run their factories means that workers do not 'belong' to the company. This arm's-length relationship facilitates the closure of factories when labor costs rise prohibitively and another country becomes more attractive. In these cases, the social contract between employer and employee is limited to the simplest, most expedient transaction – pay for work, which is a stripped-down version of the social contract that exists in most developed countries (albeit with the exception of temporary workers). There have been instances of unscrupulous foreign factory operators in export processing zones who have closed down and fled the country without any warning or termination pay to employees.

Moving jobs offshore also affects the social contract that firms have with domestic employees. Boeing's engineers' union threatened to strike in December 2002 if the company didn't decrease the number of engineers working in the firm's Russian facility. The union's concerns were job loss and the potential danger of sharing technology; management's interests were significantly lower wages for engineers ($5,400 yearly) and entry into the Russian market (Holmes and Ostrovsky, 2003). Such disparate goals do not fit the preexisting social contract.

The onset of globalization served as a trigger event in some companies – a wake-up call that people must work more efficiently and more intelligently, which resulted in increased productivity (Evenett, 1999). The threat of globalization has, however, also been held over workers' heads. According to Longworth (1999),

> " The rhetoric is probably a more potent force than globalization itself. An employer doesn't have to move jobs to Asia to persuade those left behind to take pay cuts. The mere possibility that, in this global age, he can do it is enough. (p. 10) "

Interestingly, other aspects of globalization – worldwide telecommunications and the Internet – have contributed to calls for basic labor standards. The increased publicity and communications about poor working conditions in other countries, which is known as the *CNN effect*, has resulted in greater pressure from human rights groups and labor unions (Lawrence et al., 1996). The threat of Internet-driven international boycotts of goods made by offending multinationals exerts a counterbalancing force for better labor practices in some cases. Companies that engage in exploitative practices are subject to boycotts, negative publicity, and loss of both good will and revenue (Dohrs & Garfunkel, 1999). Widespread criticism from consumers and protesters induced some MNEs like Nike to demand that their subcontractors provide better working conditions in overseas factories. To avoid bad publicity, firms like Nike, Mattel, and Levi Strauss have established guidelines and invited monitors to inspect their operations.

In sum, there is both positive and negative evidence concerning the impact of globalization on labor conditions, as shown in Table 2.

Positive effects	Negative effects
Increased job opportunities in some countries	Certain industries and companies were forced out of business
Upgraded educational system and more training in some countries	Job displacement affected some individuals
Increased labor standards or no change due to globalization[a]	Decreased labor standards[a]
Increased labor productivity	Caused downward pressure on benefits and pensions
CNN effect pressures firms to correct labor abuses	Decreased power of unions
Some firms taking proactive steps to avoid labor abuses	Child labor, unhealthy work conditions, and forced overtime in export processing zones (EPZs)
	Diminished social contract between employer and employee

Table 2 The impact of globalization on labor conditions
[a] Contradictory findings.

The impact of globalization on governments

The key question regarding globalization and governments is whether or not globalization threatens national sovereignty. Historically, governments played a major role in promoting their country's economic development and managing its economy, albeit in quite varied forms. Today, however, some critics argue that government matters less and less in a global economy. Nation-states are simply other actors on the global stage rather than its directors. Aggressive global production systems and capital markets now occupy the 'commanding heights' of global development, forcing governments on the defensive and pressuring them to deregulate, downsize, and privatize many of the social management functions they assumed during the past century (Yergin & Stanislaw, 2000). The political boundaries that define nation-states place them at a disadvantage when confronting the unique pressures of a boundaryless global economy. There is a 'jurisdictional asymmetry' between an economic system composed of centrally controlled, transnational MNEs on one hand and a political system structured into geographically defined sovereign states on the other (Kobrin, 2001b). Yergin and Stanislaw (2000) argued:

> Information technology – through computers – is creating a 'woven world' by promoting communication, coordination, integration, and contact at a pace and scale of change that far outrun the ability of any government to manage. The accelerating connections make national borders increasingly porous – and, in terms of some forms of control, increasingly irrelevant. (p. 215)

The growing power of globalized financial markets limits the scope of national policy (Lee, 1996). Because the world has become so interdependent and networked, nation-states are criticized if the 'playing field' for business is not level, which limits the degree of freedom in their decision making. This brings us to the key question: 'Who governs MNEs and a global economy?' 'The market' is not a satisfactory answer for globalization critics and some governments, and the sense that globalization is out of control creates a feeling of powerlessness and resentment in protesters. Nation-states are not designed to govern MNEs, but the idea of yielding their power to international governing bodies is perceived by some countries as yet another threat to national sovereignty (Longworth, 1999).

On the positive side of the ledger, for some governments, globalization has resulted in expanded infrastructure, more jobs, and more economic development for their citizenry. Certain countries have benefited from the transfer of modern, more effective management techniques to their business sector. Furthermore, some observers believe that the increased interdependence of trading and investment partners will draw countries closer together and serve as a deterrent against war (Harris & Goodwin, 1995; Tyson, 1999).

On the negative side, MNEs have exerted pressure on governments in several ways. International competitiveness has influenced public policy in some countries by encouraging government officials to lower labor standards (Lee, 1997). Because governments may view themselves in competition with others in a race to the bottom to attract MNEs to their country, foreign firms can have the upper hand in negotiations unless governments have something unique to offer (such as rare natural resources, highly trained people, and a large consumer market). Singapore, for example, invested heavily in education, attracting high-tech and professional industry rather than limiting its population to employment in low-wage factories.

George Soros (2002) criticized globalization for making the provision of private goods more important than public goods such as peace, the eradication of poverty, the protection of human and labor rights, and the environment. Governments of developed countries with extensive entitlement programs – social security systems, health care programs, and unemployment pay or welfare systems – are experiencing greater pressure to decrease such expenditures because they raise the rate of corporate taxation (Longworth, 1999). Nevertheless, Lee (1996) concluded that in spite of increasing globalization, national policies still determine levels of employment and labor standards. He warned, however, that there is a worldwide trend toward smaller government, which is evident in public expenditure reductions, lower taxes, less support for redistributive measures, and greater deregulation of markets, including the labor market. Thus, governments are less likely to compensate the losers from globalization at a time when globalization increases the demand for social insurance (Sutherland, 1998). A global economy allows companies (and the wealthiest citizens) to spread their tax liability to countries with the lowest rates and thereby decrease the taxes that national governments receive from formerly 'local' companies. Capital mobility weakens the tax base, which means that there are less funds available for social insurance (Sutherland, 1998) in countries that previously received tax payments.

The blueprint for economic development promoted by the International Monetary Fund and World Bank decreased the role of government with calls for privatization, deregulation, and the reduction of corporate, trade, and capital gains taxes (United Nations Conference, 1999; United Nations Development, 1999). Not only did this make some government functions irrelevant, but it also left governments with less money in their coffers. Grunberg (1998) reported that governments have fewer funds available as a result of globalization. The proportion of corporate taxes has decreased as a percentage of the total revenues in the United States, and it has also decreased relative to the share of corporate profits in all of the Organization for Economic Cooperation and Development countries (Kobrin, 2001a).[5] Hines (1999) found complex reasons for this phenomenon but also found evidence of aggressive tax avoidance behavior by MNEs and a race to the bottom by governments who reduced corporate tax rates to attract investment. Many EPZs grant tax-free status for the first years, but some MNEs shut down operations and leave as soon as the period is over, because they can take advantage of the same tax-free status elsewhere (Klein, 2000). Furthermore, MNEs sometimes influence local government policy and threaten to leave if their demands are not met. In this way, corporations externalize their costs to others.

Globalization makes it more difficult for governments to exercise their regulatory powers (Cox, 1996) and maintain their autonomy and independent decision making (Kobrin, 1997). In a literature review that examined whether globalization undermines the authority of nation-states, Guillén (2001) found mixed results. Some research concludes that MNEs have the upper hand with governments that now have less autonomy, whereas political scientists contend that the role of government has simply changed to include dealing with the problems of globalization. Kobrin (2001b) concluded that governments are not irrelevant, but they have been weakened as a result of globalization; they will continue to play a major role, but instead of exercising supreme authority, a nation may find that its sovereignty comes to mean simply being one of several prominent parties involved in international negotiations.

There is widespread agreement that governments are not designed or structured to deal with the problems of global business (Giddens, 2000), particularly problems like global warming and environmental degradation, that have accompanied economic development (Lechner & Boli, 2000). Partially to fill this gap, a growing number of nongovernmental organizations (NGOs) are trying to counterbalance the power of MNEs (Dohrs & Garfunkel, 1999). Nongovernmental organizations that focus on topics like human rights and environmental issues have organized themselves to exert pressure on MNEs, governments, and international organizations to ensure their agenda is heard. If one looks at globalization solely in terms of power, it has shifted from governments and organized labor to MNEs, markets, and international organizations (Kobrin, 2001a). This shift took place without a democratic vote – a silent coup that rankles protesters (Clarke, 2001). International organizations like the International Monetary Fund, World Bank, and World Trade Organization are not trusted by some factions of the antiglobalization protest movement because of the partiality these organizations show toward corporate interests and powerful governments. Stiglitz (2002), a former senior vice president and chief economist at the World Bank, claims that some of the protesters' complaints about the International Monetary Fund are based in fact – namely, that free-trade agreements primarily benefit the rich, that privatization has not proved successful in many countries, and that the IMF's vaunted structural adjustment programs have resulted in hardship for many.

UN Secretary-General Kofi Annan (1999) gave this warning at Davos:

> The spread of markets outpaces the ability of societies and their political systems to adjust to them, let alone to guide the course they take. History teaches us that such an imbalance between the economic, social and political worlds can never be sustained for very long.

Table 3 summarizes the positive and negative impacts of globalization on governments.

Positive effects	Negative effects
Increased economic development benefits some governments	Power of multinational enterprises (MNEs) increased at the expense of government power, sovereignty, and ability to regulate business
Increased jobs and expanded infrastructure benefit some countries	MNEs externalize some of their costs to countries
Transfer of modern management techniques into business sector	Competition for factories and foreign direct investment (FDI) result in too many concessions to MNEs by some governments
Greater interdependence among trading and investment partners may deter war	Some MNEs influence local government policy and threaten to leave if their demands are not met
Proliferation of nongovernmental organizations (NGOs) to counterbalance decreased governmental power	MNEs pay fewer taxes to governments and incorporate where the tax rate is lowest, depriving their own country of revenue
	Governments are pressured to reduce tax rates and decrease social benefits that may affect stability

Table 3 The impact of globalization on government

The impact of globalization on culture and community

Globalization may be a positive force for greater cross-cultural understanding via more cross-cultural exposure and closer cross-border ties. As Tomlinson (1999) stated,

> A world of complex connectivity (a global marketplace, international fashion codes, an international division of labor, a shared ecosystem) thus links the myriad small everyday actions of millions with the fates of distant, unknown others and even with the possible fate of the planet. (p. 25)

Tomlinson (1999) referred to the increased connectivity of the world as a double-edged sword that provides new and wider understanding at the same time that it takes away the securities of one's local world.

Critics claim that globalization is creating a monoculture that is rapidly spreading around the world. MTV culture, for instance, offends social conservatives in many countries. By this view, weakened cultural traditions combined with the importation of foreign media, stores, and goods encourage cultural homogenization. Multinational news outlets, like CNN and Rupert Murdoch's News Corporation, provoked the complaint that the 'flow of information' (a term that includes both ideas and attitudes) is dominated by multinational entities based in the most powerful nations (MacBride & Roach, 2000, p. 286). Chains like Wal-Mart, with lower prices and extensive, standardized inventory, force uniquely local small stores out of business because consumers prefer the service and prices at Wal-Mart. Monbiot (1995) claimed that the use of English as the language of business and in the media drives out and threatens minority languages. As transnational corporations grow and become more powerful, there is a concern that the culture of capitalism, which is heavily influenced by Western or U.S. culture and commoditization, will develop into a world monoculture. *Commoditization* is the process by which market capitalism transforms things that were previously not viewed as economic goods (such as human genes) into something with a price. In fact, many aspects of culture have been *commodified* as evidenced in the shopping opportunities incorporated into experiences in which they previously did not exist (Tomlinson, 1999) such as visits to natural wonders or religious ceremonies. Cultures have always influenced one another, often enriching each other in the process, but some observers conclude that cultural synchronization has been occurring at an unprecedented rate and that 'never before has one particular cultural pattern been of such global dimensions and so comprehensive' (Hamelink, 1988).

Not all communication experts, however, share this opinion. Some maintain that the media have been decentralizing with the development of regional centers (e.g., Mexico for Spanish television, India for film, and Hong Kong for East Asian film and television) and indigenized programming. Thus, they argue that the homogenizing forces of the media like satellite television exist in tension with *heterogenization* (Sinclair, Jacka, & Cunningham, 1996). Tomlinson (1999) agreed with Hamelink that cultural synchronization is an unprecedented feature of global modernity but argued, 'Movement between cultural/geographical areas always involves interpretation, translation, mutation, adaptation, and "indigenisation" as the receiving culture brings its own cultural resources to bear, in dialectical fashion, upon "cultural imports"' (p. 84). And as Howes (1996) noted,

> 66 No imported object, Coca-Cola included, is completely immune from creolization. Indeed, one finds that Coke is often attributed with meanings and uses within particular cultures that are different from those imagined by the manufacturer. These include that it can smooth wrinkles (Russia), that it can revive a person from the dead (Haiti), indigenised through being mixed with other drinks, such as rum in the Caribbean to make Cuba Libre or aguardiente in Bolivia to produce Ponche Negro. Finally it seems that Coke is perceived as a 'native product' in many different places – that you will often find people who believe the drink originated in their country not in the United States. (p. 6) 99

Pressures for a global monoculture are counterbalanced by greater attention and efforts to maintain ethnic identity. Karliner (2000) argued that globalization may be responsible for the increasing popularity of indigenous movements to maintain ethnic identity. Although globalization was not the only cause of the Islamic revolution in Iran, it provided a target for rebellion and also forced the Muslims to 'identify' themselves and determine how they wanted to live in a global society (Lechner & Boli, 2000). Anthropologist Clifford Geertz (1998) wrote that the world is 'growing both more global and more divided, more thoroughly interconnected and more intricately partitioned at the same time' (p. 107). Although few social scientists support the creation of a monoculture (Guillén, 2001), this is a common fear among protesters.

Critics claim that globalization has irrevocably changed the social landscape of communities and constitutes a threat to national culture in various ways. For example, transnational agribusiness has replaced family farms in some areas, and cutting down forests inhabited by indigenous people makes it difficult if not impossible for them to maintain their traditional way of life (Brown, Renner, & Flavin, 1998; Keck & Sikkink, 2000). The spread of newer cultures and technologies may result in the loss of knowledge about traditional practices and arts more compatible with natural systems. EPZs draw people from rural areas, moving them out of reach of their traditional safety nets. It is difficult to pinpoint how much of this migration from their traditional communities and ways of life can be attributed directly to globalization versus traditional economic development and a desire to better one's life. People, particularly men, have been forced to migrate to find work throughout history. In the case of the Mexican maquiladoras (a type of EPZ) along the U.S. border, however, the primary employees are young women, which has had a marked impact on the social structure.

Table 4 summarizes the positive and negative impacts of globalization on culture and community.

The impact of globalization on environmental sustainability

Sustainability is defined as meeting the needs of present generations without compromising the ability of future generations to meet their own needs. The moral basis for sustainability is the ethical position that destroying Earth's future capacity to support life is wrong. Global environmental issues such as global warming, deforestation,

Positive effects	Negative effects
Increased cultural exposure, understanding, and cross-border ties	More mobility and disruption of rural life away from traditional safety nets
Encouraged proliferation of indigenous organizations and movements to preserve ethnic identity	Increased exposure to cultural homogenization
	Disintegration of some local communities

Table 4 The impact of globalization on culture and community

ozone depletion, reduction of biodiversity, degradation of ocean habitats (Lawrence et al., 1996), and pollution are the key areas affected by globalization.[6] Most of the empirical studies found in a literature review on globalization's impact on the environment, which are summarized below, focused on small pieces of the puzzle – they are 'local' in nature due to the difficulty of studying the environment as a whole (Osland, Dhanda, & Yuthas, 2002).

On the positive side of the ledger, globalization has caused some countries to make a narrower range of products more efficiently; in other words, it has given them a comparative advantage. It has been responsible for creating and exporting technologies that use fewer natural resources and result in less waste and pollution.[7] Globalization has facilitated the dissemination of practices like improved energy efficiency, lowered carbon combustion, dematerialization (reducing overall use of materials), substitution of resources with reduced environmental impact, and metal recovery technologies (Allenby & Richards, 1994; Graedel & Allenby, 1995; Socolow, Andrews, Berkhout, & Thomas, 1994). The industrial ecology movement has sought to improve environmental responsiveness at the same time that it reduces the global cost of production for corporations.

On the negative side, because of globalization, harmful technologies and activities have also been exported. Although better technology is available, companies do not always use it because it can be highly capital intensive (Socolow et al., 1994).

Globalization is blamed as a source of pollution. For instance, industrial toxic effluents and pesticide runoffs from agribusiness have destroyed river fish (Khor, 1996). A recent study overseen by the UN Environment Program warns of the danger of the *Asian cloud*, which may be causing premature death, flooding, and drought. Not all of the two-mile-thick cloud is a direct result of increased industrialization and globalization; traditional practices and forest clearing are also responsible in addition to auto emission, factories, and waste incineration.[8] Since prevailing winds can carry pollution clouds around the world in a short period, they are becoming a global environmental problem (United Nations Environment, 2002).

The spread of factories around the world has made more infrastructure necessary, which requires extracted substances from the earth. Globalization promotes the transportation of raw materials and goods using nonrenewable resources. Increased travel by workers seeking jobs (Brown, Renner, & Flavin, 1998) and by MNE employees uses fossil fuel and contributes to global warming. Additionally, because MNEs have moved their operations to countries where environmental laws are absent or not enforced, greater environmental degradation has occurred. Some MNEs have taken advantage of lowered environmental protection to sell harmful products abroad that are banned in more developed countries.

Critics claim that countries are more likely to export more commodities that increase the exploitation of natural resources as a result of globalization (French, 1993). There are numerous examples of environmental degradation such as deforestation, threats to biodiversity, and depletion of fish stocks (French, 1993; Goldsmith, 1997; Wilkes, 1995). Some of these problems stem from inappropriate use or overuse, whereas others involve inappropriate modern technologies such as modern trawl fishing that scrapes the bottom of the seabed and disturbs breeding grounds (Khor, 1996). Deforestation and technological innovations in agriculture have also resulted in habitat damage and extinction of species (Rackham, 1986).

Wackernagel and Rees (1996) popularized the concept of the *environmental footprint*. They demonstrated that developed countries require greater per capita material and energy flows, and therefore greater land surface, than do developing countries. The per capita effect on the earth's crust is greatest in the wealthiest countries that extract resources at a far greater rate than they can be replaced. The globalization of materially affluent lifestyles promulgated by the media and increased travel intensifies the demand for extracted materials (Duchin, 1996).

A conflict has arisen over the view of many developing countries that it is their turn to develop, as the more advanced developed countries did, without the constraints of environmental regulations. This dilemma pits the principle of equal capacity for economic development against the competing value of environmental sustainability.

The 1992 GATT annual report laid out the argument that increased trade will produce increased incomes, which will then result in more concern about the environment (Lawrence et al., 1996). Environmentalists, however, worry that globalization will encourage greater consumption as more goods are marketed to more people, creating artificial needs and using more natural resources (Mander & Goldsmith, 1996). Although globalization theoretically should result in greater efficiency in production, it has caused more surplus and scarcity (Brown, Renner, & Flavin, 1998), which points to a less than perfect use of resources.

It would be impossible to calculate the total impact of globalization on the environment, but there is a growing body of evidence documenting its harmful effects (Osland et al., 2002). Table 5 summarizes the positive and negative impacts of globalization on environmental sustainability.

Conclusions

The current debate raging on globalization and the explosion of publications on this topic reflect the importance this phenomenon has gained in recent years. When we expand the boundaries of the debate beyond the merits of free trade, a picture emerges of globalization as an uneven process that has resulted in both positive and negative consequences, both winners and losers. Thus, the quick answer to the question 'What is

Positive effects	Negative effects
Countries make a narrower range of products more efficiently	Caused surplus and scarcity
Relative efficiency of energy use is improving	Development and increased affluence lead to larger demands for materials and energy as well as increased waste and energy-related pollution
More systematic dematerialization through manufacturing changes	Export of damaging extraction technologies continues despite existence of alternative technologies
Substitution of harmful materials by resources with reduced environmental impact	Spread of factories requires increased infrastructure that uses more extracted materials
Some firms do environmental impact studies of product's entire lifecycle	Increased travel of workers and multinational enterprise employees uses fossil fuel and contributes to global warming
Transfer of efficient technologies to assist developing countries to increase production	Some developing nations are exposed to toxic or dangerous products and technologies
Creation and transfer of more efficient technologies to some countries	Increased consumption uses more natural resources
Use of alternative energy sources decreased carbon combustion	Increased advertising creates artificial needs
Increased income may lead to concern for environmental protection	Increasing fossil fuel combustion emits gases and particles into the atmosphere
	Increased transportation of raw materials uses nonrenewable resources
	Increased environmental degradation from factories in countries without enforced environmental protection laws
Modern trawl fishing maximizes the catch for maximum immediate revenue	Degradation due to agribusiness, logging, commercial fishing, and industrial waste
	Deforestation threatens species survival

Table 5 The impact of globalization on environmental sustainability

the impact of globalization?' is 'It's mixed.' Globalization is neither a panacea nor an unmitigated plague. Given the complexity and scope of the topic, it is difficult to determine with precision whether some of the problems linked to globalization would exist independently and to what degree. We can conclude, however, that globalization in its current state often involves serious tradeoffs such as economic development and jobs at the cost of environmental degradation and weakened labor protection. One important lesson is to include these tradeoffs in the debate and in calculating the total cost of global business.

Where people stand with regard to these tradeoffs often depends on their values and mindsets – in particular their beliefs regarding free markets, government intervention, the importance of local versus global concerns, and individualist versus communitarian views about the common good (Gladwin, 2002). Understanding these differences in basic assumptions is the first step in creating a civil discourse on the topic. Although businesspeople may disagree with antiglobalization protesters' rhetoric or tactics, another key lesson is that some of their criticisms are valid and should be taken into consideration. In Kobrin's (2001a) description of the antiglobalization protest movement, he concluded that their protests may be 'the canary in the mine' – the warning signal about globalization and the role of MNEs.

A third lesson is that businesspeople (and academics) should take a systems approach to globalization to avoid problems. Customers and protesters often see more linkages than some firms seem to consider, and many consumers do care about where their purchases come from. For example, the employees of a major company warned top executives about problems in overseas factories that could result in bad publicity. The person in charge ignored the warning, insisting, 'These are just contract workers – they aren't really a part of our company.' Years later, the company is still dealing with the PR fallout and targeting by protest groups. To the public, the distinction about whose employees they were was both legalistic and irrelevant. To avoid such problems, some MNEs are now entering into dialogue with all their various stakeholders, including nongovernmental organizations.

The accounting systems used by governments and businesses discourage a systems perspective. As long as accounting systems fail to take into consideration the environmental and social costs of doing business, firms can 'look good' while doing a fair amount of harm to the larger society. Social accounting is admittedly difficult, but its advantages may now outweigh its disadvantages (Sherman, Steingard, & Fitzgibbons, 2002).

As teachers, we need to make sure our students learn about the whole picture of globalization, including its unintended consequences. Yet my examination of international business textbooks yielded virtually no mention of the impact of globalization on the environment. Globalization is one of the most challenging and complex issues humans have ever faced. The way we teach it should reflect its requisite variety – a multidisciplinary focus including all stakeholders, understanding both the abstract as well as the human and environmental impact, teaching a thorough understanding of the pros and cons, and examining the solutions offered to counteract its problems.

Globalization is driven in large part by a mindset – the belief in the sanctity of markets, which Soros (1998) called 'market fundamentalism.' Some obvious caveats come to mind, however. First, some economists question whether markets are really 'free' (see Stiglitz, 2002, for an alternative view).

Second, once we broaden the globalization debate to include more than economic arguments, it seems obvious that free trade without any regulations or constraints has not been wholly successful (Giddens, 2000). The nations that have prospered under free trade have done so in part because they have laws and institutions that serve as checks and balances. In Giddens's (2000) view,

> Trade always needs a framework of institutions, as do other forms of economic development. Markets cannot be created by purely economic means, and how far a given economy should be exposed to the world market-place must depend upon a range of criteria. … Opening up a country or regions within it to free trade can undermine a local subsistence economy. An area that becomes dependent upon a few products sold on world markets is very vulnerable to shifts in prices as well as to technological change. (p. 35)

Business scholars could help identify the criteria that Giddens mentioned and conceptualize globalization as occurring with a broader systemic context. Cookie-cutter approaches to economic development seldom work. Strategies have to fit the local context of each country with its unique institutions and historical, political, and social context.

Third, in addition to a framework of institutions, trade has to be embedded in a broader framework of shared social values that include at least some degree of concern for social justice and the common good.[9] Privatization has been successful in some countries but not where government officials or their cronies bought undervalued state assets and established monopolies. Either the rule of law or shared values is needed to prevent a winner-takes-all mentality. In their absence, perhaps MNEs have to accept that they too have social responsibilities and a broader role to play in society than maximizing shareholder wealth.[10] Concentration solely on economic growth no doubt made sense in an earlier time, but given what is known today about globalization and its impact, our focus should broaden to include a more balanced, integrated approach to economic development (United Nations Development, 2002).

If we needed further convincing that globalization demands a systems view, we might be persuaded by the backlash and counterbalancing forces it has provoked. The protest movements,[11] the growth of nongovernmental organizations, and the movements affirming ethnic identity are all reactions in part to globalization or perhaps an inherent part of globalization. It is more difficult to forecast how the nature of globalization might change in response to these forces. Some observers assume that the current state of globalization is akin to the robber baron era in the United States – a period of excess and abuse that eventually sparked a backlash resulting in policies and laws. Kell and Levin (2002) described globalization as an incomplete experiment in human history with systemic deficiencies that cause instability and social injustice. A consensus of sorts seems to be building around the need to somehow 'tame' globalization, but there is no clarity yet about how this will occur, what form it will take, and who has the requisite authority to pull it off.[12]

One interesting response to globalization is the United Nations' Global Compact. This initiative, led by Secretary-General Kofi Annan, consists of a global network of companies, nongovernmental organizations, major international labor federations, and several UN agencies. Its objective is to 'create a more stable, equitable and inclusive global market by making its nine principles an integral part of business activities everywhere' (United Nations, 2002). These principles, which involve human rights, labor standards, and environmental practices, are an attempt to establish a universal standard.

> Principle 1: Support and respect the protection of international human rights within their sphere of influence.
>
> Principle 2: Make sure their own corporations are not complicit in human rights abuses.
>
> Principle 3: Uphold freedom of association and the effective recognition of the right to collective bargaining.
>
> Principle 4: Uphold the elimination of all forms of forced and compulsory labor.
>
> Principle 5: Uphold the effective abolition of child labor.

Principle 6: Uphold the elimination of discrimination in respect of employment and occupation.

Principle 7: Support a precautionary approach to environmental challenges.

Principle 8: Undertake initiatives to promote greater environmental responsibility.

Principle 9: Encourage the development and diffusion of environmentally friendly technologies (United Nations, 2002).

The Global Compact is attempting to build shared values and create a forum for dialogue and institutional learning that will result in social change. In addition to recruiting companies who agree to integrate the nine principles into their business operations, the program's goals are to establish a learning bank that shares lessons on applying the principles, conducts issues dialogues, and generates partnership projects among the different stakeholders. Such partnerships could theoretically decrease the polarization among various groups. The architects of the Global Compact hope that it will be part of the solution to globalization's problems but do not view it as the definitive solution. To date, 700 companies have voluntarily joined the compact.

As stated in the introduction, much of the globalization literature has an ideological bent, which means there is a need for objective research on globalization's impact and for more questioning about the basic assumption of globalization itself. The U.S. acceptance of globalization as the status quo may reflect cultural and historical influences. In his Pulitzer Prize-winning book, *The Global Squeeze*, journalist Richard Longworth (1999) concluded:

> The global economy is not an act of God, like a virus or a volcano, but the result of economic actions taken by human beings and thus responsive to human control. There is no need to say, as many American economists and businesspeople do, that the market knows best and must be obeyed. This cultural capitalism is confined mostly to the United States and the other English-speaking nations. Other nations, in Europe and in Asia, see the market as the source of both bountiful benefits and lethal damage, and are determined to temper this force to their own priorities. (pp. 4–5)

Given the ever-evolving history of economic development, trade, and international relations, there is little reason for scholars to assume that globalization as we know it today is the final version. Such an assumption is dangerous if it prevents us from seeing other possibilities and the systemic consequences of the current system. Business scholars have made good progress in describing this system and documenting what it takes to be profitable. Now it's time for us to consider what else we can contribute to the debate on globalization and whether we can take a stronger leadership role in influencing the way people think about and practice global business in the future.

Notes

[1] The World Trade Organization's major functions are to administer trade agreements, serve as a forum for trade negotiations, settle trade disputes, review national trade policies, and assist developing nations in trade policy issues.

[2] Having warned you about the potential biases of globalization writers, it's only fair to explain my own stance and my impetus for writing this article. At the behest of the Northwest Earth Institute, I joined a discussion group on the impact of globalization on the environment and commenced reading. I began with few preconceived notions and with no strong inclination either for or against globalization. If anything, I was positively disposed to creating jobs in lesser developed countries, since I had learned during a previous career in international development that providing employment goes a long way toward solving a variety of social ills for poor people. In the conclusion, I will explain the position my reading led me to.

[3] Simon Valaskakis is Canada's ambassador to the Organization for Economic Cooperation and Development (OECD) in Paris and a professor of economics at the University of Montreal.

[4] As of 2002, there were more than 850 export processing zones in the world employing 27 million workers (Drezner, 2000). See International Labour Organization, *Labour and Social Issues Relating to Export Processing Zones* (1998), for information on conditions.

[5] The Organization for Economic Cooperation and Development is an international organization that consists of 30 industrialized, market-economy countries. Their representatives meet 'to exchange information and harmonize policy with a view to maximizing economic growth within Member countries and assisting non-Member countries develop more rapidly' (Organization, 2003). For more information, see http://www.oecdwash.org/ABOUT/aboutmain.htm.

[6] Bioengineering is another controversial topic. Genetic engineering can preserve existing species and create new varieties, but the impact of the latter on biological systems is still unknown. There are also ethical concerns about the ability to patent genetically engineered species and human tissues, cells, and organs.

[7] See the United Nations Conference on Environment and Development (1992) for information on the successful transfer of technological innovations. For a more complete analysis of the environmental impact of globalization, see J. Osland, K. Dhanda, and K. Yuthas (2002).

[8] The Asian cloud is the result of traditional practices such as wood- and dung-burning stoves, cooking fires, and forest clearing as well as auto emissions, factories, and waste incineration.

[9] See John Ruggie's (1982) description of embedded liberalism, which was originally conceptualized as a compromise of multilateral trade and domestic stability.

[10] *Business Week* devoted its cover story to 'Global Capitalism: Can It Be Made to Work Better?' in its November 6, 2000, issue (Engardio & Belton, 2000). Its conclusions are similar to those found here and acknowledge the need for more social responsibility on the part of multinationals and a more realistic view of economic policy that has driven globalization.

[11] For an interesting account of this movement, see Kobrin (2001a).

[12] Articulating the suggested solutions lies outside the scope of this article, but one starting point is to look at the lessons learned from 50 years of tackling various global problems in Simmons and Oudraat (2001).

References

Allenby, B. R., & Richards, D. (1994). *Greening of industrial ecosystems.* Washington, DC: National Academy Press.

Annan, K. (1999, January 31). *Address to Davos World Economic Forum*, Davos, Switzerland.

Baldwin, R. E., & Martin, P. (1999). *Two waves of globalization: Superficial similarities, fundamental differences* (NBER Working Paper Series 6904). Cambridge, MA: National Bureau of Economic Research.

Berry, A. (1996, January). *Distributional impact of market-oriented reforms.* Paper prepared at the Association for Comparative Economic Studies, San Francisco.

Brown, C. R., Renner, M., & Flavin, C. (1998). *Vital Signs.* New York: Norton.

Brown, J. (1992). Corporation as community: A new image for a new era. In J. Renesch (Ed.), *New traditions in business* (pp. 123–139). San Francisco: Barrett-Kohler.

Champlin, D., and Olson, P. (1999). The impact of globalization on U.S. labor markets: redefining the debate. *Journal of Economic Issues, 33*(2), 443–451.

Charnovitz, S. (1992, May). Environmental and labour standards in trade. *The World Economy, 15*(8), 343.

Clarke, T. (2001). *Silent coup: Confronting the big business takeover of Canada.* Retrieved January 12, 2001, from www3.simpatico.ca/tryegrowth/MAI_can.htm

Cox, R. W. (1996). A perspective on globalization. In J. H. Mittelman (Ed.), *Globalization: Critical reflections* (pp. 21–30). Boulder, CO: Lynne Rienner.

Daly, H. (1996). *Beyond growth.* Boston: Beacon.

Dohrs, L., & Garfunkel, J. (1999, February). *Time to talk about trade and human rights? Trade and human rights: A Pacific Rim perspective, a source handbook.* Seattle, WA: Global Source Education.

Drezner, D. W. (2000, November/December). Bottom feeders. *Foreign Policy,* 64–70.

Duchin, F. (1996). Population change, lifestyle, and technology: How much difference can they make? *Population and Development Review,* 22(2), 321–330.

Duin, S. (2000, December 3). Reich displays designer hips and a deft mind. *The Oregonian,* B-1.

Engardio, P., & Belton, C. (2000, November 6). Global capitalism: Can it be made to work better? *BusinessWeek,* 72–76.

Engardio, P., Bernstein, A., & Kripalani, M. (2003, February 3). Is your job next? *BusinessWeek,* 50–60.

Evenett, S. J. (1999). The world trading system: The road ahead. *Finance & Development,* 36(4), 22.

Frank, R. H., & Cook, P. J. (1995). *The winner-takes-all society.* New York: Free Press.

French, H. (1993). *Costly tradeoffs reconciling trade and the environment.* Washington, DC: World Watch Institute.

Gaunt, J. (2002, July 7). Globalization has helped the poor, study says. Reuters.

Geertz, C. (1998). The world in pieces: Culture and politics at the end of the century. *Focaal: Tigdschrift voor Antropologie,* 32, 91–117.

Giddens, A. (2000). *Runaway world: How globalization is reshaping our lives.* New York: Routledge.

Gladwin, T. (2002, March). *Keynote address presented at the Western Academy of Management,* Santa Fe, New Mexico.

Goldsmith, E. (1997). Can the environment survive the global economy? *The Ecologist,* 27(6), 242–249.

Gottschalk, P., & Smeeding, T. (1997). Cross national comparisons of earnings and income inequality. *Journal of Economic Literature,* 35(2), 633–687.

Graedel, T. E., & Allenby, B. R. (1995). *Industrial ecology.* New York: Prentice-Hall.

Graham, E. M., & Krugman, P. R. (1991). *Foreign direct investment in the United States* (2nd ed.). Washington, DC: Institute for International Economics.

Grunberg, I. (1998). Double jeopardy: Globalization, liberalization and the fiscal squeeze. *World Development,* 26(4), 591–605.

Guillén, M. F. (2001). Is globalization civilizing, destructive or feeble? A critique of six key debates in the social science literature. *Annual Review of Sociology,* 27, 235–260.

Hamelink, C. J. (1988). *Cultural autonomy in global communications.* New York: Longmans.

Harris, J. M., & Goodwin, N. R. (1995). *A survey of ecological economics.* Washington, DC: Island Press.

Hirschman, A. O. (1982, December). Rival interpretations of market society: Civilizing, destructive, or feeble? *Journal of Economic Literature,* 20, 1463–1484.

Holmes, S., & Ostrovsky, S. (2003, February 3). The new cold war at Boeing. *BusinessWeek,* 58–59.

Howes, D. (Ed.). (1996). *Cross-cultural consumption: Global markets, local realities.* London: Routledge.

International Labour Organization. (1998). *Labour and social issues relating to export processing zones.* Geneva: Author.

International Monetary Fund. (1999, May). *World economic outlook: A survey by the staff of the International Monetary Fund.* Washington, DC: Author.

Joint Venture. (2003). *Joint Venture's 2003 index of Silicon Valley.* San Jose, CA: Author.

Karliner, J. (2000). Grassroots globalization: Reclaiming the blue planet. In F. J. Lechner & J. Boli (Eds.), *The globalization reader* (pp. 34–38). Oxford: Blackwell.

Keck, M. E., & Sikkink, K. (2000). Environmental advocacy networks. In F. J. Lechner & J. Boli (Eds.), *The globalization reader* (pp. 392–399). Oxford: Blackwell.

Kell, G., & Levin, D. (2002, August). *The evolution of the global compact network: An historic experiment in learning and action.* Paper presented at the Academy of Management meeting, Denver, Colorado.

Khor, M. (1996). Global economy and the third world. In J. Mander & J. Goldsmith (Eds.), *The case against the global economy and for a turn toward the local* (pp. 47–59). San Francisco: Sierra Club.

Klein, N. (2000). *No logo.* New York: Picador.

Kobrin, S. J. (1997). The architecture of globalization: State sovereignty in a networked global economy. In J. H. Dunning (Ed.), *Governments, globalization, and international business* (pp. 146–171). New York: Oxford University Press.

Kobrin, S. J. (2001a, February). *Our resistance is as global as your oppression: Multinational corporations, the protest movement and the future of global governance.* Paper presented at the meeting of the International Studies Association, Chicago.

Kobrin, S. J. (2001b). Sovereignty @ bay: Globalization, multinational enterprise, and the international political system. In A. Rugman & T. Brewer (Eds.), *The Oxford handbook of international business* (pp. 181–205). New York: Oxford University Press.

Krishnan, R. (1996). December 1995: The first revolt against globalization. *Monthly Review*, 48(1), 1–23.

Krugman, P. (1994). Does third world growth hurt first world prosperity? *Harvard Business Review*, 72(4), 113–121.

Lavelle, L., Jespersen, F., Ante, S., and Kerstetter, J. (2003, April 21). Executive pay. *Business Week*, pp. 86–90.

Lawrence, R. A. (1995, January). U.S. wage trends in the 1980s: The role of international factors. *Federal Reserve Bank of New York Economic Policy Review*, 2(1), 18–25.

Lawrence, R. Z., Rodrik, D., & Whalley, J. (1996). *Emerging agenda for global trade: High stakes for developing countries.* Washington, DC: Overseas Development Council.

Lawrence, R. Z., & Slaughter, M. (1993). Trade and U.S. wages in the 1980s: Giant sucking sound or small hiccup? *Brookings Papers on Economic Activity: Microeconomics*, 2, 161–210.

Leamer, E. (1998). In search of Stolper-Samuelson linkages between international trade and lower wages. In S. Collins (Ed.), *Imports, exports, and the American worker* (pp. 141–214). Washington, DC: Brookings Institution Press.

Lechner, F. J., & Boli, J. (Eds.). (2000). *The globalization reader.* Oxford: Blackwell.

Lee, E. (1996). Globalization and employment: Is anxiety justified? *International Labour Review*, 135(5), 486–497.

Lee, E. (1997). Globalization and labour standards: A review of issues. *International Labour Review*, 136(2), 173–189.

Levi, M. (2000, February). *Labor unions and the WTO.* Speech given at the University of Washington, Seattle.

Longworth, R. C. (1999). *The global squeeze.* Chicago: Contemporary Books.

MacBride, S., & Roach, C. (2000). The new international information order. In F. J. Lechner & J. Boli (Eds.), *The globalization reader* (pp. 286–292). Oxford: Blackwell.

Mander, J., & Goldsmith, E. (Eds.). (1996). *The case against the global economy and for a turn toward the local.* San Francisco: Sierra Club.

Marquand, D. (1998). *The new reckoning.* Cambridge: Polity.

Monbiot, G. (1995, August 13). Global villagers speak with forked tongues. *Guardian*, 24.

Murphy, K., and Topel, R. (1997). Unemployment and nonemployment. *American Economic Review* 87(2), 295–300.

Ohmae, K. (1995). *The end of the nation state.* New York: Free Press.

Organization for Economic Cooperation and Development (OECD). (1996). *Trade, employment, and labour standards: A study of core workers' rights and international trade.* Paris: Author.

Organization for Economic Cooperation and Development (OECD). (1997). Trade, earnings and employment: Assessing the impact of trade with emerging economies on OECD labour markets. *OECD Employment Outlook*, 93–128.

Organization for Economic Cooperation and Development (OECD). (2003). *About the OECD.* Retrieved on March 27, 2003, from http://www.oecdwash.org/ABOUT/aboutmain.htm

Osland, J. S., Dhanda, K., & Yuthas, K. (2002). Globalization and environmental sustainability: An analysis of the impact of globalization using the Natural Step framework. In S. Sharma & M. Starik (Eds.), *Research in corporate sustainability: The evolving theory and practice of organizations in the natural environment* (pp. 31–60). Cheltenham, UK: Edward Elgar.

Press, E. (2002, June 10). Rebel with a cause: The re-education of Joseph Stiglitz. *The Nation*, 11–16.

Pritchett, L. (1997, 3rd trimester). La distribution passee et future du revenu mondial. [The once (and future) distribution of world income]. *Economie Internationale*, 0(71), 19–42.

Rackham, O. (1986). *The history of the countryside.* London: J. M. Dent & Sons.

Renesch, J. (Ed.). (1992). *New traditions in business.* San Francisco: Barrett-Kohler.

Robbins, D. J. (1995). *Trade, trade liberalization and inequality in Latin America and East Asia: Synthesis of seven country studies.* Unpublished manuscript, Harvard University.

Rodrik, D. (1997). *Has globalization gone too far?* Washington, DC: Institute for International Economics.

Ruggie, J. (1982). International regimes, transactions and change: Embedded liberalism in the postwar economic order. *International Organization*, 36(2): 379–415.

Sachs, J., & Schatz, H. (1994). *Trade and jobs in US manufacturing* (Brookings Papers on Economic Activity, 1, pp. 1–84). Washington, DC: Brookings Institution.

Schmidheiny, S. (1992). *Changing course*. Cambridge, MA: MIT Press.

Scott, R. E., Lee, T., & Schmitt, J. (1997). *Trading away good jobs: An examination of employment and wages in the US 1979-94*. Washington, DC: Economic Policy Institute.

Sherman, R.W., Steingard, D. S., & Fitzgibbons, D. E. (2002). Sustainable stakeholder accounting: Beyond complementarity and towards integration in environmental accounting. In S. Sharma & M. Starik (Eds.), *Research in corporate sustainability: The evolving theory and practice of organizations in the natural environment* (pp. 257–294). Cheltenham, UK: Edward Elgar.

Simmons, P. J., & de Jonge Oudraat, C. (Eds.). (2001). *Managing global issues: Lessons learned*. Washington, DC: Carnegie Endowment.

Sinclair, J., Jacka, E., & Cunningham, S. (1996). *New patterns in global television: Peripheral vision*. Oxford: Oxford University Press.

Slaughter, M. J., & Swagel, P. (2000). Does globalization lower wages and export jobs? In F. J. Lechner & J. Boli (Eds.), *The globalization reader* (pp. 177–180). Oxford: Blackwell.

Socolow, R., Andrews, C., Berkhout, F., & Thomas, V. (1994). *Industrial ecology and global change*. New York: Cambridge University Press.

Soros, G. (1998). *The crisis of global capitalism*. New York: Public Affairs.

Soros, G. (2002). *George Soros on globalization*. New York: Public Affairs.

Stiglitz, J. (2002). *Globalization and its discontent*. New York: Norton.

Sutherland, P. D. (1998, November 1). Sharing the bounty. *Banker*, 148(873).

Takashi, I. (1997). Changing Japanese labor and employment system. *Journal of Japanese Trade & Industry*, 16(4), 20–24.

Temple, J. (1999). The new growth evidence. *Journal of Economic Literature*, 37, 112–156.

Tisdell, C. (1997). Local communities, conservation and sustainability: Institutional change, altered governance and Kant's social philosophy. *International Journal of Social Economics*, 24(12), 1361–1320.

Tomlinson, J. (1999). *Globalization and culture*. Chicago: University of Chicago Press.

Tyson, D. L. (1999, May 31). Why the US should welcome China to the WTO. *BusinessWeek*, 30.

United Nations. (2002). *Global compact*. Retrieved on August 29, 2002, from http://65.214.34.30/un/gc/unweb. nsf/webprintview/thenine.htm

United Nations Conference on Trade and Development (UNCTAD). (1992). *World investment report*. Geneva: Author.

United Nations Conference on Trade and Development (UNCTAD). (1995). *World investment report*. Geneva: Author.

United Nations Conference on Trade and Development (UNCTAD). (1997). *Trade and development report*. Geneva: Author.

United Nations Conference on Trade and Development (UNCTAD). (1998). *World investment report*. Geneva: Author.

United Nations Conference on Trade and Development (UNCTAD). (1999). *North-south trade, employment and inequality: The social responsibility of transnational corporations*. Geneva: Author.

United Nations Development Programme (UNDP). (1996). *Human development report 1996*. New York: Oxford University Press.

United Nations Development Programme (UNDP). (1999). *Human development report 1999*. New York: Oxford University Press.

United Nations Development Programme (UNDP). (2001). *Human development report 2001*. New York: Oxford University Press.

United Nations Development Programme (UNDP). (2002). *Human development reports – fast facts*. Retrieved on September 9, 2002, from http://www/undp.org/dpa/publications

Valaskakis, K. (1998, Summer). The challenge of strategic governance: Can globalization be managed? *Optimum*, 28(2), 26–40.

Wackernagel, M., & Rees, W. (1996). *Our ecological footprint*. Gabriola Island, BC: New Society Publishers.

Waters, M. (1995). *Globalization*. New York: Routledge.

Wilkes, A. (1995). Prawns, profits and protein: Aquaculture and food production. *Ecologist*, 25, 2–3.

Wood, A. (1994). *North-south trade, employment and inequality: Changing fortunes in a skill-driven world*. Oxford: Clarendon.

Wood, A. (1995, Summer). How trade hurt unskilled workers. *Journal of Economic Perspectives*, 9(3), 57–81.

Wood, A. (1997). Openness and wage inequality in developing countries: The Latin American challenge to East Asian conventional wisdom. *World Bank Economic Review*, 11(1), 33–57.

Wood, A. (1998, September). Globalization and the rise in labour market inequalities. *Economic Journal*, 198(450), 1463–1483.

World Trade Organization. (2003). Retrieved March 28, 2003, from http://www.wto.org

Yergin, D., & Stanislaw, J. (2000). The commanding heights: The battle between government and the marketplace that is remaking the modern world. In F. J. Lechner & J. Boli (Eds.), *The globalization reader* (pp. 212–220). Oxford: Blackwell.

Zhao, L. (1998, April). The impact of foreign direct investment on wages and employment. *Oxford Economic Papers*, 50(2), 284–302.

JOYCE S. OSLAND is professor of management at San Jose State University, California. Her current research and consulting focus includes expatriates, cultural sense making, global leadership, Latin American management, and globalization. Her research appears in journals such as *Academy of Management Review*, *Academy of Management Executive*, *Journal of Management Inquiry*, and *HR Management*. Dr. Osland is the author of *The Adventure of Working Abroad* (Jossey-Bass, 1995) as well as *Organizational Behavior: An Experiential Approach* (Prentice Hall, 2001) and *The Organizational Behavior Reader* (Prentice IIall, 2001), both in their seventh editions. Prior to becoming an academic, She worked in Latin America and West Africa in the field of international development. She is currently president of the Western Academy of Management and was awarded their President's Award for service and leadership in 2002. Her e-mail address is osland_j@cob.sjsu.edu.

READING 2
Cultivating a global mindset*

Anil K. Gupta and Vijay Govindarajan

The economic landscape of the world is changing rapidly and becoming increasingly global. For virtually every medium-sized to large company in developed as well as developing economies, market opportunities, critical resources, cutting-edge ideas, and competitors lurk not just around the corner in the home market but increasingly in distant and often little-understood regions of the world as well. How successful a company is at exploiting emerging opportunities and tackling their accompanying challenges depends crucially on how intelligent it is at observing and interpreting the dynamic world in which it operates. Creating a global mindset is one of the central ingredients required for building such intelligence. In this article, we address the following issues: why mindset matters, what a global mindset is, the value of a global mindset, and finally, what companies can do to cultivate a global mindset.

Heterogeneity across cultures and markets is a pervasive feature of the global economic landscape. As illustrated by the initial failure of many American firms in the Japanese market,[1] ignoring such heterogeneity can be a costly mistake for any company trying to build and successfully exploit a presence across borders. Importantly, however, in dealing with heterogeneity across cultures and markets, going to the other extreme and becoming its prisoner can be an equally costly mistake. As Percy Barnevik, the architect of ABB and its first CEO, aptly observed:

> Global managers have exceptionally open minds. They respect how different countries do things, and they have the imagination to appreciate why they do them that way. But, they are also incisive; they push the limits of the culture. Global managers don't passively accept it when someone says, 'You can't do that in Italy or Spain because of the unions,' or 'You can't do that in Japan because of the Ministry of Finance.' They sort through the debris of cultural excuses and find opportunities to innovate.[2]

As the previous observations suggest, how multinational companies and their managers perceive and interpret the global social and economic environment around them has a major impact on the strategies that they pursue and the success of these strategies. Building on this premise, our goal in this article is to explore the concept of global mindset, differentiate it from alternatives such as parochial or diffused mindsets,

---

* *Academy of Management Executive*, 2002, vol. 16, no. 1.

discuss why a global mindset is important in the business world of today, and present guidelines regarding what managers and companies can and should do to cultivate a global mindset.

What is a global mindset?

The concept of mindset

In order to understand the meaning of the term global mindset, it is important first to achieve clarity regarding the underlying core concept of mindset. Generically, the mindset concept has had a long history in the fields of cognitive psychology and, more recently, organization theory, where scholars have focused on the question of how people and organizations make sense of the world with which they interact.[3] The basic research findings can be summarized as follows:

1 As human beings, we are limited in our ability to absorb and process information. Thus, we are constantly challenged by the complexity, ambiguity, and dynamism of the information environment around us.[4]

2 We address this challenge through a process of filtration. We are selective in what we absorb and biased in how we interpret it.[5] The term mindset refers to these cognitive filters.

3 Our mindsets are a product of our histories and evolve through an iterative process. Our current mindset guides the collection and interpretation of new information. To the extent that this new information is consistent with the current mindset, it reinforces that mindset. From time to time, however, new information appears that is truly novel and inconsistent with the existing mindset. When this happens, we either reject the new information or change our mindset. The likelihood that our mindsets will undergo a change depends largely on how explicitly self-conscious we are of our current mindsets: the more hidden and subconscious our cognitive filters, the greater the likelihood of rigidity.[6]

4 Every organization is a collectivity of individuals. Each individual has a mindset which continuously shapes and is shaped by the mindsets of others in the collectivity. How this shaping and reshaping of mindsets occurs depends crucially on who has how much power and who interacts with whom, in what context, for what purpose, and so forth. Hence, how the firm is organized and how decision-making power and influence are distributed within the organization play a decisive role in the shaping of the collective mindset.

5 Organizational mindsets can change and evolve in four primary ways:[7] (1) new experiences which cause a change in the mindsets of organizational members, (2) a change in the relative power of different individuals, (3) a change in the organizational and social processes through which members meet and interact with each other, and (4) a change in the mix of members comprising the firm such that the mindsets of new members differ from those departing. As illustrated by the mid-1990s shift from John Akers to Lou Gerstner at IBM,[8] the need for a different mindset is one of the most common reasons for involuntary changes in CEO positions.

Mindsets as knowledge structures

Research in cognitive psychology has also revealed that mindsets exist in the form of knowledge structures and that the two primary attributes of any knowledge structure are differentiation and integration.[9]

Differentiation in knowledge structures refers to the narrowness vs. breadth of knowledge that the individual or organization brings to the particular context. Consider, for example, the proverbial functional expert with almost no exposure outside the functional area. In colloquial terms, we would say that this person has tunnel vision – a classic case of low differentiation in knowledge structure. In contrast, a manager with significant experience in multiple functional areas has a more highly differentiated knowledge structure and is unlikely to exhibit the tunnel-vision syndrome.

Integration in knowledge structures refers to the extent to which the person or organization can integrate disparate knowledge elements. For organizations or people with low differentiation, integration is not an issue; there is no need to integrate if the knowledge is not differentiated. Integration is a critical attribute of mindsets in those contexts where differentiation is high.

Each of us, at one time or another, probably has met someone who appears to swing from one position to another as a result of being heavily influenced by whoever the person happens to meet last. Using our terminology, such a person is exhibiting a combination of high differentiation coupled with low integration (High D-Low I). In contrast, a person who seeks and values multiple opinions but then is able to develop an integrative perspective has a combination of high differentiation and high integration (High D-High I).

At the organizational level, consider a team of technical experts strongly focused on new product development. The mindset of such a team, operating in the silo of its members' expertise, would be Low D-High I. Compare this team to a cross-functional team whose composition includes experts from several functional areas such as R&D, manufacturing, marketing, after-sales service, and accounting but that has no strong leadership. The mindset of such a diffused/unfocused team would be High D-Low I. Finally, consider another team that in addition to being multifunctional has a strong leader who helps the team synthesize the diverse perspectives. The mindset of such a team would be High D-High I.

The concept of global mindset

Building on the language of differentiation and integration, we define global mindset as a High D-High I mindset in the context of different cultures and markets.[10] More concretely, we would define a global mindset as one that combines an openness to and awareness of diversity across cultures and markets with a propensity and ability to synthesize across this diversity.[11] The simultaneous focus on developing a deep understanding of diversity and an ability to synthesize across diversity is illustrated well by Home Décor Inc. (disguised name), a U.S.-based household accessories company. Founded barely five years ago, the company is one of the fastest growing manufacturers of household accessories, with a five-star customer base that includes some of the most prestigious retail chains in the United States. The CEO, an immigrant from China, summarizes the company's strategy succinctly as 'combining Chinese costs with Japanese quality, European design, and American marketing. There are other Chinese competitors in the market, but along with Chinese costs, what they bring is Chinese quality. On the other hand, our American competitors have excellent product quality but their costs are too high. We can and do beat both of them.'

As depicted in Figure 1, it is useful to compare and contrast a global mindset (High D-High I situation) with two alternative mindsets regarding the global economic environment: a parochial mindset (Low D-High I situation), and a diffused mindset (High D-Low I situation).[12] As an illustration of a parochial mindset, consider the situation at Ikea, the world's largest furniture retailer. Until as recently as a decade ago, Swedish nationals constituted virtually the entire top management team of the company. Fluency in the Swedish language was considered essential at the senior levels. And, when the company entered foreign markets, for example, the United States, it replicated its traditional Swedish concepts such as no home delivery, a Swedish cafeteria, beds that required sheets conforming to Swedish rather than U.S. standards, and so forth. In short, Ikea saw the world through a Swedish filter; it was almost blind to alternative views of market reality. Not surprisingly, the outcome was a very disappointing performance and unambiguous feedback that this mindset would be a major barrier to success in the U.S. market.

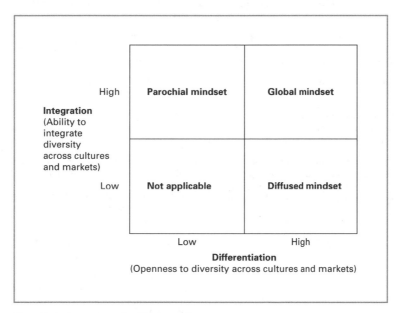

Figure 1 Alternative mindsets: a conceptual framework

As Ikea re-examined its format for U.S. operations, it faced two challenges: first, to develop a better understanding of how the needs and buying behavior of American customers differed from those it had served in the past, and second, to synthesize this understanding with its beliefs and competencies pertaining to the furniture business. Without the former, the company would continue to suffer from a misalignment between its product and service offerings and market needs; without the latter, it would be unable to develop competitive advantage over incumbent players. For Ikea, the shift from a parochial to a more global mindset required an understanding of differences between Europe and the U.S. and, equally important, also a commitment to synthesize these differences and develop a more integrative perspective on the global furniture retailing industry.

In contrast to a parochial mindset, we have observed a diffused mindset most often in the case of professional service firms (e.g., in accounting, advertising, and management consulting). These firms are often structured as networks of local partner-owned organizations. In such contexts, the power of the CEO and even the senior management team is severely constrained. While certain individual executives at the top may have highly developed global mindsets, the firm as a whole behaves as if it has a diffused mindset. The appreciation for and understanding of local issues and local differences is great, but often the ability to see the bigger global picture is inadequate.[13]

Figure 2 presents sets of diagnostic questions that managers and organizations can use to assess the extent to which they have a global mindset.

Assessing individuals

1. In interacting with others, does national origin have an impact on whether or not you assign equal status to them?

2. Do you consider yourself as open to ideas from other countries and cultures as you are to ideas from your own country and culture of origin?

3. Does finding yourself in a new cultural setting cause excitement, or fear and anxiety?

4. When you are in another culture, are you sensitive to the cultural differences without becoming a prisoner of these differences?

5. When you interact with people from other cultures, what do you regard as more important: understanding them as individuals or viewing them as representatives of their national cultures?

6. Do you regard your values to be a hybrid of values acquired from multiple cultures as opposed to just one culture?

Assessing organizations

1. Is your company a leader or a laggard in your industry in discovering and pursuing emerging market opportunities in all corners of the world?

2. Do you regard all customers wherever they live in the world as important as customers in your own domestic market?

3. Do you draw your employees from the worldwide talent pool?

4. Do employees of every nationality have the same opportunity to move up the career ladder all the way to the top?

5. In scanning the horizon for potential competitors, do you examine all economic regions of the world?

6. In selecting a location for any activity, do you seek to optimize the choice on a truly global basis?

7. Do you view the global arena as not just a 'playground' (i.e., market to exploit) but also a 'school' (i.e., source of new ideas and technology)?

8. Do you perceive your company as having a global identity with many homes, or do you instead perceive your company as having a strong national identity?

Figure 2 Assessing the global mindset of individuals and organizations

The value of a global mindset

The central value of a global mindset lies in enabling the company to combine speed with accurate response. It is easy to be fast, simplistic, and wrong. It also is easy to become a prisoner of diversity, get intimidated by enormous differences across markets, and stay back, or if the company does venture abroad, to end up reinventing the wheel in every market. The benefit of a global mindset derives from the fact that, while the company has a grasp of and insight into the needs of the local market, it is also able to build cognitive bridges across these needs and between these needs and the company's own global experience and capabilities.

These benefits can manifest themselves in one or more of the following types of competitive advantage:

- An early-mover advantage in identifying emerging opportunities;
- Greater sophistication and more fine-grained analysis regarding the trade-off between local adaptation and global standardization;
- Smoother coordination across complementary activities distributed across borders;
- Faster roll-out of new product concepts and technologies; and
- More rapid and efficient cross-border sharing of best practices across subsidiaries.

As an illustration of how valuable a global mindset can be, let us examine how its presence or absence might affect Microsoft's strategy regarding the Chinese market. In China, there is obviously a huge market for software today with an even larger market tomorrow. However, the promise of the Chinese market is accompanied by perils. Software piracy has been rampant. Public policy tends to be unpredictable and often favors local over foreign enterprises. The market's sophistication level lags a few years behind that of the more economically developed countries, but this gap is closing. And, the use of Chinese characters requires, at the very least, a major adaptation of the software's user interface and possibly even the internal code. We would contend that when Microsoft formulates and reformulates its strategy for China, it will not be successful if its mindset vis-à-vis China is lacking along either of the two dimensions; if it is shallow in its understanding of what is happening in China and/or if it is not sufficiently able to see events in China from a more integrative global perspective. China is not the only country where Microsoft faces dedicated pirates, nor is it the only one with a nationalistic public-policy regime.

Can Microsoft bring to bear lessons learned from other markets as it analyzes China? Alternatively, might lessons from China be relevant in other markets? What does Microsoft's experience in other countries say about the rate at which the sophistication of the Chinese market might evolve and about how quickly the company should bring leading-edge products and services to China? Might China be one of the best global centers for Microsoft's research into voice and character recognition technologies? Given a global mindset, these are just some of the fundamental questions that would be raised in the process of developing the company's China strategy. In the absence of a global mindset, on the other hand, few if any of these questions would be identified or addressed.

The quest for a global mindset

In thinking about how to achieve a global mindset, it is critical to remember that the key word is cultivation and that the quest for a global mindset is a ceaseless journey. Living in a complex and dynamic world as we do, the extent to which one could continue to explore the world's diversity as well as the linkages across this diversity has no upper limit. No matter how developed the global mindset of a Nokia, a Toyota, or a Cisco Systems may appear today, twenty years from now their current mindsets are, in relative terms, likely to appear quite limited.

Building on ideas from cognitive psychology and organization theory regarding development of knowledge,[14] we would contend that the speed with which any individual or organization can cultivate a global mindset is driven by four factors: (1) curiosity about the world and a commitment to becoming smarter about how the world works, (2) an explicit and self-conscious articulation of current mindsets, (3) exposure to diversity and novelty, and (4) a disciplined attempt to develop an integrated perspective that weaves together diverse strands of knowledge about cultures and markets. We shall explore these factors in turn.

Cultivating curiosity about the world

Curiosity and openness about how the world works reflect an attitude, an element of the individual's personality makeup. Like other elements of personality, it is shaped heavily by early childhood experiences and becomes more resistant to change with age. Thus, while a company does have some maneuvering room in further cultivating curiosity among its existing employees, its greatest degrees of freedom lie at the point of employee selection and in managing the company's demographic makeup.

In situations where a company has the luxury of hiring a younger workforce (e.g., Nokia, where the average age across the entire company is around 30), it may be able to develop an inherent corporate advantage in the degree to which its employees will strive to develop a global mindset. In any case, every company has a good deal of discretion in hiring people who are curious about diverse cultures and markets and in promoting those who have shown this desired curiosity.

These considerations appeared to lie behind DaimlerChrysler's appointment of Andreas Renschler as the head of executive management development in 1999, a role which gave him broad power to help shape the careers of the top 2000–3000 managers in the merged corporation. Renschler came to this job not with a background in human resource management but with a track record of having successfully managed the launch of Daimler-Benz's M-class sports utility vehicle out of a newly built Alabama car plant, a challenge that required effectively melding a team of managers from diverse national and corporate backgrounds. According to Renschler, what he looked for was 'people who were willing to change.'[15]

Promoting people to senior executive levels who place high value on global experience and global mindsets sends strong signals regarding the importance of openness to diverse cultures and markets. As an example, consider the case of Douglas N. Daft who was appointed as the chairman and CEO of Coca-Cola Company in February 2000. Born in Australia, Daft had worked outside the company's U.S. operations for almost his entire career prior to being selected for the CEO position. Daft's predecessor, Douglas Ivester, was forced out by the board partly because of insensitivity to diversity issues both outside and within the U.S. Reflecting his own background. Daft has started to steer Coca-Cola strongly in the direction of a local focus and greater regional- and country-level autonomy. The company's emphasis is more along the lines of 'think local, act local,' hoping to take advantage of country-level differences in areas such as consumer preferences for carbonated soft drinks versus other beverages, the way products are sold and distributed, pack sizes, and the sovereign risk.[16]

Articulating the current mindset

Mindsets evolve through a process of interaction between people and the environment. Our current mindsets shape our interpretations of the world around us; in turn, these interpretations affect whether or not our mindsets change or remain unaltered. Unless this iterative process allows for new learning, it is easy to get trapped in one's own mental web. A powerful way to reduce the likelihood of this entrapment is to cultivate self-consciousness about one's mindset. Doing so requires accepting the possibility that our view of the world is just one of many alternative interpretations of reality. Accepting this possibility significantly enhances the likelihood of new learning.[17]

How might an individual manager or team of managers cultivate self-consciousness regarding their current mindsets? In our experience, two approaches work best. The first approach is to ask managers or teams to articulate their beliefs about the subject domain (e.g., at Hewlett-Packard, what are our beliefs regarding the structure of the personal computer market in Europe?). In contrast, the second approach is to conduct a comparative analysis of how different people or companies appear to interpret the same reality (e.g., at Hewlett-Packard, how does our view of the European personal computer industry compare with that of Compaq, IBM, Intel, and Microsoft?). Since the comparative-analysis approach rests on the premise that any particular mindset is just one of several possibilities, our experience has been that it is the more effective of the two approaches for helping a manager, a team, or a company to uncover their often deeply buried current mindsets.

Consider, for example, the experience of one company where we succeeded in persuading the CEO that, at least once every quarter, the agenda for the board meeting must include a strategic review of why a different competitor behaves the way that it does. After a year of this relatively simple exercise, the quality of discussions in the board meetings changed dramatically. It became clear that the company's own perspective on the market potential of different countries and on whether or not joint ventures were a sensible entry mode in this particular industry were not necessarily shared by some of the industry's key players. As a byproduct, board deliberations on action issues facing the company became more comprehensive and even led to the abandonment of what the CEO had earlier believed to be some of the seemingly 'obvious' rules of this industry. In fact, this comparative-analysis approach resulted in the CEO becoming a proponent rather than an opponent of strategic alliances in this industry.

Cultivating knowledge regarding diverse cultures and markets

Companies can cultivate exposure to and increase knowledge of diverse cultures and markets in two ways: (1) facilitate such knowledge building at the level of individuals, and (2) build diversity in the composition of the people making up the company. These approaches complement each other: the former focuses on building cognitive diversity inside the mindsets of individuals, and the latter focuses on assembling a diverse knowledge base across the organization's members. Both approaches are essential for every multinational company. Cultivating a global mindset at the level of individuals is a slow process that can take years of learning through experience in multiple cultures; thus, relying exclusively on the globalization of individual mindsets would be woefully inadequate vis-à-vis industry and competitive imperatives.

Building on the widely accepted idea that people learn through both formal education and on-the-job experience, we describe and illustrate below several mechanisms that companies can use to cultivate literacy about and enthusiasm for diverse cultures and markets at the individual level.

Formal education

Formal education (language skills and knowledge building regarding diverse cultures and markets) can take place through self-study courses, university-based education, or in-company seminars and/or management development programs. For example, at its Global Management Development Institute, South Korea's Samsung Group has routinely offered substantive courses in international business management; country histories, cultures, and economies; and foreign languages. In-company programs have the added advantage that the learning occurs at multiple levels – not only in the classroom but through interactions with colleagues from other locations around the world as well.

Participation in cross-border endeavors

Companies can participate in cross-border business teams and projects. Consider, for example, a leading U.S. bank creating a 'Euro' team to coordinate the company's response to the introduction of the new European currency. Should such a team be composed only of selected managers from the company's European units, or should the team also include a very small number of Americans from the company's U.S. operations? The latter approach, in our view, can be extremely effective in building in-depth knowledge regarding diverse cultures and markets – in addition to the obvious benefits of byproducts such as development of interpersonal ties.

Utilization of diverse locations for team and project meetings

This approach has been used successfully by VeriFone, a global market leader in the automation and delivery of secure payment and payment related transactions. In the late 1990s, the company had nearly 3000 employees based at more than 30 facilities around the world. As one of several mechanisms to become more attuned to the global environment, the company's top-management team instituted a policy of meeting for five days every six weeks at a different location around the globe. This generic approach can be implemented easily at any level of the corporate hierarchy, from the board of directors to a multinational R&D team within one of the business units.

Immersion experiences in foreign cultures

Immersion experiences can range from two- to three-month training assignments to more extensive cultural learning programs. Standard Chartered, a London-based global bank, has used the former approach, sending trainees recruited in London to Singapore and those recruited in Singapore to London. The Overseas Area Specialist Course, initiated by South Korea's Samsung Group in 1991, is an example of an extensive program. Every year, over 200 carefully screened trainees selected one country of interest, underwent three months of language and cross-cultural training, and then spent a year in the chosen country devoted solely to understanding it. Trainees had no specific job assignment and were forbidden to make contact with the local Samsung office. While abroad, they were even encouraged to use modes of travel other than airlines, to achieve a deeper immersion in the local culture. At the end of the immersion period, trainees returned to headquarters in Seoul and reported on their experiences during a two-month debriefing period.[18]

Expatriate assignments

Multi-year expatriate assignments are by far the most intensive mechanism through which employees can learn about another culture and market. However, this mechanism can be the most expensive for cultivating a global mindset – for the company and, given the increasing preponderance of dual-career marriages, often for the individual. Accordingly, companies need to target expatriate assignments toward high-potential managers (as distinct from the common practice of selecting people that you don't want to see too much of) and also to ensure that their stay abroad fosters cultural learning rather than cultural isolation. As Gurcharan Das, former head of Procter & Gamble India, observed astutely:

> There are powerful ... rewards for an international manager on transfer overseas who chooses to get involved in the local community. When such people approach the new country with an open mind, learn the local language, and make friends with colleagues and neighbors, they gain access to a wealth of new culture. ... Unfortunately, my experience in Mexico indicates that many expatriate managers live in 'golden ghettos' of ease with little genuine contact with locals other than servants. ... The lesson for global companies is to give each international manager a local 'mentor' who will open doors to the community. Ultimately, however, it is the responsibility of individual managers to open their minds, plunge into their local communities, and try to make them their own.[19]

Cultivating geographic and cultural diversity among the senior management ranks

Notwithstanding the value of the various mechanisms discussed above, limits do exist on the speed with which a company can cultivate a global mindset among its employees, the number of employees that it can efficiently target for this objective, and the rate of success in cultivating their global mindsets. Accordingly, virtually all multinational companies must also expand the cognitive map of the organization by creating geographic and cultural diversity among senior management. Such efforts can be targeted at many executive levels, from the composition of the board of directors and the office of the CEO to the composition of business-unit management teams. For example, in recent years, IBM elected Minoru Makihara, the president of Mitsubishi, to its board, and General Motors elected Sweden's Percy Barnevik, first president and CEO of ABB, to its board. Similarly, in the early 1990s, of the 22 people on Dow Chemical's senior-most management committee, 10 were born outside the U.S. and 17 had had significant international experience. At the level of individual lines of business, Hoechst, the

German pharmaceutical company, serves as a good example of diversity. In the late 1990s, Hoechst's pharmaceutical business was led by an American CEO, a French CFO, and a Canadian COO.

Location of business-unit headquarters

By dispersing business-unit headquarters to carefully selected locations around the world, companies can also further the differentiation of their organizational mindset (i.e., their knowledge about diverse cultures and markets). Among major corporations, ABB was perhaps the pioneer in dispersing the locations of business-area headquarters away from the corporate center. Other more recent examples would include Eaton Corporation, which has shifted the worldwide headquarters of its light/medium truck transmission business to Amsterdam, Holland and moved the world headquarters of its automotive controls business to Strasbourg, France.

Cultivating the ability to integrate diverse knowledge bases

Notwithstanding the fact that cognitive diversity is critical for navigating in today's complex and dynamic global environment, it also can be paralyzing. A management team composed of seven people representing four nationalities adds value only when the diverse perspectives can be integrated into a coherent vision and a coherent set of decisions and actions. Otherwise, what you get is conflict, frustration, delay, and at best either a forced or a compromise decision.

In order to cultivate the ability to integrate diverse knowledge bases, the organization needs to act on two fronts: one, ensure that people will view such integration as a rewarding endeavor, and two, ensure that people will be given ample opportunity to engage in such integration as a part of their on-the-job responsibilities. The following are some of the mechanisms that companies can use to accomplish both of these goals.

Definition and cultivation of a set of core values throughout the corporation

By definition, core values are those values that cut across subsidiaries no matter where located. A set of deeply ingrained and widely shared core values (as in the case of companies such as Marriott, GE, Unilever, and Honda) can serve as an organizational as well as a social integrating mechanism. Belief in a set of core values implicitly requires people to make sense of their local observations from the perspective of the company's global agenda. And, on a social level, shared values give people with diverse cultural backgrounds and knowledge bases a common mindset on which to build a constructive rather than unproductive, conflict-ridden dialog.

Widespread distribution of ownership rights on a global basis

Ownership rights in the global parent are a powerful mechanism to ensure that every employee, regardless of location or nationality, will be inclined to look at local opportunities, local challenges, and local resources from a global perspective. Companies such as Eli Lilly (which issues stock options to every employee worldwide through the company's GlobalShares program)[20] significantly increase the likelihood that every employee will be more cosmopolitan, more global in mindset.

Cultivation of an internal labor market driven by pure meritocracy

Companies such as Cisco, McKinsey, and Ford, which are committed to using merit rather than nationality as the prime driver of career mobility right up to the CEO level, create an environment in which all managers see themselves as global resources. Such an environment goes a long way toward removing the tendency to view local knowledge as idiosyncratic and of only local value, and building a global mindset.

Job rotation across geographic regions, business divisions, and functions

Job rotations across countries have long served as an effective mechanism to promote openness to and knowledge about diverse cultures and markets. If well planned, they also help cultivate an ability to integrate across this diversity. Consider the approach adopted by Nokia. CEO Jorma Ollila systematically and periodically switches the jobs of his key managers right up to very senior levels. In 1998 Sari Baldauf, formerly the head of Nokia's Asia-Pacific operations, was appointed the new head of corporate R&D. Similarly, Olli-Pekka Kallasvuo, the former head of Nokia's U.S. operations, became the new corporate chief financial officer.[21] From a management-development perspective, one major outcome of these shuffles is to cultivate a thorough understanding of diversity (through regional responsibilities for Asia or North America) as well as an ability to integrate across this diversity (through global responsibilities for R&D or finance).

Cultivation of interpersonal and social ties among people based in different locations

Typically, the frequency and openness of interaction between two people is a function of how strong their interpersonal and social ties are. Accordingly, the more successful a company is at cultivating interpersonal and social ties among people based in different subsidiaries, the more effective it should be at integrating their diverse perspectives and knowledge bases. For instance, in France's Rhone-Poulenc Group, the top 50 managers from across the world meet three to four times every year to socialize as well as to discuss business issues. In addition, people from various subsidiaries meet with each other through their involvement in cross-border business teams. As observed by Peter Neff, the president and CEO of Rhone-Poulenc Inc., the company's U.S. operations:

> I sit on the boards of three worldwide business groups, and the leaders of these groups sit on the advisory board for the American company. These councils bring different perspectives to major decisions, considering such questions as whether a particular strategy is viable, the nature of product and business portfolios, and the potential for competitive leadership. They also decide on major capital expenditures. And, finally, they are a tool to facilitate socialization and alignment within the leadership structure.[22]

Figure 3 presents a detailed and comprehensive example of how VeriFone, a Silicon Valley-based company, utilized a variety of mechanisms to cultivate a global mindset among its people as well as the company as a whole.

Emerging opportunities and a global mindset

The world's economic landscape is changing rapidly and becoming increasingly global. For virtually every medium- to large-size company in developed as well as developing

VeriFone was a market leader in the automation and delivery of secure payment and payment-related transactions. Officially headquartered in Redwood City, California, the company was founded in 1981 and was acquired by Hewlett-Packard in June 1997 for $1.29 billion. VeriFone's stated mission was 'To create and lead the transaction automation industry worldwide.' In 1997, the company had 3000 employees based at more than 30 facilities in North America, South America, Asia and Australia, Europe, and Africa. Given below are highlights of how VeriFone cultivated a global mindset among its people and more broadly at the level of the entire company.

- Hatim Tyabji, VeriFone's CEO, disdained the idea of an all-powerful corporate headquarters and preferred to view the company as a network of locations. He likened the company to a blueberry pancake where all berries were created equal and all had the same size. Many corporate functions {e.g., human resource management and management information systems) were managed in a decentralized fashion out of multiple global locations such as Dallas (Texas), Bangalore (India), Taipei (Taiwan), and Honolulu (Hawaii).

- Virtually all employees of the company were provided with laptops and were connected to each other electronically. Every company facility was also equipped with videoconferencing facilities. When employees signed on to their email systems, a list of holidays and local times at various VeriFone locations automatically appeared on the screen.

- The top-management team, consisting of the CEO and his ten direct reports, met for five days every six weeks at a different location around the globe.

- The leadership was dedicated to instilling the company's core values (commitment to excellence, dedication to customer needs, promotion of teamwork, recognition of the individual, a global mindset, and ethical conduct) among all employees. The CEO wrote the corporate philosophy manual himself. It was translated into a number of languages including English, Chinese, French, German, Japanese, Portuguese, and Spanish. When the company rolled out corporate programs, senior managers traveled personally to various locations in order to get local input and to provide guidelines regarding how the program could be tailored to the local context.

- Prior to its acquisition by Hewlett-Packard, VeriFone published the CEO's Letter to Shareholders (in its Annual Report) in multiple languages.

- The company conducted recruitment on a global basis and instituted a uniform performance-assessment system and incentive structure around the globe.

- One of the company's recognized core competencies was its ability to leverage know-how from various locations in order to serve customers or pursue new opportunities. As an example, one of the company's sales reps in Greece learned from a large customer that a competitor had raised concerns about VeriFone's expertise in debit cards. The sales rep sent out an email request to colleagues within the company for information and references on debit installations. Within 24 hours, he had 16 responses and 10 references, including the names and phone numbers of established customers with debit-card installations. The next day, armed with this information and able to say that VeriFone had 400,000 installations worldwide, the rep closed a major deal with this customer. Stories such as this one not only provide a concrete illustration of VeriFone's already well-developed global mindset but also serve to reinforce the notion of what constitute desirable attitudes and behaviors within the company, thereby leading to a further deepening of the global mindset.

Abstracted from Stoppard, D. B., Donnellon, A., & Nolan, R. L. 1997. *VeriFone*, HBS Case No. 9-398-030. Boston: Harvard Business School Publishing.

Figure 3 Cultivating a global mindset: the Verifone approach—circa 1997

economies, market opportunities, critical resources, cutting-edge ideas, and competitors lurk not just around the corner in the home market but increasingly in distant and often little-understood regions of the world as well. How successful a company is at exploiting emerging opportunities and tackling their accompanying challenges depends crucially on how intelligently it observes and interprets the dynamic world in which it operates. Creating a global mindset is a central requirement for building such intelligence. The conceptual framework and mechanisms provided in this article can guide companies in moving systematically toward this goal.

Notes

[1] For example, see Gandz, J., Smith, M., Wali, A., & Conklin, D. W. 1992. *Procter & Gamble Japan (A)*. HBS Case No. 9-391-003. Boston: Harvard Business School Publishing.

[2] Taylor, W. E. 1991. The logic of global business: An interview with ABB's Percy Barnevik. *Harvard Business Review*, 69(2): 93–105.

[3] See Walsh, J. P. 1995. Managerial and organizational cognition: Notes from a trip down memory lane. *Organization Science*, 6(3): 280–321 for a comprehensive review of the literature on managerial and organizational cognition that builds on the work of pioneers such as Bartlett, F. C. 1932. *Remembering*, Cambridge, MA: Harvard University Press; Festinger, L. 1957. *A theory of cognitive dissonance*. Evanston, IL: Row Peterson; and Neisser, U. 1967. *Cognitive psychology*. New York: Appleton-Century-Crofts. Other classic works include Porac, J. F., & Thomas, H. 1990. Taxonomic mental models in competitor definition. *Academy of Management Review*, 15(2): 224–240; and Tversky, A., & Kahneman, D. 1986. Rational choice and the framing of decisions. *Journal of Business*, 59(4): 251–278.

[4] See Argyris, C, & Schon, D. A. 1978. *Organizational learning*. Reading, MA: Addison Wesley; Newell, A. 1990. *Unified theories of cognition*. Cambridge, MA: Harvard University Press; and Simon, H. A. 1955. A behavioral model of rational choice. *Quarterly Journal of Economics*, 69(1): 99–118.

[5] See Simon, H. A., op. cit.; and Starbuck, W. H., & Milliken, F. J. 1988. Executives' perceptual filters: What they notice and how they make sense. In Hambrick, D. C. (Ed.), *The executive effect: Concepts and methods for studying top managers*. Greenwich, CT: JAI Press.

[6] See Walsh, J. P., & Charalambides, L. C. 1990. Individual and social origins of belief structure change. *Journal of Social Psychology*, 130(4): 517–532.

[7] For research on how organizational-level cognitive schemas can change, see Bartunek, J. M. 1984. Changing interpretive schemes and organizational restructuring. *Administrative Science Quarterly*, 29(3): 355–372; Greenwood, R., & Hinings, C. R. 1988. Organizational design types, tracks, and dynamics of strategic change. *Organization Studies*, 9(3): 293–316; Hopfl, H. 1992. *Judgment and choice: The psychology of decision*. New York: John Wiley; and Lyles, M. A., & Schwenk, C. R. 1992. Top management, strategy, and organizational knowledge structures. *Journal of Management Studies*, 29(2): 155–174.

[8] Austin, R. D., & Nolan, R. L. 2000. *IBM turnaround*. HBS Case No. 9-600-098. Boston: Harvard Business School Publishing.

[9] See Nisbet, R., & Ross, L. 1980. *Human inference: Strategies and shortcomings of social judgment*. Englewood Cliffs, NJ: Prentice Hall; and Schank, R. P., & Abelson, R. P. 1977. *Scripts, plans, goals, and understanding*. Hillsdale. NJ: Lawrence Erlbaum Associates.

[10] Here we use the term markets broadly. Any particular country or region can potentially be a market for the sales of the company's products and services, for accessing technology and talent, for tapping into higher-quality or lower-cost labor, for the purchasing of raw material and components, and for the sourcing of capital.

[11] Our dual emphasis on cognitive diversity as well as integrative ability is fully consistent with the perspectives reflected in Murtha, T. P., Lenway, S. A., & Bagozzi, R. P. 1998. Global mind-sets and cognitive shifts in a multinational corporation. *Strategic Management Journal*, 19(2): 97–114; and Kobrin, S. J. 1994. Is there a relationship between a geocentric mind-set and multinational strategy? *Journal of International Business Studies*, 25(3): 493–511.

[12] These classifications parallel Perlmutter's notion of geocentric, ethnocentric, and polycentric organizations. See Perlmutter, H. V. 1969. The tortuous evolution of the multinational corporation. *Columbia Journal of World Business*, 4(1): 9–18.

An organization would be termed as having a global mindset when it demonstrates deep knowledge of diverse cultures and markets as well as an ability to synthesize across this diversity. As an example of a company with such a mindset, see the description of VeriFone in Figure 3.

An organization would be termed as having a parochial mindset when it is blind to diversity across cultures and markets. Such an organization makes little, if any, effort to adapt its products and processes to local conditions in foreign markets. As discussed in the text, Ikea appeared to have a parochial mindset at the time of its entry into the U.S. in the mid-1980s.

An organization would be termed as having a diffused mindset when it behaves as a loose federation of geographic units such that each local unit has a deep understanding of the local culture and market, yet the organization as a whole lacks the ability to synthesize across this diversity and therefore is unable to reap the benefits of global scale and scope. Many professional service firms structured as global federations of local partnerships (e.g., KPMG in the early 1990s) serve as good examples of organizations with diffused mindsets.

One cell is labeled 'not applicable' because an organization that is closed to diversity always has a highly integrated perspective regarding the external environment.

[13] See, for example, Ibarra, H., & Sackley, N. 1999. *Charlotte Beers at Ogilvy & Mather (A)*. HBS Case No. 9-495-031. Boston: Harvard Business School Publishing.

[14] See Walsh, op. cit.; Argyris & Schon, op. cit.; Walsh & Charalambides, op. cit.; and Murtha, et al., op. cit.

[15] See Ball, J. DaimlerChrysler's Renschler holds job of melding officials into cohesive team. *Financial Times* (London), 12 January 1999, B7.

[16] James, D. 20–26 September 2001. Local Coke. *BRW*. 70–74.

[17] This conclusion is consistent with research findings by, among others, Eden, C. 1992. On the nature of cognitive maps. *Journal of Management* Studies, 29(3): 261–265; Mitchell, R. 1986. Team building by disclosure of internal frames of reference. *Journal of Applied Behavioral Science*. 22(1): 15–28; and Walsh, J. P., & Charalambides, L. C, op. cit.

[18] See Govindarajan, V., & Gupta, A. K. *Global mindset of Samsung*. Tuck School Case Study. Hanover: Tuck School of Business; and Dragoon, A. 1996. Samsung Electronics: Not accidental tourists. *CIO*. 9(19): 62,

[19] Das, G. 1993. Local memoirs of a global manager. *Harvard Business Review*, 71(2): 38–47.

[20] Flynn, G. 1996. Lilly prepares its people to take on the world. Personnel *Journal,* 75(1): 58.

[21] Baker, S. Nokia: Can CEO Ollila keep the cellular superstar flying high? *Business Week*, 10 August 1998, 54–60.

[22] Neff, P. 1995. Cross-cultural research teams in a global enterprise. *Research Technology Management*. 38(3): 15–19.

ANIL K. GUPTA is a Distinguished Scholar-Teacher and Professor of Strategy and Global E-business at the Robert H. Smith School of Business, University of Maryland at College Park. He received his D.B.A. from the Harvard Business School. His research interests focus on managing in the digital age, managing globalization, and the quest for synergy. He is coauthor, with Vijay Govindarajan, of *The Quest for Global Dominance*. Contact: *agupta@rhsmith.umd.edu.*

VIJAY GOVINDARAJAN is the Earl C. Daum 1924 Professor of International Business and director of the William F. Achtmeyer Center for Global Leadership at the Tuck School of Business at Dartmouth College. He is also the faculty director for the Global Leadership 2020 Program. He is coauthor, with Anil K. Gupta, of *The Quest for Global Dominance*, published by Jossey-Bass in 2001. Contact: *vg@dartmouth.edu.*

CASE 1: ICICI BANK: PATH TO GLOBALIZATION

It was 11 April 2006 when KV Kamath, Managing Director and CEO of ICICI Bank, was reflecting on the past ten years at ICICI. Much had changed since he assumed his leadership role at ICICI in 1996. Recently, the business press had reported that, at the age of 57, he was very soft-spoken to the extent of being shy, but was a man of extraordinary vision and leadership. A mechanical engineer and an MBA from IIM Ahmedabad (see Exhibit 1.1 for Mr Kamath's biography), Kamath was not only credited with driving ICICI's growth, but also with transforming and rejuvenating the entire banking sector in India. He thought about his accomplishments in leading the bank to its path to globalization.

Mr K. Vaman Kamath is the Managing Director and Chief Executive Officer of ICICI Bank Limited. ICICI Bank (NYSE: IC) functions as a universal bank through itself and its associate companies in the areas of corporate finance, commercial banking, investment banking, asset management, non-banking finance, investor services, broking and insurance.

Mr Kamath was born on 2 December 1947, in Mangalore, Karnataka, where he spent most of his early years. After completing higher secondary and pre-university from St Aloysius, he joined the Karnataka Regional Educational College (KREC) for a Bachelor's Degree in Mechanical Engineering. After graduating from KREC in 1969, he joined the prestigious Indian Institute of Management, Ahmedabad (IIM-A) for a Master's Degree in Business Administration. The two-year curriculum at IIMA served as a valuable input in the process of his development as a manager and future business leader.

After graduating from IIMA in 1971, Mr Kamath started his career with ICICI in the Project Finance division, and moved on to different departments to gather a rich and varied experience, which included the setting up of new businesses such as leasing, venture capital and credit rating, as well as handling general management positions. As part of his general management responsibilities he initiated and implemented ICICI's computerization programme. Substantial investments in technology right from the early years have resulted in systems that are today a competitive advantage for ICICI.

In 1988, Mr Kamath joined the Asian Development Bank, Manila, in its Private Sector Department. His principal work experience at ADB was in various projects in China, India, Indonesia, Philippines, Bangladesh and Vietnam. He was the ADB representative on the boards of several companies and this experience offered him considerable insight into the working of global firms. During his years in South East Asia, Mr Kamath worked in most of the developing countries in the region, including China, Thailand, Philippines, Indonesia and Vietnam, and this provided a rich experience in terms of exposure to a variety of business situations, many of them typical to emerging markets.

Boris Tsypin, while on his MBA exchange programme from Chicago GSB, prepared this case under the supervision of Professor Ashok Som. The case was developed from generalized experience, published sources and the cooperation of the organization as a basis for class discussion rather than to illustrate either effective or ineffective handling of an administrative situation.

> In May 1996, Mr Kamath returned to ICICI as its Managing Director and Chief Executive Officer. He initiated a process of consolidation in the Indian financial sector through a series of acquisitions of non-banking finance companies during 1996–98. With the acquisition of a private bank in March 2001, and the reverse merger between ICICI Limited and ICICI Bank, Mr Kamath had achieved the objective of creating the first universal bank in India. The strategic initiatives and structural changes subsequently instituted by him across the ICICI Group have helped ICICI to re-draw its boundaries and increase its business potential. A firm believer in the concept of Universal Banking – the ability to provide complete financial services to different classes of customers – Mr Kamath had been instrumental in expanding the Group's services to retail customers and building the personal financial services business. ICICI had made substantial efforts to strengthen its relationship with the customer, enabling it to build a strong retail franchise with about five million retail customer accounts, five million bond holders and an established market presence.
>
> Mr Kamath presently resides in Mumbai, is married, and has a son and a daughter. He is an avid reader and has lectured extensively both in India and abroad. Mr Kamath is a Member of the Governing Board of various educational institutions, including the Indian Institute of Management-Ahmedabad, Indian School of Business, National Institute of Bank Management and Manipal Academy of Higher Education. Mr Kamath is also a Member of the National Council of Confederation of Indian Industry (CII). The *Asian Banker Journal of Singapore* had voted Mr Kamath the most e-savvy CEO among Asian banks. Recently, the Mumbai Management Association conferred him with the Finance Man of the Year award, and the World HRD Congress, in its Mumbai session in November 2000, voted Mr Kamath the best CEO for Innovative HR practices. Mr Kamath was recently named Asian Business Leader of the Year at the Asian Business Leader Award 2001, organized by the business television network CNBC Asia Pacific and the leading business logistics solutions company TNT.

Exhibit 1.1 Mr K. V. Kamath, MD and CEO, ICICI Bank Limited
Source: ICICI corporate website

Prior to his arrival, ICICI Bank was an old-fashioned, bureaucratic, term-lending institution lacking innovative and professionalized people processes. He and his team had effectively transformed ICICI from an industrial finance project institution into India's most comprehensive financial service powerhouse with interests in retail banking, insurance and online services, among others. Today, ICICI is India's largest private bank with assets of about $60 billion, turnover of $3.2 billion and a market value of more than $11 billion. The bank had more than 600 branches and offices, more than 2,000 ATMs and an international presence in the UK, Hong Kong, Singapore, Canada, the USA, Sri Lanka, Bangladesh, UAE, Bahrain, China, South Africa and Russia (see Exhibit 1.2 for key financial data on ICICI Bank).

Kamath was thinking of a request he had received from ESSEC Business School in Paris to showcase ICICI Bank to a group of executives from Caisses d'Epargne, the third largest bank in France. He knew that the next five years, before he retired, were going to be crucial to the bank's success in the international arena. He forwarded the French Business School's request to Lalit Gupte[1] and Bhargav Dasgupta,[2] while reflecting that his goals were to maintain the bank's momentum, continue international expansion, expand product offerings, improve technological innovation and nurture young talent to take over his vision of a truly customer-driven, technologically superior bank with a global footprint. That would be a great challenge …

	03/31/06	03/31/05	03/31/04
Sales	19,86	23,88	23,69
Operating income	13,63	15,65	15,66
Net income	2,89	3,22	3,96
Total assets	7,50	7,10	7,20
Total liabilities	38,90	37,40	31,00
EBITDA	18,36	17,04	14,99

Financial ratios analysis

Profitability	**03/31/06**	**03/31/05**	**03/31/04**
Return on total equity	19,86	23,88	23,69
Reinvestment rate	13,63	15,65	15,66
Return on assets	2,89	3,22	3,96
Return on invested capital	7,50	7,10	7,20
Cash earnings return on equity	38,90	37,40	31,00
Cash flow to sales	18,36	17,04	14,99
Operating profit margin	11,83	13,96	13,92
Pre-tax margin	11,85	13,96	13,89
Net margin	9,38	10,88	11,45

Asset utilization	**3/31/2006**	**3/31/2005**	**3/31/2004**
Assets per employee	2 725 523,98	2 476 013,76	2 393 355,80
Assets turnover	0,09	0,10	0,11
Capital expend pct total assets	0,24	0,33	0,48

Exhibit 1.2(a) Key financials of ICICI*

*Figures are in USD: 1USD = 40 INR
Source: Thompson One Banker

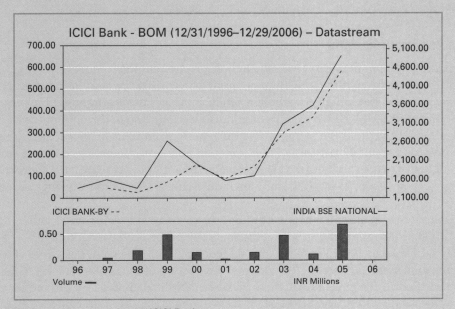

Exhibit 1.2(b) Interactive price chart of ICICI Bank
Source: Datastream

► The history of banking in India

The banking industry in India had gone through broadly four transformation phases from its inception in 1786 to the latest changes in the new millennium: Phase 1 – origination; Phase 2 – nationalization; Phase 3 – liberalization; Phase 4 – current state.

Phase 1: origination

The Indian banking industry emerged in the eighteenth century with the creation of the General Bank of India in 1786. It was the beginning of commercial banking by the British agency houses, to help finance their growing business in India. The creation of several other banks, which no longer exist, followed. The oldest bank that still existed was the State Bank of India, which was established in 1806 as the Bank of Calcutta in Calcutta. At that time, Calcutta was the most active trading port in India and, several decades later, foreign banks like HSBC and Credit Lyonnais established branches there as well. In 1865, Allahabad Bank, known as the first fully Indian bank, was established.

By the 1900s, the market had expanded, with the establishment of such banks as Punjab National Bank in Lahore and Bank of India in Mumbai, both of which were under private ownership. In 1935, the Reserve Bank of India was created to regulate the expanding banking industry.

The origination phase was characterized by relatively slow growth and periodic bank failures. There were approximately 1,100 banks and such fragmentation did not add to consumer confidence. Bank deposits were low and the funds were mostly given to traders. In fact, the savings facility of the Indian Post Office department was more trusted, more popular and more widely used.

Phase 2: nationalization

After gaining independence in 1947, the Indian government focused on promoting industrialization through the growth of domestic enterprises. To facilitate this process, in the early 1950s, the Indian government set up a number of Development Finance Institutions with the objective of providing subsidized finance to develop industrial organizations throughout the country. The three most prominent finance institutions, which provided about 67 per cent of medium- and long-term financing to the nascent Indian industry, were the Industrial Development Board of India (IDBI), the Industrial Finance Corporation of India (IFCI) and the Industrial Credit and Investment Corporation of India (ICICI).

Together with creating finance institutions, in an attempt to bring order and credibility to the banking industry, the Indian government privatized 14 major commercial banks in 1959 and 1969, and six more in 1980. The main objectives of bank nationalization were: (a) to make the administrative set-up of the banks conform to the norms specified by the government; (b) to make easy credit available to neglected sectors (or 'priority sectors') like agriculture, small-scale industry, export-orientated sectors, etc.; (c) greater mobilization of savings through bank deposits; and (d) widening of the branch networks of banks, especially in rural and semi-urban areas.

The government formed the State Bank of India to take the role of principal agent of the Reserve Bank of India and to handle the banking transactions of state governments throughout the country. At the end of the nationalization process, 80 per cent of the banking industry fell under state control.

The nationalization process, based on the stated objectives, proved to be a success. About 58,000 new branches were added across the length and breadth of the country in the next three decades. The banking industry, backed by the Indian government, gave the public implicit faith and immense confidence about the sustainability of these institutions. As a result, public-sector bank deposits rose approximately 800 per cent and advances increased by an incredible 11,000 per cent.

To summarize, over the three decades following the start of India's nationalization, the country witnessed spectacular progress in its banking system. This included: (a) massive branch expansion, especially in rural areas; (b) diversification of an increasing portion of bank credit to priority sectors, such as agriculture, small industry and transport – priority sector credit rose from 14 per cent to 41 per cent over the last two decades; and (c) greater involvement in relatively 'under-banked' states – the expansion of priority-sector lending and the emphasis on area approach had almost evened out regional disparities, and the concentration of the banking business became relatively equal.

Though the success of the nationalization programme was undeniable, the competitive efficiency of the nationalized banks had deteriorated over time. The functioning of the banks backed by the government had become bureaucratic, gaining slack and accruing high non-performing assets (NPAs) in the process of evolution. With increased geographical coverage, lines of supervision and control had lengthened. Inefficiency, productivity, profitability, capital adequacy and the financial position record of the nationalized banks had fallen well below international standards.

Phase 3: liberalization

In order to rectify some of these inefficiencies, solve the balance of payments crisis and spur growth, the Indian government,[3] under Prime Minister Narasimha Rao and Finance Minister Manmohan Singh, began to reform the banking industry, giving licences to a small number of private and foreign banks. The growth came not only from private banks but also government and foreign banks. The new generation of tech-savvy and customer-friendly banks, such as ICICI Bank and HDFC Bank, kick-started the rapid growth of the industry, together with foreign banks such as Citibank, HSBC and Standard Chartered, which already had a presence in India. During liberalization, which started in 1991, the government gradually freed interest rates and also reduced the volume and burden of directed credits in order to increase credit to the private sector.[4]

With increasing numbers of private banks, foreign banks and ATM machines, stronger competition forced the Indian banking industry to offer more competitive rates and to focus more on addressing customer needs. Telephone and internet banking were introduced. Great efforts were put forth to give customers better service, making the entire banking system more customer sensitive, convenient and swift.

▶ Phase 4: the current state

Currently, the Indian banking industry (see Exhibit 1.3) was considered mature in urban India in terms of supply, product range and reach. However, expansion into rural India still remains a challenge for private and foreign banks. Compared to other emerging markets in terms of quality of assets and capital adequacy, Indian banks have clean, strong and transparent balance sheets. The main purpose of the Reserve Bank of India was to manage the volatility of the Indian rupee, and the central bank had been able to achieve this goal by functioning autonomously, with minimal pressure from government. The Reserve Bank of India is one of the more independent central banks in the world.

Indian banking industry at a glance (2004–2005)

- 84 per cent of the survey respondents described the performance of the banking industry as 'Very Good' in the fiscal period 2004–05.
- Newly granted autonomy would certainly make the PSBs more competitive and profitable, said 88 per cent of respondents, though some more changes considered desirable.
- 48 per cent of overall respondents and 67 per cent of private bank respondents expressed the need to relax the prescribed limit of single ownership and cross-holding cap in the Ownership and Governance Guidelines for Private Sector Banks.
- Although 72 per cent of public- and private-sector bank respondents expressed their satisfaction with the recently devised road map for the foreign banks, the majority of foreign bank respondents (75 per cent) expressed complete dissatisfaction with this roadmap.
- 75 per cent of the foreign bank respondents expressed that the time frame prescribed to expand through mergers & acquisitions should have been less, and an equal number voiced that the guidelines are not in line with international norms.
- Consolidation in the banking industry followed by technological upgradation were considered key factors currently required to enhance the international competitiveness of the Indian banks.
- Free trade agreements (FTAs) considered a positive step in the area of banking by almost all respondents. The available market size and the level of access provided to Indian banks in foreign countries should be the key factors in consideration while entering into such agreements, as highlighted by 76 per cent of banks.
- Rise in the interest rates imminent, say 64 per cent of survey respondents. Majority expect increase by 0.5 per cent.
- 88 per cent of public- and private-sector banks considered HRD-related issues one of the biggest challenges in the process of consolidation.
- 83 per cent of respondent banks claim to have more than 85 per cent level of technological advancements in their banks, with remaining banks stating it to be around 65–85 per cent.
- All respondents emphasized that customer retention is significantly important for the profitability of the banks.
- More than 70 per cent of banks felt the need for advanced security software and stricter security policies to safeguard and ensure the security of customer information.
- 53 per cent of respondent banks considered six months' transition period to shift from MIFOR rupee benchmarks for interest rate derivatives to be inadequate.
- Majority of banks felt that their risk management framework for implementation of BASEL II was well in place.
- 53 per cent of survey respondents intend to increase their retail portfolio by more than 25 per cent in the year 2005–06.
- Rising indebtedness followed by lack of technological advancements were identified as biggest challenges that could affect the future growth of retail banking.
- 80 per cent of survey respondents did not agree with the notion that housing loans are creating a bubble.
- Substantial progress made by banks in cleaning up the NPAs from their balance sheets, was largely attributed to SARFAESI Act and increased provisioning on doubtful debts by majority of survey respondents.

- Absence of secondary market for the trading of security receipt issued by ARCs was identified as one of major problems in the Indian Model of NPA management.
- Separate NPA norms for the farm and the SME sector were recommended by a large number of respondents.
- 96 per cent of all banks claim that the current growth of non-food credit is sustainable for about 3–5 years.
- Detailed information on banks' sectoral exposure of credit reveals that over two-thirds of the credit flow has been on account of retail, housing and other priority-sector loans. Banks credit flow exposure to large enterprises continues to remain buoyant, with recent indications that credit to agriculture and micro credit have also picked up.
- 71 per cent of survey respondents did not consider SMEs as an avenue of forced lending.
- 95 per cent of banks intend to increase their exposure further in the area of micro credit financing.

Exhibit 1.3a The status of the Indian banking sector and challenges facing the industry
Source: Federation of Indian Chambers of Commerce and Industry (FICCI) Survey

Rank 2004	Rank 2005	Bank	Size and strength					
			Deposits	Average working funds	Net profit	Growth in path %	Growth in business %	Growth in share of total %
i	i	HDFC Bank	36,354	44,335	666	31	30	3
7	2	*HSBC*	17,013	23,570	337	71	14	−11
3	3	*ABN AMRO*	7,077	13,003	195	0	38	6
6	4	Corporation Bank	27,233	30,444	402	−20	23	−1
15	5	Andhra Bank	27,551	28,718	520	12	26	2
2	6	*Citibank NA*	21,484	30,129	600	5	12	−10
21	7	Punjab National Bank	103,167	106,302	1410	27	20	−1
9	8	*Standard Chartered*	22,522	34,801	602	1	18	−4
13	9	UTI Bank	31,712	29,846	335	20	53	24
12	10	Vijaya Bank	25,618	26,666	381	−7	25	3
28	11	Indian Overseas Bank	44,241	47,058	651	27	12	−10
4	12	State Bank of Patalia	26,496	29,200	287	−33	18	0
24	13	ICICI Bank	99,819	131,075	605	22	47	26
27	14	Allahabad Bank	40,762	38,600	542	17	32	10
5	15	Oriental Bank of Commerce	47,850	46,066	761	11	32	13
25	16	State Bank of Travancore	24,133	25,129	247	1	27	4
31	17	State Bank of Mysore	13,585	14,582	206	17	27	3
23	18	Canara bank	96,908	99,584	1110	−17	17	−5
44	19	Karnataka Bank	10,837	11,376	147	10	22	−3
33	20	Union Bank of India	61,831	62,101	719	19	28	3

Exhibit 1.3b 2005 *Business Today* survey of the best banks in India

* Bold italics are foreign banks
** Figures are in USD: 1USD = 40 INR
Source: Business Today, 26 February 2006

Analysts forecast that the growth of the Indian economy was expected to be strong and steady in the near future, the demand for banking services, especially retail banking, mortgages and investment services, were expected to be strong too. Due to liberalization, strong growth and deregulation, more and more banks were expected to enter the Indian market. To facilitate this process, the minimum capital requirement set by the Indian government was only Rs300 crores ($65 million). Also, to further facilitate the process, private banks were exempt from the Securities and Exchange Board of India (SEBI) guidelines relating to the public issue of equity, which meant that new banks could raise capital from the capital market to achieve the required equity. While, theoretically, raising money from the capital market could lead to new banks being established in India, commissioning branches throughout the length and breadth of India was a challenge for any new entrant, which had to compete with the vast branch network of existing banks (especially nationalized banks). The costs involved in building such a network were very high.

On the other hand, any new entrant that started its operations from scratch would have certain advantages. First, it would have access to the latest technology widely available in India and abroad in the banking sector. This could prove to be a source of a competitive advantage, as nationalized banks had to restructure their whole systems and processes and retrain their staff to incorporate new technologies. This would take time. Second, the new banks would enjoy a clean balance sheet with no non-performing assets, something not evident for the nationalized banks. This factor could prove to be important as the existing banks begin to feel the burden of over-extending credit, which had fuelled their recent growth.

As the Indian economy and banking industry become more developed, the banks continued to have a hard time competing for corporate and private business. For example, the availability of financial instruments for the short-term financing (like commercial paper and fixed deposits), available mostly to blue-chip corporations, had put some pressure on the banking sector. Second, the development of the capital markets had enabled corporations to access funds through equity, debt or mixed issues. Third, leasing and hire purchase had emerged as an attractive option for companies that could not raise debt or equity so easily. This option reduced the companies' large capital requirements. Finally, on the retail side, the greater availability of various securities such as bank deposits, Bombay Stock Exchange (BSE) Sensex, corporate debentures and corporate fixed deposits had given Indian customers more options to maintain and invest their wealth. Retail banks had to deliver even more value when high-liquidity and high-yield securities such as open-ended mutual funds became more and more available and accepted.

With these developments, the Indian banking industry reported that customers enjoyed a more transparent, competitive and customer-friendly banking experience than they had during the pre-liberalization period. Since the procedure for opening savings accounts had been standardized and also governed by regulations, customers could choose banks mostly on customer service and access to branch networks. Due to the proliferation of various financial instruments mentioned above, the rates offered by banks were also competitive among banks. On the other hand, though interest rates might be attractive and customer service friendly, Indians historically had a strong preference for tangible assets like gold. In fact, India is the world's largest gold jewellery market by volume, accounting for around 520 tons in 2004.[5] The challenge for all banks hoping to succeed in India was to educate the consumer, transform a country of disciplined savers into a country of investors and to change consumers' negative perception of debt.

On the corporate side, banks faced stiff competition for so called 'blue-chip'[6] accounts because of their strong cash position and, thus, lower risk. However, smaller businesses did not enjoy this privilege. India has traditionally been a capital-starved country. Thus the demands for loans were high. These firms, with much lower credit ratings, had to face much more stringent lending terms and higher interest rates. Banks had to be cautious in terms of extending credit to lesser-known companies or new ventures and a growing number of credit-hungry retail clients, especially due to the lack of expert credit reporting agencies for small and medium-scale industries.

ICICI Bank: history and evolution

Shortly after India gained its independence in 1947, ICICI Limited was established by the World Bank and the Indian government in 1955 to promote industrial development. The main objective of the institution was to provide short- and medium-term project financing to Indian business. In the 1990s, ICICI transformed itself from a development financial institution offering simple project financing to a diversified institution offering a broad range of financial products and services, either directly or through its various subsidiaries and affiliates like ICICI Bank. In 1999 ICICI became the first Indian company and first non-Japanese or non-Asian financial institution to be listed on the New York Stock Exchange.

As the banking industry went through deregulation and became more competitive, ICICI Limited and ICICI Bank looked at various restructuring alternatives. The ultimate goal was to create a universal banking institution, and the managements of ICICI Ltd and ICICI Bank concluded that the reverse merger of ICICI with ICICI Bank would be the optimal strategic and legal alternative for both entities. The merger promised to unlock synergies between the two entities and to add value to both groups of shareholders. The merger would enhance value for shareholders of ICICI Ltd through the merged entity's access to low-cost deposits, greater opportunities for earning fee-based income and the ability to participate in the payments system and provide transaction-banking services. For ICICI Bank shareholders, the merger would unlock value through a stronger balance sheet, a larger scale of operations, seamless access to ICICI's strong corporate relationships built over five decades, entry into new business segments, higher market share in various business segments – particularly fee-based services – and access to the vast talent pool of ICICI and its subsidiaries. In October 2001, the boards of directors of ICICI Ltd and ICICI Bank approved the merger of ICICI Ltd and two of its wholly owned retail finance subsidiaries, ICICI Personal Financial Services Limited and ICICI Capital Services Limited, with ICICI Bank. After the merger, ICICI's financing and banking operations, both corporate and retail, had been incorporated as a single entity.[7] Exhibit 1.4 lists a summary of key dates for ICICI.

1955	The Industrial Credit and Investment Corporation of India Limited (ICICI) incorporated at the initiative of the World Bank, the Government of India and representatives of Indian industry, with the objective of creating a development financial institution for providing medium- and long-term project financing to Indian businesses.
	ICICI emerges as the major source of foreign currency loans to Indian industry. Besides funding from the World Bank and other multi-lateral agencies, ICICI is also among the first Indian companies to raise funds from international markets.
1956	ICICI declared its first Dividend at 3.5 per cent.
1958	Mr G.L. Mehta was appointed the 2nd Chairman of ICICI Ltd.
1960	ICICI building at 163 Backbay Reclamation was inaugurated.
1961	The first West German loan of DM5 million from Kredianstalt was obtained by ICICI.
1967	ICICI made its first debenture issue for Rs6 crore, which was oversubscribed.
1969	First two regional offices in Calcutta and Madras were opened.
1972	Second entity in India to set up merchant banking services.
	Mr H.T. Parekh appointed as the third Chairman of ICICI.
1977	ICICI sponsors the formation of Housing Development Finance Corporation. Managed its first equity public issue.
1978	Mr James Raj appointed as the fourth Chairman of ICICI.
1979	Mr Siddharth Mehta appointed as the fifth Chairman of ICICI.
1982	Becomes the first ever Indian borrower to raise European Currency Units.
	ICICI commences leasing business.
1984	Mr S. Nadkarni appointed as the sixth Chairman of ICICI.
1985	Mr N. Vaghul appointed as the seventh Chairman and Managing Director of ICICI.
1986	ICICI first Indian Institution to receive ADB loans. First public issue by an Indian entity in the Swiss Capital Markets.
	ICICI along with UTI sets up Credit Rating Information Services of India Limited (CRISIL), India's first professional credit rating agency.
	ICICI promotes Shipping Credit and Investment Company of India Limited (SCICI).
	The corporation made a public issue of 75 million Swiss francs in Switzerland, the first public issue by any Indian equity in the Swiss capital market.
1987	ICICI signed a loan agreement for 10 million sterling pounds with the Commonwealth Development Corporation (CDC), the first loan by CDC for financing projects in India.
1988	ICICI promotes TDICI – India's first venture capital company.
1993	ICICI sets up ICICI Securities and Finance Company Limited in joint venture with J.P. Morgan.
	ICICI sets up ICICI Asset Management Company.
1994	ICICI sets up ICICI Bank.
1996	ICICI becomes the first company in the Indian financial sector to raise GDR.
	ICICI announces merger with SCICI.
	Mr K.V. Kamath appointed the Managing Director and CEO of ICICI Ltd.
1997	ICICI was the first intermediary to move away from single prime rate to three-tier prime rates structure, and introduced yield-curve based pricing.
	The name 'The Industrial Credit and Investment Corporation of India Limited' was changed to 'ICICI Limited'.
	ICICI announces takeover of ITC Classic Finance.
1998	Introduced the new logo symbolizing a common corporate identity for the ICICI Group.
	ICICI announces takeover of Anagram Finance.

1999	ICICI launches retail finance – car loans, house loans and loans for consumer durables.
	ICICI becomes the first Indian company to list on the NYSE through an issue of American depositary shares.
2000	ICICI Bank becomes the first commercial bank from India to list its stock on NYSE.
	ICICI Bank announces merger with Bank of Madura.
2001	The boards of ICICI Ltd and ICICI Bank approve the merger of ICICI with ICICI Bank.
2002	Moodys assign higher than sovereign rating to ICICI.
	Merger of ICICI Limited, ICICI Capital Services Ltd and ICICI Personal Financial Services Limited with ICICI Bank.

Exhibit 1.4 History of ICICI

Home market battleground

Entry strategy of Citibank

With few entry barriers, high-profile banks with deep pockets, like Citibank, entered the Indian market with modern, air-conditioned branches and friendly staff. Citibank was the first bank to set up ATMs in Mumbai and New Delhi. However, such new attractive banking offerings were reserved solely for the affluent. Citibank was very cautious in extending banking and credit services to the Indian private sector because there were no credit reporting agencies to validate customer attractiveness. Since Citibank instituted a minimum balance for ATM use (as well as branch use), the plastic debit card branded the rich with the distinction of technological superiority and high class.

However, convincing anybody in India, affluent or not, to use ATMs proved to be a formidable task for 'first-mover' Citibank. The simple service westerners take for granted was still viewed as something out of a science fiction movie. The concept of using a piece of plastic to withdraw cash from a savings account was exciting for a few but scary for the masses. To get customers to try the ATMs, Citibank had to educate the Indian consumer on the security processes and the safety of the funds from outside intruders.

Besides combating the fear of losing money in an ATM transaction, Citibank faced a much more difficult issue that it needed to overcome within Indian culture. Most of the early adopters viewed ATMs as a source for emergency cash, for an unexpected hospital visit, car repair or trip out of town. The prospect of being stuck without cash or delaying gratification was a new concept for those of the Indian culture. Years of fiscal discipline and stringent savings patterns demanded that people went to the bank only on a periodic basis, carefully planning out their use of cash.

While convincing people to take money out was difficult, persuading people to deposit money proved even more of a challenge. Customers were used to the traditional way of waiting in line, using their pay-in-slip books and getting a comforting blue stamp confirming the deposit. Simply dropping cash or a cheque into an ATM slot and getting a small confirmation receipt proved too daring for most Indians. To reassure customers, Citibank installed telephones on all ATMs that could be used to call a clerk in case of an emergency. Furthermore, security cameras, keeping track of any unauthorized activities, were installed for customers' peace of mind. Despite all these efforts, in the early years, ATM transactions were heavily skewed towards withdrawals.

The domestic strategy of ICICI

After attaining 'first mover' status, decades of consumer education and an incredible balance sheet, Citibank, by standard competitive strategy theory, should have solidified itself as the premier private bank in India. However, to everyone's surprise, this did not happen. ICICI's unique indigenous strategy proved much more successful and helped the Indian bank catch up to Citibank and, eventually, overcome it.

The new luxuries offered by Citibank and other foreign banks, such as HSBC and Standard Chartered, targeted the small segment of wealthy Indians, effectively neglecting nearly 30 to 60 million bankable households. While the western banks saw the middle class as an unattractive and risky market, K.V. Kamath of ICICI Bank saw it as an opportunity. These people kept whatever savings they had at home or in local banks and borrowed only for special occasions like weddings, education, emergencies, etc. Due to high economic growth, this growing segment of middle-class consumers saw their wealth continue to increase and, more and more, they wanted banking services that fitted their needs. 'We recognized the changing demographics and growth of a service sector [now constituting more than half of India's output],' says Chanda Kochhar, ICICI's Executive Director for Retail Banking.[8]

However, at that time, a simple transaction like cashing a cheque or making a bank deposit could mean standing in a long queue, then waiting days for multiple signatures and approvals. One senior manager at ICICI Bank commented, 'Branches themselves were often dark and literally piled high with dusty ledgers. Byzantine rules meant exasperated customers could spend hours being shuffled from desk to desk, watching cantankerous staffers sip tea and erect bureaucratic obstacles.'[9]

ICICI began to aggressively target middle-class Indians, those earning around $4,500 per year, by offering a more customer-friendly banking experience: 'We hired [international bankers] from the market and learned from what the foreign banks had been doing,' says Kalpana Morparia, Deputy Managing Director of ICICI.[10]

To serve the up-and-coming customers, ICICI opened branches that were not only clean, well lit and air-conditioned, but also computerized, enabling staff to make simple decisions, and dispense cash, loans and account statements more quickly than rivals. Furthermore, building on Citibank's introduction of ATMs, ICICI took the ATM service to another level by pushing their use beyond what is typical in the western world. For example, customers could not only withdraw and deposit funds, but also pay their bills, transfer money and even give donations to their favourite religious institutions.

While ICICI made huge strides in terms of building a customer-friendly banking institution, at the end of the century brand visibility was still poor. Only a few people knew ICICI, and maybe some had heard of the tongue-twister Industrial Credit & Investment Corp. of India. Realizing that having superior service and product offerings was not enough to build a strong brand, ICICI spent 16 times more on advertising than did the State Bank of India, the largest bank in India. As a result, the percentage of customers showing awareness of the bank shot up to 96 per cent in 2003 from just 20 per cent in 1999.[11] In fact, in 2001 ICICI received a prestigious marketing excellence award for the 'Most Recalled Advertisement on Television' from the *Indian Express*.[12] Kamath believed that brand building was important to the future of the bank, for a strong 'brand will facilitate ICICI's entry into all geographies and all different types of business'.[13]

ICICI's strategy paid off. After a new stock issue in Mumbai and New York in December 2005, ICICI Bank overtook State Bank of India Ltd to become India's largest bank in terms of market value, and the strongest player in the sweet spot of the Indian economy: *the growing middle-class market*. While ICICI enjoyed a steady growth in customer numbers, more than 15 million accounts in 2006, the growth in assets had been proportionally slow. ICICI's customer base was equal to the combined customer base of the three largest banks in Singapore. However, in terms of assets, ICICI was only one-tenth their size. To address this issue, ICICI was betting on the growing Indian economy to increase its customers' wealth, and the bank's ability to sell more, higher-margin products to its customers.

ICICI sets its sights on rural India

Much to the disapproval of foreign banks and many Indian banks, ICICI, in its typical aggressive style, began to go after India's rural population of 600 million people, who have only recently begun turning to banks (see Exhibit 1.5). Considering the difficulties of assessing credit-worthiness in a country that still does not have individual credit rating companies, the strategy of going after rural customers was viewed by many as risky. Investors, for example, were concerned about ICICI's portfolio integrity, as the bad loan balance could surge with the addition of riskier clients.

To address these concerns, ICICI once again revolutionized banking processes by developing an innovative way of checking the credit-worthiness of first-time borrowers. The bank deployed an army of specifically trained personnel to visit potential clients' homes and workplaces, and verify their personal information, assets, liabilities and salaries. 'Labour costs are low in India,' says Ms Morparia, 'so every person that comes to us, we can scrutinize their statements thoroughly before extending credit or issuing a credit card.'[14]

While ICICI was partly obliged by the Indian government to cater to this 'priority' sector, K.V. Kamath believed that getting rural customers to bank could be transformed from an isolated philanthropic activity with the hope of profit to a real business with a hint of compassion. As a sign of commitment to rural India, the rural banking

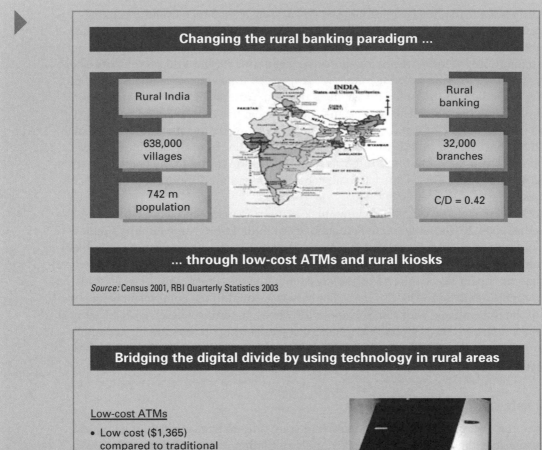

Changing the rural banking paradigm ...

Rural India		Rural banking
638,000 villages		32,000 branches
742 m population		C/D = 0.42

... through low-cost ATMs and rural kiosks

Source: Census 2001, RBI Quarterly Statistics 2003

Bridging the digital divide by using technology in rural areas

Low-cost ATMs

- Low cost ($1,365) compared to traditional ATM ($25,000)

- To provide most basic service of deposits and withdrawals

- Facilitating a chip card for all financial transactions and data storage

Exhibit 1.5 Rural banking paradigm
Source: WWB Global Network for Banking Innovation in Microfinance: Innovation Brief Challenges Moving Forward

division became a stand-alone business unit, independent from its original Social Development Group. The division over rural banking, microfinance and agricultural lending generated over 1.4 billion rupees ($32 million) and comprised about 5 per cent of the bank's net interest income in 2005.

In addition to assessing clients' credit-worthiness, ICICI bank had to deal with other challenges, like reaching customers in areas with no infrastructure and those who were often too poor to buy banking products, as well as helping customers deal with the difficult task of repaying loans (especially during bad climatic seasons caused by events such as drought, floods, etc.). To create its presence in rural regions of India that were characterized by unreliable or non-existent telephone communications, ICICI developed chip-embedded cards that could verify a depositor's identity offline by storing the person's thumbprint. To induce customers to buy banking products, ICICI began rethinking traditional banking offerings by shrinking products like insurance and mutual funds. Packaged goods companies (like Hindustan Levers) realized that the poor would buy products like shampoo if they were brought to them in small, affordable packets one could buy for a single use, instead of spending a lot on a whole bottle. In the same vein, ICICI started selling personal accident insurance at its rural branches for $2 a year, which paid out about $2,200 in case of death. Finally, ICICI took a more personal approach to banking by establishing relationships with its clients through the role of financial counsellor. 'We can't simply go there and say, "I'm a financier; I don't know anything else". If you don't know anything else, the customer is going to give you the residual of whatever happened to his life. If he's not able to sell his sugar cane, if he's not able to sell his grain, if he's not able to get good value for his milk, he suffers and you know what? You suffer,' commented Nachiket Mor, Head of Rural Banking at ICICI.

To protect farmers from bad monsoons that ruin their harvest and cause them to default on their loans, ICICI started selling the farmers rainfall insurance that offered bridge loans and even helped with administrative issues so that farmers did not miss valuable work time.

The role of technology

From the beginning of ICICI's transformation, technology played a central role. Going after millions of people who complete many small transactions (in terms of currency) would have been impossible with the traditional banking systems and procedures.

Five decades of government control had left an enduring legacy of outdated networks and information systems. ICICI had multiple reporting systems for each business unit, which were becoming cumbersome to maintain. Since IT undertook the role of information provider, the process was ad hoc and inconsistent. Furthermore, as the bank continued to grow, legacy processing and reporting systems did not have enough bandwidth to handle all the transactions. 'Coupled with this, bandwidth issues (MIS over email), security concerns with enterprise data lying on desktops, and exponentially increasing data established a distinct need for a solution that can integrate all data sources across the enterprise, in user-friendly and above-all a scalable solution that could support the growing business needs of ICICI Bank.'[15]

With the help of SAS systems, ICICI implemented an enterprise-wide reporting system that enabled synergetic reporting from multiple applications within a single business unit and, at the same time, was flexible enough to cater to the reporting needs of various business units.

▶   These investments in continuous technology upgrades had an immediate impact on the work culture and performance of the bank. For example, when other banks (especially nationalized banks) took months to approve short-term loans, ICICI began to make decisions within a week. By doing this, ICICI serviced the masses and met the long-unmet demand for reliable short-term borrowing. Its short-term lending grew rapidly, gaining market share at the expense of the technologically slow nationalized banks.

With ICICI's expansion of its ATM and branch locations to rural areas and other countries, it invested heavily in its communication network. The bank created a complex web of its own lines as well as various leased lines and switches. Kamath says that this critical infrastructure had 'given us the opportunity to scope, scale and change'.[16]

The far-reaching, high-bandwidth network enabled ICICI to push back-office processing from branches to central and regional processing hubs. 'Technology was an enabler for us to reach the stars. It gave us the possibility to extend our geographic reach without actually putting a physical bank in place in most locations,' says Vinod Easwaran, ICICI's Head of Retail Banking for Russia. 'It improved our product delivery to customers and led to a tremendous increase in efficiency in back-office processing.'[17]

According to ICICI's own benchmarking research, technology operating expense per customer was 5 per cent to 10 per cent of that of ICICI's global competitors.

Innovations at ICICI

Driven by the desire to grow and reach millions of customers, ICICI bank revolutionized Indian banking with a number of technological, product and process innovations. In order to reach rural customers, ICICI installed solar-powered ATMs that operated using wireless technology and used biometric technology instead of the standard PIN cards.[18] The ATMs were also more sophisticated in terms of available transactions, and more accessible with Braille and voice-enabled input for the blind and/or illiterate.[19] In rural areas, ICICI created 'low-cost' ATMs to provide the most basic services of deposits and withdrawals. These ATMs also operated on chip cards and cost only $1,365 instead of $25,000 for a traditional ATM.[20] Finally, in 2002, ICICI launched a so-called 'ATM on wheels'. These full-featured and networked mobile ATMs were placed at certain locations at predetermined times. The 'ATMs on wheels' were connected to the bank's central database through GPRS (general packet radio service) technology, which enabled real-time information exchange through wireless media. The movement of the mobile ATM was tracked using global positioning system (GPS) technology, and monitored by a 24-hour ICICI Bank ATM help desk.[21]

In an effort to make banking even more accessible, ICICI created a multi-channel strategy to be where the customer was. ICICI customers enjoyed various channels of banking, like 8–8 banking (branches open from 8 am to 8 pm), free internet banking, free mobile and phone banking and bank@home. For example, the bank@home concept allowed customers to drop transaction slips into a special drop box at certain defined locations. These slips were picked up by the bank every day and serviced by the local branch. These were called remote service delivery (RSD) transactions. The customer could also request to have cash delivered to him by simply calling the local branch. This service was called 'Cash on Tap' (CoT). These services aimed to reduce customers' travel time to and from the branches, and were like banking from one's home.

ICICI also pioneered a new type of branch – the rural kiosk. These low-cost kiosks took many forms (a makeshift stall, a room in a village bungalow or a multi-purpose store that also offered movies and online medical advice) and were owned by entrepreneurs. ICICI trained them, connected them to the internet and used them as conduits to sell banking products or simply to inform locals about them. By leaving kiosk ownership to others who could sell other products and services, ICICI avoided heavy overheads and created local employment.[22]

In a recent move that stunned the Indian banking industry, ICICI began offering free credit cards that were good for life. ICICI Bank had taken a substantial lead since it overtook Citibank to become the number one credit card issuing bank. The bank had issued over 35 lakh (3.5 million) credit cards against Citibank's 27 lakh.[23] Citibank, as well as other foreign banks, had questioned the sustainability of such aggressive credit lending, specifically calling attention to the integrity of the bank's assets and the potential default rates.

Wide distribution through an aggressive rollout also enabled ICICI to overtake Citibank in the auto loan market. Citibank was the pioneer in the domestic automobile loan market and enjoyed the premier position with 27 per cent share in the late 1990s. In 2005, Citibank's share fell to only 8 per cent, while ICICI's share increased from less than 10 per cent to almost 30 per cent in the same time period.[24]

Human resources: leadership redefined

Along with strategic and technological transformations, ICICI also redefined internal employee relations. When Kamath became CEO of ICICI in the late 1990s, he quickly diagnosed a problem of atrophy at the bank. Kamath spoke about the young talent at the bank: 'They were a small group of twenty, all from the top 10 per cent of the four major B-schools. One day I asked one of these youngsters to mail merge 25 letters. Two days later I asked what happened to those letters. He made some excuse. I went back to my room and in twenty minutes I did the mail merge, printed out the letters, signed them, and left them on his table.'

ICICI was a favourite recruiter at the Indian business schools. Young, ambitious, hungry and talented people would come in and, within a year, lose their motivation and leave the organization. This problem ran deep, affecting all levels, functions and business units.

In order to remedy the chronic atrophy, Kamath implemented the so-called 'parking lot' theory, whereby seniors were moved to one side after some years so that younger talent could move up. Kamath explained: 'In any organizational change, you give people a golden handshake but there will still be people working in areas from which you want to push them in or out. So you park them in other spots, you remove the blockage, and get the flow going the way you want it.'[25]

Kamath realized that, to be competitive, ICICI had to rejuvenate its organizational culture and grow out of its heritage. According to Kamath: 'We put in place a voluntary retirement scheme. Together with it we put in a new performance appraisal system and gave explicit feedback.'

Despite Kamath's efforts to explain the changes during countless meetings, five structural changes in eight years had created tensions and low morale among employees. In the words of Kamath:

> The foremost ingredient for ICICI Group's success had been the ability to continuously evolve both organizational structure and product offerings, thereby remaining on the cutting edge of financial services. The robust growth achieved during a period otherwise marked by modest economic growth, had been entirely on account of capitalizing market opportunities. With the environmental changes that had happened in the banking sector in India, financial, human, technology and speed capital, would drive the financial services sector in the future and draw the boundaries for achieving leadership in this business. My strategy has therefore revolved around augmenting these capitals.

ICICI brought back lateral recruitment, something that hadn't been done for decades. The goal was to bring new skills, competencies and experience into the organization and meet the requirements of rapidly growing businesses.[26] ICICI had even implemented a Six Sigma initiative for the lateral recruitment process, to improve capabilities in this area.

ICICI built strong capabilities in training and development, with training and leadership programmes at a dedicated training facility. ICICI Bank also used the best available training programmes and personnel, both Indian and foreign, to build skills and capabilities to a global standard.[27] In addition to world-class training, the bank encouraged cross-functional movement in order to enhance employees' knowledge and experience, as well as provide a holistic view of the organization.

Kamath also made changes at the top, creating an 'A Team' to champion his vision, a concept borrowed from GE's Jack Welch, who had been an important influence on Kamath. He also tied pay to performance and cut back the dead wood.[28] However, Kamath's 'A Team' (Lalita Gupte, S.H. Bhojani, S. Mukherji, Kalpana Morparia and Shikha Sharma), who are responsible for actually implementing Kamath's vision, was scheduled to retire before or with him.

Organizational changes did not happen overnight, or even over years. According to some analysts and banking professions, ICICI still bore the burden of atrophy that had been nurtured for years before Kamath took over: 'Young MBAs use ICICI as a training ground before moving to greener pastures. Those who stick, their biggest problem is that they are middle and junior management professionals today who are aloof from reality but bask in the glory of its leader. It's almost a sense that others do not know anything and that just by being in ICICI, you're the most knowledgeable,' said an HR consultant.

International expansion at ICICI

ICICI's venture outside India was not the first of its kind. In the 1990s, the State Bank of India, Bank of Baroda and Bank of India, all government-owned lenders, expanded into the USA, UK or France, where they had short-term success. However, due to a number of reasons, like the real estate crisis and changing organizational structures, many of these banks had not been able to succeed in the long run. ICICI's success in international expansion could be attributed to a number of unique characteristics. First, ICICI utilized various entry strategies depending on the local conditions and regulations. Many countries, for example, required banks to first run either representative offices or offshore branches for a few years before a subsidiary was allowed[29] (see Exhibit 1.6). Second, ICICI did not attempt to build a branch network from scratch. The bank made strategic acquisitions and rebranded the organizations to maintain consistency. In the same vein, ICICI encouraged its partners in local banks to leverage their network and keep costs down. Third, ICICI maintained a unique organizational strategy that differed from those of other Indian banks that have attempted to globalize. Unlike public-sector banks, which post an official overseas for two or three years, ICICI Bank aimed to identify the performers and keep them overseas to grow the business. ICICI Bank sent a local to head the operation as country head and build a local team around him – British, Chinese, American, and so on. The local heads are trained in India and absorb the parent company's culture.[30]

Where the global push is taking ICICI Bank		
Singapore	Offshore branch	N.A.
Dubai	Representative office	N.A.
London	Subsidiary	$50 million
Shanghai	Representative office	N.A.
Toronto	Subsidiary	$20 million
Bahrain	Offshore branch	N.A.
New York	Representative office	N.A.

Exhibit 1.6 Structure of international presence

Note: Some of the representative offices and offshore branches may later be converted into fully fledged subsidiaries, subject to regulatory approval. They will then need to be capitalized.

Source: ICICI Bank: The Global Gambit (http://www.businessworldindia.com/oct1303/indepth02.asp)

ICICI's international strategy can be separated into two distinct phases. During the first phase, the bank tried to capitalize on its Indian connections. In this so-called 'follow the customer' strategy, ICICI specifically targeted Indian citizens wherever they were. During the second phase, ICICI expanded its appeal to the broader public, taking advantage of its economies of scale and value propositions. The two phases of the international expansion are described below.

Follow the Indian: focus on global Indians

ICICI established its International Banking Group in 2002 in hopes of extending its successful domestic branchless expansion: 'We started with the premise that we would follow the Indian diaspora, which was located in various countries outside India, which led us to look at markets like Canada, the UK and the USA, where we initially established our footholds,' said Vinod Easwaran, ICICI's Head of Retail Banking for Russia.[31]

The strategic focus in these countries had been fee-based services such as remittances (rather than deposit expansion). ICICI saw an opportunity to help these customers, who were supporting families back home as well as buying properties there. ICICI later expanded its product/service offering by adding India-centric products for mortgages and car loans. For customers living abroad who wanted to buy a car or a house for their parents, these types of services proved invaluable, especially since local banks practically ignored this need. ICICI also offered online share trading in Indian stock exchanges for these customers.

The results were spectacular. According to ICICI Bank Deputy Managing Director Kalpana Morparia, the bank had already achieved a leadership position in the $20 billion annual remittance market with a share of nearly 20 per cent.[32] Currently, ICICI offers a number of online and offline remittance products to cater to different geographic markets. Exhibit 1.7 outlines Indian remittances in more detail.

Besides being a financial success, the strategy of following and serving the NRI (non-resident Indian) segment enabled ICICI to establish a foothold in the financial sectors of the world: 'London and Singapore are money centres but we also have linkages there. For instance, we use Singapore for raising foreign currency syndicated loans for Indian businesses,' commented Bhargava Dasgupta, Head of the International Banking Group.

On the corporate side, ICICI leveraged its corporate lending heritage to service Indian corporations doing business abroad. As in the retail sector, ICICI had been able to create a comprehensive suite of products and services to cater to the needs of this. ICICI had helped Indian companies in raising trade finance, letters of credit or project finance for their investments abroad.[33]

Follow the customer: a universal value proposition

K.V. Kamath realized that simply banking on Indian customers worldwide could not be a sustainable growth strategy in the long-run: 'We initially thought let's follow the Indian consumer, the Indian corporate, but over a period of time we realized that it is not just about following the Indian consumer and the Indian corporate,' Easwaran said.

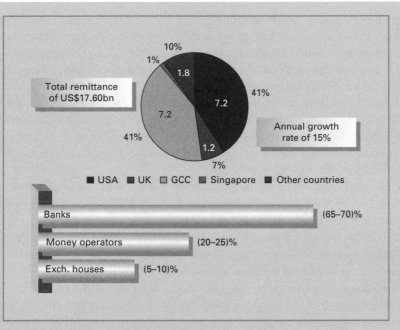

Exhibit 1.7 Pattern of remittances to India
Source: The WWB Global Network For Banking Innovation in Microfinance: Innovation Brief Challenges Moving Forward

'Being a global bank is about following the consumer wherever he is, whatever nation he belongs to.'[34]

In the second phase of international expansion, the focus shifted from following/ serving the NRI segment to attempting to export the bank's successful domestic mass-market model to certain markets abroad. ICICI's strategy was to capitalize on its economies of scale to reduce operating costs and offer better rates than competing banks in the regions.

'Our competitive advantage in mass banking lies in handling high volumes of low-ticket transactions. We have developed extensive technology capabilities to handle these low-ticket transactions,' said Morparia.[35]

ICICI was able to cut costs by pushing all the back-office processes to the central unit in India. Furthermore, ICICI did not only outsource local IT and processing to India, but also used low-cost factors of production for product development, marketing and human resources.

ICICI leveraged its information systems and networks to get close to the customer without an extensive branch presence. This goal was achieved in two ways. First, ICICI had been very successful in channelling customers away from the branches and towards ATMs, the internet and call centres. For example, in Canada in 2004, branches accounted for 29 per cent of customer banking transactions, while ATMs, the internet and telephone banking account for 34 per cent, 23 per cent and 8 per cent of transactions, respectively.[36]

▶   Just like in rural India, geographic challenges were overcome with technological innovation and creativity. For example, ICICI pioneered the staffless branch concept, allowing customers to visit unmanned branches but still talk to a representative via a video link.[37] For more sophisticated products like mortgages and insurance, ICICI set up a network of direct selling agents and dealers.

Second, ICICI had been trying to extend its reach without spending on building its own network, by tying up with big banks such as Wells Fargo, Lloyds, Emirates and DBS. For example, ICICI's British subsidiary formed a strategic alliance with Lloyds TSB to offer a host of India-linked banking services such as mortgages, remittances, NRI savings accounts and other NRI deposit products.

ICICI acquired banks, when needed, if time to market was essential. However, Kamath ruled out 'the transformational acquisition', saying 'domestic opportunity is enough and, anyway, there are still plenty of [other] things to do with our capital'.[38]

In 2006, ICICI acquired a Russian bank, Investitsionno-Kreditny Bank (IKB), which enabled ICICI to acquire an extensive network very quickly. IKB had assets of about $4.4 million and loans of $2.5 million, and ranked just outside Russia's top 1,000 banks. IKB had two branches in the Kaluga region, one in Moscow, and a staff of around 30. ICICI intended to use IKB to engage in both retail and corporate banking business. It planned to increase the bank's capital from $1.2 million to $15 million, and build a network of branches in Moscow and St Petersburg, which would operate under the ICICI brand.[39]

Currently, according to Kamath, the biggest roadblock to international growth is the absence of operations in the USA. While ICICI had a representative office in New York, it was still awaiting permission from the Federal Reserve to start banking operations in the USA. But the US regulator had become very cautious after 9/11 and was reluctant to grant licences until the foreign bank's home country's regulators adopted processes that are in line with those prescribed by the USA.[40]

Future outlook

As Kamath thought about the next five years, he wondered if the incredible growth of his bank could be sustained. Where would the next growth spurt come from? Could it be that his success was due to favourable economic conditions in India (much higher interest rates) and an outsourcing boom that had taken the world by storm right in his backyard? Kamath worried that while ICICI had managed to grow its customer base, it had not been able to grow its asset base accordingly. Furthermore, as many analysts were quick to point out, the effects of the aggressive expansion strategy on the integrity of the bank's assets were still largely unknown. Finally, Kamath wondered whether or not ICICI Bank would be able to develop a new breed of young talent to carry forward his vision after he retired.

He looked at his watch, noted the date of Caisses d'Epargne's visit to ICICI and considered whether he would have time to welcome them personally, to showcase the bank that he had created over the last 25 years …

Notes

1. Joint Managing Director & Head of International Operations.
2. Senior General Manager & Head International Banking Group.
3. Congress led central government during 1991–1996, when India took the path to liberalization.
4. *Indian Banking: Market Liberalization and the Pressures for Institutional and Market Framework Reform*, James A. Hanson, August 2001, Stanford University.
5. World Gold Council.
6. Favoured long-term equities for companies like TATAs, Reliance, Hindustan Levers, ITC etc.
7. Information in this section is taken from corporate website: www.icicibank.com.
8. 'ICICI, India's largest bank in the private sector, is growing apace with the ranks of the consumer society', Forbes.com: 22 July 2005.
9. 'ICICI banks on a new India – Focus on consumers reflects rapid shift in nation's economy', *Wall Street Journal Asia*, December 2005.
10. *Ibid.*
11. Research conducted by IMRB – Millward Brown.
12. 2001 annual report.
13. 'Cross-border strategies – ICICI: Technology powers expansion at ICICI', *Retail Banker International*, 30 November 2005.
14. 'ICICI banks on a new India – Focus on consumers reflects rapid shift in nation's economy', *Wall Street Journal Asia*, December 2005.
15. SAS case study on ICICI.
16. 'Timing and technology put bank ahead of the global game – ICICI'S annual IT operating cost per customer is just 5 to 10 per cent of its international competitors' costs', *Financial Times*, 26 January 2006.
17. 'Cross-border strategies – ICICI: Technology powers expansion at ICICI', *Retail Banker International*, 30 November, 2005.
18. 'Generating rural wealth by marrying commerce, tech.', *Indian Express*, 8 January 2006.
19. Best Multi-Channel Strategy, by Technology Awards, 3 September 2003.
20. The WWB Global Network For Banking Innovation in Microfinance: Innovation Brief.
21. ICICI press release, December 2002.
22. 'In India, thinking big by thinking small Banks aim for profits in a new market: The rural poor', Anand Giridharadas, *International Herald Tribune*, 1 October 2005.
23. 'Rivals cock a snook at ICICI credit card move', *Business Standard*, 10 August 2005.
24. 'ICICI Bank pips Citibank in automobile loan race', *Business Standard*, 10 August 2005.
25. K.V. Kamath on How To Manage Change, 9 February 2005.
26. ICICI 2002 annual report.
27. *Ibid.*
28. 'Big is beautiful', Forbes.com, 22 July 2005.
29. ICICI Bank: The Global Gambit (http://www.businessworldindia.com/oct1303/indepth02.asp).
30. 'Cross-border strategies – ICICI: Technology powers expansion at ICICI', *Retail Banker International*, 30 November 2005.
31. *Ibid.*
32. 'ICICI Bank set to boost overseas presence', *Hindustan Times,* 24 October 2005.
33. *Ibid.*
34. 'Cross-border strategies – ICICI: Technology powers expansion at ICICI', *Retail Banker International*, 30 November 2005.
35. 'ICICI Bank set to boost overseas presence', *Hindustan Times*, 24 October 2005.
36. 'Cross-border strategies – ICICI: Technology powers expansion at ICICI', *Retail Banker International*, 30 November 2005.
37. Best Multi-Channel Strategy. Technology Awards, 3 September 2003.
38. 'Timing and technology put bank ahead of the global game – ICICI'S annual IT operating cost per customer is just 5 to 10 per cent of its international competitors' costs', *Financial Times*, 26 January 2006.

[39] 'Cross-border strategies – ICICI: Technology powers expansion at ICICI', *Retail Banker International*, 30 November 2005.
[40] 'The price warrior', *Economic Times*, 25 March 2005.

? Case questions

Read the case carefully and then answer the following questions.

1 Describe the banking industry in India. How did the changes in the industry induce ICICI to become a top player domestically?

2 Compare and contrast ICICI's and foreign banks' (Citibank) strategies in India. What would you advise any new entrant in this context (BNP, for example)?

3 Discuss ICICI's globalization strategy. Why has ICICI been successful when other Indian banks have not?

4 What are the current challenges faced by ICICI and how should ICICI address them?

CHAPTER 2

Developing strategic capability: evolution of the multinational corporation

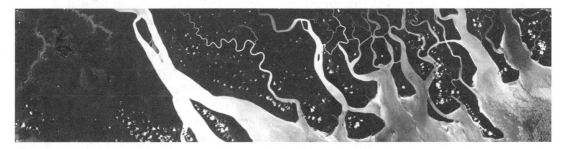

The first chapter discussed *global corporations* in a broad sense. But international business (IB) and strategy research involves more narrow terminology, which defines global companies as multinational enterprises (MNEs) or multinational companies (MNCs). This chapter shall dwell briefly on these definitional issues before moving on to the evolution of MNCs, their strengths and weaknesses, their biases, their tensions, and how they can develop multi-level competencies and interrelated capabilities. Following these discussions, the chapter will refer to the strategy literature to enumerate the linkage of national competitive advantage, industry analysis, strategy formulation and implementation in the international business landscape.

Definitional issues: MNCs

International, global, MNC, transnational

Global corporations are those whose activities are carried out across national borders, and have standardized and integrated operations worldwide. This means that necessary conditions for a global corporation to exist include land, labour, capital and entrepreneurial ventures in more than one market, and the customization of products for different markets. Sufficient conditions for global corporations to exist include asset specificity, avoidance of uncertainty, localized decision making, and sharing of intangible assets such as knowledge, resources and firm-specific skills. In the late 1980s, research termed these global companies MNCs or MNEs. For example, in the *Forbes* 2007 MNCs, the top ten corporations (by sales, profits, assets and market value) were CitiGroup, Bank of America, HSBC Holdings, General Electric, JP Morgan Chase, American Intl Group, ExxonMobil (all American companies), Royal Dutch Shell (Netherlands), UBS (Switzerland) and ING Group (Netherlands).

To be an MNC meant that there was more than just trade happening; there was more than a traditional ownership structure between the parent company and its global operations. The corporation had to decide where to locate its operations, its assets and its employees, and understand how to overcome respective conflicting demands. For example, the MNC's strategy should include overcoming the liability of its 'foreignness' (i.e. the disadvantages of being a new player in a new market, coupled with not knowing the local market). It also should include the costs associated with learning, coordination and governance. Depending on the degree of geographic dispersion, local responsiveness and national differentiation of its markets, plus organizational or global coordination and integration, the corporation must adopt one of four mentalities and strategic postures: international, multinational, global or transnational.

Figure 2.1 denotes the evolution of the theory of the multinational corporation. The pioneering work of Prahlad and Doz (1987) referred to four such strategies depending on the integration-responsiveness framework which is depicted in Figure 2.1(a). During the same period, Porter (1987) and, later, Bartlett and Ghoshal (1989) built on this framework to propose the theory and classification of MNCs that became well accepted, widely diffused and popular in the IB literature, referred to as the transnational corporation and depicted in Figures 2.1(b) and 2.1(c) respectively.

Bartlett and Ghoshal defined the *International* corporation as one in its earliest stages of internationalization, where overseas operations were labelled as 'distant outposts' that existed to supply raw materials, support manufacturing operations, and strengthen, by building new markets, the domestic parent company. Managers expatriated to these foreign units, referred to as 'appendages', were often local misfits and the decision processes for these units were usually opportunistic or ad hoc. These corporations exploited their parent company knowledge and capabilities through worldwide diffusion and adaptation, and centralized their sources of core competencies. Not only corporations but also whole industries, such as telecommunication switching instruments, had an international mentality as their technological innovations occurred in their homeland and were subsequently appropriated to other multiple markets. This strategic posture was common among US-based corporations such as GE, Procter & Gamble, Pfizer and others.

Multinational corporations understood and recognized that there are differences across national markets, and differentiation was required to be successful in these diverse markets. These corporations were more flexible, and were ready to adapt and modify their offerings, strategy, structure and management styles in their respective national markets. They understood that the skill sets needed to manage these markets were different, and

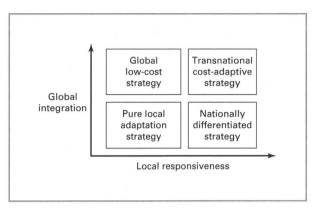

Figure 2.1(a) The integration-responsiveness framework[1]

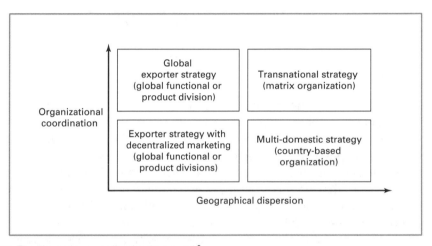

Figure 2.1(b) The dispersion-coordination framework[2]

that they needed entrepreneurs and their best talents to manage these markets. Their strategies were geared to be nationally responsive and they had the willingness to invest in the growth of these markets while learning to be self-sufficient and independent from their parent company. Some industries, like book publishing, commercial banking and laundry detergents, had multinational characteristics. In the laundry detergent sector, toothpaste R&D and manufacturing costs were relatively small compared to costs associated with adapting to local forces such as national laundry practices, laundry perfume preferences, the political nature of phosphate legislation, local distribution norms and other attributes

[1] Prahlad, C.K. and Doz, Y. (1987) *The Multinational Mission: Balancing Local Demands and Global Vision.* New York: Free Press.

[2] Porter, M.E. (1987) 'Changing patterns of international competition', in *The Competitive Challenge*, edited by David. J. Teece. Cambridge, MA: Ballinger, 27–57.

of different national markets, which necessitated differentiating strategies and products for country-specific benefits. These corporations build flexibility through national differentiation and local response mechanisms with a decentralized, self-sufficient, resourceful, entrepreneurial national organization. Traditional European companies like Nestlé, Philips and Unilever adopted this strategic posture.

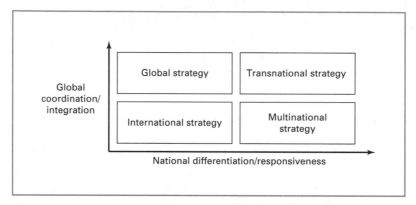

Figure 2.1(c) The global coordination/integration–national differentiation/responsiveness framework[3]

Global corporations were those that adopted an exactly opposite strategic posture to that of the multinationals. These corporations, largely Japanese, believed that the world was the market and not many differences existed in individual markets if the product was world class. They depended on global-scale efficiency, centralized R&D, often at their headquarters (HQ), and believed in providing standardized products with adequate cost and quality advantages that would overcome national differences. Here more control and coordination was required from the HQ and usually entailed a worldwide product division with global functional responsibility (see Figure 2.1b). Some industries, like aircraft manufacturing, computer hardware/software, credit cards and consumer electronics, were born global in that sense, where the forces of globalization outpaced national preferences. In these global industries, global strategies of economies of scale, centralized R&D, worldwide distribution and exports of standardized products gave the necessary leverage. These corporations depended on building cost advantages through centralized, global-scale operations and control of key decisions such as R&D, product specifications and marketing from the HQ. This strategic posture had been the classic approach of many Japanese companies, such as Matsushita, Komatsu and Canon.

Theodore Levitt (1983)[4] aptly explained the difference between a Global corporation and a MNC:

> 66 The difference between the hedgehog and the fox, wrote Sir Isaiah Berlin, is that the fox knows a lot about a great many things, but the hedgehog knows everything about one great thing. The MNC knows a lot about a great many

---

[3] Bartlett, C.A. and Ghoshal, S. (1989) *Managing Across Borders: The Transnational Solution*. Boston, MA: Harvard Business School.

[4] Levitt, T. (1983) 'The globalization of markets'. *Harvard Business Review*, May–June, 92–102.

countries and congenially adapts to supposed differences ... By contrast, the global corporation knows about the absolute need to be competitive on a worldwide basis as well as nationally and seeks constantly to drive down prices by standardizing what it sells and how it operates. **99**

Transnational corporations understood that demands to be responsive to local markets and the national environment, together with pressures to develop global-scale efficiency, were more often than not conflicting. Under this situation, either the global or multinational posture might be inappropriate and, to achieve both, a corporation had to adopt an emerging transnational mentality as its strategic posture. In this posture, key activities were neither fully centralized in the HQ, nor fully decentralized in the strategic business units (SBUs). Instead, resources and activities were dispersed and specialized. This duality leads to efficiency and flexibility at the same time. The dispersed geographic resources, assets and activities were integrated into an interdependent network of operations for sustainable advantage. However, responsiveness and differentiation were not enough to achieve the transnational mentality. Corporations had to learn from local markets, and integrate and share this learning globally to build a worldwide competitive advantage. Once this was done, transnational corporations would achieve competitive advantage by developing global-scale efficiency, flexibility and worldwide learning with dispersed, interdependent and specialized assets and capabilities. To become a member of the translational industry, Barlett and Ghoshal (1989) portrayed the logic of the global chess game that corporations had to play by – building and defending profit sanctuaries, leveraging existing strengths, cross-subsidizing weaker markets, attacking emerging markets with cross-market cash flows, forming alliances or coalitions, and merging with or acquiring competitors. Very few corporations followed this approach to begin with, but intuitively Nike and GE Medical Systems adopted this strategy where they coordinated R&D, marketing and other key decision processes from the HQ while sourcing their production capabilities from low-cost Asian and eastern European countries.

In early 2000, researchers became intrigued by new organizational forms that would co-locate and move into new types of global strategies. Two such types of corporation that would do business globally, within the context of the twenty-first century, were coined as *born global* corporations and *meta-national* corporations.

Born global corporations

With the emergence of the internet age at the beginning of the twenty-first century, the business environment looked different. This landscape was new and unexplored, and created new opportunities and threats. There was increasing scope for scale economies due to the globalization of consumer preferences, mobile consumers, the opening of new markets, low-cost manufacturing destinations and the diffusion of national boundaries. In addition, the pervasiveness of the internet age had ushered in a new breed of corporations, referred to as 'born global.' *Born global corporations* are those corporations that highlight their innovative culture, worldwide knowledge, regional expertise and multiple capabilities in order to succeed in diverse international markets.

Usually these firms thrive on global technological competence, multiple expertises in product development and world-class quality, and seek knowledge from regional knowledge sources. The operations of these born global corporations often span the globe early in their life cycle, counter to the traditional product life cycle theory. These corporations – mostly internet corporations taking advantage of their global IT infrastructure – offered products and services across the globe with relative ease because their core business model and business offering were somewhat uniform across national boundaries. By virtue of their core business, the conflicting demands of responsiveness and coordination did not affect them to a great extent. Examples of born global corporations are Amazon.com (and its various sites in different countries such as Amazon.fr), eBay.com and Skype, which have been able to diffuse their business models on a global scale from the very beginning. Following the huge success of Skype, which uses VOIP (Voice-Over-IP), it was acquired by eBay. Though regional specificities, buyer behaviour, internet usage and technological sophistication impact these type of dotcom companies to a certain extent, it is much easier to transact business globally on the internet.

Another interesting example is that of Suzlon, a provider of total solutions in wind power generation with cohesive integration of consultancy, design, manufacturing, installation, operation and maintenance. The company was incorporated in India in 1995 and, since then, has grown by more than 100 per cent in sales each year for the last five years due to significant investor interest in wind energy. More than 85 per cent of its business from its inception has been global. Driven by its core philosophy to vertically integrate manufacturing and allied capabilities in order to reduce costs, assure quality and secure the supply chain, the company has set up manufacturing operations in Belgium, China, India and the USA. The company also has R&D centres in Belgium, India, Germany and the Netherlands. Finally, sales operations for European and other international markets are located in Aarhus, Denmark. Suzlon acquired REpower, a German wind energy company, for $1.8 billion in 2007 and Hansen Transmissions, a Belgian manufacturer of wind and industrial gearboxes, in 2006, which not only provided it with both technological and market access, but also control of its wind power manufacturing value chain.

Meta-national[5] corporations

Meta-national corporations were defined as those corporations that possess 'superior capability to access, mobilize and leverage untapped pockets of knowledge scattered around the world'.[6] These companies by definition did not draw their competitive advantage from their home country, nor even from a set of national subsidiaries. Meta-nationals viewed the world as a global canvas dotted with deep pockets filled with

---

[5] Doz, Y., Santos, J. and Williamson, P. (2001) *Global to Metanational: How Companies Win in the Knowledge Economy*. Cambridge, MA: Harvard Business School Press.

[6] *Ibid.*

untapped potential in technology, market intelligence and capabilities. By sensing and mobilizing these scattered knowledges, they were able to innovate more effectively than their rivals. Some corporations, such as the Singapore-based semiconductor giant ST Microelectronics, the Japan-based luxury company Shiseido, the world's largest record company Polygram, and flat-panel display company PixTech, have showcased such a strategy of tapping localized innovations across the globe.

To end this discussion about the definitional issues of the MNCs, global corporations with the capability to balance conflicting tensions and develop a competitive advantage at each stage of their value chain have to build a concerted step-by-step strategy by building on their strengths and overcoming their weaknesses. They have to develop multi-level capabilities and strategic assets of global-scale efficiency and competitiveness, national responsiveness and flexibility, and a worldwide innovation and learning capability.[7]

An apt quote to define 'transnational' can be found in the writings of UK-based journalist, Arundhati Roy, who states, 'Terrorism is the symptom, not the disease. Terrorism has no country. It's transnational, as global an enterprise as Coke or Pepsi or Nike. At the first sign of trouble, terrorists can pull up stakes and move their "factories" from country to country in search of a better deal. Just like the multi-nationals.'

The next section looks at how nations are involved in creating and nurturing these (national) global corporations, sometimes referred to as *national champions*. It discusses how these global corporations formulate their strategies, fully utilize global opportunities, and develop multi-level competencies and interrelated capabilities for superior performance.

How do global corporations formulate their strategies?

In his seminal article, Perlmutter (1969)[8] described the strategies of MNCs as a three-stage process. The process focused on management attitudes, the nationality of executives and their biases. In his classification, the tortuous evolution is from an ethnocentric strategy (home-country attitudes with most important decisions taken at the HQ) to a polycentric strategy (host country attitudes with local responsiveness and differentiation in the decision-making process). The ultimate goal was to achieve a geocentric strategy (global attitude with an integrated and comprehensive approach to global operations). This global strategy was imperative due to the competitive advantage that accrued from it. To harness this advantage, the global corporations had to ask themselves *where in the world* shall inputs be procured, *where in the world* shall capital be raised, *where in the world* should manufacturing be located, *where in the world* should R&D centres and product development be located, and so on. For this, the global corporation had to formulate its strategies, aligning them with its competencies and capabilities. The discussion that follows draws extensively on the strategic management literature.

---

[7] Bartlett, C.A. and Ghoshal, S. (1989) *Managing Across Borders: The Transnational Solution.* Boston, MA: Harvard Business School.

[8] Perlmutter, H. (1969) 'The tortuous evolution of the multinational corporation.' *Columbia Journal of World Business,* Jan–Feb, 9–18.

Strategy formulation and implementation

To begin with, in order to evolve their strategy, be it global or local, corporations have to link their *vision*[9]*-mission-goal/objectives* and *shared values*.[10] They have to be clear with questions such as: *In what business will we compete? How do we add value to the various lines of business?* Jack Welch had a set of five questions to help GE formulate and implement its strategies:

1 What are your market dynamics globally today, and where are they going over the next several years?

2 What actions have your competitors taken in the last three years to upset those global dynamics?

3 What have you done in the last three years to affect those dynamics?

4 What are the most dangerous things your competitors could do in the next three years to upset those dynamics?

5 What are the most effective things you could do to bring your desired impact on these dynamics?

Having said that, a detailed discussion of strategy formulation and implementation is outside the scope of this book, but a powerful tool to analyse these processes is that of the McKinsey 7S model, which links the *strategy-structure-systems* paradigm with *staff* (people and rewards)*-skills-style* (of top management) and the *shared values* of the organization.

Strategic management focuses on explanations of competitive advantage, and the analysis, to begin with, boils down to *internal analysis* that focuses on the corporation's resources, strengths, weaknesses and its uniqueness, and the *external analysis,* which focuses on the opportunities, threats and industry dynamics within which the corporation is operating.

Internal analysis: core competencies, capabilities, competitive advantage and the resource-based view

The *internal analysis* is sometimes referred to as the resource-based view (RBV) of the firm. Resources are sources of inputs available to the economy for use in producing goods and services. A resource can be defined as an observable (but not tangible) asset that can be valued and traded – for example, brands, patents, land, labour and, capital licence. The RBV spoke of corporations as a bundle of unique resources and relationships. To be a source of sustained competitive advantage, resources and capabilities should be **V**aluable (can improve market position), **R**are (in short supply relative to demand), isolated from

---

[9] See Hamel, G. and Prahalad, C.K. (1989) 'Strategic intent'. *Harvard Business Review*, May–June, 63–76.

[10] A *vision* statement is likely to persist for a significant period of time as a 'beacon in the distance' towards which an organization can strive. A *mission* statement is a generalised statement of the overriding purpose of an organization. It can be thought of as an expression of its *raison d'être*. Whereas, *goals/objectives* statements are of specific outcomes that are to be achieved both at corporate and business unit level. For example, financial – desired sales or profit levels, rates of growth, dividend levels, share valuations; market based – market share, customer service, repeat business, etc. And these have to be linked in some way to the shared values of the corporation, which are its attitudes towards stakeholders and ethical agenda.

Imitation or substitution (costly to imitate or replicate) and **O**rganized (corporation should be readily able to exploit the resource and capability). J. Barney's VRIO Framework[11] stated that resources that are the same as those of a competitor, or easy to imitate, are called *necessary resources*. Those that are better than the competitor's and difficult to imitate are called *unique resources*. The task of management was to renew these resources and relationships as time and competition erode their value. Corporations added value when they matched their unique competencies to the environments they faced. Resources were utilized to build competence. These competencies existed in activities. Competencies that were better than a competitor's and difficult to imitate were called *core competencies*.[12] Competencies build capabilities.

Capabilities cannot be observed (and hence are a necessarily intangible asset), cannot be valued and can change hands only as part of the entire unit. A mixture of people and practices continuously enacts capabilities. Capability can also be defined as a routine or a collection of routines that, together with its implementing input flows, confers upon the firm's management a set of decision options for producing outputs. Capability creates competitive advantage and, with competitive advantage, strategy is formulated. Examples are the yield management system of American Airlines, the docking system and point-of-purchase inventory control system of Wal-Mart, Dell's logistics system (Direct Model), the special design and manufacturing skills involved in building machines that break down less frequently of Komatsu (strategic substitute for Caterpillar's worldwide service and supply network), and the special management and coordination skills that enable Sony to conceive, design and manufacture high-quality, miniaturized products.

To summarize, according to Barney (1991), 'in the end, this discussion reminds us that sustained competitive advantage cannot be created simply by evaluating environmental opportunities and threats, and then conducting businesses only in high-opportunity, low-threat environments. Rather, creating sustained competitive advantage depends on the unique resources and capabilities that a firm brings to competition in its environment. To discover these resources and capabilities, managers must look inside their firm for valuable, rare and costly-to-imitate resources, and then exploit these resources through their organization.'

External analysis: structure-conduct-performance (S-C-P)

External analysis was initially developed in the 1930s by a group of economists, to understand the relationship between a corporation's environment, its behaviour and

---

[11] Barney, J. (1991) 'Firm resources and sustained competitive advantage'. *Journal of Management*, 7, 49–64.

[12] Hamel and Prahalad (1989) in their article 'The core competence of the corporation'. *Harvard Business Review*, May–June, 79–92; define core competence as the 'combination of individual technologies and production skills that underly a company's myriad product lines'. They go on to say that only some competencies are core, core varies with strategy, core varies with time and core can be exploited in several ways. Core competencies underpin competitive advantage. For example, Sony's core competency in miniaturization, allows the company to make everything from the Sony Walkman to video cameras to notebook computers. Canon's core competencies in optics, imaging and microprocessor controls have enabled it to enter markets as seemingly diverse as copiers, laser printers, cameras and image scanners. In 2003, in a talk at the Advanced Management Programme, Osaka, at the Graduate School of Business, Keio University, Prahalad defined core competence as *a function of multiple technology, learning as a family* and shared across business units. Examples are integration of the acquisitions of Oracle and the innovations of Microsoft.

performance. Industry *structure* was measured by factors such as the number of competitors in the industry, the heterogeneity of products in that industry, the cost of entry to and exit from that industry, and so on. *Conduct* referred to strategies that corporations pursued in order to gain competitive advantage. *Performance* denoted both corporation-level performance and that of the economy as a whole. Michael Porter's seminal work over the last 30 years has resulted in influential models (see Figure 2.2) that link nations' competitiveness (diamond model),[13] industry attractiveness and threats (five forces),[14] corporations' strategies (generic strategies)[15] and advantage within corporations (value chain analysis).[16]

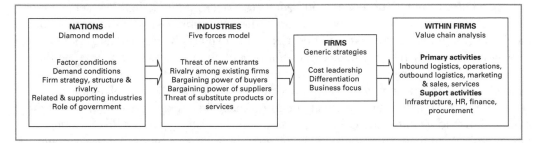

Figure 2.2 Seminal work of Michael Porter[17]

To conclude, global corporations needed to develop their strategies not only in their home market but for each market in which they were operating, in tune with their industry specificities. For example, some industries are more stable than others. Industries such as cement, steel and chocolate are more stable than telecommunications, computer chips and medical appliances. To understand fast-moving industries or more technology-driven industries, a more dynamic perspective was needed to better understand the market forces. The *dynamic capability perspective* suggested that a corporation's current position was not an accurate predictor of future performance. This was because current market position was not a competitive advantage but rather an outcome of past competitive activities. The dynamic perspective searched for clues about how the corporation had arrived at its current state and looked to the future in an effort to predict the strategy landscape.

The final section, below, examines how national corporations have evolved to be today's global corporations and how they have gained competitive advantage within their industries.

[13] Porter, M.E. (1990) 'The competitive advantage of nations'. *Harvard Business Review*, March–April, 79–91; Porter, M.E. (1990) *The Competitive Advantage of Nations*. New York: Free Press.

[14] Porter, M.E. (1979) 'How competitive forces shape strategy'. *Harvard Business Review*, March–April, 137–45.

[15] Porter, M.E. (1980) *Competitive Strategy*. New York: Free Press.

[16] Porter, M.E. (1985) *Competitive Advantage*. New York: Free Press.

[17] For a vivid and interesting discussion of corporate strategy, see Ghemawat, P. (2001) *Strategy and Business Landscape*. NJ: Prentice Hall.

The competitive advantage of nations, the role of the state and 'locally rooted' global corporations

A brief glance at the *Fortune* Global 500 corporations (based on revenues) suggests that, among the 50 largest corporations worldwide in 1990, 49 were still the largest in 2000. In 1990, 382 of the top 500 corporations originated from five countries. After a decade, in 2000, 398 of the worlds largest 500 corporations originated from the same five countries. In 2006, among the *Fortune* Global 500 corporations,[18] 300 were from just five countries.

The above necessitates a brief discussion of the competitive advantage of nations, the role of the state, the origins of today's global corporations and the creation of national champions. Industrialized nations are still at the root of most global corporations. This can be explained by revisiting Porter's work on the *competitive advantage of nations* (see Reading 3). Porter's diamond model (see Figure 2.2) gives a clear indication that the nation states had to be strong in providing and building demand conditions, factor conditions, supporting industries and adequate firm structure, strategy and rivalry. Together with these favourable conditions and ushering in an environment of free market rivalry, corporations needed to innovate in order to survive in their home markets and, with some luck and government support, nations become competitive in certain industries. For example, France dominates the tourism, luxury, agri-food (wine, cheese), nuclear energy, cement and defence industries, among others. Germany dominates industries such as automobiles, chemicals, heavy engineering and insurance. The UK dominates industries such as banking, financials, oil, telecoms, defence and others, while Japan dominates in automobiles, electronics, flat panels, and so on. The USA dominates in most of these sectors.

Thus, the role of the state often plays a crucial part in the rise and existence of some national companies, which go on to become global corporations. For example, the luxury industry in France has historically been developed due to innovations ensuing from intense rivalry between the key players in the industry, namely LVMH Group, PPR-Gucci Group, Chanel, Hermès and others. Chanel and Hermès grew exclusively by internal growth, while LVMH and PPR-Gucci grew by acquisition. Lafarge, a local French corporation, became global leader by first building a strong presence in its domestic market and, within a span of 16 years, it became global leader by pursuing a strategic posture of profitable growth primarily through acquisitions in the building/construction materials industry. Thus, the role of the state is that of catalyst and challenger, with a focus on specialized factor creation by increasing investment in education, investment and basic research, and adopting policies that promote strong competition within domestic markets. It is also intended to protect jobs, preserve national security, avoid intervening in factors and

---

[18] Five were oil companies, four automobile manufacturers and one retailer. They were ExxonMobil, Wal-Mart, Royal Dutch Shell, BP, General Motors, Chevron, DaimlerChrysler, Toyota Motor, Ford Motor Company and ConocoPhilips. The details of country of origin of the *Fortune* 500 companies in 2006 were as follows: USA (114 corporations), Japan (70), UK (40), France (40), Germany (30), China (20), Canada (14), The Netherlands (14), South Korea (12), Switzerland (12), Italy (10), Spain (9), Australia (8), India (6), Sweden (6), Belgium (5), Mexico (5), Russia (5) and others. The EU in total had 172 corporations. The location of their HQs seems also to change, with Tokyo (52 global corporations), Paris (27), New York (24), UK (23), Beijing (15) and others.

currency markets, enforce strict product, safety, and environmental standards, sharply limit direct cooperation among industry rivals, promote goals that lead to sustained investment, deregulate competition, enforce strong domestic antitrust policies, and reject managed trade. But this is usually not the case.

By the turn of the twenty-first century, the opening up of eastern Europe, the creation of the European Union, phenomenal growth opportunities in emerging markets such as India and China, and deregulation and liberalization in these nations had created immense opportunities for global corporations. But those opportunities are not without challenges and threats for both global and local corporations. Global corporations have to understand and play by the new rules of the game in these different national markets, and local companies must brace themselves for competition from these global corporations with superior resources, assets, capabilities and multi-layered competitive advantages. Most nation states, quite rationally, want to support their national companies in the face of this external competition and promote them as 'national champions'. They want to provide assistance and support by helping to turn around their close to bankrupt corporations or save them from being taken over by other global corporations. These moves go against free market competition rules, and create rivalry within industries for innovation, as proposed by Porter's diamond model (see Figure 2.2). Theoretically, these national champions can prosper and compete globally.

An example of such a promoter of national champions is France. In 1997, France's socialist government restarted a process of privatization and the opening of government-controlled firms to private investment that had begun in the 1980s. This privatization continued until 2002. In 2003 and 2004, the government reduced its stakes in large companies such as Air France-KLM (to 44.6 from 54.0 per cent), France Telecom (to 42.2 from 54.5 per cent), Renault (to 15.6 from 26.0 per cent) and Thomson (to 2.0 from 20.8 per cent), among others, though the French government still held stakes in Bull and Safran, and in 1,280 other national corporations.

Despite its privatization programme, the French government continues to promote national champions and 'economic patriotism', a concept that has been used to justify opposition to foreign takeovers of French firms. This tendency has been apparent in an effort by the government to strengthen a French takeover law and a parallel effort to scrutinize sensitive foreign investments more closely. In implementing the EU's Takeover Directive in 2005, France's National Assembly adopted provisions that would allow French companies to ignore their shareholders when trying to mount a defence against a takeover bid by a US firm. This action came just months after Pepsi, a US company, was rumoured to be preparing a takeover bid for Danone, the French food and beverage company. To prevent such takeovers, the French government employed its political arsenal – crafting legislation on corporate 'poison-pill' rules or labelling certain industries as 'vital to national security'.

The French state has always felt that it is its role to intervene in the business of French corporations, rather than to let French companies flourish – or fold – on their own. It has done this throughout history and more so in the past five years. It had bailed out Alstom,[19]

---

[19] For a detailed analysis see Gbahoué, B. and Som, A. (2004) 'Evolution of Alstom: role of the French state', ECCH Case #204-021-1.

the creator of its fastest trains, TGV, from near bankruptcy although the European Commission cried foul over this issue. Still, the French state prevailed. In 2006, after a thorough portfolio restructuring and turnaround, the French state offloaded its 21.03 per cent stake in Alstom to Bouyges Group. Similarly, it intervened to create the third largest pharmaceutical corporation globally by facilitating the merging of Sanofi-Aventis, while literally blocking the bid of Novartis, the Swiss contender.

In another manifestation of the French state's *dirigiste* policies, the government announced in 2006 a proposed $80 billion merger between Gaz de France (GDF), a state-owned gas utility, and Suez, a publicly traded Franco-Belgian water and power corporation, which would create Europe's second-biggest utility company and a huge buyer of natural gas. The merger was reportedly forged to block a takeover bid for Suez by Enel, an Italian energy company. This action led a number of prominent Italians and EU officials to accuse the French government of being protectionist. In fact, the merger plan epitomizes the 'national champion' policy that the French government has pursued for years. Certainly, a successful French firm can no longer be a national champion if it is bought by a foreign company – even if the buyer in question is also European. The French government plans to hold 34 per cent of the merged company's shares, allowing it to retain a strong decision-making role in the proposed French energy champion. Enel eventually abandoned its bid for Suez.

From the above discussion, it seems clear that, though corporations such as Alstom, GDF, Suez and Sanofi-Aventis are global corporations of today, they remain rooted locally and are helped by their nation state to achieve competitive advantage.

The next chapter discusses the evolution and development of different organizational structures, their strengths and weaknesses and how global companies are managing these organizational structures in tandem with their growth objectives.

Case introduction: Airbus and Boeing in China: risk of technology transfer

The case discusses the evolution, growth and divergent strategies of two national champions, Boeing and Airbus. Airbus is often labelled as a European champion. The case discusses the growth of divergent assets and capabilities in the same industry. The case shifts to China, the demand created by the specificities of the Chinese market and the role of the Chinese state in both attracting global leaders while ensuring protection of intellectual property rights.

This case appears after the readings for this chapter.

READING 3
The competitive advantage of nations**

*Michael E. Porter**

National prosperity is created, not inherited. It does not grow out of a country's natural endowments, its labor pool, its interest rates, or its currency's value, as classical economics insists.

A nation's competitiveness depends on the capacity of its industry to innovate and upgrade. Companies gain advantage against the world's best competitors because of pressure and challenge. They benefit from having strong domestic rivals, aggressive home-based suppliers, and demanding local customers.

In a world of increasingly global competition, nations have become more, not less, important. As the basis of competition has shifted more and more to the creation and assimilation of knowledge, the role of the nation has grown. Competitive advantage is created and sustained through a highly localized process. Differences in national values, culture, economic structures, institutions, and histories all contribute to competitive success. There are striking differences in the patterns of competitiveness in every country; no nation can or will be competitive in every or even most industries. Ultimately, nations succeed in particular industries because their home environment is the most forward-looking, dynamic, and challenging.

These conclusions, the product of a four-year study of the patterns of competitive success in ten leading trading nations, contradict the conventional wisdom that guides the thinking of many companies and national governments – and that is pervasive today in the United States. (For more about the study, see the insert 'Patterns of National Competitive Success.') According to prevailing thinking, labor costs, interest rates, exchange rates, and economies of scale are the most potent determinants of competitiveness. In companies, the words of the day are merger, alliance, strategic partnerships, collaboration, and supranational globalization. Managers are pressing for more government support for particular industries. Among governments, there is a growing tendency to experiment with various policies intended to promote national

* Harvard Business School professor Michael E. Porter is the author of *Competitive Strategy* (Free Press, 1980) and *Competitive Advantage* (Free Press, 1985) and will publish *The Competitive Advantage of Nations* (Free Press) in May 1990.

** *Harvard Business Review*, March–April 1990. Copyright ©2001. All Rights Reserved.

competitiveness – from efforts to manage exchange rates to new measures to manage trade to policies to relax antitrust – which usually end up only undermining it. (See the insert 'What is National Competitiveness?')

These approaches, now much in favor in both companies and governments, are flawed. They fundamentally misperceive the true sources of competitive advantage. Pursuing them, with all their short-term appeal, will virtually guarantee that the United States – or any other advanced nation – never achieves real and sustainable competitive advantage.

We need a new perspective and new tools – an approach to competitiveness that grows directly out of an analysis of internationally successful industries, without regard for traditional ideology or current intellectual fashion. We need to know, very simply, what works and why. Then we need to apply it.

How companies succeed in international markets

Around the world, companies that have achieved international leadership employ strategies that differ from each other in every respect. But while every successful company will employ its own particular strategy, the underlying mode of operation – the character and trajectory of all successful companies – is fundamentally the same.

Companies achieve competitive advantage through acts of innovation. They approach innovation in its broadest sense, including both new technologies and new ways of doing things. They perceive a new basis for competing or find better means for competing in old ways. Innovation can be manifested in a new product design, a new production process, a new marketing approach, or a new way of conducting training. Much innovation is mundane and incremental, depending more on a cumulation of small insights and advances than on a single, major technological breakthrough. It often involves ideas that are not even 'new' – ideas that have been around, but never vigorously pursued. It always involves investments in skill and knowledge, as well as in physical assets and brand reputations.

Some innovations create competitive advantage by perceiving an entirely new market opportunity or by serving a market segment that others have ignored. When competitors are slow to respond, such innovation yields competitive advantage. For instance, in industries such as autos and home electronics, Japanese companies gained their initial advantage by emphasizing smaller, more compact, lower capacity models that foreign competitors disdained as less profitable, less important, and less attractive.

In international markets, innovations that yield competitive advantage anticipate both domestic and foreign needs. For example, as international concern for product safety has grown, Swedish companies like Volvo, Atlas Copco, and AGA have succeeded by anticipating the market opportunity in this area. On the other hand, innovations that respond to concerns or circumstances that are peculiar to the home market can actually retard international competitive success. The lure of the huge U.S. defense market, for instance, has diverted the attention of U.S. materials and machine-tool companies from attractive, global commercial markets.

Information plays a large role in the process of innovation and improvement – information that either is not available to competitors or that they do not seek. Sometimes it comes from simple investment in research and development or market research; more often, it comes from effort and from openness and from looking in the right place unencumbered by blinding assumptions or conventional wisdom.

This is why innovators are often outsiders from a different industry or a different country: Innovation may come from a new company, whose founder has a nontraditional background or was simply not appreciated in an older, established company. Or the capacity for innovation may come into an existing company through senior managers who are new to the particular industry and thus more able to perceive opportunities and more likely to pursue them. Or innovation may occur as a company diversifies, bringing new resources, skills, or perspectives to another industry. Or innovations may come from another nation with different circumstances or different ways of competing.

With few exceptions, innovation is the result of unusual effort. The company that successfully implements a new or better way of competing pursues its approach with dogged determination, often in the face of harsh criticism and tough obstacles. In fact, to succeed, innovation usually requires pressure, necessity, and even adversity: the fear of loss often proves more powerful than the hope of gain.

Once a company achieves competitive advantage through an innovation, it can sustain it only through relentless improvement. Almost any advantage can be imitated. Korean companies have already matched the ability of their Japanese rivals to mass-produce standard color televisions and VCRs; Brazilian companies have assembled technology and designs comparable to Italian competitors in casual leather footwear.

Competitors will eventually and inevitably overtake any company that stops improving and innovating. Sometimes early-mover advantages such as customer relationships, scale economies in existing technologies, or the loyalty of distribution channels are enough to permit a stagnant company to retain its entrenched position for years or even decades. But sooner or later, more dynamic rivals will find a way to innovate around these advantages or create a better or cheaper way of doing things. Italian appliance producers, which competed successfully on the basis of cost in selling midsize and compact appliances through large retail chains, rested too long on this initial advantage. By developing more differentiated products and creating strong brand franchises, German competitors have begun to gain ground.

Ultimately, the only way to sustain a competitive advantage is to *upgrade it* – to move to more sophisticated types. This is precisely what Japanese automakers have done. They initially penetrated foreign markets with small, inexpensive compact cars of adequate quality and competed on the basis of lower labor costs. Even while their labor-cost advantage persisted, however, the Japanese companies were upgrading. They invested aggressively to build large modem plants to reap economies of scale. Then they became innovators in process technology, pioneering just-in-time production and a host of other quality and productivity practices. These process improvements led to better product quality, better repair records, and better customer-satisfaction ratings than foreign competitors had. Most recently, Japanese automakers have advanced to the vanguard of product technology and are introducing new, premium brand names to compete with the world's most prestigious passenger cars.

The example of the Japanese automakers also illustrates two additional prerequisites for sustaining competitive advantage. First, a company must adopt a global approach to strategy: It must sell its product worldwide, under its own brand name, through international marketing channels that it controls. A truly global approach may even require the company to locate production or R&D facilities in other nations to take advantage of lower wage rates, to gain or improve market access, or to take advantage of foreign technology. Second, creating more sustainable advantages often means that a company must make its existing advantage obsolete – even while it is still an advantage. Japanese auto companies recognized this; either they would make their advantage obsolete, or a competitor would do it for them.

As this example suggests, innovation and change are inextricably tied together. But change is an unnatural act, particularly in successful companies; powerful forces are at work to avoid and defeat it. Past approaches become institutionalized in standard operating procedures and management controls. Training emphasizes the one correct way to do anything; the construction of specialized, dedicated facilities solidifies past practice into expensive brick and mortar; the existing strategy takes on an aura of invincibility and becomes rooted in the company culture.

Patterns of National Competitive Success

To investigate why nations gain competitive advantage in particular industries and the implications for company strategy and national economies, I conducted a four-year study of ten important trading nations: Denmark, Germany, Italy, Japan, Korea, Singapore, Sweden, Switzerland, the United Kingdom, and the United States. I was assisted by a team of more than 30 researchers, most of whom were natives of and based in the nation they studied. The researchers all used the same methodology.

Three nations – the United States, Japan, and Germany – are the world's leading industrial powers. The other nations represent a variety of population sizes, government policies toward industry, social philosophies, geographical sizes, and locations. Together, the ten nations accounted for fully 50% of total world exports in 1985, the base year for statistical analysis.

Most previous analyses of national competitiveness have focused on single nation or bilateral comparisons. By studying nations with widely varying characteristics and circumstances, this study sought to separate the fundamental forces underlying national competitive advantage from the idiosyncratic ones.

In each nation, the study consisted of two parts. The first identified all industries in which the nation's companies were internationally successful, using available statistical data, supplementary published sources, and field interviews. We defined a nation's industry as internationally successful if it *possessed competitive advantage relative to the best worldwide competitors.* Many measures of competitive advantage, such as reported profitability; can be misleading. We chose as the best indicators the presence of substantial and sustained exports to a wide array of other nations and/or significant outbouud foreign investment based on skills and assets created in the home country. A nation was considered the home base for a company if it was either a locally owned, indigenous enterprise or managed autonomously although owned by a foreign company or investors. We then created a profile of all the industries in which each nation was internationally successful at three points in time: 1971, 1978, and 1985. The pattern of competitive industries in each economy was far from random: the task was to explain it and how it had changed over time. Of particular interest were the connections or relationships among the nation's competitive industries.

In the second part of the study; we examined the history of competition in particular industries to understand how competitive advantage was created. On the basis of national profiles, we selected over 100 industries or industry groups for detailed study; we examined many more in less detail. We went back as far as necessary to understand how and why the industry began in the nation, how it grew, when and why companies from the nation developed international competitive advantage, and the process by which competitive advantage had been either sustained or lost. The resulting case histories fall short of the work of a good historian in their level of detail, but they do provide insight into the development of both the industry and the nation's economy.

We chose a sample of industries for each nation that represented the most important groups of competitive industries in the economy. The industries studied accounted for a large share of total exports in each nation: more than 20% of total exports in Japan, Germany, and Switzerland, for example, and more than 40% in South Korea. We studied some of the most famous and important international success stories – German high-performance autos and chemicals, Japanese semiconductors and VCRs, Swiss banking and pharmaceuticals, Italian footwear and textiles, U.S. commercial aircraft and motion pictures – and some relatively obscure but highly competitive industries – South Korean pianos, Italian ski boots, and British biscuits. We also added a few industries because they appeared to be paradoxes: Japanese home demand for Western-character typewriters is nearly nonexistent, for example, but Japan holds a strong export and foreign investment position in the industry. We avoided industries that were highly dependent on natural resources: such industries do not form the backbone of advanced economies, and the capacity to compete in them is more explicable using classical theory. We did, however, include a number of more technologically intensive, natural-resource-related industries such as newsprint and agricultural chemicals.

The sample of nations and industries offers a rich empirical foundation for developing and testing the new theory of how countries gain competitive advantage. The accompanying article concentrates on the determinants of competitive advantage in individual industries and also sketches out some of the study's overall implications for government policy and company strategy. A fuller treatment in my book, *The Competitive Advantage of Nations*, develops the theory and its implications in greater depth and provides many additional examples. It also contains detailed descriptions of the nations we studied and the future prospects for their economies.

– Michael E. Porter

Successful companies tend to develop a bias for predictability and stability; they work on defending what they have. Change is tempered by the fear that there is much to lose. The organization at all levels filters out information that would suggest new approaches, modifications, or departures from the norm. The internal environment operates like an immune system to isolate or expel 'hostile' individuals who challenge current directions or established thinking. Innovation ceases; the company becomes stagnant; it is only a matter of time before aggressive competitors overtake it.

The diamond of national advantage

Why are certain companies based in certain nations capable of consistent innovation? Why do they ruthlessly pursue improvements, seeking an ever-more sophisticated source of competitive advantage? Why are they able to overcome the substantial barriers to change and innovation that so often accompany success?

The answer lies in four broad attributes of a nation, attributes that individually and as a system constitute the diamond of national advantage, the playing field that each nation establishes and operates for its industries. These attributes are:

1 *Factor Conditions.* The nation's position in factors of production, such as skilled labor or infrastructure, necessary to compete in a given industry.

2 *Demand Conditions.* The nature of home-market demand for the industry's product or service.

3 *Related and Supporting Industries.* The presence or absence in the nation of supplier industries and other related industries that are internationally competitive.

4 *Firm Strategy, Structure, and Rivalry.* The conditions in the nation governing how companies are created, organized, and managed, as well as the nature of domestic rivalry.

These determinants create the national environment in which companies are born and learn how to compete. (See the diagram 'Determinants of National Competitive Advantage.') Each point on the diamond – and the diamond as a system – affects essential ingredients for achieving international competitive success: the availability of resources and skills necessary for competitive advantage in an industry; the information that shapes the opportunities that companies perceive and the directions in which they deploy their resources and skills; the goals of the owners, managers, and individuals in companies; and most important, the pressures on companies to invest and innovate. [...]

When a national environment permits and supports the most rapid accumulation of specialized assets and skills – sometimes simply because of greater effort and commitment – companies gain a competitive advantage. When a national environment affords better ongoing information and insight into product and process needs, companies gain a competitive advantage. Finally, when the national environment pressures companies to innovate and invest, companies both gain a competitive advantage and upgrade those advantages over time.

Factor Conditions. According to standard economic theory, factors of production – labor, land, natural resources, capital, infrastructure – will determine the flow of trade. A nation

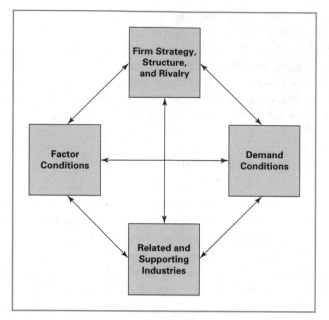

Figure 1 Determinants of national competitive advantage

will export those goods that make most use of the factors with which it is relatively well endowed. This doctrine, whose origins date back to Adam Smith and David Ricardo and that is embedded in classical economics, is at best incomplete and at worst incorrect.

In the sophisticated industries that form the backbone of any advanced economy, a nation does not inherit but instead creates the most important factors of production – such as skilled human resources or a scientific base. Moreover, the stock of factors that a nation enjoys at a particular time is less important than the rate and efficiency with which it creates, upgrades, and deploys them in particular industries.

The most important factors of production are those that involve sustained and heavy investment and are specialized. Basic factors, such as a pool of labor or a local raw-material source, do not constitute an advantage in knowledge-intensive industries. Companies can access them easily through a global strategy or circumvent them through technology. Contrary to conventional wisdom, simply having a general work force that is high school or even college educated represents no competitive advantage in modern international competition. To support competitive advantage, a factor must be highly specialized to an industry's particular needs – a scientific institute specialized in optics, a pool of venture capital to fund software companies. These factors are more scarce, more difficult for foreign competitors to imitate – and they require sustained investment to create.

Nations succeed in industries where they are particularly good at factor creation. Competitive advantage results from the presence of world-class institutions that first create specialized factors and then continually work to upgrade them. Denmark has two hospitals that concentrate in studying and treating diabetes – and a world-leading export position in insulin. Holland has premier research institutes in the cultivation, packaging, and shipping of flowers, where it is the world's export leader.

What is not so obvious, however, is that selective disadvantages in the more basic factors can prod a company to innovate and upgrade – a disadvantage in a static model of competition can become an advantage in a dynamic one. When there is an ample supply of cheap raw materials or abundant labor, companies can simply rest on these advantages and often deploy them inefficiently. But when companies face a selective disadvantage, like high land costs, labor shortages, or the lack of local raw materials, they *must* innovate and upgrade to compete.

Implicit in the oft-repeated Japanese statement, 'We are an island nation with no natural resources,' is the understanding that these deficiencies have only served to spur Japan's competitive innovation. Just-in-time production, for example, economized on prohibitively expensive space. Italian steel producers in the Brescia area faced a similar set of disadvantages: high capital costs, high energy costs, and no local raw materials. Located in Northern Lombardy, these privately owned companies faced staggering logistics costs due to their distance from southern ports and the inefficiencies of the state-owned Italian transportation system. The result: they pioneered technologically advanced minimills that require only modest capital investment, use less energy, employ scrap metal as the feedstock, are efficient at small scale, and permit producers to locate close to sources of scrap and end-use customers. In other words, they converted factor disadvantages into competitive advantage.

Disadvantages can become advantages only under certain conditions. First, they must send companies proper signals about circumstances that will spread to other nations, thereby equipping them to innovate in advance of foreign rivals. Switzerland, the nation that experienced the first labor shortages after World War II, is a case in point. Swiss companies responded to the disadvantage by upgrading labor productivity and seeking higher value, more sustainable market segments. Companies in most other parts of the world, where there were still ample workers, focused their attention on other issues, which resulted in slower upgrading.

The second condition for transforming disadvantages into advantages is favorable circumstances elsewhere in the diamond – a consideration that applies to almost all determinants. To innovate, companies must have access to people with appropriate skills and have home-demand conditions that send the right signals. They must also have active domestic rivals who create pressure to innovate. Another precondition is company goals that lead to sustained commitment to the industry. Without such a commitment and the presence of active rivalry, a company may take an easy way around a disadvantage rather than using it as a spur to innovation.

For example, U.S. consumer-electronics companies, faced with high relative labor costs, chose to leave the product and production process largely unchanged and move labor-intensive activities to Taiwan and other Asian countries. Instead of upgrading their sources of advantage, they settled for labor-cost parity. On the other hand, Japanese rivals, confronted with intense domestic competition and a mature home market, chose to eliminate labor through automation. This led to lower assembly costs, to products with fewer components and to improved quality and reliability. Soon Japanese companies were building assembly plants in the United States – the place U.S. companies had fled.

Demand Conditions. It might seem that the globalization of competition would diminish the importance of home demand. In practice, however, this is simply not the case. In fact, the composition and character of the home market usually has a disproportionate effect on how companies perceive, interpret, and respond to buyer needs. Nations gain competitive advantage in industries where the home demand gives their companies a clearer or earlier picture of emerging buyer needs, and where demanding buyers pressure companies to innovate faster and achieve more sophisticated competitive advantages than their foreign rivals. The size of home demand proves far less significant than the character of home demand.

Home-demand conditions help build competitive advantage when a particular industry segment is larger or more visible in the domestic market than in foreign markets. The larger market segments in a nation receive the most attention from the nation's companies; companies accord smaller or less desirable segments a lower priority. A good example is hydraulic excavators, which represent the most widely used type of construction equipment in the Japanese domestic market – but which comprise a far smaller proportion of the market in other advanced nations. This segment is one of the few where there are vigorous Japanese international competitors and where Caterpillar does not hold a substantial share of the world market.

More important than the mix of segments per se is the nature of domestic buyers. A nation's companies gain competitive advantage if domestic buyers are the world's most sophisticated and demanding buyers for the product or service. Sophisticated, demanding buyers provide a window into advanced customer needs; they pressure companies to meet high standards; they prod them to improve, to innovate, and to upgrade into more advanced segments. As with factor conditions, demand conditions provide advantages by forcing companies to respond to tough challenges.

Especially stringent needs arise because of local values and circumstances. For example, Japanese consumers, who live in small, tightly packed homes, must contend with hot, humid summers and high-cost electrical energy – a daunting combination of circumstances. In response, Japanese companies have pioneered compact, quiet air-conditioning units powered by energy-saving rotary compressors. In industry after industry, the tightly constrained requirements of the Japanese market have forced companies to innovate, yielding products that are *kei-haku-tan*-sho – light, thin, short, small – and that are internationally accepted.

Local buyers can help a nation's companies gain advantage if their needs anticipate or even shape those of other nations – if their needs provide ongoing 'early-warning indicators' of global market trends. Sometimes anticipatory needs emerge because a nation's political values foreshadow needs that will grow elsewhere. Sweden's long-standing concern for handicapped people has spawned an increasingly competitive industry focused on special needs. Denmark's environmentalism has led to success for companies in water-pollution control equipment and windmills.

More generally, a nation's companies can anticipate global trends if the nation's values are spreading – that is, if the country is exporting its values and tastes as well as its products. The international success of U.S. companies in fast food and credit cards, for example, reflects not only the American desire for convenience but also the spread of these tastes to the rest of the world. Nations export their values and tastes through media, through training foreigners, through political influence, and through the foreign activities of their citizens and companies.

Related and Supporting Industries. The third broad determinant of national advantage is the presence in the nation of related and supporting industries that are internationally competitive. Internationally competitive home-based suppliers create advantages in downstream industries in several ways. First, they deliver the most cost-effective inputs in an efficient, early, rapid, and sometimes preferential way. Italian gold and silver jewelry companies lead the world in that industry in part because other Italian companies supply two-thirds of the world's jewelry-making and precious-metal recycling machinery.

Far more significant than mere access to components and machinery, however, is the advantage that home-based related and supporting industries provide in innovation and upgrading – an advantage based on close working relationships. Suppliers and end-users located near each other can take advantage of short lines of communication, quick and constant flow of information, and an ongoing exchange of ideas and innovations. Companies have the opportunity to influence their suppliers' technical efforts and can serve as test sites for R&D work, accelerating the pace of innovation.

The illustration of 'The Italian Footwear Cluster' offers a graphic example of how a group of close-by, supporting industries creates competitive advantage in a range of

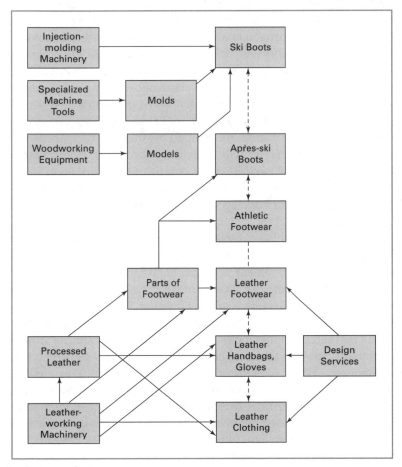

Figure 2 The Italian footwear cluster

interconnected industries that are all internationally competitive. Shoe producers, for instance, interact regularly with leather manufacturers on new styles and manufacturing techniques and learn about new textures and colors of leather when they are still on the drawing boards. Leather manufacturers gain early insights into fashion trends, helping them to plan new products. The interaction is mutually advantageous and self-reinforcing, but it does not happen automatically: it is helped by proximity; but occurs only because companies and suppliers work at it.

The nation's companies benefit most when the suppliers are, themselves, global competitors. It is ultimately self-defeating for a company or country to create 'captive' suppliers who are totally dependent on the domestic industry and prevented from serving foreign competitors. By the same token, a nation need not be competitive in all supplier industries for its companies to gain competitive advantage. Companies can readily source from abroad materials, components, or technologies without a major effect on innovation or performance of the industry's products. The same is true of other generalized technologies – like electronics or software – where the industry represents a narrow application area.

Home-based competitiveness in related industries provides similar benefits: information flow and technical interchange speed the rate of innovation and upgrading. A home-based related industry also increases the likelihood that companies will embrace new skills, and it also provides a source of entrants who will bring a novel approach to competing. The Swiss success in pharmaceuticals emerged out of previous international success in the dye industry, for example; Japanese dominance in electronic musical keyboards grows out of success in acoustic instruments combined with a strong position in consumer electronics.

Firm Strategy, Structure, and Rivalry. National circumstances and context create strong tendencies in how companies are created, organized, and managed, as well as what the nature of domestic rivalry will be. In Italy; for example, successful international competitors are often small or medium-sized companies that are privately owned and operated like extended families; in Germany, in contrast, companies tend to be strictly hierarchical in organization and management practices, and top managers usually have technical backgrounds.

No one managerial system is universally appropriate – notwithstanding the current fascination with Japanese management. Competitiveness in a specific industry results from convergence of the management practices and organizational modes favored in the country and the sources of competitive advantage in the industry. In industries where Italian companies are world leaders – such as lighting, furniture, footwear, woolen fabrics, and packaging machines – a company strategy that emphasizes focus, customized products, niche marketing, rapid change, and breathtaking flexibility fits both the dynamics of the industry and the character of the Italian management system. The German management system, in contrast, works well in technical or engineering-oriented industries – optics, chemicals, complicated machinery – where complex products demand precision manufacturing, a careful development process, after-sale service, and thus a highly disciplined management structure. German success is much rarer in consumer goods and services where image marketing and rapid new-feature and model turnover are important to competition.

Countries also differ markedly in the goals that companies and individuals seek to achieve. Company goals reflect the characteristics of national capital markets and the compensation practices for managers. For example, in Germany and Switzerland, where banks comprise a substantial part of the nation's shareholders, most shares are held for long-term appreciation and are rarely traded. Companies do well in mature industries, where ongoing investment in R&D and new facilities is essential but returns may be only moderate. The United States is at the opposite extreme, with a large pool of risk capital but widespread trading of public companies and a strong emphasis by investors on quarterly and annual share-price appreciation. Management compensation is heavily based on annual bonuses tied to individual results. America does well in relatively new industries, like software and biotechnology, or ones where equity funding of new companies feeds active domestic rivalry, like specialty electronics and services. Strong pressures leading to underinvestment, however, plague more mature industries.

Individual motivation to work and expand skills is also important to competitive advantage. Outstanding talent is a scarce resource in any nation. A nation's success largely depends on the types of education its talented people choose, where they choose to work, and their commitment and effort. The goals a nation's institutions and values set for individuals and companies, and the prestige it attaches to certain industries, guide the flow of capital and human resources – which, in turn, directly affects the competitive performance of certain industries. Nations tend to be competitive in activities that people admire or depend on – the activities from which the nation's heroes emerge. In Switzerland, it is banking and pharmaceuticals. In Israel, the highest callings have been agriculture and defense-related fields. Sometimes it is hard to distinguish between cause and effect. Attaining international success can make an industry prestigious, reinforcing its advantage.

The presence of strong local rivals is a final, and powerful, stimulus to the creation and persistence of competitive advantage. This is true of small countries, like Switzerland, where the rivalry among its pharmaceutical companies, Hoffmann-La Roche, Ciba-Geigy and Sandoz, contributes to a leading worldwide position. It is true in the United States in the computer and software industries. Nowhere is the role of fierce rivalry more apparent than in Japan, where there are 112 companies competing in machine tools, 34 in semiconductors, 25 in audio equipment, 15 in cameras – in fact, there are usually double figures in the industries in which Japan boasts global dominance. (See the table 'Estimated Number of Japanese Rivals in Selected Industries.') Among all the points on the diamond, domestic rivalry is arguably the most important because of the powerfully stimulating effect it has on all the others.

Conventional wisdom argues that domestic competition is wasteful: it leads to duplication of effort and prevents companies from achieving economies of scale. The 'right solution' is to embrace one or two national champions, companies with the scale and strength to tackle foreign competitors, and to guarantee them the necessary resources, with the government's blessing. In fact, however, most national champions are uncompetitive, although heavily subsidized and protected by their government. In many of the prominent industries in which there is only one national rival, such as aerospace and telecommunications, government has played a large role in distorting competition.

Static efficiency is much less important than dynamic improvement, which domestic rivalry uniquely spurs. Domestic rivalry like any rivalry creates pressure on companies to innovate and improve. Local rivals push each other to lower costs, improve quality and service, and create new products and processes. But unlike rivalries with foreign competitors, which tend to be analytical and distant, local rivalries often go beyond pure economic or business competition and become intensely personal. Domestic rivals engage in active feuds; they compete not only for market share but also for people, for technical excellence, and perhaps most important, for 'bragging rights.' One domestic rival's success proves to others that advancement is possible and often attracts new rivals to the industry. Companies often attribute the success of foreign rivals to 'unfair' advantages. With domestic rivals, there are no excuses.

Air Conditioners	13
Audio Equipmemt	25
Automobiles	9
Cameras	15
Car Audio	12
Carbon Fibers	7
Construction Equipment*	15
Copiers	14
Facsimile Machines	10
Large-scale Computers	6
Lift Trucks	8
Machine Tools	112
Microwave Equipment	5
Motorcycles	4
Musical Instruments	4
Personal Computers	16
Semiconductors	34
Sewing Machines	20
Shipbuilding[†]	33
Steel[‡]	5
Synthetic Fibers	8
Television Sets	15
Truck and Bus Tires	5
Trucks	11
Typewriters	14
Videocassette Recorders	10

Estimated number of Japanese rivals in selected industries

Sources: Field interviews; *Nippon Kogyo Shinbun, Nippon Kogyo Nenkan,* 1987; Yano Research, *Market Share Jitan.* 1987; researchers' estimates.

* The number of companies varied by product area. The smallest number, 10, produced bulldozers. Fifteen companies produced shovel trucks, truck cranes, and asphalt-paving equipment. There were 20 companies in hydraulic excavators, a product area where Japan was particularly strong.

[†]Six companies had annual production exports in excess of 10,000 tons.

[‡]Integrated companies.

Geographic concentration magnifies the power of domestic rivalry. This pattern is strikingly common around the world: Italian jewelry companies are located around two towns, Arezzo and Valenza Po; cutlery companies in Solingen, West Germany and Seki, Japan; pharmaceutical companies in Basel, Switzerland; motorcycles and musical instruments in Hamamatsu, Japan. The more localized the rivalry, the more intense. And the more intense, the better.

Another benefit of domestic rivalry is the pressure it creates for constant upgrading of the sources of competitive advantage. The presence of domestic competitors automatically cancels the types of advantage that come from simply being in a particular nation – factor costs, access to or preference in the home market, or costs to foreign competitors who import into the market. Companies are forced to move beyond them, and as a result, gain more sustainable advantages. Moreover, competing domestic rivals will keep each other honest in obtaining government support. Companies are less likely to get hooked on the narcotic of government contracts or creeping industry protectionism. Instead, the industry will seek – and benefit from – more constructive forms of government support, such as assistance in opening foreign markets, as well as investments in focused educational institutions or other specialized factors.

Ironically, it is also vigorous domestic competition that ultimately pressures domestic companies to look at global markets and toughens them to succeed in them. Particularly when there are economies of scale, local competitors force each other to look outward to foreign markets to capture greater efficiency and higher profitability. And having been tested by fierce domestic competition, the stronger companies are well equipped to win abroad. If Digital Equipment can hold its own against IBM, Data General, Prime, and Hewlett-Packard, going up against Siemens or Machines Bull does not seem so daunting a prospect.

The diamond as a system

Each of these four attributes defines a point on the diamond of national advantage; the effect of one point often depends on the state of others. Sophisticated buyers will not translate into advanced products, for example, unless the quality of human resources permits companies to meet buyer needs. Selective disadvantages in factors of production will not motivate innovation unless rivalry is vigorous and company goals support sustained investment. At the broadest level, weaknesses in any one determinant will constrain an industry's potential for advancement and upgrading.

But the points of the diamond are also self-reinforcing: they constitute a system. Two elements, domestic rivalry and geographic concentration, have especially great power to transform the diamond into a system – domestic rivalry because it promotes improvement in all the other determinants and geographic concentration because it elevates and magnifies the interaction of the four separate influences.

The role of domestic rivalry illustrates how the diamond operates as a self-reinforcing system. Vigorous domestic rivalry stimulates the development of unique pools of specialized factors, particularly if the rivals are all located in one city or region: the University of California at Davis has become the world's leading center of wine-making research, working closely with the California wine industry. Active local rivals also upgrade domestic demand in an industry. In furniture and shoes, for example, Italian consumers have learned to expect more and better products because of the rapid pace of new product development that is driven by intense domestic rivalry among hundreds of Italian companies. Domestic rivalry also promotes the formation of related and supporting industries. Japan's world-leading group of semiconductor producers, for instance, has spawned world-leading Japanese semiconductor-equipment manufacturers.

The effects can work in all directions: sometimes world-class suppliers become new entrants in the industry they have been supplying. Or highly sophisticated buyers may themselves enter a supplier industry, particularly when they have relevant skills and view the new industry as strategic. In the case of the Japanese robotics industry, for example, Matsushita and Kawasaki originally designed robots for internal use before beginning to sell robots to others. Today they are strong competitors in the robotics industry. In Sweden, Sandvik moved from specialty steel into rock drills, and SKF moved from specialty steel into ball bearings.

Another effect of the diamond's systemic nature is that nations are rarely home to just one competitive industry; rather, the diamond creates an environment that promotes *clusters* of competitive industries. Competitive industries are not scattered helter-skelter throughout the economy but are usually linked together through vertical (buyer-seller) or horizontal (common customers, technology; channels) relationships. Nor are clusters usually scattered physically; they tend to be concentrated geographically. One competitive industry helps to create another in a mutually reinforcing process. Japan's strength in consumer electronics, for example, drove its success in semiconductors toward the memory chips and integrated circuits these products use. Japanese strength in laptop computers, which contrasts to limited success in other segments, reflects the base of strength in other compact, portable products and leading expertise in liquid-crystal display gained in the calculator and watch industries.

Once a cluster forms, the whole group of industries becomes mutually supporting. Benefits flow forward, backward, and horizontally. Aggressive rivalry in one industry spreads to others in the cluster, through spin-offs, through the exercise of bargaining power, and through diversification by established companies. Entry from other industries within the cluster spurs upgrading by stimulating diversity in R&D approaches and facilitating the introduction of new strategies and skills. Through the conduits of suppliers or customers who have contact with multiple competitors, information flows freely and innovations diffuse rapidly. Interconnections within the cluster, often unanticipated, lead to perceptions of new ways of competing and new opportunities. The cluster becomes a vehicle for maintaining diversity and overcoming the inward focus, inertia, inflexibility, and accommodation among rivals that slows or blocks competitive upgrading and new entry.

The role of government

In the continuing debate over the competitiveness of nations, no topic engenders more argument or creates less understanding than the role of the government. Many see government as an essential helper or supporter of industry, employing a host of policies to contribute directly to the competitive performance of strategic or target industries.

Others accept the 'free market' view that the operation of the economy should be left to the workings of the invisible hand.

Both views are incorrect. Either, followed to its logical outcome, would lead to the permanent erosion of a country's competitive capabilities. On one hand, advocates of government help for industry frequently propose policies that would actually hurt companies in the long run and only create the demand for more helping. On the other hand, advocates of a diminished government presence ignore the legitimate role that government plays in shaping the context and institutional structure surrounding companies and in creating an environment that stimulates companies to gain competitive advantage.

Government's proper role is as a catalyst and challenger; it is to encourage – or even push – companies to raise their aspirations and move to higher levels of competitive performance, even though this process may be inherently unpleasant and difficult. Government cannot create competitive industries; only companies can do that. Government plays a role that is inherently partial, that succeeds only when working in tandem with favorable underlying conditions in the diamond. Still, government's role of transmitting and amplifying the forces of the diamond is a powerful one. Government policies that succeed are those that create an environment in which companies can gain competitive advantage rather than those that involve government directly in the process, except in nations early in the development process. It is an indirect, rather than a direct, role.

Japan's government, at its best, understands this role better than anyone – including the point that nations pass through stages of competitive development and that government's appropriate role shifts as the economy progresses. By stimulating early demand for advanced products, confronting industries with the need to pioneer frontier technology through symbolic cooperative projects, establishing prizes that reward quality, and pursuing other policies that magnify the forces of the diamond, the Japanese government accelerates the pace of innovation. But like government officials anywhere, at their worst Japanese bureaucrats can make the same mistakes: attempting to manage industry structure, protecting the market too long, and yielding to political pressure to insulate inefficient retailers, farmers, distributors, and industrial companies from competition.

It is not hard to understand why so many governments make the same mistakes so often in pursuit of national competitiveness: competitive time for companies and political time for governments are fundamentally at odds. It often takes more than a decade for an industry to create competitive advantage; the process entails the long upgrading of human skills, investing in products and processes, building clusters, and penetrating foreign markets. In the case of the Japanese auto industry; for instance, companies made their first faltering steps toward exporting in the 1950s – yet did not achieve strong international positions until the 1970s.

But in politics, a decade is an eternity. Consequently, most governments favor policies that offer easily perceived short-term benefits, such as subsidies, protection, and arranged mergers – the very policies that retard innovation. Most of the policies that would make a real difference either are too slow and require too much patience for politicians or, even worse, carry with them the sting of short-term pain. Deregulating a protected industry, for example, will lead to bankruptcies sooner and to stronger, more competitive companies only later.

Policies that convey static, short-term cost advantages but that unconsciously undermine innovation and dynamism represent the most common and most profound error in government industrial policy. In a desire to help, it is all too easy for governments to adopt policies such as joint projects to avoid 'wasteful' R&D that undermine dynamism and competition. Yet even a 10% cost saving through economies of scale is easily nullified through rapid product and process improvement and the pursuit of volume in global markets – something that such policies undermine.

There are some simple, basic principles that governments should embrace to play the proper supportive role for national competitiveness: encourage change, promote domestic rivalry, stimulate innovation. Some of the specific policy approaches to guide nations seeking to gain competitive advantage include the following:

Focus on specialized factor creation. Government has critical responsibilities for fundamentals like the primary and secondary education systems, basic national infrastructure, and research in areas of broad national concern such as health care. Yet these kinds of generalized efforts at factor creation rarely produce competitive advantage. Rather, the factors that translate into competitive advantage are advanced, specialized, and tied to specific industries or industry groups. Mechanisms such as specialized apprenticeship programs, research efforts in universities connected with an industry, trade association activities, and, most important, the private investments of companies ultimately create the factors that will yield competitive advantage.

Avoid intervening in factor and currency markets. By intervening in factor and currency markets, governments hope to create lower factor costs or a favorable exchange rate that will help companies compete more effectively in international markets. Evidence from around the world indicates that these policies – such as the Reagan administration's dollar devaluation – are often counterproductive. They work against the upgrading of industry and the search for more sustainable competitive advantage.

The contrasting case of Japan is particularly instructive, although both Germany and Switzerland have had similar experiences. Over the past 20 years, the Japanese have been rocked by the sudden Nixon currency devaluation shock, two oil shocks, and, most recently, the yen shock – all of which forced Japanese companies to upgrade their competitive advantages. The point is not that government should pursue policies that intentionally drive up factor costs or the exchange rate. Rather, when market forces create rising factor costs or a higher exchange rate, government should resist the temptation to push them back down.

Enforce strict product, safety, and environmental standards. Strict government regulations can promote competitive advantage by stimulating and upgrading domestic demand. Stringent standards for product performance, product safety, and environmental impact pressure companies to improve quality, upgrade technology, and provide features that respond to consumer and social demands. Easing standards, however tempting, is counterproductive.

When tough regulations anticipate standards that will spread internationally, they give a nation's companies a head start in developing products and services that will be valuable elsewhere. Sweden's strict standards for environmental protection have promoted competitive advantage in many industries. Atlas Copco, for example, produces quiet compressors that can be used in dense urban areas with minimal disruption to residents. Strict standards, however, must be combined with a rapid and streamlined regulatory process that does not absorb resources and cause delays.

Sharply limit direct cooperation among industry rivals. The most pervasive global policy fad in the competitiveness arena today is the call for more cooperative research and industry consortia. Operating on the belief that independent research by rivals is wasteful and duplicative, that collaborative efforts achieve economies of scale, and that individual companies are likely to underinvest in R&D because they cannot reap all the benefits, governments have embraced the idea of more direct cooperation. In the United States, antitrust laws have been modified to allow more cooperative R&D; in Europe, mega-projects such as ESPRIT, an information-technology project, bring together companies from several countries. Lurking behind much of this thinking is the fascination of Western governments with – and fundamental misunderstanding of – the countless cooperative research projects sponsored by the Ministry of International Trade and Industry (MITI), projects that appear to have contributed to Japan's competitive rise.

But a closer look at Japanese cooperative projects suggests a different story. Japanese companies participate in MITI projects to maintain good relations with MITI, to preserve their corporate images, and to hedge the risk that competitors will gain from the project – largely defensive reasons. Companies rarely contribute their best scientists and engineers to cooperative projects and usually spend much more on their own private research in the same field. Typically, the government makes only a modest financial contribution to the project.

The real value of Japanese cooperative research is to signal the importance of emerging technical areas and to stimulate proprietary company research. Cooperative projects prompt companies to explore new fields and boost internal R&D spending because companies know that their domestic rivals are investigating them.

Under certain limited conditions, cooperative research can prove beneficial. Projects should be in areas of basic product and process research, not in subjects closely connected to a company's proprietary sources of advantage. They should constitute only a modest portion of a company's overall research program in any given field. Cooperative research should be only indirect, channeled through independent organizations to which most industry participants have access. Organizational structures, like university labs and centers of excellence, reduce management problems and minimize the risk to rivalry. Finally, the most useful cooperative projects often involve fields that touch a number of industries and that require substantial R&D investments.

Promote goals that lead to sustained investment. Government has a vital role in shaping the goals of investors, managersv, and employees through policies in various areas. The manner in which capital markets are regulated, for example, shapes the incentives of investors and, in turn, the behavior of companies. Government should aim to encourage sustained investment in human skills, in innovation, and in physical assets. Perhaps the single most powerful tool for raising the rate of sustained investment in industry is a tax incentive for long-term (five years or more) capital gains restricted to new investment in corporate equity. Long-term capital gains incentives should also be applied to pension funds and other currently untaxed investors, who now have few reasons not to engage in rapid trading.

Deregulate competition. Regulation of competition through such policies as maintaining a state monopoly, controlling entry into an industry, or fixing prices has two strong negative consequences: it stifles rivalry and innovation as companies become preoccupied with dealing with regulators and protecting what they already have; and it makes the industry a less dynamic and less desirable buyer or supplier. Deregulation and privatization on their own, however, will not succeed without vigorous domestic rivalry – and that requires, as a corollary, a strong and consistent antitrust policy.

Enforce strong domestic antitrust policies. A strong antitrust policy – especially for horizontal mergers, alliances, and collusive behavior – is fundamental to innovation. While it is fashionable today to call for mergers and alliances in the name of globalization and the creation of national champions, these often undermine the creation of competitive advantage. Real national competitiveness requires governments to disallow mergers, acquisitions, and alliances that involve industry leaders. Furthermore, the same standards for mergers and alliances should apply to both domestic and foreign companies. Finally, government policy should favor internal entry, both domestic and international, over acquisition. Companies should, however, be allowed to acquire small companies in related industries when the move promotes the transfer of skills that could ultimately create competitive advantage.

Reject managed trade. Managed trade represents a growing and dangerous tendency for dealing with the fallout of national competitiveness. Orderly marketing agreements, voluntary restraint agreements, or other devices that set quantitative targets to divide up markets are dangerous, ineffective, and often enormously costly to consumers. Rather than promoting innovation in a nation's industries, managed trade guarantees a market for inefficient companies.

Government trade policy should pursue open market access in every foreign nation. To be effective, trade policy should not be a passive instrument; it cannot respond only to complaints or work only for those industries that can muster enough political clout; it should not require a long history of injury or serve only distressed industries. Trade policy should seek to open markets wherever a nation has competitive advantage and should actively address emerging industries and incipient problems.

Where government finds a trade barrier in another nation, it should concentrate its remedies on dismantling barriers, not on regulating imports or exports. In the case of Japan, for example, pressure to accelerate the already rapid growth of manufactured imports is a more effective approach than a shift to managed trade. Compensatory tariffs that punish companies for unfair trade practices are better than market quotas. Other increasingly important tools to open markets are restrictions that prevent companies in offending nations from investing in acquisitions or production facilities in the host country – thereby blocking the unfair country's companies from using their advantage to establish a new beachhead that is immune from sanctions.

Any of these remedies, however, can backfire. It is virtually impossible to craft remedies to unfair trade practices that avoid both reducing incentives for domestic companies to innovate and export and harming domestic buyers. The aim of remedies should be adjustments that allow the remedy to disappear.

The company agenda

Ultimately, only companies themselves can achieve and sustain competitive advantage. To do so, they must act on the fundamentals described above. In particular, they must recognize the central role of innovation – and the uncomfortable truth that innovation grows out of pressure and challenge. It takes leadership to create a dynamic, challenging environment. And it takes leadership to recognize the all-too-easy escape routes that appear to offer a path to competitive advantage, but are actually short-cuts to failure. For example, it is tempting to rely on cooperative research and development projects to lower the cost and risk of research. But they can divert company attention and resources from proprietary research efforts and will all but eliminate the prospects for real innovation.

Competitive advantage arises from leadership that harnesses and amplifies the forces in the diamond to promote innovation and upgrading. Here are just a few of the kinds of company policies that will support that effort:

Create pressures for innovation. A company should seek out pressure and challenge, not avoid them. Part of strategy is to take advantage of the home nation to create the impetus for innovation. To do that, companies can sell to the most sophisticated and demanding buyers and channels; seek out those buyers with the most difficult needs; establish norms that exceed the toughest regulatory hurdles or product standards; source from the most advanced suppliers; treat employees as permanent in order to stimulate upgrading of skills and productivity.

Seek out the most capable competitors as motivators. To motivate organizational change, capable competitors and respected rivals can be a common enemy. The best managers always run a little scared; they respect and study competitors. To stay dynamic, companies must make meeting challenge a part of the organization's norms. For example, lobbying against strict product standards signals the organization that company leadership has diminished aspirations. Companies that value stability, obedient customers, dependent suppliers, and sleepy competitors are inviting inertia and, ultimately, failure.

Establish early-warning systems. Early-warning signals translate into early-mover advantages. Companies can take actions that help them see the signals of change and act on them, thereby getting a jump on the competition. For example, they can find and serve those buyers with the most anticipatory needs; investigate all emerging new buyers or channels; find places whose regulations foreshadow emerging regulations elsewhere; bring some outsiders into the management team; maintain ongoing relationships with research centers and sources of talented people.

Improve the national diamond. Companies have a vital stake in making their home environment a better platform for international success. Part of a company's responsibility is to play an active role in forming clusters and to work with its home-nation buyers, suppliers, and channels to help them upgrade and extend their own competitive advantages. To upgrade home demand, for example, Japanese musical instrument manufacturers, led by Yamaha, Kawai, and Suzuki, have established music schools. Similarly, companies can stimulate and support local suppliers of important specialized inputs – including encouraging them to compete globally. The health and strength of the national cluster will only enhance the company's own rate of innovation and upgrading.

In nearly every successful competitive industry, leading companies also take explicit steps to create specialized factors like human resources, scientific knowledge, or infrastructure. In industries like wool cloth, ceramic tiles, and lighting equipment, Italian industry associations invest in market information, process technology, and common infrastructure. Companies can also speed innovation by putting their headquarters and other key operations where there are concentrations of sophisticated buyers, important suppliers, or specialized factor-creating mechanisms, such as universities or laboratories.

Welcome domestic rivalry. To compete globally, a company needs capable domestic rivals and vigorous domestic rivalry. Especially in the United States and Europe today, managers are wont to complain about excessive competition and to argue for mergers and acquisitions that will produce hoped-for economies of scale and critical mass. The complaint is only natural – but the argument is plain wrong. Vigorous domestic rivalry creates sustainable competitive advantage. Moreover, it is better to grow internationally than to dominate the domestic market. If a company wants an acquisition, a foreign one that can speed globalization and supplement home-based advantages or offset home-based disadvantages is usually far better than merging with leading domestic competitors.

Globalize to tap selective advantages in other nations. In search of 'global' strategies, many companies today abandon their home diamond. To be sure, adopting a global perspective is important to creating competitive advantage. But relying on foreign activities that supplant domestic capabilities is always a second-best solution. Innovating to offset local factor disadvantages is better than outsourcing; developing domestic suppliers and buyers is better than relying solely on foreign ones. Unless the critical underpinnings of competitiveness are present at home, companies will not sustain competitive advantage in the long run. The aim should be to upgrade home-base capabilities so that foreign activities are selective and supplemental only to over-all competitive advantage.

The correct approach to globalization is to tap selectively into sources of advantage in other nations' diamonds. For example, identifying sophisticated buyers in other countries helps companies understand different needs and creates pressures that will stimulate a faster rate of innovation. No matter how favorable the home diamond, moreover, important research is going on in other nations. To take advantage of foreign research, companies must station high-quality people in overseas bases and mount a credible level of scientific effort. To get anything back from foreign research ventures, companies must also allow access to their own ideas – recognizing that competitive advantage comes from continuous improvement, not from protecting today's secrets.

Use alliances only selectively. Alliances with foreign companies have become another managerial fad and cure-all: they represent a tempting solution to the problem of a company wanting the advantages of foreign enterprises or hedging against risk, without giving up independence. In reality, however, while alliances can achieve selective benefits, they always exact significant costs: they involve coordinating two separate operations, reconciling goals with an independent entity, creating a competitor, and giving up profits. These costs ultimately make most alliances short-term transitional devices, rather than stable, long-term relationships.

Most important, alliances as a broad-based strategy will only ensure a company's mediocrity, not its international leadership. No company can rely on another outside, independent company for skills and assets that are central to its competitive advantage. Alliances are best used as a selective tool, employed on a temporary basis or involving noncore activities.

Locate the home base to support competitive advantage. Among the most important decisions for multinational companies is the nation in which to locate the home base for each distinct business. A company can have different home bases for distinct businesses or segments. Ultimately, competitive advantage is created at home: it is where strategy is set, the core product and process technology is created, and a critical mass of production takes place. The circumstances in the home nation must support innovation; otherwise the company has no choice but to move its home base to a country that stimulates innovation and that provides the best environment for global competitiveness. There are no half-measures: the management team must move as well.

The role of leadership

Too many companies and top managers misperceive the nature of competition and the task before them by focusing on improving financial performance, soliciting government assistance, seeking stability, and reducing risk through alliances and mergers.

Today's competitive realities demand leadership. Leaders believe in change; they energize their organizations to innovate continuously; they recognize the importance of their home country as integral to their competitive success and work to upgrade it. Most important, leaders recognize the need for pressure and challenge. Because they are willing to encourage appropriate – and painful – government policies and regulations, they often earn the title 'statesmen,' although few see themselves that way. They are prepared to sacrifice the easy life for difficulty and, ultimately, sustained competitive advantage. That must be the goal, for both nations and companies: not just surviving, but achieving international competitiveness.

And not just once, but continuously.

Author's note: Michael J. Enright, who served as project coordinator for this study, has contributed valuable suggestions.

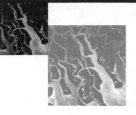

READING 4
Horses for courses: organizational forms for multinational corporations**

*Sumantra Ghoshal and Nitin Nohria**

ONE OF THE MOST ENDURING IDEAS OF ORGANIZATION THEORY IS THAT AN ORGANIZATION'S STRUCTURE AND MANAGEMENT PROCESS MUST 'FIT' ITS ENVlRONMENT, in the same way that a particular horse might be more suited to one course than another. Ghoshal and Nohria show the continued relevance of this classic insight for the organization of multinational corporations. They offer a simple scheme to classify the environment and structure of MNCs. Then, based on data on forty-one large MNCs, they show how some combinations of environment and structure fit better than others. What drives fit is the principle of requisite complexity – the complexity of a firm's structure must match the complexity of its environment. Though developed for MNCs, their argument can also apply to multidivisional firms that operate in different markets or business segments.

About two decades ago, business academics told managers that when it came to organization design, one size did not fit all. Different companies, facing different business demands, needed different kinds of organizations. More complex and turbulent environments called for more complex organizational approaches, and the nature and extent of organizational complexity had to match the firm's strategic complexity. In its initial formulation, before the hedge that 'it all depends' made it too complicated to mean anything at all, this contingency theory of organizations provided managers with some simple guidelines to help them decide on the kind of organization they should adopt.[1]

For multinational corporations (MNCs), such guidelines were available in the 'stages model' proposed by Stopford and Wells[2] (see Figure 1). This model defined the strategic complexity faced by an MNC in terms of two dimensions: the number of products sold internationally ('foreign product diversity,' shown on the figure's vertical axis) and the importance of international sales to the company ('foreign sales as a percentage of total sales,' shown on the horizontal axis). Stopford and Wells suggested that at the early stage of foreign expansion, when both foreign sales and the diversity of products sold abroad were limited, worldwide companies typically managed their international operations

---

* Sumantra Ghoshal is associate professor of business policy, INSEAD. Nitin Nohria is assistant professor at the Harvard Business School.

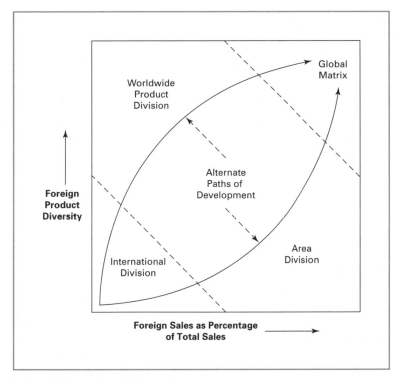

Figure 1 The Stopford and Wells model of MNC organizations

through an international division. Subsequently, some companies expanded their sales abroad without significantly increasing foreign product diversity; they typically adopted an area structure. Companies facing substantial increases in foreign product diversity tended to adopt the worldwide product division structure. Finally, when both foreign sales and foreign product diversity were high, companies resorted to the global matrix.

Over the two decades since Stopford and Wells presented this simple, descriptive model, academic research on MNCs has developed a far more elaborate understanding of MNC organizations. It is increasingly clear, for example, that the formal macrostructure described in the stages model is only a partial representation of a worldwide organization. To use a biological metaphor suggested by Christopher Bartlett, organizations have an anatomy (formal structure), but they also have a physiology (core management processes) and a psychology (the mind-sets of their managers). To analyze the organizational capabilities a company needs, one must look not only to the anatomy but also to the physiology and psychology.[3]

Further, the prescription of matching organizational characteristics to environmental and strategic demands is also under challenge. Environments do not stand still for organizations to catch up, and organizations themselves, as organic entities, are in a continuous state of flux. Instead of a mechanistic and static view of fit, one needs to recognize the fluid, multidimensional, and changing nature of both environments and organizations. What is needed is not just fit but fit and flexibility.[4]

Unfortunately, academic research and conclusions are inevitably simplified and stripped of nuances. Just as the earlier stages model was converted into a set of simplistic prescriptions, so has this new research been recast as an orgy of complexity. Bartlett and Ghoshal, for example, have repeatedly argued that companies must simplify wherever possible to protect clarity of responsibility and initiative and that the more complex or 'transnational' integrated network organization should be used only for MNCs operating in highly complex environments.[5] Yet their findings have often been interpreted as an all-or-nothing call for this 'transnational' structure in all companies.[6]

In this article we wish to make the following two points. First, although the Stopford and Wells model has its deficiencies, it does not follow that MNCs are too organizationally complex for any meaningful yet simple classification. Managers need simple organizational models and classification schemes as a starting point for thinking about the core attributes of their organizational needs. Similarly, academics need them in order to build theory and develop analytical and testable propositions. Therefore, we will propose here a useful classification scheme for MNC organizations, one that is not defined in terms of traditional structural forms (e.g., area, product, matrix, etc.), but that is based on the company's internal pattern of headquarters – subsidiary relations. Any organizational model or classification scheme is built on simplifications and, therefore, suffers from some deficiencies. Our scheme is no exception. However, in this paper we will demonstrate its usefulness for both managers and academics.

Second, although flexibility is important, so is fit. Organizational complexity is costly and difficult to manage, and simplicity, wherever possible, is a virtue. Just as a company can suffer from too simple an organization if it is operating in a complex and turbulent environment, so can it also pay an efficiency penalty for adopting an organization too complex for its environmental demands. Although insensitive to the reality of constant flux in both environments and organizations and, therefore, somewhat unfashionable in current organization research, the concept of fit remains one of the relatively few simple and robust findings in organization theory.[7] We will demonstrate here the continued validity of this concept of environment-organization fit and of the positive relationship of such fit with firm performance.

The empirical database

Our empirical analysis is based primarily on a database that has been described fully elsewhere.[8] This database consists of information on all wholly-owned subsidiaries of sixty-six large MNCs in ten prespecified countries. It was obtained from a mailed questionnaire survey completed by one correspondent from each firm, typically a senior headquarters manager with responsibility for the firm's international operations. These managers assigned values, on a scale of one (low) to five (high), to a number of variables indicative of the local context (competitive intensity in the local market, technological dynamism of the local environment, extent of local government regulations, and local resources available to the subsidiary) and the structure of the headquarters-subsidiary relation (extent to which its governance is based on centralization, formalization, and normative integration). Although each variable was measured through a single indicator, the reliability and validity of the measures were tested through a multiple-indicator, multiple-respondent survey administered at the headquarters and subsidiary levels in three large MNCs.[9] In the following analysis, we rely wholly on this database to measure structural attributes of MNCs.

We obtained additional measures, following the framework proposed by Prahalad and Doz, to classify MNC environments in terms of the twin demands of global integration and national responsiveness.[10] To measure global integration, we use Kobrin's 'index of integration,' which we consider a theoretically well-grounded and empirically precise measure of this complex construct.[11] To measure national responsiveness, we use two indicators. The first, extent of government regulations, comes from our questionnaire data. The second, advertising intensity, is computed from the industry averages published in *Advertising Age*.

Finally, we use three different economic indicators – average annual return on net assets, average revenue growth, and average annual growth in return on net assets to measure company performance. Specifically, we compute average values of these three variables for the period 1982 to 1986 as they appear in the relevant annual reports (the company survey was conducted in 1986). Corporate performance can be measured in different ways corresponding to the firms' different goals, but we employ these three economic measures because our purpose is to explore performance difference across a broad sample of firms and because these measures are recognized as both fairly comprehensive and highly important to the companies themselves.[12]

We have complete data (including Kobrin's index) for only forty-one of the sixty-six companies in the database. Accordingly, data on only these forty-one companies are used in the empirical analysis reported in this paper. Table 1 lists these companies and their principal businesses.

The paper is organized as follows. First, we draw on the existing literature to classify the environments of the forty-one companies into four categories. These categories reflect firms' varying needs to respond to distinct local conditions and to integrate across national boundaries. Second, we use Lawrence and Lorsch's dimensions of structural differentiation and integration to classify the forty-one companies into four structural categories. Finally, we hypothesize a one-to-one fit between the environmental and structural categories and test this hypothesis against the information in our database.

Classifying the environments of MNCs

Each MNC subsidiary operates in a different national environment. In each country, the local subsidiary must be responsive to local customers, governments, and regulatory agencies for its ongoing institutional legitimacy and economic success. To some extent, then, the MNC must respond to the different contingencies presented by the multiple environments in which it operates. Such contingencies have been categorized in the multinational management literature as 'forces for national responsiveness.'[13]

These different local environments may also be linked to each other – because there are common customer preferences across countries; because economies of scale, scope, and national comparative advantage create incentives for specialization and interdependence; because knowledge developed in one environment is transferable or adaptable in another; or because key players in the MNC's environment are transnational,

Name of company	Home country	Principal industry
1. Air Products and Chemicals	United States	Industrial chemicals
2. Alcan	Canada	Nonferrous metals
3. Baker International	United States	Machinery
4. Bertelsmann	Germany	Printing and publishing
5. Blue Bell	United States	Textiles
6. British-American Tobacco (BAT)	United Kingdom	Tobacco
7. BSN Groupe	France	Food
8. Caterpillar	United States	Construction and mining machinery
9. Colgate-Palmolive	United States	Drugs and pharmaceuticals
10. Continental Group	United States	Metals
11. Cummins	United States	Engines
12. Deere & Co.	United States	Construction and mining machinery
13. Digital Equipment Corp.	United States	Computers
14. DuPont	United States	Chemicals
15. Electrolux	Sweden	Household appliances
16. Emhart Corporation	United States	Machinery
17. Firestone	United States	Rubber
18. Freuhauf Corporation	United States	Automobiles
19. Friedrich Krupp	Germany	Metals
20. General Foods	United States	Food
21. General Motors	United States	Automobiles
22. Glaxo	United Kingdom	Drugs and pharmaceuticals
23. Hoechst AG	Germany	Chemicals
24. Honeywell	United States	Scientific measuring instruments
25. ICI	United Kingdom	Chemicals
26. Jacobs Suchard	Switzerland	Food
27. Kodak	United States	Photographic equipment
28. Mannesmann	Germany	Metals
29. Norsk Hydro	Norway	Chemicals
30. Norton	United States	Machinery
31. R.J. Reynolds	United States	Tobacco
32. Reckitt & Colman	United Kingdom	Drugs and pharmaceuticals
33. Rio Tinto-Zinc	United Kingdom	Metals
34. Schneider	France	Machinery
35. Seagram	Canada	Beverages
36. Siemens	Germany	Machinery
37. Solvay & Cie	Belgium	Chemicals
38. Swedish Match	Sweden	Paper and forestry
39. Timken	United States	Machinery
40. United Biscuits	United Kingdom	Food
41. Volvo	Sweden	Automobiles

Table 1 The companies surveyed and their principal businesses

such as its multinational clients, suppliers, competitors, and even regulatory agencies (such as the EEC). These linkages across national boundaries pressure the subsidiaries to coordinate their activities; they have been described as 'forces for global integration.'[14]

These two forces – for national responsiveness and for global integration – are not opposite ends of a spectrum. Although they are related, we can consider them as separate dimensions. Thus, a company with a weak force for national responsiveness does not automatically have a strong force for global integration and vice versa. For instance, businesses such as pharmaceuticals, telecommunications, and computers may simultaneously face strong demands for both global integration and local responsiveness. In computers, the growing commoditization of hardware combined with high capital intensity and scale economics constitute powerful forces for global integration. At the same time, the increasing market demands for integration of hardware from diverse sources with software and services to provide 'solutions' to customer problems create equally strong needs for local responsiveness.

The weak-weak combination is also possible. The business of producing and marketing cement is an example. Cement products are highly standardized, and marketing and distribution systems are similar across countries. Thus demands for local responsiveness are weak. However, the trade-offs between the economics of cement production and transport costs are such that global integration is not attractive.

Of course, weak-strong combinations of both sorts are possible as well. Semiconductors and airplane engines confront strong forces for global integration, given their high capital intensities and significant scale economies, but relatively weak forces for national responsiveness because product standardization is relatively high and customer demands are relatively uniform in different geographic markets. In contrast, businesses such as legal services or nonbranded foods are likely to face weak forces for global integration and strong demands for national responsiveness.

Four types of MNC environments

The environmental contingencies faced by the MNC as a whole can, therefore, be conceived in terms of the extent to which it must respond to strong and unique national environments and the extent to which it must respond to the linkages across these national environments. Adopting the terms used by Bartlett and Ghoshal, we broadly distinguish among four environmental conditions faced by MNCs: (1) a *global environment* in which the forces for global integration are strong and for local responsiveness weak, (2) a *multinational environment* in which the forces for national responsiveness are strong and for global integration weak, (3) a *transnational environment* in which both contingencies are strong, and (4) a placid *international environment* in which both contingencies are weak (see Figure 2).[15]

We adopted the following procedure to classify the environment of each of the forty-one MNCs in our sample as one of these four types. Kobrin's index of integration, which we use to measure the forces of global integration in different business environments is the ratio of the total intrafirm trade (the sum of affiliate-to-affiliate, affiliate-to-parent, and parent-to-affiliate sales) to the total international sales (sum of total sales of parent and of all affiliates) of all the MNCs in an industry. As Kobrin argues, global integration cannot be measured simply on the basis of bilateral flows. One must consider the overall system

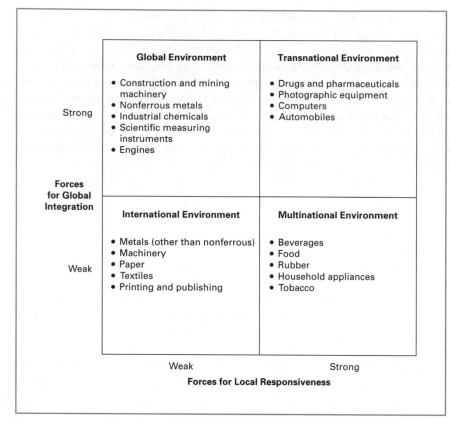

Figure 2 The environment of MNCs: classification of businesses

of interdependencies: 'Transnational integration implies mote than interdependence in the sense that events in one business environment significantly influence those in another; it implies dependence of subsidiaries on the multinational system.' According to Kobrin, cross flows of products within the total MNC system, aggregated to all MNCs in the industry, is one of the most effective ways to measure the forces of global integration. It allows for a systematic and datadriven specification of global industries and avoids the pitfalls of anecdotal and descriptive evidence. Also, the actual measures correlate highly with industry research and development (R&D) intensity – another widely used proxy for the forces of global integration – and are 'certainly in accord with an intuitive, case-study-based concept of global integration.' Kobrins index is a continuous variable and, as he notes, any particular cutoff point to delineate 'high' and 'low' categories is bound to be somewhat arbitrary. We use 20 percent (intrafirm trade as a percentage of total sales) as our cutoff point; we classify businesses such as automobiles (44 percent), computers (38 percent), photographic equipment (32 percent), engines (30 percent), scientific measuring instruments (29 percent), industrial chemicals (26 percent), nonferrous metals (23 percent), pharmaceuticals (21 percent), and construction and mining machinery (21 percent) as confronting strong forces of global integration. The remaining businesses confront weak forces for global integration.

We use two indicators to distinguish between businesses facing strong and those facing weak, forces of national responsiveness. The first is the advertising-to-sales ratio of the industry, as published in *Advertising Age*. The second is an average of the values we received on our questionnaire for the extent of local regulation, by industry (for example, we averaged the ratings given by computer companies on the extent of local regulations to come up with the computer industry average). The two measures are only weakly correlated (rank correlation 0.32, $\varnothing = 0.11$). Given that both regulations and customer preferences can act as powerful forces for local responsiveness, we categorize any business that falls above the sample mean on either of these two indicators as facing strong forces of national responsiveness and one that falls below on either indicator as facing relatively weak forces of national responsiveness.

Figure 2 shows how juxtaposition of these two indicators leads to the categorization of the different business environments into international, multinational, global, and transnational.

Structure classifications

The main criticism of models that define MNC structure in terms of function, geography, product division, or as a matrix has been that the formal organization chart is a poor representation of how an organization really functions. Organizations represent a set of relationships among individuals, groups, and units, and very different relationship patterns can flourish within the same formal structure. To understand, describe, or categorize organizations, therefore, one must focus on the pattern of these relationships. Accordingly, we suggest that an MNC's structure may be conceived more fruitfully as a nexus of the relationships between its different national subsidiaries and its headquarters.

The nature of each headquarters-subsidiary relationship is the basic unit in this conceptualization. These relationships can be described in terms of the three basic governance mechanisms that underlie them. The first of these is *centralization*, which concerns the role of formal authority and hierarchical mechanisms in the company's decision-making processes. The second is *formalization*, which represents decision-making through bureaucratic mechanisms such as formal systems, established rules, and prescribed procedures. The third is *normative integration*, which relies neither on direct headquarters involvement nor on impersonal rules but on the socialization of managers into a set of shared goals, values, and beliefs that then shape their perspectives and behavior. We believe that centralization, formalization, and normative integration, collectively, constitute a fairly comprehensive characterization of the mechanisms by which corporate-division relations may be governed in multi-unit organizations such as MNCs.[16]

Analyses of MNC organizations have often assumed that headquarters-subsidiary relationships are identical for all subsidiaries throughout the company. There is growing evidence, however, that each headquarters-subsidiary relation can be governed by a different combination of the above-mentioned three mechanisms.[17] Therefore, we conceptualize the MNC's overall structure in terms of the pattern of variation in its different headquarters-subsidiary relationships.

Four structural patterns

Using Lawrence and Lorsch's dimensions of differentiation and integration, we envision MNC structures in terms of four patterns. In the first structure – *structural uniformity* – there is little variance in how the different subsidiaries are managed, and a common 'company way' is adopted for the governance of all headquarters-subsidiary relationships. The emphasis may be on one of the three governance types or a combination. Of central importance is a strong and uniform governance mechanism for the whole company; overall integration is high, and there is little attention to differentiation.

A second structure – *differentiated fit* – represents companies that adopt different governance modes to fit each subsidiary's local context. The local context can vary in a number of ways. Two of the most important ways are environmental complexity (the level of technological dynamism and competitive intensity) and the amount of local resources available to the subsidiary.[18] When a company recognizes these differences, it can explicitly differentiate its headquarters-subsidiary relationships to ensure that the management processes fit each local context. We have previously developed a scheme that matches structures to subsidiary contexts.[19] Briefly, this scheme is as follows:

1 Low environment complexity and low levels of local resources dictate a high level of centralization and low levels of formalization and normative integration;

2 Low environment complexity and high levels of resources dictate a low level of centralization and high levels of formalization and normative integration;

3 High environment complexity and low resource levels indicate a moderate level of centralization, a low level of formalization, and a high level of normative integration; and

4 High environment complexity and high resource levels indicate a low level of centralization, a moderate level of formalization, and a high level of normative integration.

Based on the theoretical justification and empirical support provided for this scheme in our earlier paper, we use this logic to describe and identify companies adopting the differentiated fit structure. Note that differentiation is the dominant characteristic of this structure and that it lacks a strong firmwide integrative mechanism.

A third structural pattern is when a firm adopts the logic of differentiated fit but overlays the distinctly structured relationships with a dominant overall integrative mechanism – whether through strong centralization, formalization, or normative integration. We call such structures *integrated variety*.

Finally, a fourth pattern is one in which there is neither a dominant integrative mechanism nor an explicit pattern of differentiation to match local contexts. We call this pattern *ad hoc variation*.

We adopted the following procedure to classify each of the forty-one companies into these four structural categories. We aggregated the measures of centralization, formalization, and normative integration for all of a company's subsidiaries to arrive at a firmwide average of these measures. These averages were used as indicators of the strength of the firm's integrative mechanisms. When a firm's average measure for any of these three structural variables exceeded the median value across all the firms in the sample, the company was considered to have a strong integrative mechanism along that dimension; otherwise it was considered to have a weak, integrative mechanism along that dimension (see Figure 3).

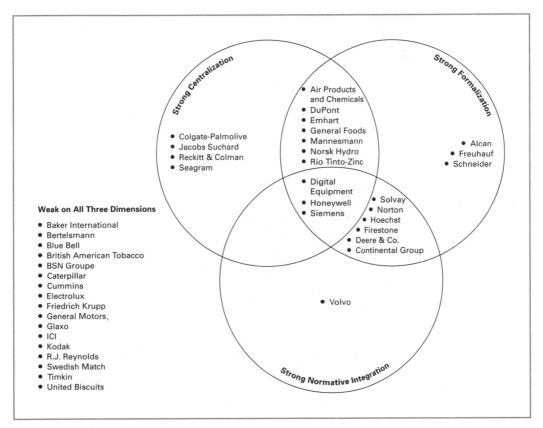

Figure 3 Companies with strong integrative mechanisms

Some of the companies appear to have strong integration mechanisms along a single dimension.[20] For example, Seagram, Jacobs Suchard, Reckitt & Colman, and Colgate-Palmolive appear to have a high level of centralization; Alcan, Freuhauf, and Schneider demonstrate a high level of formalization; whereas Volvo appears to have strong normative integration throughout the company. We do not have detailed case studies on all of the companies to cross-check these survey findings, but the results are consistent with some widely known management systems in these firms. Seagram, for example, is well known for its extremely strong and highly centralized financial control system; all sales proceeds deposited in its subsidiaries' bank accounts are transferred daily to a central account managed by corporate headquarters while the central account remits to each local bank account the amounts required to cover specific operating expenses. Alcan's worldwide planning systems are well known, as are Volvo's decade-long efforts to pioneer a new work style and corporate culture that have often been hailed as unique among Western automobile companies.

Other firms appear to have strong integrative mechanisms along multiple dimensions. DuPont, Air Products and Chemicals, Mannesmann, General Foods, Emhart, Norsk Hydro, and Rio Tinto-Zinc appear to have strong levels of both centralization and formalization; Deere & Co., Firestone, Continental Group, Hoechst, Norton, and Solvay & Cie appear to combine formalization with strong firmwide normative integration. Others like Digital Equipment Corporation, Siemens, and Honeywell appear to have high levels of all three mechanisms. Again, the findings are consistent with what little we know about some of these companies. Digital, for example, has long had highly centralized engineering, product development, and base product marketing functions; has built elaborate formal rules and systems for revenue and profit planning, pricing and discounts, and manufacturing; and has enjoyed a strong set of shared values concerning management of people, commitment to individual initiatives, and working through consensus.

The remaining companies in the sample appear to lack strong, firmwide integration along any of the three dimensions. They do not have uniform, centralized control over their worldwide activities to any significant extent. They appear to lack institutionalized rules and procedures as well as the glue of any strongly shared norms, values, and culture.

We measured the extent of structural differentiation by comparing the fit between each subsidiary's local context and the type of relationship it had with headquarters. For each company, each subsidiary was classified as high or low on the measures of environmental complexity and local resources. Each subsidiary was then classified as high, moderate, or low on the levels of centralization, formalization, and socialization that characterized its relationship with headquarters. If the headquarters-subsidiary relationship was suited to the subsidiary context (as described above), we considered the subsidiary to represent appropriate differentiation and counted the case as a 'fit.' If not, we counted the case as a 'misfit.' For each company, the extent of differentiation was measured as the ratio of the number of its 'fit' to its 'misfit' subsidiaries. When this ratio for a company exceeded the median value for the sample, it was classified as strongly differentiated in its structure; otherwise, the company was classified as weakly differentiated.

Figure 4 shows the results of this analysis, superimposed on the preceding analysis of integrative mechanisms. Some of the companies in the sample, such as Caterpillar, Cummins, Baker International, Bertelsmann, Blue Bell, Friedrich Krupp, Kodak, Timken, and Electrolux appear to lack systematic differentiation and, at the same time, do not have any strong integrative mechanism. These, then, correspond to the overall category we have characterized as *ad hoc variation*. Others, such as General Motors, Glaxo, BSN Groupe, British-American Tobacco, ICI, RJ. Reynolds, Swedish Match, and United Biscuits appear to have strong and systematic internal differentiation but lack strong firmwide integration; these correspond to our *differentiated fit* category. Firms such as Digital, Siemens, General Foods, Emhart, Norsk Hydro, Rio Tinto-Zinc, Colgate-Palmolive, Freuhauf, Schneider, Deere & Co., Hoechst, Norton, and Solvay have strong differentiation as well as strong integration (through one or more of the three integration mechanisms); these we place in the *integrated variety* category. Finally, the remaining companies demonstrate high integration through one mechanism or a combination of the three mechanisms but are not systematically differentiated internally. These firms belong to the category we have described as *structural uniformity*.

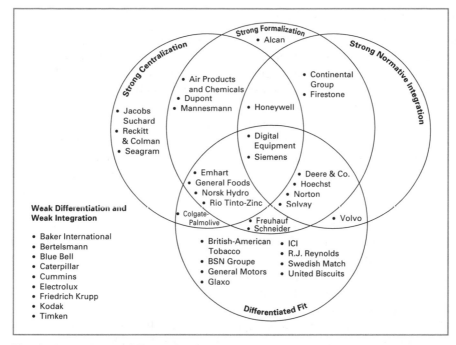

Figure 4 Mapping integration and differentation

Figure 5 summarizes these findings, showing how the forty-one companies distribute among the four structural categories we have proposed.

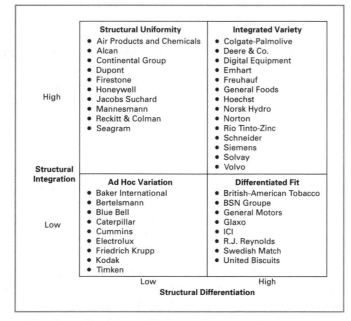

Figure 5 The structure of MNCs: classification of companies

Organization–environment fit

Our basic argument is that for effective performance, the MNC's organizational structure should fit its overall environmental contingencies. We hypothesize that structural uniformity is best suited to global environmental conditions, differentiated fit to multinational environments, integrated variety to transnational environments, and ad hoc variety to international environments.

The logic underlying these hypotheses is straightforward. In global environments, the cross-national linkages create forces for firmwide coordination that predominate over the local environmental forces. Having a common integrative structure in these situations not only enables the MNC to respond to these linkages across these environments, it also economizes on the administrative burden that managing a highly differentiated system imposes.

In multinational environments, in contrast, the MNC must respond to the local environments to be competitive. The most effective structures are likely to be those that are differentiated to respond to the local environments' needs. Here, the administrative burden of a complex differentiated system is almost a cost of doing business, but the MNC must avoid the additional administrative complexity of a strong overlying integrative mechanism.

In transnational environments, it is important for the MNC to be responsive not only to local contingencies but also to cross-national linkages. As such it needs a structure of requisite differentiation overlaid with a strong companywide integrative mechanism. Here the administrative costs of such a complex system are both necessary and justified.

In contrast, placid international environments have neither strong forces of differentiation nor strong forces of integration, and a company in such a situation might derive little benefit from systematic organizational design. Such a firm can probably avoid the costs of both differentiation and integration.

It is important to note that it is the competing costs and benefits of differentiation and integration that underlie these issues of fit. In principle, if there were no administrative cost associated with organizational complexity, one might always recommend a structure of integrated variety, because such a structure would be best able to respond to minor variations in environments as well as to a great variety of linkages. But the costs associated with administrative complexity are significant and thus lead us to the idea of requisite complexity.

To test these hypotheses, we juxtaposed the environmental (Figure 2) and structural (Figure 5) classifications of the forty-one companies, as shown in Figure 6. Each cell in this figure represents a particular environment-structure combination. Cell 1, for example, identifies those companies that, during the study period, confronted an environment of relatively weak forces of both global integration and local responsiveness and whose organizations were neither strongly differentiated internally nor strongly integrated through firmwide mechanisms. Such a combination – an international environment and an ad-hoc variation organization – represents a good fit and, according to our theory, should on average outperform firms in Cells 2, 3, and 4, which operate with the same relatively simple organizational approach but face the more complex multinational, global, or transnational environments. Similarly, the firms in Cell 1 should also outperform, on average, firms in Cells 5, 9, and 13 because these companies adopt the more complex organizational approaches, thereby expending effort and resources on organizational integration and differentiation that are not necessary for responding to the demands of their relatively simple international environment.

Structure	International	Multinational	Global	Transnational
Integrated Variety	• Emhart • Norton • Rio Tinto-Zinc • Schneider • Siemens (Cell 13)	• General Foods (Cell 14)	• Deere & Co. • Hoechst • Norsk Hydro • Solvay (Cell 15)	• Colgate-Palmolive • Digital Equipment • Freuhauf • Volvo (Cell 16)
Structural Uniformity	• Continental Group • Mannesmann (Cell 9)	• Firestone • Jacobs Suchard • Seagram (Cell 10)	• Air Products and Chemical • Alcan • Dupont • Honeywell (Cell 11)	• Reckitt & Colman (Cell 12)
Differentiated Fit	• Swedish Match (Cell 5)	• British-American Tobacco • BSN Groupe • R.J. Reynolds • United Biscuits (Cell 6)	• ICI (Cell 7)	• General Motors • Glaxo (Cell 8)
Ad Hoc Variation	• Baker International • Bertelsmann • Blue Bell • Friedrich Krupp • Timken (Cell 1)	• Electrolux (Cell 2)	• Caterpillar • Cummins (Cell 3)	• Kodak (Cell 4)

Environment

Figure 6 Mapping of environment and structure

Following this logic, it becomes clear that the seventeen companies in the four diagonal cells (1, 6, 11, and 16) – all of which represent good environment-structure fits – should, on average, outperform the twenty-four companies in the other twelve cells, all of which represent misfits. As shown in Table 2, actual performances of these forty-one companies conform to our prediction. On all three dimensions of performance – average return on net assets, growth in these returns, and revenue growth – the seventeen companies representing good environment-structure fit outperform by statistically significant margins the twenty-four companies that lack such fit.

Performance measures	Companies in cells 1, 6, 11, & 16 (diagonal = fit)	Companies in cells 2, 3, 4, 5, 7, 8, 9, 10, 12, 13, 14, & 15 (others = misfit)	p-value difference
1. Average RONA (1982–1986)	5.72	3.69	< 0.001
2. RONA Growth (1982–1986)	6.41	2.32	< 0.001
3. Revenue Growth (1982–1986)	7.19	4.98	< 0.001

Table 2 Performance of companies with environment-structure fit and misfit

Conclusion

Empirical results from a correlational analysis do not provide proof of a causal argument. In this case, our ability to draw any conclusive inferences from the findings is additionally constrained because of the small and nonrandom sample of companies we have considered and because of our relatively simple and coarse-grained measurement procedure. Despite these limitations, we do believe that we have provided some preliminary evidence for our proposition that the appropriate level of organizational complexity leads to effective performance in multiunit organizations like MNCs. In this process, we have also suggested a useful way to classify the environment and structure of MNCs. Our findings, we believe, provide some justification for the approach we have advocated.

In the recent past, MNC managers have been at the receiving end of a diverse and often conflicting set of organizational prescriptions. On the one hand, influential academics and consultants have been urging them to abandon simplistic structures and processes and instead to build multidimensional network organizations with distributed management roles and tasks, overlapping responsibilities and relationships, and built-in ambiguity and redundancy.[21] On the other hand, equally strong voices have been arguing that the performance problems faced by many large MNCs are often attributable to the complexities of their organizations and that managers must have the courage to reestablish organizational simplicity by reverting to direct decision making and unambiguous accountability.[22] Admittedly, these prescriptions are more complex than we are painting them. Nevertheless, the intense advocacy accompanying these arguments has made it difficult for managers to get a perspective on such diverse prescriptions.

We believe that the issues we have raised in this paper will be useful to these managers, if only to structure internal debate and discussions on organizational choices. To reiterate, managers need a detailed understanding of their companies' environmental demands to evaluate the kind of organizational capabilities they need to build. Unnecessary organizational complexity in a relatively simple business environment can be just as unproductive as unresponsive simplicity in a complex business environment. To return to the title of this paper, companies require different organizational horses to manage superior performance in different environmental courses. What we have proposed here is a method for analyzing these environmental courses and for selecting the appropriate organizational horses.

We need to point out that the part of our study reported in this paper took a static picture of these companies. In reality, environmental demands evolve over time and managers need to adopt a dynamic view about organizational capabilities. Even though we have not carried out detailed case research on how the different industries coveted in this study have been evolving, the limited information we have suggests that the environmental demands in at least some of them may be becoming more complex. In the food and beverages businesses, for example, the forces of global integration appear to be getting stronger, driven, among other factors, by the growing proliferation of regional and global brands. In the scientific measuring instrument business, on the other hand, the need for local responsiveness is increasing as stand-alone products are giving way to integrated systems consisting of packages of hardware, software, and related services.

As a result, these and many other businesses may be evolving to the more complex transnational category, and companies competing in these businesses may need to build the kind of organizational form we have described as 'integrated variety.' Managers need to be sensitive to such changes in environmental demands – indeed, they should drive such changes when appropriate – and must develop the ability to differentiate and integrate their organizations to lead or respond to such evolving business conditions.

We focused here on the MNC. Our argument can easily be extended, however, to any multidivisional firm. Consider, for instance, the case of a firm in which each division operates in a different market or business segment. Once again, the overall environmental contingencies faced by such a firm can be characterized in terms of the extent to which each of its business segments have unique and strong forces for local responsiveness and the extent to which these businesses are linked. In a sense, this is similar to identifying the nature of the firm's diversification, whether it is in related or unrelated business segments. Similarly the firm's overall structure can be conceived in terms of the pattern of variation in the governance of the different corporate-division relationships. Again the same four structural patterns may be identified, and we would expect the environment-structure fit to follow the logic of requisite complexity. In this situation, then, all we have done is change the source of environmental variation from geography, in the case of MNCs, to different business segments, in the case of the multiproduct firm. Of course, in some situations, the source of environmental variation in the firm's different units may well be driven by both geography and product markets. Though operationally more complex, this situation can just as easily be accommodated under the same general theoretical rubric.

Finally, let us emphasize once again that in reiterating the two-decade-old notion of environment-organization fit, we do not wish to detract from the much more sophisticated analysis of organization-environment interactions that is the focus of current research on the topic. The perspectives in these studies add richness to our understanding of the underlying processes of influence and adaptation and of the limits of those processes. However, in focusing on those processes and in highlighting the second-order benefits from characteristics such as deliberate misfit and organizational ambiguity, what we often tend to overlook are the first-order benefits of fit and organizational simplicity. We take them for granted, perhaps, but an occasional reminder of these taken-for-granted aspects of organizational analysis may help in placing the rest in proper perspective.

Notes

[1] This contingency theory had two separate roots. Lawrence and Lorsch stated it as a set of environment-organization contingencies, as did Thompson. See:

P.R. Lawrence and J.W. Lorsch, *Organization and Environment* (Boston: Graduate School of Business Administration, Harvard University, 1967); and

J.D. Thompson, *Organizations in Action* (New York: McGraw-Hill, 1967).

Alfred Chandler, on the other hand, suggested the need for a match between strategy and organization as he described the rationale for and process of evolution of the multidivisional organization in corporate America. See:

A. Chandler, *Strategy and Structure: Chapters in the History of the American Industrial Enterprise* (Cambridge, Massachusetts: MIT Press, 1962). The subsequent literature on contingency theory adopted one or both sets of views, building in this process a model of environment-strategy-organization linkages.

[2] See J. Stopford and L.T. Wells, Jr., *Managing the Multinational Enterprise* (New York: Basic Books, 1972). This research followed the work of Chandler, focusing on strategy-organization contingencies.

[3] See C.A. Bartlett, 'Building and Managing the Transnational: The New Organizational Challenge,' *Competition in Global Industries*, ed. M.E. Potter (Boston; Harvard Business School Press, 1986).

[4] See Bartlett (1986); and:
C.A. Bartlett and S. Ghoshal, *Managing across Borders: The Transnational Solution* (Boston: Harvard Business School Press, 1989).

[5] See Bartlett and Ghoshal (1989).

[6] This interpretation is manifest, for example, in:
W.G. Egelhoff, 'Exploring the Limits of Transnationalism' (Paper presented at the annual meeting, Academy of International Business, Toronto, 11–14 October 1990).

[7] For a comprehensive review and a spirited defense of the concept of fit and the contingency perspective that underlies it, see:
L. Donaldson, *In Defense of Organization Theory* (Cambridge: Cambridge University Press, 1985).

[8] This database was developed in the course of the first author's doctoral dissertation work and is fully described in his unpublished thesis: 'The Innovative Multinational: A Differentiated Network of Roles and Relationships' (Boston: Harvard Business School, 1986).
Parts of the database relevant to the analysis presented in this paper have also been described in:
S. Ghoshal and N. Nohria, 'Internal Differentiation within Multinational Corporations,' *Strategic Management Journal* 10 (1989): 323–337.

[9] The 438 companies in the database are those that responded to the questionnaire we sent to the 438 North American and European MNCs listed in:
J. Stopford, *World Directory of Multinational Enterprises* (Detroit, New Jersey: Galo Research Company, 1983). While we are not aware of any specific bias in the sample that would *a priori* invalidate any of our findings, the generalizability of our conclusions remains constrained because of the small size and potential non-representativeness of the sample. For a detailed description of the sample and of the reliability and validity of our measures, see:
Ghoshal and Nohria (1989).

[10] See C.K. Prahalad and Y.L. Doz, *The Multinational Mission: Balancing Local Demands and Global Vision* (New York: The Free Press, 1987).

[11] See S.J. Kobrin, 'An Empirical Analysis of the Determinants of Global Integration,' Special Issue, *Strategic Management Journal* 12 (1991): 17–31.

[12] Steers describes some of the different performance measures and their relevance and implications. See:
R.M. Steers, 'Problems in the Measurement of Organizational Effectiveness,' *Administrative Science Quarterly* 20 (1975): 546–558.
Venkatraman argues for the appropriateness of the measures we adopt. See:
N. Venkatraman, 'A Concept of Fit in Strategy Research: Toward Verbal and Statistical Correspondence,' *Academy of Management Review* 14 (1989): 423–444.

[13] See Prahalad and Doz (1987).

[14] For one of the earliest descriptions of MNC environments in these terms, see:
J. Fayerweather, *International Business Strategy and Administration* (Cambridge, Massachusetts: Ballinger Press, 1978).
For one of the most recent and comprehensive elaborations, see:
Prahalad and Doz (1987).
For a discussion of the factors that drive the needs for global integration and national responsiveness, see:
G.S. Yip, 'Global Strategy ... In a World of Nations?' *Sloan Managemmt Review*, Fall 1989, pp. 29–41.

[15] Our characterization and terminology need some clarifications. Bartlett and Ghoshal (1989) considered three sets of environmental forces: those of global integration, national responsiveness, and worldwide learning. Strong demands along each of these dimensions were characterized as 'global,' 'multinational,' and 'international' industries, respectively, whereas 'transnational' industries were defined as those facing strong demands simultaneously along all three dimensions. In this paper, we use the relatively simpler two dimensional conceptualization proposed by Prahalad and Doz (1987). In our framework, global and multinational industries are defined the same way as in Bartlett and Ghoshal (1989), but international and transnational industries are defined as those facing weak-weak and strong-strong combinations of the forces of global integration and national responsiveness. This characterization is consistent with the use of the terminology in Bartlett (1986), except that he did not define the 'international' industry environment explicitly in that paper.

[16] There is well-established support for these mechanisms in organization theory. Since the landmark studies of the Aston Group, centralization and formalization have been central constructs in analyzing the structure of complex organizations. See:

D.S. Pugh, D.J. Hickson, C.R. Hinings, and C. Turner, 'The Dimensions of Organization Structure,' *Administrative Science Quarterly* 13 (1968): 65–105.

Van Maanen and Schein have since argued that normative integration should be considered as another primary element in the structure of organizational relations. See:

J. Van Maanen and E.H. Schein, 'Toward a Theory of Organizarional Socialization' in *Research in Organizational Behavior*, ed. B.M. Staw (Greenwich, Connecticut: JAI Press, 1979).

[17] For a recent review of the evidence and arguments for internal differentiation in headquarters-subsidiary relationships, see:

A.K. Gupta and V. Govindarajan, 'Knowledge Flows and the Structure of Control within Multinational Corporations,' *Academy of Management Review* 16 (1991): 768–792.

[18] See Ghosbal and Nohria (1989).

For alternative conceptualizations of subsidiary context, see:

T.A. Poynter and A.M. Rugman, 'World Product Mandates: How Will Multinationals Respond?' *Business Quarterly* 47 (1982): 54–61:

and:

Gupta and Govindarajan (1991).

[19] See Ghoshal and Nohria (1989).

[20] It is interesting to observe that there is one null set in this analysis: one of the companies combines high levels of centralization and socialization while lacking formalized systems. Perhaps this is merely an artifact of the sample or a reflection of measurement error. Or perhaps this combination is administratively infeasible.

At this stage we can only speculate on this issue, but it may be a starting point for an interesting future study.

[21] For the most provocative and articulate statement of this view, see: G. Hedlund, 'The Hypermodern MNC: A Helterarchy?' *Human Resource Management* 25 (1986): 9–35.

[22] See N. Tichy and R. Charan, 'Speed, Simplicity, and Self-Confidence: An Interview with Jack Welch,' *Harvard Business Review*, September–October 1989, pp. 112–120.

CASE 2: AIRBUS AND BOEING IN CHINA: RISK OF TECHNOLOGY TRANSFER

Gustav Humbert, ex-CEO of Airbus, was once proud of his position. Under his leadership, Airbus performed well. It was even more satisfying when he considered that Airbus was a consortium led by France, the United Kingdom, Germany and even Spain. Barely six decades before, the countries were involved in World War II. Now the European group was one of only two global players in the industry. He thought of the impressive growth history of Airbus. During early 1970s, the European aircraft industry represented only 10 per cent of the global aircraft market that was primarily controlled by American companies such as Boeing and McDonnell Douglas (MDD). And, in just three decades, the leaders of the European Union could collaborate and cooperate in this highly complex technological field.

But that was history. Today, the A380 was another challenge[1] for which he had to resign, ushering in Christian Streiff, the new head of Airbus. On his recruitment to this coveted seat, at the Farnborough International Air Show Streiff spoke bombastically of doing 'a vertical take-off with full thrust'. China was the key strategic marketplace for both Airbus and Boeing. China's GDP had grown at more than 8 per cent over the past decade and showed no signs of stopping. Regarding airspace and the aircraft industry, China was expected to become the world's largest aviation market after the United States, and hence would become the next battlefield. The weapons were already chosen. Boeing, after its merger with MDD, was the undisputed challenger to Airbus with its 787s and the new 747s. Airbus, though recently experiencing some hitches, had its A380s and A350s. Their business models were as different as their aircraft. Airbus focused on a hub-to-hub strategy, whereas Boeing favoured a point-to-point strategy. Their business strategy regarding China was also entirely different. Airbus favoured an early-entrant strategy whereas Boeing favoured a late-entrant strategy. Both had their strategists racking their brains to develop a strategy for entering China. ...

The history of Airbus

A European company built with American investment

After World War II (1939–45), Europe needed to be rebuilt. Germany was devastated after three years of intensive war. France was in a difficult economic situation because of the German occupation. The United Kingdom had to switch from a war economy to a peace economy. In contrast, the United States ended the war as the strongest economy in the world in the fields of technological knowledge, investment capacities and production capacities. By the end of the war, the American economy had 52 per cent of worldwide industrial goods production and almost half the world's gold reserves. But, from an another angle, the rise of the erstwhile USSR was setting in motion geopolitical events that would become the Cold War by the late 1940s.

In this context, western European countries began to cooperate in some key sectors. They wanted to avoid any transnational competition and to cooperate in earnest to rebuild Europe. American economic support made this 'dream' possible with the Marshall Plan of 1947. Also, in 1951, the European Cooperation on Steel and Coal emphasized the convergence of political and economic interests in this area.

In 1957, Jean Monnet and Robert Schumann, known as the 'founders of modern Europe', managed to make their dreams come true with the Treaty of Rome, leading to the first European Union with six members (West Germany, France, Italy, Belgium, Luxembourg and the Netherlands). This was the beginning of the initiation of many industrial cooperations; one of the most important involved the aircraft industry. It has often been said that Airbus was a European company built with American investment.

Consolidation of clusters within the aircraft industry

In the mid-1960s, there were almost 20 different aircraft programmes under various stages of development within the European nations. The best engineers were proudly trying to rebuild their national industry with their own national technology. Due to an atmosphere of war for more than 50 years on the continent, national engineers had secretly developed diverse technologies for the aircraft industry that were incompatible with one another.

During this time, the movement towards having a single European company for the aircraft industry gained momentum. Funding was an issue for this European company, but there was a will, and so there was a way. This challenging situation led the governments of the European countries to come together to underline the necessity of a European cooperation. A project was launched to build a 300-seat aircraft. The tasks were divided: 37.5 per cent for Hawker of the UK, 37.5 per cent for Sud Aviation of France and 25 per cent for Arge Airbus. The engines were to be constructed by the British Rolls-Royce (75 per cent), the French Snecma (12.5 per cent) and the German Man (12.5 per cent). This kind of division of labour was necessary to cement a cooperation between the different stakeholders and the different nations. Regarding political stakes, the balance was respected between the European powers, the projects were subsequently merged and Airbus was born (see Exhibit 2.1 for a full history of Airbus).

Strategy of Airbus to become a world leader

During the early stages, there were difficulties with respect to funding and cooperation between the companies and the countries. But what saved Airbus was the will of the partners to continue and pitch in funds from the companies that were involved. In that sense, Airbus was not completely a greenfield operation and began operating with some success. The English presence, which was necessary at the beginning, always remained a

▶ **Airbus began with a bold decision to challenge American domination of the skies. Today, some 35 years later, Airbus is one of the world's leading aircraft manufacturers.**

Airbus was officially formed in 1970 as a consortium of France's Aerospatiale and Deutsche Airbus, a grouping of leading German aircraft manufacturing firms. Together the companies had decided to build the A300, the first twin-engine widebody airliner, to fill a gap in the market and to challenge American supremacy in the aviation industry. Shortly afterwards Spain's CASA joined the consortium and in 1974 the Airbus Industrie GIE, as it was known – Groupe d'Intérêt Economique – moved its headquarters from Paris to Toulouse.

British Aerospace joined Airbus Industrie in 1979. Each of the four partners, known as Airbus France, Airbus Deutschland, Airbus UK and Airbus España, operated as national companies with special responsibilities for producing parts of the aircraft, to be transported to Toulouse for final assembly. The GIE provided a single face for sales, marketing and customer support.

Airbus developed a deserved reputation for innovation and for listening to the needs of its customers. As Airbus's success took hold with the A300/A310 Family, the A320 Family – with its landmark fly-by-wire technology, which established commonality as key appeal of Airbus aircraft – and the long-range A330/A340 Family, the need to streamline operations to meet growing demand increased. The drive towards closer working across national boundaries also intensified as the practical benefits became clear: better quality, faster production, reduced costs and a workforce that felt part of an international family. So, in 2001, Airbus became a single fully integrated company. The European Aeronautic Defence and Space Company (EADS), a merger of the French, German and Spanish interests, acquired 80 per cent of the shares and BAE Systems, the successor to British Aerospace, 20 per cent.

Another bold step in the evolution of Airbus was taken in 2004, by which time the company had overtaken its main rival by delivering more aircraft and by securing more orders. In a major reorganisation, designed to equip the company to maintain its lead in the industry, Centres of Excellence were set up to simplify and unify the design and production management processes. Each CoE is responsible for specific parts of the aircraft and has its own chain of decision making and command.

Airbus put the seal on its successful evolution with the unveiling, in January 2005, of the A380, the world's largest and most advanced passenger aircraft. In April 2005, the A380 performed its first flight. Seating typically 555 passengers, the A380 is being hailed as the 'future of flying'. It is certainly Airbus's answer to the needs of its customers for a very large aircraft able to cope with rising demand on high-density major hub routes without increasing the number of flights. But Airbus has also addressed the needs of operators seeking to service demand on long-range point-to-point routes. The A380's unveiling was preceded by an announcement that Airbus is to build the A350, a longer-range mid-size twin engine aircraft that will bring unprecedented levels of efficiency and comfort to the long range market.

Source: http://www.airbus.com/en/corporate/people/Airbus_short_history.html

Exhibit 2.1 Short history of Airbus

sensitive issue. The British were never willing to 'dilute' (as they said) either their knowledge or their influence in the group. They did not agree to be part of the GIE Airbus that was founded in 1969, and let Sud Aviation and Deutsch Airbus manage and control the company. British suppliers became suppliers or stakeholders but they were not part of the new top management. Due to this history, Airbus, which became a public company in 1999, was jointly owned by EADS, the European defence and military giant, with an 80 per cent stake, and by BAE Systems (British Aerospace Systems), which owned the rest. Airbus founders were stakeholders of EADS and thus controlled Airbus. Lagardere of France and the French state represented French interests; Daimler represented German interests; while CASA represented Spanish interests.

Within 50 years of its inception, Airbus became the leader, overtaking its arch-rival Boeing. Airbus and Boeing together shared about 50 per cent of the world market in demand, while Airbus had a slight advantage over Boeing on deliveries. Each company had its own heritage and its own natural geographic market. For instance, American political influence in Japan had led to a skewed ratio of 7 : 3 in favour of Boeing. While, in European markets, Airbus clearly had the advantage. These positions evolved year after year, but the real differences in numbers were coming from the new developing and emerging markets.

In 2006, BAE decided to sell its shares to EADS and the entire power structure in the company was to change. It was envisioned that the public part would increase, with each founding member decreasing its participation. The balance between French and German stakeholders had to remain equal for political reasons.

Airbus was headquartered in Toulouse, France, and in Frankfurt, Germany, because the two main plants were historically present in these two regions. It was a global enterprise of about 53,000 employees, with fully owned subsidiaries in the United States, China and Japan; spare parts centres in Hamburg, Frankfurt, Washington, Beijing and Singapore; training centres in Toulouse, Miami, Hamburg and Beijing; and 130 field service offices around the world. Airbus also relied on industrial cooperation and partnerships with major companies all over the word, and a network of some 1,500 suppliers in 30 countries (see Exhibit 2.2). Gustav Humbert was named CEO in 2004 and remained in charge in 2005. This was a symbolic gesture of high reputation as, for the first time, a German became CEO of Airbus. The counterpart was the nomination of Noël Forgeard, of France and former CEO of Airbus, as co-CEO of EADS.

Exhibit 2.2 The worldwide presence of Airbus

In less than 40 years of existence, Airbus had set standards by the quality of its aircrafts. Its technological advances in avionics, use of composites, innovations in design and the continual promotion of aircraft safety had placed Airbus at the forefront of a fiercely competitive duopolistic sector. The 'Airbus spirit' was that of teamwork between nations and cultures. In 2005, Airbus booked 1,111 new gross orders, delivered a total of 378 aircraft totalling revenues of $28.4 billion (€22.3 billion) with customers from 210 countries. Airbus employed more than 55,000 employees (and supported 140,000 jobs in the USA), of 80 nationalities working in 160 offices in 20 languages. It had about 1,500 suppliers and industrial partners spanning 30 countries.

The history of Boeing

Boeing 'enjoyed' World War II and its consequences

Boeing was founded in 1916 in Puget Sound, Washington. After World War II, the American economy was flourishing and almost every industry was benefiting from a kind of golden age. The aircraft industry had boomed during the war, as it supported the war against the Axis. With contracts from the government to support the war, some aircraft companies emerged as leaders. Three of the more prominent ones were Boeing, Lockheed and McDonnell Douglas (MDD). During the war, German engineers had discovered and developed to near perfection the turbo reactor, which subsequently became the key to the profitable development of long-range commercial lines.

After the war, this technology was transferred from the ashes of the Reich to the United Kingdom and the United States by German scientists, like the famous von Braun,[2] who decided to work for the Allies. The United States took this opportunity to build a successful plan for the aviation and space sector, which was possible because the internal market was also the biggest market available for airliners, and American companies such as Boeing, MDD and Lockheed could therefore strengthen their business with national clients even before contemplating starting business across borders.

Boeing and the other American companies catapulted a European new entrant to the position of leader

In the 1970s, Airbus, the new competitor from Europe, emerged, progressively conquering markets, competing globally with the American giants and ultimately displacing Boeing from its number-one position. Airbus was not taken seriously at the beginning by Boeing, and its strategy was underestimated. Airbus took this opportunity and created some new clusters without any real reaction from its competitor in the USA. For example, it created the concept of the 'aircraft family' with its A300 and A320 series. Since the Americans took this strategy with a pinch of salt, Airbus had no competitors in the existing range of aircraft products when it attacked the market with its new innovative offerings. American companies were competing on cost leadership and hence were not really looking to innovate. To fight this impending threat of an innovative product portfolio, Boeing undertook a series of strategic mergers and acquisitions to broaden its own portfolio, which included acquiring McDonnell Douglas, the space and defence business of Rockwell International, and Hughes Space & Communications, among others. Moreover, this lack of anticipation led to a gap between the expectations of airliners and what was available in the market. Progressively the market share of Airbus increased and American companies understood they had a real competitor with a new range of products. Boeing started to revisit its strategy and tried to strengthen its offers, which led to clear competition on almost every cluster (see Exhibit 2.3 for more details).

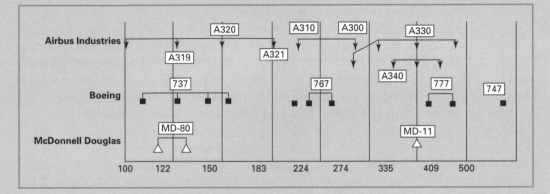

Exhibit 2.3 Direct competition between Airbus, Boeing and McDonnell Douglas

After 90 years of existence, the American giant was positioned as a broad, balanced and global enterprise, aiming at defining the future of aerospace. The commercial part of the group competed with Airbus but it represented only 40 per cent of its income, whereas 60 per cent was generated by the 'Integrated Defense Systems', the 'Boeing Capital Corporation' and the 'Connection by Boeing' subsidiaries of the group. In 2005, Boeing's revenue was $54.8 billion, with customers in 145 countries ($22.5 billion from the commercial airplanes). International sales were more than 30 per cent and 70 per cent from sales of commercial airplanes (by value). Boeing employed more than 153,300 employees in 48 US states and 67 countries. It had about 6,450 suppliers in more than 100 countries.

The aircraft industry

Aircraft production began in earnest at the start of the twentieth century, with the Wright brothers trying their first flight in December 1903. It was not a success by any means but it started the airline industry. The widespread adoption of ailerons made aircraft much easier to manage, and only a decade later, at the start of World War I, aircraft were widely used as a military tool for reconnaissance, artillery spotting and even attacks against ground positions.

Commercial aircraft were an offshoot from technology obtained from military R&D. At the beginning, the number of products was limited, as was the technology. Airlines were buying aircraft that engineers could make and that flew safely. Between the wars, with advancements in technology, aircraft grew larger and more reliable, and began to be used to transport people and cargo. In the 1930s, the Douglas DC-3 was the first airliner that was profitable carrying passengers exclusively, starting the modern era of passenger airline service. By the beginning of World War II, many towns and cities had built airports and there was a large number of qualified pilots available. The war brought many innovations to aviation, including the first jet aircraft and the first liquid-fuelled rockets.

After the war, especially in North America, there was a boom in general aviation, both private and commercial, as thousands of pilots were released from military service, and many inexpensive war surplus transport and training aircraft were available. Small aircraft manufacturers such as Cessna, Piper and Beechcraft expanded production to provide small aircraft for the new middle-class market.

As technology became advanced and more reliable, airlines had more product options to choose from. By the 1950s, the development of civil jets grew, beginning with the de Havilland Comet, though the first widely used passenger jet was the Boeing 707. At the same time, turboprop propulsion began to appear for smaller commuter planes, making it possible to serve small-volume routes in a much wider range of weather conditions.

From the 1960s, composite airframes and quieter, more efficient engines became available. Aircraft manufacturers wanted to use different aircraft for different purposes, to save costs. For example, they started differentiating between routes where the flight was full, overbooked or almost empty. They started using different aircraft for long- and short-haul distances, and also for domestic and intercontinental flights. This meant that pilots had to be specialized for different types of aircraft. These changes led to the modern classification of aircraft, which are on two variables: number of seats and the plane's flight range.

The most important innovations in the aircraft industry were in instrumentation and control. The arrival of solid-state electronics, the global positioning system (GPS), satellite communications, and increasingly small and powerful computers and LED displays dramatically changed the cockpits of airliners and, increasingly, of smaller aircraft as well. Pilots could navigate much more accurately and view terrain, obstructions and other nearby aircraft on a map or through synthetic vision even at night or in low visibility. This led to increasing production cycles; the design phase took between four and six years and the test phase took three to four years, following which aircraft had to receive certifications from external security agencies. It required thousands of flight hours before they were authorized to fly worldwide. The whole process, from design to commissioning of an aircraft, easily took seven to ten years and could cost from €2 to €6 billion. After the delivery (95 per cent of the price was paid on delivery), an aircraft would cost as much as 60 per cent of its original price again, due to maintenance costs. Hence, maintenance platforms and liability remained the cornerstones of any commercial deal.

Airbus products

Airbus started with a weak conglomerate structure of existing companies meant to cooperate as a single entity. Historically, these companies had different competencies and business models. Moreover, the industry was quite young (the first flight taken by a human was less than a hundred years earlier) and scientists and engineers working within the companies had various theories according to their own personal experiences. At the beginning, it was an uphill struggle for Airbus's top management to get engineers from France, West Germany and Great Britain to collaborate.

The first plane made by Airbus was in the upper-middle cluster and was designed to be as polyvalent as possible. This plane, the A300B, which first flew in 1972 – only three years after the project was launched and only two years after the Consortium was created – was meant to compete with the old 717 made by Boeing. This plane was a technological challenge for Airbus. With the launch of the A300B, Airbus never looked back.

After the launch of the A300B and the subsequent launch of the A320 Family, from 1974 to 1984 Airbus launched five different planes. They were the A300B4, the A310, the A310-300, the A300-600 and the A320. The first four were competing with Boeing and MDD on an empty cluster, but the A320 opened a new strategic battle and a cluster where Boeing was a leader with its 737 and MDD with its MD80. Though Airbus was a late entrant to the market, it took on Boeing head on and was proposing an extra value proposition: fly-by-wire technology, which provided better security and a smaller cost/passenger ratio for airline companies.

Next in the stable came the all-time best-selling A320 Family, with models called the A318, A319, A320 and A321. With 40 million flight hours to date, more than 2,500 aircraft were delivered to almost 160 operators. In addition, this family of aircraft provided operators with great flexibility in matching the right aircraft to specific route requirements through Airbus's Dynamic Capacity Management (DSC) system. All A320 Family aircraft shared the same type rating, allowing pilots to fly all of them after attending only one training course, and enabling the same team of mechanics to maintain the aircraft. With only minimal additional training, pilots could transition from single-aisled to larger, long-range aircraft quickly and simply. This was due to Airbus's unique 'family' product strategy.

The next innovation for Airbus was the launch of the A330/1340 Family of aircraft. This offered four families of aircraft ranging from 107 to 555 seats, the single-aisle A320 Family (A318/A319/A320/A321), the wide-body A300/A310 Family and the long-range A330/A340 Family. Later, the A330/340 Family was extended to the latest A350 Family, with models known as A350 XWB (XW denoting eXtra Wide) that would carry between 270 and 350 passengers. The A350-1000 is the largest version in this category. The A350 Family gave way to the ultra-long-range, high-capacity A380 Family.

Boeing products

In the beginning, Airbus was not considered a serious competitor and Boeing concentrated its efforts on expanding its 7 series aircraft. Boeing had the best reputation for its aircraft in every cluster. The stars for Boeing were the 717, the 737 and the famous 747 Jumbo Jet. Competition from McDonnell Douglas was easily managed, as in comparison, the Boeing 7 series was superior to the MD 8 series. For example, in comparing the MD80 with the 737, Boeing was bigger than MDD for the same cluster and more fuel efficient. With the number of seats a key variable, Boeing was ahead of MDD for all practical purposes. Boeing and MDD finally merged.

Boeing offered airplane models that served passenger markets from 100 seats to well over 500 seats, as well as the most complete line of cargo freighters. The first model in Boeing's offering was the 717-200 Family, which is a jetliner specifically designed for the short-haul, high-frequency 100-passenger airline market. After careful assessment of the challenging 100-seat market, Boeing announced that it would conclude 717 production in 2006 after delivering current customer commitments. The 737 family (737-600/-700/-800/-900 models) is a short- to medium-range airplane, based on the key Boeing philosophy of delivering added value to airlines with reliability, simplicity, and reduced operating and maintenance costs. It had sold over 6,000 units. The Boeing 747 Family and 747-8 Family are long-haul aircraft that integrate advanced technology into one of the world's most modern and fuel-efficient airplanes. The Boeing 767 Family (passenger models 767-200ER, 767-300ER and 767-400ER, and a freighter) caters to the 200- to 300-seat market. Market demand sized, shaped and launched the newest member of the Boeing twin-aisle family – the 777 Family (with six models: 777-200, 777-200ER (extended range), 777-200LR (longer range), the 777-300 and 777-300ER, and the 777 freighter). The Boeing 777 was reported to be the first jetliner to be 100 per cent digitally designed using three-dimensional computer graphics. Throughout the design process, the airplane was 'pre-assembled' on the computer, eliminating the need for a costly, full-scale mock-up. The latest in the family of Boeing was the 787 Dreamliner, classified as a super-efficient airplane with unmatched fuel efficiency. The airplane uses 20 per cent less fuel for comparable missions than similarly sized airplanes at the speed of Mach 0.85 and has more cargo revenue capacity. The 787-8 Dreamliner carries 210 to 250 passengers on routes of 8,000 to 8,500 nautical miles (14,800 to 15,700 kilometres), while the 787-9 Dreamliner carries 250 to 290 passengers on routes of 8,600 to 8,800 nautical miles (15,900 to 16,300 km). A third 787 family member, the 787-3 Dreamliner, accommodates 290 to 330 passengers and is optimized for routes of 3,000 to 3,500 nautical miles (5,550 to 6,500 km).

With the advent of Airbus's A300 series, Airbus had cleverly managed to take Boeing by surprise. Boeing did not have any competitive offer in the A300 cluster, and Airbus had changed the rules of the game before Boeing could react. This cluster was not controlled well by Boeing. Airbus's innovation with its flexibility of products to serve short- medium- and extended-range routes (the A310 and A300-600 series form Airbus's wide-body twin family, providing operators with a combination of versatility, economy and reliability). These aircraft were immensely profitable in freighter versions, either new or as converted second-hand aircraft, with more than 260 already in operation as freighters or on order. This adaptability had been key to sustaining the high residual value of the aircraft and in boosting Airbus's share of the wide-body, mid-size freighter market to over 50 per cent.

With the A300 assault from Airbus, Boeing tried to react. When the A320 arrived, Boeing modernized its 737 and the competition continued with a new 737 against each aircraft of the A320 family. Boeing was not the trend-setter at that time and because of the time necessary to launch a plane, Airbus could control every new market space as it was ahead in its planning by at least five years.

Airbus also attacked another empty cluster with its A330-A340 Family. These aircraft were complementary to the 747, which was equipped for long haul. The A330-A340

Family were better designed, more modern and could capture a large market share at the cost of Boeing's 747. Boeing retaliated with its 777. It was a winner for Boeing and a disaster for Airbus. It was the last resort that Boeing could come up with to counter the continuous onslaught by Airbus. The 777 was a huge commercial success and soon became the main cash cow for Boeing. Each 777 was sold at around $220 million (against $60 million for a 737) and Boeing sold 154 in 2005 against Airbus's 12 A340s that year. The 777 family had six different models and provided flexibility both in capacity and in range (see Exhibit 2.4 for details about the 777 Family).

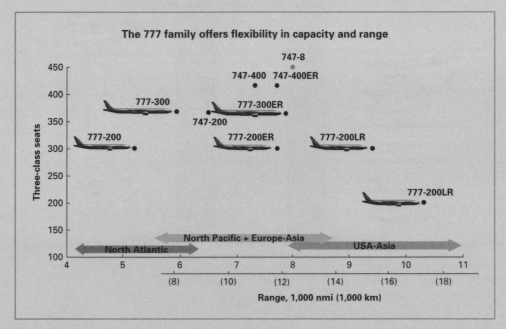

Exhibit 2.4 Reasons for the success of the 777

With the evolution of technology, competition between Boeing and Airbus extended to a new cluster, the 787 Family of Boeing. Boeing came head on with this model and challenged the A350 Family of Airbus. Boeing had in the meantime greatly improved its offer with innovations in its design. Boeing launched its 737 (737-8) and 747 (747-8) Family with new specifications that included modern elements and a reduced usage of steel and aluminium. These new specifications were supposed to reduce fuel consumption per passenger by about 20 per cent (the main criteria for airlines today due to the meteoric rise in the cost of fuel). It was reported that Boeing had mastered the state of the art in this technological field on its 787 family offerings. It was a blow for Airbus as its new A350 was not as sophisticated as Boeing in its design and fuel efficiency.

The range of products from Airbus and Boeing were success stories of innovation, but there were three major concerns. The first was a 200-seat gap between the A340-600 and the A380 (which had been criticized for its fuel consumption). In this gap, Boeing proposed three airplanes, namely the 777-300, the 747 and the new 747-800 (see Exhibit 2.5). Second, the choice of the 'hub to hub' strategy championed by Airbus (with its A380 model) had been challenged by the 'point to point' strategy that was championed by Boeing with its 787. The figures tend to show that Airbus would have to convince airlines since, in 2005, 235 planes of the 787 Family were ordered, whereas only 20 were ordered for the A380 model. The third concern was that airlines had to compare the A350 vs 787 and the biggest question would be whether the A380 would reach its break-even point of 300 units.

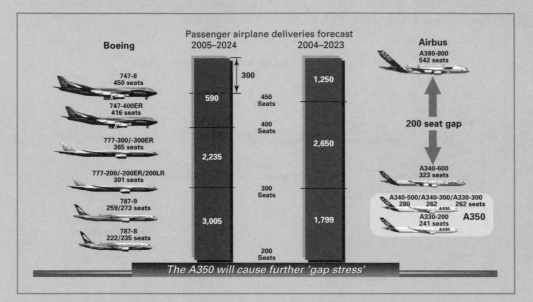

Exhibit 2.5 Perspectives for Boeing and Airbus in the battle 787 vs A 350

Demand

Demand existed both for military and civilian aircraft. Competition between Airbus and Boeing started with commercial planes and later spilled over to military clusters. One reason for this was that airline companies could order any number of aircraft from either Boeing or Airbus according to their needs and budget. But companies preferred to 'bulk' buy due to the high fixed costs involved in aircraft. For example, an airline would prefer to buy ten Airbus A320s, rather than five Airbus A320s and five Boeing 737-800s. Though the two families of aircraft from Boeing and Airbus competed in the same cluster, they were different in their specificities. Theoretically, they were both believed to be complementary to each other but, in reality, that was not so. Two kinds of aircraft implied two maintenance platforms, and maintenance accounted for about 60 per cent of the cost of each aircraft during its lifetime, which ranged from 20 to 30 years. Thus maintenance was a sunk cost and, over and above that, it was expensive for an airline to insure its planes, whether two or twenty. To buy both types of aircraft meant insuring one set with Boeing and another set with Airbus. Therefore, smaller airlines tended to deal with Boeing or Airbus at the beginning in one of the category of aircraft. Once they were hooked to one aircraft provider, switching became difficult.

This reasoning was questioned by analysts, who argued about what an airline company should do when it planned to buy both short- and long-haul aircraft. Both Airbus and Boeing negotiated on maintenance costs and tried to put together a package deal if they had more orders from a particular client. Both tried to lure customers by investing and focusing on customer service, and pushed fleet sales rather than only a few units. The family concept was at the heart of this commercial negotiation. It had begun with the A320 Family and it continued to be crucial with the A330-A350 vs Boeing 787-300, 787-800 and 787-900 battle.

A second reason for the demand had to do with the business cycle of airlines, which had been on the rise since World War II. Yet, the environment too could turn the screw. This occurred during the Asian crisis of 1998–99, the 9/11 terrorist attacks, the SARS attack, and natural calamities like earthquakes, tsunamis, hurricanes, etc.

Third, aircraft companies, in order to raise demand from emerging markets, argued that they would transfer integrated technology to these countries, especially China, as they had to maintain and upgrade the fleet bought by the national and private airlines of these countries. Developing and emerging countries that had not yet mastered the up-to-date aircraft technology saw incentives in this and eagerly negotiated for such integrated technology transfer. This transfer could be done at different levels but that was often the key to entering a new market or expanding in an existing market. Airbus's strategy was to push the option of technology transfer and act as first mover in emerging markets like China, whereas Boeing was more conservative and followed a late mover strategy.

Fourth, the aircraft industry required many high-tech elements to ensure the quality of aircraft and their safety for 20 to 30 years. Steel corroded over time. Liability was the key. Any crash of an aircraft due to a technical snag or for maintenance reasons had far-reaching effects on the company's image and credibility. Passengers frequently flying on the same international routes compared and contrasted the aircraft and usually shifted to those airlines that had better aircraft. Both Boeing and Airbus tended to be very sensitive to customer service and quality on competitive routes because a lost client was lost for almost 15 years when an aircraft from the Airbus or Boeing stable was valued at over 50 million dollars.

Finally, in this competition airlines had increasing influence on the design of aircraft. The clients were trying to squeeze out the best design possible by making Boeing and Airbus compete with one another. This was exactly what was happening with the new generation of twin-aisle aircraft: the A350, which was supposed to replace the A330/A340 or the Boeing 787. Airlines could choose one or the other family to change their fleets, but could not afford both. That was the reason why Boeing and Airbus tried their best to compete on making their offers as attractive as possible, even to the extent of modifying the design of the aircraft to suit the needs of their customers. Airbus faced an interesting problem and even Noël Forgeard, former co-CEO of EADS, recognized it in 2006 and commented, 'Two years ago we underestimated the new Boeing 787 and, according to our clients, with whom we keep on working, our offer with the A350 had to be improved in order to reach the standards set by our competitor.'

Airbus decided to improve its new offering, the A350, to satisfy its clients. An analyst had commented, '*airlines today want a Boeing made by Airbus*'. This decision required a $4 billion cost over run and a two-year delay, Airbus thought it was necessary to compete with Boeing on this family of products, which was a 2,000-aircraft market for the next 20 years, a ballpark estimation shared by both companies. But this was not enough. Boeing, after five years of trailing, had captured 75 per cent of new aircraft orders in 2006 with its latest medium-sized, long-haul 787. In various versions, carrying from 220 to 260 passengers, Boeing had about 400 orders. Airbus was losing out on this booming medium-sized long-haul jet; it scrapped its previous $4 billion update of the A330, and went in favour of the new, extra-wide-bodied planes, the A350 XWB, which would cost around $10 billion to develop. Under this revised strategy, the A350 XWB would compete with two different models of Boeing, the 787 and, the larger version, the A350-1000 with Boeing's 777-300ER.

Supply

The imperatives of the airlines industry provide a rationale as to why Airbus and Boeing tended to integrate the supply in their value chain so as to control quality and liability at each and every step of production.

From a geographical point of view, Airbus and Boeing had to deal with their respective heritages, and their plants were located next to their headquarters, Airbus at Toulouse (but also in Frankfurt because of its European origins), and Boeing in Seattle, WA. Suppliers were clustered next to these plants for many industrial reasons: size and fragility of components were at the top of the list. For Airbus, there had always been an obligation to share its activities between founders. This started to change as big contracts were based on a technology transfer deal to the country concerned. This actually started to become prominent in the Chinese case because the Chinese government knew how to bargain with the two companies by leveraging the potential of its domestic market over the next 50 years. Both Airbus and Boeing had to relocate some industrial activities to China, but they did so in very different ways. Supply activities were the first to be relocated, but not always the only aspect, and transfer was undertaken in a progressive fashion. For instance, in China, Airbus had undertaken to transfer the technology required for the manufacturing of the complete wing of the A320 Family aircraft. This started in 2000 with the first two phases, including manufacture of the leading and trailing edges. This cooperation accelerated, with Airbus placing more engineers in the Chinese factories and moving to Phase 3, which was the manufacture of the wing box. It was a major project since Airbus wings were the most advanced in the world and this family was the best-selling product for Airbus. But more than 1,000 aircraft were still to be delivered. Airbus had no comparable project with any other country.

The Chinese challenge

According to Airbus, the Chinese market would need about 1,790 aircraft by 2022, of all sizes and capabilities. Domestic traffic was expected to continue to account for the largest portion of traffic at the beginning of the twenty-first century (see Exhibit 2.6).

Population	1,313,973,713 (July 2006 est.)
Age structure	0–14 years: 20.8% 15–64 years: 71.4% 65 years and over: 7.7%
Population growth rate	0.59%
Life expectancy at birth	total population: 72.58 years male: 70.89 years female: 74.46 years
Total fertility rate	1.73 children born/woman
Literacy	definition: age 15 and over can read and write total population: 90.9% male: 95.1% female: 86.5% (2002)
GDP (purchasing power parity)	$8.182 trillion (2005 est.)
GDP (official exchange rate)	$1.79 trillion (2005 est.)
GDP – real growth rate	9.3% (official data) (2005 est.)
GDP – per capita	$6,300 (2005 est.)
GDP – composition by sector	agriculture: 14.4% industry: 53.1% services: 32.5% note: industry includes construction (2005 est.)
Labour force	791.4 million (2005 est.)
Labour force – by occupation	agriculture 49%, industry 22%, services 29% (2003 est.)
Unemployment rate	4.2% official registered unemployment in urban areas in 2004; substantial unemployment and underemployment in rural areas; an official Chinese journal estimated overall unemployment (including rural areas) for 2003 at 20% (2004)
Population below poverty line	10% (2001 est.)
Household income or consumption by percentage share	lowest 10%: 2.4% highest 10%: 30.4% (1998)
Inflation rate (consumer prices)	1.9% (2005 est.)
Currency	yuan (CNY); note – also referred to as the renminbi (RMB)

Exhibit 2.6 China: key figures (2006 estimation)
Source: CIA, *The World Factbook*, http://www.cia.gov/cia/publications/factbook/index.html

The Chinese market was also a challenge interms of the influence and role of the state in decision making in businesses. Even with deregulation and liberalization, some practices remained, and both Boeing and Airbus knew that, first, the state controlled the airlines and hence their decisions involved the state; and, second, the Chinese state tended to favour technology transfers and not just transfers categorized as low value added activities.

Airbus had a competitive advantage in this market but with only one particular cluster – the growing international traffic favouring the 'hub to hub' strategy, bolstered by the Olympics in Beijing and the World Expo in Shanghai in 2008. The flow of international delegates would be partly accommodated by airlines flying the A380s into China. The Olympics would give a stimulus to aviation development in China, and Airbus believed the 555-seat A380 was the ideal vehicle to transport tens of thousands of athletes and sports fans to Beijing. The A380, its flagship of the twenty-first century, was supposed to make its important contribution to the fast development of the aviation market in China. The rapidly growing freight operations out of China were also stimulating much interest in the A380F (cargo version) by airlines both in China and overseas. For the domestic sector, the largest demand was in the 100- to 200-seat category, like the A320 Family or the 737.

Although the A380 cluster had no immediate threat from Boeing, there was a major battle that loomed on another cluster. Trunk routes between cities such as Beijing, Shanghai and Guangzhou required optimized medium-range twin-aisle aircraft like the A330 or the new Boeing 787 Dreamliner. The competition was getting tougher, which was quite clear in Noël Forgeard's statement:

> Airbus is optimistic about this market segment, which was originally started 30 years ago with the early versions of the A300. They continue to review the best way to serve the airline's needs in this area, and their conclusion is that the A350 and the A330-200 remain the optimum combination to meet the very different range requirements of the medium-capacity sector. Both aircraft are in extensive use in Asia, including China, and frequent re-orders by operators confirm their 'best in class' status. On a worldwide basis, the A350 and A330-200 now dominate a market, which had previously been served with competitor products. Despite much current focus on this middle market segment by a potential competing project, Airbus is highly confident that the economics of the A330s and A350s will remain unchallenged.

Boeing's assumption to beat Airbus was its focus on cost leadership, which its 787 could provide vis-à-vis the A330-200. It was more so due to the escalating prices of crude. Improvements in efficiency would come in the way the 787 had been designed and built. Boeing had announced that as much as 50 per cent of the primary structure – including the fuselage and wing – on the 787 would be made of composite materials, the lightest and most corrosion-resistant materials, which would require less maintenance. It had been designed with General Electric with synergies between aerodynamics and engines that were designed by Rolls-Royce. It was expected that advances in engine technology would contribute as much as 8 per cent of the increased efficiency of the new airplane, representing a nearly two-generation jump in technology for the middle of the market. New technologies and processes are in development to help Boeing and its supplier partners achieve unprecedented levels of performance at every phase of the programme. For example, by manufacturing a one-piece fuselage section, it eliminated 1,500 aluminium sheets and 40,000–50,000 fasteners. Boeing named the 787 the 'Dreamliner'.

From a technical point of view, it seemed that the 787 was more complete than the A350, which critics commented was actually an upgrade of the A330. But the battle was not only a technical one.

Airbus's way in China

Airbus was committed to the development of aviation in China. As the rivalry intensified, Airbus tried to differentiate by providing additional services. In China, the company not only sold aircraft, but also made efforts to provide the best training and support services. The CASC/Airbus Customer Services Training and Support Center, which represented an $80 million investment by Airbus, was fully operational in Beijing.

Airbus also had designated customer support managers and representatives for all operators. They regularly visited the airlines to ensure the perfect performance of Airbus aircraft and to provide operational analysis. The customer services department provided onsite technical support to airline operations in 20 Chinese cities, including Beijing, Chengdu, Fuzhou, Gansu, Guangzhou, Nanjing, Qingdao, Shanghai, Shenyang, Shenzhen and Xi'an. In addition, Airbus regularly held seminars on flight operation, maintenance, material and management, and other fields with the General Administration of Aviation of Chain (CAAC) and airlines, with the goal of sharing experiences and providing technical expertise. In order to improve safety and management standards, Airbus developed a number of state-of-the-art software tools, such as Less Paper Cockpit (LPC), Airbus On-line Services (AOLS), Fight Operation Monitoring (FOM) and Airman. Some of these systems had been widely introduced in the Chinese airlines.

Airbus started cooperating with the Chinese authorities at different levels. Cooperation with China was primarily carried out at three levels: first, with regulators such as the CAAC; second, with airlines; and, third, with aviation industry manufacturers. Airbus saw opportunities to further develop its industrial cooperation with Chinese industry and to integrate new suppliers in its network. Four Chinese manufacturers in Shenyang, Xi'an, Chengdu and Guizhou were already involved in manufacturing parts, such as wing components, emergency exit doors and maintenance tools for Airbus aircraft.

Airbus also increased its industrial procurement from China. Its procurement from China aimed to reach an annual volume of $60 million by 2007 and double to $120 million by 2010, including a substantial amount of A380 work.

On 21 April 2005, Airbus and the China Aviation Industry Corporation II (AVIC II) agreed to set up an engineering centre in the form of a joint venture in Beijing. About two months later, Airbus and the China Aviation Industry Corporation I (AVIC I) signed an agreement at the 46th International Paris Air Show in Le Bourget for AVIC I to become a new partner in Airbus's Engineering Centre in China. The Airbus Engineering Centre was to be located in the Tianzhu Airport Industrial Zone, adjacent to the offices of Airbus China. The facility would perform aircraft-specific design work for the A350 programme at the beginning, then later ramp up to increase the number of engineers at the Engineering Centre to 50 by the end of 2005, and to 200 by 2008. As Gustav Humbert explained at a committee meeting:

> The setting up of the centre further enhanced and developed a close relationship between Airbus and the Chinese aerospace industry, with a view to China becoming a full risk-sharing partner in a future Airbus programme for new-generation aircraft. A risk-sharing partner takes complete responsibility for a part of a programme, from design to manufacturing, including the corresponding investment and profit sharing.

In 2005, more than 3,880 Airbus aircraft were in operation with 240 operators worldwide. Half of Airbus's worldwide fleet had components produced in China. Airbus was looking forward to carrying out more projects with Chinese aviation industry partners.

Airbus not only worked closely with Chinese aviation manufacturers, but also encouraged other foreign companies to get involved in industrial cooperation with China. For instance, the Jinling Shipyard had built a roll-on roll-off vessel for the transportation of A380 components (the ship owner was FRET/CETAM). China's involvement in the A380 programme marked a significant milestone in the cooperation between Airbus and China.

Boeing's way in China

In 2000, Boeing held about 75 per cent of the Chinese aircraft market, but that was mainly due to second-hand aircraft that were growing old. One analyst who followed the strategies of the two competitors in China closely, commented:

> If we were having a look at new orders, the situation was more complicated for Boeing with a great strength, the 777, and a big concern, the A320 Family. There were also two big challenges: (1) Was the market meant to plebiscite the A380 strategy of Airbus or the middle-size 787 strategy? (2) Would Boeing win this battle or would the A350 manage to overcome its technical weakness with better cooperation?[3]

The situation for Boeing was quite difficult. Dealing with the Chinese government was not exactly what an American military giant expected it would have to do. Yet, Boeing could not afford to miss out on this market, so a balance had to be found between close cooperation and sharing military intelligence by way of technology transfer.

The result was that Boeing accepted having to transfer some supply activities to China in order to reduce costs and to please the Chinese government, which had strong bargaining power with the two companies (see Exhibit 2.7). Yet it decided not to transfer high technology activities out of its US territory. Boeing had a centre in Beijing to train pilots and to educate maintenance labour but nothing like Airbus.

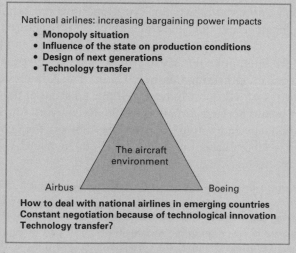

Exhibit 2.7 The aircraft environment and the influence of national airlines

Conclusion

Although Airbus claimed to be the world leader in 2005, with 51 per cent of the volume, it was actually Boeing, after five consecutive years of difficulties, that led the market, claiming 56 per cent. An analyst summed up the situation thus: 'Boeing managed to sell mainly aircraft at US$200 million whereas Airbus sold planes from the A320 Family, which are around US$60 million. And that will probably impact the profitability of both firms.'

Regarding the next-generation aircraft, the 787 remained ahead of the A350. The 787 was due to be released in 2008, while the new A350, after its redesign, will not be released until 2012. On the other hand, the A380, which was supposed to be delivered by the end of 2006, was delayed by technical glitches. Nevertheless, with reinforced trust from its clients, notably Singapore Airlines, total sales of more than 400 units of the A380 have been booked by Airbus.

As for future battles, R&D budgets continue to increase because of booming oil prices – for example, Airbus decided to increase its R&D budget from €200 million in 2005 to €450 million in 2006.

The future is not easy to predict. The battle will continue and it should remembered that the '8' in the names A380 and 787 was not a logical progression of the series of A340, A350 and 737 ... it actually referred to an Asian superstition which says that the number 8 is lucky. It will be interesting to see how these arch-rivals will act and what divergent strategies they will use to seduce and control a market that was estimated to be worth $221.3 billion (€174 billion) in 2005.

Notes

[1] A 12-month delay on the A380 had created turmoil deep within the Airbus management system. Airbus already faced cost overruns of $2 billion. Noël Forgeard, co-CEO of the European Aeronautic Defence and Space Company (EADS) had to leave and Gustav Humbert, CEO of Airbus, resigned. Mr Streiff replaced Mr Humbert, and Louis Galoos, a Frenchman, replaced Mr Forgeard to join Tom Enders, a German, at the helm of EADS. The bicephalic structure of EADS – two Chairman, two CEOs – reflects its Franco-German origins. Also Airbus (still 20 per cent owned by BAE Systems, a British firm that wants to sell its stake to EADS) is not fully integrated into the parent company, and works as if it is a state within a state.

[2] Wernher von Braun (1912–77) was one of the most important rocket developers and champions of space exploration. Von Braun is well known as the leader of what has been called the 'rocket team' which developed the V–2 ballistic missile for the Nazis during World War II. The V–2s were manufactured at a forced labour factory called Mittelwerk. Before the Allied capture of the V–2 rocket complex, Von Braun engineered the surrender of 500 of his top rocket scientists, along with plans and test vehicles, to the Americans. For 15 years after World War II, von Braun worked with the US Army in the development of ballistic missiles. Von Braun's extraordinary contribution was launching the first US satellite, hurling the first American astronauts into space, and winning the 'moon race' with the Saturn V super-booster, which powered Armstrong, Aldrin, Collins and their successors to the lunar surface. A gregarious, whisky-drinking night owl who could out-cuss any of his friends, von Braun also played the piano and cello, mastered scuba diving, flew an array of aircraft, spoke several languages, became a serious amateur astronomer, and was an avid reader and conversationalist, as much at ease discussing Nietzsche as nuclear fission.

[3] On this point it must be underlined that, under pressure from the airlines, Airbus decided to change the specification of the A350 to get closer to that of the 787. It could be considered as a victory for Boeing and evidence of the strategic importance of this cluster according to both companies.

▶

? *Case questions*

Read the case carefully and then answer the following questions.

1 Analyse briefly Airbus and Boeing's respective global strategies. Discuss why they have followed such divergent strategies, which apparently led to success for both companies?

2 Comment on the strategy adopted by Boeing and Airbus with respect to China. How should China take advantage of the situation?

3 Do you think there is a risk of technology transfer in China? If yes, how do you justify Airbus's strategy? If not, how do you justify Boeing's strategy?

4 What do you think will be the future strategy of Airbus and Boeing in the Chinese market?

5 What would be your recommendations for the two companies?

PART 2
The Organizational Imperative

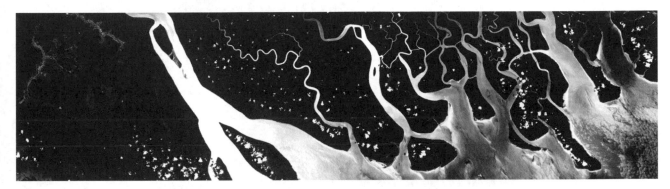

Part Contents

CHAPTER 3

Managing organizational design for global operations

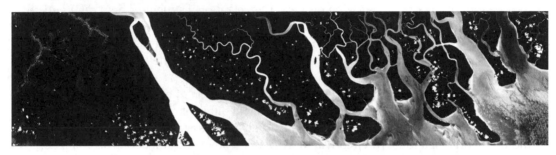

Part 2 draws on the preceding discussion to further develop how global companies organize themselves. The previous chapter dealt with definitional issues of the global corporation, and identified their strengths and weaknesses, their biases, their tensions. It discussed how these global corporations developed multi-level competencies and interrelated capabilities, often growing to be national champions, for sustained competitive advantage. This chapter dwells on the evolution and development of different organizational structures, their strengths and weaknesses, and how global companies are designing their organizational structures in tandem with their growth objectives.

Throughout most of modern business history, corporations have attempted to add value by matching their structures to their strategies.[1] At the beginning of the last century, corporations, in a quest to create efficiency through economies of scale, centralized key functions like marketing, sales, finance and operations. With diversification and the growth of business globally, a competing model emerged by which global corporations created business units structured around products and geographic markets. The smaller business units sacrificed some economies of scale but were more flexible and adaptable to local conditions.[2] These two structures – centralized by function versus relatively decentralized by product and region – was the norm until the late 1970s. With a changing business landscape during the 1980s, however, the disadvantages of these two structures became apparent, and companies tried to amass the advantages of both. That was the time when

---

[1] Kaplan, R.S. and Norton, D.P. (2006) 'How to implement a new strategy without disrupting your organization', *Harvard Business Review*, March, 100–9.

[2] *Ibid.*

many global corporations, such as ABB, shifted to the matrix structure, with the assumption that they could retain both the economies of scale of centralized functions and the flexibility of their product line and geographic business units. Also it was very easy to draw up a matrix and pinpoint responsibilities. But matrix organizations were difficult to coordinate. Managers operating at a matrix intersection had to juggle the demands of two masters, which led to conflict and delay[3]. At the end of the century, the matrix structure gave way to a networked structure, where organizations operated virtually across traditional structures and boundaries. Today, new organizational forms, such as hybrid structures, are being created to match the nature of competition and the economy.

Organizational structures define roles, relationships and procedures, and help corporations in the decision-making process. Organizational structures help *differentiate* the specialization, standardization and departmentalization of tasks and functions, while helping to coordinate *integrating mechanisms* such as hierarchical supervision, formal rules and procedures, training and socialization. They also help define the boundaries of the corporation and its interfaces with the environment.[4]

Gareth Morgan (1989)[5] denoted pictorially the evolution of organizational structures. He showed that corporations evolved over time with different organizational structures (see Figure 3.1). He defined his first model as Weber's classical 'rigid bureaucracy': the traditional organizational pyramid with a CEO at the helm and strict controls in place. Model 2 comprised a senior management team with a CEO and heads of department that

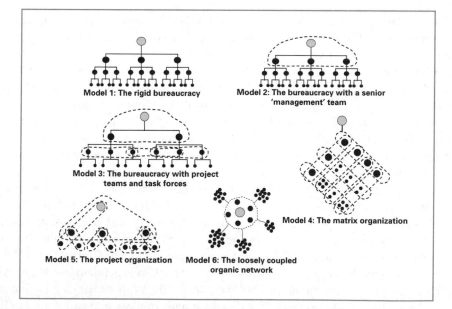

Figure 3.1 Schematic illustration of Morgan's six models

---

[3] *Ibid.*

[4] Nohria, N. (1995) *Note on Organizational Structure*. HBS 9-491-083.

[5] Morgan, G. (1989) *Creative Organization Theory*. Thousand Oaks, CA: Sage.

held weekly meetings. This style of management did not rely entirely on control by the CEO, but by the management team. Model 3 comprised project teams and task forces, with information passed up the hierarchy and decisions passed down. Model 4 was a matrix form with equal priority given to functional departments and the product portfolio. In model 5, the work was carried out by project teams; most of the core activities were tackled through project teams that were specialized; teams were dynamic and innovative. Model 6 was a loosely linked networked organization, which worked under a subcontracting mode with core staff from headquarters focused on strategy and brand management.

This evolution leads to the definitional issues connected with the different structures.

The most basic structural form is the *functional structure*. As the name suggests, it is organized according to bureaucratic principles. Offices are differentiated by functions such as sales, marketing, production, finance, engineering and R&D. Integration occurs at the senior management level. This structure is mostly suited to stable environments. Corporations like AT&T still follow this basic functional structure. Figure 3.2(a) illustrates a functional structure.

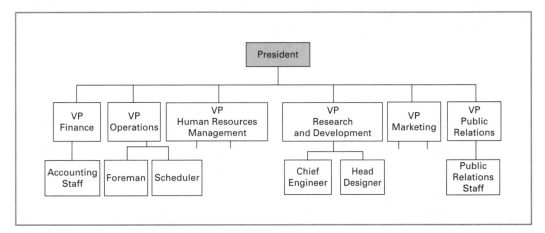

Figure 3.2(a) A functional structure

As corporations become larger and more complex in terms of products and services, or with regard to markets and clients they serve, a *divisional structure* emerges, perhaps with some centralized functional departments. This structure combines bureaucracy within divisions with internal markets and financial controls. Offices are differentiated by divisions, such as product or geography. Integration of the business strategy occurs at the divisional level. A functional structure entails the decentralization of business strategies and the implementation of strategies by each division, together with allocation of capital, technology and human resources by senior management. Attention is focused on division to markets, technology and financial controls. This type of structure is usually adapted to innovations in technology and marketing. Examples of companies that follow this type of structure include Johnson & Johnson and Unilever. Figure 3.2(b) depicts a divisional structure.

When the business landscape demands pressure dimensions such as product and function or product and geography, corporations adapt a *matrix structure*. Here, differentiation occurs by division and function. Usually the integration process is unclear and highly political.

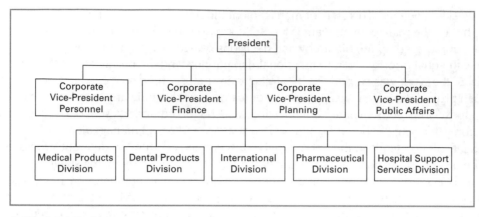

Figure 3.2(b) A divisional structure.

The structure has a dual focus, with high political conflict and administrative costs. Usually the advantages of a functional and divisional structure are not realized. Examples of corporations that has incorporated a multi-dimensional matrix structure include ABB, Lafarge, LVMH, Boeing, BP and Michelin. Figure 3.2(c) illustrates a matrix structure.

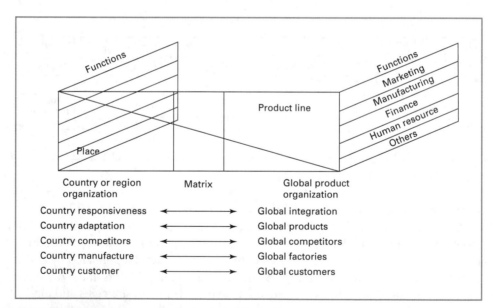

Figure 3.2(c) A matrix structure
Source: adapted from J.R. Galbraith and R.K. Kazanjian (1986) *Strategy Implementation: Structure Systems and Process* (2nd edn). St Paul: West, 159.

The *network structure* departs from the traditional bureaucratic model as there is no stable, clearly defined hierarchy. It is usually characterized by a complex network of vertical and horizontal relationships. These are called intra- and inter-organizational networks. Differentiation and integration occur through temporary cross-functional project teams or cross-company teams, which are usually relied upon, adopted by and are suited to strategic alliances and joint ventures. This structure combines both the processes and characteristics of formal and informal organization. Examples of corporations that have adopted this structure include Nike, DKNY, Reebok and Cisco.

When any of the three basic structures – functional, divisional and matrix – is combined with a network structure, it generates a *hybrid structure*. When global corporations intertwine a formal multi-divisional structure or a matrix structure with informal working groups that are spaced as networks, a hybrid structure is generated. Usually, cross-functional teams, informal teams and/or temporary work groups are formed with the creation of hybrids. Here there is no optimal structure but there are constant changes in the mode of functioning. The emphasis is on getting things done. This structure is more suited to an inter-organizational network and alliances as in Renault-Nissan and, AF-KLM, or where there is increased outsourcing of work processes.

Table 3.1 summarizes the characteristics, and the advantages and disadvantages of the different structures.

	Functional	Divisional	Matrix	Network
Environment	Stable	Heterogeneous	Complex with multiple demands	Volatile
Flexibility and adaptability	Poor	Good	Moderate	Excellent
Firm boundaries	Core/periphery	Internal/external markets	Multiple interfaces	Porous and changing
Efficiency	Excellent	Poor, repetition	Moderate	Good
Responsibility/ accountability	Exact: pinpointed	Excellent: local products and markets	Dual: poor	Moderate
Power and authority	Positional and functional expertise	General management responsibility and resources	Negotiating skills and resources	Knowledge and resources
Control and coordination	At the top, hierarchical: poor	At the level of division: moderate	Dual: poor	Multiple, cross-functional teams: moderate
Communication and decision making	Centralized, formal, top-down	Top-down, formal, separation of strategy and execution	Dual, shared, informal, top-down and bottom-up	Multi-sided, informal, decentralized
Specialization	Silos and over-specialized	Product orientated	End result orientated	Market orientated
Training	Easy and logical reflection	Difficult, general managerial	Difficult, human relations	Difficult, knowledge and communication
Politics	Inter-functional	Within/inter-division	Product/function/ place orientated	Shifting coalitions
Strategy	Focused, low cost, mono brand	Diversified, conglomerates	Multi-local, multi-divisional, multi-product	Innovative, outsourcing

Table 3.1 General characteristics, and relative advantages and disadvantages of different organizational structures[6]

[6] Adapted from Nohria, N. (1995) *Note on Organizational Structure*. HBS 9-491-083.

Organizational design for international operations

Organizational design must encompass different differentiation and integration mechanisms in order for corporations to operate effectively. It is a complex process, and more so for global corporations. This complexity arises due to the tortuous evolution of the global corporation, as it has not only to respond to the changing demands of the environment, but also to efficiently and effectively reconfigure assets, competencies and capabilities throughout its business units. As global corporations try to balance the conflicting demands of global integration and local responsiveness, they usually adopt a contingency-based approach. For example, pressures of global integration are considerably high in industries such as aircraft manufacturing, consumer electronics and computers, while pressures for local responsiveness are considerably high in industries such as publishing, branded packaged goods and clothing. Corporations in these diverse industries align their organizational design to the conflicting demands to which they are accustomed.

When local corporations expand their operations globally, they usually set-up overseas subsidiaries that cater to all global operations of a division. With expanding operations, these subsidiaries are usually grouped into one *international division*. A vice president of international operations is responsible for the subsidiaries and reports directly to the CEO. With this design, international operations receive due attention from top management. A breed of global managers is nurtured within these operations, and the corporation follows a unified, centralized approach towards all its global operations. However, this design might lead to the creation of two groups of managers – one with 'favoured' global status and the other with local status. With growth, the corporation might face difficulty in adequate resource allocation and, as functions such as R&D are mostly dispersed and localized, there are chances of replication and reduced coordination. According to Bartlett and Ghoshal's classification, the design of such corporations, with a multinational mentality is called the 'decentralized federation'.[7]

Some corporations, however, consider it important to exercise strict control in allocating resources, and favour coordinating all global operations from headquarters (HQ). Such corporations envisage the threats to business more than opportunities, and favour a design that will allow them to coordinate operations and react from HQ. Usually, this design can be of three types – *product division, functional division* and *geographic division* – which ultimately converge to form the global matrix structure.[8] Out of the three divisions, the functional division is uncommon in a global operation and can be observed only in oil and mining corporations. Geographic division is more common, where the focus is more on geographic spread rather than on products, and is mainly found in corporations with mature products and narrow product ranges, such as Alcatel, Airbus and Boeing. Out of these three designs, the most prevalent is the product division. In the product division, global responsibility rests with the product groups. For example, the DVD product division of Sony has worldwide responsibilities. This means that the head of

---

[7] Bartlett, C.A. and Ghoshal, S. (1989) *Managing Across Borders: The Transnational Solution.* Boston, MA: Harvard Business School.

[8] Stopford, J. and Louis, T.W. (1972) *Strategy and Structure of the Multinational Enterprise.* New York: Basic Books.

the DVD product division controls finance, production, marketing, sales and people development globally, and runs the division as a profit centre with close control by HQ on budget issues and the bottom line. In this type of design, the world is the unit of analysis, and corporations (Japanese companies are good examples) think in terms of creating highly standardized products with adequate cost and quality advantages, and manufacturing them on a global scale in a few highly efficient plants, often at the corporate centre. This design harnesses economies of scale and scope, but may be too far from local tastes, preferences and customers. According to Bartlett and Ghoshal's classification this design of corporations encompasses those with a global mentality, and is referred to as the 'Centralized Hubs'.

The evolution of the traditional international divisional design has given way to the so-called *network structure* of corporations operating globally. Corporations need to be responsive to local market and political needs, while dealing with the pressure of developing global-scale competitive efficiency. Thus, the key activities and resources should neither be centralized nor decentralized, allowing flexibility for each subsidiary to carry out its own tasks on a local-for-local basis. The resources and activities are dispersed but coordinated, and these dispersed resources are integrated into an interdependent network of worldwide operations, which leads them to achieve efficiency and flexibility at the same time. The differentiated units, whether subsidiaries, R&D centres or cross-functional teams, process and act upon specialized and generalized information in an entrepreneurial fashion. The centre of the network coordinates strategic objectives and operational policies throughout the differentiated units, ensures an efficient flow of resources and re-channels the corporation's accumulated knowledge and experience. The channels facilitate interaction, coordination and integration among the differentiated yet independent product, geographic and functional divisional units. Nohria, and Bartlett and Ghoshal classified the design of these types of corporation, with a transnational mentality, as the 'integrated network'.

The next chapter discusses the challenges of managing across cultures. As global companies become bigger and bigger, the effective management of different subsidiaries becomes a challenge. And more so due to the strong national heritages of companies that, although they have become global in their operations today, may still operate with a nationalistic mindset.

Case introduction: Vodafone: out of many, one

In 2004, Vodafone Group plc was the world's largest cell phone provider by revenue. From 1999, Vodafone had invested $270 billion (€225 billion) mostly in stock, building an empire spanning 26 countries. It controlled cell phone operations in 16 countries and had minority stakes in companies in ten others. The case traces the history of Vodafone's growth and its capacity to transform and adapt itself to the dramatically changing market environment in the dynamic telecommunications sector. The case analyses Vodafone's growth through acquisitions and the subsequent integration of acquired units, with a key focus on how it manages its structure by coordinating its businesses on a global scale.

This case appears after the readings for this chapter.

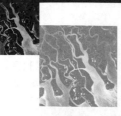

READING 5
Changing perspectives on global strategy and organization*

Thomas Malnight

Traditionally, companies have evolved their international strategies based on leveraging their existing strengths globally through either centralized or decentralized structures. In today's competitive environment, however, this is no longer enough. As Thomas Malnight explains, firms need to develop fundamentally new approaches to structuring and managing worldwide operations, creating flexible, global networks where the emphasis is on value creation.

Overview

As earlier chapters discussed, there are various motivations for international growth. For example, in some industries competitive pressures *require* companies to grasp global opportunities at some or all stages of the value chain. In other industries, while global strategies are not such an essential requirement, they can nevertheless offer *rewards* to the expanding firm.

There are also distinctions to be made in terms of how companies approach new markets. One of the oldest motivations for foreign investment was to *seek natural resources.* Over time this has evolved into categories such as *market seekers,* where emphasis is put on factors such as market size and disposable income, *cost seekers,* who move abroad more for the ability to produce high-quality goods at low prices, and, most recently, *knowledge seekers,* where tapping into know-how becomes the prime motivation.

What this chapter sets out to do is to take this perspective to the level of the firm and its organization, addressing how individual firms build strategies to enhance their competitive advantage, and the organizational challenges of effectively building and leveraging global networks of operations. It will discuss how being global offers an expanding array of opportunities for enhancing firm competitive advantage based on leveraging these global networks of operations.

Background

In a study of the evolution of modern global competition, Alfred Chandler, the renowned business historian, highlighted the emergence of firms operating across national borders

---

* Malnight, T. (2001) Changing Perspectives on Global Strategy and Organization, Chapter 11 in *Accelerating International Growth*, by Rosenzweig, P., Gilbert, X., Malnight, T. and Puick, V., Sussex, UK: IMD/Wiley (ISBN: 0-471-49659-6).

Reproduced with permission of John Wiley & Sons Ltd.

resulting from the development of mass transportation, communication and production technologies beginning in the 1850s and 1860s. As a result, the early development of firms with international operations concentrated in industries with high volume production or distribution processes, a situation that remained even through the early 1970s. As late as 1973, 65% of the largest industrial corporations in the world were concentrated in a few industrial sectors – food, chemicals, oil, machinery and primary metals.

However, there have been dramatic changes in the form and focus of international trade and competition since the 1970s, driven by the new technologies – including communication and information, and product-specific production technologies – as well as the transfer of managerial methods across borders as sources of firm advantage. The number of industries affected today by the potential for global strategies has expanded dramatically, as has the mix of strategic opportunities for firms operating globally. As a result, the need for companies to have global strategies has become an accepted wisdom in most industries, with management at more and more firms having to address the impact on their company's competitive advantage of how and where they operate globally.

This acceptance has brought recognition of both the opportunities and the challenges of operating globally, not only for firms with established networks of worldwide operations but also for small-to-medium-sized companies. The complexity of these opportunities reflects the fact that there is no single ideal approach for operating globally. Companies like ABB, Intel, McDonald's, Yahoo! or Gillette are global in different ways, and the opportunities and challenges for each firm to benefit from being global clearly need to be analysed within the context of their environment. Intel has an integrated worldwide organization to develop, produce and sell highly innovative components around the world. What would not work for Intel is the McDonald's model of providing a worldwide formula for franchising locally.

On its part, the ABB approach of occupying over 5000 'local' markets is the antithesis of a company like Gillette, which is based on selling almost identical products globally. Yahoo! typifies how the Web has enabled even very young companies to exploit global expansion from a very early stage by developing a global brand with local content, by leveraging the company's common technology platform. In all of these companies, the issue is not a question of *if* they need to be global or not, but rather how operating globally can enhance their competitive advantage and how they can structure and manage their operations to capture these potential advantages.

Case Study: Yahoo!: Going Global and Acting Local

Yahoo! is a global internet communications, commerce and media company offering a branded network of services to more than 166 million individuals each month all over the world. Having begun as an [*sic*] free online navigational guide in 1995, when two Stanford University doctoral students decided to turn what was a hobby into a business, Yahoo! has served as a prominent example of how a young brand can exploit the global reach offered by the internet and rapidly emerge into a multinational player by bypassing the slower, step-by-step approach to internationalization which has characterized global expansion in the past. Whatever happens to the brand, its growth is still instructive.

According to a research report on Yahoo! by Lehman Brothers (29 June, 2000) the portal is one of the few companies that has lived up to what it calls the mythical 'internet business model' or a virtual business with highly scaleable revenue streams, a large amount of operating revenue, strong profits and a cash flow. Revenues in 2000 were $1.1 billion, up 88% from 1999. Its growth is mainly the result of online advertising from both online and offline companies; it continues an aggressive programme of investing in new services and initiatives, including the business-to-business area, focused brand-building and accelerated entry into new markets.

It is its global capabilities which have been one of its greatest strengths. Yahoo!'s strategy has been international in outlook from the early days of its founding. That strategy has combined exploiting a consistent brand identity with a common design and services, and establishing local offices to create local content. It had already set up satellites in Canada and Japan within a year of its emergence, and by September 1996 it made its first foray into Europe with the launch of a localized version in the UK, quickly followed by sites for France and Germany. Yahoo! has an audience of more than 30 million in Europe, including 9–10 million in the UK.

Although it is such a stalwart member of the new dot.com fraternity, Yahoo!'s approach to global expansion is in some ways not that different from its bricks and mortar counterparts. For example, its entry into markets has often been done in alliances with partners: it launched in Europe with Ziff-Davis, a leading publisher of computer magazines and online computing content. It also faces local regulations and restrictions: in France its ability to conduct online auctions was delayed because of complex legal issues, while the slowness of many countries to come to terms with online shopping puts a brake on revenues.

Nevertheless, exploiting its first-mover advantage, it is now in first or second place in all the main markets around the world, including Europe, Canada, Korea and Japan. Having built up strong audience figures by acting as a free-to-users content aggregator and thus generating substantial online advertising, Yahoo!, like other portals, has embarked on a number of strategic initiatives to find more sustainable revenue streams from more value-added activities such as e-commerce, and differentiate itself from its competitors both in the old and new economy. The challenge will be to maintain its momentum as the market matures and big companies in sectors like telecommunications get to grips with their internet strategies.

Yahoo!'s management have outlined five key initiatives in order to capitalize on the next wave of internet growth:

- Leverage further the e-commerce opportunities throughout its network.
- Extend the depth and breadth of services on its international properties and monetize its global reach.
- Integrate more broadband content into its sites.

- Make Yahoo! services ubiquitous across platforms and devices.
- Develop additional services for small and mid-sized businesses.

Yahoo!'s vision is to be the world's portal, so it aims at providing a similar home page to internet users across the world. This determination to build a global brand is tailored to the local language, culture and legislative framework, however. In France, for example, the management style is modelled as much as possible on that of its Silicon Valley parent, but adapted to the French work culture as well as legislation. And while what [*sic*] the French users see almost exactly what their American counterparts see, the content is very much geared to a French audience.

Country	Launched	Country	Launched
Yahoo! UK and Ireland	4Q96	Yahoo! Asia	4Q97
Yahoo! France	4Q96	Yahoo! EN	4Q97
Yahoo! Germany	4Q96	Yahoo! Italy	2Q98
Yahoo! Japan	4Q96	Yahoo! Spain	4Q98
Yahoo! Canada	4Q96	Yahoo! Taiwan	1Q99
Yahoo! Australia (incl. NZ)	2Q97	Yahoo! Singapore	1Q99
Yahoo! Korea	3Q97	Yahoo! Hong Kong	1Q99
Yahoo! Sweden	4Q97	Yahoo! Brazil	3Q99
Yahoo! Norway	4Q97	Yahoo! China	3Q99
Yahoo! Denmark	4Q97	Yahoo! Mexico	4Q99
		Yahoo! Argentina	1Q00
		Yahoo! India	2Q00

Table 1 Yahoo! – global expansion at blistering pace
Source: Lehman Brothers (2000).

Traditional approaches to global strategy: value-leveraging strategies and organizations

Initially many companies expand around the world for two major reasons, both of which focus on primarily *leveraging* existing company strengths. These two interrelated reasons are:

- reducing costs through increasing volume or accessing low-cost labour or other resources; and/or
- expanding sales of existing products or know-how.

Underpinning these motivations is a belief that the centre, the headquarters and home market operations are the primary source of a company's 'value' creation. Company advantage focuses on the strength of the domestic operations and the ability to manage the transfer of products and know-how across national markets (Figure 1). Managing the transfer of products involves developing the capacity to sell and distribute products, with these products often produced by home market operations. Managing the transfer of know-how involves developing the capacity to set up local operations that can mimic or duplicate domestic operations, thus leveraging such know-how within multiple local markets.

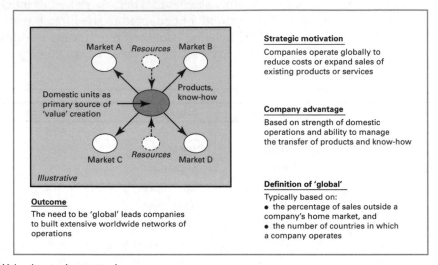

Figure 1 Value-leveraging strategies
Source: Adapted from Bartlett and Ghoshal (1989).

At this stage of expansion, the definition of a company being 'global' is often measured based on the percentage of its sales outside its home market and the number of countries in which it operates. In both cases, the higher these numbers the more 'global' a firm is considered. Thus a firm having 60% of its sales outside its home market and with operations in 80 countries is more 'global' than one having only 30% of its sales outside its home market and operations in only 20 countries. An important result of these 'global' expansion strategies is the building of extensive worldwide networks of operations.

What is Globalization?

One of the most frequently used, and often abused, terms describing business challenges todays is globalization. The world is globalizing!! Firms are globalizing!! Managers need to globalize!! The challenges associated with globalization are very real, but it is important for managers to understand and consider more carefully what is meant by the term globalization and how it affects the way they operate. Although much has been written about globalization, no clear definition has emerged, and, as a result, significant confusion exists about the topic.

Globalization is not a single, monolithic trend but occurs at multiple levels (Figure 2). At the macro level, globalization of industries involves how the external and competitive environment facing firms is changing and how these changes impact the competitive requirements, opportunities and challenges facing firms. As a result of industry trends, emerging competitive requirements are changing to include a growing emphasis on speed and flexibility, an expanded focus on learning and innovation, and the ability to draw and integrate information from multiple sources to create organizational knowledge. In many cases the requirements are a direct result of changes in the competitive environment.

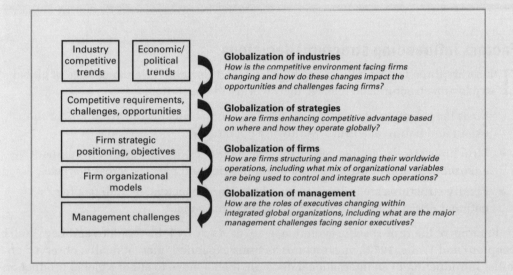

Figure 2 Globalization: a multi-level phenomenon

Globalization of strategies concerns how firms are enhancing their competitive advantage based on where and how they operate globally, and the specific strategic objectives and positioning firms can develop to meet the requirements arising from changes in their industry.

Globalization of firms is about the organizational model itself. What operational models will allow firms to structure and manage their worldwide operations in line with their changing strategies? There has been much discussion on the need to move toward global models shifting from a traditional vertical, hierarchical structure to a growing horizontal orientation across dispersed and interdependent worldwide operations. Frequently these new models fundamentally alter how managers structure, control and integrate their worldwide operations.

Globalization of management centres on how the roles of executives are changing within integrated global organizations. What are the major management challenges facing senior executives?

Why is this integrated perspective important? Because it helps move beyond broad generalizations to address the specific challenges facing an individual firm. For example, when asking what types of managers a firm needs to run its overseas operations, there is not a single correct answer. It depends on the type of organization it is trying to create, which subsequently depends on its strategy. When asking what type of organizational model is appropriate, it depends on a firm's strategy and its specific competitive environment. When asking what is an appropriate global strategy for a firm, it depends on a combination of the specific competitive requirements in its environment, as well as an assessment of its own resources and know-how.

Factors influencing structural decisions

There are three factors influencing how firms in this value-leveraging stage of global expansion structure and manage their worldwide operations.

- First, the selection of a structure is influenced by firm-specific *evolution*, or the extent and nature of a firm's worldwide operations.
- Structures are also influenced by the characteristics of the worldwide competitive *environment*, including the extent of similarities and barriers across markets.
- Finally structures are influenced by *administrative* factors, including a firm's national origin or the mindset of its senior management.

In terms of the firm-specific evolution, a 1970s study by John Stopford and Lew Wells (Stopford and Wells, 1972), on structures as firms expanded internationally, observed an initial introduction of an international division, then a move to either a global product or geographic based (e.g., Europe, Asia, etc.) structure, then a move to a matrix or grid-type structure (Figure 3). In the initial stages of expansion, international divisions are often used to manage and control small and relatively simple 'foreign' operations, minimizing the disruption to other busy units. These international divisions have the dual advantages of concentrating expertise on operating within 'foreign' markets within one unit, as well as freeing other management to concentrate on their primary domestic market operations.

As international business grows in either importance (percentage of a company's sales) or complexity (e.g., number of businesses or markets), firms introduce new structures. If business grows in importance, but remains largely concentrated within a few products or businesses, companies tend to introduce geographic or area-based structures. Area-based structures reflect a high degree of decentralization within regions and provide the management of each territory autonomy over its value-creation activities to adapt to local or regional conditions. If international business grows in importance and complexity, firms tend to introduce global product or functional structures, reflecting a high degree of centralized controls within globally focused units. These structures are based on the notion that each product division should have full authority to rationalize and coordinate its value creation activities, improve communication and resource transfers, and strategically respond to the competitors globally. If international operations

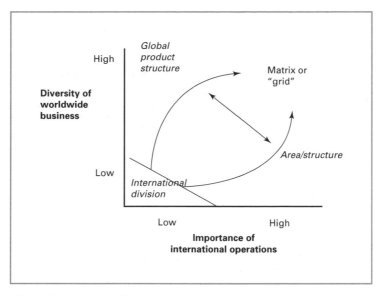

Figure 3 Patterns of organizational evolution
Adapted from Stopford and Wells (1972) with the permission of Perseus Books, from *Managing the Multinational Enterprise* by Stopford, John M. & Wells, L.T., Basic Books, New York.

grew in both importance and diversity, Stopford and Wells found that firms employed some type of matrix or grid structure.

A second factor influencing structural choices within value-leveraging strategies is the nature of the industry competitive environment. Prahalad and Doz (1987) characterized these environments based on two conflicting pressures, for both 'global integration' and 'local responsiveness'. Some environments reflect relatively independent national markets, with primary pressures for local responsiveness. These environments typically have high barriers between and significant differences across markets, and competition occurs largely within each national market. Other environments reflect integrated world markets, with few and falling barriers between and growing similarity across national markets, with competition occurring across large continuous world markets. Strategies and organizations will vary dramatically across these environments. With high pressures for responsiveness and few for integration, firms tend to introduce decentralized, geographic-focused structures. When pressures for integration are high and there are perceived to be few benefits from local responsiveness, firm structures tend to reflect globally centralized product or functional structures (Figure 4).

The third set of factors involves firm choices, often influenced by management or cultural styles or preferences. For instance, US or Japanese multinationals have traditionally been more likely to employ structures with stronger centralized controls. On the other hand, European multinationals have been more likely to employ decentralized structures, with higher autonomy given to national affiliates. In terms of the mindset of senior management, Perlmutter (1969) distinguished between ethnocentric (i.e., home-country), polycentric (i.e., host-country), and geocentric (world) orientations, with a significant influence on resulting strategies and organizations.

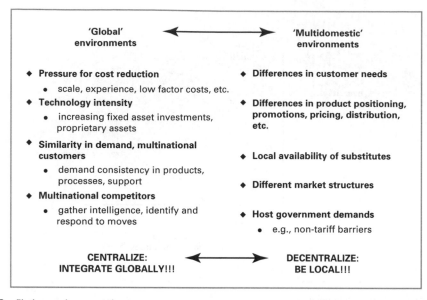

Figure 4 Conflicting environmental pressures
Adapted from Prahalad and Doz (1987) with the permission of The Free Press, a Division of Simon Schuster, Inc., from *The Multinational Mission: Balancing Local Demands and Global Vision* by C.K. Prahalad and Yves Doz. Copyright © 1987 by The Free Press.

Traditional value-leveraging structures

Overall these factors result in two primary approaches to structuring and managing worldwide operations within a value-leveraging global strategy. The first approach reflects a *centralized* globally focused organization, while the second reflects a *decentralized* (Figure 5) or geographic-focused organization. The strategic objectives and associated organizations of centralized and decentralized approaches vary dramatically. Centralized approaches focus on the benefits of global structures and are associated with environments emphasizing the benefits of global integration. Organizational characteristics of centralized structures include having strategic, value-creating resources and operations that reside in the home market with tight centralized formal controls over foreign operations. There are frequently separate domestic and international units, with a one-way flow of products, resources and ideas, and with the international units at both a strategic and geographic distance.

The decentralized structure reflects the benefits of geographic-oriented structures and environments emphasizing the need for local responsiveness. Foreign markets are seen as different and unique, with a strategic focus on transferring know-how within national markets, and locally adapted to reflect differences across markets.

Organizational characteristics include operating as a portfolio of autonomous affiliates in major markets. Most value-creating operations are duplicated within national markets, which are monitored through financial controls focusing on affiliate profitability. There is a tendency to emphasize the use of local executives in decision-making positions within each market.

Competitive environment
- Primary pressures for global integration

Global strategy
- Primary focus on domestic operations with incremental, but opportunistic approach to expansion
- Foreign strategy to leverage domestic resources

Organization
- Separate domestic and international units
- Primary value-creating, strategic operations centralized in domestic market with dispersed supporting operations
- Strong centralized formal controls over international operations
- Key decision-making positions held by home-country executives, often with we/they (home country-foreigner) mindset
- One-way flow of products, technologies, staff, ideas from domestic to foreign operations

Figure 5 Centralized strategy and organization
Adapted from *Managing Across Borders: The Transnational Solution* by C. Bartlett & S. Ghoshal, 1989.

Competitive environment
- Country markets perceived as different and unique, with each market requiring local customization and expertise

Global strategy
- Foreign strategy to transfer know-how within national markets and value-creating activities to adapt and exploit this expertise within national markets
- Strategy to operate as portfolio of largely national focused affiliates

Organization
- Autonomous affiliates in each market
- Primary value-creating operations duplicated within major national markets
- Control systems focused on profitability, with measurement and rewards based on local results
- Key decision-making positions held by local executives
- Limited flows of products, technologies, staff, ideas from domestic to foreign operations

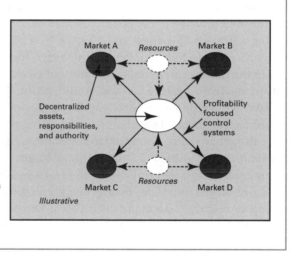

Figure 6 Decentralized strategy and organization
Adapted from *Managing Across Borders: The Transnational Solution* by C. Bartlett & S. Ghoshal, 1989.

Advantages and disadvantages of traditional structures

Centralized and decentralized structures offer the management of firms operating within value-leveraging strategies numerous benefits, but also have important limitations as well. While centralization can be an effective structure to manage worldwide flows of standardized products, decentralization can be effective for managing flows of know-how to each national market, allocating largely autonomous operational management to local executives. Within both approaches, structuring decisions are typically made at the level of the firm and this consistency of structure across operations simplifies the management of worldwide operations, with clear roles and responsibilities across the organization. Global controls in centralized firms are managed through direct reporting relationships, while in decentralized organizations national affiliates are measured and controlled based on local profitability. Both structures also are associated with an alignment of responsibility and accountability. Finally each approach has a clear set of strategic benefits, with centralized structures focused on developing the advantages of global integration, and decentralized structures the benefits of local responsiveness. Both structures enable firms to build significant international sales and operations across world markets.

However, there are also important limitations for these structures. Both centralized and decentralized structures focus on making decisions on strategy and organization *at the level of the firm,* with this selection involving a balancing or trade-off among various opportunities. Both structures emphasize some motivations from operating globally, trading off against other potential benefits. As will be discussed later in this chapter, in many industries firms are now focused on simultaneously pursuing multiple strategic opportunities from operating globally, as opposed to selecting among potential benefits.

There are additional important limitations for both type of structures. Centralized structures emphasize home-country resources, personnel and market requirements, limiting a firm's willingness and capacity to access local personnel, resources, or know-how or respond to local market requirements. Innovations – or market requirements – outside the home market are frequently not given adequate weight in the company strategic decision-making process. Additionally, there is a clear limitation on the ability of a firm to develop and utilize operations outside the home market, with executives and operations frequently delegated to a supporting position.

On the other hand, decentralized structures have similar limitations. While offering important opportunities to strengthen positions within national markets, the organization results in duplication and fragmentation across markets. Duplicating operations across countries results in a high cost structure, limiting a firm's capacity to develop economies of scale in critical cost-focused operations. This fragmentation also limits a firm's ability to leverage expertise, innovations or resources across markets, with exchanges primarily being financial in nature. Finally the structure limits a firm's opportunity to develop advantages associated with flexibility from coordinating operations across markets.

Current debate on global operating structures

Thus, overall traditional structures for operating globally offer numerous benefits, but with severe constraints as well. The current debate on structuring decisions reflects this situation (Figure 7). Many firms, especially during the initial stage of building international operations, elect either the centralized or decentralized structures. While often effective during the value-leveraging stage of development, these single-minded approaches to structure often result in frequent reorganizations.

Both structures focus on some strategic advantages at the cost of others, essentially focusing the organization on the primary challenges or opportunities a firm faces at any time. As the mix of these challenges and opportunities changes, many firms have been found to respond by undergoing frequent reorganizations, moving between product and geographic structures. Other firms respond to growing strategic complexity by introducing a matrix structure. However, for many firms, matrices have been associated with bureaucratic conflict and power struggles.

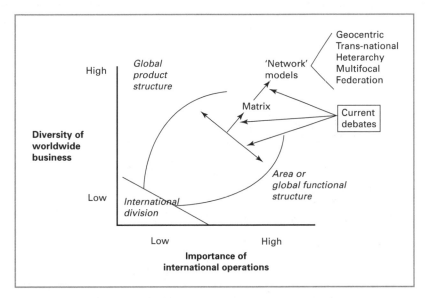

Figure 7 Debate on patterns of organizational evolution, including the emergence of potential new organizational models

Adapted from Stopford and Wells (1972) with the permission of Perseus Books, from *Managing the Multinational Enterprise* by Stopford, John M. & Wells, L.T., Basic Books, New York.

A further option under development at many firms involves the introduction of fundamental new approaches to structuring and managing worldwide operations. These emerging structures are associated with leveraging the advantages of a firm's network of operations, and are often associated with new strategic challenges and opportunities from operating globally that will be described in the section on value-creating global strategies.

Emerging challenges and opportunities in operating globally: value-creating strategies and organizations

Today many firms – large and small – compete globally with established networks of worldwide operations. These networks include both operations owned and operated by the firm, as well as strategic alliances and other partner firms. The opportunities associated with operating an established network of operations extend beyond those reflected in value-leveraging strategies. But also so do the challenges

(Figure 8). Today many firms globally perform a series of *functions* to produce multiple *products* with operations spanning multiple *geographic markets* and serving the needs of different *customer* types. There are strategic and organizational pressures and opportunities across each of these dimensions of a firm's operations: today, firms simultaneously face pressures to develop leading edge functional skills, to develop and manage expertise and operating scale within and across major product areas, to develop and leverage expertise within major geographic markets, and to develop the capacity to serve a wide range of customers. For many firms, the need to *simultaneously* pursue each of these objectives has become critical, directly impacting their strategies and structures for operating globally.

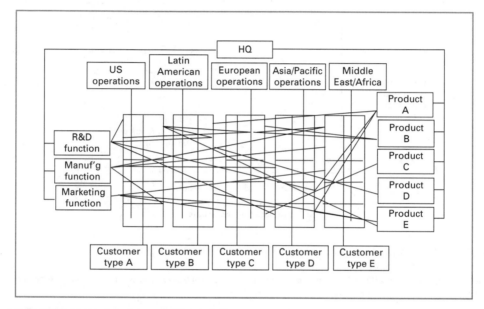

Figure 8 Emerging strategic and organizational challenges

In this increasingly complex global competitive environment, there is a fundamental transition taking place in the way companies of all sizes need to think about their strategies and organizations for operating globally. Moving beyond value-leveraging strategies and centralized or decentralized structures, firms are compelled to take new approaches to operating globally. This new approach involves shifting focus from not just *where* a firm operates and sell its products, but also *how* it structures and manages all of its worldwide operations to capture and create value across all activities. *The strategic pressures and opportunities for firms operating globally, both through their internal operations and through external partners, are accelerating over time.*

Building and managing process networks

In addressing strategies and structures for effectively competing globally today, companies have moved beyond looking for a single global strategy and structure for all their operations, and are rather focusing on discrete *processes* that cumulatively result in a firm developing, producing and supplying products to markets. Processes involve multiple operations that combine to perform a series of tasks or activities that create something of value (an 'output'). Processes are distinguished to divide the overall industry value chain based on variations in the nature of work performed and objectives pursued.

A typical process flow (Figure 9) within many industries involves *creating*, *developing*, *making* and *selling* products or services. Each process can involve either individual or multiple functions, can impact individual or multiple products, can impact multiple types of customers, and can involve individual or multiple geographic markets. Both vertically integrated and specialized firms typically perform processes. In the pharmaceutical industry, for example, the drug discovery process (creating new compounds) is performed not only by integrated pharmaceutical firms, but also by specialized (e.g., biotechnology) firms, research institutes, and universities. Overall, focusing on processes involves taking a managerial approach to global strategies and structures, by focusing on patterns of variations in objectives and tasks within and across firms in an industry. *Firm competitive advantage is based on building and integrating effective process strategies and structures.*

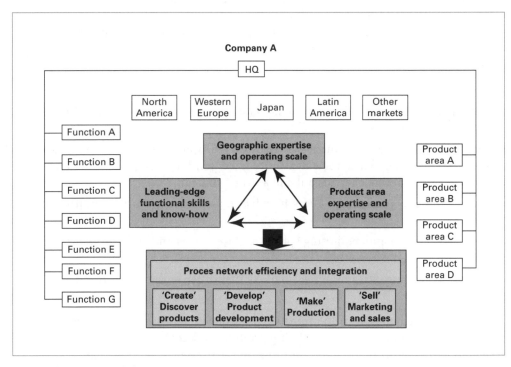

Figure 9 Typical process chain

For building and managing effective process networks, firm management should ask three questions:

- *What* are our overall strategic objectives and how can we enhance these objectives based on operating globally?

- How can we enhance our overall competitive advantage based on *where* we should perform each operation, including how each process enhances our performance?
- How can we enhance our overall competitive advantage based on *how* we coordinate, integrate and manage both within and across processes to capture value?

Value-creating strategies: from strategic trade-offs to managing strategic tensions

As we have seen, one important limitation of traditional global strategies is that they involve trading off one set of strategic objectives for another. In the most basic sense, centralized strategies optimized value and efficiency in standardized products at the expense of local responsiveness and flexibility. Decentralized strategies focused primarily on local responsiveness and flexibility. As described earlier, there is an expanding array of potential strategic advantages associated with operating globally. The challenge facing management today is to focus simultaneously on multiple and often conflicting strategic objectives. For example, increasingly firms need to be efficient, flexible, responsive and innovative all at the same time.

Operating a global network of operations opens up a host of additional strategic opportunities for established multinationals. Some additional potential advantages include:

- serving the worldwide needs of customers;
- anticipating and responding to the movements of global competitors within and across national markets;
- locating facilities or sourcing materials from multiple locations, not only to lower costs but also to enhance their flexibility to respond to changes in foreign exchange rates or other market changes outside a firm's control;
- innovating new products or know-how based on their exposure to multiple national markets;
- gaining access to and exploiting specialized resources and skills from around the world;
- balancing revenue streams across markets that differ in their growth rates or risk profiles.

Reflecting these emerging opportunities, the strategic motivations for operating globally extend beyond leveraging existing products or know-how across national markets, to *value-creating* strategies building on the existence and management of a worldwide network of operations. *Value-creating strategies focus not only on enhancing the strength of each operations, which are increasingly dispersed globally, but also the ability to create and manage expanding flows and exchanges across these operations* (Figure 10). In other words, being global offers an expanding array of opportunities for enhancing firm's competitive advantage based on leveraging the global network of operations.

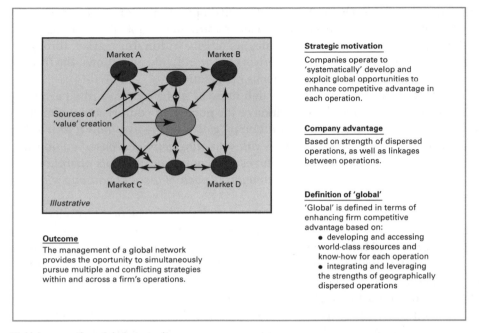

Strategic motivation

Companies operate to 'systematically' develop and exploit global opportunities to enhance competitive advantage in each operation.

Company advantage

Based on strength of dispersed operations, as well as linkages between operations.

Definition of 'global'

'Global' is defined in terms of enhancing firm competitive advantage based on:
- developing and accessing world-class resources and know-how for each operation
- integrating and leveraging the strengths of geographically dispersed operations

Outcome

The management of a global network provides the oportunity to simultaneously pursue multiple and conflicting strategies within and across a firm's operations.

Figure 10 Value-creating global strategies

In terms of moving beyond strategic trade-offs to pursuing multiple objectives simultaneously, the company needs to ask what its overall strategic challenges are both as a firm and for each process. What is happening in the environment? What are my objectives? What are the processes and challenges that I am facing across different parts of the business and what are the tensions that I am going to focus on? Then, once those tensions have been identified, the company can look at what kind of organizational structure is needed in terms of products, functions and geographies to make the most of each particular business stream, including the roles and responsibilities each part should play in pursuing these objectives.

Process networks focus on creating and capturing value based on advantages derived not just from the centre but from the strength of each dispersed operation and, importantly, the *linkages* between the process networks. As a result, these networks offer an effective potential mechanism for moving beyond single strategic objectives and the traditional approach of trading off some advantages against others. Within network approaches, different nodes or operations can focus on different and distinct potential strategic advantages offering the firm the potential to pursue multiple and often conflicting objectives simultaneously.

The emergence of a value-creating approach to operating means that traditional measures of the 'globality' of firms may no longer be appropriate. Can we consider a company to be global if, although a large percentage of its sales are 'international', the primary source of its value creation resides in a single home-market driven brand, with an assumption that as long as the world wants to consume this existing brand growth opportunities continue? Or are there fundamental opportunities for value creation that this firm is missing? Likewise, can we consider a firm to be 'global' if, although it has operations only in one market and its sales are largely within this market, through linkages to other firms, with existing networks of worldwide operations, the firm captures the value associated with its focus of operations?

Within this perspective, an effective definition of 'globality' has shifted away from the percentage of sales outside a home market or the number of countries in which a firm operates. *Increasingly an effective definition of 'globality' involves how a firm enhances its overall competitive position, in all its value-creating activities, based on how it develops and accesses world-class resources and know-how for all its operations, as well as how it integrates and leverages the strengths of each of these operations within and across world markets.*

The limitations of traditional definitions of 'globality' can be demonstrated by the recent comments of a senior executive of a leading US pharmaceutical company. This executive commented that the company was witnessing 'reverse globalization' as sales and profit growth were increasingly driven by the company's home market. But what this executive had not considered was that the new products behind the company's success had been discovered using *worldwide* information and laboratories, had been rapidly developed and launched by using *worldwide* markets for rapid approval, and were produced in multiple worldwide locations to enhance tax and other cost considerations. So even though sales were accruing in the US, the company had enhanced its overall competitive advantage by operating around the world.

Strategic and organizational challenges in the pharmaceutical industry

The world market for pharmaceuticals, which totalled $303 billion in 1997, has long been considered attractive and highly profitable, with the average profit margin of the ten largest pharmaceutical companies being 30 per cent in 1997. Competing in this industry, integrated pharmaceutical companies discover, develop, manufacture and sell products. Discovery involves chemical, biological and pharmacological activities to identify and synthesize new compounds for the potential treatment of various diseases or medical conditions. The resulting 'lead compounds' are tested to investigate efficacy, toxicity and potential side effects, and subsequently studied through a series of clinical trials as part of receiving regulatory approval. Data from all trials are included in a New Drug Application (NDA) that is submitted to regulatory officials. It has been estimated that for every 5000 to 10 000 compounds initially evaluated in laboratories one product is approved.

A series of new technologies have been fundamentally altering the drug discovery and development process, suggesting the potential for continued growth of the industry. These technologies include genomics (study of the way that genes interact to impact human development, health and sickness), combinatorial chemistry (combining known molecular building blocks to quickly create gigantic libraries of compounds for screening), high-throughput screening (robotic techniques for testing drug candidates against biological targets) and bio-informatics (using computers to collect and store huge volumes of data generated by biomedical research). These advances are expected to lead to an increasing flow of new product candidates, with one industry expert in the late 1990s commenting, 'More drugs will be discovered in the next 10 years than have been discovered in the last 100 years.'

Industry challenges

At the same time, a number of trends are challenging the traditional structure and profitability of the industry. These pressures are associated with rising R&D costs, lengthening development and approval times for new products, growing competition from generics and follow-on products, and rising cost containment pressures. Pharmaceutical companies spend about 20% of sales on R&D, and the cost of developing new products has skyrocketed. A 1992 study by the US Office of Technology Assessment estimated the pretax cost of a single new drug at $359 million, compared with $231 million in the late 1980s and $125 million in the early 1980s. Subsequent studies have estimated these development costs for a new drug at between $350 and $500 million.

Simultaneous with escalating costs has been a lengthening of the time required for development and regulatory approval. New regulations have increased the average time for obtaining regulatory approval in the United States to 8 to 10 years. Given the fixed patent life for products[1], these increases have had a direct impact on a product's effective patent life, the period in which the patent holder has enjoyed market exclusivity.

Once new products are launched, further pressures result from the growth of so-called 'follow-on' products and generics. Follow-on products result from the incredibly rapid exchanges of information and the increasing focus of pharmaceutical research on common therapeutic indications and disease pathways. Following the expiration of a product patent, pressures result from the rapid entry of generic products. According to industry sources, it is not unusual for sales of a drug to drop by more than 50 per cent in the first year after patent expiration as a result of generic competition, and they continue to decline rapidly thereafter.

Finally, health-care expenditures represent a large and growing portion of the gross domestic product (GDP) of most major markets, resulting in growing cost containment efforts in most world markets. Examples of cost-control mechanisms have included reference pricing (establishing a fixed reimbursement based on therapeutic equivalence) and establishing budgets for individual physicians. In the United States, managed-care organizations and government national insurance programs (e.g., Medicare) increasingly emphasize total cost management.

Cumulatively these trends pressure pharmaceutical firms to innovate in developing a continual flow of new products, to speed the development and launch of new products, to improve the cost efficiency of all operations, and to be aggressive in selling products to major world markets. These challenges and opportunities directly affected how pharmaceutical firms operate globally.

---

[1] US manufacturers typically file a patent application when submitting an Investigational New Drug (IND) application, protecting themselves for 17 years from the date the patent was actually issued.

Process-level global strategies and organizations

This section examines the global strategic and organizational challenges facing pharmaceutical companies, focusing on the processes of discovering new compounds, developing and launching these products, and marketing and selling these products within world markets. (The processes associated with producing and supplying the products are not addressed.) Each of these processes involves multiple functional-, geographic-, and product-focused units.

The challenges facing pharmaceutical companies in *discovering new products* have reflected the need to ensure a continual flow of innovative new potential products (Figure 11). Operating globally has offered a number of potential opportunities to enhance these processes. Generally there are three different types of units involved in the discovery process: therapeutic area units responsible for overall innovation within a product area, functional units that provide common technologies and supporting tools to all research efforts, and research laboratories that may perform research activities for multiple therapeutic areas. Companies enhance their potential for innovation by accessing the best scientists, irrespective of national origin or geographic location, to oversee research efforts in each therapeutic area in which it operates. At the same time, research is conducted in pharmaceutical and biotechnology companies, universities and research laboratories around the world. In order to enhance innovation, companies need to access leading-edge knowledge and expertise, not just that located in their home country. Finally given the rising investment costs in supporting technologies and research tools, companies need to develop and leverage growing investments in these tools.

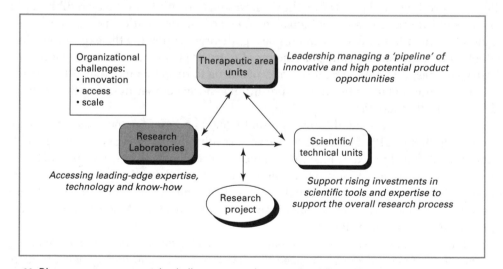

Figure 11 Discovery process strategic challenges: ensuring a continual flow of innovative new potential compounds

The overall challenges facing pharmaceutical companies in the *development process*, associated with obtaining regulatory approval for new products, involve increasing the speed of securing regulatory approval and launching new products in the world market (Figure 12). According to one industry estimate, each year that the development time of an average product can be shortened results in an additional cash flow of $150 million. For 'blockbuster' products, these gains in incremental cash flow could be substantially higher, reflecting both incremental patent-protected sales revenue and opportunities associated with beating competitive products to market.

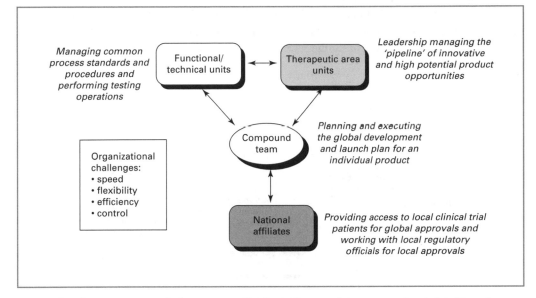

Figure 12 Development process challenges: speeding the testing, regulatory approval and global launch of new products

Global opportunities for speeding the development and launch include accessing a larger number of clinical trial patients and leveraging regulatory variations across markets. For example, in some markets there are regulatory waiting periods for conducting some tests that can delay the development process by one or more months. Operating globally can allow a company to continue working on development testing, without compromising quality standards or procedures, by globally allocating these testing requirements. Similarly it is possible to more quickly access a large number of patients working across world markets, as opposed to duplicating the trials within each market or within a single market. Securing these benefits requires the standardization of testing procedures and standards, at the most stringent levels, to share the resulting data across markets.

Organizationally there are four types of units active in the development process. Functional and testing units (toxicology, etc.) establish and manage global development standards and procedures for all trials, as well as providing technical expertise to product teams, and performing testing and supporting services as required for the development of individual compounds. Therapeutic area units manage the overall development portfolio of the products under development in any area. Product-focused (cross-functional) teams are responsible for planning and executing the rapid global development and launch of new products across world markets. National affiliates are responsible for securing, as requested by the product teams, clinical trial patients for different products under development, as well as working with local regulatory officials to secure national approvals.

The process of *marketing and selling* pharmaceutical products globally also faces conflicting global strategic pressures and opportunities (Figure 13). On the one hand, pharmaceutical companies face pressures to maximize the returns on new products within a fixed, but shortened product patent-protected marketing periods. On the other hand, companies face pressure to maximize the returns on their portfolio of products within national markets that can vary significantly in local market characteristics (e.g., medical care systems, etc.). Maximizing global product returns and national product portfolio returns is a classic challenge facing companies in many industries.

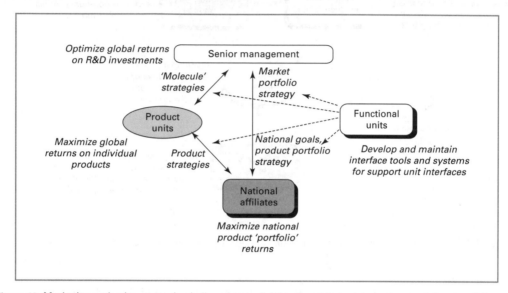

Figure 13 Marketing and sales strategic challenges: maximizing the global returns on new products and the local returns on the product portfolio

Organizationally there are several types of units involved in responding to these challenges. Senior management is responsible for ensuring the overall returns across products that vary in their life cycle and the potential across markets that vary in their characteristics. Product units focus on maximizing the returns on individual products (even though they do not 'own' the ultimate sales forces within the national affiliates), while national affiliates focus on maximizing the national returns on the company's total portfolio of products (even though they do not have critical expertise on individual products). Functional units play a critical role in developing the supporting interface systems for managing these interfaces. These include, for example, product strategy systems that support management in the evaluation of potential across products, as well as national market strategy systems that support the evaluation of differences in market opportunities in markets that vary in their characteristics.

These strategic challenges facing pharmaceutical companies vary dramatically across processes, and operating globally has a major impact on a company's ability to develop advantage in each process. Organizationally, however, the challenges involve developing multiple types of process networks within the firm, with each integrating the roles and contributions of multiple types of units and pursuing a mix of strategic objectives. Although the strategic and organizational challenges are severe, a company's ability to understand and respond to them will directly impact a firm's competitiveness. There is often a well known and common understanding across firms in terms of the challenges – often the issue is being able to effectively build, and establish and manage the organization.

Network structures: building efficient and effective process networks

Since the 1980s, many consultants and academics have developed a number of organizational models, accompanied by futuristic sounding names: heterarchy, transnational, multifocal, horizontal and federation, to name but a few. Most of these models have a few characteristics in common, suggesting approaches for managers to disperse their operations globally and manage expanding horizontal flows and exchanges of products, people, information and other resources. These models all build on the notion of the firm becoming a global network.

Overall the network approach calls on managers to look beyond transferring their traditional home-based products and know-how to worldwide markets. Instead, companies need to look to how they can enhance their ability to respond to growing competitive pressures by tapping into opportunities associated with value-creating global strategies, and then install organizations that optimize both their dispersed operations *and* the linkages between them. Structurally network challenges encompass two primary issues: *optimizing each operation for each task or activity and then managing and optimizing linkages between these operations.*

In terms of optimizing the performance of each unit within a firm's network of operations, process network structures dramatically increase the ability of managers to allocate flexibly roles and responsibilities globally. Some operations can be centralized at a single location, potentially at locations designed to enhance the performance of such operation. Other operations can be distributed across multiple locations, allowing managers to source flexibly from across these operations to respond to market changes outside its control (e.g., changes in foreign exchange rates). Other operations can be decentralized to serve the needs of local national markets.

These network configuration decisions involve a series of decisions by managers on how to structure the nodes of the network. These network configuration decisions include the following:

- location of worldwide facilities;
- roles of worldwide facilities;
- nature and extent of exchanges among worldwide facilities.

Subsequently the management of process networks often appears to be moving toward a loosely coupled organization that can be likened to a form of controlled anarchy. It can appear that each part of an organization in and of itself is strong but the linkages between them are also stronger across markets than they would be in more traditional models. An important shift has occurred in the notion of linkages between worldwide operations, moving from management and control toward alignment and integration, where the focus is on enhancing potential advantages of the entire network, as opposed to those of individual operations.

At the same time, increasingly, managers are recognizing a wide range of organizational variables that can be used to *align and integrate* worldwide operations, including the following:

- human resources, staff;
- reporting channels;
- decision authority allocation;
- management control systems;
- operating standards and procedures;
- planning and information systems;
- measurement and evaluation systems;
- corporate culture;
- informal communications and linkages.

Combinations of these organizational variables offer managers a wide range of structural alternatives. For example, for many processes, companies are centralizing operating standards and procedures (around best practices) and planning systems (to align and allocate activities globally), but employing dispersed operations with extensive decentralization of decision authority without defined boundaries. Is this centralized or decentralized? Other processes can be managed globally through decentralized operations, planning and decision making, but with a strong centralized culture and tight communication. Again, is this centralized. or decentralized? Managers today have a wide array of structural alternatives – between traditional centralized and decentralized structural approaches – to integrate and align worldwide operations.

Determining your Mix of Strategic Motivations for Operating Globally

As has been highlighted throughout this chapter, there is a wide and growing range of strategic opportunities for firms operating globally. Given the relationship between the strategic motivations for operating globally and the organizational challenges of doing so, it is important for executives to develop a clear understanding of their motivations and opportunities for operating globally across the different parts of their operations. To help determine the nature of opportunities facing your firm, the following list of opportunities can be used to understand the nature of the current potential global strategy, and thus the nature of your subsequent organizational challenges. In considering these opportunities, it is useful to consider these motivations at multiple levels, first at the level of the firm as a whole and then across your different functions, markets, and products or services.

Rank each motivation on a scale of 1 (low) to 5 (high)

Motivations for operating globally	*Rank*
Reducing costs	
• Reduce costs through increasing volume	_____
• Reduce costs through accessing low-cost labour	_____
• Access commodities or other standard inputs	_____
• Minimize logistics costs	_____
Expanding sales	_____
• Access new markets for existing products	_____
• Meet unique local market requirements and build strong local relations	_____
• Build presence in established and emerging markets	_____
Average value-leveraging objectives	
Enhancing operations, accessing specialized resources	
• Access skilled labour resources or professional staff	_____
• Access unique or specialized technologies	_____
• Access other unique specialized resources or inputs	_____
Leveraging a global network	_____
• Enabling flexibility to shift operations (e.g., production) among dispersed facilities	_____
• Innovate products or processes by operating across multiple markets	_____
• Speed development and launch of new products	_____
• Serving the worldwide needs of customers	_____
• Optimizing regulatory variations across markets	_____
• Enhancing the ability to anticipate and respond to global competitors	_____
Average value-creating objectives	_____

The more your motivations for operating globally across your operations (at the level of the firm, functions, markets and product) are associated with value-leveraging objectives, the more your organizational choices should likely be between the traditional centralized or decentralized structure. However, if your motivations are increasingly associated with value-creating objectives, the more the nature of your organizational challenges should involve introducing and managing global network-type structures.

Emerging management challenges: building and integrating process networks

Within individual firms today, there are multiple types of networks emerging that can directly enhance firm's competitive advantage. Some of these networks focus on accessing and leveraging knowledge and information, others on building and leveraging common data and information, and others on leveraging common facilities globally. Table 2 provides examples of the overall characteristics of these various types of networks.

Overall, management challenges today involve building and managing effective process networks, as well as sharing resources and integrating across process networks. In the pharmaceutical industry, firm competitive advantage is based on firms developing effective process networks to discover new compounds, develop and launch new products and produce, market and sell these products in worldwide markets. There is extensive sharing of resources across each of these processes, and management of each process is dependent on the inputs (requirements) and outputs of other processes.

	Knowledge-sharing networks	Data-sharing networks	Facility-sharing networks
Global dispersion of operations: responsibility and location	Global product structure	Global process structure	Global functional structure
	Dispersed global product-area responsibility for process output	Dispersed global product-specific responsibility for process output	Single unit with global process responsibility for all operations
	Dispersed and specialized operational facilities	Dispersed and duplicated operations for undertaking common activities within markets	Dispersed and specialized facilities with global-product type responsibility.
Cross-unit interdependence: exchanges and flows	Exchanges of know-how and expertise	Exchanges of data and know-how for individual products	Primary flows of intermediate products to global markets
	Global sharing of technology 'tools' across units	Operations aligned through common operating standards and procedures to ensure global process consistency	Operational planning integrated through technical and operating standards focused on worldwide requirements
	Operations coordinated within overall corporate strategy		
Structural flexibility: structures and linkages	Primary operational and budget flexibility within global product-area units	Primary operational and budget flexibility within product-specific teams	Primary flexibility within global functional unit
	Focus on identifying and sharing innovations arising globally and across centres	Focus on identifying and sharing of information and expertise for individual compounds	Sharing of best practices for common tasks across facilities
	Internal 'contracting' system for cost transfers	Internal 'contracting' system for cost transfers	Internal 'contracting' through transfer price systems

Table 2 Structural characteristics of a sample network-based multinational

Summary

This chapter has addressed the movement from value-leveraging toward value-creating global strategies, and the associated movement from traditional centralized or decentralized structures toward network-type structures. More and more firms have to build an effective global network that will be able to deal with and manage the multiple and conflicting objectives of being efficient, flexible, innovative and responsive – *at the same time* – and be global, regional and local – *at the same time.*

It will be based on answering questions such as:

- What is the objective of each process network across our overall value-creating activities?
- What tensions is it trying to manage?
- What different units need to be involved, both internally and externally?
- What kind of organization are we trying to create?
- What are the roles and responsibilities across the different units?
- What kind of mechanisms can we develop for both formal and informal linkages?
- How can I do this quickly?

Building and optimizing these process networks obviously require moving beyond incremental change to fundamental strategic and organizational design. Firms do not have the luxury of evolving this structure over a period of years;. they need to move toward an optimum position for value creation as quickly as possible.

Networks are not for every company and they can also be organizationally costly to set up and run. So if you are simple, stay simple. But if your firm faces increasing external pressures along functional, product and geographic positions, has growing needs to share resources across businesses, and has pressures to improve flexibility and response time to market opportunities, then installing and managing a network-type approach arc critical to a firm's overall competitive strategy, not just its global one.

Learning points

- Traditional strategies for international expansion are no longer effective in an environment of increasing complexity and speed.
- Firms now have to look beyond a single global strategy and structure, whether centralized or decentralized, to create new sources of value.
- In this process-based approach, firms should determine how to enhance their strategic objectives in terms of *where* they perform each operation and *how* they coordinate, integrate and manage both within and across processes to capture value.
- Network structures offer value-creating opportunities based not just on the centre and the strength of the dispersed operations, but on the linkages between them.

- This begins to shift the way firms oversee dispersed operations, from management and control towards alignment and integration, to enhance the potential advantages of the entire network.
- The challenge is to focus on multiple and often conflicting strategic objectives in the search for efficiency, flexibility, responsiveness and innovation – at the same time.

References

Bartlett, C.A. and Ghoshal, S. (1989) *Managing Across Borders: The Transnational Solution,* Harvard Business School Press, Boston.

Perlmutter, H.V. (1969) The Tortuous Evolution of the Multinational Corporation. *Columbia Journal of World Business,* January–February, pp. 9–18.

Prahalad, C.K. and Doz, Y. (1987) *The Multinational Mission: Balancing Local Demands and Global Vision,* The Free Press, New York.

Stopford, J.M. and Wells, L.T. (1972) *Managing the Multinational Enterprise,* Basic Books, New York.

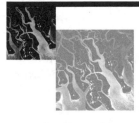

READING 6
Causes of failure in network organizations*

Raymond E. Miles and Charles C. Snow

It is widely recognized that we are in the midst of an organizational revolution. Throughout the 1980s, organizations around the world responded to an increasingly competitive global business environment by moving away from centrally coordinated, multi-level hierarchies and toward a variety of more flexible structures that closely resembled networks rather than traditional pyramids. These networks – clusters of firms or specialist units coordinated by market mechanisms instead of chains of commands – are viewed by both their members and management scholars as better suited than other forms to many of today's demanding environments.[1]

However, despite the current success of network organizations, the most likely forecast is that their effectiveness will decline rather than improve over time, In fact, there is already evidence of deterioration in some network organizations – failures caused not by the inappropriateness of the network form but because of managerial mistakes in designing or operating it.

Indeed, the evolution of the network form of organization appears to be following a familiar pattern. Historically, new organizational forms arise to correct the principal deficiencies of the form(s) currently in use. As environmental changes accumulate, existing organizational forms become less and less capable of meeting the demands placed on them. Managers begin to experiment with new approaches and eventually arrive at a more effective way of arranging and coordinating resources. The managers who pioneer the new organizational form understand its logic and are well aware of its particular strengths and weaknesses. However, as the use of the new form increases, so too does the potential for its misuse. When design and operating flaws multiply, the form loses its vitality and begins to fail.

The evolution of the network form

Over the course of American business history, four broad forms of organization have emerged. First, the *functional organization* appeared in the late nineteenth century and flourished in the early part of the twentieth. This new organizational form allowed many firms to achieve the necessary size and efficiency to provide products and services to a growing domestic market. An early vertically integrated functional organization was designed by Andrew Carnegie who applied ideas about functional specialization from the

* *California Management Review*, Summer 1992.

Copyright © 1992, by The Regents of the University of California. Reprinted from the *California Management Review*, Vol. 34, No. 4. By permission of The Regents.

railroads to steel production. By controlling both raw materials supplies and distribution, he was able to keep his mills running efficiently on a tightly planned schedule. A current example of the functional organization is Wal-Mart, Inc., one of the nation's largest retailers. Across the country, Wal-Mart focuses on a well-defined and socio-economically homogeneous target market as it locates its stores in small towns and suburbs of medium-sized cities. For these highly similar markets, Wal-Mart makes maximum use of on-line computerized sales data from over 1,200 stores to feed what is recognized as one of the most efficient inventory and distribution systems in the country. Like its functional predecessors, Wal-Mart performs a limited set of functions extremely well, using the specialized talents of planners, logistics specialists, and store personnel. However, while Wal-Mart is tightly integrated from its warehouses through its store shelves, the company does not attempt to actually produce the goods it sells. Nevertheless, because of its buying power, Wal-Mart can centrally coordinate an army of suppliers eager to respond to its forecasts and schedules.

Next, the *divisionalized organization* appeared shortly after the end of World War I and spread rapidly in the late 1940s and into the 1950s. Among the earliest divisionalized structures was that designed by Alfred Sloan at General Motors, where specific automobile brands and models were aimed at distinct markets differentiated primarily by price. Product divisions (Chevrolet, Pontiac, Cadillac, etc.) operated as nearly autonomous companies, producing and marketing products to their respective targeted customers while corporate management served as an investment banker for growth and redirection. A modern divisionalized firm is Rubbermaid, whose ten operating divisions account for over 200 new products a year. Each division has its own target market and its own R&D team focused exclusively on that market, allowing maximum responsiveness in a diversified product arena.[2]

The third organizational form was the *matrix*, which evolved in the 1960s and the 1970s, and combined elements of both the functional and divisional forms. An early matrix structure was created at TRW, which sought to make both efficient use of specialized engineers and scientists while adapting to a wide range of new product and project demands. Technical and professional personnel moved back and forth from functional departments to product or project teams, and from one team to another, as their skills were needed. Many modern matrix organizations are even more complex, such as the one used by Matsushita, which combines global product divisions with geographically based marketing groups.

Movement toward the *network* form became apparent in the 1980s, when international competition and rapid technological change forced massive restructuring across U.S. industries and companies. Established firms downsized to their core competence, de-layering management hierarchies and outsourcing a wide range of activities. New firms eschewed growth through vertical integration and instead sought alliances with independent suppliers and/or distributors.

Within this general trend toward disaggregation and looser coupling, managers experimented with various organizational arrangements. Instead of using plans, schedules, and transfer prices to coordinate internal units, they turned to contracts and other exchange agreements to link together external components into various types of network structures.[3] As illustrated in Figure 1, some networks brought suppliers, producers, and distributors together in long-term stable relationships. Other networks

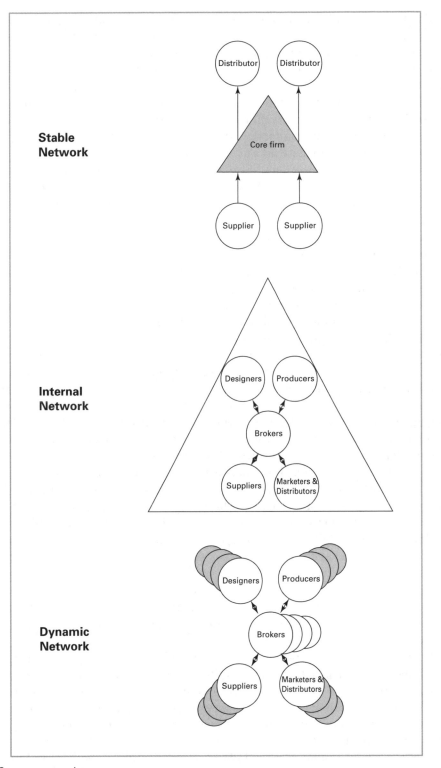

Figure 1 Common network types

were much more dynamic, with components along the value chain coupled contractually for perhaps a single project or product and then decoupled to be part of a new value chain for the next business venture. Finally, inside some large firms, internal networks appeared as managers sought to achieve market benefits by having divisions buy and sell outside the firm as well as within.[4]

Network organizations are different from previous organizations in several respects. First, over the past several decades, firms using older structures preferred to hold in-house (or under exclusive contract) all the assets required to produce a given product or service. In contrast, many networks use the collective assets of several firms located at various points along the value chain.[5] Second, networks rely more on market mechanisms than administrative processes to manage resource flows. However, these mechanisms are not the simple 'arm's length' relationships usually associated with independently owned economic entities. Rather, the various components of the network recognize their interdependence and are willing to share information, cooperate with each other, and customize their product or service – all to maintain their position within the network. Third, while networks of subcontractors have been commonplace in the construction industry, many recently designed networks expect a more proactive role among participants – voluntary behavior that improves the final product or service rather than simply fulfills a contractual obligation. Finally, in an increasing number of industries, including computers, semiconductors, autos, farm implements, and motorcycles, networks are evolving that possess characteristics similar in part to the Japanese *keiretsu* – an organizational collective based on cooperation and mutual shareholding among a group of manufacturers, suppliers, and trading and finance companies.[6]

Although the network organization exhibits characteristics that are different from previous forms, the stable, dynamic, and internal networks shown in Figure 1 nevertheless incorporate elements of the prior organizational forms as their main building blocks. For example, a functionally organized firm may realize that it needs to outsource the manufacture of certain components, or ally with specific distributors, in order to focus its attention only on those operating activities for which it is best equipped. The result of such changes is a stable network organization: a core firm linked forward and backward to a limited number of carefully selected partners. Upstream stable networks linking suppliers to a core firm are common in the automobile industry. Downstream networks often link computer hardware manufacturers and value-added retailers.

Alternatively, a large multinational matrix organization made up of various design, manufacturing, and distribution units, may decide to replace centrally determined transfer prices with genuine buying and selling relationships among these units. The result is an internal network.[7]

Lastly, in some industries, rapid technological and market changes may encourage a divisionalized firm to disassemble into a multi-player dynamic network of designers, suppliers, producers, and distributors instead of holding all of these assets internally. This is what has occurred over the past twenty years in most publishing firms.

In sum, the network organization in its several variations has sought to incorporate the specialized efficiency of the functional organization, the autonomous operating effectiveness of the divisional form, and the asset-transferring capabilities of the matrix organization – all with considerable success. However, the network form itself has inherent limitations and is vulnerable to misapplication and misuse. To understand the real and potential weaknesses of the network, we need to examine the problems that have plagued (and continue to befall) its predecessor forms.

Causes of failure in earlier organizational forms

As noted above, a similar evolutionary pattern can be seen in each of the earlier organizational forms. Widespread initial success occurred as the new form provided an innovative arrangement of a firm's resources and a new operating logic responsive to the emerging environment. However, a growing list of failures eventually followed. Some of the causes of failure were obvious – for example, the new form was increasingly, perhaps faddishly, applied in settings for which it was never intended or suited.

The more intriguing failures are those that arise from two types of subtle managerial 'mistakes': individually logical *extensions* of the form which in the aggregate push the form beyond the limits of its capability; and *modifications* of the form which, while reasonable on the surface, nevertheless violate the form's operating logic. To fully understand these causes of failure, it is necessary to first restate the logic of the functional, divisional, and matrix forms and then examine major types of preventable failures against that logic. (See Table 1.)

The functional form

The functional form of organization can be thought of as a special-purpose machine designed to produce a limited line of goods or services in large volume and at low cost. The logic of the functional form is *centrally coordinated specialization*. Departments, each staffed with specialized experts in numbers established by a central budget, repeatedly make their contribution to the firm's overall effort in accordance with a common schedule. To be successful, the functional form's specialized skills and equipment must be fully and predictably operated. Firms in the late nineteenth and early twentieth century frequently integrated forward, creating new wholesaling and retailing channels to assure that their output could be efficiently distributed and sold. Similarly, these firms often integrated backward to assure themselves the steady flow of materials and components essential to efficient operation. Today's functional paragons, such as Wal-Mart, are masters at obtaining these kinds of efficiencies, but typically they are not as vertically integrated.

Although vertical integration assures functionally structured firms input and output predictability, it does not come without costs. The further backward and forward a firm integrates, the greater the costs of coordination and the larger the number of specialized assets demanding full utilization. Ultimately, it becomes difficult to determine whether any particular asset along the value chain is making a positive contribution to overall profitability. In fact, the recent trend toward disaggregation (e.g., buying rather than making components, outsourcing sales or distribution) reflects the recognition by many firms that coordination costs and asset underutilization are offsetting the benefits of predictability and hierarchical control.

An example that illustrates these tradeoffs involves the turnaround efforts made at Harley-Davidson in the early 1980s. The motorcycle manufacturer discovered that much of its production inflexibility, along with excessive costs, was caused by attempting to produce virtually all of its own parts and components. A move to a just-in-time inventory system allowed Harley-Davidson to outsource many parts and supplies, reducing its total cycle time and bringing new products to the market quicker while lowering overall costs. What is interesting about organizational 'failures' such as that at Harley-Davidson is that managers need not do anything wrong – at Harley, the company's functional structure encouraged internal production of parts and components to assure control. Rather, such systems often fail because managers do too many things right![8]

Alternatively, the functional organization form will also fail if it is modified inappropriately. The functional organization's logic of centrally controlled, specialized assets does not easily adapt to product or service diversity. A functionally structured manufacturing firm can efficiently produce a limited array of products if demand for the various products can be forecast and productions runs strictly scheduled. However, if the number of products offered becomes too large, or if demand variations interfere with efficient scheduling, the functional form begins to prove inflexible and costly to operate.

Organizational form	Functional	Divisional	Matrix
Primary Application	Efficient production of standardized goods and services	Related diversification by product or region	Shared assets between standardized products and prototype contracts (e.g., many aerospace firms)
			Shared assets between worldwide product divisions and country-based marketing divisions (e.g., some global firms)
Extension Failure	Vertical integration beyond capacity to keep specialized assets fully loaded and/or to evaluate contributions	Diversification (or acquisitions) outside area of technical and evaluative expertise	Expanding number of temporary contracts beyond ability of allocation mechanisms
			Search for global synergy limits local adaptability
Modification Failure	Product or service diversification that overloads central planning mechanisms	Corporate Interventions to force coordination or obtain efficiencies across divisions	Modifications that distort the dual focus (i.e., favor one type of market or product over another)

Table 1 Causes of failure in traditional organizational forms

For example, after World War II, the Chrysler Corporation rapidly expanded its product line in an attempt to match General Motors' strategy of a 'product for every pocketbook.' However, while its models proliferated (actually exceeding the number of GM models at one point), Chrysler did not adopt the divisional structure then used by its competitors. Chrysler's mostly functional structure ultimately suffered from losses in efficiency and from added coordination costs as the company attempted to accommodate increasing product variability and complexity. Here, managers modified key aspects of Chrysler's functional structure for apparently logical reasons, moves that probably were initially successful. However, an eventual array of over seventy different models demanded not just continued structural modification but total restructure – the adoption of a new (the divisional) form.

The divisional form

The divisional form of organization can be thought of as a collection of similar special-purpose machines, each independently operated to serve a particular market and all evaluated centrally on the basis of economic performance for possible expansion, contraction, or redirection. The operating logic of the divisional form is thus *the coupling of divisional autonomy with centrally controlled performance evaluation and resource allocation.* The divisional form achieves both flexibility and economies of scope by its ability to rapidly focus clusters of assets on new or expanding markets. It develops a unique competence for evaluating divisional performance in a given set of related markets and for investing pooled returns to promote growth in existing divisions and to create or acquire new divisions. The divisional form also may develop mechanisms for transferring new technology and managerial knowhow across divisions as well as to newly created or acquired operations. Overall, the divisional form's ability to reallocate management knowhow and emerging technology, along with resources generated from existing operations, gives it an advantage in responding to new opportunities and in the cost of startup.

Markets for differentiated goods and services grew rapidly in the 1920s and again after World War II. As described above, the early divisionalized organization at General Motors focused different automobile models on distinct markets, differentiated primarily by price. Similarly, Du Pont identified different types of markets in which its several divisions could use their technical and managerial knowhow in applied chemistry, and Sears Roebuck challenged managers across the country to independently operate 'hometown stores with nationwide buying power.'

Although divisionalized firms are adept at moving incrementally into related areas, they are also vulnerable to overextension. Most divisionalized firms have had the experience of moving into markets that initially appeared to be appropriate but ultimately turned out to fall outside their area of expertise. Entry into unrelated markets weakens the divisionalized firm's ability to appraise performance and make investment decisions. As the firm moves further away from its unique informational base, its decisions become no more efficient, perhaps even less so, than those the market might make. For example, General Mills, a highly successful divisionalized firm, at least twice extended itself into areas that proved to be beyond its zone of technical and investment expertise, first into electrical appliances and later into toys and fashion goods. In both cases, the firm recognized its own shortcomings and either divested the divisions or moved back from direct operation.[9]

Divisionalized firms are also vulnerable to modifications that begin with good reason but subsequently undermine the form's operating logic. For example, the creation of cross-division committees to share technology, or the creation of a corporate staff group to help coordinate process improvements, may genuinely prove valuable. However, excessive coordination requirements across divisions eventually constrain the divisions' flexibility to meet the demands of their respective markets. Similarly, corporate staff enforcement of interdivisional planning gradually undermines corporate management's ability to accurately assess the individual effectiveness of each division. Both types of modification, though successful when carefully applied, may expand until they violate the logic of divisional independence and corporate appraisal. Just such extensive coordination requirements constrained, in fact destroyed, the operating autonomy of the separate automobile divisions of General Motors. Initially, in a period of weak competition, the firm enjoyed cross-divisional scale economies without major losses from decreased flexibility and responsiveness. However, under growing competition, GM's complex, interdivisional planning process delayed new product development, and its intrusive coordination mechanisms contributed to unit costs above those of its competition. Most recently, in order to produce a 'truly new' car (Saturn), GM had to circumvent its own convoluted structure by creating an entirely new division.

Clearly, in a divisionalized firm, broad operating freedom creates the opportunity for divisions to suboptimize – to take actions that improve their own profitability at the expense of possible overall corporate gains. However, such possibilities are simply part of the normal costs of using the divisional form, offset in the longer run by the benefits gained from well-made local decisions. Unfortunately, fewer and fewer firms today appear to be willing to leave the logic of the divisional form intact. Indeed. many firms that refer to themselves as divisionalized in fact have extensive corporate staff coordination and minimal divisional autonomy. Such operations actually produce all the costs and rigidity of the functional form while adding the cost of divisional duplication of resources. Again, individually sound decisions may add up to overall operating inefficiencies and ineffectiveness.

The matrix form

The matrix organizational form can be thought of as a complex machine simultaneously generating two or more outputs for a set of both stable and changing markets. The operating logic of the stable portion of the matrix form is similar to that of the functional form, centrally coordinated specialization. Not surprisingly, the portion responding to unique or changeable markets emphasizes local operating autonomy as is the case in the divisional form. To these dual aspects of its operating logic, the matrix form adds the requirement for *balance among the components to produce mutually beneficial allocations of resources.*

For example, in one type of matrix, an aerospace firm may fulfill a number of long-term contracts to produce a line of standard products in the functionally structured, stable portion of the organization. Simultaneously, the firm may group a series of project teams around contracts for customized products or prototypes. In this type of matrix, the key contribution of the form is its ability to supply the members of the various project teams through temporary assignment of personnel from the stable departments of the firm. Then, when a project is completed, personnel return to their home departments to work on standard product needs and perhaps await reassignment to another project team. The matrix form gives a firm the capacity to expand and contract and to constantly address new market opportunities while holding key human assets.

In another matrix application, a multi-product, multinational firm may combine worldwide product divisions with national or regionally based marketing groups. Again, the key in a global matrix is to gain the benefits of local operating flexibility while employing resources 'owned' by the product divisions.

As with the functional and divisional forms, the matrix form can be overloaded by simply extending a firm's operations beyond the capability of its structure. For example, in the aerospace matrix, each additional project places new demands on the resource-allocation capacity of the firm. Ultimately, resources are held but are not kept fully employed, and the firm achieves something akin to negative synergy – each new logical addition brings with it coordination costs which exceed its benefits.

Equally troublesome are failures of the matrix form resulting from modifications that violate its operating logic. Recall that the purpose of the matrix form is to let two different types of market forces help shape the operation of the firm. However, many firms are unwilling or unable to maintain balance between or among their market foci and functional components. For example, if worldwide product divisions have no means of influencing the marketing priorities of national or regional marketing groups, operating efficiency may be totally subordinated to local responsiveness. Alternatively, if managers of functional departments have full say over assignments to project teams, the needs of the stable portion of the organization will dominate those of the flexible side, making it difficult for project team managers to meet customer needs for both technical sophistication and timeliness.

In sum, there is considerable historical evidence to suggest that an organizational form performs optimally only within certain limits. When a particular form's operating logic is violated, even by apparently reasonable extensions or modifications of the form, failure may result.

Potential causes of failure in network organizations

Like its predecessor forms, the network organization can fail because of alterations made by well-intentioned managers. The network form has an operating logic associated with each of its variations, and violations of this logic are likely to limit the form's effectiveness and, in the extreme, cause it to fail.

The stable network

The stable network has its roots in the structure and operating logic of the functional organization. It is designed to serve a mostly predictable market by linking together independently owned specialized assets along a given product or service value chain. However, instead of a single vertically integrated firm', the stable network substitutes a set of component firms, each tied closely to a core firm by contractual arrangement, but each maintaining its competitive fitness by serving firms outside the network.

Given its logic, the most common threat to the effectiveness of the stable network is an extension that demands the complete utilization of the supplier's or distributor's assets for the benefit of the core firm. If the several suppliers and distributors in the stable network focus their assets solely on the needs of a single core firm, the benefits of broader participation in the marketplace are lost. Unless suppliers sell to other firms, the price and quality of their output is not subject to market test. Similarly, unless multiple outlets are used, the value actually added by distributors must be set by judgment rather than by market-driven margins. The process of asset overspecialization and overdedication by network partners is frequently incremental and can therefore go unnoticed. Continued, step-by-step customization of a supplier's processes, either voluntarily or at the core firm's insistence, can ultimately result in the inability of the supplier to compete in other markets and an obligation on the part of the core firm to use all of the supplier's output. (See Table 2.)

Another reason for network members to participate in the market outside their relationship with the core firm is to force these components to maintain their technological expertise and flexibility. Suppliers come into contact with innovations in product or service designs and develop their adaptive skills by serving various clients. Overspecialization and limited learning can easily occur if both the core firm and its components are not alert. In fact, for maximum effectiveness, both the core firm and its stable partners must explicitly consider the limits of allowable dedication – forcing themselves to set restrictions on the proportion of component assets that can be utilized.

An enormously effective stable network has been put together by Nike, the athletic shoe and apparel giant. Founded in 1964, as a U.S. dealer for a Japanese shoe firm. Nike began developing its own product line in 1972 and has built a $3 billion business on a clear strategy of working closely with, but not dominating, a wide range of suppliers in Korea, Taiwan, Thailand. and the Peoples Republic of China. Nike wants its suppliers to service other designers so that they can enhance their technical competence and so that they will be available when needed but not dependent on Nike's ability to forecast and schedule their services. A major factor in Nike's continuing market leadership is its ability to introduce new models quickly to meet (or create) market trends. Perhaps most importantly, Nike has maintained its technical competence and leads the industry in R&D investment.[10] Nike personnel work directly with suppliers to build and maintain their capability, verifying product quality in-process as well as after the fact. To assure their own expertise in manufacturing (and to prevent costly design mistakes), Nike has continued a small domestic manufacturing operation focused on leading-edge designs.

The stable network can also be damaged by unthoughtful or even inadvertent modifications. In the search for assurance that suppliers can meet quality standards and delivery dates, some core firms attempt to specify the processes that the network member must use. Deep involvement in a supplier's or distributor's processes can occur through innocent zeal on the part of the core firm's staff and may be enthusiastically endorsed by the component's staff. Within limits, close cooperation to assure effective linkage is valuable. However, the core firm can ultimately find itself 'managing' the assets of its partners and accepting responsibility for their output. Moreover, when the operating independence of the network member is severely constrained, any creativity that might flow from its managers or staff is curtailed – and the core firm is not getting the full

Type of network	Stable	Internal	Dynamic
Operating Logic	A large core 'firm creates market-based linkages to a limited set of upstream and/or downstream partners	Commonly owned business elements allocate resources along the value chain using market mechanisms	Independent business elements along the value chain form temporary alliances from among a large pool of potential partners
Primary Application	Mature industries requiring large capital Investments. Varied ownership limits risk and encourages full loading of all assets.	Mature industries requiring large capital Investments. Market-priced exchanges allow performance appraisal of internal units.	Low tech Industries with short product design cycles and evolving high tech industries (e.g. electronics, biotech, etc.)
Extension Failure	Overutillization of a given supplier or distributor leading to unhealthy dependence on core firm	Extending asset ownership beyond the capacity of the internal market and performance appraisal mechanisms	Expertise may become too narrow and role in value chain is assumed by another firm
Modification Failure	High expectations for cooperation can limit the creativity of partners	Corporate executives use 'commands' instead of influence or incentives to intervene in local operations	Excessive mechanisms to prevent partners' opportunism or exclusive relationships with a limited number of upstream or down-stream partners

Table 2 Causes of failure in network organizations

benefit of the component's assets. In effect, the core firm is converting the network into a vertically integrated functional organization.

The internal network

The logic of the internal network requires the creation of a market inside a firm. Here organizational units buy and sell goods and services among themselves at prices established in the open market. Obviously, if internal transactions are to reflect market prices, the various components must have regular opportunity to verify the price and quality of their wares by buying and selling outside the firm. The purpose of the internal network, like its predecessor, the matrix form, is to gain competitive advantage through shared utilization of scarce assets and the continuing development and exchange of managerial and technological knowhow. But, also like the matrix, the internal network can be damaged by extensions that overload its internal market mechanisms and by modifications that unbalance the relationships between buyers and sellers.

For example, the giant multinational firm ABB Asea Brown Bovari has grown quickly to over $25 billion in revenues and nearly a quarter of a million employees through a concerted program of mergers and acquisitions which has given it unmatched local and global synergy in the electrical systems and equipment market. To this point, the firm has increased shareholder value by thoughtfully specifying the market domain of each of its components and creating the internal mechanisms by which they can exchange goods and services in mutually beneficial ways under overall market discipline. However, it would be easy for such a firm to be seduced by its current success into an attempt to move further and further afield. At the moment, the CEO and key managers of ABB have a well-articulated concept of how the firm's global internal market operates.[11] However, each new business line, and each new geographic area addressed, must be carefully interconnected throughout the global grid, a task whose difficulty increases not arithmetically but geometrically.

Internal networks thus can fail from overextension, but they can fail perhaps even faster because of misguided modification. The most common managerial misstep in internal networks is corporate intervention in resource flows or in the determination of transaction prices. Not every interaction in the internal network can and should flow from locally determined supply and demand decisions. Corporate managers may well see a benefit in having internal units buy from a newly built or acquired component, even though its actual prices are above those of competitors in the marketplace. Such prices may be needed to sort out the operation and develop full efficiency. However, the manner in which corporate management handles such 'forced' transactions is a crucial factor in the continuing health of the network. Ideally, corporate executives will manage the internal economy rather than simply dictate the transfer price and process. This can be accomplished by providing a 'subsidy' to the startup component to allow it to sell at market prices while still showing a profit, or by providing buyers with incentives that keep their profits at rates which would occur if they were free to buy from lower priced competitors. Obviously, such subsidies or incentives should be time bound and carefully monitored to prevent abuses. Although this process is demanding, it serves to protect the logic of market-based internal transactions rather than reverting to centrally determined transfers. Unfortunately, as indicated, instead of influencing the internal market and preserving the ability to evaluate components on actual performance, many corporate managers 'command' component behaviors and risk destroying agreement on the criteria for performance evaluation.

Despite potential problems, the shift from complex, centrally planned hierarchies to internal market structures is a growing movement, and IBM's recent announcements provide one more large, highly visible example. IBM's plan is to turn each of its major units into self-managed businesses, free to buy and sell goods and services with one another and ultimately with outside buyers and sellers as well. A 1991 conference reported experiments in building internal networks in organizations ranging from services (Blue Cross-Blue Shield), to materials (Alcoa), to low (Clark Equipment) and high tech (Control Data) manufacturers. Not surprisingly, these applications tend to demonstrate both the benefits and the types of resistance anticipated here. However, it is too early to tell whether these and other internal network structures will avoid major managerial mistakes.[12]

The dynamic network

The operating logic of the dynamic network is linked to that of the divisional form of organization. Recall that the divisionalized organization emphasized adaptability by focusing independently operated divisions on distinct but related markets. The combination of central evaluation and local operating autonomy is reflected in the dynamic network where independent firms are linked together for the one-time (or short-term) production of a particular good or service. For the dynamic network to achieve its full potential, there must be numerous firms (or units of firms) operating at each of the points along the value chain, ready to be pulled together for a given run and then disassembled to become part of another temporary alignment.

The availability of numerous potential partners eager to apply their skills and assets to the upstream or downstream needs of a given firm is not only the key to success of the dynamic network, it is also a possible source of trouble. For example. if a particular firm in the value chain over-specializes – refines but also over time restricts its expertise – it runs the risk of becoming a 'hollow' corporation, a firm without a clearly defined. essential contribution to make to its product or service value chain.[13] Firms need to occupy a wide enough segment of the value chain to be able to test and protect the value of their contribution. A designer needs to retain its ability to build prototypes, a producer may need to experiment with new process technologies, and so on. Firms with a contribution base that is either too narrow or weakly defined are easily overrun by their upstream and/or downstream neighbors. Indeed, examples of firms (and industries) pushed into decline and ultimate failure by excessive outsourcing abound. From radios to television sets to video recorders, outsourcing decisions by U.S. corporations allowed foreign suppliers to acquire the technical competence to design and sell their own products, eventually capturing the bulk of U.S. domestic markets.[14]

Conversely, firms with a clear competence-based position on the value chain, a base maintained by continuing investment in technology and skill development, can afford to interact confidently with upstream and downstream partners. Nevertheless, there is a constant temptation for firms to go beyond the development of their own competence as the means of insuring their viability. They may seek to add protection through an excessive concern for secrecy, heavy emphasis on legalism in contractual relations, a search for preferential relationships with particular partners, and so on. In fact, potentially dysfunctional network behaviors are currently multiplying across the personal and business computer industry as firms, including industry giants IBM and Apple, build an almost undecipherable maze of interconnected agreements and alliances to protect market share, enter new arenas, search for technical innovations, and promote the adoption of technical and/or system standards. Each of these efforts is designed to give the newly formed partners a competitive advantage over those players not included (who are instead building their own web of alliances).[15] Such protective modifications can constrain the primary strength of the dynamic network – its ability to efficiently allocate member firms, uncoupling and recoupling them with minimum cost and minimum loss of operating time.

In sum, the dynamic network places demands on its component firms to continually reappraise their technical competence and the scope of their activities, not only to maintain their own well-being but that of the broader network as well. No one component can know everything that is happening or everything that is needed in the broader network. However, each component can preserve its own competence and refrain from behaviors which are a threat to network performance.[16]

Avoiding failure: developing the competence for self-renewal

In the preceding sections, we have outlined how organizational forms may lose their vitality over time as managers make what appear to be logical extensions or modifications. However, rather than improving performance, these actions may gradually obscure and subvert the operating logic of the form. Few organizations appear to have the capacity for self-renewal – the ability to adapt without losing effectiveness. What is needed is the competence to not only make adjustments to environmental shifts, but to do so either: within the constraints of the operating logic of the existing organizational form; or by adopting a new form to fit a new market strategy. Obviously, the ability of an organization to self-renew is easier to describe than achieve. However, such competence may be enhanced as a firm increasingly adopts characteristics of one of the three network types (stable, internal, or dynamic).

The possibility that firms adopting network structures will improve their self-renewal competence flows from two unique characteristics of the network form: the essential relationships among components are *external* (and thus highly *visible* to all parties) and these relationships are *voluntary* (and thus must reflect *explicit* commitments).

Dynamics of external relationships

Even when a network's components are commonly owned, the essential structure of the organization is external – an exoskeleton of clearly specified, objectively structured contracts and buy-and-sell agreements that guide interactions rather than internal schedules, procedures, and routines. Conversely, in purely internal communication and reporting channels, every interaction is colored by the hidden threat of hierarchical politics, the likelihood that power and influence rather than performance are guiding behavior. In older organizational forms, for example, cost data and/or performance measures may be manipulated by simply changing accounting conventions – such as the way in which overhead expenses are accumulated and assigned. With external linkages, attempts at personal gain may be made, but the behavior will be much more transparent.

Of course, the fact that network linkages are external does not guarantee that they will always be efficacious to each of the parties, but it does push the parties toward performance-based equity. A number of years ago, we predicted that network organizations would create 'full-disclosure information systems' to assure that all decisions were made objectively and fairly.[17] Such practices are now quite common. As the CEO of Excel Industries, a major supplier of Ford, states: 'They know every cost we incur.'[18]

In sum, visible, external linkages among network components have perceptual as well as substantive benefits. A faulty external coupling must be dealt with, while purely internal mechanisms can be eroding or even broken for some time before the damage demand, the affected parties' attention.

Dynamics of voluntary relationships

External, visible relationships, as suggested, tend to be explicit. They specify the performance that is expected from each partner and how that performance will be measured and compensated. Explicitness, however, doe not require complex, legalistic, or highly formal contracts. A contract can be as simple as a due date and a price based on disclosed costs. In the construction industry, 'partnering' sessions are held among network members at the beginning of major projects to clarify responsibilities and relationships and to agree on methods of resolving disputes. Similarly, General Electric's Workout Program is designed to bring GE's managers, customers, and vendors together to create effective working relationships.[19]

Most importantly, the fact that network relationships are explicit does not mean that they are dictated by one party or another. In fact, underlying all or the positive characteristics of network structures is the dynamic of voluntarism. If voluntarism is not present – if partners are not free to withdraw from relationships they believe are unfairly structured – then the value or openness and explicitness is compromised. Of course, such compromises can and do occur, as noted earlier. For example, in stable networks, components may become overly dependent on one another, and in internal networks corporate interventions may force components into relationships that are neither fair nor appropriately subsidized.

Nevertheless, U.S. firms are gaining experience at creating and maintaining fair and voluntary relationships. For example, Harley-Davidson claims it is no longer 'waging war' with its suppliers. Harley's managers reportedly 'threw the lawyers out' and produced a simple contract that clarified goals for suppliers and outlined how disputes could be resolved.[20]

In sum, the unique, positive characteristics of the network organization discussed here can assist managers in making adaptations by enabling them to test their proposed modifications and extensions against the operating logic of the form. Because changes are visible and clear to all parties in the network, there are likely to be multiple players tracing the impact of any change. Moreover, the key characteristic of the network form, voluntarism, is in itself a litmus test of logic violation – *any* change that reduces voluntarism is a potential threat to the overall efficiency of the network.

Conclusion

Research over the past decade has increasingly confirmed what managers and organizational theorists have long understood – organizations, particularly large, complex firms, have a difficult time responding to changes in their competitive environment. Instead of adapting incrementally as market and/or technological changes occur, managers tend to wait until environmental demands accumulate to crisis proportions before attempting a response, and then they often fail. When managers do behave incrementally, they frequently make patchwork alterations to the existing organization as each new market or technological shift occurs but without considering the ultimate systemic impact. Such adjustments gradually move the organization away from its core structural logic, creating an idiosyncratic system highly dependent on a few key individuals or units to function. These organizations are not only unstable and costly to operate, they often are so convoluted that it is difficult even to determine where major change might begin – to get to the center of a complex organizational knot.

Our premise here has been that organizational forms, particularly the network form, need not be so prone to failure. If managers understand the logic of the form their organization employs, and if they keep that logic visible to themselves and others associated with the organization, the benefits of proposed changes can be weighed against the strains they impose on the total system. In fact, we believe that it is possible to anticipate how and why each organizational form is likely to fail. Moreover, if managers understand the operating logic of alternative forms, they can explore the possibility that environmental changes have pushed their organization outside the boundaries of one form and into those of another.

Finally, we have tried to illustrate how the network form should help make the manager's task of successful adaptation easier. By its very nature, the network organization is always in the process of renewal – its important elements are in a constant state of adjustment to market, technological, and other forces in the environment. This continual process of adaptation, coupled with the fact that network components are typically smaller and more focused than those of integrated firms, should help managers deepen their understanding of the form's operating logic and develop their renewal skills.

Whether the network form of organization is less prone to internally generated failures than its predecessors is ultimately determinable only over time. Nevertheless, its evolution provides managers the opportunity to explore and test their understanding of organizations from a new vantage point, and the continued study of networks should contribute to a better understanding of the causes of success and failure in all organizational forms.

Notes

[1] During the early and middle 1980s. articles began to appear (a) *forecasting* network forms of organization [e.g., Raymond Miles and Charles Snow, 'Fit, Failure and the Hall of Fame,' *California Management Review* (Spring 1984)]; (b) *describing* the form's key characteristics [e.g., Hans Thorelli, 'Networks: Between Markets and Hierarchies,' *Strategic Management Journal* (January/February 1986); and Raymond Miles and Charles Snow, 'Network Organizations: New Concepts for New Forms,' *California Management Review* (Spring 1986)]; and (c) *debating* the costs and benefits of network structures [e.g., 'The Hollow Corporation', *Business Week*, March 3, 1986]. A few years ago, a rash of books and articles appeared exploring and generally endorsing various types of network, structures, including strategic alliances, value-added partnerships, global market matrices, and so on [e.g., Peter Drucker, *The New Realities* (New York, NY: Harper & Row, 1989); Charles Handy, *The Age of Unreason* (Boston, MA: Harvard Business School Press, 1990); Robert Reich, *The Work of Nations* (New York, NY: Knopf, 1991); Russell Johnson and Paul Lawrence, 'Beyond Vertical Integration – The Rise of the Value Added Partnership,' *Harvard Business Review* (1988)]. Most recently, a cover story in *Business Week* ['Learning From Japan,' January 27, 1992, pp. 52–60) details numerous examples of U.S. firms creating and benefiting from network structures.

[2] For a brief description of both Rubbermaid and Wal-Mart, see the Special Report, *Business Month* (December 1988), pp. 38 and 42.

[3] For an early discussion of how large firms have disaggregated their operations and spread them across multiple, smaller elements along the value chain, see Michael J. Piore and Charles E. Sabel, *The Second Industrial Divide* (New York, NY: Basic Books, 1984). See also Johnson and Lawrence, op. cit.

[4] A more detailed description of these three types of networks, and the forces shaping them, is provided in Charles C. Snow, Raymond E. Miles, and Henry J. Coleman, Jr., 'Managing 21st Century Network Organizations,' *Organizational Dynamics* (Winter 1992), pp. 5–20.

[5] Cooperative, entrepreneurial behavior of this sort is being increasingly encouraged both inside and across firms. See James Brian Quinn and Penny C. Paquette, 'Technology in Services: Creating Organizational Revolutions,' *Sloan Management Review,* 31 (Winter 1990): 67–78.

[6] There are two main types of *keiretsu*. Many stable networks in the U.S. resemble 'supply' *keiretsu,* which are groups of companies integrated along a value chain dominated by a major manufacturer. To date there are no American counterparts to 'bank-centered' *keiretsu,* which are industrial combines of 20–45 core companies centered around a bank. For discussions of *keiretsu-like* networks to the U.S., see Charles H. Ferguson, 'Computers and the Coming of the U.S. *Keiretsu,'* *Harvard Business Review* (July/August 1990), pp. 55–70; and 'Learning From Japan,' *Business Week,* op. cit. See also 'Japan, All in the Family,' *Newsweek,* June 10, 1991, pp. 37–40.

[7] IBM announced a major restructuring along these lines late in 1991. See 'Out of One Big Blue, Many Little Ones,' *Business Week*, December 9, 1991, p. 33. For a complete description, see David Kirkpatrick, 'Breaking Up IBM,' *Fortune,* July 27, 1992, pp. 44–58.

[8] Thomas Gelb, 'Overhauling Corporate Engine Drives Winning Strategy,' *The Journal of Business Strategy* (November/December 1989), pp. 91–105.

[9] See General Mills, Annual Report, 1985.

[10] See Nike, Annual Report, 1991.

[11] See William Taylor, 'The Logic of Global Business: An Interview with ABB's Percy Barnevik,' *Harvard Business Review* (March/April 1991), pp. 91–105.

[12] See, Jason Magidson and Andrew Polcha, 'Creating Market Economies Within Organizations: A Conference on Internal "Markets",' *Planning Review,* 20 (January/February 1992): 37–40.

[13] *Business Week* used the term 'hollow corporation' pejoratively in its March 3, 1986 cover story, op. cit. However, recognizing that thoughtful outsourcing does not cause an organization to lose its critical expertise, Quinn, Doorley, and Paquette discuss how firms are 'learning to love the hollow corporation.' See James Brian Quinn, Thomas L. Doorley, and Penny C. Paquette, 'Technology in Services: Rethinking Strategic Focus,' *Sloan Management Review,* 31 (Winter 1990), p. 83.

[14] These and other examples are discussed in companion articles in the February 1992 issue of *The Academy of Management Executive* [Richard A. Bettis, Stephen P. Bradley, and Gary Hamel, 'Outsourcing and Industrial Decline,' pp. 7–22; and James A. Welch and P. Ranganath Nayak, 'Strategic Sourcing: A Progressive Approach to the Make-or-Buy Decision,' pp. 23–31]. However, while both pieces bemoan the negative impact of faulty outsourcing decisions on U.S. competitiveness, each recognizes that outsourcing, if properly handled, can be an important management tool, and Welch and Nayak propose models to assist with strategic outsourcing decisions.

[15] See James Daly and Michael Sullivan-Trainor, 'Swing Your Partner, Do-Si-Dough,' *Computerworld*, December 23, 1991/January 2, 1992, pp. 21–25.

[16] In contrast to the widely publicized and potentially damaging alliances emerging among major computer firms, many small Silicon Valley firms have built profitable dynamic network relationships. In these networks, many firms do nothing but design custom computer chips while others specialize in manufacturing these designs. In some instances, designers have even shared some of their expertise with large concerns in return for access to manufacturing competence. Such networks emerge and are maintained by trust and by the recognition of unique competencies and mutual dependencies. See John Case, 'Intimate Relations,' *INC.* (August 1990), pp. 64–72.

[17] Miles and Snow (1986), op. cit., p. 65.

[18] 'Learning From Japan,' *Business Week,* op. cit., p. 59. Similar relationships based on full cost and profit information sharing among Silicon Valley chip designers and manufacturers are described in John Case, op. cit.

[19] Snow, Miles, and Coleman, op. cit.

[20] 'Learning From Japan,' op. cit., p. 59.

CASE 3: VODAFONE: OUT OF MANY, ONE*

Arun Sarin reclined in his seat in a first-class compartment en route to London. The CEO of Vodafone, the world's largest mobile telephone operator, began reflecting on the events of the past few days, in particular Vodafone's decision to exit the Japanese market by selling Vodafone's stake in Japan Telecom to Tokyo-based Softbank in a deal valued at $15.4 billion. After the sale, the company would return $10.5 billion to its shareholders. Vodafone had trailed behind NTT DoCoMo and KDDI since its entry into Japan in 2001, thanks to fickle consumers, the lack of a low-end tier in the segment, and the challenge of coordinating terminals and technologies across borders. The time had come to make a hard decision, and Sarin had made it.

It was not the first time he had been faced with such a decision. Two years earlier Vodafone had made headlines in the financial press with its failed attempt to takeover the US mobile operator, AT&T Wireless. After a long takeover battle, Vodafone's American rival Cingular Wireless had offered $41 billion in cash for AT&T Wireless.[1] At the time, Sarin had not been sure whether to regret the failed takeover. He could easily have financed a larger sum for the bid, but major shareholders had been very explicit that anything beyond an offer of $38 billion would be detrimental to their interests.[2] Vodafone's offer had forced Cingular to increase its bid from $30 billion to $41 billion, meaning it could take Cingular many years to digest the merger (refer to Exhibit 3.1 for share prices of Vodafone since 1989). There might yet come more promising and cheaper ways for Vodafone to enhance its presence in the world's largest economy with huge growth potential.

Sarin knew he could not afford to alienate Vodafone's shareholders by pursuing growth at all costs. However, Vodafone's current hold in the American market (the non-controlling stake in Verizon Wireless – the only one in the USA) was not comforting either. The relationship with the other main shareholder, Verizon, was quite strained, management had refused to adopt the single Vodafone brand and had insisted on using the outdated American CDMA network standard instead of the group-wide GSM/UMTS standard.[3]

Being CEO was definitely not an easy job, with so many things to consider and the shadow of his larger-than-life predecessor Sir Chris Gent looming over him. But this was exactly the reason why he was being paid £1.2 million a year as base salary.[4]

Johannes Banzhaf, while on his double-degree ESSEC-Mannheim management programme prepared this case under the supervision of Ashok Som. The case was made possible by the permission of Mr Arun Sarin, CEO, and the active participation of Mr Alan Harper, Director, Group Strategy and Business Integration. The case was developed as a basis for class discussion rather than to illustrate either effective or ineffective handling of an administrative situation.

*'Out of many, one' comes from the Latin *E Pluribus Unum* signifying the harnessing of global scale and scope synergies of One Vodafone.

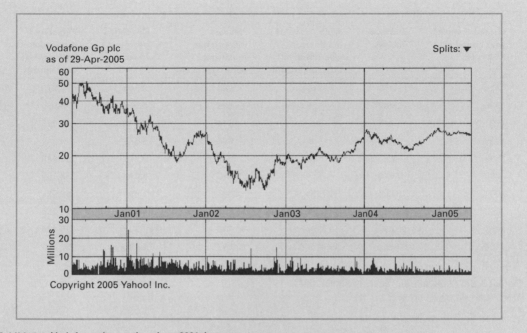

Exhibit 3.1 Vodafone share price since 2001, in pence
Source: http://finance.yahoo.com

Company overview: Vodafone group plc

In 2005, Vodafone was the leading mobile phone operator in the world. It had more than 150 million customers in 26 different countries.[5] Vodafone employed approximately 67,000 people around the world and had its headquarters in Newbury, England. Being listed on the stock exchanges of New York (ticker: VOD), London and Frankfurt, it boasted a market capitalization of $165.7 billion[6] – making it the 11th most valuable company in the world. In fiscal year 2003, it suffered a loss of $15.5 billion (on revenue of approximately $48 billion) – a figure that was the result of large write-downs on the goodwill of acquired companies and huge amortization charges related to the acquisition of other mobile operators like Mannesmann D2. These charges amounted to $18.8 billion.[7] In fact, if one excluded these extraordinary non-cash charges, Vodafone was very profitable, as indicated by its gross margins and capacity to generate huge positive cash flows: the cash flow from operating activities (before capital expenditure and other outflows) amounted to £12.3 billion (approximately $22.7 billion) in fiscal year 2004, while free cash flow exceeded an unbelievable £8 billion ($15.7 billion – refer to Exhibit 3.2 for an overview of Vodafone Group's financials).[8] Vodafone had been consistently paying dividends and had recently announced a £3 billion share repurchase programme.[9]

For the financial year ended 31 March	Turnover (in £m)	Profit (loss) for the financial year (after taxation, in £m)	Net cash inflow from operating activities (in £m)	Dividends per share (pence)	Registered proportionate customers (in thousands)
1995	1,153	238	386	3.34p	2,073
1996	1,402	311	615	4.01p	3,035
1997	1,749	364	644	4.81p	4,016
1998	2,408	419	886	5.53p	5,844
1999	3,36	637	1,045	3.77p	10,445
2000	7,873	487	2,510	1.34p	39,139
2001	15,004	(9,763)	4,587	1.40p	82,997
2002	22,845	(16,155)	8,102	1.47p	101,136
2003	30,375	(9,819)	11,142	1.70p	119,709
2004	33,559	(9,015)	12,317	2.03p	133,421

Exhibit 3.2(a) Vodafone key financials 1995–2004
Source: company annual reports

	2003	2002
Mobile telecommunications:		
Northern Europe	6,057	
Central Europe	4,775	
Southern Europe	8,051	
Americas	5	
Asia Pacific	8,364	
Middle East and Africa	290	
= Total mobile operations	**27,542**	**20,742**
Other operations:*		
Europe	854	
Asia Pacific	1,979	
= Total group turnover	**30,375**	**22,845**

Exhibit 3.2(b) Group turnover for the year ended 31 March 2003, in £m, by geographic region
*'Other operations' mainly includes the results of the group's interests in fixed-line telecommunications businesses in Germany (Arcor), France (Cegetel) and Japan (Japan Telecom). The turnover figure for the Americas does not include the 45 per cent stake in Verizon Wireless (USA).
Source: adapted from company annual report, 2003

History of Vodafone[10]

The company was formed as Racal Telecom Limited in 1984 as a subsidiary of Racal Electronics plc, a British electronics manufacturing company. It successfully bid for a private-sector UK cellular licence in 1982 and hosted the first ever mobile phone call in the UK in 1985. The customer base stood at 19,000 on 31 December 1985.

In October 1988, Racal Telecom Ltd went public by offering approximately 20 per cent of the company's stock. Three years later, it was fully de-merged from Racal Electronics and became an independent company with a different name, Vodafone Group plc, and was listed on the London and New York Stock Exchanges. Corporate legend states that the 'founders had the foresight to realize that people would do more than talk over their phones and so created a future-proof name that would embrace both VOice and DAta mobile communication: Vodafone'.[11] Due to its early start, it managed the largest mobile network in the world by 1987.

In 1992, Vodafone pioneered again when it signed the world's first international 'roaming' agreement with Telecom Finland, allowing Vodafone's customers to use their phones on a different network while still being billed in their home country. Four years later, Vodafone became the first operator in the UK to offer so-called 'pre-paid' packages that do not require customers to sign a long-term contract.

Christopher Gent succeeded Sir Gerald Whent at the helm of the company on 1 January 1997. Gent was responsible for shifting Vodafone's growth strategy from organic to aggressive external, orchestrating its move towards globalization. In the same year, Vodafone's 100th roaming agreement was signed.

In early 1999, Vodafone signed up its 10-millionth customer, half of them in the UK. Vodafone's growth reached the next level when it successfully merged with AirTouch Communications Inc. of the USA – a $61 billion deal. Vodafone renamed itself briefly Vodafone AirTouch and more than doubled its customer base to more than 31 million customers worldwide (September 1999) in 24 countries across five continents.[12] In the late 1990s and early in the new millennium, stock markets were steering towards a bubble, with 'mobile' being the latest hype and insane sums being paid for mobile operators and the licences to operate mobile networks. At the end of November 1999, the company had a market capitalization of approximately £90 billion. Vodafone's North American branch was integrated into a new entity branded Verizon Wireless together with Bell Atlantic's mobile business, with Vodafone retaining a 45 per cent stake in the new venture. Verizon Wireless was the largest mobile phone operator in 2003 in a very fragmented North American market (36 million customers and 24 per cent market share as of 30 September 2003).[13]

In a move that sent shockwaves through corporate Germany in 1999, Vodafone launched a €100 billion takeover bid for Mannesmann in order to get hold of its D2 mobile phone business, the private market leader in Germany. A bitter struggle for Mannesmann's independence ensued, but finally the board of Mannesmann gave in and the deal was closed in 2000: €190 billion paid in stocks – Germany's largest ever takeover.[14] Vodafone's customer base once again doubled and the company found itself among the ten largest companies in the world in terms of market capitalization. The mobile telephony boom reached its peak and former national providers (such as Deutsche Telekom, France Télécom and Telefonica) embarked on a buying binge that brought them to the verge of bankruptcy when the bubble finally burst (Deutsche Telekom shares fell from more than €100 to €15).

The year 2001 saw a consolidation and restructuring within Vodafone, which reported 82.9 million customers for the financial year ending 31 March 2001. It grew at a

▶

▶ somewhat slower pace than in previous years, about half of it generated by internal growth and the other half by acquisitions (e.g. acquiring Ireland's Eircell and increasing its stake in Spanish AirTel Movil to 91.7 per cent). However, 'slower growth' still meant that Vodafone had added approximately 20 million customers by the end of 2002. At that time, the company board announced that the Indian-born American Arun Sarin would takeover as CEO on 30 July 2003.

There were no large-scale acquisitions in 2002 and 2003, but instead a host of smaller deals and partnership agreements. In February 2004, Vodafone's bid for AT&T Wireless in the USA failed against a higher offer by Cingular, yet clearly indicated that Vodafone had all but renounced its growth ambitions.

Growth at Vodafone

Traditionally, growth at Vodafone was by acquisition rather than organic. It had a track record in takeovers and their subsequent successful integration, Germany's Mannesmann being the most prominent example. Today branded as Vodafone Germany, Mannesmann was the group's most profitable venture (in terms of EBIT, which surpassed £2 billion in 2003) and its largest subsidiary. On the mobile telephony acquisition strategy, Alan Harper, Group Strategy and Business Integration Director, commented:

> In the past ten years there had been a sea change in the evolution of the telecommunications industry. The rule in this industry has been 'hunt or be hunted'. The strategy of the global players had been mobile-centric, multi-market strategies. Most of the companies, like Hutchison, Mannesmann and AirTouch, started much smaller, like a start-up, and did not have any history as an operator and the parent company was usually a trading company. Vodafone acquired Mannesmann, AirTouch and the rest of the small players. FT acquired Orange. DoCoMo was restructured back into NTT.

Unlike many of its competitors, Vodafone used shares for its acquisitions. This might be one of the reasons it emerged from the telecoms crisis relatively early and could concentrate on growth again, while virtually all of its competitors were still occupied in trying to reduce their debt burden (e.g. Deutsche Telekom, France Télécom, MMO2, KPN).[15] However, as Vodafone's shares had shown only lacklustre performance in prior months, it increasingly had to use hard cash to increase its holdings in subsidiaries or for new acquisitions. As Vodafone did not want to compromise its very good credit ratings (by industry standards) under any circumstances, it had slowed down on acquisitions and had been focusing on internal growth for the past two years (refer to Exhibit 3.3 for Vodafone's strategic intent).

Vodafone had acquired other businesses along with the mobile phone business as in the case of Japan Telecom and Mannesmann, where it got ownership of fixed-line operations; however, it had always been explicit in its concentration on its core business of mobile telecommunications. Usually it started looking for potential buyers for the other businesses. In the words of Alan Harper, Group Strategy and Business Integration Director: 'We had been always mobile focused. In 1995, when I joined Vodafone,

The company had maintained a strategy of focusing on global mobile telecommunications and providing network coverage to allow its customers to communicate using mobile products and services. The company's strategy was increasingly focused on revenue growth and margin improvement from providing enhanced services to its customer base. This growth strategy had three principal components:

1 to grow voice and data revenues through an increased marketing focus on our established high-quality customer base

2 to extend our operational leadership of the industry through maximizing the benefits of scale and scope, through the use of partner network agreements, by increasing equity interests in businesses where the group had existing shareholdings and by promoting the Vodafone brand, and

3 to extend service differentiation, investing in delivering Vodafone branded, easy to use, customer propositions for mobile voice and data.

Where appropriate, and if circumstances allow, the company may also make further acquisitions or disposals of businesses.

Exhibit 3.3 Vodafone's strategic intent
Source: www.vodafone.com

it was mobile focused. It has a turnover of €8 billion, it was the third largest mobile operator in UK and had 80 per cent business in the UK. Today, in 2005, we are still mobile focused, with a turnover of €100 billion, the biggest in the world and only 10 per cent in UK.'

Vodafone balanced its investment options by taking its time to ensure a good investment and disinvestment option. For example, it sold Japan Telecom's fixed-line operations in 2003 for ¥261.3 billion (£1.4 billion),[16] while it reinforced its long-term commitment to Japan in 2005 by making a further investment of up to £2.6 billion. As Arun Sarin, pointed out, 'Our transactions in Japan will simplify the structure, confirm our commitment to the Japanese marketplace and enable us to deliver on the changes needed to improve our position.'

Arcor was not divested and was still part of Vodafone Germany as of 2005. Arcor might even serve as a strategic weapon to cannibalize on incumbent Deutsche Telekom's profitable fixed-line business.[17]

From mid-2001, Vodafone had entered into arrangements with other network operators in countries where it did not hold any equity stake. Under the terms of so-called 'Partner Network Agreements', Vodafone cooperated with its counterparts in the development and marketing of global services under dual-brand logos. By 2003, Vodafone had extended its reach into 11 other countries, thus establishing a first foothold in these markets.[18] Such an agreement was a classic win-win situation: Vodafone not only gained new market insight with little risk but at the same time was able to assess the quality of the partner in order to identify possible takeover targets, while the partner benefited from Vodafone's unique marketing and technological capabilities.

Vodafone's acquisition strategy always followed a similar pattern: first, the number one or two player within a national market was identified, while it carefully avoided acquiring the incumbent mobile operator that was linked to the state-owned telecom monopoly (like T-Mobile, which was the mobile division of Deutsche Telekom, or

▶ Orange, a business unit of France Télécom). It seems that Vodafone feared the bureaucratic inertia of these organizations and would rather focus on more flexible, entrepreneurially minded challengers (with Mannesmann's D2 once again being a good example, or France's SFR) that would challenge the incumbents in different local markets. Referring to this strategy Alan Harper explained:

> Our vision has been to leverage scale and scope benefits, reduce response time in market, and ensure effective delivery to customers. This we have achieved by collecting or acquiring national (operational) companies and [giving] them a mission as a 'challenger company' in each of the national markets. For example, Vodafone with SFR is a challenger to France Télécom in France, Vodafone UK is a challenger to British Telecom in the UK, and Vodafone Germany a challenger to Deutsche Telecom in Germany. Together with this challenger mindset, we nurture and instil an entrepreneurial spirit inside Vodafone Group companies, and in this respect we do not behave as a traditional telephone company. Since we differ from being a traditional company, the cultural alignment of people working for Vodafone is a key issue in sustaining this challenger and entrepreneurial mindset. To focus on this cultural alignment, we give autonomy to the local entity and reiterate that the local entity did not join a global company like IBM or HP. The local entity has to work in a matrix structure and keep alive the 'challenger mindset' on fixed-line telephony and other incumbents, challenge the status quo every day and evolve by being local entrepreneurs.

Branding, identity and pricing

After a successful bid for a takeover target, Vodafone followed a diverse strategy in terms of branding, creating its identity and its own pricing models. As Alan Harper explained:

> We play different models of creating Vodafone's identity in the market. Which way we adapt depends on a number of factors and considerations, such as the strength of the local brand, the prevalent company culture and the general fit between Vodafone's processes and the acquired business's processes. But frankly, at the end of the day, it comes down to a question of management judgement. For example, in New Zealand, when we acquired Bellsouth, we changed Bellsouth almost overnight to Vodafone New Zealand. Similarly, in Portugal, we undertook an overnight integration of Telecel to Vodafone Portugal. Telecel transformed into Vodafone Portugal and became challenger to the traditional PTT. Whereas in Italy, when we acquired Omnitel, it took us two and a half years to change Omnitel to Omnitel Vodafone. Omnitel colours were green and white, and we could not change them to Vodafone red immediately. This was because Omnitel had a strong brand image, very well known, and we had to be very cautious during the transition. The market would never have accepted it. The same was the case with DT in Germany.

The management judgement of fast or slow rebranding focused on the customer and organizational response of the acquired market and acquired company. Usually the national brand was kept alive for some time until the dust of the takeover battle had settled. Vodafone then carefully launched its phased rebranding campaign to bring the

new subsidiary under the 'Vodafone' umbrella. Usually, it added 'Vodafone' to the original corporate brand. To better coordinate these branding efforts, Vodafone appointed David Haines, a former Coca-Cola manager, as global brand director.[19]
As he explained,

> For example 'D2' became 'D2 Vodafone'. Within a year, Vodafone modified the logo to its typical red colour and changed the order of company name, for example 'D2 Vodafone' to 'Vodafone D2'. During the last phase, the original 'national' name was eliminated completely and only the global brand and logo remained. This process could take more than two years and usually passed almost unnoticed by the customers, who got accustomed to the new logo due to the extensive branding campaigns, often in conjunction with the launch of a new global product (like Vodafone's Mobile Connect Card, enabling emailing and internet access via a laptop and the mobile network) or service (e.g. Vodafone live! mobile internet portal). Following this pattern, Vodafone Omnitel in Italy and J-Phone Vodafone in Japan became a single brand in May 2003 and October 2003, respectively.[20]

Vodafone launched its first truly global communications campaign at the beginning of August 2001 to reinforce its brand awareness and a global brand identity. Arun Sarin reiterated:

> Throughout the past few years, Vodafone has done a terrific job of building brand awareness as we have moved towards a single global brand. Beyond brand awareness, we want people to understand that the Vodafone name represents great service, great value and great innovation. When our name becomes synonymous with these attributes we will achieve brand preference and expect to see our market share climb as a result.

Across all media, a homogenous corporate brand and identity was communicated including the slogan 'How are you?' and introduced the inverted comma as logo. To stay in sync with Vodafone's global aspirations, the group selected two globally recognized brands: it sponsored Manchester United Football Club and the Ferrari Formula One team to improve awareness and perception of the brand. In addition, it supported its brand by individual sponsorship contracts and other marketing communication programmes at the local level. According to a Vodafone statement: '*An audit of the first year of sponsorship of Scuderia Ferrari reveals that the sponsorship had outperformed all the annual targets set internally by Vodafone and helped establish exceptional global brand awareness.*'[21]

Being number one or number two in most markets[22] it had entered, Vodafone never used 'low prices' to attract new customers. Instead, it focused on creating and marketing new value-added services that enticed customers to sign up with Vodafone, even if this implied that customers were not paying the lowest rates available. According to Arun Sarin:

> We have rededicated ourselves to delighting our customers because we believe this is the foundation for our continued success. We recognize that every customer interaction provides another opportunity to win loyalty and that's why we continue to raise standards on the quality of customer care in our call centres and our stores, and the quality of our networks. Key to delighting our customers is our ability to deliver superior voice and data services according to differing customer needs.

Vodafone was not immune to the pricing policies of its competitors, which meant that it lowered its tariffs whenever the price differential became too great and the new subscriber market share dropped below a critical level. Given its size and healthy finances, it could usually weather price wars and simply waited until the aggressive player lost its thrust. Appendix 1 explores in some detail the role of fixed costs and their impact on pricing in the mobile telecommunications market.

Integrating to one Vodafone

Vodafone realized that real business integration extends far beyond having a single brand. Critics had pointed out that establishing a global brand and logo is among the easier tasks of managing a multinational corporation. Alan Harper stressed:

> The careful rebranding policy not only targeted customers, but also tried to address the needs and concerns of employees. The employees had to adjust to the fact that though they were 'national challengers with an instilled entrepreneurial spirit' they were also part of the family of the global Vodafone Corporation based in Newbury, England. It was perceived that most employees were proud of having contributed to the success of challenging the incumbent operator and were reluctant to be incorporated into a larger corporation that they perceived as 'distant'.

After the heady days of Chris Gent and acquisitions by the dozen, Arun Sarin had to find innovative ways to integrate 'a disparate group of national operations' into one company. He recognized that winning over the hearts of employees and achieving cultural alignment was perhaps the 'biggest challenge of all'. An analyst at Merrill Lynch praised Arun Sarin as 'smart' and 'strategically as good as it gets'.[23] Sarin seemed to be a good fit for the extraordinary task ahead, as he was described as 'an operating man rather than a dealmaker' and 'the archetypal international executive'.[24] The portrait of Sarin went on like this:

> Born and brought up in India, but now an American citizen, Mr Sarin's background was an asset. There might seem to be a certain irony in putting an Indian-American in charge of the world's biggest mobile-phone operator, each of these countries had made a mess of introducing wireless telecoms. But Vodafone was a British company that aspired to be a true multinational. It had large operations in Germany, where it bought Mannesmann in 2000, in Italy and in Japan. To put another Brit into the top job might have bred resentment. ... The son of a well-to-do Indian military officer, he went to a military boarding-school, but his mother encouraged him not to follow his father's career. Instead, he took an engineering degree at the Indian Institute of Technology, the country's equivalent of MIT. From there he went to the University of California at Berkeley on a scholarship, to earn a further degree in engineering and an MBA. He had lived in America ever since. The main remnants of his origins were an Indian wife (whom he met at Berkeley), a touch of an accent and a passion for cricket, which he shares with Sir Chris [Gent, his predecessor].[25]

Sarin, however, was not the only director on Vodafone's board with a distinct international background. As a result of Vodafone's past acquisitions and their pragmatic integration into the group, many skilled foreign (non-British) managers had been retained and had since joined the board, including two German, one Italian, one South African and one Swede, among others (see Exhibit 3.4).

As of 30 July 2005, Vodafone had six executive directors and eight non-executive directors, including the Chairman, Lord MacLaurin.

- **Lord MacLaurin of Knebworth**, Chairman
- **Paul Hazen**, Deputy Chairman and Senior Independent Director
- **Arun Sarin**, Chief Executive (Indian-born and raised, graduated from the Indian Institute of Technology), but now an American citizen. Former Chief Executive Officer for the United States and Asia Pacific region until 15 April 2000, when he became a non-executive director. Former director of AirTouch from July 1995, and President and Chief Operating Officer from February 1997 to June 1999. Appointed Chief Executive on 30 July 2003.
- **Peter R. Bamford**, Chief Marketing Officer
- **Thomas Geitner**, Chief Technology Officer
- **Julian M. Horn-Smith**, Group Chief Operating Officer
- **Kenneth J. Hydon**, Financial Director
- **Sir John Bond**
- **Dr Michael J. Boskin**
- **Professor Sir Alec Broers**
- **Dr John Buchanan**
- **Penelope L. Hughes**
- **Sir David Scholey, CBE**
- **Professor Jürgen Schrempp**
- **Luc Vandevelde**

Exhibit 3.4(a) Vodafone's executive and non-executive directors on the board

- **Arun Sarin**, Chief Executive
- **Sir Julian Horn-Smith**, Deputy Chief Executive
- **Ken Hydon**, Financial Director
- **Peter Bamford**, Chief Marketing Officer
- **Thomas Geitner**, Chief Technology Officer
- **Jürgen von Kuczkowski**, Chief Executive Germany
- **Pietro Guindani**, Chief Executive Italy
- **Bill Morrow**, Chief Executive United Kingdom
- **Paul Donovan**, Regional Chief Executive
- **Brian Clark**, Chief Executive Asia Pacific and Group Human Resources Director Designate
- **Shiro Tsuda**, Chief Executive Japan
- **Alan Harper**, Group Strategy and Business Integration Director
- **Phil Williams**, Group Human Resources Director
- **Stephen Scott**, Group General Counsel and Company Secretary
- **Simon Lewis**, Group Corporate Affairs Director

Exhibit 3.4(b) Vodafone's operational executive heads
Source: www.vodafone.com

At the annual general meeting in July 2003, Sarin emphasized the need to benefit from economies of scale and scope. In June, 2004, Arun Sarin redefined this as follows:

> At Vodafone, everything we do furthers our desire to create mobile connections for individuals, businesses and communities. Our Vision is to be the world's mobile communications leader and we're delighted by the prospects for the future of our industry. Our commitment to this industry is underlined by our company values, which state that everything we do is driven by our passion for customers, our people, results and the world around us ... Operating in 26 markets (together with partner networks in a further 14 countries, with approximately 151.8 million registered customers, and approximately 398.5 million total venture customers puts us in an enviable position to leverage our global scale and scope ... Another competitive advantage is our leadership position on cost and time to market. From network services to sales, and marketing to customer care and billing, we have many varied systems in use across the business. With strong cooperation between our various operating companies we can achieve further savings.

To coordinate, restructure and integrate its various systems across 26 countries, Vodafone launched its 'One Vodafone' initiative, which aimed to boost annual pre-tax operating profits by £2.5 billion by FY2008.[26] Alan Harper explained in detail:

> We are in a period when we are integrating our company. With acquisitions all over the world, one of our challenges is to integrate seamlessly not only technology (which by the way is more or less similar across the world) but people. And this is a key part of the branding evolution that we have witnessed. The challenge of this restructuring programme is to balance the need for coordination and synergies while encouraging local initiatives.
>
> The One Vodafone programme is a business integration activity and we are in the process of 'gradual integration of our business architecture'. For example, we are running down a real-time billing system to an integrated system for 28 million customers. It is a very difficult task if one tries to understand the billing system of mobile telephones. Under One Vodafone, there are currently eight programmes, networks (design and supply procurement, coordination and consolidation initiatives), IT (design, back office, billings, ERP/HR, operations – data centre processes), service platforms, roaming (mapping footprints), customer (next practice services), handset portfolio, MNC accounts, retailing (one won't believe, we are the eighth largest retailer in the world taking together our stores that are owned or franchised) ... We are trying to integrate national operating units across footprints and trying to leverage scale and scope while trying to retain the local autonomy and responsiveness of our challenger national units.

Alan Harper agreed that implementation of One Vodafone was a challenge. He explained:

> To implement One Vodafone, we have undertaken a change in the organizational structure of the group [refer to Exhibit 3.5]. We still operate in a matrix format. What One Vodafone tries to achieve is to simplify the integration issues in terms of brand strength and integrating local culture and processes. We centralize all our

marketing efforts, branding and product development. Technology is standardized. Network design (switching, radio) are coordinated. Best practices are benchmarked by Advance Services such as service platforms and portals (Vodafone live!). Knowledge is shared via the HQ, HR, strategy and marketing departments, through lateral processes, including our governance processes. We keep and encourage local initiatives such as customer services, sales, network billing, IT systems. We are trying to incorporate the best of all the cultures to the maximum extent possible, and in this way … we have tried to transform Vodafone UK into a new Vodafone. "

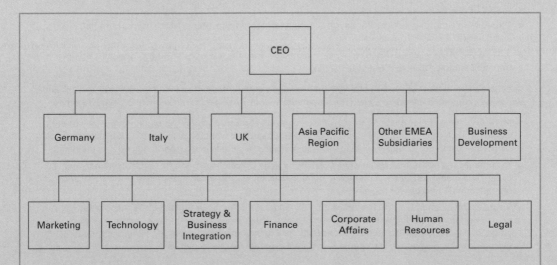

Vodafone Group plc ('Vodafone') announces board changes and a new organisational structure which will enable continued improvement in the delivery of the Group's strategic goals. This structure will become effective as from 1 January 2005.

The new organization is designed to:

- Focus more attention on customers in Vodafone's local markets;
- Enhance Vodafone's ability to deliver seamless services to corporations;
- Facilitate co-ordinated delivery of 3G across all markets;
- Function as an integrated company, delivering on One Vodafone; and
- Simplify decision-making, accountabilities and governance structures to speed up execution

Vodafone will simplify its existing regional structure with major countries and business areas reporting into the Chief Executive. All first line management functions in the Operating Companies will have a dual reporting line to the respective functions at Group level.

Arun Sarin, Chief Executive said: 'We are creating an organisation that is better positioned to respond to the high expectations of our customers. Faster execution will enable us to extend our lead within the mobile industry and deliver the benefits to our customers, our employees and our shareholders.'

Main Board Appointments
Sir Julian Horn-Smith will be appointed Deputy Chief Executive with effect from 1 January 2005. Vodafone separately announces that Andy Halford has been appointed Financial Director Designate. Andy will succeed Ken Hydon when he retires on 26 July 2005.

Operating Company Structure

Vodafone's operating company structure will be streamlined to ensure effective and fast decision-making, enabling improved time to market across a number of business initiatives. Consequently, the following operating companies and business areas will report directly into the Chief Executive:

- European Affiliates (Belgium, France, Poland, Romania and Switzerland) and Non-European Affiliates (China, Fiji, Kenya, South Africa and United States), led by Sir Julian Horn-Smith;
- Germany, led by Jürgen von Kuczkowski;
- Italy, led by Pietro Guindani;
- United Kingdom, led by Bill Morrow;
- Other EMEA Subsidiaries (Albania, Egypt, Greece, Hungary, Ireland, Malta, Netherlands, Portugal, Spain and Sweden), led by Paul Donovan;
- Asia Pacific (Australia, Japan and New Zealand), led by Brian Clark who will also be appointed Group Human Resources Director Designate

Vodafone's Group functions will be strengthened to support the delivery of seamless global propositions and Vodafone's continued integration. The following functions will also report directly into the Chief Executive:

- Marketing, led by Peter Bamford, the Chief Marketing Officer. This function will be reinforced by a newly created Multi National Corporates unit which will assume full accountability for serving Vodafone's global corporate customers. Group Marketing will also manage the global handset portfolio and procurement;
- Technology, led by Thomas Geitner, the Chief Technology Officer. In addition to standardized network design and global supply chain management, this function will introduce the concept of shared service operation for IT and service delivery;
- Business Development, a new function led by Sir Julian Horn-Smith. Sir Julian will be responsible for driving Vodafone's product and services portfolio into Vodafone's affiliates and the Partner Networks. In addition, this function will assume responsibility for expanding and consolidating Vodafone's footprint through the Partner Network programme and any Corporate Finance activities

New Governance Structure

Vodafone also announces changes to its governance process. The Group will have two management committees which will oversee the execution of the Main Board's strategy and policy.

- The Executive Committee
  Chaired by Arun Sarin, this committee will focus on the Group's strategy, financial structure and planning, succession planning, organizational development and Group-wide policies.
- The Integration and Operations Committee
  Chaired by Arun Sarin, this committee will be responsible for setting operational plans, budgets and forecasts, product and service development, customer segmentation, managing delivery of multi-market propositions and managing shared resources.

Exhibit 3.5 Board changes and new organizational structure as of January 2005
Source: www.vodafone.com

One Vodafone was clearly communicated across the company via internet, intranet and different training programmes, as well as a monthly employee magazine called *Vodafone life! The global magazine for all Vodafone people.* The HR department prepared special 'initiation' training programmes to acquaint new employees with the Vodafone way, labelled the 'Vodafone footstep', which included its vision and values (see Exhibit 3.6)

We have one vision and a set of values that underpins everything we do. Both our vision and our values were shared throughout the global organization.

Our vision
To be the world's mobile communications leader – enriching customers' lives, helping individuals, businesses and communities be more connected in a mobile world.

- Our customers use mobile communications to make their lives richer, more fulfilled, more connected. They will prefer Vodafone because the experience of using Vodafone will be the best they can find.
- We will lead in making the mobile the primary means of personal communications for every individual around the world.
- Through our leadership, our scale, our scope and our partnerships, we will bring online mobile services to the world.

Our values
Passion for customers
Our customers have chosen to trust us. In return, we must strive to anticipate and understand their needs and delight them with our service.

- We value our customers above everything else and aspire to make their lives richer, more fulfilled and more connected.
- We must always listen and respond to each of our customers.
- We will strive to delight our customers, anticipating their needs and delivering greater quality and more value, faster than anyone else.

Passion for our people
Outstanding people working together make Vodafone exceptionally successful.

- We seek to attract, develop, reward and retain outstanding individuals.
- We believe in empowerment and personal accountability.
- We enjoy what we do.
- We believe in the power of our teams.

Passion for results
We were action-oriented and driven by a desire to be the best.

- We were committed to be the best in all we do.
- We all play our part in delivering results.
- We seek speed, flexibility and efficiency in all we do.

Passion for the world around us
We will help people of the world to have fuller lives – both through the services we provide and through the impact we have on the world around us.

- We recognize the responsibilities that accompany the growth we have achieved.
- We will be a force for good in the world.
- A spirit of partnership and mutual respect was critical in all our activities.

Exhibit 3.6 Vodafone's vision & values
Source: www.vodafone.com

and the 'Ten Business Principles'.[27] On translating the vision and values alongside changes in structure and systems, Vodafone witnessed the revamping of people processes within the organization. Commenting on employees, Arun Sarin explained:

> As the business expands and the environment around us evolves, it is crucial for us to develop, recruit and retain the people that will lead us into this new world. We are working hard to make sure our employees have the right skills and knowledge to anticipate our customers' needs. We are identifying new ways to share the best of what we do on a global basis. We continue to reap the benefits of a motivated team with a strong customer service culture, which will help earn a reputation for Vodafone that is second to none.

The HR Department had set up a fast-track career path (the Global Leadership Programme, GLP) for high-potential managers, rotating them across business functions and countries, and equipping them with crucial multicultural skills.

Despite the integration and standardization efforts, the corporate headquarters had to ensure a certain level of independence for individual country subsidiaries to take into account differing business models and customer expectations. For example, 48 per cent of Vodafone's customers in Germany had a contract, while this kind of long-term commitment to an operator was almost unheard of in Italy (92 per cent were pre-pay customers).[28]

To orchestrate the move towards greater coordination, as well as to identify and disseminate best practices, the group had created two new central functions, Group Marketing (to drive revenue growth), and Group Technology and Business Integration (to drive cost and scale benefits).[29] Communicating Vodafone's new focus on integrating the bits and pieces resulting from past acquisitions was clearly a top management task. The Integration and Operations Committee was instituted, staffed with members of the Executive Board and chaired by Arun Sarin. This committee was responsible for 'setting operational plans, budgets and forecasts, product and service development, customer segmentation, managing delivery of multi-market propositions and managing shared resources' across geographies.[30] Alan Harper, who had been heading the group strategy department at Vodafone since 2000, saw his job title changed to Group Strategy and Business Integration Director. Simultaneously, Vodafone restructured itself at the corporate level to include the two new functions, which directly reported to the group's COO, Julian Horn-Smith.

Thomas Geitner was appointed head of the new unit, Group Technology & Business Integration, as Chief Technology Officer: 'The purpose of Group Technology will be to lead the implementation of a standardized architecture for business processes, information technology and network systems. This will support the next generation of products and services and the critical role of introducing and operating 3G capacity.'[31]

A key focus of Group Technology activities was the management and control of Group-wide projects in relation to the ongoing rollout of 'third generation' (3G) networks, the enhancement of Vodafone live! and the development of the Group's business offerings. This work included the continued development of technical specifications, the creation and management of global contracts with suppliers, as well as the testing of terminals.[32]

It was committed to providing underlying terminal and platform technologies on a global basis. Within the mobile phone industry, a shift of power away from handset makers (Nokia, Siemens, Ericsson, etc.) could be observed. Global operators such as Vodafone had increasingly succeeded in forcing the producers to offer specially designed and branded products: the thriving Vodafone live! multimedia service was launched on Sharp GX-10 handsets exclusively manufactured and branded for Vodafone.[33] If this trend persisted, Vodafone would be the first to benefit from its huge purchasing power and could even force Nokia (which had an almost 40 per cent world market share) to cater more towards Vodafone's needs.[34] Vodafone could also use its unrivalled clout when negotiating with network equipment suppliers (such as Alcatel, Nokia and Siemens) to squeeze their margins.

Peter Bamford was appointed Chief Marketing Officer and head of the Group Marketing department, which was in charge of 'providing leadership and coordination across the full range of marketing and commercial activities including brand, product development, content management, partner networks and global accounts'.[35]

For Vodafone, the question was how customers could derive a benefit from Vodafone's increasingly global reach, ultimately driving top-line growth. Alan Harper explains:

> We are a technology and sales and distribution group focused on local companies winning market share against incumbents in respective countries. We do not develop technology but we are users of technology. Technology is developed by companies such as Nokia, Ericsson and Nortel. We buy their technology – and technology evolution in our sector is more or less standard, it evolves, grows without major differentiations and after a period of time it is standardized. Now the challenge is how best we can leverage using and integrating the technology across our companies … With the evolution and growth of our company we are today more of a company that prides itself on the differentiation of the services that we bring to our customers. We are still 100 per cent sales driven but we are much more customer-centric and customer service orientated, and take pride in understanding customer needs as we graduate to offering our customers the next best service and focusing on customer delight (like, say, Amazon). We now execute much better and this is due to the shift in our competencies.

Vodafone started creating service offerings and product packages directly leveraging Vodafone's network and delivering tangible value to customers. For example, it created a tariff option that enabled customers to seamlessly roam the globe, on a special per-minute rate, on the same network, without having to worry about high interconnection fees or differing technical standards. A new unit within Group Marketing was created to develop and market services specifically tailored to the needs of global coordination, such as seamless wireless access to corporate IT systems and special rates for international calls on the network. Such a global service offering could clearly serve as a differentiating factor to competitors that could not match Vodafone's global footprint.

▶ ## Woes in the USA and France

There were still two nagging issues for Arun Sarin: Vodafone's 45 per cent stake in Verizon Wireless and the unresolved issues about control in France's SFR, for which Vodafone had been at loggerheads with Vivendi for several years. Vodafone was far from happy about these minority stakes, because they did not fit with its single-brand 'One Vodafone' strategy.

In the USA, Vodafone customers still could not use their cell phones on the Verizon Wireless network, because it operated under a different standard. It was indicated that this situation was likely to continue well into the era of 3G, because Verizon planned to adopt an incompatible standard.[36] Without a single technological platform and a uniform brand, Vodafone could extract little value from its American venture (except the cash dividend of $1 billion a year it received).[37] After the failed bid for AT&T Wireless, Vodafone had several options at its disposal, all of them with their own pros and cons.

Probably the most obvious option would be to takeover Verizon (the parent company of Verizon Wireless) completely, including its fixed-line business, in order to force it to adopt Vodafone standards. It was deemed likely that such a bid could escalate to a $150 billion hostile takeover battle, a figure that might be too large even for juggernaut Vodafone.[38] Verizon's management clearly was not willing to cede the wireless operations to Vodafone, but dreamt of becoming the single owner of Verizon Wireless itself.

Alternatively, Vodafone could buy another operator outright. But regulatory constraints would require it to sell its stake in Verizon Wireless first, because it was prohibited to own more than a 20 per cent stake in two competing operators at once. Under the current agreement with Verizon, Vodafone held a put option, which allowed it to sell some of the holdings each year at a fixed price to Verizon. If Vodafone decided to exercise this option, it had to do so by July 2006 in order to realize a maximum value of $20 billion. Verizon could choose to pay Vodafone either in cash or stock, although Vodafone had the right to a minimum cash sum of $7.5 billion.[39]

Some observers questioned the idea of selling Verizon and buying another operator, as Verizon Wireless was the most successful and profitable one – why swap 'a minority stake in a very good operator for a controlling stake in a less good one'?[40]

In France, Vodafone was in an equally uncomfortable position. It shared ownership of Cegetel, the parent company of France's number two mobile phone business SFR (35 per cent market share with 13.3 million customers), with Vivendi having the majority stake in the venture. On 31 March 2003, Vodafone's ownership interest in SFR was approximately 43.9 per cent, comprising a direct holding of 20 per cent in SFR and an indirect holding through its stake in Cegetel.[41] Commenting on Vodafone's struggle with Vivendi about SFR, an analyst at Global Equities SA joked, 'We have a saying: small minority shareholdings for little idiots; big minority shareholdings for big idiots.'[42]

While Vodafone managers had a certain say in the operations and strategy of SFR (SFR launched the co-branded multimedia services of Vodafone live!), Vivendi continued to refuse to sell SFR to Vodafone. Talks between Sarin and Fourtou, the CEO of Vivendi, did not yield any results, and Vivendi's true strategic intentions with SFR remained unclear.[43] The remaining 56 per cent stake in SFR was valued at roughly £8 billion ($13 billion).[44] After Vivendi declined Vodafone's offer for SFR in 2002, Vodafone issued a statement claiming that it was 'a long-term investor in Cegetel and SFR' and that it 'looks forward to continuing its successful partnership with Vivendi'.[45]

'France is a very simple market for us,' noted Alan Harper in April 2005. 'We know the market, we know the business model and we know the management of SFR, which takes part in routine Vodafone management meetings.' Pugnaciously, he added: 'The natural home of SFR is Vodafone. We are a very patient company.'

It remains to be seen whether Vivendi wants to keep its cash cow or if it was simply trying to push the price in this cat-and-mouse game.

Challenges ahead

Arun Sarin knew that his job would not become uninteresting anytime soon as many challenges lay ahead. Certainly, Vodafone was the largest player in the industry, but being active in 26 countries out of 200 left a lot of room to grow. As he closed his eyes and thought of Vodafone's global footprint, he was instantly reminded that Vodafone was not present in Latin America and in many African countries. Then there was the Middle East. Vast untapped markets lay ahead with today's mobile penetration of about 1.7 billion potential customers, of which Vodafone had about 3.5 million; in five years it would be 2.5 billion, half the world's population. And then there was his native country, India, where he invested $1.5 billion to buy a 10 per cent stake in Bharti Tele-Ventures, the largest mobile operator in the country. Countries in eastern Europe, many of which had recently entered the EU, should definitely be added to Vodafone's turf: Vodafone had just announced that it would be willing to invest up to $18 billion on acquisitions in Russia and other eastern European countries.[46] The 2005 acquisition of the mobile operators MobiFon (Romania) and Oskar (Czech Republic) was certainly just the first step in enlarging Vodafone's footprint.[47] Not to mention China. The sheer size of the market was awe-inspiring. Vodafone's strategic partner, China Mobile, alone had more than 150 million customers, but Vodafone only had a minuscule 3.27 per cent stake in the company.[48] For Vodafone, according to Alan Harper, this stake served as a:

> strategic foothold in a very important market with a relatively small-scale investment. China Mobile is the fastest-growing mobile company in the world today, connecting about 2–3 million customers a month. It has 70 per cent of the Chinese market share. Vodafone clearly understands that China Mobile can never become Vodafone China. That is a reality due to investment options and the quasi-political situation of the Chinese mobile telephony market. Knowing all

▶ this, we still invested in China Mobile because we feel that ... We learn everyday from China Mobile and our intention is to have regular knowledge flow between Vodafone and China Mobile. This is because our strategy is to make the technology standardized so that the learning between us is much faster ... Our investment in China Mobile is through China Mobile HK. We have a clear exit strategy with liquid assets, if our investment does not do well in the future. If it does well, we might think of increasing our foothold, but not to a sizeable extent. We are happy to have a foothold in one of the largest and fastest-growing markets of the world, with our investment we have an insider position, we have a position of influence with the operator, with the Chinese government, we have seat on the board, we have regular dialogue and our interest is to make China use the same technology as ours so that we can benefit from the scale and scope. **"**

At the same time, significant business risks lurked in all markets and Arun Sarin was well aware of them. In 2006, the merger of AT&T with Bellsouth Corp. had put pressure on Verizon Wireless to buy out Vodafone and force it to exit the US market. The introduction of 3G, which had a very promising start in Germany with good sales of mobile connect cards, might shift the focus of the whole industry away from networks to content. Revenue from voice traffic was flat or even declining due to competing technologies like internet calling, which was fundamentally changing the telecoms industry. Sarin knew that most of the growth would have to come from new data services. Competitors had also begun to get their feet on the ground again, with rumours about a merger between MMO$_2$'s German operations (O$_2$ Germany) and KPN's E-Plus.

Nokia had just presented its first WiFi-powered phone that did not need the traditional mobile network but a wireless LAN hotspot. If this technology should become popular, it would undermine Vodafone's current business model and could turn billions of fixed assets into worthless electronic scrap.[49]

At the beginning of 2006, Arun Sarin made some tough decisions. He faced up to slowing growth in his core market by unveiling an impairment charge of £23 billion to £28 billion ($40 billion to $49 billion) and exited the Japanese market by selling its stake to Tokyo-based Softbank in a deal valued at $15.4 billion, confirming that after the sale it would return $10.5 billion to its shareholders. Vodafone had trailed behind NTT DoCoMo and KDDI since its 2001 entry into Japan, due to fickle consumers, the lack of a low-end tier in the segment, and the challenge of coordinating terminals and technologies across borders. He managed to tighten his grip on the company and put down a boardroom revolt that had questioned his leadership. He not only won a public expression of support from Lord Ian MacLaurin, the company's Chairman, but also forced out Sir Christopher Gent, the Honorary Life President and former Chief Executive.

Arun Sarin thought Vodafone could have the best of both worlds. Now was the time to combine Vodafone's superior skills in acquiring companies with best-of-breed business integration and operational capabilities. He could ensure Vodafone's exceptional profitability for many years to come by keeping Vodafone a wireless company to the core, and also using innovations such as broadband wireless technology, known as WiMAX, to offer new services. It was now up to him to shape Vodafone's future.

Appendix 1: the economics of the mobile phone market: the role of fixed costs

The mobile phone market was characterized by extremely high fixed costs. The setting up of a nationwide network could require significant investments running into billions of euros.[50] Usually, an operator did not have the choice to offer network coverage limited to metropolitan areas (which would dramatically reduce the scale of initial investment required), either because of regulation prohibiting such a selective offer, or simply because national coverage was a key success factor for literally 'mobile' customers.

In some countries, the licences to operate using a certain bandwidth cost as much as €8 billion (the record price each operator in Germany paid for its UMTS licence to the government), adding huge financing charges to the already existing fixed costs.[51] However, once capacity was installed, the cost of an additional customer using the network was virtually zero, while every euro of revenue adds to the company's bottom line. An installed and running network was a foundation for reaching very high operating margins. Vodafone, for example, estimates that once the initial investments had been made, less than 10 per cent of revenues were needed to maintain the network.[52] Even the marketing campaigns benefited from the economies of scale: the larger an operator's customer base, the lower its per-user cost of such advertising efforts.

A substantial proportion of the costs described here were not only fixed, but also sunk, further aggravating the problem of price pressure. The investment into network could hardly be sold to anybody else (because of differing technological standards) and hence the initial cost was 'sunk'. Companies realize that they cannot undo their decision to invest, because the infrastructure is already there – it is rational for companies to act as if their initial investment was zero.

The existence of high fixed costs explained the periodic price wars that had driven prices down ever since mobile telecommunications started. Some operators had begun offering free calls or flat rates at the weekend (when capacity utilization was at the lowest). Usually, it was the smaller operators and the new market entrants that offered lower prices to reach a critical mass as quickly as possible. In Germany, which had one of the largest markets for mobile telephony with more than 60 million customers and a high population density, the threshold for an acceptable return on investment was estimated to be around 20 per cent of the total market share, which had neither been attained by O_2 (a subsidiary of MMO_2) nor by E-Plus (KPN).

The economics of the market necessitated that there were no more than three or four operators in a country (see Exhibit 3.7). In Germany, Mobilcom and Quam never reached critical size and had to exit the market in 2003 and 2002, respectively, writing off their individual investments of €8 billion each in 3G licences.[53]

Country	Service name:	Ownership (%):	Subsidiary (S), Associate (A) or Partner (P):	Proportionate customers (1000s):	No. of competitors:
			Europe		
Albania	Vodafone Albania	83.0	S	472 (31 Dec 2003)	1
Austria	A1	n/a	P	n/a	n/a
Belgium	Proximus	25.0	A	1,067 (31 Mar 2003)	2
Croatia	VIP	n/a	P	n/a	n/a
Cyprus	Cytamobile	n/a	P	n/a	n/a
Denmark	TDC Mobil	n/a	P	n/a	n/a
Estonia	Radiolinja	n/a	P	n/a	n/a
Finland	Radiolinja	n/a	P	n/a	n/a
France	SFR	43.9	A	5,931 (30 Jun 2003)	2
Germany	Vodafone Germany	100.0	S	24,668 (31 Dec 2003)	3
Greece	Vodafone Greece	98.2	S	2,373 (30 Jun 2003)	2
Hungary	Vodafone Hungary	87.9	S	1,170 (31 Dec 2003)	2
Iceland	Og Vodafone	n/a	P	n/a	n/a
Ireland	Vodafone Ireland	100	S	1,871 (31 Dec 2003)	2
Italy	Vodafone Italy	76.8	S	15,852 (31 Dec 2003)	3
Lithuania	Bit GSM	n/a	P	n/a	n/a
Luxembourg	LUXGSM	n/a	P	n/a	n/a
Malta	Vodafone Malta	100.0	S	162 (31 Dec 2003)	1
Netherlands	Vodafone Netherlands	99.8	S	3,400 (31 Dec 2003)	4
Poland	Plus GSM	19 Jun	A	949 (31 Mar 2003)	2
Portugal	Vodafone Portugal	100.0	S	3,332 (31 Dec 2003)	2
Romania	Connex	20 Jan	A	537 (31 Mar 2003)	3
Slovenia	Si.mobil	n/a	P	n/a	n/a
Spain	Vodafone Spain	100.0	S	9,685 (31 Dec 2003)	2
Sweden	Vodafone Sweden	99.1	S	1,409 (31 Dec 2003)	3
Switzerland	Swisscom Mobile	25.0	A	3,635 (31 Mar 2003)	3
United Kingdom	Vodafone Group	n/a	n/a	n/a	n/a
United Kingdom	Vodafone UK	100.0	S	13,947 (31 Dec 2003)	4
			Americas		
United States	Verizon Wireless	44.3	A	16,638 (31 Dec 2003)	Various
			Africa and Middle East		
Bahrain	MTC-Vodafone Bahrain	n/a	P	n/a	n/a
Egypt	Vodafone Egypt	67.0	S	1,838 (31 Dec 2003)	1
Kenya	Safaricom	35.0	A	303 (31 Mar 2003)	1
Kuwait	MTC-Vodafone	n/a	P	n/a	n/a
South Africa	Vodacom	35.0	A	2,756 (31 Mar 2003)	2
			Asia Pacific		
Australia	Vodafone Australia	100.0	S	2,676 (31 Dec 2003)	4
China	China Mobile (Hong Kong) Ltd	3.3	Investment	4,048 (31 Mar 2003)	2
Fiji	Vodafone Fiji	49.0	A	44 (31 Mar 2003)	None
Japan	Vodafone K.K. (Japan)	69.7	S	10,268 (31 Dec 2003)	3
New Zealand	Vodafone New Zealand	100.0	S	1,527 (31 Dec 2003)	1
Singapore	M1	n/a	P	n/a	n/a

Exhibit 3.7 Vodafone's subsidiaries, partners and investments around the globe

Source: adapted from corporate website (www.vodafone.com), accessed on 10 March 2004

Growth for a mobile phone company had so far mainly come from increased penetration, which stood at around 80 per cent in most mature markets (e.g. Germany: 74 per cent). With new customers becoming increasingly rare (see to Exhibit 3.8 for customers of Vodafone by country), operators were constantly searching for new sources of revenues and had introduced text messaging and other basic value-added services, such as downloadable ringtones and logos.[54] The standard measure in the industry to assess the quality of the customer base was average revenue per user (ARPU).[55]

Country	Customers
UK	13,313
Ireland	1,765
Germany	23,261
Hungary	952
Netherlands	3,312
Sweden	1,331
Italy	15,044
Albania	364
Greece	2,373
Malta	126
Portugal	3,129
Spain	9,184
United States	15,332
Japan	10,035
Australia	2,593
New Zealand	1,349
Egypt	1,609
Others	17,614
Group total	122,686

Exhibit 3.8 Customers by country (in '000s), as of 30 June 2003
Source: adapted from interim report, November 2003

As the new 3G networks (third generation, enabling high-speed data transmission) go online, available capacity will take another quantum leap, with unpredictable consequences for pricing. There seem to be promising opportunities to concentrate on the huge market for fixed-line telephony. Not surprisingly, there was a clear relation between the per minute price of a call and the average amount of cell phone usage. Conversely, there was no relation between the ARPU and the average price per minute charged, which indicated that customers substituted their fixed-line minutes with cell phone minutes whenever a price drop occurred. In other words, the increased quantity usually compensated the operator for the lower revenue per minute (see Exhibit 3.9).

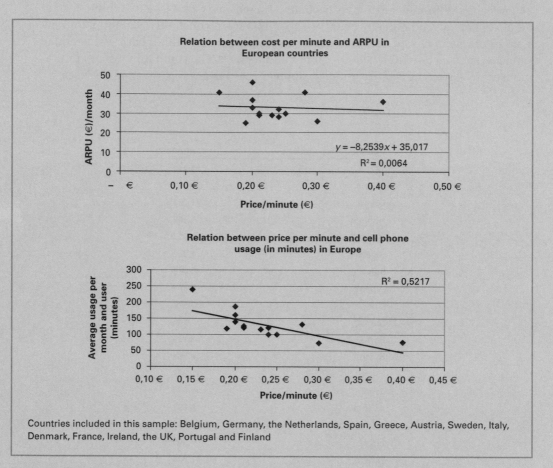

Relation between cost per minute and ARPU in European countries

$y = -8,2539x + 35,017$

$R^2 = 0,0064$

Relation between price per minute and cell phone usage (in minutes) in Europe

$R^2 = 0,5217$

Countries included in this sample: Belgium, Germany, the Netherlands, Spain, Greece, Austria, Sweden, Italy, Denmark, France, Ireland, the UK, Portugal and Finland

Exhibit 3.9 The relationships between per-minute prices and ARPU in European countries
Source: own analysis based on data by Merrill Lynch, Diamond Cluster; published in the *Frankfurter Allgemeine Zeitung*, 27 October 2003, p. 21

Another key performance indicator that had attracted management attention in recent years was the so-called 'churn rate', a percentage of the customer base being lost to competitors each year. In competitive markets with high handset subsidies, the churn rates of operators could be anywhere between 19 per cent (Germany) and 30 per cent (UK).[56] In other words, on average after three to five years, an operator had churned its entire customer base! These churn rates carried high costs for the operators, because they had to spend heavily, mainly on marketing and handset subsidies to attract new customers and to retain the old ones. Customer acquisition costs easily exceeded €100 per new customer or made up to 12.4 per cent of service revenue (figure for Vodafone Germany).[57] If an operator added low-value customers (i.e. those with a low monthly ARPU), it could take many months until the operator could break even on a customer.

Notes

[1] The scenario described herein was fictional. However, all data relating to the AT&T Wireless deal was factual: *Financial Times Deutschland*, 17 February 2004, www.ftd.de.

[2] *Financial Times Deutschland*, 12 February 2004, www.ftd.de.

[3] *Financial Times Deutschland*, 17 February 2004, www.ftd.de.

[4] Equal to Christopher Gent's compensation as reported in the Company Annual Report 2003. This figure does not include stock options and performance-based pay.

[5] Corporate website (http://www.vodafone.com/), data current as of 31 December 2003.

[6] Yahoo! Finance (http://finance.yahoo.com), 13 March 2004.

[7] Annual Report 2003, available at www.vodafone.com.

[8] Interim results for the six months to 30 September 2003, published 18 November 2003; available at www.vodafone.com.

[9] Company annual report 2004.

[10] This historic overview follows information provided at http://www.vodafone.com/, accessed on 5 March 2004.

[11] www.vodafone.com.

[12] Reportedly, Sir Christopher Gent closed the deal with AirTouch via his cell phone from Australia, where he was watching a game of cricket: *Independent* (London), 17 January 1999: 'Vodafone's boss realises long-held ambition with the acquisition of AirTouch'.

[13] *Financial Times Deutschland*, 17 February 2004, www.ftd.de.

[14] A chronology of the takeover battle was provided at http://www.manager-magazin.de/unternehmen/artikel/0,2828,242161-2,00.html.

[15] 'A New Voice at Vodafone', *The Economist*, 2 August 2003, Vol. 368.

[16] Interim Results for the six months to 30 September 2003, published 18 November 2003; available at www.vodafone.com.

[17] 'Vodafone starts wireline attack, first in Germany', *Dow Jones International News*, 10 March 2005.

[18] *Ibid.*

[19] 'Keeping pole position', *Total Telecom Magazine*, August 2003.

[20] *Ibid.*

[21] www.vodafone.com.

[22] With Australia and Japan being notable exceptions.

[23] Quoted in 'Vodafone dominance tipped to keep rolling', *Utility Week*, 31 January 2003.

[24] 'A new voice at Vodafone', *The Economist*, 2 August 2003, Vol. 368.

[25] *Ibid.*

[26] Presentation to analysts and investors on 27 September 2004, available at www.vodafone.com.

[27] www.vodafone.de and www.vodafone.com.

[28] *Ibid.*, p. 8.

[29] Press release on 23 June 2003, available at www.vodafone.com.

[30] www.vodafone.com.

[31] *Ibid.*

[32] Interim results for the six months to 30 September 2003, p. 16.

[33] According to the Key Performance Indicators for the quarter ended 31 December 2003, released on 28 January 2004; available at www.vodafone.com. Vodafone live! had over 4.5 million customers in 15 countries as of 13 November 2003.

[34] 'Keeping pole position', *Total Telecom Magazine*, August 2003.

[35] *Ibid.*

[36] 'A New Voice at Vodafone', *The Economist*, 2 August 2003, Vol. 368.

[37] 'Where does vodafone turn now?' *Business Week Online*, 18 February 2004. 'Keeping pole position', *Total Telecom Magazine*, August 2003, quotes £564 million as cash dividend in financial year 2002/2003, equivalent to 11 per cent of Vodafone's free cash flow. This arrangement expires in April 2005.

[38] 'Where does vodafone turn now?' *Business Week Online*, 18 February 2004.

[39] 'Keeping pole position', *Total Telecom Magazine*, August 2003.

[40] Bob House of Adventis, a consultancy, quoted in: 'Vodafone's dilemma', *The Economist*, 12 February 2004.

[41] Annual report 2003.

[42] Laurent Balcon, quoted in: 'Keeping pole position', *Total Telecom Magazine*, August 2003.

[43] 'Clear as mud: Vodafone versus Vivendi', *The Economist*, 7 December 2002.

[44] *Euromoney*, November 2003, Vol. 34 Issue 415.

[45] 'Clear as mud: Vodafone versus Vivendi', *The Economist*, 7 December 2002.

[46] www.Vwd.de Vereinigte Wirtschaftsdienste GmbH, 26 February 2004.

[47] According to a Vodafone press release on 15 March 2005, the Group paid approximately US$3.5 billion in cash for the transaction and thus could add 6.7 million customers.

[48] Annual Report 2004, p. 8.

[49] 'Nokia takes leap into Wi-Fi Phones', *Wall Street Journal Europe*, 23 February 2004.

[50] Vodafone for example had £24.1 billion as gross fixed assets in its balance sheet, 83 per cent of which were accounted for by network infrastructure. Annual Report 2003, p. 90.

[51] 'Vodafone prescht im Rennen um UMTS-Einführung vor', *Handelsblatt*, 13/14 February 2004.

[52] Annual Report 2003, p. 94

[53] 'Vodafone prescht im Rennen um UMTS-Einführung vor', *Handelsblatt*, 13/14 February 2004.

[54] In some instances, these new services already generate up to 20 per cent of revenues. *Ibid.*

[55] For example, Vodafone's ARPU in the UK was £297 and €312 in Germany for the year, according to the 'Interim results for the six months ended 30 September 2003'; available at www.vodafone.com.

[56] Data for Vodafone, which can be considered as representative for the industry. *Ibid.*

[57] *Ibid.*

? *Case questions*

Read the case carefully then answer the following questions.

1 What are Vodafone's core competencies? How can you explain its success over the past two decades?

2 Describe and analyse the impact of the economics of the mobile phone industry on the market structure and the strategies of the operators.

3 Can and/or should Vodafone continue growing by acquisition? Why or why not? What are the implications for managing its organizational design for its operations?

4 Try to locate Vodafone in the Local Responsiveness/Global Coordination matrix. Where is it now? Where will it move? How and why should it get there?

5 What was the cause for failure in Japan? What would you recommend Arun Sarin to do in the USA, France, India and China?

CHAPTER 4

Managing across cultures

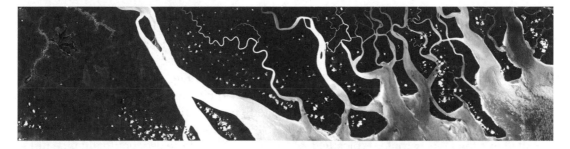

The previous chapter discussed the evolution and development of different organizational structures, their strengths and weaknesses and how global companies are designing their organizational structures in tandem with their growth objectives. This chapter continues the discussion, focusing on the challenges of managing across cultures. As global companies become bigger and bigger, the effective management of different subsidiaries becomes a challenge. This is mostly due to the companies' strong national heritages: while they have become global in their operations, they still operate from a nationalistic mindset.

Culture has been defined in many ways. Most believe that it arises out of acquired knowledge and experience over generations. This knowledge and experience generates social behaviours such as aesthetics, morals, values, norms, attitudes, beliefs, law, customs and religion. Culture is not innate; it is learned. It is not inherited; it is passed down from generation to generation, and is cumulative. It is symbolic, patterned, interrelated and adaptive. It has a structure. It is integrated and shared between individuals, groups, organizations, societies and nations. These characteristics are manifested in the forms of education and language, as well as the political and societal framework within a nation. Anthropologists interpret the societal framework in two ways: based on kinship and on associations between individuals that give rise to a country's national culture.

Managing a corporation across cultures necessitates the balancing of similarities and differences. Global managers sometimes cater to *parochialism* or *simplification* to manage these similarities and differences. Parochialism is a way of looking at the world through one's own lens, background and perspectives. On the other hand, simplification is a way of understanding that human beings who come from different cultures are still similar in their basic nature, relationships, modes of behaviour and activities in time and space. For example, an MBA student who was born in Spain and has lived for a considerable portion of his life in Russia and France perceives these two cultures differently. From living in

Russia, he learned never to be late, not to open gifts in front of the host, to shake hands with men only once inside the house or before entering the house (since Russians believe that it brings bad luck to the house if one shakes hands at the door or while entering), never to refuse to drink vodka, to always compliment the cook, and not to be impatient. In France, he learned that power is centralized, value is placed on unwritten customary rules, administrative processes are rigorous and can be compared to those in the army, to enjoy life, to stay close to friends, and to speak the 'French way' and not like a foreigner. His home country of Spain is influenced by the Roman Catholic church: envy is a national illness, leading to complaints and comparisons with neighbours, success is attributed to luck and not hard work, laziness is valued, siesta time is observed, and life is full of cooking, sun, beaches and nightlife.

The above examples corroborate Perlmutter's seminal article,[1] in which he identifies three cultural attitudes or states of mind of managers working for global corporations. They are **e**thnocentric (or home country orientated), **p**olycentric (or host country orientated), **r**egion-centric (or regional orientated) and **g**eocentric (or world orientated). He called this the EPRG profile. Typically, R&D turns out to be more geocentric, finance turns out to be more ethnocentric, while marketing functions are more polycentric, particularly in developed economies. In most global corporations, this profile generates tensions as corporations try to seek the dominant cultural mix but often fall short of providing one due to the orientation of top management.

Managing a business globally requires the management of diverse conflicting tensions, one of them being host country culture vs the national culture. The key argument is that the national cultural roots partly determine a global corporation's behaviour. This implies that a global corporation has to understand the cultures of the different nations where it operates and learn how to adapt to those cultures. For example, it is generally concluded that the USA, France and Japan have different national cultures. France and Japan tend to have a centralized decision-making process, while the USA tends to favour decentralized decision making. The USA prefers risk-taking, innovation, a short-term orientation and low organizational loyalty, whereas France and Japan favour stability, a long-term orientation and high organizational loyalty. The USA and France favour competition and individual rewards, while Japan favours cooperation and group rewards. The USA and Japan favour strict formal procedures, while France favours more informal work processes. A variety of research recommendations have pointed out that US corporations focus on lower quality and lower price, European corporations pursue a strategy of high quality and price, while Japanese corporations focus on high value and low price. Thus, it can be concluded that inter-country differences are substantial and global corporations have to manage these differences.

Three milestone studies on national cultures have been conducted in the last three decades, by Geert Hofstede, Fons Trompenaars and a group of researchers around the world, commonly referred to as the GLOBE study. In his study with more than 116,000 respondents from more than 70 countries, Hofstede identified five major dimensions of culture: power distance, uncertainty avoidance, individualism, masculinity and long-term

[1] Perlmutter, H.V. (1969) 'The tortuous evolution of the multi-national', *Journal of World Business*, 4, 9–18.

orientation. In his work, he proposes that his dimensions are indicative of and affect the political and social system of a nation. Table 4.1 gives an example of the highest and lowest Hofstede index scores in his first four dimensions.

	Power distance	Uncertainty avoidance	Individualism	Masculinity
Highest three	Mexico [81]	Belgium [94]	USA [91]	Japan [95]
	India [77]	Japan [92]	Australia [90]	Austria [79]
	Singapore [74]	France [86]	UK [89]	Italy [70]
Lowest three	Denmark [18]	Greece [11]	Singapore [20]	Netherlands [15]
	Israel [13]	Portugal [10]	S. Korea [18]	Norway [8]
	Austria [11]	Singapore [8]	Pakistan [14]	Sweden [5]

Table 4.1 Highest and lowest Hofstede (2003)[2] index scores in four dimensions

Another Dutch researcher, Fons Trompenaars,[3] in his study with 15,000 managers from 28 countries conducted over a period of ten years, derived five relationship orientations (somewhat similar to Hofstede's dimensions) that address how people deal with one another. His dimensions were based on 23 countries from which he had at least 500 respondents. The dimensions were universalism–particularism, individualism–communitarianism, neutral–emotional, specific–diffuse and achievement–ascription. Table 4.2 gives the highest and lowest Trompenaars (1994)[4] scores in four dimensions.

	Universalism	Individualism	Neutral	Specific	Achievement
Highest three	USA	USA	Japan	Australia	Australia
	Australia	Czech	UK	UK	USA
	Germany	Argentina	Singapore	USA	UK
	Particularism	**Communitarianism**	**Emotional**	**Diffuse**	**Ascription**
Lowest three	Venezuela	Singapore	Mexico	Venezuela	Venezuela
	CIS	Thailand	Netherlands	China	Indonesia
	Indonesia	Japan	Switzerland	Spain	China

Table 4.2 Highest and lowest Trompenaars (1994)[5] scores in four dimensions

---

[2] Hofstede, G. (2003) *Comparing Values, Behaviors, Institutions and Organizations across Nations.* Thousand Oaks, London and New Delhi: Sage.

[3] Trompenaars, F. (1994) *Riding the Waves of Culture: Understanding Diversity in Global Business.* New York: Irwin.

[4] *Ibid.*

[5] *Ibid.*

The Global Leadership and Organizational Behavior Effectiveness (GLOBE)[6] study was an attempt to integrate and extend previous research on cultural attributes and leadership. The study comprised nine different cultural attributes in three industries (financial services, food processing and telecommunications), with more than 17,000 respondents. The respondents were middle managers from 825 organizations in 62 countries. The nine cultural attributes were: uncertainty avoidance (UA), power distance (PD), societal collectivism (SC), in-group collectivism (I-GC), gender egalitarianism (GE), assertiveness (A), future orientation (FO), performance orientation (PO) and humane orientation (HO). The GLOBE study reinforced Hofstede and Trompenaars' conclusion, and extended it by certain dimensions while focusing more on differences in managerial leadership styles. Table 4.3 gives the highest and lowest GLOBE scores in four dimensions.

	UA	PD	SC	I-GC	GE	A	FO	PO	HO
Highest three	Spain	Denmark	South Korea	Austria	Russia	Austria	Singapore	USA	Philippines
	USA	Canada	Egypt	Denmark	Spain	Greece	Switzerland	Taiwan	Ireland
						USA	Netherlands	NZ	Malaysia
	UA	PD	SC	I-GC	GE	A	FO	PO	HO
Lowest three	Sweden	Russia	Sweden	Russia	Denmark	Sweden	Kuwait	Russia	Brazil
	NZ	Argentina	Denmark	Hungary	Netherlands	NZ	Italy	Argentina	Singapore
						Japan	Poland	Greece	France

Table 4.3 Highest and lowest GLOBE scores

In conclusion, national differences like autocratic or participative, implementation of rules and cooperation–competition norms exist in management styles. There are differences in the degree to which people trust one another and believe in externalities like luck or fate. The ability to plan for the uncertain future is another variable. Processing of subtle information, communication styles and the notion of time are important to understanding differences in cultures. Born in Brazil to Lebanese parents and educated in France, Carlos Ghosn, CEO of Renault-Nissan sums it up thus:[7]

> ❝ Renault remained sensitive to Nissan's culture at all times, allowing the company room to develop a new corporate culture that built on the best elements of Japan's national culture ... I dismantled Nissan's *keiretsu* investments, ditched the seniority rule, revamped compensation system to one that focused on performance, eliminated the position of 'advisors' (deep culture change) and gave operating responsibility, built trust through transparency, mobilized cross-functional teams that transitioned to cross-company teams which focused on mingling of culture rather on positions ... On the whole, I think Nissan's

[6] House, R., Hanges, P.J., Javidan, M. and Gupta, V. (2004) *Culture, Leadership and Organizations: The GLOBE Study of 62 Societies.* London: Sage.

[7] Ghosn, C. (2002) 'Saving the business without losing the company', *Harvard Business Review*, 80(1), January, 3–10.

identity and culture as a company have been far more important factors in its performance than its country of origin … In fact, looking to national culture for an explanation of a company's failure or success almost always means you are missing a point. All that a national culture does is provide the company with the raw human resources for competing … no matter how promising your resources, you will never be able to turn them into gold unless you get the corporate culture right. A good corporate culture taps into the productive aspects of a country's culture, and in Nissan's case we have been able to exploit the uniquely Japanese combination of keen competitiveness and sense of community that has driven the likes of Sony and Toyota – and Nissan itself in earlier times. **"**

Case introduction: Lafarge: from French cement company to global leader

Lafarge is a French company that has become the largest building and construction material company in the world. In the last decade, Lafarge accelerated the pace of its growth into new countries by acquiring companies, and expanding into new businesses and new products through its four divisions: cement, aggregates and concrete, roofing and gypsum. Numerous acquisitions and joint ventures in all four divisions and on every continent, particularly Asia, have allowed Lafarge to continue consolidating its position as a world leader in cement. Lafarge, in 2002, operated in 75 countries with 77,000 employees and posted €14.6 billion of annual sales through its four divisions. Just five years earlier, in 1997, Lafarge operated in only 35 countries with 35,000 people and had sales of €6.4 billion. This case describes Lafarge's policy of 'growth and profitable growth' by successful acquisitions and post-merger integration. The case deals with the issues of internal restructuring to fuel its external strategy of growth, and traces the process of internationalization of a French cement producer. The case also examines the basis for globalization of what many would think of as a very 'local business'. It presents an opportunity to examine the logic of global competitive moves. Lafarge, with its transfer of best practices, managing its people the 'Lafarge Way' and the way it manages cultural diversity, provides a basis for discussing the sources of superior performance in a global context. In addition, the wide array of benefits that Lafarge derives from its operations in different countries broadens conventional notions of why firms globalize.

This case appears after the readings for this chapter.

Leading by leveraging culture*

Jennifer A. Chatman and Sandra Eunyoung Cha[†]

We occasionally get calls from prospective clients who, having heard that we consult with organizations to improve their cultures, ask us, 'Come on down to our organization and get us a better one.' Perhaps they are thinking that, somehow, after we have worked our culture magic, employees will be singing and dancing in their cubicles. Although this is a nice image, simply trying to make employees happy misses the power of leveraging culture. The problem is that organizational culture has become faddish; and, as such, it has been over-applied and underspecified. Our goal here is to precisely clarify why culture is powerful and to provide specific criteria for developing a strong, strategically relevant culture that is likely to enhance an organization's performance over the long haul.

We will not claim that by simply managing culture, leaders will be assured of organizational success, or that by neglecting culture, they will be doomed to failure. Leveraging culture is but one of a number of key leadership tools. We *will* claim, however, that by actively managing culture, an organization will be more likely to deliver on its strategic objectives over the long run.

Why is organizational culture powerful?

Focusing people intensely on strategy execution

A 1999 *Fortune* magazine article highlighting pathbreaking research by Ram Charan and Geoffrey Colvin began with a provocative title: 'Why CEOs Fail.'[1] The definitive answer had been found, and it was notoriously simple: CEOs failed when they were unable to fully execute their strategy. This was an amazing conclusion because it stood in contrast to what industrial economists have been telling us for years – that firms with well-formulated and hard-to-imitate business strategies emerge as the winners.[2] Charan and Colvin's article suggested that firms whose strategies were merely reasonable but were executed fully could be the most successful.

California Management Review, 45(4), Summer 2003.

Copyright © 2003 by The Regents of the University of California. Reprinted from the *California Management Review*, Vol. 45, No. 4. By permission of The Regents.

California Management Review, University of California ■ F501 Haas School of Business #1900 ■ Berkeley, CA 94720-1900 (510) 642-7159 ■ fax: (510) 642-1318 ■ e-mail: cmr@haas.berkeley.edu ■ web site: www.haas.berkeley.edu/cmr/

Copyright ©2003 EBSCO Publishing

[†]The first author wrote this article while a Marvin Bower Fellow at the Harvard Business School and is grateful for their support.

This shifts the focus from strategy formulation to strategy *execution* – and culture is all about execution. Consider the often-cited example of Southwest Airlines, a company with a transparent, almost simple, strategy: high volume along with short and convenient flights using only fuel-efficient 737s, culminating in low costs and the ability to offer customers low-priced tickets. As a result, Southwest has been the only U.S. airline to be profitable for 28 consecutive years.[3] One key to Southwest's success is its remarkably short turnaround time, 15 minutes versus competitors' average of 35 minutes.[4] Planes don't sit long at the jet way. Instead, employees across functional lines band together to get the planes out quickly. This results in an average plane utilization of around 12 hours at Southwest versus the industry average of closer to 9 hours. Southwest's success hinges not on how brilliant, unique, or opaque their strategy is, but on the alignment between their culture and strategy, on how clearly employees understand the culture and how intensely they feel about it.

Culture is a system of shared values (defining what is important) and norms (defining appropriate attitudes and behaviors).[5] Strong cultures enhance organizational performance in two ways. First, they improve performance by energizing employees – appealing to their higher ideals and values and rallying them around a set of meaningful, unified goals. Such ideals excite employee commitment and effort because they are inherently engaging[6] and fill voids in identity and meaning.[7] Second, strong cultures boost performance by shaping and coordinating employees' behavior. Stated values and norms focus employees' attention on organizational priorities that then guide their behavior and decision making. They do so without impinging, as formal control systems do, on the autonomy necessary for excellent performance under changing conditions.[8]

An effective culture is closely related to business strategy. Indeed, a culture cannot be crafted until an organization has first developed its business strategy. The first criterion for using culture as a leadership tool is that it must be *strategically relevant*.

Formal versus social control: the power of shared norms

Norms – legitimate, socially shared standards against which the appropriateness of behavior can be evaluated – are the psychological bases of culture.[9] Norms influence how members perceive and interact with one another, approach decisions, and solve problems.[10] Norms are distinct from rules, which are formal, codified directives. The concept of norms also implies social control – that is, norms act as positive or negative means of ensuring conformity and applying sanctions to deviant behavior.[11]

Roethlisberger and Dickson's classic research showed that group norms shaped employee's behavior more powerfully than either monetary rewards or physical work environments.[12] Employees at Western Electric's Hawthorne Plant developed norms that dictated the acceptable amount of work each employee should complete. Unfortunately, this constrained many employees' productivity. Just as those who worked too little, those who worked *too much* were shunned by other members of the work unit. As a result, few employees deviated from the norm. We are so influenced by other's expectations, specifically their expectations that we uphold shared social norms, that we are willing and likely to *alter our behavior* in their presence – that is, to do something different than we would do if we were alone. We assimilate because the consequences of violating strong norms – at best, embarrassment, and, at worst, exclusion or alienation from the social group – threaten our ability to survive in an interdependent world.

How then, do norms work in today's organizations? Consider an example from the first author's personal experience while shopping at Nordstrom, a strong culture organization known for its emphasis on customer service. Lance, a polite and attentive sales associate showed her nine pairs of shoes. Unfortunately, the store did not have the size/color/style combination that she wanted. As she was leaving, another sales associate, Howard, approached and suggested that he could call a few other Nordstrom stores to find the shoes. Ten minutes later, Howard excitedly informed her that, though he had not found the shoes at another Nordstrom store, he did find them at a nearby Macy's (a primary Nordstrom competitor). Rather than sending her to Macy's, Howard had already arranged for the shoes to be overnight mailed to her home. 'Of course,' Howard informed her, 'Macy's will bill you for the shoes, but Nordstrom will pay for the overnight delivery charge.' Howard understood the importance of customer service and was willing to go above and beyond the call of duty to ensure that even Lance's customer was completely satisfied. Furthermore, while leaving Nordstrom, the first author overheard an interaction that she was, clearly, not supposed to hear. Howard had gone back to Lance and said, 'I can't believe you didn't work harder to find those shoes for her. You really let *us* down.' Remember, Howard is not Lance's boss – they are peers – and yet, the norms encouraging customer service at Nordstrom are so strong that members are willing to sanction each other, regardless of status, for a failure to uphold those norms.

Nordstrom prides itself on providing, not average or good, but *outstanding* customer service. The problem is that relying on formal rules, policies, and procedures will not result in outstanding anything, be it customer service, innovation, or quality. Think back to the last time you had a peak consumer experience – when you were 'wowed' by someone or an organization. What impressed you? When we ask people this question, they typically talk about how someone went above and beyond the call of duty to solve *their specific problem*. Formal rules are useful for standardizing performance and avoiding having to relearn things each time. However, they are only useful for addressing situations that are *predictable and regular*.[13] In contrast, outstanding service is determined, in customer's eyes, by how organizations deal with situations that are nearly impossible to anticipate, unique to a particular person, and difficult to solve.

The irony of leadership through culture is that the less formal direction you give employees about how to execute strategy, the more ownership they take over their actions and the better they perform. New employees at Nordstrom are told simply to 'use your good judgment in all situations.'[14] At Southwest, they are encouraged to 'do what it takes to make the Customer happy.'[15] Employees have to be freed up from rules in order to deliver fully on strategic objectives; they have to understand the ultimate strategic goals and the norms through which they can be successfully achieved, and they must *care* about reaching those goals and what their coworkers will think of them if they don't. Strong norms increase members' clarity about priorities and expectations as well as their bonds with one another. Unlike formal rules, policies, and procedures, culture empowers employees to think and act on their own in pursuit of strategic objectives, increasing their commitment to those goals.[16] Violations are considered in terms of letting their colleagues down rather than breaking rules. The payoff is huge. If Howard is monitoring his own behavior against Nordstrom's strategic objectives – *as well as Lance's* – their manager does not have to spend time looking over their shoulders and can, instead, focus on the really important work of leadership: planning for the next strategic challenge and supporting employees so they can do an outstanding job. Thus, the second criterion for using culture as a leadership tool is that it be *strong*.

What makes culture strong?

Strong cultures are based on two characteristics, high levels of agreement among employees about what's valued and high levels of intensity about these values. If both are high, a strong culture exists; and if both are low, the culture is not strong at all. Some organizations are characterized by high levels of intensity but low levels of agreement, or what could be called 'warring factions.'[17] Such intensity exists within many high-tech firms, but groups disagree about priorities. For example, marketing groups typically focus on customer-driven product features while engineering groups focus on elegant product designs.

More common, however, are organizations in which members agree about what's important, but they don't much care and, as such, are unwilling to go the extra mile (e.g., take a risk, stay late) to deliver on strategic objectives or to sanction others for a failure to uphold those norms. These are called 'vacuous' cultures and their prevalence probably reflects the faddish nature of organizational culture and the lip service such organizations pay to it.[18] Most organizations are aware of the importance of managing culture, but in their attempt to jump on the culture bandwagon they are unable to develop the clarity, consistency, and comprehensiveness that encourage employees to care intensely about executing strategic objectives.

Though strong organizational cultures have long been touted as critical to bottom-line performance in large organizations,[19] newer evidence from a unique sample suggests that developing a strong, strategically relevant culture may be best accomplished when an organization is young. In a longitudinal study of 173 young high-technology companies, founders' initial model of the employment relation dramatically influenced their firms' later success.[20] Firms that switched models as they aged were less successful. Firms that were built around the commitment model, which emphasizes a strong culture and hiring based on culture fit, stood out from those founded on the engineering or bureaucracy models by completing initial public stock offerings sooner.[21]

Emphasizing innovation

The final criterion for using culture as a leadership tool involves the content of organizational culture. Though organizational norms revolve around many dimensions,[22] only one appears to be universally applicable across organizations regardless of their size, industry, or age and that is innovation.[23] In a comprehensive longitudinal study of 207 large firms over an 11-year period, Kotter and Heskett found that firms that developed a strong, strategically appropriate culture performed effectively over the long run only if their culture also contained norms and values that promoted innovation and change.[24]

Most creativity research has focused on hiring creative people, but innovation may depend more on whether cultural norms support risk-taking and change.[25] Consider the following study. Outside observers were asked to evaluate the intelligence of product development team members engaged in meetings in which one member was pitching a product idea to the other members. Guess whose intelligence was rated the lowest by the outside observers time and again? It was the person pitching the product idea. Why would this be the case? Imagine what team members are saying – things like: 'Didn't you think of ... ?' and 'We already tried ... .' The product pitcher is responding with phrases such as 'Um, I'm not sure' and 'I don't know.' Not only are critical skills valued more than creative skills, but also creativity and wisdom are inversely related in people's minds.[26] Expressing a creative idea is, therefore, risky – since a person suggesting one can end up being perceived as unintelligent.[27] The lesson for organizations is clear: employees may refrain from generating creative ideas because the cost of expressing them is too high. Managers can bet on their employees having creative ideas in their head – about how to do their jobs better, improve a system, or develop a new product. The question is: Are they willing to say their ideas out loud?

Establishing these norms and promoting innovation may require thinking unconventionally and adopting some 'weird' ideas such as 'ignore people who have solved the exact problem you face' and 'find some happy people and get them to fight.'[28] Three times a year, executives at Walt Disney Company host a 'Gong Show' in which everyone in the company – including secretaries, janitors, and mailroom staff – gets to pitch movie ideas to the top executives.[29] Structured brainstorming groups can also create an environment where publicly raising creative ideas is not only acceptable, but also rewarded socially. At IDEO, one of the most successful product development companies in history, brainstorming sessions take on the character of a 'status auction' where the more creative the idea, the higher the bid.[30]

Leaders also promote innovation by creating a shared belief that team members are safe to take interpersonal risks. When employees feel psychologically safe, they engage in learning behavior – they ask questions, seek feedback, experiment, reflect on results, and discuss errors or unexpected outcomes openly.[31] Leaders create these norms by influencing the way creative ideas and errors are handled, which, in turn, leads to shared perceptions of how consequential it is to make a mistake. These perceptions influence employees' willingness to report mistakes and ultimately can feed into a more lasting culture of fear or of openness that will influence employees' ability to identify and discuss problems and develop new ideas.[32]

Finally, leaders must move quickly to implement promising ideas. Consider Charles Schwab's foray into Internet stock trading – or, rather, their near-invention of this entire category of trading.[33] In late 1995, one of CIO Dawn Lepore's research groups developed experimental software that would allow Schwab's computer systems to talk to one another. The research team was aware that it would be difficult to explain to Lepore the merits of this rather unsexy middleware project. Therefore, they put together a separate piece of front-end software that would demonstrate one of many possible applications. The demo was scheduled, and Lepore by chance brought along Charles Schwab, a self-described techno-buff. The front-end software the engineers put together was a simple web-based software trade. They were, of course, less interested in pursuing an online brokerage than in gaining Lepore's approval to continue working on their obscure project. However, Lepore and Schwab instantly recognized the value of this technology, with Schwab recalling that 'I fell off my chair.'[34]

Within weeks, Schwab had put together a team to commercialize an online brokerage. The team was fed resources and protected from the larger bureaucracy, reporting directly to Schwab President David Pottruck. As Pottruck said, 'We needed a group that felt like they were nimble, unshackled from the larger bureaucracy.'[35] Within three months the team had developed a commercial product, and within two weeks of introducing it, Schwab amassed 25,000 online brokerage subscribers, their goal for the entire year. By 1998, Schwab had captured 30% of the online market share, roughly equal to the next three online competitors combined (E*Trade, Fidelity, and Waterhouse Securities). Two lessons are relevant here. First, developing a culture that encourages employees to express creative ideas may cause good ideas to crop up from unexpected places. Second, and more importantly, once managers spot a good idea, norms that emphasize urgency and speed will ensure its implementation.

Leadership tools to manage and change organizational culture

These three criteria for using culture as a leadership tool are supported by substantial empirical and applied evidence.[36] The question, however, is how can leaders develop, manage, and change their culture to meet these criteria and promote extraordinary performance? There are three key managerial tools for leveraging culture for performance.[37]

Tool #1: recruiting and selecting people for culture fit

Selection is the process of choosing new members (for organizations) and choosing to join a particular organization (for job candidates). Our approach to selection contrasts with typical approaches by emphasizing person-culture fit in addition to person-job fit.[38] This requires anticipating whether the culture a firm emphasizes will be rewarding for potential recruits.

First, consider General Electric's description of desirable candidates, who 'stimulate and relish change and are not frightened or paralyzed by it, see change as an opportunity, not a threat,' and 'have a passion for excellence, hating bureaucracy and all the nonsense that comes with it.' Note the intensity of the language, which does not focus on which computer programs people know or their geographic preferences, but rather their thirst for challenge and change. These are qualities that differentiate between people who are, and are not, successful at GE. Firms often get caught focusing exclusively on hiring people whose skills fit their entry-level jobs, and yet, if a person is successful, he or she will hold multiple jobs within the firm. These jobs are linked by the organizational culture. Therefore, it makes sense to hire people who will fit the culture, possibly even trading off some immediate skills necessary for the specific entry job for better culture fit. People can learn new skills; establishing culture fit is much harder.

Second, be mindful of recruiter characteristics.[39] A fundamental theory in psychology is the 'similarity-attraction effect.'[40] We are attracted to people who are similar to ourselves. Why? Well, most of us like ourselves, think we're doing a pretty good job, and wouldn't mind having lunch with ourselves now and then. Therefore, when you ask us to recruit new members, we are likely to pick people just like us. The message is simple but important: Be careful which people you send out to do your recruiting because you will get more of them back.

Third, consider the selection process in light of the organizational culture. How, for example, did Cisco Systems ensure high culture fit despite facing Silicon Valley's brutally competitive labor market in the late 1990s, hiring an average of 1000 new employees through small acquisitions and individual recruiting *every month?* First, they developed culturally consistent selection criteria targeting candidates who were frugal, enthusiastic about the future of the Internet, smart, and not obsessed with status.[41] Second, they conducted benchmarking studies and focus groups so that the selection process was maximally effective in getting the people they wanted.[42] Third, they targeted 'passive applicants,' people who are satisfied in their current jobs and not job hunting but who might be lured to Cisco, and developed a convenient web site for them to learn about Cisco. Noticing that they were getting over 500,000 hits per month during work hours, Cisco made sure that the web site was fast and easy to use; for example, the initial application took 5 minutes to complete. Applicants who pressed a 'friends@Cisco' hot key got a call from a current Cisco employee at a comparable level within 24 hours.[43] These discussions typically focused on the hard-to-convey culturally relevant information that, because of the similarity of the source to the candidate, provided credible information about what it is really like to work at Cisco. Cisco aggressively pursued and won desired candidates by constructing a comprehensive, culturally relevant selection process.

Tool #2: managing culture through socialization and training

Socialization is the process by which an individual comes to understand the values, abilities, expected behaviors, and social knowledge that are essential for assuming an organization role and participating as an organization member. Socialization and selection processes are somewhat substitutable.[44] In tight labor markets, firms need to rely more on socializing people once they join, and, conversely, when labor is more freely available and firms can be highly selective, they will not need to invest as much in socialization practices. Much is known about effective socialization practices.[45] Two key aspects of socialization are ensuring that employees acquire cultural knowledge and that they bond with one another.

At E*Trade, which was founded in 1996 and grew to become the #2 online brokerage by 1999, new employees are asked to stand up on a chair at their first staff meeting and tell everyone something embarrassing about themselves.[46] Though a slightly bizarre practice, it jibes with sound psychological logic. Once newcomers disclose this embarrassing thing about themselves, asking questions about their new job or company won't be nearly as embarrassing. Newcomers will be much more likely to ask their new colleagues for the information they need to hit the ground running in their new job without worrying about a loss of face since they already lost their face at that first meeting. Newcomers are grateful that their new colleagues accept them despite their faults. Further, knowing that others have gone through this unique initiation rite creates a bond that allows members to work together more effectively and, by increasing their accountability to others, makes it more likely that newcomers will work hard to uphold established organizational norms. E*Trade's CEO, Christos Cotsakos, has also taken his executive team Formula One racing to make them 'move faster' and has enrolled them in cooking school to increase their agility in working together.[47] These practices promote the two goals of socialization: clarifying the cultural values and creating strong bonds among employees so that they are accountable to one another for upholding those values.

Tool #3: managing culture through the reward system

Culture is an organization's informal reward system and needs to be intricately connected to formal rewards. At CompUSA, the largest retailer and reseller of personal computer related products and services in the United States, CEO James Halpin has created 'a cross between a college fraternity and a military boot camp.'[48] The company's strategic focus on revenue is extremely salient, sometimes encompassed in rather uncomfortable practices. For example, regional sales managers attending quarterly meetings are assigned a seat at the U-shaped table according to their store sales, with those with the lowest sales being assigned to the tables nearest the front because, as Halpin says, 'they have to listen to everything we've got to say.'[49] Name badges include a person's name and their stores' 'shrink number,' or inventory losses due to theft or accounting errors. On the positive reinforcement side, when employees make large commissions – such as when a young employee made $50,000 in commission in one month – Halpin travels to their store to deliver the cash to them personally, in front of customers and other employees. Though these specific rewards (and punishments) may be inappropriate for some organizations, the lesson is that rewards need to be clear, consistent, and comprehensive – the focus on generating revenues at CompUSA is simply impossible for employees to miss.

Pitfalls inherent in leading through culture

It is extremely important that organizational leaders cultivate their organizational culture. Employees attend vigilantly to leaders' behavior, even to the rather mundane aspects such as what they spend time on, put on their calendar, ask and fail to ask, follow up on, and celebrate.[50] These behaviors provide employees with evidence about what counts and what behaviors of their own are likely to be rewarded or punished. They convey much more to employees about priorities than do printed vision statements and formal policies. Once leaders embark on the path to using culture as a business tool, it is critical that they regularly review their own behavior to understand the signals they are sending to members.

Ironically, leading through culture can set leaders up to be vulnerable to a problem created by a series of psychological processes, recently labeled the 'hypocrisy attribution dynamic.'[51] Cultural values are powerful because they inspire people by appealing to their ideals, and they clarify expectations by making salient the consistency between these values and each member's own behavior.[52] However, just as emphasizing cultural values inherently alerts us to our own behavior, it makes others' behavior salient too, giving us high standards for judging them as well. We then become particularly attentive to possible violations, especially by leaders, who are highly visible based on their power over our fate at work. When we detect potential inconsistencies between stated values and observed actions, our cognitive tendency to judge others harshly kicks in.

Leaders who emphasize cultural values should expect employees to interpret those values by adding their own layers of meaning to them. Over time, an event inevitably occurs that puts leaders at risk of being viewed as acting inconsistently with the very values he or she has espoused. Employees are driven by the actor observer bias,[53] the human tendency to explain one's own behavior generously (viewing good outcomes as caused by one's own enduring dispositional attributes and bad outcomes as caused by situational influences) and to explain others' behavior unsympathetically (attributing good outcomes to situational influences and bad outcomes to others' enduring dispositional traits). When leaders behave in ways that appear to violate espoused organizational values, employees conclude that the leader is personally failing to 'walk the talk.' In short, organization members perceive hypocrisy and replace their hard-won commitment with performance-threatening cynicism. Worse yet, because such negative interpersonal judgments are inherently threatening, employees say nothing publicly, precluding a fair test of their conclusions and disabling organizational learning from the event. The process cycles as subsequent events are taken to confirm hypocrisy, and eventually a large number of employees may become disillusioned.

To avoid this undermining dynamic, leaders need to uphold their commitment to their culture even in the most trying times. Consider a pivotal moment at Dreyer's Grand Ice Cream, a $1 billion company.[54] In June of 1998, a set of unexpected events coincided to make it the toughest period the company had ever faced. First, the investments and actions to implement Dreyer's brand-building and national expansion goals took longer than expected and also substantially increased Dreyer's cost structure, thus affecting profitability. Second, Dreyer's CEO, Gary Rogers, had been diagnosed with a brain tumor and had undergone neurosurgery and radiation treatment earlier that spring. A number of unexpected external challenges surfaced as well. Butterfat, the key ice cream ingredient, rose to a record high of $2.91 per pound, costing the company an unanticipated $22 million in gross profits in 1998; but aggressive discounting by their competitors made it difficult for Dreyer's to raise prices by an amount sufficient to compensate for higher dairy costs. Further, the entire 'Better-For-You' segment (healthier low-fat desserts), in which Dreyer's had invested heavily, began to reverse its upward trajectory. Finally, Ben & Jerry's, the socially conscious superpremium ice cream company, was threatening to terminate its long-term distribution contract (and subsequently did so in August 1998), influencing Dreyer's national distribution system, which required distributing significant volumes of their own and competitors' ice cream to offset the cost of building such a system.

Rather than engaging in the kind of panicked cost-cutting common among organizations in tough situations like this, Dreyer's executive team intentionally handled this near-crisis period in a way that was consistent with the culture in which they had long invested. They started with honest and open communication, emphasizing how much they valued their employees. This message was taken seriously by employees because Gary Rogers and Rick Cronk (Dreyer's President) had spent decades consciously building the core components of their culture from their own personalities of openness and accessibility. As soon as they were prepared to announce the restructuring to the financial community and their employees, executive committee members were on planes, flying across the country, and by the end of that week they had met with every one of their more than 4000 employees. As Cronk put it, 'we know our limits and understand the law, but we tend to be very open with our employees, we communicate a lot.' An account executive recalled that 'they reassured us by calling it straight ... they informed us of their game plan and that they needed us and counted on us ... you looked at these [senior managers] and thought, you'd run through a wall for this guy.' Dreyer's executive staff and employees were motivated by senior executive visits to rally around the company.

Rogers also instituted '1-800 calls' to reinforce Dreyer's strategy. Employees could call in to hear pre-recorded speeches by Rogers, which humanized the leadership and ensured that employees had an avenue to learn about Dreyer's strategy and plans directly from the leader. Rogers' speeches had an honest tone that celebrated successes and disclosed shortcomings, and they were exceptionally popular with employees.

In June 1998, Dreyer's executive team made a key financial decision to continue to invest in the Dreyer's Leadership University (DLU), providing unequivocal evidence that Dreyer's cared about employee development, even during difficult times. They hoped to 'reinvent and rejuvenate the Dreyer's leadership,' said Cronk. They knew that they would reap the benefits of such training in the longer term. 'There was a real foundational understanding that [DLU] was an investment in the future,' said the Director of People Support and Development, 'you have to make an investment in your people and they'll deliver in the future.' The VP of sales agreed: 'when people heard that we were investing another million dollars into the [culture] and DLU it created a high degree of comfort and confidence that we're focused on what's really important and that it's not just talk.'

These culturally consistent actions paid off for Dreyer's. By the fall of 2000, the company had rebounded with its robust premium and superpremium product lines (e.g., Dreamery). Even though Dreamery only launched in September 1999, it successfully captured 11.5 percent of the superpremium category. Dreyer's entire superpremium portfolio had a 31.3 percent volume share, while Haagen Dazs had a 34.1 percent share and Ben & Jerry's had a 33.4 percent share.[55] The company also reported positive earnings and analysts estimated revenue to be $1.2 billion in 2000 and $1.4 billion in 2001 with earnings per share of $.80 and $1.33 respectively. Dreyer's stock price, down as low as 9.88 in September 1998 at the time of the restructuring announcement, reached over 36 by January 2001. Despite the recession and the typical ice cream slow down in winter, Dreyer's stock price closed on January 2, 2003 at a whopping 71.23 after agreeing to merge with Nestlé (pending FTC approval). Dreyer's also signed a new agreement with Ben & Jerry's to distribute its products nationally (after Unilever's purchase of Ben & Jerry's was finalized). Finally, Dreyer's acquired a number of distributors to expand its presence in non-grocery outlets. The acquisitions would provide Dreyer's with substantial synergies and cost savings.

Reflecting on that period, Cronk said, 'It was a common trust and of sharing the facts – openness ... we weren't sugarcoating anything, putting a Hollywood spin on anything ... we were honest and clear ... people believed the story and they understood ... there was an enormous amount of pride and optimism.' Another senior executive recalled his confidence in his sales team to help Dreyer's through difficult times. 'We've invested in the culture, I know my people, my people are winners, not losers ... we've hired people with the right personalities and we've instilled in them the Dreyer's culture and we have the confidence that they will do the right thing.'

To succeed, leaders must instill their employees with confidence and clarity about key cultural values just as the executive team at Dreyer's did. They must make the time to help employees interpret key events and changes in light of cultural values on an ongoing basis. If they do not, employees will provide their own explanations; and when leader behaviors are ambiguous or beloved structures are axed, the explanations that employees spontaneously generate are not likely to be charitable.

The three C's of culture

Organizational culture can be a powerful force that clarifies what's important and coordinates members' efforts without the costs and inefficiencies of close supervision. Culture also identifies an organization's distinctive competence to external constituencies. Managing culture requires creating a context in which people are encouraged and empowered to express creative ideas and do their very best. Selection, socialization, and rewards should be used as opportunities to convey what's important to organizational members. Organizational cultures that are strategically relevant, strong, and emphasize innovation and change are most effective. Three levers exist for forming, strengthening, and changing culture, how organizations: recruit and select; socialize, orient, and train; and reward and lead people. Paradoxically, the very strength of cultural values can also be a leader's downfall. However, leaders who embrace cultural values when threatening events occur can avoid this risk. Culture 'works' when it is clear, consistent, and comprehensive.

One thing is guaranteed: A culture will form in an organization, a department, and a work group. The question is whether the culture that forms is one that helps or hinders the organization's ability to execute its strategic objectives. Organizational culture is too important to leave to chance; organizations must use their culture to fully execute their strategy and inspire innovation. It is a leader's primary role to develop and maintain an effective culture.

Notes

[1] Ram Charan and Geoffrey Colvin, 'Why CEOs Fail,' *Fortune*, June 21, 1999, pp. 68–78.

[2] E.g., M.E. Porter, *Competitive Strategy: Techniques for Analyzing Industries and Competitors* (New York, NY: Free Press, 1980).

[3] J.R. Laing, 'Nothing but Blue Skies,' *Barron's*, July 2, 2001, pp. 25–29.

[4] C. O'Reilly and J. Pfeffer, 'Southwest Airlines: Using Human Resources for Competitive Advantage (A),' HR-1A, Graduate School of Business, Stanford University, 1995.

[5] R.E. Walton, 'Establishing and Maintaining High Commitment Work Systems,' in J.R. Kimberly, R.H. Miles, and Associates, eds., *The Organizational Life Cycle: Issues in the Creation, Transformation, and Decline of Organizations* (San Francisco, CA: Jossey-Bass, 1980), pp. 208–290.

[6] C. O'Reilly and J. Chatman, 'Cultures as Social Control: Corporations, Cults, and Commitment,' in L. Cummings and B. Staw, eds., *Research in Organizational Behavior*, Vol. 18 (Greenwich, CT: JAI Press, 1996), pp. 157–200, at 166.

[7] R.F. Baumeister, 'The Self,' in D.T. Gilbert, S.T. Fiske, and G. Lindzey, eds., *The Handbook of Social Psychology*, 4th ed. (New York, NY: McGraw-Hill, 1998), pp. 680–740.

[8] M.L. Tushman and C.A. O'Reilly, *Winning Through Innovation: A Practical Guide to Leading Organizational Change and Renewal* (Boston, MA: Harvard Business School Press, 1997).

[9] A. Birenbaum and E. Sagarin, *Norms and Human Behavior* (New York, NY: Praeger, 1976).

[10] K.L. Bettenhausen and J.K. Murnighan, 'The Development of an Intragroup Norm and the Effects of Interpersonal and Structural Challenges,' *Administrative Science Quarterly*, 36/1 (March 1991): 20–35, at 21.

[11] E.g., O'Reilly and Chatman, op. cit.

[12] F.J. Roethlisberger and W. J. Dickson (with H.A. Wright), *Management and the Worker: An Account of a Research Program conducted by the Western Electric Company, Hawthorne Works, Chicago* (Cambridge: MA, Harvard University Press, 1939).

[13] C. O'Reilly, 'Corporations, Culture, and Commitment: Motivation and Social Control in Organizations,' *California Management Review*, 31/4 (Summer 1989): 9–25.

[14] R. Spector and P.D. McCarthy, *The Nordstrom Way* (New York, NY: John Wiley & Sons, 1995), p. 16.

[15] O'Reilly and Pfeffer, op. cit., p. 7.

[16] O'Reilly and Chatman, op. cit.

[17] O'Reilly, op. cit.

[18] Ibid.

[19] E.g., J.C. Collins and J.I. Porras, *Built to Last: Successful Habits of Visionary Companies* (New York, NY: HarperBusiness, 1994).

[20] E.g., J.N. Baron, M.T. Hannan, and M.D. Burton, 'Labor Pains: Change in Organizational Models and Employee Turnover in Young, High-Tech Firms,' *American Journal of Sociology*, 106 (2001): 960–1012.

[21] M.T. Hannan, M.D. Burton, and J.N. Baron, 'Inertia and Change in the Early Years: Employment Relations in Young, High Technology Firms,' *Industrial and Corporate Change*, 5 (1996): 503–537.

[22] E.g., J.A. Chatman and K.A. Jehn, 'Assessing the Relationship between Industry Characteristics and Organizational Culture: How Different Can You Be?' *Academy of Management Journal*, 37 (1994): 522–553.

[23] D. Caldwell and C.A. O'Reilly, 'Norms Supporting Innovation in Groups: An Exploratory Study,' working paper, University of Santa Clara, Santa Clara, CA, 1995.

[24] J.P. Kotter and J.L. Heskett, *Corporate Culture and Performance* (New York, NY: Free Press, 1992).

[25] T.M. Amabile, Motivating Creativity in Organizations: 'On Doing What You Love and Loving What You Do,' *California Management Review*, 40/1 (Fall 1997): 39–58.

[26] R.J. Sternberg, L.A. O'Hara, and T.I. Lubart, 'Creativity as Investment,' *California Management Review*, 40/1 (Fall 1997): 8–21.

[27] T.M. Amabile, 'Brilliant but Cruel: Perceptions of Negative Evaluators,' *Journal of Experimental Social Psychology*, 19 (1983): 146–156.

[28] R.I. Sutton, 'The Weird Rules of Creativity,' *Harvard Business Review*, 79/8 (September 2001): 94–103, at 97.

[29] S. Wetlaufer, 'Common Sense and Conflict: An Interview with Disney's Michael Eisner,' *Harvard Business Review,* 78/1 (January/February 2000): 114.

[30] A. Hargadon and R.I. Sutton, 'Building an Innovation Factory,' *Harvard Business Review*, 78/3 (May/June 2000): 157–168.

[31] A. Edmondson, 'Psychological Safety and Learning Behavior in Work Teams,' *Administrative Science Quarterly*, 44 (1999): 350–383.

[32] A.C. Edmondson, 'Learning from Mistakes Is Easier Said than Done: Group and Organizational Influences on the Detection and Correction of Human Error,' *The Journal of Applied Behavioral Science*, 32 (1996): 5–28.

[33] E. Schonfeld, 'Schwab Puts It All Online,' *Fortune*, December 7, 1998, pp. 94–100.

[34] Ibid., p. 95.

[35] Ibid., p. 96.

[36] E.g., Kotter and Heskett, op. cit.

[37] For greater detail on these three tools, see J.A. Chatman, 'Matching People and Organizations: Selection and Socialization in Public Accounting Firms,' *Administrative Science Quarterly*, 36 (1991): 459–484; O'Reilly (1989), op. cit.; O'Reilly and Chatman, op. cit.; Tushman and O'Reilly, op. cit.

[38] Chatman, op. cit.

[39] M.L. Connerley and S.L. Rynes, 'The Influence of Recruiter Characteristics and Organizational Recruitment Support on Perceived Recruiter Effectiveness: Views from Applicants and Recruiters,' *Human Relations*, 50 (1997): 1563–1586.

[40] E.g., E. Berscheid and H.T. Reis, 'Attraction and Close Relationships,' in D.T. Gilbert, S.T. Fiske, and G. Lindzey, eds., *The Handbook of Social Psychology*, 4th ed. (New York, NY: McGraw-Hill, 1998) pp. 193–281.

[41] C. O'Reilly, 'Cisco Systems: The Acquisition of Technology Is the Acquisition of People,' Case # HR-10, Graduate School of Business, Stanford University, 1998).

[42] B. Beck, 'Cisco Systems,' class presentation, Haas School of Business, Berkeley, CA, March 2000.

[43] O'Reilly (1998), op. cit.

[44] Chatman, op. cit.

[45] E.g., J. Pfeffer, *The Human Equation: Building Profits by Putting People First* (Boston, MA: Harvard Business School Press, 1998).

[46] L. Lee, 'Tricks of E*Trade: In His Drive to Create a Net Powerhouse, Christos Cotsakos Is Building a Culture that's Edgy, a Bit Bizarre – and Often Brilliant,' *Business Week*, February 7, 2000, p. EB18.

[47] Ibid.

[48] S. Puffer, 'CompUSA's CEO James Halpin on Technology, Rewards, and Commitment,' *Academy of Management Executive*, 13 (1999): 29–36, at 29.

[49] Ibid., p. 33.

[50] J. Pfeffer, *Power in Organizations* (Marshfield, MA: Pitman Publishing Co., 1981).

[51] S.E. Cha and A. Edmondson, 'How Strong Organizational Values Can Inhibit Learning,' working paper, Harvard University, Cambridge, MA, 2001.

[52] M. Rokeach, *The Nature of Human Values* (New York, NY: Free Press, 1973).

[53] E.E. Jones and R.E. Nisbett, *The Actor and the Observer: Divergent Perceptions of the Causes of Behavior* (Morristown, NJ: General Learning Press, 1971).

[54] V. Chang, J. Chatman, and G. Carroll, 'Dreyer's Grand Ice Cream (A) & (B),' OB-35 (A) & (B), Graduate School of Business, Stanford University, 2001.

[55] G.L. Teitelbaum and D. Geissler, 'Dreyer's Grand Ice Cream,' Merrill Lynch, October 27, 2000, p. 2.

JENNIFER A. CHATMAN is the Paul J. Cortese Distinguished Professor of Management at the Haas School of Business, University of California. <chatman@haas.berkeley.edu>

SANDRA EUNYOUNG CHA is a doctoral candidate in organizational behavior at the Harvard Business School. scha@hbs.edu

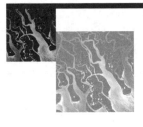

READING 8
The many dimensions of culture*

Academic Commentary by Harry C. Triandis

I first met Geert Hofstede in 1973, at the Congress of the International Association of Applied Psychology in Liege, Belgium. He mentioned to a group of delegates at the Congress that he had a large data set that he was going to analyze and offered to take us to Brussels to look at it. We were quite impressed.

A few years later. Sage Publications asked me to review the manuscript that became the 1980 book. I recommended publication most enthusiastically. I found the individualism-collectivism dimension particularly helpful, because it organized many of the observations of research I had done in the 1960s in traditional Greece and in Illinois.[1] For instance, I observed that Greeks behaved much more differently when they interacted with an ingroup (e.g., the family) than with an outgroup (e.g., strangers) than did the samples from Illinois. The Greeks behaved much more under the influence of norms (what should I do?) than of attitudes (what would I like to do?) than was true for Americans. They defined who they were in more social terms. Many social behaviors were associated with intimacy in Greece to a greater extent than was the case in Illinois. For example, upon meeting a 'new friend,' the Greeks might ask: 'How much do you earn per month?' which was not a likely question in Illinois.

At the time I reviewed the Hofstede book, I was also studying Hispanics in the USA. Many of the findings could be understood much better if the individualism-collectivism dimension was taken into account. For example, we found when we presented several hundred situations to our samples of Hispanics and non-Hispanics and asked them to rate the probability of different behaviors in those situations that the answers fell into a particular pattern. When the behavior was *positive*, the Hispanic average rating of the probability was higher than the rating of the non-Hispanics, but when the behavior was *negative*, the Hispanic average rating of the probability was lower than the rating of the non-Hispanics. We called this the *simpatia* script,[2] because it is characteristic of people who want to have good relationships with others, i.e., want others to see them as 'simpatico.'

The other dimensions of Hofstede's 1980 book – Power Distance, Uncertainty Avoidance, and Masculinity-Femininity – are also interesting. In what follows I will first make some general comments about Hofstede's work, then will discuss the

* Academy of Management Executive, 2004, 18(1).

individualism-collectivism dimension and stress its importance in the recent literature in psychology and organizational studies, and finally I will touch on the other dimensions.

The importance of Hofstede's work

When I started working as a psychologist, in the mid-1950s, the study of culture was of marginal significance. Psychologists favored cross-cultural studies only as a means of confirming that their findings were universal and eternal. By contrast, I felt that culture was a central topic for psychology because, like Hofstede, I am multicultural and multilingual and I reacted to many of the 'important' findings of social psychology by saying to myself: 'This would not make sense in X culture.' Most psychologists in the 1950-80 period held the view that 'cultural differences are for anthropologists to work on.' While there were some psychologists who paid serious attention to culture, such as Klineberg whose text on social psychology included much cultural material, and some who collaborated with anthropologists, like Jerry Bruner and Bill Lambert and Wally Lambert, the majority view was that 'culture is none of our business.' The minority view held, by contrast, that culture is so pervasive that all psychology should be a cultural psychology.

Culture 'inside' the person

The Hofstede book increased the influence of the minority. But culture was still thought of as 'out there' and thus of little importance for psychologists. A major turning point occurred when culture started to be conceived of as 'inside' the person. This view argues that all psychological processes have a cultural component. This perspective was common in the Soviet Union, among the followers of Vygotsky, Luria, and Leontiev, and it entered psychology when Michael Cole,[3] who had studied there, insisted that a 'cultural psychology' should be added to the 'cross-cultural psychology.' But Cole was not 'mainstream.' The change occurred when well-established mainstream psychologists like Hazel Markus[4] and Dick Nisbett[5] of the University of Michigan became converted. The conversion occurred when their students, such as Kitayama and Peng, convinced them that what was true in Michigan was not true in Japan or China. When these mainstream psychologists went to the Far East, they became fascinated and converted.

The turning point

I think that in the field of psychology a critical turning point occurred with the publication of the Markus & Kitayama[6] review, which essentially showed that there are major cultural differences in cognition, emotion, and motivation. Psychologists suddenly realized that what was considered universal in psychology is true only in the West, e.g., in individualist cultures; it is not valid everywhere. Of course this work required antecedents, and Hofstede, as well as Triandis,[7] was among the antecedents needed to make that argument. In any case, the Markus and Kitayama paper shifted the field. Instead of culture being something at the margin of psychology, it became a vital topic. Between 1984 and 2000 the number of papers in the major psychology journals that were concerned with culture increased seven-fold![8] Many mainstream psychological findings were no longer eternal verities, but depended on time and place.

An interesting indication of the change in the 'culture of psychology' was the story of the writing of the chapter on culture for the *Handbook of Industrial and Organizational Psychology* (Dunnette & Hough). Dunnette asked me to write it in 1985. I wrote the first draft, but the volume that was to include it was delayed because the other authors were late in delivering their chapters. A couple of years later, I was asked to update the culture chapter, which I did. Again the others were late, and a couple of years later Dunnette asked me to update it again, which I did. By 1992 the field had changed so much that Dunnette asked me to edit a whole international volume (!) for the *Handbook*.[9] Hofstede's work was referenced almost 70 times in that volume.

The cultural and individual levels of analysis

An important contribution of Hofstede's work was the emphasis on the distinction between the cultural and individual levels of analysis. His work was at the cultural level, and at that level individualism and collectivism are on opposite poles. But when serious work at the individual level of analysis was undertaken. Individualism was split into several facets (such as Distance from Ingroups, Hedonism, and Competition), and Collectivism was split into such factors as Family Integrity and Sociability. These factors were no longer on opposite poles but could be correlated, so that a person could be high in both collectivist and individualist tendencies. For example, one study has shown that people who were raised in a collectivist culture and then lived in an individualist culture for several years were high in both collectivism and individualism.[10] Other studies suggested that people who were high on both individualism and collectivism were better adjusted and could deal with adversities more successfully. It is almost like the argument that one should invest in a diversified portfolio!

The detractors

Hofstede has had his detractors. Scholars come in at least two varieties: Those who are creative and those who are critical. Hofstede is creative and, while he tries to be methodologically sophisticated, there are places where he can be criticized. The critics[11] are usually not creative, and they do inflate themselves by disparaging others. My reaction to McSweeney's paper was that he made some valid points but 'the perfect is the enemy of the good.'

I see no point in rehashing the arguments of the critics. I think they are summarized by the previous quote.

In short, Hofstede's work has become the standard against which new work on cultural differences is validated. Almost every publication that deals with cultural differences and includes many cultures is likely to reference Hofstede.

Individualism and collectivism: the most important dimension

In 1980 I started studying the individualism-collectivism dimension in greater detail. Over the years this dimension has become the most important in studying cultural differences, though the other four Hofstede dimensions also deserve attention.

In a paper I wrote on the occasion of the publication of the second edition of Hofstede's book,[12] I argued that there are scores of dimensions of cultural variation. Some dimensions are 'primary' and directly linked to variations in ecology. Other dimensions are 'secondary' having evolved from the primary dimensions, the way *homo sapiens* has evolved from *homo habilis*. Hofstede has identified many of the primary dimensions.

The research

In the course of the last 25 years, many people have worked on the individualism-collectivism dimension, and some of the findings are worth recording. First, the perceptions and behavior of people in collectivist cultures are different from the perceptions and behavior of people in individualist cultures.[13] Among the most important characteristics of people in collectivist cultures relative to those in individualist cultures is the emphasis on *context* more than on *content*. For instance, in communication they pay more attention to *how* something is said (tone of voice, gestures) than to *what* is said. This can lead to catastrophic results, as happened in Geneva in 1991. Secretary of State James Baker told the Iraqis 'We will attack you if you do not get out of Kuwait,' and they understood that the Americans would not attack, because Baker was calm and did not seem to be angry! What a mistake!

In addition, collectivists see people as relatively mutable and the environment as relatively immutable; individualists see individuals as stable entities, no matter what the environment. Collectivists see behavior as due to external factors, such as norms and roles, more than due to internal factors, such as attitudes and personality. Furthermore, they see the self as interdependent with ingroups. But the self changes depending on the ingroup one is with. In individualist cultures the self is stable.

In collectivist cultures people give priority to ingroup goals rather than to personal goals. They pay more attention to norms than to attitudes. They see interpersonal relationships as more stable than do people in individualist cultures.[14] There is now also considerable information about cultural differences in thought patterns.[15]

As we studied individualism and collectivism in different cultures, we realized that within culture there are individuals who are *idiocentric* (think, feel, and behave like people in individualist cultures) as well as individuals who are *allocentric* (like people in collectivist cultures). Collectivist cultures have somewhere between 30 and 100 per cent allocentrics; individualist cultures have somewhere between zero and 35 per cent allocentrics. Individualist cultures have somewhere between 35 and 100 per cent idiocentrics, while collectivist cultures have somewhere between zero and 35 per cent idiocentrics. Idiocentrics in collectivist cultures feel dominated by the culture and want to escape it. The democracy movement in Tian an Men Square in China is an example. Allocentrics in individualist cultures feel the need to join groups – associations, unions, social movements, a kibbutz, a commune.

Idiocentrics were found to be high in expressiveness, dominance, initiation of action, aggressiveness, logical arguments, regulation of flow of communication, eye contact, tended to finish the task, and had strong opinions. Allocentrics were high on accommodating and avoidance of argument, and they shifted their opinions more easily than did idiocentrics.

Tendencies toward idiocentrism or allocentrism are influenced by many factors. Idiocentrism increases with affluence, when the person has a leadership role, much education, has done much international travel, and has been socially mobile. In addition, it is more likely if the person has migrated to a culture other than the culture of upbringing and has been socialized in a bilateral family (where both the mother's and father's relatives were influential). Furthermore, idiocentrism increases when the person has been greatly exposed to the Western mass media or has been acculturated for years to a Western culture.[16]

Allocentrism is more likely if the person has been financially dependent on some ingroup, is of low social class, has had limited education, has done little travel, has been socialized in a unilateral family (e.g., where only the father's family norms are present), is traditionally religious, and has been acculturated to a collectivist culture.[17]

Research showed that allocentrics in collectivist situations are especially cooperative, but idiocentrics are not, and no one is very cooperative in individualistic situations.[18] Thus the kind of situation in which one is interacting with another person must also be considered.

Noting the number of topics that have been found to be relevant to individualism and collectivism, we can see the importance of this dimension. Unfortunately, however, most of the research was done in East Asia and North America, and we are not yet sure that the findings that will be summarized below also apply to other collectivist and individualist cultures.

Hofstede identified Power Distance as an important dimension of cultural variation. This dimension interacts with individualism and collectivism in interesting ways, resulting in different kinds of individualism and collectivism.[19] For example, we can consider horizontal and vertical varieties of individualism and collectivism. Horizontal individualism (HI) is found most commonly in Scandinavia, where people want to do their own thing but do not want to 'stick out.' Vertical individualism (VI) is more common in the US, especially in competitive situations, where people want to be 'the best' and to be noticed by others. Americans often want to be on television and to be mentioned in the newspapers (see the crowds in front of NBC in the morning, waving at their relatives). Horizontal collectivism (HC) is typical of the Israeli kibbutz. Vertical collectivism (VC) is found in traditional cultures such as rural China or India.

A test has been developed that assesses what per cent of the time, in different situations, people use one of these four patterns. For example, in a study[20] of Danish and American students, the Danish sample used the HI pattern 49 per cent of the time, across situations; the American sample used it 44 per cent of the time. The Danish sample used HC 35 per cent of the time, while the American sample used it 28 per cent of the time. The Danes used VI 8 per cent of the time and the Americans 22 per cent of the time. The Danes used VC 8 per cent of the time and the Americans 6 per cent of the time. In these studies a difference of 2 per cent is statistically highly significant. Thus, we see rather important differences between the two kinds of individualist societies. In collectivist cultures studies have shown higher levels of VC (of the order of 15 per cent) than are shown above.

Implications for working in another culture

When teaching people to work in another culture, it is helpful to mention to them some of the findings outlined above. The individualism-collectivism framework becomes a general way of thinking about cultural differences and facilitates learning about the other culture.

In individualist cultures, studies found greater use of individualist human resource practices. For example, people were selected on the basis of individual attributes, while in collectivist cultures they were selected on the basis of group memberships. Other things being equal, there is more training in collectivist that in individualist cultures because employees are more loyal to the organization and high in organization commitment, so that they are less likely to leave the organization. Paternalism is a more common leadership style in collectivist than in individualist cultures. In fact, the boss is much more involved in the personal life of employees, knows much more about them, and does more helpful things on their behalf in collectivist than in individualist cultures. For example, a boss might find a spouse for an employee, might send congratulations when the employee's child graduates from high school, or send condolences when a member of the employee's family dies.

Managers in collectivist cultures are not as concerned with performance as managers in individualist cultures are, but they are more concerned with interpersonal relationships than managers in individualist cultures are.

As countries become more affluent, their populations become more individualist. However, this change requires several generations. We do not know how long it takes for a complete switch from collectivism to individualism, but even in individualist cultures we find collectivist elements (see above).

With the recent concern about deception in organizations around the world (Enron, etc.), it is interesting to note that the individualism-collectivism dimension has some relevance. Triandis et al.[21] found that people in vertical collectivist cultures are likely to use deception if it helps their ingroup; however, people who are vertical idiocentrics are also likely to use deception. In this case, competitiveness and the need to be 'the best' (i.e., have the most impressive organization) seem to be the factors that increase the use of deception.

In sum, the individualism-collectivism dimension has generated a great deal of research, some of which is summarized above. The Power Distance dimension was closely linked with it in Hofstede's study and was here presented as resulting in horizontal and vertical kinds of individualism and collectivism.

Uncertainty avoidance: tight and loose cultures

The Uncertainty Avoidance dimension of Hofstede has also stimulated some corresponding research. There are major cultural differences among cultures in the extent to which they are tight or loose.[22] In tight cultures there are many rules, norms, and standards for correct behavior. For example, there are strict rules about how to smile or bow. In loose cultures there are few rules, norms, or standards. Furthermore, when people do not follow a rule, when they break a norm or ignore a standard, in tight cultures they are likely to be criticized, punished, or even killed. In loose cultures people in that situation are likely to say: 'It does not matter.'

Tightness requires agreement about norms. This is more likely when the culture is isolated, so that it is not influenced by other cultures. Furthermore, cultural homogeneity is obviously needed for a culture to be tight. Finally, in cultures with high population density, tightness is particularly functional, since it helps regulate behavior so that people do the right thing at the right time and can thus interact smoothly and with little interpersonal conflict.

Japan is a tight culture; it was even tighter in the 19th century than it is now. People in Japan are often afraid that they will act inappropriately, that they will be criticized. Getting drunk in Japan is particularly helpful because it is an occasion when one can relax and break all norms, and people excuse the inappropriate behaviors.

Japanese teenagers who spend some years in the US, which is a relatively loose culture, find it very difficult to return to Japan, because they are criticized for trivial behaviors such as having too much tan (there is more sunshine in the US than in Japan) or having the 'wrong' hairdo. One major problem in Japanese high schools is that young people gang up on one fellow student who has deviated from 'proper behavior,' such as using an upper-class accent when most fellow students use a different accent.

The Taliban in Afghanistan was one of the most extreme cases of a tight society. They executed people right and left for 'offenses' such as listening to music!

Thailand is a loose culture. When people do not do what they are supposed to do, other people may just smile and let it go. Thailand is not at all isolated, since it is sandwiched between the major cultures of China and India. People have different points of view about 'correct' behavior, so there is much tolerance when others do not behave 'appropriately.'

The US is in between. However, the US in the 1940s was much tighter than it is now. One clue of tightness is the extent to which people wear more or less the same type of clothing. In the 1950s, for instance, going to a party required coat and tie. Now one can go in almost anything, except a bathing suit! Organizations also differ in how tight they are. Some require coat and tie, and others allow their employees to wear whatever they like.

Hofstede's Uncertainty Avoidance is related to tightness. In cultures high in Uncertainty Avoidance, people want to have structure, to know precisely how they are supposed to behave and what is going to happen next. Predictability of events is highly valued.

There is research on tightness. For example, across a large number of societies, there is a correlation between tightness and collectivism.[23] One study found more agreement about the meaning of concepts in Japan than in the USA.[24] Gelfand at the University of Maryland is at present summarizing data from 35 cultures that measure tightness and its societal correlates.

Other dimensions of cultural variation

A major dimension of cultural variation is cultural complexity. It contrasts hunters and gatherers with information societies. However, because organizational psychologists deal mostly with industrial societies, this dimension is not relevant. Nevertheless one can mention that in combination with tightness-looseness it seems to be related to collectivism and individualism. Collectivist cultures are both tight and simple; individualist cultures are both loose and complex.[25] Research by Carpenter[26] has supported this point.

The masculinity-femininity dimension has received less attention in the literature than the other dimensions. Masculinity is correlated with domestic political violence and other phenomena. Hofstede summarized several studies that included this dimension in his books, especially in the second edition of *Culture's Consequences*.[27] This book summarizes recent work regarding each of the Hofstede dimensions. It includes almost 900 references to recent publications that have contributed something to our understanding of these dimensions.

The influence of Hofstede's dimensions

Thus each of the important dimensions of cultural variation has been uncovered by Hofstede. The dimensions he identified are relevant to how people function in industrial societies. We can look at the way these dimensions influence psychological processes and organizational behaviors in many cultures. The dimensions have generated a tremendous amount of research and have been highly influential in all the social sciences.

Notes

[1] Triandis, H. C. 1972. *The analysis of subjective culture*. New York: Wiley.

[2] Triandis, H. C., et al. 1984. *Simpatia* as a cultural script of Hispanics. *Journal of Personality and Social Psychology*, 47: 1363–1375.

[3] Cole, M. 1996. *Cultural psychology: A once and future discipline*. Cambridge, MA: Harvard Press.

[4] Markus, H., & Kitayama, S. 1991. Culture and self: Implications for cognition, emotion, and motivation. *Psychological Review*, 98: 224–53.

[5] Nisbett, R. 2003. *The geography of thought*. New York: Free Press.

[6] Markus & Kitayama.

[7] Triandis, H. C. 1989. Self and social behavior in differing cultural contexts. *Psychological Review*, 96: 506–520.

[8] Hong, Y-y. 2003. Biculturalism. Lecture given at the University of Illinois Psychology Department, April.

[9] Triandis, H. C., Dunnette, M., & Hough, L. (eds.). 1994. *Handbook of industrial and organizational psychology* (second edition. Vol. 4). Palo Alto, CA: Consulting Psychologists Press.

[10] Yamada, A., & Singelis, T. 1999. Biculturalism and self-construal. *International Journal of Intercultural Relations*, 23: 697–709.

[11] McSweeney, B. 2002. Hofstede's model of national cultural differences and their consequences: A triumph of faith – a failure of analysis. *Human Relations*, 55: 89–118.

[12] Triandis, H. C. 2003. Dimensions of culture beyond Hofstede. In Vinken, H., Soeters, J., & Ester, P. (eds.). *Comparing cultures: Dimensions of culture in a comparative perspective*. Leiden, The Netherlands: Brill Publishers.

[13] Triandis, H. C. 1995. *Individualism and collectivism*. Boulder, CO: Westview Press.

[14] Triandis, H. C., & Suh, E. M. 2002. Cultural influences on personality. *Annual Review of Psychology*, 53: 133–160.

[15] Nisbett.

[16] Triandis, H. C., & Trafimow, D. 2001. Cross-national prevalence of collectivism. In C. Sedikides & M. B. Brewer (eds.). *Individual self, relational self, collective self.* (pp. 259–276). Philadelphia: Psychology Press.

[17] Ibid.

[18] Chatman, J. A., & Barsade, S. G. 1995. Personality, organizational culture, and cooperation: Evidence from a business simulation. *Administrative Science Quarterly,* 40: 423–443.

[19] Triandis, 1995.

[20] Nelson, M. R., & Shavitt, S. 2002. Horizontal and vertical individualism and achievement values: A multimethod examination of Denmark and the United States. *Journal of Cross-Cultural Psychology,* 33: 439–458.

[21] Triandis, H. C., et al. 2001. Culture, personality and deception: A multilevel approach. *International Journal of Cross-Cultural Management,* 1: 73–90.

[22] Triandis, Dunnette, & Hough.

[23] Carpenter, S. 2000. Effects of cultural tightness and collectivism on self-concept and causal attributions. *Cross-Cultural Research,* 34: 38–56.

[24] Chan, D. K-S., et al. 1996. Tightness-looseness revisited: Some preliminary analyses in Japan and the United States. *International Journal of Psychology,* 31: 1–12.

[25] Triandis, Dunnette, & Hough.

[26] Carpenter.

[27] Hofstede, G. 2001. *Culture's consequences,* second edition. Thousand Oaks, CA: Sage.

HARRY C. TRIANDIS **is professor emeritus at the University of Illinois in Urbana-Champaign. He received his Ph.D. in psychology from Cornell. He has lectured in more than 40 countries and has published about 200 journal papers and book chapters and seven books. He has received numerous awards and citations for distinguished contributions to international psychology. Contact:** *triandis@uiuc.edu.*

CASE 4A: LAFARGE: FROM FRENCH CEMENT COMPANY TO GLOBAL LEADER

Lafarge – the company

Léon Orvin began producing industrial limestone in 1833 after acquiring a limestone quarry in south-eastern France. He took over the business, acquired by his family in 1749, with the purchase of the Lafarge domain in south-eastern France, an area known for generations for the quality of its limestone deposits. That was history. From a local French cement company, today Lafarge is the world leader in construction materials, covering 75 countries. Over the last five years, sales increased from 6.413 million euros in FY1997 to 14.610 million euros in FY 2002. Net income for the group increased from 371 million euros in FY1997 to 756 million euros in FY2002. Lafarge grew from 37,097 employees in 1997 to 77,000 in 2002, more than 100 per cent growth. However, the transformation was not an easy task. Over the last decade, as Bertrand Collomb, who was chairman and CEO of Lafarge from 1989, pointed out in 2000:

> Following prolonged recession in Europe, which lasted from 1991 until 1996, and the Asian crisis of 1998, worldwide economic trends now appear positive. World growth was 4 per cent in 2000, and is forecast to continue at about 3 per cent per year. But we must remain on our guard because interest rates are on an upward swing, oil prices are rocketing, growth in the United States is expected to slow and the German construction market remains sluggish. Most importantly, the process of worldwide consolidation in our industries is gaining pace, and this is why it is necessary for us to ensure we have the means to stay among the top-ranking world groups and be the pre-eminent player in our sector. ... In 2001, Lafarge strengthened its position as world leader in building materials thanks to a vigorous policy of acquisition and development on every continent.

History

Lafarge Group, incorporated in 1833, is currently the world leader in cement and building materials. Lafarge started in France as a local cement company and undertook its first international business in 1864 by delivering limestone to help construct the Suez Canal. Lafarge established a research laboratory in 1887 that developed Ciment Fondu, a rapidly hardening and weather resistant cement, in 1908. The following decade saw

---

Ashok Som wrote this case. The case was written with the active support and permission of Dr Bertrand Collomb, Chairman and CEO, Lafarge. The case was developed as a basis for class discussion rather than to illustrate either effective or ineffective handling of an administrative situation.

This case is prohibited from any type of reproduction, storage or transmittal without permission. To order copies contact European Case Clearing House, Case #304-019-1.

Lafarge concentrating on horizontal integration by acquiring limestone and cement companies throughout France.

The period from 1914 to 1955 witnessed rapid growth at Lafarge. It set up operations in North Africa and soon became the leading cement producer in Algeria, Morocco and Tunisia. In 1926, Lafarge expanded to the United Kingdom. By 1939, Lafarge was the leading cement producer in France. Production doubled from 1945–55 due to post-war rebuilding boom.

The years from 1955 to 1981 was a phase of mergers, acquisitions and growth of Lafarge, mostly in the Americas. In 1956, Lafarge constructed its first North American cement plant, creating Lafarge Cement of North America with the start of the Richmond plant in Canada. In 1959, Lafarge began operations in Brazil. By the end of the 1960s, Lafarge Canada had become the third-largest cement producer in the country, with an annual production capacity of 900,000 tons. In 1980, a merger agreement was signed between Lafarge and Coppée, forming Lafarge Coppée. Acquisitions in the United States and Canada established Lafarge Coppée as the number one cement producer in North America. The size of the group increased from 12,000 to 17,000 employees.

During the 1980s, Lafarge focused its growth in Europe, a single market representing more than 300 million people. The group acquired interests in Asland (Spain), Aslan (Turkey) and Perlmooser (Austria), and invested in East Germany, the Czech Republic (1991), then Poland, Romania, Russia and Ukraine.

In the last decade, Lafarge accelerated the pace of its growth into new countries by acquiring companies, and expanding into new businesses and new products through its four divisions: cement, aggregates and concrete, roofing and gypsum. Numerous acquisitions and joint ventures in all four divisions, on every continent, particularly Asia, saw Lafarge consolidating its position as a world leader in cement.

In 1994, Lafarge established a foothold in China; today, all four of the group's divisions operate there. The group's expansion in Poland began in 1995 with the acquisition of a 75 per cent stake in Kujawy. Lafarge acquired Redland of the UK in 1997, positioning itself strongly in aggregates and concrete, and gaining entry into the roofing market. There have been further developments throughout Asia during the late 1990s (1998: Indonesia and the Philippines; 1999: India and South Korea). With the acquisition of Warren in Canada in 2000, Lafarge became one of the leading aggregate producers in North America. Lafarge divested its speciality products businesses in 2000, which became Materis, to fund its grand growth plan of acquiring Blue Circle. In 2001, following the acquisition of Blue Circle, Lafarge became the world's leading cement producer and undisputed leader in the business of building materials.

In July 2001, Lafarge was listed on the New York Stock Exchange (NYSE). Today, Lafarge operates in 75 countries with 77,547 employees, has 178,000 shareholders and posts €14.610 billion of annual sales through its four divisions. Exhibit 4a.1 displays the main divisions of Lafarge group.

	Cement	Aggregates and concrete	Roofing	Gypsum
Profile	44% of group sales 32,238 employees	35% of group sales 16,942 employees	12% of group sales 12,362 employees	8% of group sales 3,661 employees
Business	Ranges of cements	Aggregates, ready-mix concrete	Ranges of roof tiles	Gypsum wallboard systems
International scope	W. Europe (40%), N. America (32%), Asia-Pacific (8%), Latin America (6%), Mediterranean Basin (5%), Africa-Indian Ocean (5%), Central & Eastern Europe (4%)			
Objectives	Consolidate its positions	Achieve operational excellence	Strengthen its world leadership	Become a world leader

Performance
Sales: €14,610 million
Gross operating income: €2,132 million
Net income: €456 million
EPS: € 3.52

Exhibit 4a.1 Lafarge overview
Source: data published as full-year end result as of 31 December 2002

The cement industry – the product

It was in 1824 when Joseph Aspdin, an Englishman, while searching for suitable material to use in the construction of a lighthouse, developed a type of cement that would set and harden under water. He named it Portland Cement because the set and hardened look was similar in colour and texture to the stones from quarries near Portland, England. Since then, the product has seen rapid and spectacular developments. Aspdin's method of carefully proportioning limestone and clay, and pulverizing that material is still applicable today. The pulverized material is then supplemented by other raw materials, such as sand, mill scale and bauxite, to achieve the right quantities of calcium, silica, aluminium and iron (depending on the type of cement being produced). This mix is then ground further in a raw feed mill (dry process or wet process) before being 'cooked'. The raw feed then undergoes a burning process through the kiln. In the kiln, the raw materials are calcinated (heated to 1450°C) to produce clinker. The fuel required to heat the kiln accounts for almost 50 per cent of operating costs, which is the reason cement manufacturers use waste materials as fuel. A small amount (5–10 per cent) of gypsum, which improves the setting time for the concrete mix, is added to the cooled clinker and ground into a fine 'cement' powder. Exhibit 4a.2 depicts the process pictorially.

Demand

Cement is a commodity whose demand is determined by business cycles within the construction industry. If construction slows, a drop in cement prices will not help boost construction. On the other hand, if cement prices rise, there is no real impact on demand. That is, demand is inelastic to price.

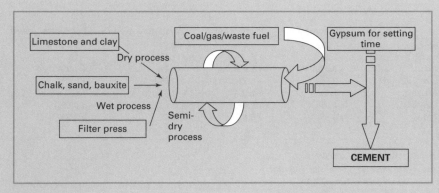

Exhibit 4a.2 How cement is made

World demand for cement is about 1.4–1.5 billion tons per annum.[1] During the last decade, this demand has grown at a compounded rate of 5.5 per cent, some 4 per cent faster than the growth in population during the same period (see Exhibit 4a.3). At the same time, the economic growth in the triad (Europe, USA and Japan) has relatively slowed down. Regional differences are quite high in terms of demand (see Exhibit 4a.4). Developed markets in Europe have been struggling to grow, while in the other parts of the world, particularly in Asia and South America, countries with high economic growth have seen rising demands for cement. For example, Asia saw a 7 per cent increase in the demand for cement during the last decade. Countries with high GDP and low growth are called mature markets, while countries with low GDP, high growth and high consumption of cement are known as emerging markets. Per capita cement consumption also shows huge differences between various regions. For example (see Exhibit 4a.5), the North American and European markets consume nearly four times as much cement per head when compared to Africa. Asia, the biggest market, currently consumes over 250 kilos per head, about 60 per cent of the European average. Within a country there is a correlation between cement consumption per capita and GDP per capita (see Exhibit 4a.6). This relationship, however, is not linear: at higher GDP levels the amount of cement consumption begins to decline and flatten out. But even at higher levels of GDP there are some markets, most notably the USA, that have seen renewed growth in cement consumption.

	1990	1991	1992	1993	1994	1995	1996	1997	1998	1999	Av. growth rate 1990–99
Production	1008	1042	1130	1206	1308	1388	1440	1473	1449	1494	4.5%
Imports	71	72	76	78	90	100	102	102	101	102	4.1%
Exports	70	72	75	81	93	101	105	105	105	110	5.1%
Consumption	1006	1037	1127	1197	1296	1376	1427	1458	1440	1483	44%
Population	4972	5075	5197	5226	5276	5360	5443	5518	5589	5663	1.5%
Kg per capita	202	204	218	229	246	257	262	264	258	262	2.9%

Exhibit 4a.3 Global cement market
Source: European Cement Review, January 2000

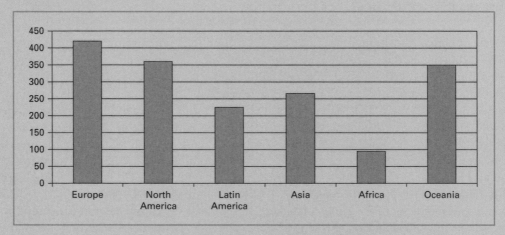

	Consumption	Production	Population growth	Per capita growth
Europe	– 0.9%	– 0.4%	0.5%	– 1.4%
North America	+ 2.1%	+ 2.7%	+ 1.1%	+ 1.0%
Asia	+ 8.9%	+ 8.9%	+ 1.6%	+ 7.1%
S & C America	+ 3.3%	+ 3.2%	+ 0.3%	+ 3.0%
Africa	+ 2.6%	+ 2.6%	+ 2.6%	n.c
Oceania	+ 2.9%	+ 2.1%	+ 2.0%	+ 0.9%
Total	**+ 5.5%**	**+ 5.6%**	**+ 1.5%**	**+ 3.9%**

Exhibit 4a.4 Regional cement trends
Note: All figures are compounded growth rates 1990–1999
Source: European Cement Review, January 2000

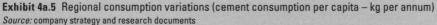

Exhibit 4a.5 Regional consumption variations (cement consumption per capita – kg per annum)
Source: company strategy and research documents

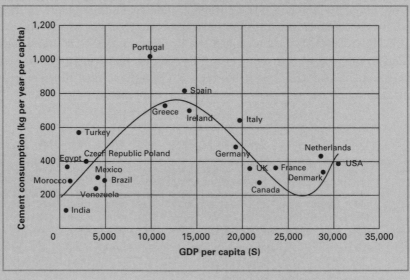

Exhibit 4a.6 GDP vs cement consumption per capita

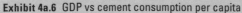

Supply

Cement is a commodity produced using limestone. Since limestone is abundant in most regions of the world, cement is produced locally. Its production requires a huge captive investment. The investment is written off after several decades. Lafarge invests in a cement plant that has limestone reserves and capacity to run for 50 years. Fixed costs in the industry are particularly high and significant relative to variable costs. Fixed costs generally account for more than 50 per cent of the overall production costs. The fixed costs are usually sunk costs. Once built, a cement plant can serve no other purpose. As fixed costs are high with respect to the variable costs, the break-even point is high. With automation, labour costs have decreased, but energy consumption is the most significant variable cost. Thus, profits in the industry are sensitive to the level of utilization of the production capacity. Significant cash flows are generated only when production increases beyond the break-even point, which depends on the efficiency of the plant. For example, in December 1995, the Lafarge group announced that it was going to rebuild the Richmond cement plant in British Columbia, which supplied the regional Vancouver market. The cement plant was set up in 1958 and was in operation for more than 30 years. Lafarge invested in a new plant, estimated to be worth more than $100 million.

The second most important feature that affects supply is transportation costs. In the USA, average transportation and distribution costs account for almost 25 per cent of the cement price. As a result, the sphere of sales is within the radius of 150–300 km from the site of production. The cost of transportation is highest when it is by road, followed by rail, and is cheapest by sea. Global cement capacity and production statistics are shown in Exhibit 4a.7.

World cement production (%)			
	2000	**2001**	**2001**
USA	89,510	91,000	5.5
Brazil	39,208	40,000	2.4
Egypt	24,143	22,000	1.3
France	20,000	21,000	1.3
Germany	38,000	40,000	2.4
India	95,000	100,000	6.1
Indonesia	27,789	28,000	1.7
Iran	20,000	23,000	1.4
Italy	36,000	36,000	2.2
Japan	81,300	82,000	5.0
South Korea	51,255	52,000	3.1
Mexico	31,677	30,000	1.8
Russia	32,400	35,000	2.1
Spain	30,000	30,000	1.8
Taiwan	18,500	18,500	1.1
Thailand	32,000	32,000	1.9
Turkey	35,825	36,000	2.2
Other countries	330,000	340,000	20.6
China	583,190	595,000	36.0
Total	1,615,797	1,651,500	100

Exhibit 4a.7 Global cement capacity and production statistics (millions)
Source: Credit Suisse First Boston Equity Research, 14 February 2002

When a buyer chooses between two cement producers, his/her decision is based primarily on price, with innovation accounting for little in the competitive process. However, differentiation between producers exists in a number of areas: (a) homogeneity of quality – the quality and the colour of cement should remain constant throughout the entire construction period; (b) delivery delays; (c) technical assistance – to choose cement suited for specific construction purposes; and (d) deliveries with greater flexibility. Service quality is the only way to influence buyers when price differences are minimal.

Increased competition

Competition in the cement industry initially occurs at the local level due to high transportation costs. Competition cannot be based on price as price cuts are easily spotted because of the nature of the product, which is undifferentiated. Competition is hence based on head-to-head market confrontation focused on price rebates and sales volume, in order to expand market share. Any substantial price cut by a competitor results in a price war. Rivalry also occurs when firms want to enhance their respective competitive advantages on the basis of improved product quality or reduced production costs.

Due to high barriers of entry and high consolidation in the industry, competition occurs at multi-point and multi-market level. Historically, cement firms entered different local markets as a business expansion strategy, to take advantage of growing markets and to hedge against local economic fluctuations. At the regional and national level, this has led to greater concentration and head-to-head confrontation between a reduced number of large multi-plant firms. Concentration in the cement industry has frequently resulted in a small number of cement groups such as Lafarge, Holcim, Cemex, Heidelberger and Italcementi dominating their domestic markets, and then entering foreign markets where they compete with other local firms.

High transportation costs make location an important factor in the pricing policy. The best location combines three advantages: (a) the plant is set up in a quarry with large quantities of high-quality and easily workable limestone; (b) the plant is close to large urban areas; and (c) the plant is near a railway line or a river network, allowing cement to be delivered to faraway places. A cement plant located inland rarely sells outside a 300 km radius and would normally sell the bulk of its production within 150 to 200 km.

Emerging industry structure: the 'six sisters' of cement

Over the last five years, a group of six multinational companies (see Exhibit 4a.8) – Lafarge (France), Holcim (Switzerland), Cemex (Mexico), Heidelberger (Germany), Taiheiyo (Japan) and Italcementi (Italy) have established the foundation of a worldwide network of plants that will eventually dominate the cement industry in most regions of the world. This concentration distinguishes the cement industry from other cyclical sectors because: (a) geographical diversification smoothes out the volatility of the earnings cycle within individual markets; (b) rational competitors operate by the same rules across a wide range of markets, with similar targets for return on capital; and (c) the certainty of retaliation and the impossibility of knocking well-capitalized competitors out of the game means that there is little point in competing on price. Thus, none tries. Each of the six major international competitors still has clearly identifiable national origins and controls a significant share of its home market. Each group also operates production facilities in more than a dozen countries around the world.

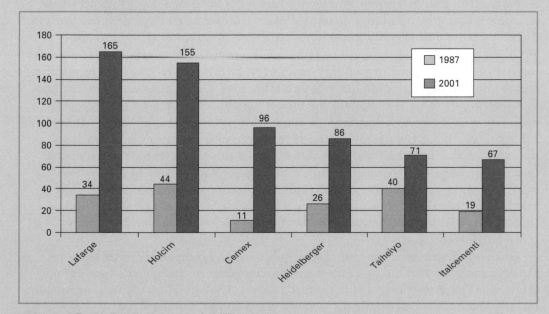

Exhibit 4a.8 Total influenced capacities in million tonnes
Lafarge: 165 mn t, including Blue Circle, excluding 25% participation in Tongyang (tot. cap. 10 mn t)
Holcim: 155 mn t, excluding 75% participation in Cibinong (tot. cap. 9.7 mn t)
Heidelberger: 86 mn t, excluding 31% participation in Indocement (tot. cap. 15.8 mn t)
Total world capacity estimated at 1310 mn t, excl. China

The strategy of the 'six sisters' is rooted in the nature of the business. In most mature markets, the surplus cash flow from established cement operations cannot be reinvested in cement in the same markets. The mature markets still offer growth potential in related businesses and the six sisters generally seek to increase production capacity in each market. This generates significant cash flows and is the main source for financing other activities. For example, Lafarge reinforces and diversifies its market share in other businesses. The acquisition of Redland is an illustration of such a strategy. This move added new products (concrete and baked clay tiles) to its existing range of offerings in building materials and enhanced its market share in concrete and aggregates.

Due to nature of the cement business, the six sisters follow each other across the globe to enter new markets and grow by acquisition, thus gaining significant market share.

▶ Regrouping the market among several large players makes for a more sustainable rise in cement prices since the main outlet for cement – ready-mixed concrete – is controlled by the cement manufacturers. Lafarge uses its acquisitions depending on the level of economic development of the country in question as a bridgehead to introduce the group's product, such as aggregates, gypsum and roofing tiles, with the aim of creating a building materials division in each country.

Greenfield investments are usually rare. In the 1990s, there were only two such instances (Holcim, in Vietnam and Egypt) where the MNC established its presence in a new country by building a greenfield plant rather than by buying an existing one. This is because building new capacity is expensive, costing between $120 and $180 per ton, depending on local factors such as cost of land, environmental legislation and the need for ancillary equipment. Infrastructure, like captive electricity generation and investment in quarries and kilns, also adds to the costs. Acquisition provides access to local markets at the lowest possible cost. Lafarge's strategy of acquisition in emerging countries is to acquire local cement manufacturers at moderate prices of less than $100 per ton.[2] After investing in modernization, it then boosts operating margins on the acquired assets by about 10 per cent to nearly 20 per cent within four years, which translates to a return on capital of about 11 per cent, or nearly 4 points more than the cost of capital. Operating margins are increased by efficiently integrating the acquired company, sharing technical global know-how, transferring best practices, internal and external benchmarking, and by putting in place an efficient IT system.

One way of measuring the cost of an acquisition is by comparing it with the replacement cost. Technology in the cement sector advances incrementally. No major innovations have been recorded in the last 20 years. The capital investment required for one ton of output is much the same as it was ten years ago. For most quoted companies, the standard valuation technique is enterprise value per ton of capacity. This is calculated as market capitalization plus debt, plus minority interests, less non-related investments, divided by the annual clinker production capacity. Acquisitions with an enterprise value per ton below replacement cost are considered cheap. Deals above parity are regarded as expensive.

When cement multinationals make an acquisition, they are paying for market access. These companies make their money by exploiting demand within a defined geographic territory, in competition with a limited number of other manufacturers. Even when profitability is low, the franchise, and the assets that serve it, still has a value. Franchise value[3] can in theory be separated from the shareholder value that the new owners hope to generate from an acquisition. The value added after a deal flows from the company's ability to operate the plant more effectively than its predecessors – to gain market share or reduce the cost of production. Franchise value is a function of the market conditions and the cost of capital in the target country at the time of the deal. It is calculated by reference to the average performance of the local industry, not the performance or profitability of the target company. The details of franchise value across countries and the way it is calculated is explained in Exhibit 4a.9.

Country	Ex-plant price per tonne (US$)	Cash cost per tonne (US$)	EBITDA margin (%)	EBITDA per tonne (US$)	Risk-free rate (%)	ERP (%)	Market gearing (%)	WACC (%)	FV per demand (US$/t)	Dom demand (mt)	Dom supply (mt)	Dom balance (%)	Franchise value (no growth) (US$/t)	Trend growth (%)	Franchise value (trend) (US$/t)
Japan	48	38	21	10	1.8	5.0	50.0	4.8	208	72.8	97.0	75	156	0.1	160
Korea	50	33	34	17	8.5	8.0	20.0	15.1	113	47.6	62.1	77	86	5.0	129
Taiwan	58	37	36	21	5.7	8.0	25.0	12.0	176	20.5	24.5	84	147	3.0	196
Indonesia	41	23	44	18	12.0	8.0	50.0	16.5	109	18.1	45.3	40	44	7.5	80
Malaysia	41	28	31	13	8.0	8.0	25.0	14.3	90	8.2	17.5	47	42	7.8	93
Philippines	49	34	31	15	14.0	8.0	50.0	18.5	81	12.5	20.4	61	50	8.0	88
Thailand	48	26	46	22	10.0	8.0	40.0	15.2	145	25.6	58.0	44	64	8.0	135
India	52	38	27	14	9.5	8.0	40.0	19.0	74	80.8	85.0	95	70	7.5	116
S Africa	55	37	33	18	15.0	6.0	15.0	20.3	89	8.8	12.0	74	65	0.9	68
Egypt	53	33	38	20	10.0	8.0	0.0	18.0	111	24.7	23.0	107	119	5.9	178
Greece	58	30	48	28	6.4	6.0	20.0	11.4	246	8.5	15.0	57	139	1.5	161
Poland	38	28	26	10	9.5	6.0	20.0	14.5	69	13.8	16.3	85	58	5.0	89
Turkey	40	26	35	14	10.3	8.0	0.0	18.3	77	36.4	61.0	60	46	6.5	71
Europe	**67**	**44**	**33**	**22**	**4.9**	**4.3**	**18.3**	**8.6**	**260**	**144.9**	**194.9**	**74**	**193**	**0.5**	**206**
France	78	49	37	29	4.7	4.0	30.0	7.8	372	19.1	28.1	68	253	−1.5	211
Germany	72	51	29	21	4.6	4.0	25.0	7.9	268	37.0	51.0	73	194	1.0	221
Italy	55	38	31	17	4.8	4.0	25.0	8.1	211	35.0	52.5	67	141	−0.3	136
Portugal	66	40	39	26	4.8	5.0	10.0	9.4	277	10.0	9.6	104	289	0.0	289
Spain	64	40	38	24	4.8	5.0	10.0	9.4	255	31.0	39.3	79	201	2.7	283
UK	74	51	31	23	5.4	4.0	10.0	9.1	253	12.8	14.4	89	225	−0.2	219
Canada	67	42	37	25	5.5	4.0	0.0	9.5	263	8.6	15.2	56	148	0.5	157
USA	69	48	30	21	5.7	4.0	0.0	9.7	216	107.1	97.3	110	238	1.0	266
Combined	**63**	**45**	**34**	**23**	**5.7**	**4.0**	**0.0**	**9.6**	**240**	**115.7**	**112.5**	**103**	**247**	**1.0**	**274**
Argentina	62	40	35	22	12.0	8.0	40.0	17.2	128	8.2	9.5	86	110	3.0	134
Brazil	59	39	34	20	13.0	8.0	40.0	18.2	110	40.1	45.8	88	96	5.0	133
Mexico	96	40	58	56	12.0	8.0	50.0	16.5	339	25.7	44.0	58	198	2.5	233
Venezuela	95	35	63	60	15.0	8.0	20.0	21.6	278	4.5	8.6	52	145	−0.5	142
Europe & US	**68**	**46**	**32**	**22**	**5.0**	**4.3**	**13.8**	**8.8**	**247**	**260.6**	**307.4**	**85**	**209**	**0.6**	**226**
RoW	53	34	35	19	10.2	7.5	29.7	16.0	117	456.8	645.0	71	83	4.8	118

Exhibit 4a.9 Franchise value*

* Franchise value is best calculated at the country level, using the following variables:

- the average cash profit per tonne, defined as EBITDA per tonne of sales
- the balance between supply and demand, defined as domestic demand as a percentage of domestic capacity excluding imports and exports (we have termed this relationship 'domestic balance')
- the weighted average cost of capital
- an estimate of expected long-run growth.

The average cash profit per ton is discounted by the weighted average cost of capital to arrive at the capital value of the cash flow generated in perpetuity by one ton of production. To arrive at the value of one ton of capacity, simply multiply this figure by domestic balance (domestic demand divided by domestic clinker capacity). If demand is higher than available supply, then the value of capacity increases. If not, it falls.

The resulting figure is effectively the theoretical value of one ton of capacity in a given country, assuming that all sales are made domestically. This figure reflects only the value of current demand, and makes no allowance for future growth. It is also a country average, which means that individual plants may be worth more or less, depending on their utilization rates and their cost of production relative to the national performance.

Source: ING Barings, February 2000

▶ ## Lafarge and globalization

The cement industry has been witnessing major diversification, takeovers, joint ventures, mergers, integration and formation of global conglomerates, and other alternative activities in order to protect itself from the adverse consequences of business cycles. Lafarge, over the last decade, has invested heavily in newly industrialized countries offering considerable medium- to long-term growth potential, such as Turkey, Morocco, eastern Europe, Brazil, Venezuela, China and India. For Lafarge, globalization means to be present in every strategic market by acquiring one or more of the local cement producers. The global competitors operate in a similar fashion. Thus, buyer bargaining power, secret rebates, price cutting, price discrimination and competition on service quality have become the norm in the global cement industry. In this sense, markets have become global. Yet in the building materials business, markets are inherently local: consumer tastes are diverse; the business strategies of firms result in the fragmentation of markets on the basis of product lines and location; trade and competition policies vary from country to country. Two factors – high transportation costs and low inventories – together mean that there is no such thing as a worldwide, market-clearing price, as distinct from a global average price. In this sense, cement is a commodity but not like grain or oil. It is not possible to build sustainable, worldwide competitive advantage by locating production in any one country. Supply and demand are matched on a local basis. At cyclical peaks and troughs the boundaries may become regional, but never global.

According to this globalization strategy, the vision, mission and values of Lafarge were as follows:

> " Our vision is to offer the construction industry and the general public innovative solutions bringing greater safety, comfort and quality to their everyday surroundings. The consumer should be placed at the heart of Lafarge's preoccupations. This vision is to be achieved by offering all construction industry sectors – from architect to tradesman, from distributor to end user – a comprehensive range of products and solutions for each stage of the building process. The company values a 'wait and see' philosophy and it includes a long-term orientation with industrial efficiency, value creation, protection of the environment, respect for people and cultures and preservation of natural resources and energy. "

Lafarge has yet to explore the full implications of its goal of globalization. Five of the key issues it will need to address in exploring globalization are:

1 continuing development of its growth strategy
2 further realization of the benefits from its restructuring programme
3 fast integration of the acquired companies to create synergy and hence value
4 internationalization of its workforce and to develop managers willing to be mobile and able to operate successfully in a wide variety of markets, and people with diverse cultural backgrounds
5 managing its human resources, which have doubled in the last five years.

Lafarge's strategy

The cement division's strategic intent was to 'keep growing and growing profitably'. The three main goals followed by the cement division of Lafarge were: (a) doubling sales within ten years (1997 to 2007) by growth in emerging markets and acquisitions in mature markets; (b) growing more rapidly than its competitors with an objective to increase capacity to 60–80 Mt between 2001 and 2005; and (c) integrating acquired units as quickly as possible.

But Lafarge did not just focus on emerging markets as did some of the other global players. In February 2000, it mounted a hostile bid for Britain's Blue Circle, the sixth-largest cement producer and, in January 2001, it bought Blue Circle at a price of €3.8 billion. With this acquisition, Lafarge became the global leader in the construction business, with one-tenth of the world market. The motives behind this acquisition included achieving a certain size in order to remain visible and attractive to investors, expanding cash flow, geographic presence and, probably, dislodging Holcim from top spot in the global cement industry. The chairman and CEO of the group commented on this acquisition thus:

> We [Lafarge] want to be the undisputed leader in all of our businesses, and, the leader in construction materials through operational excellence, growth and the creation of value. Today the construction materials market characterizes a strong movement towards worldwide consolidation. Lafarge must be able to take advantage of the best acquisition opportunities that arise; there are currently many on the market. To finance this programme, the Group has chosen to concentrate its resources on its major worldwide businesses. The introduction of financial partners will enable the Group to enjoy greater financial flexibility.

For the Lafarge Group, strategy implies ambition. The 'Principles of Action' (see Exhibit 4a.10) were drawn up in consultation with all stakeholders. As a long-term goal, the strategic intent was not only to defend and maintain the profitability of operations by continuous improvement of performances, but also to achieve profitability for new operations. To do so, Lafarge restructured its portfolio by divesting 66.67 per cent of its holding in speciality materials. It is now a partner company called Materis. Materis is composed of five businesses: admixtures, aluminates, mortars, paints and refractories.

In 2002, Lafarge's annual turnover was €1.46 billion, more than 50 per cent of which was earned outside of France. To raise funds to achieve its broader objectives, Lafarge sold the Road Making Division of Europe. Currently, Lafarge is trying to sell €700 million worth of assets to reduce debt.

For the Lafarge Group, strategy implies an ambition, some demands and a sense of responsibility. It is only when these components are brought together that actions become sustainable and long term.

Our Principles of Action have been drawn up and worked on in consultation with all concerned. They epitomize our ambitions, our convictions, our code of conduct and our values.

Our ambition

To be a world leader in construction materials

- Be recognized as an important participant and shape the future of our businesses through our capacity to innovate
- Be a leader in a competitive environment

- Pursue long-term strategies
- Adopt an international approach

Our responsibilities

To anticipate and meet our customers' needs

- Create a perceived difference and be the supplier of choice
- Serve our customers better by knowing them better
- Contribute to the development and progress of the construction industry

To enhance the value of our shareholders' investments and gain their trust

- To provide shareholders with a competitive return on their investment
- To provide them with clear information
- To respect the interests of our partners and minority shareholders

To make our employees the heart of our company

- To base legitimate authority on the ability to contribute to the company's success
- To develop mutual respect and trust
- To provide employees with equitable compensation and a fulfilling professional environment

To gain from our increasing diversity

- To make our cultural diversity an asset
- To delegate responsibility with accountability and control
- To develop an effective cross-operational management approach
- To make use of synergies and share knowhow

To respect the common interest

- To participate in the life of the communities where we operate
- To operate responsibly towards the environment
- To be guided by the principles of integrity, openness and respect in our commitments

Exhibit 4a.10 Lafarge's 'Principles of Action'
Source: company documents

Restructuring for internationalization

On internationalization Bertrand Collomb reiterated that:

> International development can be fostered through diversity and innovation. If one wants to push international development one cannot manage it from the top. Maintaining a decentralized operation is very critical. Developing international executives is the best way to become more international.

Lafarge initiated an organizational restructuring process with the help of McKinsey & Co., which began in 1999. The Group was divided into four divisions and a new organizational structure was drawn up to facilitate the change process. The clarification, simplification and formalization of Group policy in the areas of finance, human resources, research and development, corporate communication, environment, information systems, and purchasing and marketing have accompanied this decentralization. In addition, guidelines on the management style expected of all Lafarge managers was set out as 'The Lafarge Way' (see Exhibit 4a.11). Notwithstanding criticisms, alternatives and suggestions about the organizational structure, constant communication and top management's conviction in the structure has resulted in its successful implementation.

Lafarge's management style is defined as 'participative'. But this concept has sometimes been misunderstood as 'management by consensus'. Either that or participation has been forgotten because of business or time pressures. In any case the Group has changed so much recently – half of Lafarge's employees were not in the Group two years ago – that it is time to redefine its management style.

Create value while respecting the Group's guiding principles

Our 'Principles of Action' have not changed, and define our responsibilities: our overriding objective is to create value for our shareholders. To achieve this objective, we must first meet the needs of our customers. Lafarge's identity and success is also based on the importance we give to our employees, and on the strength and benefits of being a group.

Clarify our strategies and our organization

To be successful as a Group, we need shared values, clear strategies, common information and reporting systems and performance measurement criteria. Today, we have started to develop a number of these systems, such as the Cement Operations Reporting Project (CORP), Top 2000 for our ready-mix concrete, as well as the EVA (Economic Value Added) project, to improve our performance measurement and compensation systems. We are now redefining the Group's organization, by rationalizing the role of the corporate function and giving the five divisions (Cement, Aggregates & Concrete, Roofing, Gypsum and Speciality Products) more direct responsibility for strategic development and performance improvement.

To allow more decentralized initiative … with better decision processes

Our aim is to create a management framework that allows more decentralization and individual empowerment. This requires trust in people, as well as clarity in the decision processes. We need to determine at what level a decision should be taken, who is accountable and on what basis, in order to avoid pushing the decision upwards, or diluting responsibilities through a slow, inefficient process.

True participation, but not necessarily a consensus

Participative management is not decision by consensus. Rather, it means involving all those who can contribute to a better decision, while clearly recognizing who has the ultimate responsibility to decide. In this regard, our proposed reorganization is meant to streamline our decision-making processes.

Managers leading by example

Even more important than this organizational framework is the attitude of our employees. We especially want managers who are true leaders, able to drive their organizations to the highest performance level. Individuals who practise what they say, respect group disciplines, share information, and who are professional in managing employee evaluation, career management and the compensation system. Hence the renewed importance we want to give to open, frank two-way discussions in evaluation interviews.

Innovative and willing to contribute to the Group's success

We also need individuals able to innovate, to take initiative and to act decisively within their realm of responsibility. Finally, we want individuals who look beyond their particular objectives, and who are ready to contribute to the attainment of Group synergies and overall goals.

A management 'model'

In summary, the main components of our management philosophy are:

- an organized and coherent Group, with shared values and clear strategies, well-defined procedures, systems and rules
- confident in a decentralized and participative management process
- with managers who lead by example, take the initiative, and who want to contribute to the overall success of the Group.

Exhibit 4a.11 Lafarge's management style: 'The Lafarge Way'
Source: company documents

▶ ## Principles of restructuring

Restructuring was based on certain key issues: (a) to understand and implement procedures to *integrate* its worldwide operations; (b) manage dispersed, *locally responsive* interdependent business units across the globe; (c) *reduce uncertainty* within the group by introducing mechanisms which would *globally coordinate* the group's policies; and (d) synergize the *learning* within the group by jointly developing knowledge, *differentiated* contributions and sharing it worldwide.

Interestingly, Lafarge's two main competitors had entirely different global strategies regarding this issue of managing their global corporation. Holcim believed in total decentralization, whereas Cemex believed in total centralization and control through its information system network.

The key issues of differentiation, integration and uncertainty avoidance involved: (a) differentiation mechanisms – decentralization, changing of a hierarchical organizational structure to a flatter one, delegation of authority down the line and hiring, motivating and retaining specialized personnel; (b) integration mechanism – long-range planning, evolution of a shared culture within the group, formation of committees and cross-functional teams, proper information technology and control systems, and constant internal and external communication within the group; and (c) uncertainty avoidance – gathering of market information, forecasting, monitoring of internal activities, actively participating in industry activities while informally interacting with politicians, traders, dealers and bureaucrats.

Operational impact of restructuring

The new organizational structure

A global strategy of growth must be supported by an adequate organizational structure. The cement division was divided into regions, business units (BUs) and individual plants. A BU is the regional administrative body specific to a country. Each unit is responsible for its assets and returns (EVA)[4] and is presided over by a business unit manager, who usually comes under the supervision of a regional president. Lafarge divided its global operations into eight regional areas with eight regional presidents. The regions are as follows:

1 **Western Europe & Morocco** – France, Italy, Spain, UK
2 **Middle East & Trading** – Cameroon, Egypt, Greece, Jordan, Trading/Shipping
3 **Latin America** – Brazil, Chile, French Caribbean, Honduras, Mexico, Venezuela
4 **Asean** – Indonesia, Malaysia, Philippines
5 **Asia** – Bangladesh, China, India, Japan, South Korea
6 **Africa** – Benin, Kenya, Nigeria, South Africa, Southeastern Africa (Malawi, Tanzania, Zambia, Zimbabwe), Uganda
7 **Central Europe, CIS, Turkey** – Austria, Czech Republic, Germany, Poland, Romania, Russia – CIS
8 **North America** – Great Lakes region, Northeast region, Northwest region, Northwest Pacific region, River region, Southeast region.

Cement units all over the world make up the cement division, which comes under the hierarchical authority of the Group general management and the functional authority of the division executive vice president.

Regarding the divisional structure, one of the managers pointed out:

> The creation of divisions was to segregate the line of products. It was at a global level. At the local level there have not been many changes. The organizational challenge is to be a Group and not to work in silos as divisions. Our strength was to gain synergy from Lafarge resources but now there are too many internal borders and one has to go through administrative processes to harness the strength that the Group has. McKinsey's approach of SBU has very little flexibility. It needs to be clarified within the Group. With EVA, everyone thinks about one's own bottom line as it is linked with individual performance. It kills the perspective of Economic Value Added (EVA)…

Exhibits 4a.12 and 4a.13 show the organizational structure before and after the organizational restructuring process.

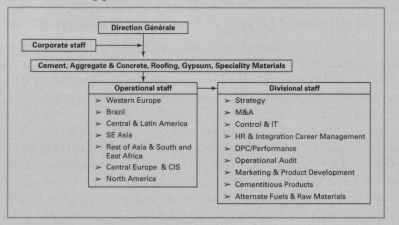

Exhibit 4a.12 Organization (before restructuring)
Source: company documents

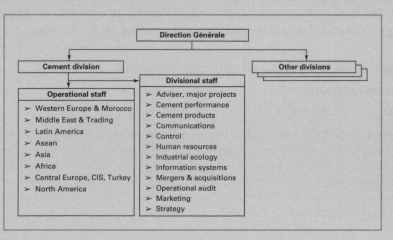

Exhibit 4a.13 Organization (after restructuring)
Source: company documents

▶ Delegation of authority is practised at Lafarge. Almost every decision is based on a project format. A project consists of a project leader who is responsible for the success of the project. For example, current projects in the organization department focus on total productivity management (TPM), safety, environment and organization methodology. Similarly, in the integration department, projects focus on integrating companies in Mexico, Honduras, Jordan, Uganda, South Africa, India, Korea and the Philippines. Each country-based job is treated like a project with the involvement of the Unit Management Committee, integration manager, Project Steering Committee and members of the Project Working Group. In addition, other active contributors to each of these projects are the Transition Team, Relation Director, Corporate & Cement Division departments and external consultants (if any).

Speaking on delegation, the VP of HR pointed out: 'People in this organization are afraid to take decisions and this can only be improved by more delegation and the right kind of delegation. The process of decision making has to be clarified so that it is simple and people will refrain from avoiding responsibility.'

The internationalization of Lafarge: 'a storehouse of best practices'

Lafarge is considered a storehouse of best practices and best specialists in the industry. The specialists of the cement industry are in the technical centre of Lafarge (Cement Technical Centre), which reports to the Cement Performance Department (DPC). The technical expertise is distributed in a two-tier structure – the first is the central laboratory, which pools together the scientific knowledge and develops synergies between materials. The second is the decentralized network of more than 25 applications laboratories supplemented by division, business and unit technical centres. The technical expertise is divided further into three professional fields of manufacturing, technical support and R&D. The technical experts are from the following areas of expertise – geology, quarry management, process, manufacturing, product quality, cement applications, engineering (mechanical/electrical), control, industrial process automation, maintenance, management of engineering projects, project design and studies, technical economic audits, performance audit and environment. The cement performance department coordinates the technical expertise with the departments of investment, industrial performance, knowledge management, process, technology and products.

Organizational implications: integrating the Group

Managing cultural diversity

Speaking about culture, one of the managers became nostalgic:

> French culture is an internal reality of Lafarge. The HQ at 61 rue des Belles Feuilles in Paris has existed for over 75 years now; 25 years ago, Lafarge was a small French cement company. People knew each other much better. It was less complicated and was divided into four regions. Today, Lafarge is much more complicated just because of its sheer size. There is a takeover announcement every day and jobs are much more functional.

Other managers differ:

> We have the knowledge, expertise and talent. Now the times are changing and Lafarge is quick to understand these changes, unlike many other French companies. That is the strength of Lafarge. Our chairman understands this and accordingly wants us to change to be global leaders and he has been pushing for the change right from the beginning. For example, we have two official languages – French and English – while the normal working language is the local language.

One of the managers explained the corporate culture:

> It is the corporate culture of Lafarge to make employees feel at home. We try to make our employees feel that the company is reliable and that they do not need to worry. This is very important to the strategic development of the enterprise. It is a challenge to make and keep them happy.

One of the managers added:

> The reason why Lafarge cares so much for people has a lot to do with the nature of the industry. The cement industry requires big investments and a long-term commitment. There are no quick returns. Therefore, to be successful in this industry, the company has to have a long-term strategic vision. Accordingly it gives a lot of consideration to the long-term development of people and community relations.

Whereas others differed:

> Though we are trying, we still lack the international culture that we should have, given our portfolio of countries. If you look and do a head-count in the Corporate HQ you will see what I mean. It is improving for sure for the last 15 years but lot needs to be done along these lines. Most of the personnel are technically orientated and we do not focus enough on the management functions like marketing, finance, IT and strategy. Though we have all these departments they do not contribute much to the final analyses. I define it as a 'technical culture', which is short-term orientated, which is not good in the long run for the global Lafarge.

Another manager continued:

> Everyone here is accustomed to do their own, good job. Everyone is waiting for the vision to be put forth, to do his or her bit and leave for the day. Very few show initiative and responsibility, and there is little scope for individual initiative, as everyone is looking up to the Direction Générale for guidance, vision and direction. Managers are there to do their duty and this is so because no one quite knows whose ideas will be implemented. The planning cycle is very long and extensively rigorous, most of the time unnecessary; when the time comes to act there is little scope to improvise and be flexible. Simply put, use of common sense is rare, everything is logical and methodical and everyone has doubts whether the documents that are produced day in and day out are implemented properly or not, or have any utility at all.

▶ Speaking about the relationship between culture, business strategy and the challenges ahead:

> " There are huge organizational challenges for the company. This is no more a French company – the organization is in 75 countries and growing by the day. How can one justify that three people run such an organization? The key question in terms of vision and leadership is how do you want to organize this company after five years? The business is relatively simple: cement. It is slow moving and technologically simple. Yet there are many drawbacks in the decision making by which we lose ground. We do better only after going through the learning curve time and again. When will the company learn? Perhaps this is the French corporate style. "

The above observation was explained by one of the managers in this manner:

> " Lafarge is full of cement people. They are Catholics. They are not business people as our competitors are. Lafarge will try to make better cement and more cement for industrial success. Lafarge exists not only for profits, as business schools teach. As in the French way they say 'the growth is to play with and not to be satisfied with'. When we acquire a company it is not to close it down and shelve its assets. It is to merge the new company and create more cement. This is what is different from our competitors' policy, which uses cement as a cash cow to reap profit and invest it elsewhere. Lafarge invests in cement again as the greenfield examples in Bangladesh and China show. "

Retired employees of Lafarge are welcome to the Lafarge cafeteria once every week to cherish the time they worked there and to take part in important events. They are still a part of the Lafarge family. The secretarial staff is also provided with opportunities for short trips to visit foreign countries.

One of the senior managers concluded: '*Relationship and personal touch is the key to success of Lafarge.*'

Style of management

The Chairman of the Group, when asked about the style of management of the group, said:

> " Participative management is not decision by consensus. Rather, it involves all those who can contribute to a better decision, while clearly recognizing who has the ultimate responsibility to decide. In this regard, the proposed reorganization is meant to streamline our decision making processes. "

The Group officially follows the 'The Lafarge Way'. As managers pointed out:

> " The culture is open and participative, although decisions are not taken in a participative way. Decisions are taken by the Direction Générale. Most of the important decisions even at the regional and country level have to be taken by the Direction Générale. Managers exist to implement the decisions of the Direction Générale. The obvious question that comes to one's mind is 'What are people working for at high positions?' "

Another observation reiterated that:

> The decision-making process is a 'little lazy'. Decisions have to be sweetened before they can be implemented. They are entirely top management orientated. The hierarchy is not that tangible and obvious as top management is easily approachable for discussions and new ideas, but top management feels that they are 'tangible gods with the ultimate decision making power'.

The VP HR pointed out:

> Changes are on the agenda to make the decision process simpler and less hierarchical. To be participative there is a lot to improve to be able to take decisions at the lowest possible level as well. On one hand we practise participative style of management but on the other hand it is not so.

On the ways of working, there were diverse opinions. But most believed that time was wasted in meetings that yielded few results: the meeting may carry on for hours without any concrete steps coming forth.

> We plan, plan and plan. Planning is an important part in the 'Lafarge Way'. Implementation and action is a slow and tedious process. Sometimes the planning process is so rigorous and in such depth that decision making becomes difficult when the time for action comes. This is the reason behind all the missed opportunities and the lost ground in most parts of the world. We usually do well after the third or the fifth attempt. Rarely do we see someone taking responsibility forthrightly and carry a business.

The management style was summed up by one of the managers:

> The style is a very traditional technology-minded one. It is slow moving, consensus minded but decisions are taken at the top. It can also be put as 'industrial minded' and is based on repeated evaluations. French people have rules for everything, accurately and methodically documented, but no one follows the rules. It is the same story here.

The Lafarge Way has evolved over many years. The practising style has been that of a family, with the Direction Générale being the head of the family. The whole group is closely knit, with 'family' ties, and much of the work before the formation of SBUs in 1999 was done on the basis of personal relationships. With the formation of SBUs, there was a change in structure, reporting and accounting policies. Any consultation or formation of teams had to be accounted for. As an example, if the HR manager from the gypsum division wanted some assistance from the HR manager of the cement division, the gypsum division had to pay for consulting time to the cement division. This is not practised, but the processes and systems are being put in place. The Lafarge Way acquired in the last ten years and a 'professional culture' is necessary to integrate the new acquisition.

The chairman and CEO is the official spokesperson for Lafarge. A coordination and liaison team deals with the companies of the Lafarge Group in 75 countries, across six continents. Constant interactions are maintained with key professionals in the industry or in the ministry in all countries in which it operates. Regular meetings are held with heads of government and with finance and industry ministers as Lafarge invests heavily in different countries. The information sharing is done through a professional and dedicated communication department, which integrates all employees through mailers, monthly news letters, emails, homepages and intranet through internet servers across the world. All internal events and happenings are mailed individually and the department integrates all divisions and plants through its network and database. Besides extensive internal communication, the communication department pays considerable attention to external communications. Press releases and external communication about Lafarge are important as Lafarge is involved in acquisitions.[5] Lafarge enjoys a unique goodwill not only in France but also wherever it has acquired companies, for its open and caring attitude towards people and community. Personnel at plants, BUs, divisions and corporate offices are always in touch with each other through state-of-the-art communication systems. The email is on Lotus Notes and has a database of 77,000 people from all over the world, which makes the communication easy, fast, cheap and reliable. The database gives addresses instantly. Together with this, there are 61 internet addresses for different countries. The intranet site, built in 2000 and known as Lafarge Employee Online (LEO), helps to connect people anywhere in the world with utilities like jobs within Lafarge Group, travel information, currency converter, time zones, group directory, etc.

Lafarge involves its personnel in committees and cross-functional teams. There are both vertical and horizontal integration mechanisms built in the organization. This is done with the help of teams and periodic group meetings. The decision process is largely top-down and is implemented by managers. Suggestions are discussed and the process is participative but not consensus orientated. The final decision always comes from the Direction Générale. The Direction Générale is a committee of three members. The Cement Executive Committee is a group of ten members. The HR Management Committee consists of ten members, and meets four times a year. It consists of all the Senior VPs of HR related to all the divisions. A good example of cross-functional teams is the integration team, which is known as the 'transition team' and consists of experts from HR, organization, control and IT, marketing and sales, maintenance, industrial and corporate finance. The IT and control department takes care of all the necessary details of this function. It is responsible for improving and controlling all transverse operations of the division by classifying proper use of language (reporting terms), methods (official procedures) and systems (implementation of these procedures). This work is accomplished through a network of regional controllers working closely with the regional presidents.

Global coordination and organizational learning

The cement strategy department is in charge of collecting information from the marketplace. Data are collected from many sources and from different parts of the world and consolidated at the HQ. The data are analysed and put in a 'Lafarge' format before using them for future presentations and monthly reports. Each year the cement strategy department prepares a strategic review for each country. The report consists of sections on plants (Lafarge and competitors), consumption forecasts, per capita income, demand–supply balance, market segmentation by usage, products, etc. market share, imports and competitive positions. Budgets are prepared for five years on the basis of these reports. This is then discussed with the strategists in each country and the group unit head when a detailed analysis of the budget is conducted. The details are then presented to the Direction Générale, which takes the decision on strategic investments. There is a yearly meeting of the strategy managers to share and learn about the different local businesses.

Lafarge is one of the best companies in the world according to its reputation in business, industry and academic circles. Its open attitude and participation in most national and international activities makes it a model organization. It is looked upon as one of the best French companies and a leader in the internationalization process. Lafarge is at least a decade ahead of similar French organizations.

Conclusion

Is growth sustainable?

Although Lafarge has grown at an alarming pace and achieved its vision of becoming the number one firm in the construction industry, senior management recognizes that there is still a long way to go in terms of managing the growth of a one time French cement company which has transformed to a global leader. The integration of Blue Circle is still in process and full synergies are yet to be attained two years after the acquisition (see Exhibit 4a.14 for a comparison of the last six years' financial statements of Lafarge). With recession in mature markets, growth by acquisition can be sustainable only in emerging markets.

Yr to Dec	1997	1998	1999	2000	2001	2002
Sales	6,413	9,802	10,528	12,216	13,698	14,610
Gross operating income	1,239	1,968	2,222	2,592	2,862	3,101
Operating income on ordinary activities	858	1,397	1,630	1,905	2,065	2,132
Operating income	842	1,418	1,707	1,927	2,171	–
Income before tax	750	1,130	1,370	1,438	1,576	–
Net income before amortization of goodwill	559	809	981	1,059	1,162	914
Net income, Group share	371	466	614	726	750	456
Earning per share (in euro)	4.1	4.9	6.2	6.7	5.9	3.5

Exhibit 4a.14 Consolidated statement income (in millions euro)
Source: annual reports, 1998, 1999, 2000, 2001, 2002

Is change sustainable?

While Lafarge faced a number of issues in 2002, perhaps the most important was how to sustain the internal change process. Lafarge's large-scale acquisitions in China, India, South Korea, Indonesia, Malaysia, Philippines and that of Blue Circle brought to the fore the concerns and difficulties of working across different cultures, languages and mindsets. However, optimism is not lacking and substantial steps in the transformation process, like the use of dual language within the Group, are pointed out as steps in the right direction. The common background of an engineering/technical education of most top management is in itself a language of sorts. Extensive internal and external communication within the group and above all Lafarge's policy of respect and care for its employees serves to manage the transition and transformation of Lafarge from local French cement company to global leader.

Notes

1 *European Cement Review*, January 2000.
2 Bank Julius Baer & Co Ltd. Sector Study, Cement Industry, 5 November, 1999.
3 ING Barings, 'European Cement Review', February 2000.
4 Economic Value Added (EVA) = Net Operating Profit After Tax – Capital Charge
   NOPAT = Sales – Operating Expenses – Depreciation – Tax
   Capital Charge = Invested Capital × Cost of Capital
5 China, 1997; Honduras, 1998; Philippines, 1998; Turkey & Morocco, 1998; Tisco & Raymond Cement, India, 1997 & 1999; Jordan Cement, 1999; Beni Suef, Egypt, 1999; Hima Cement, Uganda, 1999; Lafarge South Africa, 1998; Cemento Portland Blanco, Mexico, 1999; Blue Circle, UK, 2000.

CASE 4B: LAFARGE: LOOKING TO THE FUTURE

Introduction

A lot happened at Lafarge from 2002 onwards. In 2005, the Group posted an 11 per cent sales growth, a 7 per cent increase in operating income and a 5 per cent increase in net profit over the full year (see Exhibit 4b.1 for full details). Lafarge became the No. 1 cement company in 2001 when it bought Blue Circle Industries plc of the U.K. for 4.7 billion pounds ($8.7 billion), still the biggest acquisition in the global building materials industry. The company currently employs about 80,000 people in 76 countries.

In mid-September 2005, Bertrand Collomb, Chairman of the Lafarge Group, and Bernard Kasriel, Chief Executive Officer, announced before the opening of the annual meeting of the Group's 150 senior managers in Evian, that the Board of Directors on the recommendation of its Nominations Committee, had decided to appoint Bruno Lafont as Chief Executive Officer as of 1 January 2006. Bruno Lafont, a graduate of HEC Business School and École Nationale d'Administration (ENA), had spent his entire career within the Group, starting as an auditor in 1983 and holding posts in Germany and Turkey before making his mark in 1998 as head of gypsum, where he had doubled sales. Bertrand Collomb, Chairman of Lafarge's Board of Directors commented:

> Today's announcement is the culmination of a process that began three years ago with Bernard Kasriel, under the direction of the Board of Directors, to organize the succession of the senior management team, in keeping with the Group's spirit and traditions. I am sure the new team will remain loyal to the values of the Group even as it takes on new challenges.

New initiatives

In his first six months in the top job, Bruno Lafont eliminated a layer of senior management and bought out Lafarge's North American subsidiary's minorities for $3.5 billion. Lafarge said it aimed to maintain growth at a 'sustained pace'' by expanding a cement business that was already the world's biggest. The company would focus mainly on emerging markets, adding capacity by opening new plants and making acquisitions, it said. Lafont reiterated the main points of his strategic plan for the Group and commented:

> Our strategic plan places shareholders at the heart of our Group. Our aim is to be the best in our sector, which means achieving the best performance, attaining the highest levels of profitability and creating the most value for shareholders.

Ashok Som wrote this case. It is an update of Case 4a 'Lafarge: from French cement company to global leader' (ECCH Reference: 304-019-1). It is intended to be used as a basis for class discussion rather than to illustrate either effective or ineffective handling of a business situation.

This case is prohibited from any type of reproduction, storage or transmittal without permission. To order copies contact European Case Clearing House, Case #306-518-1.

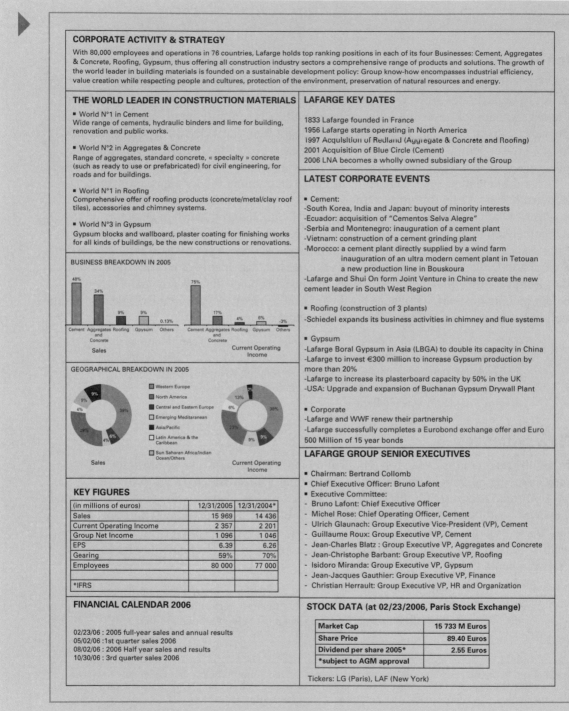

CORPORATE ACTIVITY & STRATEGY

With 80,000 employees and operations in 76 countries, Lafarge holds top ranking positions in each of its four Businesses: Cement, Aggregates & Concrete, Roofing, Gypsum, thus offering all construction industry sectors a comprehensive range of products and solutions. The growth of the world leader in building materials is founded on a sustainable development policy: Group know-how encompasses industrial efficiency, value creation while respecting people and cultures, protection of the environment, preservation of natural resources and energy.

THE WORLD LEADER IN CONSTRUCTION MATERIALS

■ World N°1 in Cement
Wide range of cements, hydraulic binders and lime for building, renovation and public works.

■ World N°2 in Aggregates & Concrete
Range of aggregates, standard concrete, « specialty » concrete (such as ready to use or prefabricated) for civil engineering, for roads and for buildings.

■ World N°1 in Roofing
Comprehensive offer of roofing products (concrete/metal/clay roof tiles), accessories and chimney systems.

■ World N°3 in Gypsum
Gypsum blocks and wallboard, plaster coating for finishing works for all kinds of buildings, be the new constructions or renovations.

BUSINESS BREAKDOWN IN 2005

GEOGRAPHICAL BREAKDOWN IN 2005

KEY FIGURES

(in millions of euros)	12/31/2005	12/31/2004*
Sales	15 969	14 436
Current Operating Income	2 357	2 201
Group Net Income	1 096	1 046
EPS	6.39	6.26
Gearing	59%	70%
Employees	80 000	77 000
*IFRS		

FINANCIAL CALENDAR 2006

02/23/06 : 2005 full-year sales and annual results
05/02/06 :1st quarter sales 2006
08/02/06 : 2006 Half year sales and results
10/30/06 : 3rd quarter sales 2006

LAFARGE KEY DATES

1833 Lafarge founded in France
1956 Lafarge starts operating in North America
1997 Acquisition of Redland (Aggregate & Concrete and Roofing)
2001 Acquisition of Blue Circle (Cement)
2006 LNA becomes a wholly owned subsidiary of the Group

LATEST CORPORATE EVENTS

■ Cement:
-South Korea, India and Japan: buyout of minority interests
-Ecuador: acquisition of "Cementos Selva Alegre"
-Serbia and Montenegro: inauguration of a cement plant
-Vietnam: construction of a cement grinding plant
-Morocco: a cement plant directly supplied by a wind farm
            inauguration of an ultra modern cement plant in Tetouan
            a new production line in Bouskoura
-Lafarge and Shui On form Joint Venture in China to create the new cement leader in South West Region

■ Roofing (construction of 3 plants)
-Schiedel expands its business activities in chimney and flue systems

■ Gypsum
-Lafarge Boral Gypsum in Asia (LBGA) to double its capacity in China
-Lafarge to invest €300 million to increase Gypsum production by more than 20%
-Lafarge to increase its plasterboard capacity by 50% in the UK
-USA: Upgrade and expansion of Buchanan Gypsum Drywall Plant

■ Corporate
-Lafarge and WWF renew their partnership
-Lafarge successfully completes a Eurobond exchange offer and Euro 500 Million of 15 year bonds

LAFARGE GROUP SENIOR EXECUTIVES

■ Chairman: Bertrand Collomb
■ Chief Executive Officer: Bruno Lafont
■ Executive Committee:
- Bruno Lafont: Chief Executive Officer
- Michel Rose: Chief Operating Officer, Cement
- Ulrich Glaunach: Group Executive Vice-President (VP), Cement
- Guillaume Roux: Group Executive VP, Cement
- Jean-Charles Blatz : Group Executive VP, Aggregates and Concrete
- Jean-Christophe Barbant: Group Executive VP, Roofing
- Isidoro Miranda: Group Executive VP, Gypsum
- Jean-Jacques Gauthier: Group Executive VP, Finance
- Christian Herrault: Group Executive VP, HR and Organization

STOCK DATA (at 02/23/2006, Paris Stock Exchange)

Market Cap	15 733 M Euros
Share Price	89.40 Euros
Dividend per share 2005*	2.55 Euros
*subject to AGM approval	

Tickers: LG (Paris), LAF (New York)

Exhibit 4b.1 Lafarge in 2006
Source: Lafarge Group, May 2006

With his succession, Lafont immediately incorporated a new management team, launched an advertising campaign and initiated a high-profile restructuring plan for the Group.

Fresh advertising campaign

The advertisement campaign targeted publications in France, the United Kingdom and the United States. It spoke about Lafarge's strengths in areas of differentiation as: 'creator of new ideas'; 'detector of growth potential'; 'extractor of value for the company and its shareholders'; 'transformer of raw materials into a futuristic vision.'

Renewed restructuring

Quickly after his succession, Bruno Lafont announced that Lafarge would harness faster-than-expected profit growth by 2008 through a programme of cost rationalization, asset sales and acquisitions. The plan was called 'Excellence 2008'. In 2005, Lafarge's EPS had grown only 2 per cent.

The key points of the plan were: (a) an accountable and mobilized management team and organization, with a performance-based culture; (b) a programme to reduce costs by €400 million by 2008; (c) the generation of €1.5 billion in additional cash flow over the next three years; (d) a strategy of profitable growth, focused on cement activity in fast-growing markets and on innovation in concrete; (e) the possible divestment of the roofing business; and (f) a renewed commitment to the Group's values, with priority given to employee safety, corporate governance and sustainable development.

As part of the plan, the Group raised its targets to an average annual EPS growth of 10 per cent by 2008 and ROCE of 10 per cent by year-end 2008, up from 8.5 per cent at the end of 2005 (see Exhibit 4b.2 for full details of the plan).

Our main growth vector in the coming years will clearly be our cement business, in particular in fast-growing markets. We will accomplish this through balancing our growth between the construction of new plants and acquisitions, building on the positions that we have built up in recent years. We will do this in strict compliance with our EPS and ROCE targets, while maintaining a strong financial structure.

The divestment of our roofing business is under consideration, on the condition that we can obtain the full valuation of our assets and maintain a minority interest in this activity, while acting in the best interests of our shareholders.

1. Accelerated transformation of the organization
We have begun to transform our organization in order to simplify our processes, accelerate decision making, make managers truly accountable for the performance of their business units and encourage cost reductions, in order to optimize the Group's development.

Already, the Group's top management structure has been simplified, with the suppression of the Direction Générale level and the reorganization of Group functions. The organization in North America is now aligned with that of the Group, by business line, resulting in the elimination of a hierarchical level. All aggregates and concrete activities, worldwide, are now directly under the authority of the Aggregates & Concrete Division. We have completed the reorganization of our cement technical centres, with a new regional breakdown and reinforced engineering capacities. We have reviewed the main levers of our information systems strategy.

All this makes it possible to launch a new phase of reorganization, towards a greater standardization of our procedures and systems and the development of synergies at country level.

2. A programme to reduce costs by €400 million by 2008

Over the past six months, we have undertaken a detailed review to identify areas for cost reductions within each of the Group's activities. The current transformation of the Group to create a more efficient organization is one of the vectors for reducing costs. Thanks to this groundwork, we are now able to announce a cost-reduction programme of €400 million, which takes into account the expected synergies from the buy-out of minority interests in Lafarge North America and €60 million in cost reductions arising from the turnaround plan of the roofing activity.

3. €1.5 billion in additional cash flow generation

We will achieve this by pursuing our programme to improve working capital requirements, by tight controls on maintenance investments, by lowering the cost of our investments to modernize existing plants or build new capacity, and through a divestment programme over €1 billion euros by the end of 2008.

4. The possible divestment of the roofing business

The turnaround plan for the roofing business, the aim of which is to reach an EBITDA of €350 million in 2008, is well under way and progressing rapidly. Lafarge announces its intention to explore opportunities to divest the roofing business, if valuation conditions are met and the Group can maintain a minority stake in this activity, in the best interests of our shareholders.

5. A strategy of profitable growth

Lafarge is determined to maintain growth at a sustained pace in the coming years. This growth will be generated first by the cement business, primarily in fast-growing markets, through the construction of new production capacity and through acquisitions, and by the aggregates business. It will also be fuelled by an acceleration in the pace and contribution of innovations in all businesses, notably in concrete.

6. The Group reaffirms its values to mark its difference and reinforce its leadership

Lafarge reaffirms its commitment to its values of respect, care and excellence. Vital for the realization of its strategic plan and inseparable from the result-orientated culture introduced at all levels of the organization, these values are crucial for the long-term leadership of the Group and for the best valuation of its shareholders' investment.

Lafarge renews its commitment to being ranked among the world's most effective industrial groups in terms of employee health and safety, protection of the environment, social responsibility and corporate governance.

Exhibit 4b.2 The future: 'Excellence 2008' will bring about 'sustainable and undisputed leadership'
Source: speech given by Bruno Lafont, Lafarge CEO

Portfolio restructuring and shareholder involvement

Bruno Lafont, during his first six months as CEO, declared that he aimed to boost Lafarge's cash flow by about 1.5 billion euros, with at least 1 billion euros coming from asset disposals (excluding the roofing business) and the rest from tightening controls on capital spending. His target for increased profit was based on earnings per share figures. The company's cost-reduction target of 400 million euros included anticipated savings from the buyout of minority interests in the North American unit and 60 million euros from a turnaround plan at the roofing unit.

The future of the roofing business division

The roofing business division, based near Frankfurt, is the world's largest maker of clay and concrete tiles and each year produces enough to cover 1.5 million houses, together with chimneys on another 165,000 houses. The division employs 12,000 people at 162 factories in 35 countries. Profitability had eroded by a decline in selling prices following a decade-long construction slump in Germany, where 25 of its plants are located, and which account for 20 per cent of sales. It had annual sales of 1.5 billion euros in 2005, less than when Lafarge acquired the operation through the £2.1 billion ($3.9 billion) purchase of Redland plc in 1998. Operating profits of 98 million euros had fallen 60 per cent since 1998.

Bruno Lafont's goals for the division included earnings of 350 million euros by 2008, compared with 222 million euros in 2005, excluding interest, tax, depreciation and amortization. He commented:

> There are no assets that must remain in the group if they can't create sustained value. We will exit operations that fail to meet growth targets. The divestment of our roofing business is under consideration, on the condition that we can obtain the full valuation of our assets and maintain a minority interest in this activity. We're not obliged to sell it, but if it's good for shareholders we'll do it.

It was reported that Lafarge had hired JPMorgan Chase & Co. to advise on a possible sale of the division but a final decision was yet to be made. Securities analysts were of the opinion that the business could fetch 2 billion euros.

Albert Frere: the Belgian billionaire

It was reported in the business press that Lafarge launched its first buy-out offer in February 2006, shortly after it became known that Belgian billionaire Albert Frere had acquired a stake in Lafarge. It was reported that Frere, who had interests in companies like Suez and Bertelsmann, would increase his 8.2 per cent stake in Lafarge to 10 per cent or more and demand a board seat to increase pressure on the company's management to work harder for shareholders. 'His presence should maintain pressure on Lafarge to reform/restructure,' said Credit Suisse, citing the Belgian investor's reputation as 'a catalyst for change' for companies in which he builds long-term stakes. In anticipation of Frere's likely demands, analysts were of the opinion that Bruno Lafont, the new boss of Lafarge, should unveil his aggressive restructuring plan.

Growth in emerging markets

With these developments, Lafarge reiterated that it aimed to maintain growth at a '*sustained pace*' by expanding its cement business, which was already the world's biggest. The company would focus mainly on emerging markets, adding capacity by opening new plants and making acquisitions (see Exhibit 4b.3 for details). Lafont commented,

> We will accomplish this through balancing our growth between the construction of new plants and acquisitions ... We will do this in strict compliance with our EPS and return on capital employed targets, while maintaining a strong financial structure.

The cement business had been pursuing its strategy of strong, value-creating growth by significantly expanding production capacity and modernizing industrial facilities (see Exhibit 4b.4). In 2005, the Group began the construction of nearly 5 million tons of additional production capacity in China, Bangladesh, Mexico, Morocco, Ecuador, Russia,

South Africa and Vietnam. These were expected to be fully operational in 2006. An amount of around €400 million was earmarked for its cement production capacity of 5 million tons by 2008 in countries such as Zambia, South Korea and Chile. But the major leap in growth came from China (see Exhibit 4b.5, which illustrates projected growth potential in emerging markets).

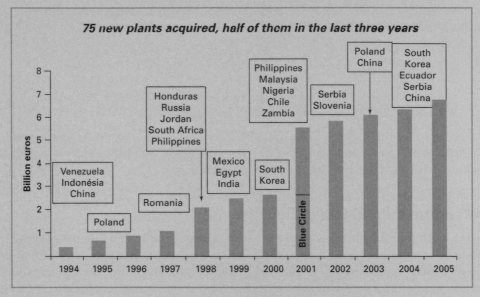

Exhibit 4b.3 Acquisitions to the tune of 7 billion euros in emerging markets

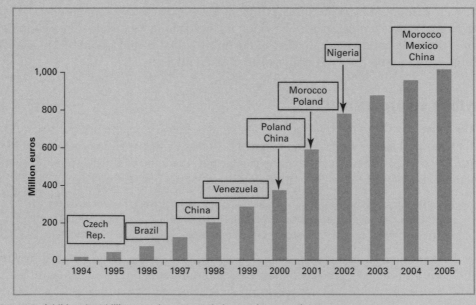

Exhibit 4b.4 Additional 1.1 billion euro investment in increasing capacity

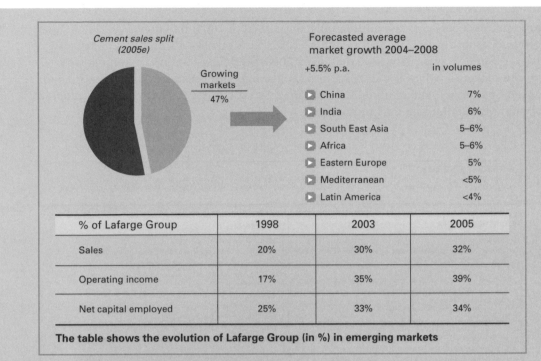

Exhibit 4b.5 Projected growth potential in emerging markets

China

Lafarge established a presence in China in 1994. The company gained valuable experience in China's divided and highly competitive market thanks to the expertise of Jean Desazars, then Regional President of Asia Operations. The Group had strategized, developed and adapted to the specific demands of the regional Chinese market, which represented around one billion tons, or half the world's tonnage. Its sustained growth remained between 7 per cent and 8 per cent per year and there was growing new demand for quality products. In February 2006, Jean Desazars was promoted at Lafarge to Directeur Général Adjoint (Executive Vice President) in charge of strategy and development (including overseeing the company's business portfolio, and directing Lafarge's M&A teams), as part of the company's reorganisation of its top management. He earned a degree in economics from Paris I University and a degree in political science from Sciences Po. He attended the École Nationale d'Administration (ENA) and worked as a diplomat before joining Lafarge in 1989.

In mid-2005, Lafarge signed a JV agreement with Shui On Construction Materials Limited (SOCAM) to create the new cement leader in south-west China, one of the three cement leaders in the whole of China. In late 2005, Lafarge Shui On Cement strengthened its presence in the Sichuan province in south-west China and announced the acquisition of 100 per cent share of the Shuangma Investment Group.

In 2006 Lafarge was present in three provinces of China with four cement plants (see Exhibit 4b.6 for full details). They were: Chinefarge, 50 km north of Beijing with a production capacity of one million tons, purchased in 1994; Dujiangyan in the Sichuan province (south-west China), a greenfield plant built in 1999; its production capacity of 1.4 million tons was planned to double by 2006; Shunfa, also north of Beijing, was purchased and modernised in 2002; and Chongqing, purchased in 2003, was a modern cement plant that had an initial production of 800,000 million tons and inaugurated its second production line for 1 million tons.

ACTIVITY & STRATEGY

Lafarge started its activity in China in 1994 with the establishment of a joint venture in Cement (Chinefarge), and is now one of the Top 2 cement players in China with the JV Lafarge-Shui On. All four of the Group's Divisions are represented in the country. All are local joint ventures partnership, where Lafarge holds a majority stake.

LAFARGE IN CHINA

- **16,000 employees**
- **Cement : Lafarge Shui On Cement (Lafarge holds 55% of the JV)**
  - 14,000 employees
  - production capacity : 21 Mt
  - 17 plants (Beijing, and the provinces of Sichuan, Yunnan, Chongqing, Guizhou)
- **Aggregates & Concrete :**
  1 readymix concrete plant (Beijing)
- **Roofing :**
  6 concrete roof tile plants (Sanshui, Shooxing, Beijing, Nanjing, Quingdao and Chengdu)
- **Gypsum : Lafarge Boral Gypsum (a 50/50 JV)**
  3 plasterboard plants (2 in Shanghai, 1 in Chongqing)

KEY DATES

1994 Chinefarge JV in Cement

1996 Construction of a plasterboard plant in Shanghai

1999 Dujiangyan JV and restructuring start

2000 Lafarge and Boral sign agreement to merge gypsum assets in Asia

2002 – Acquisition of a Cement plant in Shunfa
 – Beginning of the operations at the Dujiangyan plant

2003 Signed of a new JV in Chongqing

2004 – Lafarge invests USD 58 million to double the capacity of its Dujiangyan cement plant in China by 2006, and USD 40 million to double the capacity of its Chongqing plant by 2005
 – Lafarge concludes an exclusive partnership agreement with the Shui On Group in Yunnan province

2005 – Lafarge Boral Gypsum in Asia (LBGA) to double its capacity in China
 – Lafarge and Shui On merge their cement operations in China to create the new cement leader in South West Region
 – Acquisition of Shuangma, in Sichuan, by Lafarge Shui On
 – The second cement production line in Chongqing starts

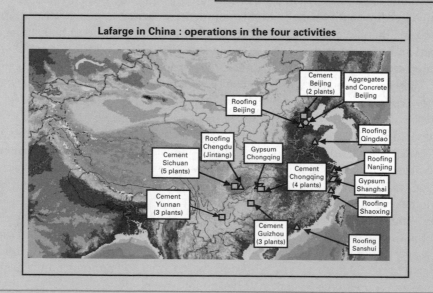

Lafarge in China : operations in the four activities

Exhibit 4b.6 Lafarge in China
Source: Lafarge Group, January 2006

Lafarge had many firsts in China. Joining the Group in June 2003, the Chongqing cement plant was situated at the heart of a market of 30 million people, an autonomous municipality located towards the south-east of Sichuan. It had a capacity of 0.8 million tons. In response to a very sharp increase in the local demand for cement, it was decided to construct a second production line. The Group took a chance by trying to adapt to the methods of Chinese manufacturers, and built a factory quickly and inexpensively. Lafont commented during the inauguration of the second production line, 'It is a first in the Group's history. The new production line at the Chongqing cement plant, operational since June 2005, was built entirely on the Chinese model.'

Lafarge's strategy in China (and India) was to target certain regional markets using large production capacities equipped with modern technologies. The Group's development was based on investments, purchasing existing sites and building new plants through joint ventures. The recruitment and training of local managers to run the plants had been the Group's main priorities.

India

The Indian cement industry had inherent attractions for MNCs after India liberalized its markets in 1991. The Indian cement industry is the second largest market in Asia after China. It is also the third largest market in the world. Demand growth in the Indian market continued to remain positive, unlike that in other Asian countries.

Lafarge's Indian operations, Lafarge India Pvt. Ltd, started in November 1999, subsequent to the takeover of Tata Steel's Cement division. In January 2001, Lafarge took over Raymond's cement plant in Bilaspur, Chhattisgarh. In total, the company acquired a total capacity of 4 million tons of cement and after de-bottlenecking, currently, has a manufacturing capacity of 5 million tons of cement and 3 million tons of clinker. Two of its plants are located in Chhattisgarh and a grinding unit is located in Jharkhand State.

Lafarge India's operations included production and retailing of Portland slag cement, ordinary Portland cement and Portland pozzolana cement, besides clinker and colour roofing products. The company developed a good social focus and some of its activities included providing training to unemployed youth, computer education for girls and computer-aided education for others, and supporting the setting up of an eye care institute in Raipur. As part of its social initiatives, Lafarge Group launched a programme in India to help provide affordable housing for low-income people. In addition, Lafarge was engaged in the rehabilitation of quarries that aid nearby villages through water harvesting. Lafarge SA at present has a 71 per cent stake in Lafarge India through its holding companies, with the balance held by other strategic investors. Lafarge enjoyed a 21 per cent market share in eastern India alone, which was growing at a healthy pace of 11 per cent to 12 per cent per annum, and planned to set up a greenfield venture at Mejia in Bankura District in the State of West Bengal. The 1 mt plant was conceived in 2004 and was expected to commence commercial production by 2008.

Lafarge's future decision to invest in India was purely dependent upon its Asian strategy. Indian companies normally commanded lower valuations because the markets were more fragmented than cement markets in the rest of the world (excluding China).

India was also perceived to be a higher-risk country than some of the other emerging markets. With the acquisition of Blue Circle in 2001, Lafarge's capacity in Asia had risen from a paltry 5 million ton to 33 million ton. One analyst commented that:

> We believed that Lafarge management would now be looking at diversifying its cement portfolio towards other markets, especially North America, Latin America and Africa, where it has lesser presence than Asia. This would mean that the company would deploy its financial resources to these markets first before considering India or any other Asian country for investments. One should not be surprised therefore if Lafarge puts its India plans on the back burner for a reasonable length of time.

Between 2001 and 2005, Lafarge missed two acquisition opportunities in India. The first was L&T cement, which was acquired by the Indian MNC, Aditya Birla Group, while the second was Associated Cement Company (ACC), which was partially bought by the key Indian player, Gujarat Ambuja Cement, and later by Holcim. Holcim subsequently bought 14.8 per cent of Gujarat Ambuja with a total investment close to $2 billion, giving them investment in two Indian companies in a matter of one year. With the Gujarat Ambuja deal, Holcim was reported in the media to have become the undisputed leader of the global cement industry, ahead of its French rival Lafarge. Lafarge countered by fully acquiring Lafarge North America. Holcim-ACC-Gujarat Ambuja and Aditya Birla Group together commanded more than 50 per cent of the Indian building-construction market share. Industry experts were of the opinion that this could result in price stability and gathering momentum for further consolidation.

After a gap of almost five years, Lafarge India was reported to be on the move for acquisitions in India. The first Indian CEO of Lafarge India, Uday Khanna, commented:

> Our vision is to build up a strong presence in an expanding market. There are various ways one can achieve growth. It could be through expansion, takeovers or by setting up greenfield projects. Our parent company is actively pursuing growth plans in India. We are moving in all directions. We are also in discussion with others, but it would be premature to reveal our plans at this juncture.

On 26 September 2006, Lafarge revealed that it had won the approval of the Indian government to invest $170 million (160 million euros) to build a 3 million-ton capacity cement plant in Alsindi, located in the northern state of Himachal Pradesh, taking its total output from 5.5 to 8.5 million tons. This greenfield project is expected to be completed in 2010.

On 10 October 2006, Lafarge announced that it had signed an MOU to construct a second production line at Lafarge's Sonadih plant in the Raipur District of the state of Chhattisgarh, increasing the plant's total clinker capacity by 1.6 million tons to 3 million tons per year. The company also planned a 1 million-ton grinding station at its plant in Mejia in the key market of West Bengal. The project represents an investment of around 140 million euros and is scheduled in two phases. It is expected to increase value starting in 2009. In total, Lafarge's production capacity in India will increase from the current 5.5 million tons to around 12 million tons. The overall project represents a total investment of around 75 euros per new ton of capacity.

? *Case questions*

Read the cases carefully and then answer the following questions.

1 What does globalization mean for Lafarge and how can it globalize effectively? What role does the nature of industry play in the globalization process?

2 Should Lafarge grow by expanding current operations or should it grow by acquiring foreign firms? Why is growth imperative in this industry? How is value created in this process?

3 Does Lafarge have an effective structure to support its growth strategy? If yes, why, if not, why not? How can the company realize the full benefits of its organizational structure?

4 Is the overall business strategy of Lafarge in tandem with its 'Principles of Action' and 'The Lafarge Way'? What is the role of organizational culture and administrative heritage in managing a global corporation?

5 How does Lafarge manage the change process internally? What is the role of the 'best practices' in driving the internationalization process?

6 Comment on the expansion strategies of Lafarge in China and India. Why was it more successful in China and less so in India?

PART 3
The Change Imperative

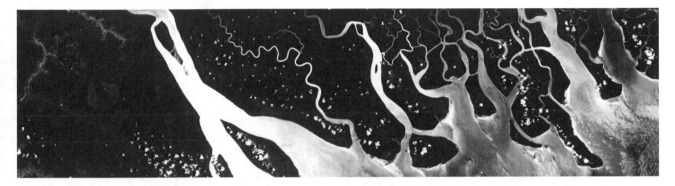

CHAPTER 5

Managing mergers and acquisitions

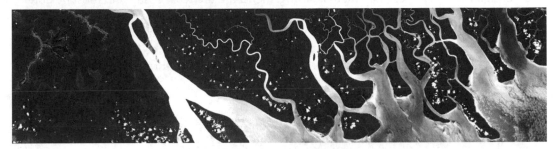

The previous chapter dealt with how global companies organize themselves. It discussed the evolution and development of different organizational structures, and the challenges of managing companies across cultures. This chapter discusses the change process that many global organizations are facing today in complex and dynamic environments. It also looks at the role of mergers and acquisitions (M&As), strategic alliances, and the pros and cons of the expansion processes of the global corporation. Finally, the chapter explores the logic of M&As and touches upon the challenges of the post-merger integration process.

Corporations can utilize a variety of modes of entry into global markets, with international expansion and growth opportunities being accomplished in three ways:

1 exporting, with contractual agreements such as licensing and franchising

2 making foreign direct investments that entail alliances, joint ventures or acquisitions

3 forming new wholly owned subsidiaries.

Each of these modes of entry has its strengths and weaknesses. Thus choosing the appropriate entry strategy is essential to superior competitive performance in global markets. For example, exporting strategy has the lowest investment and risk, but also the lowest degree of ownership and control. With the direct foreign investment approach, risk and ownership is high, whereas control is very high in the case of forming a new wholly owned subsidiary.

Exporting: licensing, franchising

*E*xporting involves the transfer of goods and services to foreign countries for their sale through a company operating in that country. Most firms begin their international expansion with exporting because it does not require an extended investment in another country. Relatively low entry and exit costs provide firms with the ability to quickly and easily establish a presence in a foreign market. On the other hand, the high costs of tariffs and transportation, the loss of control over pricing and distribution, and the inability to tailor goods and services to local markets makes it difficult to effectively compete in global markets.

Licensing is a contractual arrangement that involves selling the right to produce and/or sell products to foreign markets. *Franchising* is the counterpart of licensing, which focuses on selling the right to use a brand name and/or operating method in order to sell a service to foreign markets. These contractual arrangements are the least costly and most flexible mode of entry into and expansion of global markets since the licensee assumes the risk of investing in the manufacture, marketing and distribution of the goods and services. On the downside, profits are reduced since returns must be shared with the licensee, and the risk of the licensee becoming a serious competitor after the agreement expires may arise as they learn the business.

FDI: alliances – joint ventures, M&A, greenfield

The final mode of entry into global markets is *foreign direct investment* (FDI). The increase in FDIs by global corporations has influenced international trade patterns, although not always in ways that are straightforward; they generally result from a series of complex interactions, which may vary over time. For example, outward FDI can be a substitute for exports, with parent companies setting up affiliates to meet the local demand or to circumvent restrictive trade policies in the host country. On the other hand, foreign investment can also be undertaken in order to take advantage of more favourable conditions in the host countries, such as cheaper labour or lower taxes. It may also be associated with stronger exports in the construction phase of production facilities abroad, followed by an increase in imports of finished goods at a later stage. Finally, it may be a direct complement to exports when firms undertake investment abroad to facilitate and enhance the distribution of their products. FDI can occur in three ways: joint ventures, acquisitions and greenfield ventures.

Strategic alliances

Corporations cooperate globally to share knowledge, learning, resources, rewards and control; to spread risks; to reduce costs; to gain complementary competencies to access location-specific assets and distribution networks; and to secure vertical and horizontal linkages.

In the case of strategic alliances, corporations mutually agree to certain objectives in order to achieve a common goal. International expansion needs resources and the ability to coordinate in order to be successful. Corporations may seek partners to share these costs, and may explore synergies in areas such as R&D, co-funding research projects, cross-licensing proprietary technology, sharing production facilities, coordinating procurement and management of the supply chain, marketing existing distribution networks and sharing in making the financial decisions. The basic benefits partners gain from their strategic alliances are ease of market entry, shared risk, shared knowledge and expertise, and competitive advantage. Strategic alliances can ease market entry because they allow firms to overcome barriers such as entrenched competition and hostile government regulations, and/or reduce the cost of entry. The logic of strategic alliances is to achieve more and to compete more effectively than if each party had acted independently.

But, more often than not, a strategic alliance leads to delayed decision making, conflicts, and shared roles and authority. Some of the main causes of failure include incompatibility among the partners, limited access and sharing of information, disagreement over the distribution of earnings, a perceived loss of autonomy, and conflicting business priorities. At times, incompatibility can lead to outright conflict, although typically it leads to poor performance of the alliance. However, with this benefit comes one of the primary disadvantages of strategic alliances: the risk of giving away proprietary information.

For example, a complex maze of alliances exists in the airline industry. Star Alliance led by Lufthansa, One World led by British Airways and Sky Team led by AF-KI M are examples of such alliances. When these alliances work well, mergers take place, as happened with AF-KLM, which created the largest airline corporation by revenue. A similar example has occurred in the telecommunications industry, where with deregulation the restrictions on foreign ownership are being lifted. Corporations such as Vodafone (which acquired Mannesmann), France Télécom (acquired Orange), AT&T (acquiring Bell South to have full control of Cingular Wireless) have become global players.

Joint ventures

Joint ventures (JVs) are a special type of strategic alliance where two or more corporations cooperate and agree to share ownership of an FDI in order to pursue common business objectives in a foreign market. Usually the partners in a JV create a new business entity that is legally separate and distinct from its parents. These agreements allow firms to share the risks and resources required to expand into global markets and contribute to the development of new organizational capabilities. A JV might be a comprehensive one, whereby the partners participate jointly in most parts of the business, or it might be a focused one that concentrates on a particular facet of a business. A joint venture almost always takes the form of a corporation, usually incorporated in the country in which it will be doing business. The corporate form enables the partners to arrange a beneficial tax structure, implement novel ownership arrangements and better protect their other assets. The two primary reasons for the failure of joint ventures are incompatibility of the partners and conflict between the partners.

For example, a study cited in the *Harvard Business Review*[1] reported that, out of 49 JVs studied in 1991, only 51 per cent were successful – that is, each partner had achieved returns greater than the cost of capital. A decade later, in 2001, the same group of researchers analysed more than 2,000 alliance announcements – and found that the success rate was about 53 per cent despite studies which have found that JVs fail because of incorrect strategies, incompatible partners, inequitable or unrealistic deals, and weak management. Some of the challenges that the JVs faced were strategic misalignment, non-creation of a governance system that is shared by the partners, economic interdependencies and building a shared organization.

---

[1] Bramford, J., Ernst, D. and Fubini, D.G. (2004) 'Launching a world-class joint venture', *Harvard Business Review*, February, 91–100.

Mergers & acquisitions

In the recent past, mergers and acquisitions (M&As) have been a more popular mode of expansion than strategic alliances and greenfield investments. In Europe and the rest of the world there have been multi-billion-dollar M&As. Some noted high-profile recent M&As are Lafarge-Blue Circle, Cemex-RMC, AF-KLM, Renault-Nissan, Sanofi-Aventis, Arcelor-Mittal, and Tata-Corus, to name a few.

Mergers and acquisitions are the simplest vehicle for accelerating growth. They are also favourable as they provide immediate market access, and often immediate access to technology, patents, etc. For example, Cisco and Oracle's strategy of M&A has been to access technology. Pharmaceutical companies acquire biotech and other pharmaceuticals companies to gain immediate access to R&D and the pipeline of drugs. However, M&As also incur high risks, both in terms of industry consolidation and also strategic, organizational, cultural and people fit between the acquirer and the acquired. During an acquisition, both pre-acquisition analysis and post-acquisition management are a necessity for the success of the acquisition. Usually corporations ask themselves some very basic questions before embarking on an M&A. Those questions include:

- What are the costs and expected benefits of the acquisition?
- How will the acquisition be financed?
- What are other alternatives to achieve similar objectives?
- What are the synergies?
- How can these synergies be maximized in the shortest possible time?
- How can combined resources be allocated quickly?
- What are the means of achieving post-merger integration levels and at what speed?
- And so on.

Why do corporations pursue cross-border M&As?

Some of the reasons corporations pursue cross-border M&As are as follows:

- immediate market power and access (including distribution and channel control) without expanding capacity
- overcoming barriers to entry, and building economies of scale and scope
- fuel consolidation and competitive stabilization
- fast way of accelerating growth (difficult to do so organically in saturated markets) and revenues
- synergy in resource allocation, portfolio diversification, financial leverage through improved debt, credit and tax rationalization
- tangible and intangible resource acquisition
- immediate access to R&D, products, knowledge and talent
- ensuring survival (follow the herd, and eat or be eaten)
- free cash flows

- agency problems
- managerial belief that they can manage better
- potential for profitable growth.

Why is it so difficult to get M&As right? What should be done?

There might be many reasons why M&As fail, but some that have been consistently been referred to by researches are as follows:

- absence of clear vision, mission and objectives for the combined entity; there must be ongoing and visible involvement of top management
- high merger transition and coordination costs must be managed in phases
- lack of communication; there needs to be clarity of both internal and external communication, which should be significant, constant and consistent; a merger generates uncertainty, and constant reinforcement is needed for all stakeholders to understand and participate in the merger process
- absence of an effective post-merger integration process, including interface management (gatekeeping), specialized integration teams, learning, etc.
- too much time spent finding synergy and ways of cost rationalization such that corporations lose track of growth and opportunities for revenue generation by the combined entity; choosing the right people for different cross-functional and cross-company teams to facilitate the integration process is crucial
- loss of intangible resources such as talent, knowledge and capabilities that reside within teams and individuals; retaining the talent and learning about their needs in the new entity is critical
- issues related to strategic, organizational and cultural fit, and a lack of respect for the acquired company's employees
- a lack of commitment and trust in the merger from both sides.

What organizational architecture should the M&A entity have?

There are some options regarding the organizational architecture, depending on the strategy of integration of the acquiring corporation (see Figure 5.1). Options include holding, preservation, and absorption or symbiosis.

Holding is relatively rare. Bank One in the USA grew by buying small local banks in different regions in the country. Little autonomy was granted due to Bank One's strict control and monitoring procedures. Also little interdependence was achieved because the acquired banks rarely had any need to interact.

In *preservation*, the acquired corporation preserves the acquired corporation's independence and cultural autonomy. This usually occurs when the rationale of the merger might be to expand into new geographic areas (where its brand is not well known), to acquire a famous product line with distribution outlets, to acquire a brand or to acquire management knowledge. L'Oréal's acquisition of the UK's Body Shop is a classic example of the acquisition of a product line with distribution outlets, where the brand Body Shop was preserved. Oracle's acquisition of Peoplesoft meant acquiring management knowledge. Vodafone follows a preservation strategy for some years when it enters a new market, to allow customers to become accustomed to its brand; it did so in Japan and Italy. LVMH's acquisition of multiple brands is a similar strategy in the luxury sector. There are degrees to which strategic interdependence can be bestowed. The key success driver is to protect the boundaries of the acquired corporation, and institutionalize its routines and practices as a separate entity. A preservation strategy is usually helpful when the acquired company has a very strong administrative heritage and it would be detrimental for the merger to seek full integration.

Absorption, as the term suggests, means assimilating the acquired corporation within the acquiring corporation's fold. The acquired corporation conforms to the systems, processes and routines of the acquirer's organizational architecture. In this type of acquisition, synergies are related to cost rationalizations, improvement in the systems and processes, and the transfer of best practices. An absorption strategy is mainly used during industry consolidations. Success depends on choosing the target well for cultural compatibility, sometimes geographic distance, and moving quickly to reduce uncertainty and capture available synergies. For example, cement companies such as Cemex and Lafarge follow this strategy. GE and eBay practise this strategy regularly to integrate into their portfolios the acquired corporations' technology and R&D.

Symbiosis is a strategy often referred to as 'best of both' or as a 'merger of equals'. Usually the strategy of symbiosis comprises complex processes where the transformation of both corporations results from the merger. More often than not, both corporations learn from symbiosis and try to operate differently as they reflect on their past and try to work out an effective process for the combined entity. Examples of this type of mega-merger are many. For example, Renault-Nissan, AF-KLM, Arcelor-Mittal, Sanof-Aventis, Total-Elf-Fina, ExxonMobil, GlaxoSmithKline, AstraZeneca, DaimlerChrysler, AOL-Time Warner, to name a few.

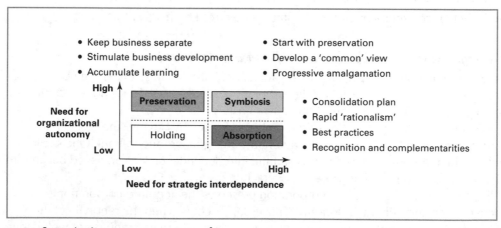

Figure 5.1 Strategies for post-merger outcomes[2]

---

[2] Haspeslagh, P. and Jemison, D. (1991) *Managing Acquisitions: Creating Value Through Corporate Renewal.* New York: Free Press.

Implementation of M&As

Building strategies is the simple part; implementation is the complex part. For example, Lafarge's strategy (see Case 4) was to become world leader in the building construction materials industry. At the time, in 2000, it was ranked third in the world. As part of its strategy, Lafarge aimed to double its sales by 2007 as it worked its way to the number one position. But it had failed in its hostile takeover attempt on the UK's Blue Circle, the number seven building construction materials corporation. Then, in 2001, it acquired Blue Circle in a friendly takeover. During the post-merger implementation, Lafarge found that most of Blue Circle's plants were at a much lower level technologically than Lafarge's facilities, which meant that the acquisition implementation would take more time than had been envisaged, and require additional investment. This was a surprise to many of the managers involved; the success of an M&A deal lies in its implementation.

A much spoken about M&A success is Renault-Nissan. In the words of Carlos Ghosn, Chairman and CEO of Renault-Nissan, some of the key success factors were first determined by laying down the right questions for every phase of the process. For example, during the strategic value analysis, corporations should ask simple questions like what are the benefits and what do they get? Second comes analysis of fit (and non-fit), where critical issues such as strategy, capabilities, culture and organizational fit have to be understood in order to determine how workable the relationship is. At this stage, national, industry and organizational cultures have to be borne in mind. In terms of organizational fit, variables such as size, structure, systems, skills, style and staff have to be matched to design the new organization. At this stage, the life cycle of the organization and its historical performance are critical in the negotiation process. Third, at the agreement and organization stage, design and negotiation and work functions have to be determined in order to set the operational scope, interface and governance. Finally, during the actual implementation stage, working methods for integration, cooperation and evolution have to be planned. For Nissan, some of the processes involved during implementation included setting up an interface management team, which led to the formation of cross-functional and cross-company teams. Vision, mission, goals and measurable objectives were restated and communicated internally and externally throughout the organization. Operations were maintained on an even keel to further mutual understanding. Priority was given to strengthening Nissan, taking stock and establishing control, in order to build credibility within top, middle and lower management.

The post-merger integration (PMI) process

The outcome of post-acquisition transformation and integration depends on managerial action taken during the process. The transformation and integration of the acquired corporation is subject to tensions between implementing radical change to match the strategy and corporate culture of the acquirer, and promoting what is valuable in terms of resources and cultural attributes in the acquired organization. Thus the PMI process is fundamentally a trade-off between the benefits of retaining various organizational routines and the benefits of disrupting them, on both the target and the acquirer side. This is done in order to best exploit the opportunity an acquisition presents. Two processes – people and systems – are crucial during the PMI. The integration of people processes appears to facilitate the effectiveness of the integration of system processes within the acquired organization. If the systems integration is pursued before the people processes are completed, the acquisition has a high likelihood of running into problems because individuals on both sides might be sceptical about the motives of the acquirer's management. The alternative might be undertaking both together, and at an equal pace, after an initial period.

The knowledge transfer required implicitly determines the appropriate degree of integration, which subsequently determines the speed of integration. In situations where it makes sense for the target either to be kept as a separate unit or be fully integrated from the outset, which is the case when the knowledge transfer required is from the acquirer to the target, the integration process can proceed immediately and quickly. Cemex and GE follow this method. In contrast, in circumstances where a knowledge transfer flow is needed from the target to the acquirer, or bidirectionally, the integration process should be slow. Corporations such as Holcim and, depending on the country, Vodafone follow this method.

Though there are numerous explanations for merger failure, some of the determinants of merger success have been identified as strategic vision, strategic fit, deal structure, due diligence, pre-merger planning, post-merger integration and the external environment. It is the actual execution of the merger strategy through pre-merger planning and the post-merger integration process that appears to be critical. Though poor performance in any one of these areas can cause merger failure, there has been significant discussion related to the drivers of success. Some of these are coherent PMI strategy, speed, a strong integration team, communication, and alignment or fit. Reinforcing a 'merger of equals' rather than an acquisition has a clear advantage as it reflects a very different set of priorities in the integration process, and has significant implications for all employees in terms of both process and content. For example, Carlos Ghosn reported that 'Renault has done everything in order to avoid hurting Nissan's pride and avoid appearing as its "saviour"... Renault was aware at all times of the risks of a merger. The loss of identity is a huge risk. The only thing we have is our capacity to motivate our people. How can we motivate them if they have lost their individuality? Renault never adopted an "arrogant" attitude. This behaviour created a climate in which trust could be built ...'.

Commitment to a successful PMI is often demonstrated through a full-time function with an ample leadership role and high-profile composition that works on the basis of projects that are separate from the core business. It is often the duty of the integration team to eliminate any culture clash in the new organization. Also the success of the PMI process depends on speed as employees may regard a slow pace as a sign of uncertainty, and may pursue opportunities with rival firms. Customers may likewise fear instability and seek competitors' products if the visible aspects of the integration are not achieved rapidly. Thus, achievable and measurable milestones need to be created in all areas, especially with regard to the measurement of synergies. The milestones also need to be monitored, and responsibility needs to be shared by the integration team, business units and functional areas. Some ways to measure success might be: the retention of key employees; goals achieved related to a time schedule, costs and revenue; the completion of integration of systems and processes; the number of best practices adopted and implemented; employee audits like moral survey results; positive stock market reaction and the satisfaction of customers.

Evolution of M&As

Haspeslagh and Jemison (1991, p. 15) recommend 'for value creation to be realized, integration must be seen as an evolutionary process of adaptation, rather than as a completely predictable, planned activity'. Corporations in dynamic environments follow the co-evolutionary framework of strategy process. Co-evolution requires the alignment and orchestration of a web of shifting networks among evolving businesses. M&As, be they horizontal, vertical or related, seek such alignment with their partners. To manage this aligned evolution, dynamic capabilities[3] are required. The set of dynamic capabilities becomes a necessity during periods of radical change, like that induced by economic transition, deregulation, liberalization, geopolitical and technological changes, when an M&A occurs. The building up of dynamic capabilities during an M&A calls upon individuals to redesign routines within the corporation. It may involve changing their routines, their patterns of interaction, and possibly even their attitudes and value systems. Building these new dynamic capabilities in an existing organization is an evolutionary process that is driven by the processes of knowledge generation and organizational learning. Organizations co-evolve, rather than reincarnate themselves overnight, when facing a change in their ownership. During ownership changes, successful learning is first a function of the corporation's absorptive capacity, which is its ability to adopt knowledge in the environment, connect it with existing knowledge and routines and thus apply it to the corporation's purposes. Where suitable routines are lacking, corporations have to engage in trial-and-error processes to explore and develop new routines. This period of experimentation is a crucial phase for firms facing an unfamiliar environment with new rules and performance criteria, especially during the M&A process. Corporations with internal processes that generate and adopt superior capabilities are more 'fit' for sustained competitive advantage.

Case introduction: Mittal-Arcelor: the bid

On 27 January 2006, Mittal Steel, the world-leading steel producer, announced it was making a hostile bid on its rival, Arcelor, the number two steelmaker. The bid was rejected by Arcelor's board and led to virulent reactions from many of those in the governments directly or indirectly involved. Mittal Steel, which is based in Rotterdam and London, was created and is still owned and managed by a steel magnate, an Indian-born self-made entrepreneur, Lakshmi Mittal. Since the 1970s, he has followed a successful strategy synonymous with early globalization: he bought several inefficient old state-owned assets cheaply in nations with weak or non-existent unions, overhauled them and turned them into cash-generating machines, which in turn helped fuel future acquisitions. On that day in January, the target had a totally different profile, however. Indeed, Arcelor was itself created in 2002 by a merger of three European steelmakers: Aceralia (Spain), Arbed (Luxembourg) and Usinor (France), which were considered national champions in their home countries.

This case appears after the readings for this chapter.

---

[3] Dynamic capabilities are 'the organizational and strategic routines by which firms achieve new resource configurations as markets emerge, collide, split, evolve, and die' (Eisenhardt, K.M. and Martin, J.A. (2000) in 'Dynamic capabilities: What are they?' *Strategic Management Journal*, 21 (10/11), 1105–21, on p. 1107.

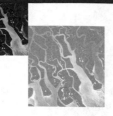

READING 9
How to make strategic alliances work*

Jeffrey H. Dyer, Prashant Kale and Harbir Singh

Developing a dedicated alliance function is key to building the expertise needed for competitive advantage.

Strategic alliances – a fast and flexible way to access complementary resources and skills that reside in other companies – have become an important tool for achieving sustainable competitive advantage. Indeed, the past decade has witnessed an extraordinary increase in alliances.[1] Currently, the top 500 global businesses have an average of 60 major strategic alliances each.

Yet alliances are fraught with risks, and almost half fail. Hence the ability to form and manage them more effectively than competitors can become an important source of competitive advantage. We conducted an in-depth study of 200 corporations and their 1,572 alliances. We found that a company's stock price jumped roughly 1% with each announcement of a new alliance, which translated into an increase in market value of $54 million per alliance.[2] And although all companies seemed to create some value through alliances, certain companies – for example, Hewlett-Packard, Oracle, Eli Lilly & Co. and Parke-Davis (a division of Pfizer Inc.) – showed themselves capable of systematically generating more alliance value than others. (See 'A Dedicated Function Improves the Success of Strategic Alliances, 1993–1997.')

How do they do it? By building a dedicated strategic-alliance function. The companies and others like them appoint a vice president or director of strategic alliances with his or her own staff and resources. The dedicated function coordinates all alliance-related activity within the organization and is charged with institutionalizing processes and systems to teach, share and leverage prior alliance-management experience and know-how throughout the company. And it is effective. Enterprises with a dedicated function achieved a 25% higher long-term success rate with their alliances than those without such a function – and generated almost four times the market wealth whenever they announced the formation of a new alliance. (See 'Research Design and Methodology.')

---

* MIT *Sloan Management Review*, Summer 2001.

How a dedicated alliance function creates value

An effective dedicated strategic-alliance function performs four key roles: It improves knowledge-management efforts, increases external visibility, provides internal coordination, and eliminates both accountability problems and intervention problems. (See 'The Role of the Alliance Function and How It Creates Value.')

Improving knowledge management

A dedicated function acts as a focal point for learning and for leveraging lessons and feedback from prior and ongoing alliances. It systematically establishes a series of routine processes to articulate, document, codify and share alliance know-how about the key phases of the alliance life cycle. There are five key phases, and companies that have been successful with alliances have tools and templates to manage each. (See 'Tools To Use Across the Alliance Life Cycle.')

Many companies with dedicated alliance functions have codified explicit alliance-management knowledge by creating guidelines and manuals to help them manage specific aspects of the alliance life cycle, such as partner selection and alliance negotiation and contracting. For example, Lotus Corp. created what it calls its '35 rules of thumb' to manage each phase of an alliance, from formation to termination. Hewlett-Packard developed 60 different tools and templates, included in a 300-page manual for guiding decision making in specific alliance situations. The manual included such tools as a template for making the business case for an alliance, a partner-evaluation form, a negotiations template outlining the roles and responsibilities of different departments, a list of ways to measure alliance performance and an alliance-termination checklist.

Research Design and Methodology

We conducted two types of research. From 1996 to 2000, we interviewed at companies such as Hewlett-Packard, Warner-Lambert (now part of Pfizer), Oracle, Corning, Lilly, GlaxoSmithKline and others that were reputed to have effective alliance capabilities. We also interviewed executives at companies that did not have a dedicated strategic-alliance function, many of which have had relatively poor success with alliances. We conducted a survey-based study of 203 companies (from a variety of industries) with average revenues of $3.05 billion in 1998. The analysis of alliance success and stock-market gain from alliance announcements is based on data from 1,572 alliances formed by the companies between 1993 and 1997.

To assess the long-term success of the alliances, we collected survey data on the primary reasons that each of the alliances was formed. We then asked managers to evaluate each alliance on the following dimensions:

- the extent to which the alliance met its stated objectives;
- the extent to which the alliance enhanced the competitive position of the parent company;

▶

▶ ■ the extent to which the alliance enabled each parent company to learn some critical skills from the alliance partner; and

■ the level of harmony the partners involved in the alliance exhibited.

Managers used a standard 1–7 (1 = low and 7 = high) survey scale. Alliances that received an above-average score on the four dimensions were rated 'successes,' and those that received scores below average were rated 'failures.' Assessments of alliance success and failure then were used to calculate an overall alliance success rate for each company. The alliance success rate is essentially a ratio of each company's 'successful' alliances to all its alliances during the study period.

In recent years, academics have begun using a market-based measure of alliance value creation and success based on abnormal stock-market gains. To estimate incremental value creation for each company, we built a model to predict stock price based on daily firm stock prices for 180 days before an alliance announcement. The model also includes daily market returns on the value-weighted S&P 500. Abnormal stock-market gains reflect the daily unanticipated movements in the stock price for each firm after an alliance announcement.

Other companies, too, have found that creating tools, templates and processes is valuable. For example, using the Spatial Paradigm for Information Retrieval and Exploration, or SPIRE, database (www.pnl.gov/infoviz/spire/spire.html), Dow Chemical developed a process for identifying potential alliance partners. The company was able to create a topographical map pinpointing the overlap between its patent domains and the patent domains of possible alliance partners. With this tool, the company discovered the potential for an alliance with Lucent Technologies in the area of optical communications. The companies subsequently formed a broad-based alliance between three Dow businesses and three Lucent businesses that had complementary technologies.

After identifying potential partners, companies need to assess whether or not they will be able to work together effectively. Lilly developed a process of sending a due-diligence team to the potential alliance partner to evaluate the partner's resources and capabilities and to assess its culture. The team looks at such things as the partner's financial condition, information technology, research capabilities, and health and safety record. Of particular importance is the evaluation of the partner's culture. In Lilly's experience, culture clashes are one of the main reasons alliances fail. During the cultural assessment, the team examines the potential partner's corporate values and expectations, organizational structure, reward systems and incentives, leadership styles, decision-making processes, patterns of human interaction, work practices, history of partnerships, and human-resources practices. Nelson M. Sims, Lilly's executive director of alliance management, states that the evaluation is used both as a screening mechanism and as a tool to assist Lilly in organizing, staffing and governing the alliance.

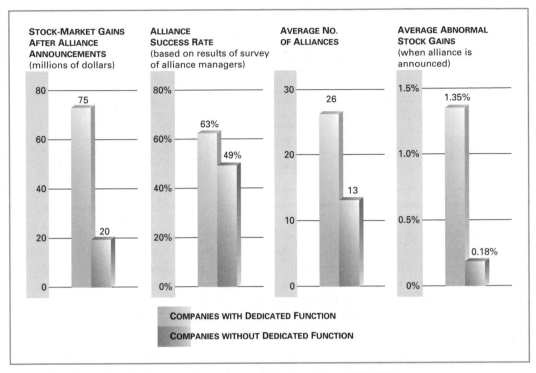

Figure 1 A dedicated function improves the success of strategic alliances, 1993–1997

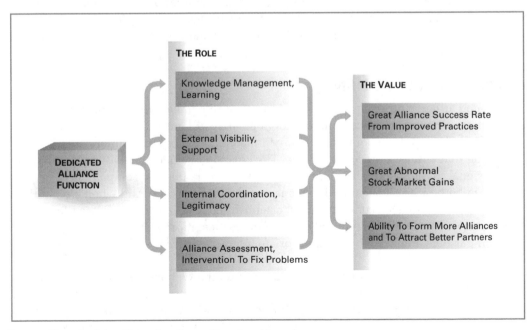

Figure 2 The role of the alliance function and how it creates value

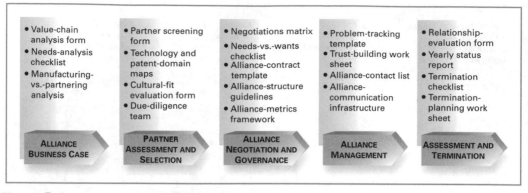

Figure 3 Tools to use across the alliance life cycle

Dedicated alliance functions also facilitate the sharing of tacit knowledge through training programs and internal networks of alliance managers. For example, HP developed a two-day course on alliance management that it offered three times a year. The company also provided short three-hour courses on alliance management and made its alliance materials available on the internal HP alliance Web site. HP also created opportunities for internal networking among managers through internal training programs, companywide alliance summits and 'virtual meetings' with executives involved in managing alliances. And the company regularly sent its alliance managers to alliance-management programs at business schools to help its managers develop external networks of contacts.

Formal training programs are one route; informal programs are another. Many companies with alliance functions have created roundtables with opportunities for alliance managers to get together and informally share their alliance experience. To that end, Nortel initiated a three-day workshop and networking initiative for alliance managers. BellSouth and Motorola have conducted similar two-day workshops for people to meet and learn from one another.

Increasing external visibility

A dedicated alliance function can play an important role in keeping the market apprised of both new alliances and successful events in ongoing alliances. Such external visibility can enhance the reputation of the company in the marketplace and support the perception that alliances are adding value. The creation of a dedicated alliance function sends a signal to the marketplace and to potential partners that the company is committed both to its alliances and to managing them effectively. And when a potential partner wants to contact a company about establishing an alliance, a dedicated function offers an easy, highly visible point of contact. In essence, it provides a place to screen potential partners and bring in the appropriate internal parties if a partnership looks attractive.

For instance, Oracle put the partnering process on the Web with Alliance Online (now Oracle Partners Program) and offered terms and conditions of different 'tiers' of partnership (http://alliance.oracle.com/join/2join_pr2_l.htm). Potential partners could choose the level that fit them best. At the tier I level (mostly resellers, integrators and application developers), companies could sign up for a specific type of agreement online and not have to talk with someone in Oracle's strategic-alliance function. Oracle also used its Web site to gather information on its partners' products and services, thereby developing detailed partner profiles. Accessing those profiles, customers easily matched the products and services they desired with those provided by Oracle partners. The Website allowed the company to enhance its external visibility, and it emerged as the primary means of recruiting and developing partnerships with more than 7,000 tier I partners. It also allowed Oracle's strategic-alliance function to focus the majority of its human resources on its higher-profile, more strategically important partners.

Providing internal coordination

One reason that alliances fail is the inability of one partner or another to mobilize internal resources to support the initiative. Visionary alliance leaders may lack the organizational authority to access key resources necessary to ensure alliance success. An alliance executive at a company without such a function observed: 'we have a difficult time supporting our alliance initiatives, because many times the various resources and skills needed to support a particular alliance are located in different functions around the company. Unless it is a very high-profile alliance, no one person has the power to make sure the company's full resources are utilized to help the alliance succeed. You have to go begging to each unit and hope that they will support you. But that's time-consuming, and we don't always get the support we should.'

A dedicated alliance function helps solve that problem in two ways. First, it has the organizational legitimacy to reach across divisions and functions and request the resources necessary to support the company's alliance initiatives. When particular functions are not responsive, it can quickly elevate the issue through the organization's hierarchy and ask the appropriate executives to make a decision on whether a particular function or division should support an alliance initiative. Second, over time, individuals within the alliance function develop networks of contacts throughout the organization. They come to know where to find useful resources within the organization. Such networks also help develop trust between alliance managers and employees throughout the organization – and thereby lead to reciprocal exchanges.

A dedicated alliance function also can provide internal coordination for the organization's strategic priorities. Some studies suggest that one of the main reasons alliances fail is that the partnership's objectives no longer match one or both partners' strategic priorities.[3] As one alliance executive complained, 'We will sometimes get far along in an alliance, only to find that another company initiative is in conflict with the alliance. For example, in one case, an internal group started to develop a similar technology that our partner already had developed. Should they have developed it? I don't know. But we needed some process for communicating internally the strategic priorities of our alliances and how they fit with our overall strategy.'

Companies need to have a mechanism for communicating which alliance initiatives are most important to achieving the overall strategy – as well as which alliance partners are the most important. The alliance function ensures that such issues are constantly addressed in the company's strategy-making sessions and then are communicated throughout the organization.

Facilitating intervention and accountability

A 1999 survey by Anderson Consulting (now Accenture) found that only 51% of companies that form alliances had any kind of formal metrics in place to assess alliance performance.[4] Of those, only about 20% believed that the metrics they had in place were really the appropriate ones to use. In our research, we found that 76% of companies with a dedicated alliance function had implemented formal alliance metrics. In contrast, only 30% of the companies without a dedicated function had done so.

Many executives we interviewed indicated that an important benefit of creating an alliance function was that it compelled the company to develop alliance metrics and to evaluate the performance of its alliances systematically. Moreover, doing so compelled senior managers to intervene when an alliance was struggling. Lilly established a yearly 'health check' process for each of its key alliances, using surveys of both Lilly employees and the partner's alliance managers. After the survey, an alliance manager from the dedicated function could sit down with the leader of a particular alliance to discuss the results and offer recommendations. In some cases, Lilly's dedicated strategic-alliance group found that it needed to replace the leader of a particular Lilly alliance.

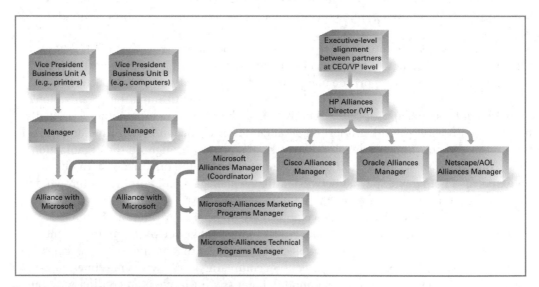

Figure 4 Hewlett-Packard alliance structure for key alliance partners

When serious conflicts arise, the alliance function can help resolve them. One executive commented, 'Sometimes an alliance has lived beyond its useful life. You need someone to step in and either pull the plug or push it in new directions.' Alliance failure is the culmination of a chain of events. Not surprisingly, signs of distress are often visible early on, and with monitoring, the alliance function can step in and intervene appropriately.

How to organize an effective strategic-alliance function

One of the major challenges of creating an alliance function is knowing how to organize it. It is possible to organize the function around key partners, industries, business units, geographic areas or a combination of all four. How an alliance function is organized influences its strategy and effectiveness. For instance, if the alliance function is organized by business unit, then the function will reflect the idiosyncrasies of each business unit and the industry in which it operates. If the alliance function is organized geographically, then knowledge about partners and coordination mechanisms, for example, will be accumulated primarily with a geographic focus.

Identify key strategic parameters and organize around them

Organizing around key strategic parameters enhances the probability of alliance success. For example, a company with a large number of alliances and a few central players may identify partner-specific knowledge and partner-specific strategic priorities as critical. As a result, it may decide to organize the dedicated alliance function around central alliance partners.

Hewlett-Packard is a good example of a company that created processes to share knowledge on how to work with a specific alliance partner. (See 'Hewlett-Packard Alliance Structure for Key Alliance Partners.') It identified a few key strategic partners with which it had numerous alliances, such as Microsoft, Cisco, Oracle and America Online and Netscape (now part of AOL Time Warner) among others. HP created a partner-level alliance-manager position to oversee all its alliances with each partner. The strategic-partner-level alliance managers had the responsibility of working with the managers and teams of the individual alliances to ensure that each of the partner's alliances would be as successful as possible. Because HP had numerous marketing and technical alliances with partners such as Microsoft, it also assigned some marketing and technical program managers to the alliance function. The managers supported the individual alliance managers and teams on specific marketing and technical issues relevant to their respective alliances. Thus HP became good at sharing partner-specific experiences and developing partner-specific priorities.

Citicorp developed a different approach. Rather than organize around key partners, the company organized its alliance function around business units and geographic areas. In some divisions, the company also used an alliance board – similar to a board of directors – to oversee many alliances. The corporate alliance function was assigned a research-and-development and coordinating role for the alliance functions that resided in each division. For instance, the e-business-solutions division engaged in alliances that were typically different from those of the retail-banking division; therefore, the alliance function needed to create alliance-management knowledge relevant to that specific division. Furthermore, to respond to differences among geographic regions, each of Citicorp's divisions created an alliance function within each region. For example, the e-business-solutions alliance group in Latin America would oversee all Citicorp's Latin American alliances in the e-business sector. The e-business division's Latin American alliance board would review potential Latin American alliances – and approve or reject them.

Organize to facilitate the exchange of knowledge on specific topics

The strategic-alliance function should be organized to make it easy for individuals throughout the organization to locate codified or tacit knowledge on a particular issue, type of alliance or phase of the alliance life cycle. In other words, in addition to developing partner-specific, business-specific or geography specific knowledge, companies should charge certain individuals with responsibility for developing *topic-specific* knowledge.

For example, when people within the organization want to know the best way to negotiate a strategic-alliance agreement, what contractual provisions and governance arrangements are most appropriate, which metrics should be used, or the most effective way to resolve disagreements with partners, they should be able to access that information easily through the strategic-alliance function. In most cases, someone within the alliance function acts as the internal expert and is assigned the responsibility of developing and acquiring knowledge on a particular element of the alliance life cycle. For some companies, it may be important to develop expertise on specific types of alliances – for example, those tied to research and development, marketing and cobranding, manufacturing, standard setting, consolidation joint ventures or new joint ventures. The issues involved in setting up such alliances can be very different. For example, whenever the success of an alliance depends on the exchange of knowledge – as is the case in R&D alliances – equity-sharing governance arrangements are preferable because they give both parties the incentives necessary for them to bring all relevant knowledge to the table. But when each party brings to the alliance an 'easy to value' resource – as with most marketing and cobranding alliances – contractual governance arrangements tend to be more suitable.

Locate the function at on appropriate level of the organization

When done properly, dedicated alliance functions offer internal legitimacy to alliances, assist in setting strategic priorities and draw on resources across the company. That is why the function cannot be buried within a particular division or be relegated to low-level support within business development. It is critical that the director or vice president of the strategic-alliance function report to the COO or president of the company. Because alliances play an increasingly important role in overall corporate strategy, the person in charge of alliances should participate in the strategy-making processes at the highest level of the company. Moreover, if the alliance function's director reports to the company president or COO, the function will have the visibility and reach to cut across boundaries and draw on the company's resources in support of its alliance initiatives.

A critical competence

Companies with a dedicated alliance function have been more successful than their counterparts at finding ways to solve problems regarding knowledge management, external visibility, internal coordination, and accountability – the underpinnings of an alliance-management capability.

But although a dedicated alliance function can create value, success does not come without challenges. First, setting up such a function requires a serious investment of the company's resources and its people's time. Businesses must be large enough or enter into enough alliances to cover that investment. Second, deciding where to locate the function in the organization – and how to get line managers to appreciate the role of such a function and recognize its value – can be difficult. Finally, establishing codified and consistent procedures may mean inappropriately emphasizing process over speed in decision making.

Such challenges exist. But the company that surmounts them and builds a successful dedicated strategic alliance function will reap substantial rewards. Companies with a well-developed alliance function generate greater stock-market wealth through their alliances and better long-term strategic-alliance success rates. Over time, investment in an alliance-management capability enhances the reputation of a company as a preferred partner. Hence an alliance-management capability can be thought of as a competence in itself, one that can reap rich rewards for the organization that knows its worth.

Acknowledgments

This research greatly benefited from the support of the Wharton Emerging Technologies Management Research Program, Mack Center for Managing Technological Innovation.

Additional resources

A helpful resource is John Harbison and Peter Pekar's 'Smart Alliances: A Practical Guide to Repeatable Success,' published in 2000. For a more scholarly development of ideas in the article, we recommend: Y, Doz and G. Hamel's 1998 book from Harvard Business School Press, 'The Alliance Advantage: The Art of Creating Value Through Partnering'; J. Dyer and H. Singh's 1998 'The Relational View' in Academy of Management Review; R, Gulati's 'Alliances and Networks,' which appeared in Strategic Management Journal in 1998; 'Building Alliance Capability: A Knowledge-Based Approach' from the 1999 Academy of Management Best Paper Proceedings and 'Alliance Capability. Stock Market Response and Long-Term Alliance Success' from the 2000 Academy of Management Proceedings, both by P. Kale and H. Singh. Also of interest are J. Koh and N. Venkatraman's 'Joint Venture Formations and Stock Market Reactions,' which appeared in 1991 in Academy of Management Journal; M. Lyles' 'Learning Among Joint-Venture Sophisticated Companies' in a 1998 Management International Review special issue, and Bernard Simonin's 1997 article, 'The Importance of Collaborative Know-How' in Academy of Management Journal.

Notes

[1] B. Anand and T. Khanna, 'Do Companies Leam To Create Value?' Strategic Management Journal 21 (March 2000): 295–316.

[2] P. Kale, J. Dyer and H. Singh, 'Alliance Capability, Stock Market Response and Long-Term Alliance Success,' Academy of Management Proceedings (August 2000).

[3] J. Bleeke and D. Emst, 'Collaborating To Compete' (New York: John Wiley & Sons, 1993); and 'The Way To Win in Cross-Border Alliances,' The Alliance Analyst, March 15, 1998, 1–4.

[4] 'Dispelling the Myths of Alliances,' Outlook (1999): 28.

JEFFREY H. DYER is a professor of international strategy at Brigham Young University's Marriott School in Provo. Utah.

PRASHANT KALE is an assistant professor at University of Michigan Business School.

HARBIR SINGH is a professor of management at the Wharton School of the University of Pennsylvania.

Contact the authors at jdyer@byu.edu, kale@umich.edu and singhh@wharton.upenn.edu.

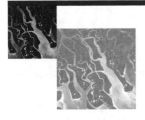

Reading 10

Making mergers and acquisitions work: strategic and psychological preparation*

Mitchell Lee Marks and Philip H. Mirvis

Three out of four mergers and acquisitions fail to achieve their financial and strategic objectives. Because the nature of the combination process – such as the secrecy that shrouds negotiations – runs counter to the requirements of rigorous research, efforts to learn why so many combinations fail, and to understand the management actions that put combinations on a successful course, have yielded limited insights. As a result, mergers and acquisitions continue to be mismanaged and to produce disappointing results. This article draws from the authors' experience in over 70 mergers and acquisitions to understand the managerial actions that distinguish successful from disappointing combinations. It focuses on early efforts in the precombination phase that steer a combination toward the successful path. Precombination preparation covers strategic and psychological matters. The strategic challenges concern key analyses that clarify and bring into focus the sources of synergy in a combination. This involves reality testing of potential synergies in light of the two sides' structures and cultures and establishing the desired relationship between the two companies. And the psychological challenges cover actions required to understand the mindsets that people bring with them and develop over the course of a combination. This means raising people's awareness of and capacities to respond to the normal and to-be-expected stresses and strains of living through a combination.

Fewer than one quarter of mergers and acquisitions achieve their financial objectives, as measured in ways including share value, return on investment, and postcombination profitability. Many factors account for this dismal track record: buying the wrong company, paying the wrong price, making the deal at the wrong time. Another factor, however, seems to be at the core of many failed combinations – the process through which the deal is conceived and executed.[1]

Academy of Management Executive, 2001, Vol. 15, No. 2.

Corporate combinations – the merger of separate entities into a new firm or the acquisition of one firm by another – have become a regular component of the managerial repertoire. Many motives prompt executives to acquire or merge with another organization. Perhaps a combination can help a company pursue a strategy that would otherwise be too costly, risky, or technologically advanced to achieve independently. Other deals are opportunistic, as when a troubled competitor seeks a savior or when a bidding war ensues after a firm is put into play. Still other acquisitions or mergers can be defensive moves to protect market share in a declining or consolidating industry.

The overarching reason for combining with another organization is that the union will provide for the attainment of strategic goals more quickly and inexpensively than if the company acted on its own.[2] In this era of intense and turbulent change, involving rapid technological advances and ever increasing globalization, combinations also enable organizations to gain flexibility, leverage competencies, share resources, and create opportunities that otherwise would be inconceivable.

Despite their frequency, corporate combinations have proven difficult events for organizational researchers to assess. The nature of doing a deal runs counter to the requirements of sound research. For both legal and competitive reasons, merger negotiations are shrouded in secrecy. This hinders data collection, but also means that researchers cannot anticipate and identify research sites before the combination occurs. Even after the announcement of a deal, more questions than answers remain. Executives are harried and employees anxious; no one has the time or the inclination to cooperate with a research program. And combinations pose some substantial methodological dilemmas. For example, when does a merger begin – as it is conceived, when it is announced, or when it receives legal approval? Similarly, there is no discrete ending to a merger.

As a result, most research investigations of the process through which combinations have been managed tend to be retrospective. A typical research design asks senior executives to assess the relative influence of various factors on the outcomes of their past combination activities. With 20/20 hindsight, executives acknowledge the human, organizational, and cultural aspects of the combination-management process. However, the lessons learned from past combinations are not being applied in a systematic manner to the management of current combinations.

Combination phases

For more than 20 years, we have been involved in an action research program investigating and addressing human, cultural, and organizational aspects of corporate combinations.[3] During this time, we have participated as researchers or consultants in over 70 mergers and acquisitions. These combinations have involved large, medium, and small companies, have been friendly and unfriendly, and have spanned a broad range of industry sectors – including financial services, telecom, high tech, health care, pharmaceuticals, manufacturing, professional services, consumer products, entertainment, and government.

Early in our research program, we collaborated with Management Analysis Center of Cambridge, MA, in a study of combinations in banking and finance.[4] This research showed that significant differences could be identified between typical and successful cases by separating the distinct phases organizations go through in the transition from independent to integrated entities:

- precombination phase, as the deal is conceived and negotiated by executives and then legally approved by shareholders and regulators;

- combination phase, as integration planning ensues and implementation decisions are made;

- postcombination phase, as the combined entity and its people regroup from initial implementation and the new organization settles in.

To be sure, these are not clear-cut phases. Integration planning increasingly occurs in the precombination phase, before the deal receives legal approval. Pfizer and Warner-Lambert launched integration planning teams before their deal closed in June 2000 and AOL's President Robert Pittman moved into an office at Time-Warner's New York City headquarters even as federal regulators were reviewing that corporate marriage. Still, some distinct emphases emerged during the earliest months as a deal was being conceived and negotiated that distinguished the combinations that did and did not meet their strategic and financial objectives.

In the precombination phase, a financial tunnel vision predominated in the typical disappointing cases. Buyers concentrated on the numbers: what the target was worth; what price premium, if any, to pay; what the tax implications were; and how to structure the transaction. The decision to do a deal was typically framed in terms of the combined balance sheet of the companies, projected cash flows, and hoped-for return on investment.

Two interrelated human factors added to this financial bias. First, members of the buy team in most instances came from financial positions or backgrounds. They brought a financial mindset to their study of a partner and their judgments about synergies were mostly informed by financial models and ratios. They often did not know very much about, say, manufacturing or marketing; nor did they bring an experienced eye to assessments of a partner's capabilities in these regards. There was also a tendency for hard criteria to drive out soft matters in these cases. If the numbers looked good, any doubts about organizational or cultural differences tended to be scoffed at and dismissed.

In the successful cases, by contrast, buyers brought a strategic mindset to the deal. They positioned financial analyses in a context of an overarching aim and intent. Successful buyers also had a clear definition of specific synergies they sought in a combination and concentrated on testing them well before momentum built and any negotiations commenced. Here, too, human factors played a part. Members of the buy team in successful cases came from technical and operational, as well as financial, positions. And during the scouting phase, they dug deep into the operations and markets of a candidate when gauging its fit. Sensible buyers considered carefully the risks and problems that might turn a strategically sound deal sour. This does not mean that the financial analyses were neglected or that they were any less important to success. To the contrary, what put combinations on the road toward success was both an in-depth financial understanding of a proposed combination, and a serious examination of what it would take to produce desired financial results.

Putting a combination on the path toward success

Steering a combination toward the successful path begins in the precombination phase. Many observers liken organizational combinations to organ transplants. The surgery must be well thought out and planned, and the surgical team and patient prepped, prior to the operation, to allow for rapid execution and minimize the likelihood of rejection. We urge clients to be proactive in the precombination phase: planning and preparation are integral to success when companies join forces.

Preparation in a combination covers strategic and psychological matters. The strategic challenges concern key analyses that clarify and bring into focus the sources of synergy in a combination. This involves reality testing potential synergies in light of the two sides' structures and cultures and establishing the desired relationship between the two companies. The psychological challenges cover the actions required to understand the mindsets that people bring with them and develop over the course of a combination. This means raising people's awareness of and capacities to respond to the normal and to-be-expected stresses and strains of living through a combination.

Purpose, partner, parameters, and people

The journey toward a successful combination begins well before dealings commence. As strategic intent and selection criteria are set, as a deal is being conceived, and as potential partners are screened, assessed, and negotiated with, executives, staff specialists, and advisors need to continuously address at least four different aspects of their potential combination: purpose, partner, parameters, and people.

Purpose: putting strategy to work

The strategic synergies in a combination should lead to a set of decisions in the precombination phase on the intentions, rationale, and criteria for the deal. They guide eventual action for excavating sources of productive combination.

Strategic intent

Strategy setting begins with scrutiny of an organization's own competitive and market status, its strengths and weaknesses, its top management's aspirations and goals. The results define a direction for increased growth, profitability, or market penetration in existing businesses, for diversification into new areas, or simply for cash investment – which may or may not involve combination activity.

In successful acquisition programs, the CEO, relevant corporate and division management, and various advisors translate these objectives into specific strategic and investment criteria. Most buying companies have standard metrics for evaluating a candidate that include its earnings, discounted cash flow, and annual return on investment. They also have objectives about the impact of a combination on profitability, the combined organization's earnings per share, and future funding requirements.

Here the typical and successful combination roads part ways. In so many cases, financial fit receives a disproportionate amount of attention and priority in the search for a partner. In successful cases, financial criteria are respected and adhered to, but are balanced by careful consideration of each of the synergies sought in a combination and what it will take to realize them. Knowledge gained from this careful look at synergies not only sharpens the parties' assessment of their potential acquisitions, it also enables leadership to put forward a clear and convincing rationale for the combination that goes beyond the numbers. Most combinations involve expense-reduction. Executives who seek to create value have to be able to demonstrate to staff on both sides that there is more to the deal than cost-cutting – and that involves a crisp statement of how synergies will be realized and what that means for the people involved. Two recent oil industry mergers illustrate how early intentions influence subsequent integrations. BP selected Amoco and ARCO as integration partners because both provided good fits with BP's retail operations and oil reserves. Exxon Mobil was a copy-cat merger. Rather than highlight strategic intent, these firms were motivated by a need to catch up with the scale of the new market leader and relied purely on financial analyses. With no strategic intent guiding integration, the result was a political free-for-all in which integration decisions were based on empire building and turf protection rather than strategy.

If the true motives underlying a combination have less to do with strategy and more to do with nonrational forces – for example, the desire to run the largest company in an industry or the fear of being swallowed up by competitors – then a successful combination is unlikely because there are no true benefits to reap by joining forces. Yet combinations based on such motives are not infrequent. A blue-ribbon panel of financial experts concluded 20 years ago that CEO ego was the primary force driving mergers and acquisitions in the United States.[5] More recently, a Columbia University business school study found that the bigger the ego of the acquiring company's CEO, the higher the premium the company is likely to pay for a target.[6]

Clear criteria

When they have a voice in and can agree on the merits of a strategy, top executives, corporate planners, and line managers operate from a common interest and perspective. To enforce this consensus, corporate leaders assert strategic criteria and make sure the acquisition team searches for candidates that fit them.

A firm first needs to know what it is looking for in an acquisition candidate or merger partner. Having a full and open review of these criteria allows for debate and consensus building between staff and line executives. If conflicts or confusion about these criteria are not fully addressed up front, they will persist down the road. Applying these criteria religiously greatly increases the likelihood of selecting a partner that will bring true productive value to the combination, rather than one that will just be an acquisition for the sake of doing a deal. Understanding precisely what synergies are sought sets the stage for subsequently mining opportunities through the combination planning and implementation phases. The more unified both sides are – within and between themselves – about what is being sought, the more focused they can be in realizing their objectives.

Two sets of criteria help here. One is a generic set of criteria that guide a firm's overall combination program and strategy. These are characteristics of organizations that must be present in any combination partner. At Emerson Electronic, a few factors guide search and selection of all alliance partners, such as not going into business with firms in turnaround situations and not straying beyond its core competency in manufacturing.[7]

The second set of criteria guide the assessment and selection of a specific partner. In its effort to acquire other healthcare providers, a southern California hospital established criteria for what it was looking for in this particular search. These included 'maintain/ enhance quality of care – bring a continually improving level of quality care to the community served by the hospital' and 'geographic distribution – enhance the geographic reach of the hospital across Los Angeles county and throughout southern California.' Some selection criteria were at odds with one another, such as finding a partner that both is the 'low-cost provider' and 'adds prestige.' The hospital's executive team prioritized the relative importance of each criterion prior to the selection process. When it came time to evaluate choices, the team then assessed the multiple candidates and weighted the high priority criteria accordingly.

Partner: search and selection

Successful acquirers know what they are looking for and conduct a thorough due diligence to ensure that they get what they want. Their screening of candidates covers the obvious strategic and financial criteria, but extends also to include assessments of the human and cultural elements that can undermine an otherwise sound deal. How deep is the management talent in the target? What labor relations issues lurk around the corner? How does the company go about doing its business? Is their culture a good enough fit with ours?

Thorough screening

The value-creating acquisition of Benham Capital Management Group by Twentieth Century Advisors began with a screening process that integrated human and cultural issues with strategic and operational criteria. Both firms meshed along operational lines in offering only no-load mutual funds and treating small shareholders well; but one senior executive told us that an exchange of corporate values statements during due diligence was among the data indicating that cultural compatibility existed as well: 'Their "Guiding Principles" and our "Statement of Beliefs" were very similar. Both companies stated honesty as a fundamental belief and you don't too often see that both stated and acted out in the financial-services industry.'

A thorough assessment of combination candidates also covers less tangible matters. First, it reveals the motives of the sellers in an acquisition or partners in a merger. Why does leadership of the target want to sell? Are they responding to a business opportunity or are they driven by more personal motives, like wanting to cash out their investment? Does senior leadership want to stay on board after the sale? Do the buyers want the seller's leadership to stay? If so, will there be good chemistry between the leaders of the two sides?

Second, thorough screening gets below the top leadership and considers the mindsets of the two management teams. How do the target's people feel about working with or for the buyer's people? Are they looking for a company with deep pockets to fund them to glory, or are they likely to fight hard to fend off any threats to their autonomy after the deal closes? Does the buyer's management team buy into this deal or do factions exist?

Where does the target's team stand? Are the technical and professional staff – who are outside the inner circle, but are needed to make the combination work – involved in the process? Are they apt to depart after a combination is announced? Even if answers to these questions are not deal killers, they indicate what has to be done to win people over during courtship phase.

A thorough precombination screening comes only from speaking directly with a good cross-section of the management team from the potential partner. Automated Data Processing CEO Art Weinbach is clear on the value of face-to-face due diligence with an array of managers from potential partners: 'The greater surprises have come to us in the people and the people relationships. We have to spend more time on the people side of the equation in the due-diligence period. That is not as simple as looking at organizational charts; it requires speaking and listening to people both for the formal business issues as well as the less formal how does it really work issues. You learn a lot by listening.'[8]

Diligent due diligence

In most combination programs, true diligence needs to be put back into due diligence. Typically, the financial people who dominate due-diligence teams get a sense of the partner they want and build a case for combination going forward. It is important to get people on the team who will probe deeply and thoroughly enough to work backward and identify faulty assumptions and what might hinder eventual success.

Take information technology as an example. Proper due diligence ascertains first the extent to which the candidate's system has the capacity to meet its own current and future business needs, and then considers the compatibility between the two sides' systems right now and following anticipated growth. If the capacity and compatibility are not there, then the cost for getting there – and the impact of that cost on the financials of the deal – needs to be determined through a realistic (as opposed to an overly optimistic) evaluation.

Broadening the membership of the team also enhances organizational due diligence. Membership can be expanded to include staff professionals from areas like human resources and information technology, and operating managers who will be working with new partners if the combination is carried out. A functional specialist provides a breadth of analysis that simply cannot be conducted by a corporate generalist. Operations managers have a particularly important role on due diligence teams. They can find many reasons why a deal that looks good on paper would crash on takeoff. In addition to reviewing operational issues, they can also assess the chemistry between themselves and their counterparts. If it is not there early on, it is not likely to be developed later. Differing viewpoints and preferences for how to conduct business are not in and of themselves reasons to negate a deal, but incongruent values, genuine distrust and outright animosity should be noted as red flags.

Some organizations we have worked with place up to 20 people on their due-diligence teams. This may be bulky in terms of scheduling logistics and organizing findings, but it pays off when a potential showstopper gets unearthed. One organization convenes two diligence teams to assess candidates and overcome the deal fever that frequently afflicts due diligence. Knowing that a poor partner can exact a huge financial toll and be a tremendous burden on management time and energy, this company goes forward only with combinations that pass muster with both teams.

Due diligence is also a time to size up the breadth and depth of managerial talent in the potential partner. A study of large combinations found that 65 percent of successful acquirers reported managerial talent to be the single most important instrument for creating value in a deal.[9] Smart buyers not only evaluate current executives but also look closely at managers not yet in leadership positions.

Parameters: defining the combination

There is a tendency for buyer and seller to get mired in the details of their transaction and lose sight of the big picture. Studies of the acquisition process have found that a fragmentation of financial, strategic, organizational, and cultural analyses leaves the executives involved with different, and often competing, perspectives on how to put their organizations together.[10] In addition, each company has its own way of doing business, its own preferences and power structure, and a history of past decisions, forsaken options, and financial and physical investments. What appears to yield strong financial and strategic synergy between, say, two manufacturing groups may not be realizable because of incompatible structures and systems or sharp differences in cultures.

Defining the end state

Partners in successful combinations share a commonality of purpose and recognize and accept the terms of their relationship. People are able to focus their energy on a common goal and let go of any wishful thinking that may run counter to the realities of the combination. Yet in so many cases, corporate marriage contracts, like those between individuals, tend to be implicit rather than explicit, and are open to interpretation and misunderstanding. Carefully defining the end state of a deal can bring the pleasantries and promises of the precombination courtship to a quick halt. Failing to do so can lead to an even more unpleasant divorce.

While the work of achieving the desired end state will involve many people, the initial step is the responsibility of senior executives involved in doing the deal. In the best cases, the senior executive from the buying side puts his or her cards on the table regarding expectations and assumptions for the combining organizations. The senior executive needs to think through and come to the precombination discussions with a clear sense of which aspects of this desired end state are open to negotiation and which are not during precombination discussions and subsequent planning.

With this in mind, executives who hope to combine their companies are well advised to consider and share their hopes, expectations, and biases for how the postcombination organization will be structured. These intentions are largely determined by the degree of integration anticipated for the combined organization. We use a grid of different types of postcombination change to help executives think through their options and clarify their intentions. (See Figure 1.)

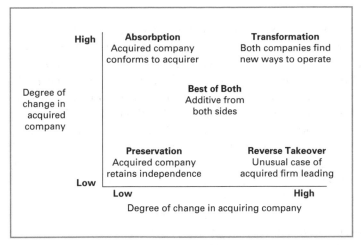

Figure 1 Defining the integration end state

Preservation

This end state where the acquired company faces a modest degree of integration and retains its ways of doing business is typically found in diversified firms that promote cultural pluralism among business units. To succeed, corporate management has to protect the boundary of the subsidiary, limiting intrusions by its corporate staff and minimizing conformance to its rules and systems. Strategic synergies generated in a preservative combination come from the cross-pollination of people and work on joint programs.

Absorption

When the acquired company is absorbed by a parent and assimilated into its culture, the lead companies generally bring in new management and conform the target to corporate reporting relationships and regimens. Acquisitions in the airline industry, such as American's absorption of Air California, Delta's of Western, and USAir's of PSA, are classic examples.

Reverse takeover

In the mirror image of the absorption combination, the acquired company dictates the terms of the combination and effects cultural change in the lead company. When this unusual type of combination occurs, it typically involves the absorption by an acquired business unit or division of a parallel unit in an acquirer. For example, Marriott Corporation acquired Saga and folded its own contract food-services business into it.

Best of both

Studies find the achieving of synergy between companies through their partial to full integration to be more successful than others – and most fraught with risk.[9] It can also be the bloodiest. Financial and operational synergies are achieved by consolidation. This means crunching functions together and often leads to reductions in force. The optimal result is full cultural integration – the blending of both companies' policies and practices. The merger of equals between Chemical Bank and Manufacturers Hanover and the combination of Canada's Molson Breweries with Carling O'Keefe are examples.

Transformation

When both companies undergo fundamental change following their combination, synergies come not simply from reorganizing the businesses, but from reinventing the company. This is the trickiest of all the combination types and requires a significant investment and inventive management. Transformation poses a sharp break from the past. Existing practices and routines must be abandoned and new ones discovered and developed. In the integration of Pfizer Animal Health and SmithKline Beecham's animal pharmaceutical business in Europe, president Pedro Lichtinger took two orthodox operations and transformed them into a new organization geared toward the emerging realities of the European Community. In doing so, he broke down traditional country-specific structures and cultures and forged a pan-European strategy, structure, team, and identity as the precombination parties merged.

A senior executive will frequently enter a combination with ideas for differing functions to end up at various points on the grid. In Pfizer's acquisition of Warner-Lambert, financial reporting systems clearly were mandated by the buyer. A reverse acquisition occurred in the consumer-products area, however, where Warner-Lambert's business was much larger. John Niblack, head of Pfizer's R&D function, used the merger to transform that organization. An executive has a picture of where he or she wants the combination to end, and makes those intentions clear to all parties. Certainly this end state may change as the partners learn more about each other, and about opportunities and challenges that arise during the combination-planning and implementation phases, but both sides enter into the combination with a shared sense of the desired end state.

Cards on the table

One of the worst moves any buyer can make is to talk merger and act acquisition. Sometimes buyers think they are doing the right thing by softening their messages and welcoming target personnel as partners. Other times, they are being outright manipulative by wooing the other side with pledges of a merger of equals when their true intention is to dominate. When postcombination parameters do not mesh with precombination promises, the result can only be disenchantment and distrust.

Whatever the intentions of the lead organization, false expectations abound in the target. Sometimes, people innocently misinterpret what they hear because of the inconsistent use of language across partners. Other times, being in a state of psychological denial interferes with partners' truly hearing what is being stated. Still other times, a partner knows quite well what is being said, but presumes that its own political skills will reign and change the situation as the organizations come together.

Announcing the desired end state provides an early opportunity to clear the air of any misperceptions or fantasies about how the two sides will coexist in the combined organization. Beyond checking misperceptions, a well articulated desired end state communicates to the work force that their leadership has a solid sense of where it wants to take the combination. This breeds employee confidence that leadership is managing the combination well. It also gives people something tangible to talk about, rather than turn to the worst-case scenarios, rumors, and naysaying that predominate in most combinations. Finally, a clear and understood desired end state guides combination planning and implementation. With the parameters established, integration planning teams and busy executives can study options and make recommendations within a realistic context rather than worry about having plans shot down by a senior executive because they did not fit preconceived expectations.

People: managing the dealings

Combination partners typically enter a deal with distinct mindsets. In an acquisition, the buyer and seller usually have very different psychological perspectives on the deal. Often they bring a one-up versus one-down outlook into their dealings, particularly when the acquiree is strapped for cash and has had a downturn in business performance. In cases where the roles of lead and target are not so well delineated, psychological factors can also influence the relationship. Members of one side may see themselves – or be seen by the other side – as more worldly, technically sophisticated, financially strong, or savvy in the marketplace. Yet the very premise for the merger – that the partners will gain access to or leverage each other's technology, patents, customers, or some other capability that they do not already possess – calls for a true meeting of the minds. The AOL-Netscape integration, for example, was slowed by Netscape's self-perceptions of technical superiority; the people who believed they had invented the Internet were dismayed at combining with a firm they considered the McDonald's of the Internet.

Psychological mindsets certainly influence early dealings and can dominate the critical months of transition planning and implementation. (See Table 1.) And they often carry over into the combined organization. Awareness of these mindsets – both one's own and one's partner's – helps both sides prepare for a successful combination.

Party	Mindset	What to expect
Buyer	Air of superiority Drive to consolidate gains Urge to dominate the action	Headiness Urgency Power moves
Seller	State of shock Defensive retreat Sense of fatalism	Anxiety and anger Resistance Hostility and defeatism

Table 1 Precombination mindsets of buyers and sellers

Mindset of the buyer

To the victors go the spoils. Bidding wars and hostile takeovers are certainly exhilarating for the winners. And even for executives involved in a friendly deal, there are few moments in a career that equal the intensity and satisfaction of buying another company.

Acquiring another organization, or assuming the role of lead party in a merger, translates into a strong air of superiority. This attitude frequently carries over into assumptions that the buying company's business acumen – and policies, procedures, people, and systems – are superior to those of the purchased firm. Being the dominant party contributes to condescending attitudes about the other side: On more than one occasion, we heard executives from buying companies crow: 'They are still battling the problems we solved five years ago. Wait until we show them how to do things.' Thus AOLers themselves felt superior to their counterparts from Netscape.

As the combination begins, lead companies are impelled to move fast and consolidate their gains. A sense of urgency prevails in the lead organization as it wants to put its plans into motion fast. There is always something uncertain about precisely what has been bought – who they are, what they do, whether they really know how to run their business. Corporate staffers pounce on the target to get their hands on things in a hurry.

This fuels managers' momentum in the lead company to dominate the action. They have studied the situation longer and have more detailed plans and priorities. Top management may have promised to go slow and honor traditions during the precombination negotiations, but vice presidents, corporate staffers, and managers get the taste of power and have their own designs. Moreover, they are rewarded for meeting budgets and producing results, not for how fairly or smoothly they manage the combination. As a result, lead managers often unilaterally dominate the action and impose their own integration plans. Prior promises mean nothing.

Mindset of the seller

Why is being acquired so debilitating to an organization? In a hostile deal or one imposed by the board, there is from the start a sense of violation: Executives we have interviewed have likened it to a rape and described their buyer as an attacker or barbarian. Even in friendly deals, acquired managers often describe themselves as being seduced by promises that changes will be minimal, and as being taken advantage of once they are forced to accommodate to the new owner's demands.

A state of shock permeates a company following an acquisition announcement. Executives wander the halls after a combination is announced, unprepared to assume new duties and responsibilities. Executive recruiter John Handy found that 90 percent of nearly one thousand senior and middle executives he studied were psychologically unprepared for the changes in status and organizational structure they would encounter following their company's acquisition.[11] Seeing and sensing the anxiety in their superiors, other employees grow anxious about the combination, how it will be managed, and their personal fate in it.

One way executives cope with their shock is by a defensive retreat. This allows acquired executives to regroup and reformulate a battle plan for countering the enemy. At one acquired manufacturing firm, this led to a strategy of noncompliance and various tactics to resist the overtures of the lead company. Even in mergers of equals, perceived fears of losing status or ways of doing things lead executives to dig in and protect their turf.

Acquirees often feel powerless to defend their interests or control their fate. Even when the deal is friendly or when a company is rescued from a hostile deal by a sympathetic third party, the consequences are frequently out of the acquirees' control. Sellers sometimes respond with passive or aggressive hostility; other times, they withdraw with a sense of defeatism.

Many managers use Elisabeth Kübler-Ross's stages of reactions to death and loss to illustrate their personal reactions to being acquired.[12] Initially, there is denial and disbelief. Upon learning they are up for sale, executives go into a state of shock, denying the reality and their own vulnerability. The work force can both under- and overreact, predicting that nothing will happen or that everything will change. People in the target company then experience anger. They will be angry at their leadership for selling out and then for cashing in. Later they will be angry with the buyer. While expressions of anger allow people to vent their emotions, many become stuck at this stage and are never able to move on to accommodate to the new situation.

For those who can psychologically move forward, next comes bargaining. People's natural tendency is to look out for themselves. Some will leave what they consider to be a sinking ship. Others will try to make themselves indispensable. Some will cozy up to new management and pitch their importance and value to the organization. Others will guard data or customer relationships as leverage for survival.

Only after time will people accept the reality of the new situation and be ready to work with counterparts in a genuine and committed way. For some, this may be a matter of weeks or months. Others take years. Some individuals never reach the stage of acceptance.

Psychological preparation

An executive we worked with suggested that preparing for a combination was like 'preparing to be hit by a Mack truck.' Maybe so, but at least it helps to know that others have gotten up off the pavement and gone on with their lives. Psychological preparation for a combination means raising awareness of the normal and to-be-expected mindsets of combination partners. Preparation alerts executives on both sides to the mindsets of the buyer and the seller, and holds up the mindset of partnership as the standard to achieve.

In many combinations in which we have been involved, employees from both sides have participated in sensitization seminars to foster dialogue about their respective mindsets. Individuals hear about combination mindsets, express their hopes and concerns going forward, and learn tactics for coping with their mindset and that of their counterparts.

Another way to raise awareness of combination mindsets is by educating people through readings, presentations, or discussions of the human realities of a combination. Many organizations distribute books and articles describing the mindsets of buyer and seller, sponsor workshops in which outside experts describe the dynamics of combining, and engage executives in discussing expectations or experiences in going through combinations. In organizations with experience in combinations, veterans of previous mergers and acquisitions can share their first-hand experiences with novices. Central to Cisco's fine reputation as a successful acquirer is its use of a buddy system to link veteran acquirees with newly acquired executives.

Combination preparation workshops

A more dynamic approach to raise awareness of these mindsets is through an experiential activity that helps people develop a true feeling of what it is like to acquire or be acquired. This proved to be a powerful intervention when two CEOs of high-technology companies shook hands on what they jointly termed 'a merger of equals.' Little did they know that they held quite different interpretations of that phrase. The target company

CEO assumed this meant that both sides would have equal say in combination decisions. The lead company CEO, however, intended it to mean that his side would have the final say, but would engage its counterparts to determine how to best implement those decisions. Both CEOs prepared their teams according to their personal interpretations and ultimately destroyed the goodwill between them.

The target CEO convened his board and asked it to negate the deal. The target company was in a weak financial condition, however, and the board could not justify that course of action. The deal remained, but so did the bad blood between the two sides.

One of us engaged executives from both sides in a two-day meeting that combined educational with experiential activities. The morning of the first day began with a discussion of human, cultural, and organizational issues in combinations, including the mindsets of buyers and sellers. After a lunch break, the two teams went to work on a business simulation. Acquired executives played the Green Widget Company and lead company executives the Red Widget Company. Being competitive business people, they threw themselves into the simulation and established strategies and tactics for maximizing their returns. Just five minutes before the close of the first day's session, however, the facilitator announced that the Green company intended to acquire the Red company, reversing their roles in the actual deal. Nothing further was said about the details of the acquisition, though more information was promised for the next morning. Day one adjourned and all were invited to cocktails and dinner.

In the lounge, it was as if the simulation were still on. Red Company executives huddled in one corner, wondering out loud what their fate might be at the hands of their new owners and plotting ways to resist any changes in control. Green Company executives, at the other end of the bar, began planning how they would establish authority in their new acquisition.

The next morning, the two groups identified their negotiating teams and readied their combination strategies. The Red team was determined to protect its independence despite the change in ownership. The Green team aimed toward consolidating operations quickly. Neither team was coached to develop these mindsets; they developed naturally based on their roles. It was then announced that the two sides would participate in a series of negotiating sessions, with time allotted for the teams to report back to their colleagues. After three rounds of negotiations, no progress had been made: target executives were obstinate in their resistance and lead executives grew increasingly disenchanted with the lack of progress in negotiations and planning. In a fit of frustration at the next negotiating session, the Green team head fired the executive who headed the Red team. The facilitators then called an end to the simulation and the two sides were brought together to discuss what they had experienced.

Green Company executives began by asserting how uncooperative and unrealistic their acquired counterparts had been. Red Company executives, in turn, complained that the Greens never intended to listen to any input from their side, were disrespectful to them and their way of doing things, and were not willing to negotiate alternative courses for approaching the combination. Red executives acknowledged that what they saw the Green team doing in the simulation reflected their own tendencies in the real acquisition: they were eager to move ahead with consolidation and assumed things would go their way. More than this, however, the Reds gained a deep understanding of what it is like to have one's organization suddenly taken away in a combination. They became more sympathetic and empathetic toward the plight of their real-life acquired counterparts. The Greens, for their part, came to see how easy it was to slip into the mindset of the buyer and dominate the action. The awareness of self and others raised in the experiential activity led to the creation of formal ground rules for combination planning.

As the combination became legal and integration planning hit full stride, no one expected a complete turnaround in people's behaviors. Yet both sides saw enough movement from their counterparts and give-and-take in their relationships to build confidence in their ability to move forward together.

Commitment from top leadership

Another way to rein in the controlling behaviors of the lead company is to have the proper outlook modeled and managed at the top. In the merger of paper producers Abitibi-Price and Stone-Consolidated, we got senior team executives to meet early in the precombination phase, well before the deal became legal. Working with internal human resources professionals, one of us designed an offsite meeting agenda that included frank discussion about the role of the group in leading the combination and the ground rules that would guide its leadership. One ground rule directed executives to reach out to the other side when as they proceeded to make staffing and integration decisions. Only if they practiced partnership and overcame the tendency to favor people and practices familiar from their side, the executives acknowledged, could middle-level managers be expected to do the same.

Middle managers who must make the deal work also manifest the mindsets of buyer and seller. Some headiness on the part of lead company managers down the line is inevitable. It is imperative, then, that senior executives set the proper tone, articulate the principles of integration, and bring those principles to life in their own actions. Senior executives must also be prepared to act accordingly when the principles are not followed. A top executive from the lead company in an entertainment merger one of us worked on recalled: 'Despite all of the urgings for partnership from our CEO, a sense of "when in doubt, go with our way" prevailed among middle-level managers from our company. It is very difficult to get people to put aside their way of doing things.' In this case, lead company executives listened and responded to complaints from acquired counterparts and spent time coaching their own middle managers. Realistically, acts of domination were not overturned, but the acquired team recognized that a genuine effort was made to counter excessive domination.

Precombination planning

Some firms are beginning to complement preparation for a specific deal with a more generic approach to precombination planning, particularly in industries, like telecom and healthcare, where combinations have become recurring events. Their aim is to have their act together when a combination opportunity arises.

As these organizations survey their competitive environments and deliberate strategic responses, they see that combinations are increasingly important for getting them where they want to go. Knowing that acquisitions and mergers are essential to meeting their strategic objectives – and in some cases necessary for their basic survival – executives take the opportunity to prepare to meet the organizational challenges in combining entities. A small but growing number of companies have either learned from their own failed combinations or taken seriously the feeble track record of other organizations and recognized the need to beef up their readiness for combining successfully.

Kaiser Permanente, the large health-maintenance organization, determined through its strategic-planning process that multiple acquisitions and strategic alliances would be essential for its long-term growth and survival in the volatile healthcare industry. Kaiser's leadership recognized that it did not have the internal competence to identify and implement combination opportunities. Advice from external consultants, coupled with the urging of an executive with considerable combination experience who had just joined Kaiser's senior team, led to the formation of an internal Acquisitions and Alliances SWAT Team. Middle-level managers from a broad array of functions and geographical units were asked to contribute their perspectives in the full combination process, from target selection to integration. Team members received a crash course in everything from valuation to culture clash. Nearly fifty managers graduated into roles to complement staff professionals and external advisors in targeting and integrating acquisition targets and alliance partners.

At Weyerhauser, the forestry and paper-products giant, consolidation among other industry players and the recognition that new ventures were likely to be pursued through acquisitions and alliances prompted senior executives to enhance their awareness of combination pitfalls and success factors and their readiness to manage a combination. Finance, strategy, and human resources executives joined with operations executives who had managed previous acquisitions in the company for an earnest assessment of their acquisition performance. The open discussion of what had and had not worked in previous combinations, both inside and outside the company, led to a more thorough and rigorous regard for the full set of organizational challenges in a combination.

At both Kaiser and Weyerhauser, organizational preparation began well in advance of combination activity. Even when organizations have not been this foresightful, there is still time to act after the initial combination announcement. In some large acquisitions, several months can pass awaiting legal approval. Most organizations waste this time. Others use it. At Pfizer, even before the Warner-Lambert acquisition received legal approval, merger-management training programs raised awareness of combination mindsets and alerted executives to the realities of the integration process. Internal facilitators participated in a day-long integration-team launch meeting that described pitfalls common to other firms' integration-team efforts and guided team members building effective teamwork in their planning groups.

A particularly in-depth precombination planning session was coordinated by internal organization development professional Ronny Versteenskitse of Seagram Spirits and Wine Group (SSWG). Soon after acquiring Seagram, French entertainment conglomerate Vivendi announced its intention to retain the target's film and music holdings, but divest its liquor and wine businesses. Employees in SSWG were in limbo as their unit was put on the auction block. Rather than wait and see what the buyer would do, Versteenskitse convened a four-day meeting of senior human-resources professionals. The meeting featured discussions of the status of major HR initiatives in the company in light of the eventual change in ownership, the fate of employees who would not be retained after the sale, success factors in mergers and acquisitions, and the human and cultural realities of joining forces. On the closing day, executives from BP and Amoco and Chemical Bank and Chase discussed their successful integrations. The meeting concluded with a discussion of strategies for actively dealing with the buyer by sharing the output produced at the meeting and reaching out to form a collaborative relationship with counterparts in the lead organization. There was no assurance that the buyer would be receptive to this outreach, but HR professionals left the conference feeling confident that they were doing the best job possible to prepare themselves, their organization, and their new colleagues for the rigors of integrating previously separate organizations.

Preparing to move forward

Actions taken – and not taken – in the precombination phase as a deal is being conceived and negotiated set a direction whereby a merger or acquisition heads down a successful path or veers off toward failure. In this phase, leadership sets its growth objectives and business strategy, and determines what kind of firm it wants to partner with, how, and why. It conducts a search, selects a partner, and negotiates a deal. To enhance the likelihood of a successful combination, leadership uses this period to prepare to join forces strategically and psychologically.

Successful combinations begin with self-scrutiny and analyses that yield a conclusion that a company can realize strategic goals more realistically, rapidly, and/or cost-efficiently through a combination than by acting on its own. This creates the basic rationale for scouting the marketplace with the intention of merging or acquiring. Fleshed out further, it also informs search criteria and is applied in screening candidates. As a partner is identified, strategy comes to life in preparing a business case for how the two parties will create value and in thoroughly analyzing potential costs and risks in putting the two together.

Companies have to organize themselves to buy and sell. On both sides, this means putting together a team that includes not only corporate staff and the CEO but also the executives who ultimately have to lead the combination. In addition to its obvious part in determining strategic and financial fit, thorough screening explores a partner's motivation for doing a deal, its culture, and the makeup of its people. Diligent due diligence, in turn, digs deep to understand if the values of the potential partner are compatible; if the bench strength exists to manage the combination while running the core business; if all parties are on the same wavelength on synergies and what it takes to combine; and if there is enough trust and chemistry to propel the combined organization into becoming more than the sum of its parts. Such diligence counters momentum and the rush to close, giving the parties a chance to get better acquainted and – when warranted – to back out gracefully.

Good strategies do not necessarily produce good combinations. Psychological preparation educates people about the mindsets of winners and losers and readies them to meet and work with their counterparts. Seminars and simulations help employees contend with the concerns that arise early on and increase once integration starts.

In the period between the announcement of a sale and its legal close, executives can begin to identify the optimal points of integration between firms, define a desired cultural end state, and prepare for the grueling work of forming transition teams. They also need to think through how to allocate executive time and talent to the combination process. Meanwhile, preparations can be made to ramp up communications, conduct training, and develop and implement retention and layoff policies.

Strategic and psychological challenges afflict all combinations, even the friendliest and most soundly conceived ones. The more these issues are raised and worked through during the precombination period, the more prepared people will be to take on the challenges of integration and contribute to mining the strategic synergies in a combination. Precombination planning readies people to move forward in their personal and organizational transitions, and establishes the dynamics that endure as the combining teams come together to manage the transition to a unified postcombination organization.

Notes

[1] For studies of postcombination financial results, see Wright, M., Hoskisson, R. E. & Businetz, L. W. 2001. Firm rebirth: Buyouts as facilitators of strategic growth and entrepreneurship. *The Academy of Management Executive,* 15(1): 111–125; Davidson, K. M. 1991. Why acquisitions may not be the best route to innovation. *Journal of Business Strategy,* 12(3): 50–52; Elsass, P. M. & Veiga, J. F. 1994. Acculturation in acquired organizations: A force-field perspective. *Human Relations,* 47(4): 431–453; Hitt, M. A., Hoskisson, R. E., Ireland, R. D., & Harrison, J. S. 1991. Effects of acquisitions on R&D inputs and outputs. *Academy of Management Journal,* 34(4): 693–706; and Lubatkin, M. H. 1983. Mergers and the performance of the acquiring firm. *Academy of Management Review,* 8(2): 218–225.

[2] The strategic role of combinations is discussed in Haspeslagh, P. & Jamison, D. B. 1991. *Managing acquisitions: Creating value through corporate renewal.* New York: The Free Press.

[3] Marks, M. L. & Mirvis, P. H. 1998. *Joining forces: Making one plus one equal three in mergers, acquisitions, and alliances.* San Francisco: Jossey-Bass.

[4] Management Analysis Center. 1985. A study of the performance of mergers and acquisitions in the financial services sector. Cambridge, MA.

[5] Boucher, W. I. 1980. The process of conglomerate merger. Washington, DC: Bureau of Competition, Federal Trade Commission.

[6] Sirower, M. L. 1997. *The synergy trap.* New York: The Free Press.

[7] Conference Board. 1994. Change management: Strategic alliances. New York.

[8] McCreight and Company. 1996. Ensuring success with mergers and acquisitions. Wilton, CT.

[9] Anslinger, P. L. & Copeland, T. E. 1996. Growth through acquisitions: A fresh look. *Harvard Business Review.* January-February.

[10] Jemison, D. B. & Sitkin, S. B. 1986. Acquisitions: The process can be a problem. *Harvard Business Review,* March-April.

[11] Handy, I. 1969. How to face being taken over. *Harvard Business Review,* November-December.

[12] Kübler-Ross, E, 1969. *On death and dying.* New York: Simon and Schuster.

MITCHELL LEE MARKS, a San Francisco-based management consultant, helps organizations plan and implement mergers and acquisitions, enhance senior team effectiveness, build desired cultures, and strengthen internal transition management capabilities. He has a Ph.D. in organizational psychology from the University of Michigan and has authored several publications. Contact: MitchLM@aoi com.

PHILIP H. MIRVIS is an organizational psychologist whose work concerns large-scale change and the character of the workforce and workplace. He has written seven books, including two on mergers. Dr. Mirvis is a fellow of the Work/ Family Roundtable and Center for Corporate Community Relations. He has a Ph.D. in psychology from the University of Michigan, where he is an adjunct professor. Contact: pmirv@aol.com.

Introduction

Lakshmi Mittal, chairman and CEO of Mittal Steel, the Netherlands-based world's top steel producer, was in a relaxed mood as he presented the company's 2005 annual results at a Park Lane hotel in February 2006. Not only were the numbers impressive, but the 55-year-old Indian-born magnate could afford to play down the political storm in Europe that had created his €18.6 billion bid for the European steel maker Arcelor, the world's number two steel producer (see Exhibit 5.1). He said the debate in Europe was moving beyond initial expressions of horror created at the thought of a firm owned by Indians, albeit ones who had lived in London for 30 years, buying a European champion:

> In the beginning there was a bit of surprise, but I'm very pleased with my meetings with politicians. They have started to realize that there is a strong industrial logic and that is good for Europe to create a global champion. We are moving away from politics.[1]

A few days later, L.N. Mittal realized that the bid battle was just starting. Arcelor had prepared a defence plan codenamed 'Project Tiger' and a highly aggressive briefing referred to the Mittals as 'the Moon family'. Along with his defence plan for shareholders, Guy Dollé, Arcelor's CEO, said he was hunting partnerships in emerging markets to thwart Mittal's approach. Meanwhile, the Autorité des Marchés Financiers, the French regulator, was approving new laws proposed by the government, which included emergency legislation to allow companies to fight hostile bids.

The bid

On 27 January 2006, Mittal Steel announced a hostile bid for Arcelor. Three days later, Mittal Steel confirmed details of the offer reported to the shareholders of Arcelor. If successful, the bid would create the world's first 100 million ton-plus steel producer. The offer valued each Arcelor share at €28.21, a 27 per cent premium over the closing price, an all-time high on Euronext Paris and a 55 per cent premium over the volume weighted average share price over the preceding 12 months. This offer valued Arcelor at €18.6 billion (see Exhibit 5.2). The bid would create an entity four times larger than its nearest rival. The new company would have leading market positions in NAFTA, the EU, central Europe, Africa and South America. In the automotive sector, it would be

Ashok Som wrote this case. The author gratefully acknowledges the contribution of Saoussane Tayaa, Maria Roshini Mathew, Pelin Atamer and Emeline Nicolas, ESSEC MBA students, for their research help. The case was based on published sources and generalized experience. It was developed as a basis for class discussion rather than to illustrate either effective or ineffective handling of an administrative situation.

▶ the leader in both the EU and NAFTA regions, and would also have leading positions in South America, eastern Europe, Africa and Asia. Mittal expected cost savings from the acquisition of $1 billion from efficiencies in purchasing, marketing and manufacturing. Moreover, Mittal Steel's stand-alone raw material (iron ore) self-sufficiency rate was about 60 per cent and the combination of Arcelor and Mittal Steel would create the world's fourth largest iron ore producer.

Top steel producers in 2004 (milions of metric tonnes crude steel output)

Rank	Company	Country	Output
1	Mittal Steel*	Netherlands	59.0
2	Arcelor**	Luxembourg	50.6
3	Nippon Steel	Japan	31.4
4	JFE Holding	Japan	31.1
5	POSCO	Korea	31.1
6	Baosteel	China	21.4
7	US Steel	U.S.	20.8
8	Corus	U.K.	19.9
9	Nucor	U.S.	17.9
10	ThyssenKrupp	Germany	17.6
11	Riva	Italy	16.7
12	Gerdau group	Brazil	13.4
13	Severstal	Russia	12.8
14	China Steel	Taiwan	12.5
15	Sumitomo Metal	Japan	12.3
16	EvrazHolding	Russia	12.2
17	Sail	India	12.1
18	Anshan	China	11.9
19	Magnitogorsk	Russia	11.3
20	Wuhan	China	9.3

Exhibit 5.1 World ranking of steel producers (2004)

  * Pro-forma ISG

** Pro-forma CST

Sources: IISI · Mittal Steel

The offer was subject to only three conditions: (1) a minimum acceptance of more than 50 per cent; (2) Mittal Steel shareholder approval and the Mittal family undertaking to vote in favour of the transaction; and (3) no change in Arcelor's substance (no disposal or acquisition) during the offer. The offer from Mittal was a mixture of cash and stock. The main offer consisted of four Mittal Steel shares plus €35.25 cash in exchange for five Arcelor shares (or 0.8 Mittal shares plus €7.05 cash for each Arcelor share). Alternative offers were a stock offer of 16 Mittal Steel shares for 15 Arcelor shares or a cash offer of €28.21 for each Arcelor share. Shareholders had the ability to elect to receive more cash or shares. Importantly, Mittal management had indicated that if the offer was successful, it may apply to list its shares on Euronext (Paris, Brussels and Madrid) and the Luxembourg stock exchange, in addition to its current listing on Euronext.

Mittal Steel also announced that it had entered into an agreement with ThyssenKrupp AG to sell the common shares of Dofasco Inc, the Canadian steelmaker that Arcelor was to acquire earlier against ThyssenKrupp itself.

Mittal Steel offers to acquire Arcelor	

Offer	• 4 Mittal Steel shares plus €35.25 cash for 5 Arcelor shares
	  - Ability to elect to receive more cash or shares,
	    subject to 25% cash and 75% stock paid to aggregate
	  - 31% premium on 1 month weighted average price [1]
	  - 55% premium on 12 month weighted average price [1]

Conditions	• Minimum acceptance >50.0% • Mittal Steel shareholder approval - Mittal family undertakes to vote in favour of transaction • No change in Arcelor substance during offer
Other	• Agreement to sell Dofasco to ThyssenKrupp for €3.8 billion (C$68/Share) • Modification of Super Voting rights upon completion • Compliance with Brazilian law with respect to Brazilian subsidiaries
Expected closing	• Q2 2006

Exhibit 5.2 Mittal Steel's offer for Arcelor
Source: Mittal Steel website, January 2006, presentation of the bid

Reactions to the bid

Arcelor

Just a few days after Mittal Steel announced its bid, the Arcelor board rejected it, denouncing several aspects:

> The board has swiftly concluded that Arcelor and Mittal Steel do not share the same strategic vision, business model and values ... The proposal could have severe consequences on the group, its shareholders, employees and customers.[2]

Arcelor's management explained that the merger did not make industrial sense. Arcelor's best tactic then was to play on shareholders' fears of alleged weak corporate governance at Mittal Steel, and that company's monocultural management and weak strategy, as well as convince them that Arcelor was much better off without Mittal Steel. The defence plan was called Project Tiger and several types of argument were put forward, as discussed below.

Incompatible corporate governance, management styles and identities?

First, on corporate governance, it was pointed out that Mittal Steel suffered a monocultural management with 87.4 per cent of the capital in the same hands and the presence of Mittal's son Aditya and his daughter on the Mittal board. Almost 97 per cent of the voting rights were controlled by the Mittal family. Shares with 'super voting rights' had been retained by the family. If the takeover was allowed, the Mittal family would exercise absolute control over the merged entity. On the other hand, Guy Dollé, Arcelor's CEO, portrayed Arcelor as a model of modern corporate governance (see Exhibit 5.3): 'Arcelor's corporate governance – with an 18-member board comprising six nationalities and a liquid shareholding in which no single organization had a large stake – is on a "different planet" to Mittal's,' said Guy Dollé, CEO of Arcelor.[3]

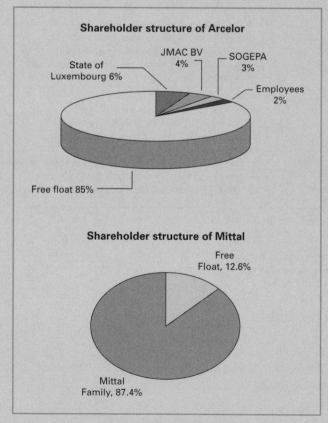

Exhibit 5.3 Shareholding structure of companies
Source: Mittal Steel website, Commerzbank Report, 2005

Guy Dollé, while opening a news conference, mocked the presence of Indian-born Mittal's son as his company's finance director: 'I'd like to present to you my fellow managers – my son isn't one of them.'[4]

But L.N. Mittal rejected this attack from Arcelor:

> Family-owned companies are not unknown in Europe, and in fact they outperform other companies … Our New York listing means that our corporate governance standards are high; we already have five independent directors out of nine, a higher proportion than Arcelor, and we will enlarge the board when the deal goes through. Our stock is covered by 10 to 12 analysts and we have got the highest market capitalization in the world of steel.[5]

Second, Arcelor noted that the corporate cultures of the two companies made for an impossible marriage. They were said to be so different that the merger would take too long and bring no benefit to the shareholders: 'It is not obvious this deal would benefit shareholders [of Arcelor]. There are enormous cultural differences between the two companies which could take up to five years to resolve,' said Valery Khoroshkovsky, CEO, Evraz, Russia's largest steelmaker.[6]

Third, corporate social responsibility was pointed out as another major difference. Arcelor had from its beginning adopted a strong ethical and social responsibility stance. Arcelor had created the 'Arcelor Principles of Responsibility', which presented the group's vision and ethical standards, dedicated to sustainable development, and summarized Arcelor's commitments towards its employees, customers, shareholders, bankers, suppliers and other stakeholders.[7] Arcelor was committed to zero accidents (since the merger, the number of work accidents had been halved and the seriousness rate has decreased from 40 per cent). The company also developed every employee, provided customers with innovative steel solutions, grew profitably, held open dialogues and partnerships with all the stakeholders, was reliable and efficient in every part of the business, protected the environment and saved scarce resources, was innovative, created value and supported sustainable development, respected cultural diversity and rejected any discrimination. 'As the world leader of steel markets, Arcelor is committed to sustainable development. We have the ambition to develop steel solutions for a better world,'[8] said Guy Dollé.

On the other hand, Mittal was well known for its drastic methods of restructuring dilapidated plants, which often included numerous layoffs and maintained a worse safety record than Arcelor.

Others gave another point of view, among them Roland Berger:

> The deal is not about job losses and restructuring; it is more of market penetration. [Mr] Mittal is not a man who has a reputation for firing people, but for delivering growth for his companies and his shareholders – who have traditionally been quite badly treated by European steelmakers.[9]

A business non-sense?

The counter-attack focused on the criticism of Mittal Steel's business model. It had been pointed out that Arcelor's turnover was the highest among the world's top steelmakers, though Mittal Steel was at the top in production. Mittal Steel's automation levels were also said to be inferior, while Arcelor focused on high-tech products (see Exhibit 5.4). 'Mittal Steel makes a steel equivalent to 'Eau de Cologne', while Arcelor is making Perfume with more expensive steel,'[10] Guy Dollé said.

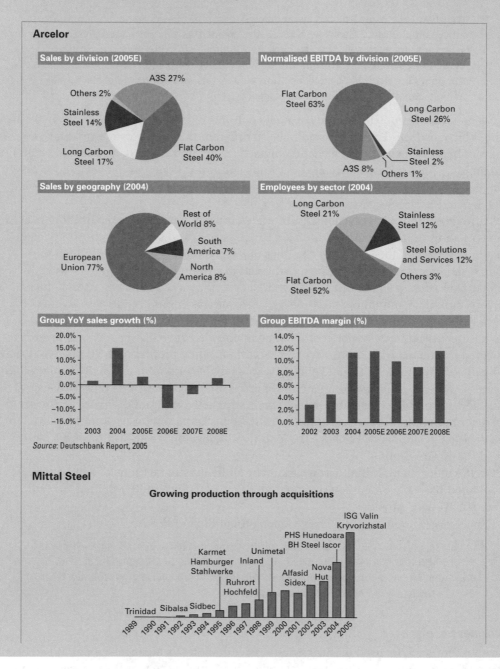

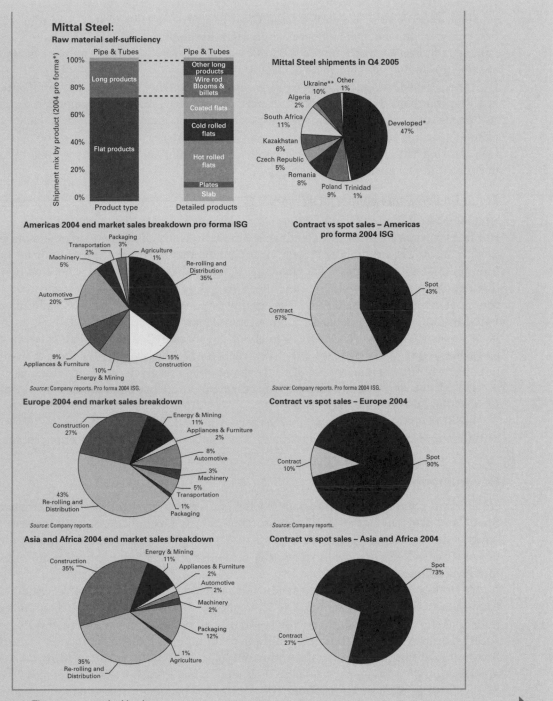

Exhibit 5.4 The two companies' business structure
Source: JP Morgan Report, 2005

▶ Some experts, such as Rod Beddows, Chief Executive of HB advisers, a London-based finance group for the metal industry, supported this analysis: 'Mittal is focused on making commercial-grade products, while Arcelor is a very technical company geared more to producing a higher value of steel.'[11]

It was alleged that Mittal Steel required huge investments to update its manufacturing facilities in eastern Europe and North America. The Mittal-owned company had a high risk profile due to cyclical-geographic exposure, and movement of its stock reflected this factor, according to the Luxembourg-based company. Also under attack was the delay in restructuring Mittal Steel, which could mean that Arcelor and its employees would have to suffer if the takeover was allowed.

Mittal, an unreliable partner for mergers?

Arcelor's board of directors underlined the problems raised by the merger of LNM Holdings (owned by the Mittals) and Ispat International (quoted assets) to create Mittal Steel in 2004. The briefing for Project Tiger claimed that the original prospectus for Ispat International made promises that were later ignored by the Mittals and it implied that the distinction between quoted assets and those owned by the family had always been a source of conflict after the merger. The attempt was made to show that, if Arcelor merged with Mittal, it would be in the same situation as Ispat. The briefing also claimed that Ispat's promise to pay dividends was frequently ignored by Mittal and that, between 1997 and 2004, it paid a dividend for only three years despite having positive income in all but one year. 'By comparison, LNM's sole shareholders received dividends totaling €2,386 million as part of the acquisition agreement with Ispat International,' the briefing says. Mittal Steel denied the claims.

Building on the arguments against the takeover itself, it was argued that the way Mittal announced the hostile bid, without 'any real' prior discussion, was unacceptable.

Governments

Arcelor was composed of former national steel interests from France, Luxembourg and Spain, and also had activities in Belgium. Though only Luxembourg state possessed Arcelor shares, France, Spain and Luxembourg had publicly and strongly opposed the takeover, with Belgium remaining neutral. Britain supported Mittal. Mittal promised there would be no job losses.

Mr Dollé's defence strategy received strong support from European public officials. Prime Minister Jean-Claude Juncker of Luxembourg was soon in the press, denouncing the bid as 'incomprehensible' and vowing to use 'all necessary means' to thwart its success. France's Prime Minister Dominique de Villepin and Finance Minister Thierry Breton joined him, questioning the 'industrial logic' behind the bid and calling for the mobilization of 'economic patriotism'. Days later, when French President Jacques Chirac met with Mr Juncker in Luxembourg, the Arcelor bid had shot to the top of their agenda. Additionally, Spain's Finance Minister announced that his ruling Socialist government had come out against the Mittal bid. The Belgian government, which owned a 2.6 per cent stake in Arcelor, appointed Lazard to help it conduct a more thorough and dispassionate analysis of the bid. Further highlighting the immense complexity of the transaction, even the US government got involved, with the Department of Justice announcing it would conduct an antitrust review of the deal. When asked about the intervention of the French government, for example, despite it not being a shareholder, Philip White of the Economist Intelligence Unit explained:

> There is a long-standing anxiety about foreign takeovers of French companies, particularly when these are either hostile, or in sectors which are deemed to be strategic. There's also a long-standing taste within official circles for promoting French national champions.[12]

France went even further as Thierry Breton proposed a law to protect French companies from takeover by foreign companies. The law was inspired by takeover practices in the United States, aiming to equip French companies with the same defence capabilities as their Anglo-Saxon peers. The new French takeover laws followed similar action taken by the Luxembourg government earlier the same month. It rushed through a new law allowing companies listed in the principality to defend a hostile bid by issuing new shares without calling for a general meeting of shareholders. The new rules included a 95 per cent threshold before predators could compel minority shareholders to sell.

As the issues of nationality, culture and patriotism had been systematically associated with the refusal of the bid, even the Indian government felt it had to defend the project of its Indian-born citizen, Mittal, over European protectionism. Indian Trade Minister Kamal Nath publicly accused European governments of discrimination and racism, and warned it could hamper India–EU talks at the World Trade Organization.

Rubbishing the perception that the opposition to the bid was 'racist' in nature because Mittal was Indian, the Luxembourg ambassador Paul Steinmetz said his government would have reacted in a similar way even if an American, Russian or any other nationality was involved in such a move. Maintaining that the issue involved thousands of jobs, he said the government in his country was wondering what Mittal's intentions were. Citing 'historical, cultural and economic attachment' to Arcelor, which was located in Luxembourg, Paul Steinmetz said Mittal should 'explain more' on why he was taking the step, which appeared more of a 'financial project rather than an industrial one'. Steinmetz also answered to the Indian threat, emphasizing that the issue concerned 'two European companies' and that the Luxembourg government had the right to intervene as it had a majority stake of 5.6 per cent in Arcelor: 'As a shareholder, we [the Luxembourg government] should raise voice … We cannot sit back,' he said, adding, however, that 'the situation is different for the Indian government, which is not a shareholder. … I don't see where India fits into it, except that Mr Mittal was born in India. … From a legal point of view, we are the only government who really has a locus stand.'[13]

Britain's piece of advice to its European partners opposing the UK-based steelmaker's bid on Arcelor was to be open-minded and remember that it was an era of globalization. Putting his point forward, British High Commissioner Sir Michael Arthur said they could learn from the British experience with globalization:

▶ 66 We as a government in the last 20 years have not resisted overseas hostile takeover bids. In the 1970s, our car industry died … but it has now been completely revived on the back of modern technology and investment from Japanese carmakers such as Honda. We as a government are quite proud of it. Britain now produces more cars than France. Last year we produced 1.6 million cars. That's the difference of vitality between Britain and those who are opposing Mittal Steel's bid.[14] 99

The steel industry in Britain was a good example of globalization, he said:

66 In Britain we used to have big steel manufacturers which produced high-steel products but we have reduced it considerably because India, China and Korea are more competitive and that's the way it will be. We are repositioning ourselves as a high-end knowledge economy because that's where we think our future is going to be … We believe in global partnership. 99

At the Senate, Thierry Breton said that it was about a fight because the bid had been declared hostile by one of the companies implicated (Mittal), but shareholders were the ones who would decide once they were provided with a detailed industrial project from Mittal Steel. He also said he was surprised by the way Mittal Steel launched the operation:

66 Mittal did not take the time, as is usual in almost all big deals, to present friendly and positively its project to all players involved in the bid. By players, I mean shareholders of course, but also employees, clients and all that feel concerned about the deal.[15] 99

No matter how the Mittal-Arcelor deal would end over time, the steel battle would remain a lesson for all deals involving the merger of giants from around the world in the new era of worldwide consolidation.

66 The Mittal bid for Arcelor could well be the template for other such hostile bids in the future. It may involve a large Indian IT services company launching a bid for a large American IT services firm. Or a Japanese carmaker for an American one. And the governments concerned may not even be shareholders (in the Arcelor-Mittal instance, the state of Luxembourg owns a 5.6 per cent stake in Arcelor). Yet, the governments involved will need to look at the merger closely simply because it will involve the fates of minority shareholders and, more importantly, employees in their countries. The final decision in the Mittal-Arcelor instance may have to be taken by shareholders, but there is a role for stakeholders such as governments to play. The sooner governments figure out just what being a stakeholder is about, the better for business.[16] 99

Mittal countered the attack from governments by playing on the same emotions and values that generated the opposition to Mittal's bid:

66 I have sought to explain to governments that this deal does not take away anything from Europe. We are not planning to cut jobs. We are not planning to shift or reduce investment. We are not taking decisions about Europe away from Europe. Rather, we are providing the opportunity – very rare – for a European company to be an undisputed global industry leader. Europe is steeped in industrial tradition and yet today few European industrial companies are sector leaders. This transaction will change that. A European company will be the undisputed number one in the steel industry. A business platform which will be able to flourish in a globalizing economy, and from which Europe can only stand to benefit.[17] 99

Rationale for the bid

The combination of Mittal Steel and Arcelor would employ 320,000 people globally, achieve an annual turnover of $69 billion, operate 61 manufacturing facilities in 27 countries, and produce 110 mtpa of steel a year, thus controlling 10 per cent of global steel production. The merger would create a steel company with unprecedented scale, a strong global presence and wide product offerings. Its world production would be more than twice that of would-be second-placed world player, Nippon Steel.

A step forward for the consolidation and improvement of the steel industry

Experts viewed the merger as helpful for the steel industry by enabling it to overcome the looming issue of overcapacity. The creation of this large player would also rebalance the power between steelmakers and their suppliers. For the moment, most of the bargaining power was on the side of the raw material suppliers. L.N. Mittal used this approach to gather support for his hostile bid: 'This deal is not about power or money; it is about the consolidation of the industry.'[18]

This stance had continuously been his vision for the steel industry: 'Do I believe that there has been enough consolidation yet? No, I do not. Mittal Steel Company is now the largest producer in the world, with only 6 per cent of total global production. When compared with other industries, it is clear that steel is still a fragmented market,'[19] said Mittal in 2004.

'Consolidation of our industry has already started, but it is important that it continues so that we can move away from being seen as a volatile and erratic sector ... Although the target is always moving, my vision for the steel industry has always remained constant. Consolidation is essential for its future,'[20] he said in December 2003.

A value-creator deal for Mittal Steel

Chairman Lakshmi Mittal declared his intention to make the group 'the lowest-cost steel producer in every market':

> " The result of the combined transactions marks a major step forward in the Company's stated objective of being a low-cost, high-margin, global steel producer. With the creation of one unified company, Mittal Steel has enhanced its ability to reap the full benefits of its unmatched size and scope.[21] "

Cost synergies

The merger would give unprecedented synergies in purchasing, manufacturing and shipping, both in scope and scale. Being by far the largest steel manufacturer would enable stronger bargaining power against raw material suppliers (iron ore and coal suppliers). These synergies were projected to reach $1 billion. Unlike Arcelor, Mittal had

▶ acquired large reserves of iron ore. With the merger, the group's iron ore self-sufficiency would thus diminish (see Exhibit 5.5).

Projected post-merger synergies

Source	Synergies	Drivers	Examples
Purchasing	$600m	• 1.25% of COGS of combined entity • Improved purchasing power • Optimised material flows to reduce landed cost • Access to non-traditional suppliers	• ISG (Achieved $67m of annualized synergies – 1.2% of COGS) • Inland (achieved $225m of synergies – 7.5% of COGS in 3 yrs)
Marketing and Trading Opportunities	$200m	• Savings in distribution costs by integrating distribution channels • Additional quantities to be available for Arcelor distribution network • Cross product flows	• Estimated cost savings of approx $10–15/t on 18mt of production in Europe • Estimated cross product flows of 2–4 mt
Manufacturing Process Optimization	$200m	• Optimize capacity utilization – right product at right mill • Specialization of facilities – larger order size per facility	• Inland/ISG capacity utilization savings of $2.50/t on 20mt forecasted • 6 months realized synergies of $13 million • 1% yield improvement in Europe will translate into $150m on 60mt of shipments

Iron ore self-sufficiency

- Iron Ore – 4th largest producer globally
- DRI – over 11mt of production capacity
- Coal – significant captive source
- Coke – self-sufficient
- Ownership of infrastructure and shipping fleet

Exhibit 5.5 Expected synergies
Source: Mittal Steel website, January 2006, presentation of the bid

However, some experts were less enthusiastic:

> Even though they [Mittal and Arcelor] will be producing 100 million tons, this won't give them pricing power because the market is still a very fragmented market. They are still too small for that, but it will give them an advantage over their competitors in terms of cost savings and know-how in the fields of automotive and construction.[22]

A richer product mix

Arcelor was producing higher-value steel products. The Mittal/Arcelor group would thus increase its average price compared to Mittal's pricing before the acquisition. Arcelor would also bring its expertise in producing these high-priced steels and provide opportunities for developing new products. Mittal/Arcelor could be the only 'one-stop shop', offering the widest range of steels.

Geographic complements

Given that Arcelor and Mittal's geographic presences did not overlap, the combination of the two would create a truly global steel company and provide the group with leadership positions in the five main regions (South America, NAFTA, European Union, central Europe and Africa), allying both developed and emerging markets. This widespread activity would help reduce the risks of volatility of the group.

Roland Berger, founder and Supervisory Board Chairman of Roland Berger, the largest Europe-based Strategy Consultancy, analysed it thus:

> The deal would create a large and really global company that can deliver real economies of scale ... with the exception of Japan, [as] they [Mittal and Arcelor] are all over the world. It would more likely create a company that is more competitive than either on its own.[23]

Opening up new opportunities

Both companies had identified China, India, Turkey and Brazil as key markets for the future (see Exhibits 5.6 and 5.7). If the merger was completed, Mittal and Arcelor would not clash on these new markets but would instead bring their assets together and conquer them. The example of the Ukrainian KryvorizhStal was self-explanatory. After Arcelor had made an aggressive bid in October 2004, Mittal Steel had to pay an additional $1.3 billion to buy and prevent Arcelor from closing the deal, while the third bidder had dropped out long before. Combined, Arcelor and Mittal would have a better chance of clinching deals without paying a premium. As stated by Lakshmi Mittal: 'With the combined force, we will be able to accelerate our presence in China.'[24]

Geographic evolution of world steel production		
	In 2000	In 2004
EU 15	19%	16%
China	15%	26%
Japan	13%	11%
USA	12%	9%
Russia	7%	6%
South Korea	5%	4%
Ukraine	4%	4%
India	3%	3%
Brazil	3%	3%
Rest of the world	19%	18%

Exhibit 5.6 World production evolution
Source: Xerfi

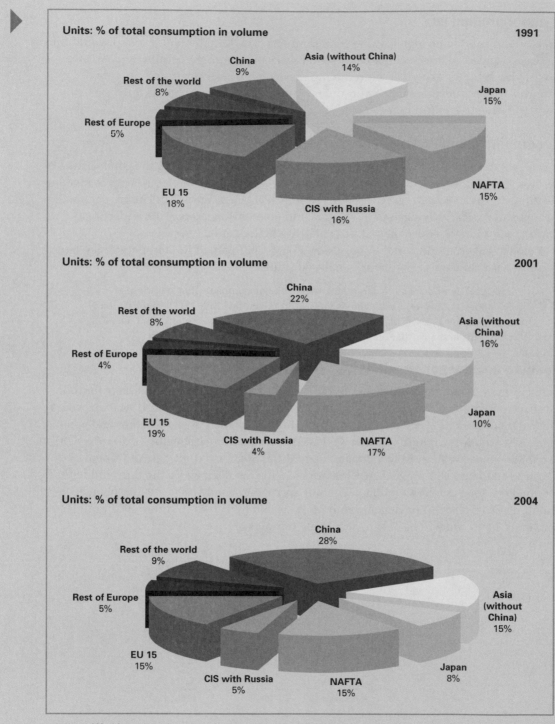

Exhibit 5.7 World consumption of steel, geographic breakdown and evolution
Source: Xerfi.com

What Arcelor did

Several defence mechanisms can be used to thwart a hostile takeover bid, sometimes referred to as 'shark repellent' strategies, and can be combined:

- deter shareholders from accepting the bid by proving that the merger would not profit shareholders because of the absence of true synergies – the difficulties of implementing the merger, for instance

- search for a friendly takeover; this is referred to as the 'white knight strategy'

- acquire another company in order to increase the price of the company and thus prevent the hostile bidder from being able to afford the deal; this is the 'defensive merger' strategy

- introduce 'poison pills' and other 'shark repellents' to create barriers and difficulties to an easy and cost-effective takeover and merger; poison pills are provisions in a company's operating documents designed to make hostile takeovers expensive. Poison pills commonly take the form of shareholder rights plans, which stipulate that existing shareholders may purchase additional shares at bargain prices if a single buyer acquires a specified percentage of the outstanding stock, thus making the acquisition of a controlling interest more difficult; poison pills are often structured to include the issuing of new shares, further diluting the stake held by a hostile bidder; 'golden parachutes' are close to the 'poison pill' mechanism (see Exhibit 5.8).

Golden parachute

This measure discourages an unwanted takeover by offering lucrative benefits to the current top executives, who may lose their job if their company is taken over by another firm. Benefits written into the executives' contracts include items such as stock options, bonuses, liberal severance pay, and so on. Golden parachutes can be worth millions of dollars and can cost the acquiring firm a lot of money, and therefore act as a strong deterrent to proceeding with their takeover bid.

Greenmail

A spin-off of the term 'blackmail', greenmail occurs when a large block of stock is held by an unfriendly company or raider, which then forces the target company to repurchase the stock at a substantial premium to destroy any takeover attempt. This is also known as a 'bon voyage bonus' or a 'goodbye kiss'.

Macaroni defence

This is a tactic by which the target company issues a large number of bonds that come with the guarantee that they will be redeemed at a higher price if the company is taken over. Why is it called macaroni defence? Because if a company is in danger, the redemption price of the bonds expands, kind of like macaroni in a pot! This is a highly useful tactic, but the target company must be careful it doesn't issue so much debt that it cannot make the interest payments.

Takeover-target companies can also use leveraged recapitalization to make themselves less attractive to the bidding firm.

People pill

Here, management threatens that, in the event of a takeover, the management team will all resign at the same time, en masse. This is especially useful if they are a good management team; losing them could seriously harm the company and make the bidder think twice. On the other hand, hostile takeovers often result in the management being fired anyway, so the effectiveness of a people pill defence really depends on the situation.

▶

Poison pill

With this strategy, the target company aims at making its own stock less attractive to the acquirer. There are two types of poison pill. The 'flip-in' poison pill allows existing shareholders (except the bidding company) to buy more shares at a discount. This type of poison pill is usually written into the company's shareholder-rights plan. The goal of the flip-in poison pill is to dilute the shares held by the bidder and make the takeover bid more difficult and expensive.

The 'flip-over' poison pill allows stockholders to buy the acquirer's shares at a discounted price in the event of a merger. If investors fail to take part in the poison pill by purchasing stock at the discounted price, the outstanding shares will not be diluted enough to ward off a takeover.

An extreme version of the poison pill is the 'suicide pill', whereby the takeover-target company may take action that may lead to its ultimate destruction.

Sandbag

With this tactic the target company stalls with the hope that another, more favourable company (like 'a white knight') will make a takeover attempt. If management sandbags for too long, however, they may be getting distracted from their responsibilities of running the company.

White knight

This is a company (the 'good guy') that gallops in to make a friendly takeover offer to a target company that is facing a hostile takeover from another party (a 'black knight'). The white knight offers the target firm a way out with a friendly takeover.

Exhibit 5.8 'Poison pills' and other defence mechanisms against hostile takeover bids
Source: The Wacky World of M&As (www.investopedia.com)

Arcelor's 'Tiger Project' was a communication plan to prove to and persuade shareholders that Arcelor and themselves were better off without Mittal. Arcelor announced on 27 February a '2006–2008 plan' to seduce its shareholders and convince them not to sell their shares. The plan's aim was 'maximizing value creation for shareholders', promising an increase in results by 24 per cent and generous dividends.

Arcelor did not adopt the 'white knight strategy'. Despite the name of Nippon Steel being cited in the press, that defence strategy was not chosen by Arcelor.

In the last week of May, the Arcelor board announced a €13.6 billion merger proposal with the largest Russian steelmaker, Severstal. It produced speciality steels and value-added steels, dominating the flat steel and carbon long steel categories. It was also one of the low-cost producers of speciality steel thanks to its recent modernization of plants in Europe and Russia. Severstal was also strongly implanted in North America.

The merger was described as a friendly transaction, which, like Mittal's offer, consisted of a cash-share swap but was 20 per cent higher than Mittal's bid. Arcelor's shares were thus valued at €44, which represented a 100 per cent premium over Arcelor's closing share price on 26 January 2006. The merger would slightly change the capital structure of Arcelor, with Alexey Mordashov becoming the single largest shareholder (32 per cent) but leave the management team unchanged, with Joseph Kinsch and Guy Dollé as Chairman and CEO of the merged entity, and Alexey Mordashov as Non-Executive President of the board.

Synergy creations were put forward with the deal. The merger between the second largest steel company and the largest Russian steel company would create globally the largest and most profitable steel company, dethroning Mittal from its number one position. Based on the company's pro forma 2005 results, the combined entity would have sales of €26 billion, EBITDA of €9 billion, 135,000 employees and a capacity to produce 70 mtpa.

Joseph Kinsch and Guy Dollé from Arcelor, along with Alexey A. Morashov, Chairman of Severstal, strongly supported the move to convince shareholders, insisting on the differences from the Mittal offer:

> Arcelor's board of directors believes that the merger with Severstal fully recognizes the value inherent in Arcelor and offers Arcelor shareholders superior industrial logic, greater value and the highest standards of corporate governance compared to Mittal Steel's offer. Therefore we believe this deal is in best interests of Arcelor's shareholders. (Joseph Kinsch)[25]
>
> The merger with Severstal represents a breakthrough transaction for Arcelor that positions the combined company at the forefront of the international industry. The transaction is consistent with Arcelor's strategy of value before volume, and was negotiated in the best interest of both groups. The merger is consistent with Arcelor's strategy in the BRIC markets. We are creating a truly extraordinary growth platform for investors and a much better choice for our shareholders. We are confident that they will support the Arcelor way. Long-lasting relationships, existing successful partnerships and a friendly approach guarantee limited risks of execution and therefore increase the chances to make this merger a massive success. (Guy Dollé)[26]
>
> I am delighted about our merger with Arcelor. Arcelor is a superb company with highly successful management and world-class assets that produces extremely high-quality products. Severstal's top management team, highly profitable assets and low-cost operations, together with Arcelor's attributes will position the combined company to lead the way in the consolidation of the steel industry. (Alexey A. Morashov)[27]

But analysts did not react positively to the offer. Indeed, the merged group of Arcelor and Severstal would not be as attractive as the Mittal-Arcelor one. Arcelor-Mittal would have a capacity of 113 mt. In terms of geographic presence, Severstal-Arcelor would be mainly restricted to the EU, Russia and Latin America, while Mittal-Arcelor would be complementary and obtain a global presence. Moreover, the choice of Mittal provided greater self-sufficiency for iron ore. Overall, higher synergies would be had with the Mittal-Arcelor merger. Mittal Steel-Arcelor was estimated to create $1 billion from operational synergies, while Arcelor-Severstal announced €505 million. L.N. Mittal had a similar point of view and expressed it bluntly thus: 'The proposed merger between Arcelor and Severstal is a second-grade merger and is like a marriage in hell.'[28]

Were the defence mechanisms useful? Time will tell. But, in general, defence mechanisms are not useless; defending oneself is also a way of bargaining. If Arcelor ended up being acquired, the battle would have increased the value of Arcelor and given leeway to management to impose some of its conditions.

▶ ## What should Mittal and Arcelor do now?

On 10 May 2006, Mittal announced that he was willing to sweeten his bid if Arcelor's board was ready to soften its opposition to the bid. Mittal also made efforts to meet Arcelor chairman Joseph Kinsch. Following this, Arcelor declared that it would be prepared to meet Mittal, provided his company gave sufficient information on the 'intentions of Mittal Steel, its business plans, value of shares and elements justifying the combination of the two groups', stating that all material sent earlier by Mittal was insufficient. To further ease the takeover, Mittal Steel announced the appointment of billionaire François Pinault as a new independent non-executive director. Mittal also offered to scrap its preferential voting rights and its two-tier system, in which Mittal's family had ten votes for every share. He also agreed to offer positions to Arcelor executives in the new company.

On 25 June, Mittal announced a sweetened offer that was 49 per cent higher than the original offer made on 26 January.

How the Arcelor shareholders would vote on the bid and whether the governments would succeed in thwarting the bid are the keys to the future of this mega-merger. What is sure is that this hostile bid will have opened a new era in and beyond the steel industry by the size of the bid and the hostility it received from Arcelor, governments and western countries.

Industry experts forecast that a steel industry of giants with a trend towards mega-consolidation is the steel industry's future.

The vision of a merged Mittal-Arcelor company puts a different perspective on what could happen next in the steel industry.[29] The question is: Is this going to create something to herald a sea-change in how these companies operate? If you were positive on the sector, you might say it could bring an end to deep cyclical peaks and troughs.[30]

One consequence of consolidation would also be the weakened power of governments and an increased role for shareholders. Analysts wondered if the historic levels of opposition reached against this hostile bid were justified. The fact that the bidder was an MNC from an emerging country had been part of the hostility it has encountered. The new aspect of globalization that was seen with this takeover bid was that it was strongly hyped in the media and thus was 'normalized' in people's minds, which may have opened the door for other bids of this type.

Appendix 1: Mittal

Lakshmi Mittal was born in India in 1950 into a family of entrepreneurs: his father, Mohanlal Mittal, ran a business called Ispat Industries, started in 1950. After graduating, Lakshmi joins his father's business and in 1976 became the Managing Director of PT Ispat Indo, a plant producing steel rods in Indonesia. This was the start of the LNM Group, part of the family business. In 1989, LNM made its first global move by acquiring the Iron & Steel Company of Trinidad & Tobago from the Mexican government, renamed Caribbean Ispat. This was the first of a series of many acquisitions throughout the world.

Key figures

By 2005 it had achieved a capacity of 70 million tons, 49.2 million tons of shipment, $28.1 billion in revenues, ROCE of 30, and employed 225,000 people. It had an enterprise value of $11.3 billion and net cash of $801.3 million. Mittal Steel was then essentially a holding company with no business operations of its own, as all of its subsidiaries are wholly or majority owned, directly or indirectly through intermediate holding companies.

The company's shares were traded on the New York Stock Exchange and Euronext Amsterdam. Lakshmi Mittal and his family owned about 87.4 per cent of Mittal Steel, with the remainder in free float divided between former shareholders in ISG (9 per cent) and Ispat (3 per cent).

Geography

Mittal Steel was called 'the only true global steel company' by the *Financial Times*, as it spanned the globe with operations in 17 countries, and 30 per cent of its assets in Europe, 30 per cent in the Americas and the remaining 40 per cent in Asia and Africa in 2005. A total of 48.2 per cent of it employees were in Europe, 5.9 per cent in the Americas and 45.9 per cent in Asia. At the same time, 41.1 per cent of it revenues came from Europe, 31.7 per cent from the Americas and 27.2 per cent from Asia.

Product offer and development

Mittal Steel had both steelmaking and steel-rolling facilities, which use mini-mill, integrated mini-mill and blast furnace processes. It served all the major steel consuming sectors, including automotive, appliance, machinery and construction, with a range of product lines: semi-finished steel, flat products, long products, wire rod, coated steels, tubes and pipes.

Mittal Steel had strong vertical integration. While many steel producers had chosen to focus solely on steelmaking, Mittal had consistently integrated backwards, investing in captive sources of raw material, more than 40 per cent of its iron ore and coal requirements from group companies and strategic contracts. In coke, it owned more than 15 million tons of annual production capacity, which met the company's overall annual requirements.

Low-value, low-margin semi-finished steel constituted 20 per cent of the overall product mix. Many of the plants that Mittal Steel had acquired were geared towards low-end steel for construction and highway barriers, not up to the specifications for the more demanding automotive and white-goods industries. Mittal Steel was investing in value-added products to meet increased demand and provide higher margins. Among finished products, flat steel constituted 66 per cent and long steel 24 per cent of the product mix in 2005.

The strategy: worldwide consolidation

Mittal's major business strategy had been to acquire sick steel plants all over the world and turn them into profitable businesses in a short period of time. The overall strategy

▶ was simple: buy underperforming mills, maximize production and upgrade the product mix. The plants were often state-owned, underinvested and with second-rate technologies. Once acquired after harsh negotiating, a team of experts was often sent to the new plant to implement modernization and production maximization, as well as severe cost control and management, including workforce downsizing and access to Mittal's worldwide supply pool.

In order to benefit fully from the acquisitions, integration and international coordination were part of Mittal's strategy. Knowledge management and best practice transfer principles were at the heart of the organization.

Appendix 2: Arcelor

Arcelor was created in 2002 from the merger of three European steel companies: Luxembourg's Arbed, Spain's Aceralia and France's Usinor.

Key figures

In 2005 Arcelor had a capacity of 55 million tons, 47 million tons of shipment, €32.6 billion in revenues, €3.85 ($4.57) billion net profit and an ROCE of 26.5. Arcelor had an enterprise value of €18.2 billion ($22.3 billion), including €2.6 billion of debt. Arcelor had more than 96,000 employees around the world.

In 2005, Arcelor's shareholder structure was as follows: 6 per cent of shares for the state of Luxembourg, 4 per cent for JMAC BV, 3 per cent for the Walloon region (SOGEPA), 2 per cent for employees and 85 per cent for free float.

Geography

Arcelor sales were deeply rooted in Europe with 77 per cent of sales to the European Union. North America and South America represented respectively only 8 per cent and 7 per cent of Arcelor's revenues. Arcelor was basing most of its American strategy on an expansion in South America in general and Brazil in particular as a regional growth driver. Arcelor already had a long-established presence in Brazil, thanks to its Arbed division.

Product offer and development

Arcelor operated in four key areas of activity: flat carbon steel, long carbon steel, stainless steel, and steel solutions & services (A3S). Accounting for 66 per cent of shipments in 2005, flat steel dominated the Arcelor product mix, which was not surprising considering the company's involvement in the automotive industry. Arcelor was the world's leading producer of flat carbon steels, in terms of volume and value.

Arcelor was known for its technological leadership. It had ten research and development facilities in France, Belgium and Spain, employing 1,300 scientists. It spent about 140 million euros on research in 2005.

The Arcelor group was a major purchaser of raw materials, particularly iron ore and coal. Despite generating one-third of its own requirements for energy, Arcelor was one of the largest energy consumers in many European countries. In order to reduce group exposure to the electricity market, Arcelor was developing its generating capacity through projects in Spain, France and Belgium.

The strategy

Arcelor was pursuing active portfolio management to reduce the volatility of earnings, and continuing previous cost-cutting and restructuring plans. It sought to progress to the upper end of value-added products with partnerships, particularly in research and development, as well as to ensure group growth through targeted acquisitions that would create value and contribute to reinforce Arcelor's geographic presence. Arcelor also had ambitions to further expand internationally in order to capture the growth potential and low-cost benefits of emerging markets. Since its creation, Arcelor had consolidated its leadership in Europe and in Latin America.

Just three days before Mittal announced its bid, Arcelor had taken over Canada's biggest flat steel maker, Dofasco, in a hostile $4.9 billion cash offer, beating Germany's ThyssenKrupp, which had tried to act as white knight. This acquisition was meant to expand Arcelor's presence in the North American automotive steel market, where margins were higher than in other sectors.

Notes

[1] www.mittalsteel.com.
[2] Cited in 'Arcelor broadly rejects Mittal bid, setting stage for long fight', by Carter Dougherty, *International Herald Tribune*, 5 June, 2006.
[3] Marsh, Peter, 'Mittal seeks to reassure over Arcelor bid', *Financial Times*, 30 January 2006.
[4] 'What they said about the Arcelor bid', *Business Times*, Malaysia, 30 January 2006.
[5] www.mittalsteel.com.
[6] Birchall, Jonathan and Marsh, Peter, 'Mittal's Arcelor deal deserves to succeed', *Financial Times*, 10 February 2006.
[7] www.arcelor.com.
[8] www.arcelor.com.
[9] Birchall, Jonathan and Marsh, Peter, 'Mittal's Arcelor deal deserves to succeed', *Financial Times*, 10 February 2006.
[10] 'Culture clash cited in Mittal's Arcelor bid', Angela Charlton, 8 February 2006.
[11] Marsh, Peter, 'Big beasts steeled for marathon bid battle', *Financial Times*, 31 January 2006.
[12] *Ibid.*
[13] *Ibid.*
[14] *Ibid.*
[15] *Ibid.*
[16] *Business Today*, 26 February 2006.
[17] Mr Mittal's speech at Gandrange, 20 April 2006.
[18] 'Consolidation good for Arcelor – Steel Biz', Chris Noon, 20 March 2006, www.forbes.com.
[19] www.mittalsteel.com.
[20] Lakshmi N. Mittal, Steel Success Strategies, December 2003.
[21] www.mittalsteel.com.
[22] Wardel, Jaim, 'Mittal unveils a $22.8 billion offer for Arcelor', http://biz.yahoo.com, 27 January 2006.
[23] Birchall, Jonathan and Marsh, Peter, 'Mittal's Arcelor deal deserves to succeed', *Financial Times*, 10 February 2006.

24 www.mittalsteel.com.

25 http://press.arcelor.com.

26 http://press.arcelor.com.

27 www.arcelor.com.

28 www.mittalsteel.com.

29 Guy de Selliers, Chairman of HB Advisers, a London-based finance group; Marsh, Peter, 'Mittal can reshape the steel industry', *Financial Times*, 30 January 2006.

30 Bertie Thompson, a fund manager at Aberdeen Asset Management, 'Mittal bids $23 billion for Arcelor in steel shake-up', http://in.news.yahoo.com, 28 January 2006.

? *Case questions*

Read the case carefully then answer the following questions.

1 What is the rationale for the bid? Evaluate the bid.

2 Analyse the pros and cons of such a merger from the perspective of 'fit' – strategic, capabilities, cultural and organizational.

3 Comment on Arcelor's defence plan. On what logic is the plan based? What other plans could it have adopted?

4 How and why did each government react to the bid? Discuss the role of nation states in this type of bid. Is protectionism and promotion of 'national champions' still relevant in today's world?

5 Comment on the recent growth and relevance of emerging-country MNCs. Are governments in developed economies ready to accept globalization of emerging-country MNCs and the specificities of their development model?

CHAPTER 6

Organizational restructuring: adapting to global challenges

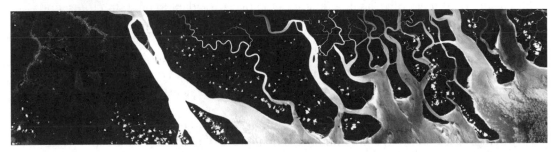

The previous chapter dealt with managing mergers and acquisitions, the pros and cons of these, and touched upon the challenges of post-merger integration in the expansion process of the global corporation. This chapter focuses on the organizational restructuring of the global corporation that is necessitated by any major external or internal adjustments. It discusses the concepts behind managing the renewal and change process effectively, and how global corporations might want to re-examine and integrate their change process with the overall design of the organization.

Corporate restructuring has been an area of great interest throughout most of modern business history. For example, the competitive implications of the changes in a global corporation's business portfolio have been central in the minds of corporate strategists, while the attempt to unlock value by matching their structures to their strategies has been of prime concern to human resource and change managers. In global corporations, headquarters (HQ) tries to align corporate and business unit strategies by first articulating its theory of synergy and then encouraging the business units to develop strategies that contribute to those enterprise-level objectives. All the while, the corporation must address the local competitive situation. It is here that the bulk of the corporation-wide systems – costs, revenue management, innovation, financial allocation, customer needs, IT – used for measuring performance and allocating responsibilities hits a bottleneck. For the sake of efficiency, most such systems have to be both locally responsive and globally controllable. But this emphasis encourages local business units to become silos that perform well on their local measures but fail to contribute to HQ synergies. For example, Philips' and Matsushita's restructuring failures can be partially attributed to the failure of identifying this balance between coordinating mechanisms from HQ and the responsiveness of its local business units, which has been reflected in their organizational structures. This requires a complex balancing act of protecting existing advantages while building the new ones needed to defend and reinforce existing capabilities.

These balancing acts often turn into nightmares if companies begin to engage in expensive and distracting restructurings. As global corporations have struggled with these issues, many have been caught up in expensive and frustrating cycles of organizational change. Philips, Matsushita and ABB are classic examples. ABB went through one reorganization after another following its first experiment with the matrix form in the late 1980s. Philips had a new restructuring agenda every time it had a new CEO, almost once every decade, while Matsushita followed suit as its bottom line was hit. Usually this restructuring churn is very expensive and often creates new organizational problems as bad as the ones they solve. It takes time for employees to adapt to new structures, and a great deal of tacit knowledge – precisely the kind that has become most valuable – gets lost in the process, as disaffected employees leave. On top of that, companies are saddled with the vestiges of previous organizational decisions, such as obsolete local and regional headquarters, and legacy IT infrastructures. Given the costs and difficulties involved in finding structural ways to unlock value, it's fair to raise the question 'Is restructuring the right tool for the job?'

But there are no easy answers to this question. A plausible explanation is that restructuring is a complex and multidimensional process. In the USA, the rationale for restructuring has been for the illusive cause of greater efficiency through downsizing the corporation. But in Europe, which has strong unions and inflexible labour laws, downsizing is not a viable option. Reconfiguration of European corporations has been mostly in response to changes in European markets and industry-wide changes.

Corporate restructuring has been defined in many ways. The simplest definition states:

> " Restructuring encompasses a broad range of transactions including selling lines of business or making significant acquisitions, changing capital structure through infusion of high levels of debt, and changing (the) internal organiza-tion of the firm. Business portfolio restructuring may occur through the sale of lines of business, which are seen as peripheral to the long-term strategy of the firm. Restructuring can also involve a sequence of acquisitions and divestitures to develop a new configuration of the lines of business of the corporation ... Organizational restructuring is intended to increase the efficiency and effec-tiveness of management teams through significant changes in organizational structure, often accompanied by downsizing.[1] "

Thus corporate restructuring encompasses both external and internal redesign of the firm. External redesign accounts for asset-based, financial/capital, portfolio and ownership structure. It is also referred to as down-scoping and leveraged buy-outs. Down-scoping refers to spin-offs, divestitures or closures that eliminate businesses that are unrelated and non-core. Thus, with down-scoping, a corporation is able to strategically refocus on its core business, which allows it to be managed more efficiently and effectively. Down-scoping has been commonly used in the USA by large firms such as AT&T and GE, while

---

[1] Bowman, E.H. and Singh, H. (1993) 'Corporate restructuring: reconfiguring the firm', *Strategic Management Journal*, 14 (S1), 5–14.

it is rarer in Asia, Latin America and Europe, where the tendency is to build diversified conglomerates, business groups or national champions. One high-profile divestiture is the case of DaimlerChryser AG, which sold 80.1 per cent of its money-losing Chrysler Group to private equity firm Cerberus Capital Management LP for $7.4 billion, unwinding a troubled 1998 combination aimed at creating a global leader. The deal is a stunning reversal of the $36 billion takeover of Chrysler by Daimler-Benz AG, which tried to set the mould for global automotive manufacturers. Chrysler was losing about $1.5 billion every year and had planned a restructuring that would eventually shed 13,000 jobs. The prospect of a sale to a private equity firm had worried unions in the United States because of the firms' tendency to slash costs and jobs. It was feared that a private equity buyer would 'strip and flip' the company by selling it off in pieces. Private equity firms typically use money provided by pension funds, hedge funds and wealthy private investors to acquire public companies or parts of companies and take them private, often to reorganize and sell later at a profit. GM also sold a majority stake in its General Motors Acceptance Corp. financing arm to a consortium of investors led by Cerberus, for about $14 billion. Analysts had said buying a big stake in Chrysler would let Cerberus combine GMAC operations with Chrysler Financial.

In the case of leveraged buy-outs (LBOs), again used frequently in the USA rather than other parts of the globe, corporations buy the assets of a firm in order to take that firm private, whereby the firm's stock is no longer traded publicly. Following an LBO, more often assets are stripped and sold, the rationale being to support debt payments, to down-scope, to refocus on the core business, to develop innovations and an entrepreneurial streak, and to grow and return to profitability in the medium term. For example, Alstom, the French heavy engineering giant, which operated in more than 70 countries and had more than 100,000 employees, was close to bankruptcy in 2004. Alstom has been known for its technological excellence, which ranged from power generation to high-speed trains (TGV) – both France's and Alstom's flagship of technological success. The French state, after a European Union-wide debate, bailed out its national champion for €772 million after giving assurances of several disposals. Alstom went through a financial restructuring process, divesting two of its divisions, Power and Marine. Power was divested to French nuclear giant Areva, while Marine was divested to Aker Yards SA. Subsequent to that, the French state offloaded its 21.3 per cent stake in the engineering group to France's third-largest mobile phone operator, Bouygues, netting a €1.26 billion (£880 million) profit.

Internal redesign occurs in the interests of organizational restructuring.[2] Here the focus is on the internal operations of the corporation, and specifically on organizational restructuring and change processes within the organization. Usually such change processes are underscored by *multi-dimensionality* and emphasize the need to redesign vision, mission, shared values, structure, strategy, systems, culture, management style, skills, incentives and human resources. Organizational restructuring is far more effective if corporations choose a design that realigns these multi-dimensional forces with one another.

---

[2] Researchers have proposed that organizational restructuring in general is disruptive and increases rate of corporate failure. Others have claimed that organizational change may be deadly, but if survived may promise good health. Some have reported that restructuring is beneficial to organizations, while most agree that organizational restructuring is the most common and predictable response to radical changes in the environment and is usually followed by a shift in business strategy.

Organizational restructuring is part of the overall design of corporations. Organizational redesign is a realignment process that ensures reorganization of global activities in an effective and efficient manner. It involves cost reduction, productivity improvement and building the new capabilities that are required to lead evolution, have high impact, are value added and increase overall shareholder value. The redesign evolves over time as corporations try to reconfigure processes to match the external demands of the environment. Specifically, restructuring is needed when new competencies are required and corporations have to find innovative ways to allocate resources, integrate processes and manage effectively across business units. This is a challenge as corporations not only have to manage this in their HQ but also in the myriad business units that are dispersed across the globe, and also subject to rapid and ongoing environmental changes. Failure to address this challenge would impact both short- and long-term performance and ultimately the survival of the corporation.

As stated above, organizational restructuring should have a positive impact on firm performance, even if only after sometime – say, three to five years. In this medium term, it is expected that the shedding of redundant resources (i.e. separation from non-core assets and excess employment) and acquisition of complementary assets through investment, training and upgrading of product range, production and technology would positively impact upon the firm's performance. Though these strategies are not well known in all parts of the globe, they are effective. For example, in the USA, restructuring is sometimes synonymous with downsizing, while in continental Europe, Japan and most countries in Asia this is not the case. Downsizing, as the name suggests, is a proactive reduction in the workforce, which might also accompany the closure of operating units, although it may or may not change the portfolio of the corporation. During the last decade, many *Fortune* 500 corporations in the USA have used downsizing as a tool for organizational restructuring. The most frequently cited reason for downsizing is cost reduction to enhance profitability and efficiency. But downsizing has inherent risks that arise from three side effects. First, downsizing can damage the social fabric of the organization and thus undermine employee motivation and cooperative values. Studies report that layoffs have a traumatic effect on employee morale, especially in Latin, east European and Asian cultures, where the norm of paternalistic leaders taking responsibility for their employees beyond a purely contractual principal–agent relationship is common. Second, downsizing can lead to the loss of people, or sale of assets, that are crucial for the firm's core capabilities and resources. In fact, the very capabilities that could generate continuous improvement may be lost. For instance, displaced top managers take with them their knowledge of local markets and networks, as well as of the organization and its technology. Third, downsizing is a legitimate action as it squeezes out any slack that had accumulated during profitable periods; downsizing can eliminate this slack. But complete elimination of slack may become counterproductive as a certain degree of slack can be an important resource for innovation and for managerial learning, and thus for transformation. Hence the crucial strategic issue in organizational restructuring is not *how much* a firm is downsized, but *how* downsizing helps to develop coherent core competences, and *how* the layoffs are managed. Figure 6.1 describes the corporate restructuring process.

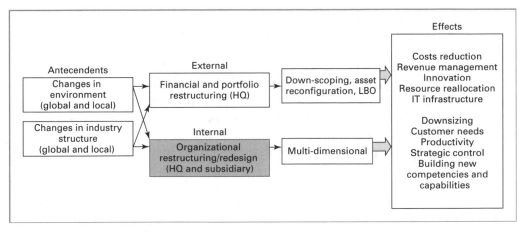

Figure 6.1 Corporate restructuring

Organizational redesign

Based on a large body of research, organizational redesign should be chosen based on a certain context and, further, the description of that context should be multi-dimensional, including both structural and human components. Structural components of organizational redesign include goals (both short- and long-term intent), strategy (refocus on core business, as discussed earlier) and structure. Human components include people, coordination, control and incentive mechanisms. Together they include, holistically, the organizational challenge.

Fundamentally, organizational redesign involves three mechanisms. The first is to process information from the environment in order to coordinate and control its activities in the face of *uncertainty*. *Uncertainty* can be defined as the difference between the amount of information required to perform the task and the amount of information already possessed by the organization. Organizations tend to reduce this uncertainty by adopting *uncertainty avoidance mechanisms* such as collecting market information, forecasting, monitoring of internal activities, vertical integration, actively participating in industry circles, and informal interaction with politicians, traders and dealers. The implementation of these mechanisms would ideally match the demands of the organization for information processing and its information-processing capacity. The second mechanism is to partition or *differentiate* a large task of the whole organization into smaller tasks of the sub-units. *Differentiation* can be defined as the state of segmentation of the organizational system into sub-systems, each of which tends to develop particular attributes in relation to the requirements posed by its relevant external environment. The differentiation mechanisms include decentralization of formal structures, reducing hierarchy in organizations, delegation and specialization. The third mechanism is to coordinate and *integrate* these smaller sub-unit tasks so that they fit together to efficiently realize the larger task: the organizational goals. *Integration* can be defined as the 'quality of the state of collaboration that exists among departments that are required to achieve unity of effort by the demands of the environment'. Integration mechanisms involve information sharing through internal and external communication, renewal of organizational culture and organizational climate, long-range planning, style of top management, coordination of liaison activities, formation of committees and cross-functional teams, management information and control systems. Differentiation and integration mechanisms are complementary to each other.

Researchers have argued that the reduction and management of uncertainty is a major organizational enterprise, particularly for global corporations. Global organizations face environmental uncertainty across borders and must develop mechanisms that reduce or structure this uncertainty so that efficient planning of operations in multiple markets becomes feasible. Having achieved at least a partial closure, they must then differentiate themselves to cope more effectively with the diverse contingencies in their internal environment, and at the same time strive to coordinate their activities by integrating their operations. Thus, the more the organization has been able to achieve closure (the greater the reduction in uncertainty it has been able to effect and the clearer the identification it has been able to make of the crucial contingencies in its environment), the more capable it will be of differentiation. The more differentiated the organization is, the more it will strive to use integrative mechanisms. Figure 6.2 depicts the model of organizational redesign.

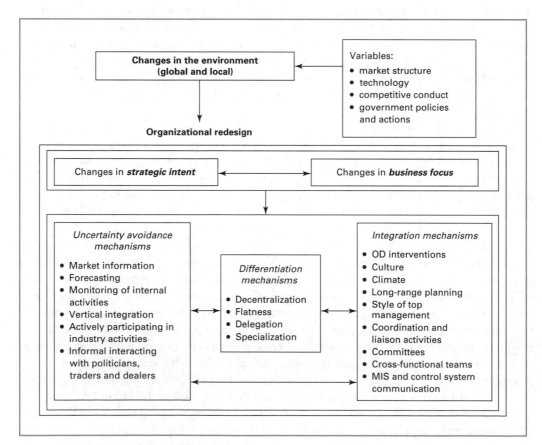

Figure 6.2 Model of organizational redesign

Corporations undergoing a flux in business environment find continuous organizational renewal and alternative adaptations are necessary. The mechanisms indicate a proactive *process* that has been well accepted and recognized in the literature, but that has been used only recently by corporations as part of their global business strategy. Corporations face a host of challenges while they engage in dynamic restructuring as part of the adaptation strategy. Some of the specific challenges that managers face are of re-engineering, with resultant alignment of the new processes within the organization, quality programmes, integration during M&As, cultural renewal, customer satisfaction and service issues, rightsizing and delayering, lack of motivation resulting in employee flight, and adequate internal and external communication due to the strategic redirection of the corporation. The Indian context provides an excellent illustration of the phenomenon of large-scale entry of MNCs and the resultant changes in the competitive structure of the markets where more creative, innovative mechanisms fuel organizational redesign. As Roberts,[3] (2004, p. 12) pointed out: 'Achieving high performance in a business results from establishing and maintaining a fit among three elements: the strategy of the firm, its organizational design, and the environment in which it operates.'

Case introduction: restructuring of Canal Plus: the beginning of a new era

André Rousselt, in late 1984 with the participation of Générale des Eaux, a French public limited company and leader in wastewater management, linked up with the Havas media group to create Canal Plus, the first pay encrypted TV in France (and in Europe). Within ten years, Pierre Lescure took over as CEO, having been the blue-eyed boy of Rousselet. For the past ten years, Canal Plus has had an increasing number of subscribers, is the undisputed market leader with no visible signs of competition, and has constant and positive EBIT, with a high level of confidence from shareholders. Between 1996 and 2000, Jean-Marie Messier, CEO of Générale des Eaux, formed Vivendi Universal, which had businesses in music, publishing, TV and film (Canal Plus, Universal Pictures, Universal Studios), entertainment parks, telecoms (Cegetel and SFR – two major mobile operators in France) and the internet, with a controlling stakes in Canal Plus. By 2002, with the internet bubble burst, the telecoms market crashed, which caused an economic slowdown in the USA and Europe. Vivendi Universal's debt level reached 13 billion euros and its share value decreased by 80 per cent. In 2002, Jean-Marie Messier was ousted by the Board of Vivendi Universal, and Jean-René Fourtou was ushered in as the new CEO. In 2002 Canal Plus had a net debt of 5.1 billion euros, despite a turnover of 4.8 billion euros, a net loss of 325 million euros. Fourtou immediately appointed new top management at Canal Plus, with Bertrand Méheut as the new CEO, who undertook a successful financial and organizational restructuring of the company in a record 18 months.

This case appears after the readings for this chapter.

---

[3] Roberts, J. (2004) *The Modern Firm: Organizational Design for Performance and Growth*. New York: Oxford University Press.

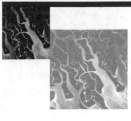

READING 11
Successful change and the force that drives it*

John P. Kotter

PEOPLE WHO HAVE BEEN through difficult, painful, and not very successful change efforts often end up drawing both pessimistic and angry conclusions. They become suspicious of the motives of those pushing for transformation; they worry that major change is not possible without carnage; they fear that the boss is a monster or that much of the management is incompetent. After watching dozens of efforts to enhance organizational performance via restructuring, reengineering, quality programs, mergers and acquisitions, cultural renewal, downsizing, and strategic redirection, I draw a different conclusion. Available evidence shows that most public and private organizations can be significantly improved, at an acceptable cost, but that we often make terrible mistakes when we try because history has simply not prepared us for transformational challenges.

The globalization of markets and competition

People of my generation or older did not grow up in an era when transformation was common. With less global competition and a slower-moving business environment, the norm back then was stability and the ruling motto was: 'If it ain't broke, don't fix it.' Change occurred incrementally and infrequently; If you had told a typical group of managers in 1960 that businesspeople today, over the course of eighteen to thirty-six months, would be trying to increase productivity by 20 to 50 percent, improve quality by 30 to 100 percent, and reduce new-product development times by 30 to 80 percent, they would have laughed at you. That magnitude of change in that short a period of time would have been too far removed from their personal experience to be credible.

The challenges we now face are different. A globalized economy is creating both more hazards and more opportunities for everyone, forcing firms to make dramatic improvements not only to compete and prosper but also to merely survive. Globalization, in turn, is being driven by a broad and powerful set of forces associated with technological change, international economic integration, domestic market maturation within the more developed countries, and the collapse of worldwide communism. [See Figure 1.]

---

* Chapter 2 in *Leading Change*, by John P. Kotter, Boston, MA: Harvard Business School Press, 1996.

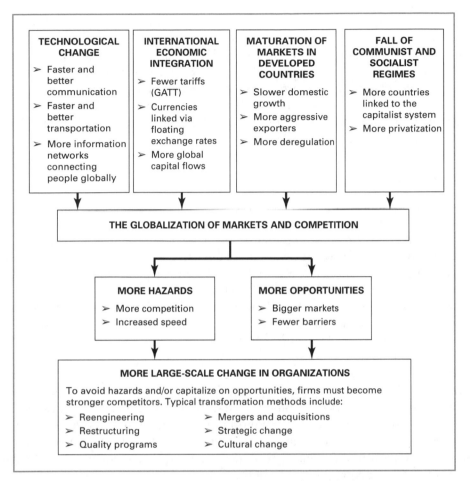

Figure 1 Economic and social forces driving the need for major change in organizations

Source: From *The New Rules: How to Succeed in Today's Post-Corporate World* by John P. Kotter. Copyright © 1995 by John P. Kotter. Adapted with permission of The Free Press, a Division of Simon & Schuster.

No one is immune to these forces. Even companies that sell only in small geographic regions can feel the impact of globalization. The influence route is sometimes indirect: Toyota beats GM, GM lays off employees, belt-tightening employees demand cheaper services from the corner dry cleaner. In a similar way, school systems, hospitals, charities, and government agencies are being forced to try to improve. The problem is that most managers have no history or legacy to guide them through all this.

Given the track record of many companies over the past two decades, some people have concluded that organizations are simply unable to change much and that we must learn to accept that fact. But this assessment cannot account for any of the dramatic transformation success stories from the recent past. Some organizations have discovered how to make new strategies, acquisitions, reengineering, quality programs, and restructuring work wonderfully well for them. They have minimized the change errors described in chapter 1. In the process, they have been saved from bankruptcy, or gone from middle-of-the-pack players to industry leaders, or pulled farther out in front of their closest rivals.

An examination of these success stories reveals two important patterns. First, useful change tends to be associated with a multistep process that creates power and motivation sufficient to overwhelm all the sources of inertia. Second, this process is never employed effectively unless it is driven by high-quality leadership, not just excellent management – an important distinction that will come up repeatedly as we talk about instituting significant organizational change.

The eight-stage change process

The methods used in successful transformations are all based on one fundamental insight: that major change will not happen easily for a long list of reasons. Even if an objective observer can clearly see that costs are too high, or products are not good enough, or shifting customer requirements are not being adequately addressed, needed change can still stall because of inwardly focused cultures, paralyzing bureaucracy, parochial politics, a low level of trust, lack of teamwork, arrogant attitudes, a lack of leadership in middle management, and the general human fear of the unknown. To be effective, a method designed to alter strategies, reengineer processes, or improve quality must address these barriers and address them well.

All diagrams tend to oversimplify reality. I therefore offer [Figure 2] with some trepidation. It summarizes the steps producing successful change of any magnitude in organizations. The process has eight stages, each of which is associated with one of the eight fundamental errors that undermine transformation efforts. The steps are: establishing a sense of urgency, creating the guiding coalition, developing a vision and strategy, communicating the change vision, empowering a broad base of people to take action, generating short-term wins, consolidating gains and producing even more change, and institutionalizing new approaches in the culture.

The first four steps in the transformation process help defrost a hardened status quo. If change were easy, you wouldn't need all that effort. Phases five to seven then introduce many new practices. The last stage grounds the changes in the corporate culture and helps make them stick.

People under pressure to show results will often try to skip phases – sometimes quite a few – in a major change effort. A smart and capable executive recently told me that his attempts to introduce a reorganization were being blocked by most of his management team. Our conversation, in short form, was this:

> 'Do your people believe the status quo is unacceptable?' I asked. 'Do they really feel a sense of urgency?'
>
> 'Some do. But many probably do not.'
>
> 'Who is pushing for this change?'
>
> 'I suppose it's mostly me,' he acknowledged.
>
> 'Do you have a compelling vision of the future and strategies for getting there that help explain why this reorganization is necessary?'
>
> 'I think so,' he said, 'although I'm not sure how clear it is.'

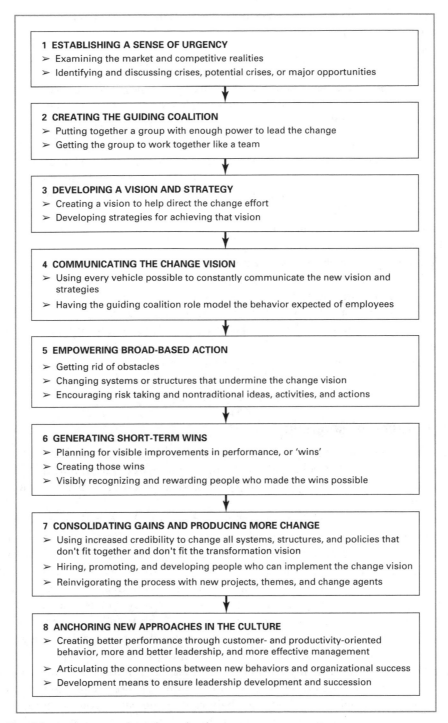

1 ESTABLISHING A SENSE OF URGENCY
➢ Examining the market and competitive realities
➢ Identifying and discussing crises, potential crises, or major opportunities

2 CREATING THE GUIDING COALITION
➢ Putting together a group with enough power to lead the change
➢ Getting the group to work together like a team

3 DEVELOPING A VISION AND STRATEGY
➢ Creating a vision to help direct the change effort
➢ Developing strategies for achieving that vision

4 COMMUNICATING THE CHANGE VISION
➢ Using every vehicle possible to constantly communicate the new vision and strategies
➢ Having the guiding coalition role model the behavior expected of employees

5 EMPOWERING BROAD-BASED ACTION
➢ Getting rid of obstacles
➢ Changing systems or structures that undermine the change vision
➢ Encouraging risk taking and nontraditional ideas, activities, and actions

6 GENERATING SHORT-TERM WINS
➢ Planning for visible improvements in performance, or 'wins'
➢ Creating those wins
➢ Visibly recognizing and rewarding people who made the wins possible

7 CONSOLIDATING GAINS AND PRODUCING MORE CHANGE
➢ Using increased credibility to change all systems, structures, and policies that don't fit together and don't fit the transformation vision
➢ Hiring, promoting, and developing people who can implement the change vision
➢ Reinvigorating the process with new projects, themes, and change agents

8 ANCHORING NEW APPROACHES IN THE CULTURE
➢ Creating better performance through customer- and productivity-oriented behavior, more and better leadership, and more effective management
➢ Articulating the connections between new behaviors and organizational success
➢ Development means to ensure leadership development and succession

Figure 2 The eight-stage process of creating major change
Source: Adapted from John P. Kotter, 'Why Transformation Efforts Fail,' *Harvard Business Review* (March–April 1995): 61. Reprinted with permission.

'Have you ever tried to write down the vision and strategies in summary form on a few pages of paper?'

'Not really.'

'Do your managers understand and believe in that vision?'

'I think the three or four key players are on board,' he said, then conceded, 'but I wouldn't be surprised if many others either don't understand the concept or don't entirely believe in it.'

In the language system of the model shown in (Figure) 2, this executive had jumped immediately to phase 5 in the transformation process with his idea of a reorganization. But because he mostly skipped the earlier steps. He ran into a wall of resistance. Had he crammed the new structure down people's throats, which he could have done, they would have found a million clever ways to undermine the kinds of behavioral changes he wanted. He knew this to be true, so he sat in a frustrated stalemate. His story is not unusual.

People often try to transform organizations by undertaking only steps 5, 6, and 7, especially if it appears that a single decision – to reorganize, make an acquisition, or lay people off – will produce most of the needed change. Or they race through steps without ever finishing the job. Or they fail to reinforce earlier stages as they move on, and as a result the sense of urgency dissipates or the guiding coalition breaks up. Truth is, when you neglect any of the warm-up, or defrosting, activities (steps 1 to 4), you rarely establish a solid enough base on which to proceed. And without the follow-through that takes place in step 8, you never get to the finish line and make the changes stick.

The importance of sequence

Successful change of any magnitude goes through all eight stages, usually in the sequence shown in [Figure] 2. Although one normally operates in multiple phases at once, skipping even a single step or getting too far ahead without a solid base almost always creates problems.

I recently asked the top twelve officers in a division of a large manufacturing firm to assess where they were in their change process. They judged that they were about 80 percent finished with stage #1, 40 percent with #2, 70 percent with #3, 60 percent with #4, 40 percent with #5, 10 percent with #6, and 5 percent with #7 and #8. They also said that their progress, which had gone well for eighteen months, was now slowing down, leaving them increasingly frustrated. I asked what they thought the problem was. After much discussion, they kept coming back to 'corporate headquarters.' Key individuals at corporate, including the CEO, were not sufficiently a part of the guiding coalition, which is why the twelve division officers judged that only 40 percent of the work in #2 was done. Because higher-order principles had not been decided, they found it nearly impossible to settle on the more detailed strategies in #3. Their communication of the vision (#4) was being undercut, they believed, by messages from corporate that employees interpreted as being inconsistent with their new direction. In a similar way, empowerment efforts (#5) were being sabotaged. Without a clearer vision, it was hard to target credible short-term wins (#6). By moving on and not sufficiently confronting the stage 2 problem, they made the illusion of progress for a while. But without the solid base, the whole effort eventually began to teeter.

Normally, people skip steps because they are feeling pressures to produce. They also invent new sequences because some seemingly reasonable logic dictates such a choice. After getting well into the urgency phase (#1), all change efforts end up operating in multiple stages at once, but initiating action in any order other than that shown in [Figure 2] rarely works well. It doesn't build and develop in a natural way. It comes across as contrived, forced, or mechanistic. It doesn't create the momentum needed to overcome enormously powerful sources of inertia.

Projects within projects

Most major change initiatives are made up of a number of smaller projects that also tend to go through the multistep process. So at any one time, you might be halfway through the overall effort, finished with a few of the smaller pieces, and just beginning other projects. The net effect is like wheels within wheels.

A typical example for a medium-to-large telecommunications company: The overall effort, designed to significantly increase the firm's competitive position, took six years, By the third year, the transformation was centered in steps 5, 6, and 7. One relatively small reengineering project was nearing the end of stage 8. A restructuring of corporate staff groups was just beginning, with most of the effort in steps 1 and 2. A quality program was moving along, but behind schedule, while a few small final initiatives hadn't been launched yet. Early results were visible at six to twelve months, but the biggest payoff didn't come until near the end of the overall effort.

When an organization is in a crisis, the first change project within a larger change process is often the save-the-ship or turnaround effort. For six to twenty-four months, people take decisive actions to stop negative cash flow and keep the organization alive. The second change project might be associated with a new strategy or reengineering. That could be followed by major structural and cultural change. Each of these efforts goes through all eight steps in the change sequence, and each plays a role in the overall transformation.

Because we are talking about multiple steps and multiple projects, the end result is often complex, dynamic, messy, and scary. At the beginning, those who attempt to create major change with simple, linear, analytical processes almost always fail. The point is not that analysis is unhelpful. Careful thinking is always essential, but there is a lot more involved here than (a) gathering data, (b) identifying options, (c) analyzing, and (d) choosing.

Q: So why would an intelligent person rely too much on simple, linear, analytical processes?

A: Because he or she has been taught to manage but not to lead.

Management versus leadership

Management is a set of processes that can keep a complicated system of people and technology running smoothly. The most important aspects of management include planning, budgeting, organizing, staffing, controlling, and problem solving. Leadership is a set of processes that creates organizations in the first place or adapts them to significantly changing circumstances. Leadership defines what the future should look like, aligns people with that vision, and inspires them to make it happen despite the obstacles (see [Figure 4]).

This distinction is absolutely crucial for our purposes here: A close look at [Figures] 2 and 3 shows that successful transformation is 70 to 90 percent leadership and only 10 to 30 percent management. Yet for historical reasons, many organizations today don't have much leadership. And almost everyone thinks about the problem here as one of *managing* change.

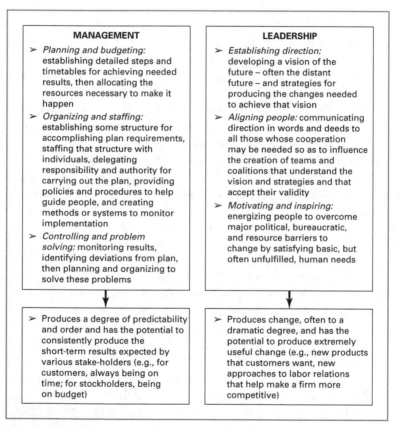

MANAGEMENT	LEADERSHIP
➤ *Planning and budgeting:* establishing detailed steps and timetables for achieving needed results, then allocating the resources necessary to make it happen	➤ *Establishing direction:* developing a vision of the future – often the distant future – and strategies for producing the changes needed to achieve that vision
➤ *Organizing and staffing:* establishing some structure for accomplishing plan requirements, staffing that structure with individuals, delegating responsibility and authority for carrying out the plan, providing policies and procedures to help guide people, and creating methods or systems to monitor implementation	➤ *Aligning people:* communicating direction in words and deeds to all those whose cooperation may be needed so as to influence the creation of teams and coalitions that understand the vision and strategies and that accept their validity
➤ *Controlling and problem solving:* monitoring results, identifying deviations from plan, then planning and organizing to solve these problems	➤ *Motivating and inspiring:* energizing people to overcome major political, bureaucratic, and resource barriers to change by satisfying basic, but often unfulfilled, human needs
➤ Produces a degree of predictability and order and has the potential to consistently produce the short-term results expected by various stake-holders (e.g., for customers, always being on time; for stockholders, being on budget)	➤ Produces change, often to a dramatic degree, and has the potential to produce extremely useful change (e.g., new products that customers want, new approaches to labor relations that help make a firm more competitive)

Figure 3 Management versus leadership
Source: From *A Force for Change: How Leadership Differs from Management* by John P. Kotter. Copyright © 1990 by John P. Kotter. Adapted with permission of The Free Press, a Division of Simon & Schuster.

For most of this century, as we created thousands and thousands of large organizations for the first time in human history, we didn't have enough good managers to keep all those bureaucracies functioning. So many companies and universities developed management programs, and hundreds and thousands of people were encouraged to learn management on the job. And they did. But people were taught little about leadership. To some degree, management was emphasized because it's easier to teach than leadership. But even more so, management was the main item on the twentieth-century agenda because that's what was needed. For every entrepreneur or business builder who was a leader, we needed hundreds of managers to run their ever-growing enterprises.

Unfortunately for us today, this emphasis on management has often been institutionalized in corporate cultures that discourage employees from learning how to lead. Ironically, past success is usually the key ingredient in producing this outcome. The syndrome, as I have observed it on many occasions, goes like this: Success creates some degree of market dominance, which in turn produces much growth. After a while, keeping the ever-larger organization under control becomes the primary challenge. So attention turns inward, and managerial competencies are nurtured. With a strong emphasis on management but not leadership, bureaucracy and an inward focus take over. But with continued success, the result mostly of market dominance, the problem often goes unaddressed and an unhealthy arrogance begins to evolve. All of these characteristics then make any transformation effort much more difficult. (See [Figure 4].)

Arrogant managers can overevaluate their current performance and competitive position, listen poorly, and learn slowly. Inwardly focused employees can have difficulty seeing the very forces that present threats and opportunities. Bureaucratic cultures can smother those who want to respond to shifting conditions. And the lack of leadership leaves no force inside these organizations to break out of the morass.

The combination of cultures that resist change and managers who have not been taught how to create change is lethal. The errors described in chapter 1 are almost inevitable under these conditions. Sources of complacency are rarely attacked adequately because urgency is not an issue for people who have been asked all their lives merely to maintain the current system like a softly humming Swiss watch. A powerful enough guiding coalition with sufficient leadership is not created by people who have been taught to think in terms of hierarchy and management. Visions and strategies are not formulated by individuals who have learned only to deal with plans and budgets. Sufficient time and energy are never invested in communicating a new sense of direction to enough people – not surprising in light of a history of simply handing direct reports the latest plan. Structures, systems, lack of training, or supervisors are allowed to disempower employees who want to help implement the vision – predictable, given how little most managers have learned about empowerment. Victory is declared much too soon by people who have been instructed to think in terms of system cycle times: hours, days, or weeks, not years. And new approaches are seldom anchored in the organization's culture by people who have been taught to think in terms of formal structure, not culture. As a result, expensive acquisitions produce none of the hoped-for synergies, dramatic downsizings fail to get costs under control, huge reengineering projects take too long and provide too little benefit, and bold new strategies are never implemented well.

Employees in large, older firms often have difficulty getting a transformation process started because of the lack of leadership coupled with arrogance, insularity, and bureaucracy. In those organizations, where a change program is likely to be overmanaged and underled, there is a lot more pushing than pulling. Someone puts together a plan, hands it to people, and then tries to hold them accountable. Or someone makes a decision and demands that others accept it. The problem with this approach is that it is

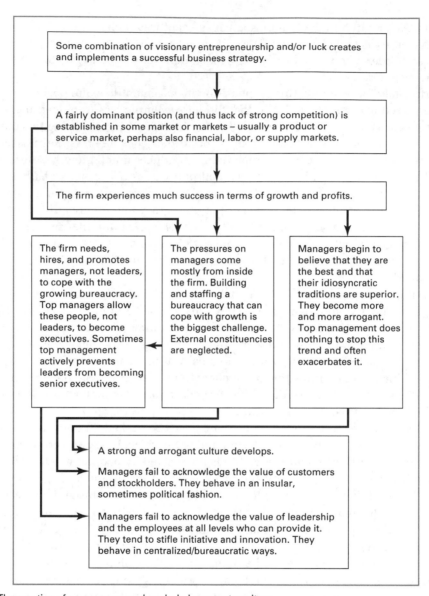

Figure 4 The creation of an overmanaged, underled corporate culture

Source: From *Corporate Culture and Performance* by John P. Kotter and James L. Heskett. Copyright © 1992 by Kotter Associates, Inc. and James L. Heskett. Adapted with permission of The Free Press, a Division of Simon & Schuster.

enormously difficult to enact by sheer force the big changes often needed today to make organizations perform better. Transformation requires sacrifice, dedication, and creativity, none of which usually comes with coercion.

Efforts to effect change that are overmanaged and underled also tend to try to eliminate the inherent messiness of transformations. Eight stages are reduced to three. Seven projects are consolidated into two. Instead of involving hundreds or thousands of people, the initiative is handled mostly by a small group. The net result is almost always very disappointing.

Managing change is important. Without competent management, the transformation process can get out of control. But for most organizations, the much bigger challenge is leading change. Only leadership can blast through the many sources of corporate inertia. Only leadership can motivate the actions needed to alter behavior in any significant way. Only leadership can get change to stick by anchoring it in the very culture of an organization.

As you'll see in the next few chapters, this leadership often begins with just one or two people. But in anything but the very smallest of organizations, that number needs to grow and grow over time. The solution to the change problem is not one larger-than-life individual who charms thousands into being obedient followers. Modern organizations are far too complex to be transformed by a single giant. Many people need to help with the leadership task, not by attempting to imitate the likes of Winston Churchill or Martin Luther King, Jr., but by modestly assisting with the leadership agenda in their spheres of activity.

The future

The change problem inside organizations would become less worrisome if the business environment would soon stabilize or at least slow down. But most credible evidence suggests the opposite: that the rate of environmental movement will increase and that the pressures on organizations to transform themselves will grow over the next few decades. If that's the case, the only rational solution is to learn more about what creates successful change and to pass that knowledge on to increasingly larger groups of people.

From what I have seen over the past two decades, helping individuals to better understand transformation has two components, both of which will be addressed in some detail in the remainder of this book. The first relates to the various steps in the multistage process. Most of us still have plenty to learn about what works, what doesn't, what is the natural sequence of events, and where even very capable people have difficulties. The second component is associated with the driving force behind the process: leadership, leadership, and still more leadership.

If you sincerely think that you and other relevant people in your organization already know most of what is necessary to produce needed change and, therefore, are quite logically wondering why you should take the time to read the rest of this book, let me suggest that you consider the following. What do you think we would find if we searched all the documents produced in your organization in the last twelve months while looking for two phrases: 'managing change' and 'leading change'? We would look at memos, meeting summaries, newsletters, annual reports, project reports, formal plans, etc. Then we would turn the numbers into percentages – X percent of the references are to 'managing change' and Y percent to 'leading change.'

Of course the findings from this exercise could be nothing more than meaningless semantics. But then again, maybe they would accurately reflect the way your organization thinks about change. And maybe that has something to do with how quickly you improve the quality of products or services, increase productivity, lower costs, and innovate.

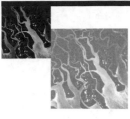

READING 12
Redesigning the human resources function at Lafarge*

Ashok Som

This article describes the detailed process of redesigning and implementing the human resources (HR) function at Lafarge. The article argues that a well-articulated and integrated approach of (1) recruitment, selection, and induction, (2) retraining and redeployment, (3) a performance appraisal system, (4) a compensation and reward mechanism, and (5) rightsizing is required to be aligned with the overall business strategy of the organization. It also reinforces that the foundation of a value-added HR function is a business strategy that relies on people as a source of competitive advantage. Key challenges for Lafarge in the future include (1) maintaining the change momentum, (2) fast and effective integration of acquired companies and transfer of 'best practices,' and (3) attracting and retaining a diverse workforce through their internationalization program. © 2003 Wiley Periodicals, Inc.

Introduction

During the last 25 years, constant marketplace discontinuities and the accelerating pace of change have seen traditional businesses and organizations redesigning themselves for superior organizational performance (Delaney & Huselid, 1996; Huselid, 1995; Huselid, Jackson, & Schuler, 1997). In this quest, human resource management (HRM) has aspired to be a business partner for more than a decade. There has been a continuous debate on how human resource strategy can be linked to the business strategy of the organization (Martell & Carroll, 1995; Pfeffer, 1994; Schuler, 1992; Ulrich, 1997; Wright, McCormick, Sherman, & McMahan, 1999; Wright & McMahan, 1992). Recently there has been an emphasis among academics and practitioners on people (and people management systems) as a source of competitive advantage (Bartlett & Ghoshal, 2002; Becker & Huselid, 1999; Ulrich, 1998). Previous empirical research has given useful insights about the linkage of HRM with firm performance (Becker & Huselid, 1998) and has consistently found that more effective HR management is associated with superior financial performance. Yet data on how organizations actually manage people to provide a source of competitive advantage are scarce. What is still missing is a clearer understanding of how these processes operate, and subsequently, how organizations

* ***Human Resource Management***, Fall 2003, Vol. 42, No. 3, pp. 271–88.

©2003 Wiley Periodicals, Inc. Published online in Wiley InterScience (www.interscience.wiley.com).
DOI: 10.1002/hrm.10085

Correspondence to: Ashok Som, Assistant Professor, Strategy and Management Area, ESSEC Business School, Paris, Avenue Bernard Hirsch–B.P. 105 95021 Cergy-Pontoise Cedex, France; email: SOM@essec.fr might actually manage their people (Becker & Huselid, 1999), and more importantly how organizations might redesign their human resource function to help provide a source of competitive advantage to keep up with the accelerating pace of change in the external and internal environment.

This article attempts to provide some insights into the redesigning of the HR functions at Lafarge through the presentation of a detailed case study describing the HRM strategies employed by Lafarge, which is known to be a leader in the management of people.

Previous research

The study began with a review of previous literature on case studies of different organizations, which have reportedly understood HRM practices and the redesign of these practices to provide a source of competitive advantage.

A detailed case study of the redesign of the HR process and structure at Whirlpool Corporation saw a multidimensional model that integrated three redesign tactics: contracting out new roles with line management for a new role for HR, identifying and developing new HR competencies, and redesigning HR work, systems, and organization (Kesler, 1995). In a case study of Albert Einstein Healthcare Network, the reason for designing and redesigning HR programs was to achieve organizational agility through contextual clarity, embedding core values, and enriching work practices (Shafer, Dyer, Kilty, Amos, & Ericksen, 2001). In the case of Northern Telecom (Kochanski & Randall, 1994), the HR function tackled the task of changing the fundamental form of the organization by reducing costs and improving performance, employee effectiveness, and satisfaction through the development of a strategic architecture that integrated workflows, structures, and the competency enhancement process. During the revitalization of Eastman Kodak, the key competencies under the rubric of HR excellence, a small number of core competencies, and an even smaller number of leverage competencies applicable to HR roles were the source of competitive advantage (Blancero, Boroski, & Dyer, 1996). Similarly, in a case study of 3M, an executive-level global competency model consisting of 12 competencies, such as developing people, inspiring others, customer orientation, and nurturing innovation and others, was the source of competitive advantage (Alldredge & Nilan, 2000).

In the critical case-study analysis of Mercantile Bancorporation Inc., Forbringer and Oeth (1998) reported that HR practices made a significant impact on business results and provided a springboard for the HR department pursuant to the findings of Ulrich (1997). Some of their findings included HR initiatives to help identify, communicate, and support core cultural competencies; expand economic literacy; expand corporate knowledge or the capture of collective wisdom; play the role of a change agent (Ulrich, 1997; Ulrich, Brockbank, Yeung, & Lake, 1995); and, overall, strive to be innovative. The linkage of employee needs satisfaction and organizational capability for competitive advantage in the case study of Southwest Airlines illustrated the role of human resources in creating and sustaining competitive advantage (Hallowell, 1996). The findings suggested that much of the value that Southwest created was through employee satisfaction, which was converted to customer and shareholder value via organizational capabilities and was captured by the firm as a result of its cost advantage and superior service.

Becker and Huselid (1999) attempted to provide insights into the 'state of practice' through the presentation of five detailed case studies describing HRM strategies employed by partnership firms (Herman Miller, Lucent, Praxair, Quantum, and Sears) known to be leaders in the management of people. The lessons learned were (1) the foundation of value-added HR function is a business strategy that relies on people as a source of competitive advantage and a management culture that embraces that belief; (2) a value-added HR function will be characterized by operational excellence, a focus on client service for individual employees and managers, and delivery of these services at the lowest possible cost; and (3) a value-added HR function requires HR managers that understand the human capital implications of business problems and can access or modify the HR system to solve those problems. In a case study of Hewlett Packard, Truss (2001) tried to contribute to this debate of the linkage of HRM and organizational performance by asking what HR policies and practices a financially successful organization like Hewlett Packard uses. Her findings seem to suggest that the notion of 'good performance' needs to be disaggregated and compared and contrasted to individual and organizational-level performance parameters.

As useful as the earlier research was in helping to identify the linkage of the role of HRM and firm performance, it also engendered several concerns. Most of the studies, for example, were anchored in the present, raising questions concerning current HR philosophies and HR practices, but not describing *how* the organizations redesigned their HR functions for competitive advantage and aligned their HR functions with overall business strategy for superior performance. Further, the studies tended to produce a list of HRM best practices or a framework for achieving HRM competencies for sustained competitive advantage. It seems likely that there is a possible convergence of the above studies, and, in particular, that the assumptions within the best-practice and HRM-competency literature can produce a universalistic set of HR practices suitable for all situations. The studies provided no apparent basis for individual HR practices. Finally, it was not clear in some of the studies that the respondents in the studies (even though the studies were company-specific) possessed the knowledge required to make accurate judgements about overall business strategy, HRM strategy, their linkage, and firm performance.

Given these concerns and keeping the limitations of the past case studies in mind, a conscious effort was made to build on previous efforts by conducting a company-specific longitudinal study of how an organization redesigns its HR functions for competitive advantage and aligns the HR function with the overall business strategy for superior performance.

Methodology

This study is exploratory in nature. Following Yin (1994) and Eisenhardt (1995), an embedded case-study design was found suitable for this study. A broad, qualitative method was deemed suitable to study the phenomenon of HRM, utilizing multiple sources that tap into the rationale of how an organization redesigns its HRM functions (Becker & Gerhart, 1996; Becker & Huselid, 1999; Gerhart, 1999; Truss, 2001).

This article reports on the findings of a longitudinal case study of a French firm, Lafarge. Lafarge was chosen for analysis specifically because it is a successful organization in terms of financial performance (i.e., it was a leader within the industry of building materials, was growing at a steady rate, and had been profitable within industry standards); it has a reputation for being excellent in terms of human resource management in France and all over the globe; and it was willing to participate in the longitudinal study.

Data were collected from December 2000 to February 2001 and from January to March 2003. More than 15 top management (including the president and CEO, regional president, executive vice president, vice president, general managers, and country heads) and nine senior and middle management executives (senior managers and managers), including HR executives, were interviewed using a detailed, semi-structured open-ended interview format. Open-ended questions involved how HR policies and practices evolved in the organization. A generic approach was adopted to analyze the HR practices, and data were collected on a wide range of HRM areas, including recruitment and selection, induction, retraining and redeployment, performance appraisal, compensation and rewards, career management, and rightsizing. The data were from the perspectives of both policymakers, that is, the HR department, and practitioners such as staff and line and senior managers, recognizing that experiences are likely to vary between levels of staff. On an average, each interview lasted from 1.5 hours to 2 hours. Extensive evaluation of archival data, company documents, media reports, consultant reports, and sector reports were undertaken. At both times, the research was carried out at the Lafarge head office in Paris.

The context: changes at Lafarge

Léon Orvin began producing industrial limestone in 1833 after acquiring a limestone quarry in southeastern France. He took over the business, acquired by his family in 1749, with the purchase of the Lafarge domain in southeastern France, an area known for generations for the quality of its limestone deposits. That was the history. From a local French cement company, Lafarge is now the world leader in construction materials, spanning 75 countries. The transformation was in no way an easy task. Bertrand Collomb, who has been the chairman and CEO of Lafarge since 1989, points out the situation over the last decade:

> Following prolonged recession in Europe, which lasted from 1991 until 1996, and the Asian crisis of 1998, worldwide economic trends now appear positive. World growth was 4% in 2000, and is forecasted to continue at about 3% per year. But we must remain on our guard because interest rates are on an upward slope, oil prices are rocketing, growth in the United States is expected to slow, and the German construction market remains sluggish. Most importantly, the process of worldwide consolidation in our industries is gaining pace, and this is why it is necessary for us to ensure we have the means to stay among the top-ranking world groups and be the preeminent player in our sector. ... In 2001, Lafarge strengthened its position as world leader in building materials thanks to a vigorous policy of acquisition and development on every continent.

Over the last five years, sales increased from 6.413 million euros in FY 1997 to 14.610 million euros in FY 2002 while net income, Group share, increased from 371 million euros in FY 1997 to 756 million euros in FY 2002. Lafarge had 37,097 employees in 1997, while in 2002 it had 77,000 employees, a growth of more than 100%.

The cement industry, globalization, and business strategy at Lafarge

The cement industry has been witnessing major shake-ups, takeovers, joint ventures, mergers, integration, and the formation of global conglomerates. The industry is also investing in alternative activities in order to protect itself from the economic impacts of business cycles. In the last decade, Lafarge has invested heavily in newly industrializing countries that offer considerable medium- to long-term growth potential, such as Turkey, Morocco, Brazil, Venezuela, China, and India. For Lafarge, globalization occurs in every strategic market by acquiring one or more cement producers in order to gain a significant market share. To gain market share, cement organizations in general are facing buyer bargaining power and have to deal with secret rebates, price cutting, price discrimination, and competition on service quality.

In this scenario, markets have become global. Yet markets are inherently local. Consumer tastes are diverse, business strategies of firms result in the fragmentation of markets according to product lines and location, and trade and competition policies vary from country to country. For the cement industry, high transportation costs and low inventories together mean that there is no such thing as a worldwide, market-clearing price, as distinct from a global average price. In this sense, cement is a commodity, but not a commodity like grain or oil. It is not possible to build sustainable, worldwide competitive advantage by locating production in any one country. Supply and demand are matched on a local basis. At cyclical peaks and troughs, the boundaries may become regional, but never global.

Keeping this globalization strategy in mind, the vision, mission, and values of Lafarge are as follows:

> Our vision is to offer the construction industry and the general public innovative solutions bringing greater safety, comfort, and quality to their everyday surroundings. The consumer should be placed at the heart of Lafarge's preoccupations. This vision is to be achieved by offering all construction industry sectors – from architect to tradesman, from distributor to end user – a comprehensive range of products and solutions for each stage of the building process. The company values a 'wait and see' philosophy and it includes a long-term orientation with industrial efficiency, value creation, protection of the environment, respect for people and cultures, and preservation of natural resources and energy. (Collomb, personal communication)

Five of the key issues it will need to address in the globalization process are (1) continuing development of its growth strategy, (2) managing its human resources, which have doubled in the last five years, (3) further realization of the benefits from its restructuring program, (4) fast integration of the acquired companies to create synergy and, hence, value, and (5) internationalization of its workforce and development of managers willing to be mobile and able to operate successfully in a wide variety of markets and with people of diverse cultural backgrounds.

The strategic intent is to 'keep growing and growing profitably.' The three main goals followed by Lafarge were (1) doubling sales within 10 years (1997 to 2007) by development in emerging markets and through acquisition in mature markets, (2) growing more rapidly than its competitors with an objective of 60 to 80 metric tons in increased capacity between now and 2005, and (3) integrating acquired units as quickly as possible.

The Lafarge Group did not focus only on emerging markets, as some of the other global players did. In February 2000, it mounted a hostile bid for Britain's Blue Circle, the sixth-largest cement competitor and, then, in January 2001, Lafarge bought Blue Circle at a price of 3.8 billion euros to become the global leader in the construction business, with one-tenth of the world market. Through this acquisition it aimed to achieve a certain size in order to remain visible and attractive to investors, to expand cash flow and geographic presence, and probably to dislodge Holceim from the top spot in the global cement industry. The Group's aim was indeed to become the world leader in cement.

> We [Lafarge] want to be the undisputed leader in all of our businesses, and, as such, the leader in construction materials through operational excellence, growth and the creation of value. Today a strong movement towards worldwide consolidation characterizes the construction materials market. Lafarge must be able to take advantage of the best acquisition opportunities that arise; there are currently many on the market. To finance this program, the Group has chosen to concentrate its resources on its major worldwide businesses. The introduction of financial partners will enable the Group to enjoy greater financial flexibility while maintaining strong links with the Division's businesses. (Collomb, personal communication)

For the Lafarge Group, strategy implies an ambition. *The Principles of Action* (Figure 1) was drawn up in consultation with all the stakeholders.

Restructuring for internationalization

> International development can be fostered through diversity and innovation. If one wants to push international development one cannot manage it from the top. Hence maintaining a decentralized operation is very critical. Developing international executives is the best way to become more international. (Collomb, personal communication)

Lafarge initiated an organizational restructuring process with the help of McKinsey and Company. The implementation process began on January 1, 1999. The Group was divided into four divisions – cement, aggregates and concrete, roofing, and gypsum. A new organizational structure was drawn up to facilitate the change process. The clarification, simplification, and formalization of Group policy in the areas of finance, human resource, research and development (R&D), corporate communication, the environment, information systems, and purchasing and marketing have accompanied this decentralization. In addition, guidelines on the management style expected of all Lafarge managers have been set out in *The Lafarge Way* (Figure 2). Though, after two years, there have been many suggestions that have been proposed about the organizational structure and constant communication, top management's conviction has made it work.

For the Lafarge Group, strategy implies an ambition, some demands, and a sense of responsibility. It is only when these components are brought together that actions become sustainable and long-term.

Our principles of action have been drawn up and worked on in consultation with all concerned. They epitomize our ambitions, our convictions, our code of conduct, and our values.

OUR AMBITION

- To be a world leader in construction materials
- To be recognized as an important participant and shape the future of our businesses through our capacity to innovate
- To be a leader in a competitive environment
- To pursue long-term strategies
- To adopt an international approach

OUR RESPONSIBILITIES

To anticipate and meet our customers' needs

- To create a perceived difference and be the supplier of choice
- To serve our customers better by knowing them better
- To contribute to the development and progress of the construction industry

To enhance the value of our shareholders' investments and gain their trust

- To provide shareholders with a competitive return on their investment
- To provide them with clear information
- To respect the interests of our partners and minority shareholders

To make our employees the heart of our company

- To base legitimate authority on the ability to contribute to the company's success
- To develop mutual respect and trust
- To provide employees with equitable compensation and a fulfilling professional environment

To gain from our increasing diversity

- To make our cultural diversity an asset
- To delegate responsibility with accountability and control
- To develop an effective cross-operational management approach
- To make use of synergies and share know-how

To respect the common interest

- To participate in the life of the communities where we operate
- To operate responsibly toward the environment
- To be guided by the principles of integrity, openness, and respect in our commitments

Figure 1 Principles of action
Source: Lafarge. (n.d.). Internal company document. Paris: Author.

Key human resource initiatives and activities

As Lafarge worked to create and broaden its identity and investor confidence, it became more innovative and proactive. The work environment was driven by a demand for operational excellence. The organization was restructured and streamlined, and over 100% more employees were added to the group through new acquisitions. In support of these changes, much of the corporate HR's time was focused on career management,

Lafarge's management style Is defined as 'participative.' But this concept has sometimes been misunderstood as 'management by consensus.' Either that or participation has been forgotten because of business or time pressures. In any case the Group has changed so much recently – half of Lafarge's employees were not in the Group two years ago – that it is time to redefine its management style.

Create value while respecting the Group's guiding principles

Our 'Principles of Action' have not changed, and define our responsibilities: our overriding objective is to create value for our shareholders. To achieve this objective, we must first meet the needs of our customers. Lafarge's identity and success is also based on the importance we give to our employees, and on the strength and benefits of being a group.

Clarify our strategies & our organization

To be successful as a Group, we need shared values, clear strategies, common information and reporting systems and performance measurement criteria. Today, we have started to develop a number of these systems, such as the Cement Operations Reporting Project (CORP), Top 2000 for our ready-mix concrete, as well as the EVA (Economic Value Added) project, to improve our performance measurement and compensation systems. We are now redefining the Group's organization, by rationalizing the role of the corporate function and giving the five divisions (Cement, Aggregates & Concrete, Roofing, Gypsum, & Specialty Products) more direct responsibility for strategic development and performance improvement.

To allow more decentralized initiative ... with better decision processes

Our aim is to create a management framework that allows more decentralization and individual empowerment. This requires trust in people, as well as clarity if the decision processes. We need to determine at what level a decision should be taken, who is accountable and on what basis, in order to avoid pushing the decision upwards, or diluting responsibilities through a slow inefficient process.

True participation, but not necessarily a consensus

Participative management is not decision by consensus. Rather, it means involving all those who can contribute to a better decision, while clearly recognizing who has the ultimate responsibility to decide. In this regard, our proposed reorganization is meant to streamline our decision-making processes.

Managers leading by examples

Even more important is that this organizational framework is the attitude of our employees. We especially want managers who are true leaders, able to drive their organizations to the highest performance level. Individuals who practice what they say, respect group disciplines, share information, and who are professional in managing employee evaluation, career management and the compensation system. Hence the renewed importance we want to give to open frank two-way discussions in the evaluation interviews.

Innovative and willing to contribute to the Group's success

We also need individuals able to innovate, to take initiative, and to act decisively within their realm of responsibility. Finally, we want individuals who look beyond their particular objectives and are ready to contribute the attainment of Group synergies and overall goals.

A management 'model'

In summary, the main components of our management philosophy are:

- An organized and coherent Group, with shared values and clear strategies, well-defined procedures, systems and rules
- Confidence in a decentralized and participative management process with managers who lead by example, take initiatives and who want to contribute to the overall success of the Group

Figure 2 Lafarge's management style – The Lafarge Way
Source: Lafarge. (n.d.). Internal company document. Paris: Author.

key-post management, development of high potential, internationalization, language skills, compensation and benefits, management development and training, postmerger integration, organizational development, employment, and safety and working conditions. The level of HR involvement in the development, redesign, and implementation of process changes, however, varied widely from one division to another, one business unit to another, and one region to another, reflecting Lafarge's regional business management approach. For example, the major focus in Asia was on business development, transfer of best practices, and quick integration of the acquired companies. In Europe and the United States, support was provided largely through delivery of training, while in Africa, many of the change-oriented activities were integrated with or led by HR.

Implementing this process of HR redesign throughout the Group required uniform operating mechanisms that were emphasized and communicated worldwide through published policies such as the *Lafarge HR Group Policy Manual and Career Management Manual.* In the words of the chairman, the priorities in the field of human resources were twofold – enhancing performance and investing in people. Lafarge plans to raise their investment in training by setting up a Group training program that will be an extension of the 'Meet the Group' (Figure 3) integration seminar and to complement training packages run by the divisions and business units. Lafarge intends to standardize career interviews for managers once every three or four years, on the occasion of every transfer. Together with the above training programs, Lafarge is also working on the leadership profiles that the Group needs.

After more than 20 years, the 'Meet the Group' seminar has been given fresh impetus and will now reflect the growing size of the Group. The new program, which will be identical on every continent, takes the 'Lafarge Way' as its central thread. These seminars target managers who have been in their jobs for between 6 and 18 months, whether they are recently recruited or have been promoted internally, along with managers who come into the Group as a result of an acquisition. The objective is to enable them to acquire a better knowledge and understanding of all the Group's businesses, the challenges it faces and its priorities for the future, to identify ways of implementing the Lafarge Way concretely, to help with the improvement of businesses by making use of Group best practices, and to develop a network beyond the frontiers of their own Business Unit and their Division people.

What has changed?
The new formula is highly interactive and is based on the participation of the group members, who are the leading players in their own training. Each session is sponsored by an operational manager who is the seminar leader, representing the Group and participating throughout the 3-day program, assisted by a professional facilitator.

The program is built on the following sequences: 'Getting to know the Group,' 'Knowing the products and their applications,' 'The Lafarge manager' (a team leader and change agent, HR and career manager), 'Improving the performance of our businesses,' and 'Creating value.' After an 'Exchange with the Direction Générale,' the seminar ends with a sequence called 'Proposals for the future.'

Figure 3 Induction program – 'Meet the Group'
Source: Lafarge. (n.d.). Internal company document. Paris: Author.

HR at Lafarge

Fundamentals of the redesign of HR infrastructure

The HR community at Lafarge has been widely identified as the single most important department in leading change efforts internally and externally, most of which have come about largely as a result of successful integration of acquired companies.

The structure of HR at Lafarge has five layers: (1) headquarters-based corporate HR, (2) divisional HR – cement, aggregates and concrete, roofing, and gypsum, (3) regional HR, (4) country HR, and (5) plant HR. The plant HR is usually run by the local personnel supervised by the country HR (preferably from the same country but belonging to the HR network of Lafarge). The country HR reports to the regional HR manager. To achieve this goal, HR functions follow an integrated and aligned approach toward (1) recruitment, selection, and induction, (2) retraining and redeployment, (3) a performance appraisal system, (4) a compensation and reward mechanism, (5) rightsizing, and (6) integration.

Recruitment, selection, and induction

Lafarge competes for the best people in the labor market with a long-term view. It recruits diversified and international profiles, which have a potential to evolve. HR believes that career development is the responsibility of both the individual and of the Group. The recruitment function is decentralized. The HR directors of the regions take the initiatives, as they understand the local and regional markets better. The central recruitment department recruits staff for the headquarters in Paris.

The establishment of the Group in a number of newly industrialized countries (India, Korea, Egypt, Jordan, the Philippines, etc.) is a source for a rich knowledge pool of international expertise and experiences. Employees of increasingly varied nationalities are being recruited, and international mobility in career paths is being stepped up. These two factors will help to promote future growth and build up a pool of international managers trained to be business heads of Lafarge.

Seminars are organized, as a part of the induction program (Figure 3), on a regular basis in all five continents in the context of integration of newly acquired companies. Similarly, 400 recently hired managers participated in the 'Meet the Group' seminar. These meetings are organized with the aim of presenting the Group, its values, its strategy, and its way of functioning.

Lafarge has special recruitment processes under three categories, which started in 1996:

1 Junior high potentials – under the age of 40 and can reach the level of general manager before 41 years. (The 'junior high potentials,' according to the director of HR, are loosely defined as 'those who will be the international managers of the Group in the future.' Identified high potentials, if French, would invariably have a background from École Polytechnique, French 'Grandes Écoles,' or École Nationalé d'Administration, and, for non-French personnel, preferably would be educated at one of the globally respected business schools in the United States, Europe, or Asia.)

2 High potentials – over 40 years and can reach the level of general managers by the age of 45.

3 Viviers – those who are under training in a mature country (like France, Spain, the United States, Brazil, Germany, or Austria) to inherit a particular position. The vivier policy allows new units to rapidly develop their competencies in different areas. The viviers can either be newly hired people or internal resources, generally trained outside the unit. Mature or existing units further develop their resources to assist in the development of the groups, complementing their immediate needs by proactive recruitment.

There is scope in Lafarge for internship and apprenticeship. The business school-to-company relationship has been forged over time as an ongoing initiative. Lafarge is in direct contact with the student population through a number of openings such as student fairs, presentations in colleges by Lafarge managers, and paid internships. Lafarge also offers limited-duration contracts to fresh graduates to provide them with professional experience, which also gives the Group a chance to talent-spot future managers.

Retraining and redeployment

Lafarge has also done a good job in retraining and redeploying people. With 50% of its employees joining the Group through different acquisitions across the globe, redeployment was a necessity in order to share and train the Lafarge Way. For retraining and redeployment, Lafarge targets all its employees and looks for both technical expertise and management perspective – the ability to work in cross-cultural teams, the ability to listen and to lead, language skills, adaptability to new environments, and an open mind-set to think in international terms. The company believes that it would be difficult to fit into the Lafarge Way without these attributes.

In addition to general training programs, specific training programs and opportunities are decided upon during the yearly appraisal and career management of individuals. The corporate headquarters, the divisions, and the business units share the training responsibilities.

Before the redesign of the HR functions, Lafarge had different training policies for top management, middle management, and lower management. The training program for top management was under the corporate HR, which identified and provided individualized training schedules in top business schools under the executive development programs. The training programs for middle management were looked after by the respective divisions (cement, aggregate, etc.). Workers were given training at the plant level. After the redesign of HR in 1999, Lafarge now follows the learning organization methodology with an emphasis on learning on the job, learning from within the group, and coaching in the field. This is done through formation of networks and by internal consultancy. The training managers act as facilitators of learning and development and help managers to learn and cooperate on the job. Some of the examples of the new training policy are to talk about dreams, send invites for training objectives, and make the managers feel that they are responsible. The training program today wants to boost performance, the real challenge being how training changes the way people work and how it influences the business results. In the words of the director of training:

> We have to understand that we are an international organization and not the old French organization taking over companies all over the world like colonizing countries. Since we are growing, we have to find ways of learning and sharing the knowledge that comes with every acquisition. Budget is an important parameter and the new policy is to learn as much from the diverse experience that the Group has from its acquired companies. There is a lot of mobility in the Group. There are 400 expatriates all over the globe with 150 of international status. Usually the newly acquired companies wait and watch instead of working with a clean slate to harness benefits from Lafarge's huge wealth of resources by putting forward their competencies and best practices. This is where the learning will take place.

The retraining and redeployment cycle is critical in Lafarge. Redeployment is linked to career development, which means that an international assignment (see Figure 4 for the process of internationalization) is taken as a career development tool rather than a reward. Expatriation or a transfer within the Group is meant to be a career move and taken as a means to gather international experience for further career growth. Compensation increases with an expatriation assignment. Employees are recruited for the home country because the Group wants to develop local people to work locally after gaining international experience if required. The home unit pays for all the costs including expatriation and training. For units still undergoing restoration (i.e., not yet up to division performance standards), requirements for the development of competencies are even more important. The newly acquired units will have to identify the necessary competencies required to be able to replace the expatriates present in their units.

Why Internationalize?

Internationalization is an essential strategic element. Its aim is to:

- Bring together the human resources necessary to take in hand the new activities and developments of the Group and the search for new opportunities. Taking into account our development objectives, we want to double the number of managers in international situations in the next five years.
- Diffuse accumulated know-how and expertise throughout the Group's diverse operating units.
- Integrate men and women of different nationalities, origins and professions.
- Develop a management style based on networking in the different domains of the company's management.
- Increase the awareness, within our management ranks, including non-expatriates, of the 'international' reality of the Group's strategy, activities, and way of functioning.

Whom to Internationalize?

- Internationalization must be a success not only for the Group but for the person who is internationalized.
- Expatriates for international assignments should have a desire to go overseas and have a recognized level of performance. The priority is to offer career development opportunities to managers and experts who have an important development potential.
- Internationalization is not only reserved for technical people.
- It is also important to diversify the origins (nationality and culture) of expatriates in order to have the necessary human resources in place, avoid the difficulties of reinsertion in the home country, and make up international teams who have good local roots.
- Internationalization also concerns the expatriate's family.

How to Internationalize?

- The Group has made a policy decision to encourage international exposure to as large a number of employees as possible.
  Internationalization can take many diverse forms depending on the objective required:
- Classic expatriation for 3–5 year period in respect to career development
- Expatriation to professionals in order to respond to precise operational needs due to international needs of the Group
- Assignments of reasonably short duration.

Figure 4 Internationalization

Performance appraisal system

Lafarge has recently tried to integrate the performance management system (PMS) and personal development plan (Figure 5) with the other elements (recruitment, selection,

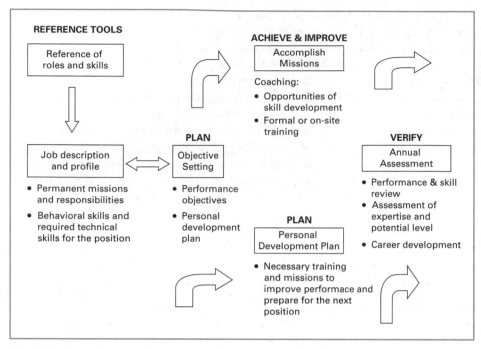

Figure 5 Individual assessment methodology: appraisal and personal development plan
Source: Lafarge. (n.d.). Internal company document. Paris: Author.

training, and compensation) of the HR system. From 1998, it has increased its emphasis on PMS and its linkage to career development. This has been the key focus area within Lafarge's new bonus plan, which started in 1999. All the HR directors from different divisions formed a central team, which is responsible for decision making regarding the implementation of the redesigned HR policies and, specifically, PMS.

Like many organizations, Lafarge has shifted from a 180-degree performance appraisal system to a 360-degree performance appraisal system for key positions including senior managers and 'cadres.' Performance is reviewed according to set objectives. To deal with any potential negative consequences arising from the process, the corporate and divisional HR departments provide coaching and training to deal with negative feedback. Overall, this process has worked well at the administrative level, but some managers think that PMS is an American concept and more effective coaching and training is needed to accustom French managers to provide and receive direct feedback.

Compensation and reward mechanism

Lafarge believes that a strong compensation-performance relationship is an essential element of a strategy that relies on people as a source of competitive advantage. Lafarge wants to attract, motivate, and retain talented people by providing competitive total remuneration (base pay, variable pay, and benefits). Lafarge's compensation policy is to target total cash compensation (base salary and bonus) between the median and upper quartile of relevant companies. Lafarge follows the Hay Scale in its compensation policy.

To support the strategy of continual performance improvement and value creation, a new bonus plan has been implemented for managers. It introduced a set of new elements, such as (1) use of EVA (economic value added) as a financial performance indicator (2) a greater focus on long-term value creation through the introduction of a long-term bonus and (3) a significant increase in the maximum bonus percentage, to allow differentiation between average performance and excellent performance. The bonus plan consists of two components – the annual bonus and the long-term bonus. The annual bonus is split into two equal parts, where one part is based on the financial success measured through EVA for the year and the rest of the bonus is based on yearly personal objectives. The personal objectives are based on the SMART methodology (specific, measurable, accountable, realistic, and time). Based on financial and personal targets that aim to foster operational excellence in each of Lafarge's businesses, the new plan has been designed to accord recognition to superior performances and forms part of a policy of equitable and competitive global remuneration.

A new employee shareholding scheme (ESOP) called *Lafarge* en action 99 was launched to give many employees the opportunity of becoming Lafarge shareholders, and 21,000 employees located in 33 countries participated, bringing total employee shareholders up to 28,000.

Rightsizing

Lafarge does not believe in downsizing but instead believes in an optimum workforce and invests in absorbing the excess workforce. Once the internal skills are developed in newly acquired units, redeployment schemes are offered. The employment units are a resource for counseling, outplacement, or retraining in order to acquire a new professional qualification. All employees who wish to start their own businesses are helped to do so at every stage, until completion of their project. Similarly, job creation is initiated and supervised by internal Lafarge teams. For example, in Romania, there were 8,000 workers in three plants. With Lafarge practices in place, the workforce is now reduced to 2,500. Most of the workers who acquired new skill sets were relocated to other plants in Central and Eastern Europe. Optimization was achieved by subcontracting peripheral jobs such as regular cleaning and maintenance.

Innovation and research and development: a storehouse of best practices

Lafarge is considered a storehouse of best practices and specialists who are the best in the industry. The specialists of the cement industry are in the CTI, the technical center of Lafarge under the cement performance department (DPC). The technical expertise is distributed in a two-tier structure – the central laboratory, which provides a source for the pooling of scientific knowledge and the development synergies between materials, and the decentralized network of over 25 applications laboratories supplemented by division, business, and unit technical centers. The technical expertise is divided further into three professional fields of manufacturing, technical support, and research and development. The technical experts are from 16 areas of expertise – geology, quarry management, process, manufacturing, product quality, cement applications, engineering (mechanical/electrical), control, industrial process automation, maintenance, management of engineering projects, project design and studies, technical economic audits, performance audits, and environment. The cement performance department coordinates the technical expertise with the departments of investment, industrial performance, knowledge management, process, technology, and products.

Corporate social responsibility and environmental protection

Lafarge places a high value on corporate social responsibility through the wealth it produces, the jobs it creates, the training it provides, or the community-oriented social, educational, and cultural initiatives that it supports. Lafarge actively participates in the development of communities that surround its employees. It is on this principle that Lafarge has founded its employment policy. For example, in October 2000, Hurricane Mitch battered Honduras and neighboring countries in Central America with torrential rains. The Direction Générale at Lafarge decided to make an initial emergency donation, and at the request of scores of employees, an appeal fund was launched enabling the Group's personnel to contribute some 190,000 euros ($200,000) to the emergency relief effort. Of the total 5,000 tons of cement donated by the Group, 1,500 tons were used by nongovernmental organizations for reconstruction, while 3,500 tons were handed over to a national foundation, Maria, which was headed by Maria Flores, the wife of the president of Honduras, to enable a hospital to be built.

Lafarge has also signed a partnership agreement with the WWF (World Wildlife Fund) to contribute to the protection of biodiversity and to raise awareness levels. Lafarge is in fact the first industrial group to sign an agreement of this type.

Challenges facing the redesign of HR at Lafarge

Maintaining the change management

While Lafarge faced a number of issues in 2002, the most important concern was how to sustain the internal change process. Lafarge's large-scale acquisitions in China, India, South Korea, Indonesia, Malaysia, and the Philippines, as well as the Blue Circle acquisition, stirred some concerns about the difficulties of working across different cultures, different languages, and different mind-sets.

Aligning with the overall business strategy of the company of growth and performance, the key challenge for HR, according to the vice president of HR is to support international growth, keeping in mind the professional and technical skill sets required by the Group. Huge effort has been put in place to hire the right people and improve their international capability. Encouragement and reward mechanisms are in place for both career and personal development through promoting, training, and coaching. The effective linkage between HR and business strategy is being constantly maintained and upgraded by means of the HR action plan at the corporate level. The HR action plan states the business needs of the individual HR business units. The cumulative plan of the different HR business units throughout the globe is reviewed to form the three-year action plan to match with the mid- and long-term strategy of the company.

The momentum of change leads to the creation of divisions. But sometimes it is felt that the role of the corporate HR and the division HR are somewhat diffused. Better integrating mechanisms between the corporate HR and the division HR are being debated. One of the senior vice presidents reflected that, overall, the HR policies and practices of the Lafarge Group are excellent and can perhaps not only be compared to the best in the industry but to the best companies in the world. What remains to be done is quick diffusion and implementation of those policies and practices.

Substantial steps have been taken in the HR redesign process, like the use of dual language within the Group. The common background of engineering or technical education of most of the top-management team was in itself a language of sorts. Extensive internal and external communication within the Group and, above all, Lafarge's continuous policy of respect and care for its employees could serve as a path to manage the transition and transformation of Lafarge from a local French cement company to a global leader.

Fast and effective postacquisition integration of acquired companies and transfer of best practices

One of the regional presidents described the overall view of the HR role in postacquisition integration:

> HR is a scarce resource for achieving success. It is more so when companies have to be integrated into Lafarge. Lafarge would like to see the acquired companies integrated as fast as possible to give returns on its investments. Often there is a wide gap in what was perceived and the reality that one encounters in the acquired companies. One has to look into the style of management, hire new blood, and train them. There is a lot of pressure during the implementation stage, and the wide gap between theory and practice is felt acutely during this process. Integration has a key role to play as it has direct linkages with the capital deployed and the ROI, which in turn is directly linked to improving operations, creating value and its reflection in the stock exchanges.

Postacquisition integration at Lafarge means getting a new unit to attain the performance levels fixed at the time of the investment, to meet Lafarge standards of operational excellence, and to assimilate an acquired company within the Group's fold to attain the Lafarge standard of performance. The redesign of the HR function in the Group witnessed the creation of an integration department in 1999 headed by an integration director, and the creation of an integration manual and an integration toolkit. The integration toolkit will provide the newly acquired companies with full information about the Lafarge Way and the best practices in areas like maintenance, HR, organization, safety, environment, process, quality, logistics, and in business functions like communication, marketing and sales, control and information technology (IT), purchasing, and technical centers.

From the HR point of view, postacquisition integration is a crucial issue. The director of integration expressed that the key success factor in a postacquisition integration phase is to keep the right balance between the transfer of softer skills such as shared values and culture and harder skill sets such as technical excellence. The right balance is critical to the success of an integration mission.

Lafarge culture is predominantly French, as its roots are French. But during postacquisition integration, Lafarge feels that the culture and values of the acquired company cannot be ignored. This feeling portrays that *shared culture* is perhaps more critical than putting the systems, procedures, policies, and practices in place. Once the shared culture is taken into consideration and there is enough respect for the acquired company by placing trust in good and talented people, the rest of the system processes are not too difficult to implement. Lafarge best practices can be transferred smoothly to make the unit on par with Lafarge standards.

While the integration department is new, Lafarge's primary concern is to find the right balance between a fast and a slow postacquisition integration process. The ongoing debate seems to be the choice between the fast, harsh, and forceful way of integration that one of Lafarge's competitors practices and the original Lafarge Way of integrating acquired companies. Historically integration by the Lafarge Way has been a slow process. Lafarge, after acquisition, starts the integration process by speaking to all the stakeholders and tries to incorporate an action plan. When the rules of the game are put in place, Lafarge invites the acquired company to play the game together according to the rules. Some of the concern is that too much time is spent on minute details, technical matters, and transfer of best practices, which results in delay in achieving the bottom line. For example, Lafarge gives a 10–15-year horizon and a long-term commitment for plowback, compared to its closest competitor, which has a 5–10-year cycle. But the general view at Lafarge is that there is enough room for local people and local culture to be integrated within the Group's fold. Also, Lafarge does not believe in firing people – it takes time to find out ways and means to invest again to absorb the excess workforce (for example as has been done in Poland, Germany, and Czechoslovakia). One of the regional presidents commented that Germany had been very well integrated by the slow process and that the country manager did a very good job together with the then regional president. Good integration has been possible in Spain, Brazil, Czechoslovakia, Poland, and Austria. With the business environment becoming harsh and fierce competition in the industry, Lafarge has to quickly heed this issue in the near future.

Attracting and retaining a diverse workforce through their internationalization program

Perhaps the biggest challenge for HR is to keep pace with Lafarge's growth strategy in its quest to shift from a French cement company to a global leader in the building-construction industry. This shift requires an ability not just to respond to business-strategy requirements, but to understand global business trends so that HR can work in partnership with top-management objectives to recruit the right people, train them with the right skills, develop the right mind-set, and navigate growth opportunities profitably and efficiently. HR believes that a productive environment built upon its strong culture and values will enhance its ability to attract and retain talent.

The challenge the company faces is the fast rate of expansion and the ability to keep pace with incoming people from the acquired units, determine their placement, and at the same time do strategic recruitment without getting overstaffed or understaffed in the process. While Lafarge has made significant progress in this area, some managers feel that there are not enough HR interventions regarding recruitment of bright people in comparison to the pace at which the Group is growing. Due to lack of talent in some specific areas, integration of the newly acquired companies perhaps takes too much time.

Lessons for redesigning the HRM function

Clearly, the implications of the Lafarge case study (and the experience of other large corporations) revolve around the ability to redesign the HRM function and align it to the overall business strategy of the organization. Notwithstanding the limitations of the study (noted below), the present study holds a number of lessons that are potentially important for researchers and practitioners, who are, or will be, trying to redesign HRM functions in the years to come.

Lafarge's successful redesigning of its HRM function speaks consistently of top management's commitment toward change and constant internal and external communication with its stakeholders regarding the change process. The philosophies at Lafarge (*Principles of Action* and *The Lafarge Way*) have been successfully transformed to HRM practices. Thus, the first implication of this study is that *deep top-management commitment and constant communication of that commitment are the key links to transform philosophies (mission, vision, goals, and business strategy) into practices.*

The second implication focuses on *the importance of alignment or fit of the redesigned HR strategy with the overall business strategy of the organization.* HRM function at Lafarge has been successfully redesigned to fit the overall ambition of Lafarge (*Principles of Action*).

The third implication of the case study is that *HR must design and redesign effective methods to anticipate business needs and provide strong leadership.* Finding the right balance between corporate, divisional, regional, country, and local HR issues is critical within the framework of today's highly competitive internal and external environment. For HR to design effective methods and provide strong leadership, appropriate skills and competencies are required: to know the business, to know how to translate the business needs to HR goals, to manage uncertainties by being present in the market, to forecast changes, and to be able to integrate and grow to create value in terms of human potential.

The fourth implication focuses on *the effort of the organization to expand the role of HR to that of a strategic partner and a change agent, without sacrificing the traditional role of HR (administrative expert and employee champion).* This finding is supported by the studies of Ulrich (1997) and later Becker and Huselid (1999).

As a corollary to the fourth implication, the fifth implication *reinforces the role of HR in change management and explains how HR can redesign itself and the organization to create a culture that supports the change process and spearheads the change momentum.*

The sixth and the final implication follows from the resource-based view, which argues that having unique, inimitable resources and the effective deployment of these resources are key to achieving sustained competitive advantage (Barney, 1991). *Competitive advantage through people and culturally entrenched HR practices is difficult to achieve and even more difficult to sustain, but once achieved, it is not easy to duplicate.* Here it is important to mention that redesigning the collective competencies of an entire HRM function is a Herculean task that requires the effective cooperation of the line managers, credibility of the redesign process, and the willingness of the HRM department to actively pursue the redesign process. As any change process suggests, generating short-term wins to consolidate gains and produce more change anchors the new approaches in the culture (Kotter, 1995).

There are, inevitably, limitations to this study. The lessons are, of course, based on the data of a single case study and there is a problem of generalizability.

Conclusion

This case study explained how an organization redesigns its human resource function to help provide a source of competitive advantage to keep up with the accelerating pace of change in the external and internal environments. As HR becomes more aligned to the business needs of organizations it becomes a competence that organizations can leverage to provide sustaining value to the needs of the organization. Three specific needs identified for Lafarge were to maintain the change momentum, create a fast and effective postacquisition integration mechanism for acquired companies and for the transfer of best practices, and attract and retain a diverse workforce through their internationalization program.

ASHOK SOM is an assistant professor of international strategy management at ESSEC Business School, Paris. He holds a PhD from the Indian Institute of Management (IIM), Ahmedabad, and M.Tech and M.Sc from the Indian Institute of Technology (IIT), Kharagpur. His current research and consulting activities focus on the role of strategy in shaping human resource practices, creation and evolution of organizational capabilities and performance during organizational design/restructuring process, cross-cultural integration and HRM innovations within firms. He has published in the *International Journal of Human Resource Development and Management, Keio Business Forum* (forthcoming) and in international conference proceedings. He is a recipient of awards such as Best Research Proposal Award, Aditya Birla (India) Center, London Business School, and McKinsey Wings of Excellence Award, University of St. Gallen, Switzerland. He is currently the country representative of France at the international management division of the Academy of Management.

References

Alldredge, M. E., & Nilan, K. J. (2000). 3M's leadership competency model: An internally developed solution. Human Resource Management, 39, 133–145.

Barney, J. (1991). Firm resources and sustained competitive advantage. Journal of Management, 17, 99–120.

Bartlett, C. A., & Ghoshal, S. (2002). Building competitive advantage through people. MIT Sloan Management Review, 43(2), 34–41.

Becker, B., & Gerhart, B. (1996). The impact of human resource management on organizational performance: Progress and prospects. Academy of Management Journal, 39, 779–801.

Becker, B., & Huselid, M. A. (1998). HR as a source of shareholder value: Research and recommendations. Human Resource Management, 36, 39–47.

Becker, B., & Huselid, M. A. (1999). Strategic human resource management in five leading firms. Human Resource Management, 38, 287–301.

Blancero, D., Boroski, J., & Dyer, L. (1996). Key competencies for a transformed human resource organization: Results of a field study. Human Resource Management, 35, 383–403.

Delaney, J. T., & Huselid, M. A. (1996). The impact of human resource management practices on perceptions of organizational performance. Academy of Management Journal, 39, 949–969.

Eisenhardt, K. (1995). Building theories from case study research. In G. Huber & A. Van de Ven (Eds.), Longitudinal field research methods. Thousand Oaks, CA: Sage.

Forbringer, L., & Oeth, C. (1998). Human resources at Mercantile Bank Corporation Inc.: A critical analysis. Human Resource Management, 37, 177–189.

Gerhart, B. (1999). Human resource management and firm performance: Challenges in making causal inferences. Research in Personnel and Human Resource Management, 4, 31–51.

Hallowell, R. (1996). Southwest Airlines: A case study linking employee needs satisfaction and organizational capabilities to competitive advantage. Human Resource Management, 35, 513–534.

Huselid, M. (1995). The impact of human resource management practices on turnover, productivity and corporate financial performance. Academy of Management Journal, 38, 635–672.

Huselid, M., Jackson, S., & Schuler, R. (1997). Technical and strategic human resource management effectiveness as determinants of firm performance. Academy of Management Journal, 40, 171–188.

Kesler, G. C. (1995). A model and process for redesigning the HRM role, competencies, and work in a major multinational corporation. Human Resource Management, 34, 229–252.

Kochanski, J., & Randall, P. M. (1994). Rearchitecting the human resources function at Northern Telecom. Human Resource Management, 33, 299–315.

Kotter, P. J. (1995, March/April). Leading change: Why transformation efforts fail. Harvard Business Review, 55–67.

Martell, K., & Carroll, S. J. (1995). How strategic is HRM? Human Resource Management, 34, 253–267.

Pfeffer, J. (1994, Winter). Competitive advantage through people. California Management Review, 9–28.

Schuler, R. S. (1992). Linking the people with the strategic needs of the business. Organizational Dynamics, 21(1), 18–32.

Shafer, R. A., Dyer, L., Kilty, J., Amos, J., & Ericksen, J. (2001). Crafting a human resource strategy to foster organizational agility: A case study. Human Resource Management, 40, 197–211.

Truss, C. (2001). Complexities and controversies in linking HRM with organizational outcomes. Journal of Management Studies, 38, 1121–1149.

Ulrich, D. (1997). Human resource champions: The next agenda for adding value and delivering results. Boston: Harvard Business School Press.

Ulrich, D. (1998, January/February). A new mandate for human resources. Harvard Business Review, 124–134.

Ulrich, D., Brockbank, W., Yeung, A. K., & Lake, D. G. (1995). Human resource competencies: An empirical assessment. Human Resource Management, 34, 473–495.

Wright, P. M., McCormick, B., Sherman, W., & McMahan, G. (1999). The role of human resource practices in petro-chemical refinery performance. International Journal of Human Resource Management, 10, 321–335.

Wright, P. M., & McMahan, G. C. (1992). Theoretical perspective for strategic human resource management. Journal of Management, 18, 295–320.

Yin, R. (1994). Case study research: Design and methods. London: Sage.

CASE 6: RESTRUCTURING OF CANAL PLUS: THE BEGINNING OF A NEW ERA

Bertrand Méheut, CEO of the Canal Plus group, was reflecting on the positive results he was about to announce to the press. In 2003, with 135,000 new subscribers in France, Canal Plus had reached a total of 8.1 million subscribers. The increase in the number of customers came from both the premium channel (in 2004 – the best result since 1994) and of Canal Satellite, the digital version of Canal Plus, which had 230,000 new subscribers in 2003.

Appointed in July 2002, first as COO of the company then as CEO, Bertrand Méheut was satisfied with the work he and his top management team had accomplished. In a short period of time, they had successfully managed to restructure the French TV group, which had had a history of being non-conventional. The restructuring affected all areas of the company, from strategic marketing to human resources, from facility management to promotional strategies. They successfully stabilized the management, divested non-profitable subsidiaries, introduced new and attractive programmes, right-sized costs … all in only 18 months.

However, despite the positive results, there were continuous rumours about the possible sale of Canal Plus by its main shareholder Vivendi Universal. The entire European media industry was keen to secure a slice of the Canal Plus pie.

Company background

In 1984, André Rousselet launched the first private TV channel in France when viewers there were unhappy with the existing channels, and were ready to pay to see attractive and exclusive programmes dedicated to the French market.

His first success was in convincing the French authorities to allow the future Canal Plus to secure a terrestrial feed. He then gathered around him talented specialists in TV programming. From the start, Canal Plus aired two different kinds of programmes. The first type, also the major part of Canal Plus, was encrypted and accessible only to subscribers. The second type was the six-hour-per-day free programming that the channel was required by the French state to broadcast.

To attract more subscribers, the channel from its inception strived to be different from the other TV channels. André Rousselet focused on pleasing French viewers by offering three specific types of programme: entertainment programmes, highlighting humour and creativity, exclusive movies, and sports (particularly the French Football League).

Frédéric Vaulpré, Director, Studio Canal Video and alumni of the ESSEC EMBA programme, wrote this case under the supervision of Ashok Som. It is intended to be used as a basis for class discussion rather than to illustrate either an effective or ineffective handling of a business situation.

In addition to this new product mix, the channel implemented an aggressive direct marketing policy, the likes of which had not been seen in the TV industry before. According to the founders of the channel, the key success factor was in establishing a strong relationship with the subscriber. At that time, direct marketing techniques were new among French companies and Canal Plus was a pioneer in this area by setting up one of the first call centres (called 'CAT' – Centre d'Accueil Téléphonique). In May 1986, Canal Plus boasted more than 1 million subscribers and, in 1987, more than 2 million households had a subscription. Canal Plus was seen as one of the fastest-growing success stories of the media industry.

The television channel industry

The television industry has developed into an intriguing worldwide business with local specificities, different strategies and a broad range of implementation issues (see Exhibit 6.1). Multinational media groups and local players have tried to balance their strategy between standardization and adaptation in this industry (see Exhibit 6.2) to gain market access. During the late 1980s, few multinational media groups existed and even fewer global brands in the television industry. Some of the best-known TV channels in the business are: news (CNN, BBC), sports (ESPN, Eurosport), music (Disney, MTV), documentaries (National Geographic Channel, Discovery), and business and finance (Bloomberg, CNBC).

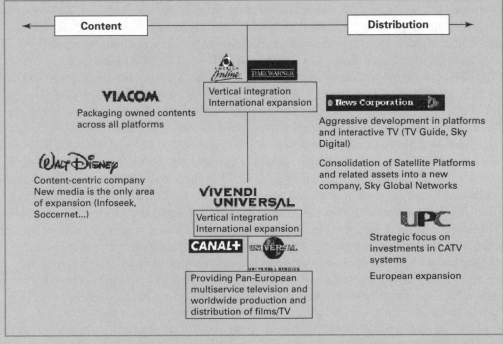

Exhibit 6.1 Major media companies: key strategies

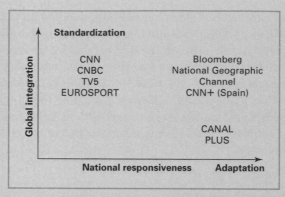

Exhibit 6.2 TV strategy: standardization vs adaption

In the news business, CNN (Cable News Network) was launched by Ted Turner in 1980 and was at that time available to 1.7 million households. But its specific content, tone and live coverage of the Gulf War in 1991 enabled the Atlanta-based group to build a worldwide leadership in the news segment. CNN was the first news channel that not only covered every event in the USA (i.e. a television version of radio's 'Voice of America'), but also delivered news about world events to the entire world – from the first Iraq war in 1991 to the student demonstration in Tiananmen Square in Beijing. CNN has been a leading player in Europe despite competition from other European networks. With approximately 25 news channels around the world, CNN can be seen in more than 200 countries. In Europe, CNN reaches more than 80 million households. By the end of the 1990s, competitors, both at the local and international levels, had emerged. Each country had its own national news channel (Fox News in the USA, Sky News in the UK, LCI in France, Nachrichten 24 in Germany, etc.) and some international channels started broadcasting 24-hour live news, like EuroNews, BBC World and Al Jazeera.

In the sports segment, Disney, a major player in terms of an international network of channels, owns ESPN, which was a pioneer in the world of sports broadcasting. The company was the leading cable sports broadcaster with seven domestic networks in the USA, including its flagship ESPN, ESPN2 (sporting events, news and original programming), ESPN Classic (historical sports footage), ESPN HD and ESPNEWS (24-hour news and information), and reaches more than 89 million American homes. It also reaches another 190 countries through ESPN International. ESPN has tried to adapt its channels by implementing a 'glocal' approach. ESPN Classic Sport, which launched its first European Channel in France in 2002, has now covered most of the key countries in continental Europe, from Italy to Spain. Though the channel broadcasts with a similar format, a homogeneous design and a standard programme grid, each channel has developed some local flavour and customer responsiveness, such as '*Platini week*' in France or '*The best of Juventus Football Club*' in Italy. This 'glocal' approach was in response to an increase in competition, particularly in Europe, and a need to adapt to different markets. The main competitor of ESPN in Europe has been Eurosport, an encrypted channel exclusively available on cable and digital satellite. Eurosport from the beginning offered extensive coverage of the most prominent national and international sports (football, tennis, golf and skiing). Eurosport reaches more than 95 million European homes and 250 million viewers in 54 countries. Additionally, one of the major strengths of Eurosport is that a large majority of European viewers can watch their favourite sports in their native languages.

The news and sports channels are followed by the music channels in popularity. In this field, MTV Networks, a subsidiary of Viacom, owns and operates cable networks like MTV, VH1 and Nickelodeon. Since Viacom acquired CBS, MTV Networks also houses CBS's former cable properties CMT (Country Music Television) and Spike TV (formerly the New TNN, renamed after a long court battle that was settled with film director Spike Lee). Other channels include Comedy Central and TV Land. The company operates MTV Films in association with sister firm Paramount Pictures. MTV Networks also licenses consumer products based on its brands. MTV channels today have a worldwide presence on all major cable and satellite operators.

Documentary channels have been an area where TV channels have been competing fiercely. The two major players are the National Geographic and Discovery Channels. Supported by the National Geographic Society based in Washington, National Geographic Channel (NGC) benefits from a unique brand that is synonymous with quality programmes designed to 'provide intelligent, factual and entertaining content across several key genres, such as adventure and exploration, human origins, natural phenomena, travel, science and technology, and wildlife'. With such a credo, NGC is available in more than 230 million homes in 153 countries on 5 continents and in 27 languages. The channel boasts a monthly audience of more than 120 million people, 58 million of whom are considered 'upscale' individuals.

The main competitor of NGC, the Discovery Channel, started its operations in June 1985 with 156,000 subscribers in the USA. Today, Discovery has grown to have operations in more than 160 countries and 1.3 billion cumulative subscribers. Discovery's more than 90 networks of distinctive programming represent 25 network entertainment brands, including TLC, Animal Planet, Travel Channel, Discovery Health Channel, Discovery Kids, Discovery Times Channel, The Science Channel, Military Channel, Discovery Home Channel, Discovery en Español, Discovery Kids En Español, Discovery HD Theater, FitTV, Discovery Travel & Living (Viajar y Vivir), Discovery Home & Health and Discovery Real Time. Other channels consist of Discovery Education and Discovery Commerce, which operates 120 Discovery Channel stores. Discovery also distributes BBC America in the United States.

Among business and finance news channels with worldwide broadcasting are Bloomberg Television and CNBC. Bloomberg TV developed its network due to its experience in financial and corporate analysis by its finance specialists working for the 'Bloomberg Terminal' (the popular database and screen used in every market room across the world by traders, fund managers and bankers). Bloomberg's management positioned and advertised its network channels as 'thought globally, impacted locally'. The Bloomberg network comprises more than 20 channels worldwide. In Europe, it had a predefined strategy that was set in motion in 1997 when it launched its first pan-European channel in English, which focused mainly on the London Stock Exchange. This catered to the UK and other English-speaking countries (particularly the Nordic

▶ countries). After the launch of this channel, Bloomberg expanded with a French and a German channel. By 2003, the 'big five' western European countries (France, Germany, Italy, Spain and the UK) had their own language-specific channels, focusing both on international and local markets, and also on international and domestic companies. This approach enabled Bloomberg to gain better advertising leverage than CNBC which could not count on local advertising campaigns because CNBC is a sister company of NBC, one of the largest US TV networks. CNBC had worldwide coverage but the channel catered to English-speaking audiences and focused mainly on American-British companies.

The Canal Plus business model, however, was different from its very inception. Even though it followed the historical model of a French channel, each country had replicated and differentiated the model simultaneously. The replication and differentiation were possible because each channel was based on two key programmes: sport (mainly football) and movies, as TV viewers from different countries had different requirements. For example, a viewer in Madrid and a viewer in Warsaw might request the same sport offering (football, for example) but they might not agree to the same movie being aired (with the exception of Hollywood hits). Other examples highlighting this specificity are the famous *Muppets* (*Les Guignols*), and the fact that adult movies were never introduced to the Polish channel to avoid offending the cultural sentiments of Polish viewers.

Competitor groups in the TV industry

News Corporation: Rupert Murdoch, born in Melbourne, Australia, founded News Corp. Now a US citizen, Murdoch manages his News Corporation Limited, which had an asset base of approximately $52 billion and annual revenue of approximately $19 billion by 2004.

A diversified international media and entertainment company, News Corporation had operations in eight segments of the industry: film entertainment, television, cable network programming, direct broadcast satellite television, magazines, newspapers, publishing and others. News Corp is spread over five continents, namely North America, Europe (Continental Europe and the United Kingdom), Australia, Asia (including the Pacific). In the direct broadcast satellite television segment, News Corp is the world leader, holding five main digital platforms: BSkyB, Direct TV, Fox Tel, Sky Italia and Star Asia.

British Sky Broadcasting service (**BSkyB**) and its subsidiaries operate the leading pay TV broadcasting service in the United Kingdom and Ireland. Sky's main objective was to build upon its position as the leading provider of multi-channel television services in the UK and Ireland in order to deliver long-term growth in shareholder value. Sky wanted to achieve this expansion in two ways: through acquisition of new DTH subscribers and through the maintenance of a low churn rate. In June 2003, the number of DTH satellite subscribers in the UK and Ireland was 6,845,000, representing a net increase of 744,000 that year. Sky achieved its target of 7 million subscribers by the end of 2003.

Direct TV is the largest multi-digital channel service provider and the second largest pay TV distributor in the USA, with more than 12.2 million subscribers and $970 million in profit in 2003. It is distributed over 850 digital video and audio channels. Direct TV enhanced its content with the use of News Corp and Fox News resources in order to offer a wide range of choices. The cable operators posed heavy competition in the industry, but Direct TV had inherent advantages over cable, such as national coverage, greater flexibility and lower costs. Besides the American core business, Direct TV Latin America had emerged from bankruptcy with 1.5 million subscribers in 28 countries.

Fox Tel, Australia's leading subscription television provider, offered consumers the choice of more than 130 digital channels. Its distribution included both cable and satellite programming. Fox Tel commenced cable services in 1995, expanding to satellite distribution in 1999 and is available to more than 70 per cent of Australian homes. Fox Tel's strategy was to penetrate into areas where there was a lack of cable network. Fox Tel was connected to more than 1 million homes, but still had potential for growth as the market was largely dominated by cable. The argument to bring new customers from cable to satellite was that new technologies (DVRs, high-definition television and WiFi) adapt more easily to satellite than to cable. Fox Tel provided programming to other communication companies for distribution in metropolitan and regional Australia.

Star Asia is Asia's leading multi-platform content and service provider, with more than 40 distributed services in seven languages. It reaches more than 300 million viewers across 53 Asian countries. By the end of 1995, Star Asia was acquired by Rupert Murdoch and became a central part of his global media empire. Star Asia's audience was originally concentrated in Taiwan, China and India, but has steadily grown as its programming began to target other cultures and languages. All of Star's channels are advertisement driven and free. Star has been working with a strategy of providing regionally focused niche or genre-focused programming. In 2003, Star Asia had 1,700 employees and its coverage reached from the Arab world to South and East Asia.

Sky Italia was born through the merger between two broadcasting companies. The satellite companies were Stream, which had approximately 600,000–700,000 subscribers, and Telepiù, which had about 1.6 million subscribers (Canal Plus Group). Sky Italia was officially launched in July 2003. Its primary challenge was to secure the network as piracy was common in the Italian market. Some 600,000 viewers have subscribed to Sky Italia since July 2003. However, according to some newspapers, the codes have been broken again, which could force the company to change its terminals. In 2003, Sky Italia had more than 2.6 million subscribers, with a target of 3 million by the end of 2004. The strategy was similar to that of BSkyB – to create a monopoly over sports (Italian league) and movies.

News Corp and Rupert Murdoch were fiscally registered in Australia (due to tax benefits) even though 75 per cent of annual revenue was from News Corp, USA. The IRS put pressure on Murdoch and threatened to levy maximum fines on him, which led him to change his fiscal address to the United States. After targeting Rupert Murdoch as an individual, the IRS took aim at News Corp, which had decided to relocate to the USA (for the fiscal address and stock market listing). This decision had been approved by regulatory authorities and News Corp shareholders. According to News Corp, this decision would result in greater access to financial resources in the USA. However, the transfer had a cost and a significant impact on the company's annual profits.

TPS was founded in 1996 by TF1 (66 per cent) and M6 (34 per cent) to fill the growing need in the French pay TV market. In 2003, TPS had more than 1.2 million subscribers. Its core competence was to broadcast direct satellite and ADSL television.

▶ Soccer and movies were 'the golden spears' of TPS, intended to increase market share. This was possible due to business partnerships with several Hollywood major companies and the French soccer national league. They also provided financial support to the French movie industry. TPS's strategy was similar to that of BSkyB – to focus on movies and sports in order to provide a larger choice for subscribers. In addition to broadcasting activity, TPS had production activity, which made investments in programme development.

TPS Casting Activity broadcasts a large choice of channels, both thematic and general, and other services in order to target the audience as a family unit. However, due to existing contracts, the company focused mainly on soccer, broadcasting 242 games each year. Besides soccer, TPS also broadcast more than 1,000 movies a year, with some exclusivity. The commercialization was done through a network of official retailers granted by TPS.

TPS Production Activity: in addition to broadcasting, TPS produced and edited programmes and services in three main areas: movies (participation in French movies), sports, and programmes for kids. These programmes were broadcast exclusively on TPS satellite and cable. TPS also produced interactive services for its subscribers such as video games and email services. In 2004, 91 per cent of subscribers were using its interactive services, according to TPS.

In 2003, the French market was a competitive battleground between TPS and Canal Satellite. One of the main areas of competition was the future auction of the French soccer league broadcasting rights. After the bankruptcy of Leo Kirch Network, which had a large stake in sports broadcasting rights, the competition in France for these rights seemed to pose a financial threat to the two pay TV companies. But both depended heavily on sport broadcasting. Canal Satellite won the November 2004 auction for the football seasons from 2005 to 2008.

Canal Satellite and TPS had different pricing strategies. TPS had a more aggressive policy, with a starting offer from €11, whereas Canal Satellite was positioned at around €15–20. They had a different communication approach as well. TPS had a price-orientated communication – 'you have got TPS all for €11' – whereas Canal Satellite had a quality-orientated communication approach: 'Canal Satellite the best of digital TV', with exclusive channels orientated to value-added programmes.

New entrants

Historically, the number of potential new entrants in this market has been very limited. Nevertheless, the pay TV market has attracted some challengers. An example is the case of Mr Saban, born in 1944 in Alexandria, Egypt, and now a US citizen living in Los Angeles. In 1988, Saban founded Saban Entertainment, an international television, production, distribution and merchandising company. He started his entertainment company by providing the market with *Power Rangers*, a Japanese serial for kids. Saban formed a partnership with Rupert Murdoch in order to create a fully integrated entertainment company that brought together Saban's content and merchandising strengths with Fox Broadcasting's network distribution. In 1997, the Saban-Fox partnership acquired the Fox Family Channel, a fully distributed cable network reaching 81 million homes in the USA. Saban and Rupert Murdoch joined forces in the sale of Fox Family Worldwide to the Walt Disney Company. The deal, spearheaded by Saban, was the largest cash transaction ever executed by a single individual in the history of Hollywood. The transaction closed on 24 October 2001 and made ripples in the media industry, with $1.5 billion for Saban and Murdoch.

In August 2003, Saban and his partner, French TV group TF1, bought a controlling stake in Germany's largest commercial broadcaster, Group Kirch Media, ProSiebenSat.1 Media, as well as a film rights library, in a deal worth about 2 billion euros ($2.2 billion). With this deal, Saban became a heavyweight challenger in the European media field and was now in a position to diversify his group. He declared in German newspapers that it might make business sense for his company to enter the pay TV sector, especially in Germany, the biggest European TV market. At that time, the German market had only one pay TV channel (Premiere), so he had the choice to either buy Premiere or develop his own channel in order to enlarge the market.

According to some analysts, Saban was weighing up the pros and the cons of selling ProSiebenSat.1 Media after returning it to profit. In addition, he was planning to enter the pay TV market in Europe (he did not mention anything about how and when). With his extended film rights library, he was now in a good position to feed a new pay TV channel.

The strategy of Canal Plus

André Rousselet founded Canal Plus on 4 November 1984. His vision was to set up a new terrestrial television channel in France. He succeeded. Rousselet's vision took shape due to the participation of Générale des Eaux, a French public limited company and a leader in wastewater management, and the Havas media group in which it had a stake of 15 per cent. His television channel ushered in an era of pay encrypted TV in France and in Europe.

André Rousselet's first challenge was to create the first pay TV channel to survive and then to make it profitable. He had two main strategies he planned to use to achieve these objectives. First, Rousselet knew the importance of attracting highly competent and motivated talent and, therefore, he hired sports specialists (either commentators, production specialists or rights negotiators), famous journalists (like Pierre Lescure, who later became CEO of Canal Plus), and artistic directors to set up specific logo and graphic guidelines for the channel. Second, Rousselet decided to implement a 'cutting edge' marketing strategy. His logic was that Canal Plus was a premium product based on exclusive rights; hence, the channel should benefit from premium marketing campaigns. Canal Plus rapidly became a distinctive, attractive brand recognized by its own characteristics (for the timeline see Exhibit 6.3).

Inspired by US channel HBO, Canal Plus developed a series of programmes to strengthen its relationship with subscribers. Within three years, Rousselet had not only achieved his objectives, but surpassed them.

From the beginning of 1986, the management of Canal Plus focused on entertainment and sports coverage. In November 1987, Havas – the main shareholder of Canal Plus – introduced Canal Plus on the stock market. The positioning of the channel immediately showed its positive effect in increased sales. Buoyed by this success, the group set up an

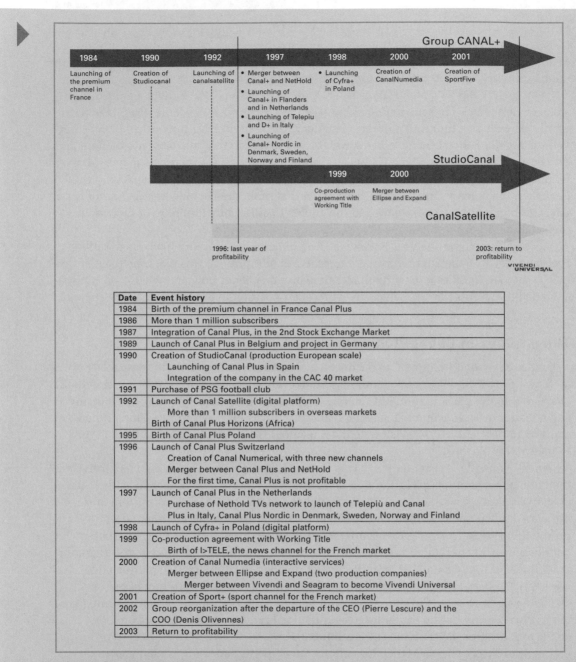

Date	Event history
1984	Birth of the premium channel in France Canal Plus
1986	More than 1 million subscribers
1987	Integration of Canal Plus, in the 2nd Stock Exchange Market
1989	Launch of Canal Plus in Belgium and project in Germany
1990	Creation of StudioCanal (production European scale) Launching of Canal Plus in Spain Integration of the company in the CAC 40 market
1991	Purchase of PSG football club
1992	Launch of Canal Satellite (digital platform) More than 1 million subscribers in overseas markets Birth of Canal Plus Horizons (Africa)
1995	Birth of Canal Plus Poland
1996	Launch of Canal Plus Switzerland Creation of Canal Numerical, with three new channels Merger between Canal Plus and NetHold For the first time, Canal Plus is not profitable
1997	Launch of Canal Plus in the Netherlands Purchase of Nethold TVs network to launch of Telepiù and Canal Plus in Italy, Canal Plus Nordic in Denmark, Sweden, Norway and Finland
1998	Launch of Cyfra+ in Poland (digital platform)
1999	Co-production agreement with Working Title Birth of I>TELE, the news channel for the French market
2000	Creation of Canal Numedia (interactive services) Merger between Ellipse and Expand (two production companies) Merger between Vivendi and Seagram to become Vivendi Universal
2001	Creation of Sport+ (sport channel for the French market)
2002	Group reorganization after the departure of the CEO (Pierre Lescure) and the COO (Denis Olivennes)
2003	Return to profitability

Exhibit 6.3 Canal plus group history, 1984–2002

International Development Department to plan out its European expansion. The strategy was based on the fact that similar offerings did not exist in other European countries and that there were possible unexploited economies of scale, especially in buying movie rights. The new challenge for Canal Plus was to expand into Europe.

European expansion

The year 1989 was the starting point for Canal Plus's internationalization. A channel was first launched in Belgium, followed by Spain, Germany and Poland. In 1991, the expansion continued with the launch of a channel that covered North Africa, then other channels for the French regions of the Caribbean and New Caledonia. In each region, the group positioned itself as a premium channel similar to the French model but responsive to the specifics of each country. For example, in Spain, in order to establish Canal Plus as a key player in the pay TV segment and to respect local habits, the management decided that the channel would have a 30-minute news programme at 9pm (common in Spain for other channels), which was an exception among other Canal Plus channels in Europe.

The European expansion strategy was based on different economic and competitive criteria. For example, in Spain, Canal Plus rapidly attracted new subscribers and succeeded in positioning itself as a specific channel with French roots, whereas in Germany, Canal Plus was never launched (the presence of two major players Bertelsmann and Kirch in this country made it impossible for a foreign group to launch its own channel).

In 1992, parallel to the European expansion, the company decided to launch a digital platform in France, called Canal Satellite. Dedicated to theme channels, Canal Satellite offered channels with a large variety of programmes (news, sports, documentaries, cartoons, etc.) for a price below that of Canal Plus, its premium channel. The shift to digital platforms was implemented in other European countries with the launch of Cyfra+ (Poland), D+ (Italy), CanalDigital (Spain), etc. In France, where this initiative was introduced first, the digital platform maintained the lead in the market (see Exhibits 6.4 and 6.5).

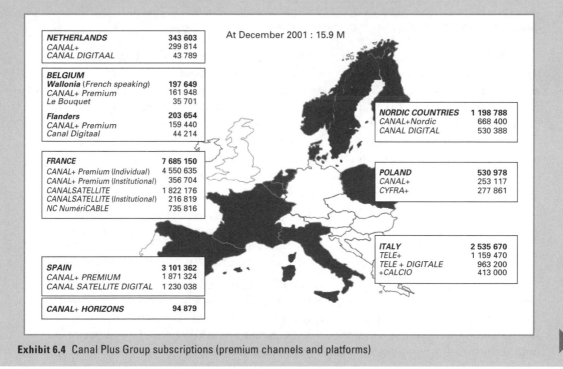

NETHERLANDS	**343 603**
CANAL+	299 814
CANAL DIGITAAL	43 789

BELGIUM	
Wallonia (French speaking)	**197 649**
CANAL+ Premium	161 948
Le Bouquet	35 701
Flanders	**203 654**
CANAL+ Premium	159 440
Canal Digitaal	44 214

FRANCE	**7 685 150**
CANAL+ Premium (Individual)	4 550 635
CANAL+ Premium (Institutional)	356 704
CANALSATELLITE	1 822 176
CANALSATELLITE (Institutional)	216 819
NC NumériCABLE	735 816

SPAIN	**3 101 362**
CANAL+ PREMIUM	1 871 324
CANAL SATELLITE DIGITAL	1 230 038

CANAL+ HORIZONS	**94 879**

At December 2001 : 15.9 M

NORDIC COUNTRIES	**1 198 788**
CANAL+Nordic	668 400
CANAL DIGITAL	530 388

POLAND	**530 978**
CANAL+	253 117
CYFRA+	277 861

ITALY	**2 535 670**
TELE+	1 159 470
TELE + DIGITALE	963 200
+CALCIO	413 000

Exhibit 6.4 Canal Plus Group subscriptions (premium channels and platforms)

Country	2002	2003	2004	2005	2006	2007	CAGR
Germany	4,883	7,117	10,410	14,143	18,090	21,859	35%
UK	10,924	13,817	16,742	19,184	20,758	21,590	15%
Italy	3,010	3,598	5,188	6,553	7,953	9,393	26%
Spain	2,946	3,626	4,504	5,568	6,878	8,290	23%
Netherlands	610	915	1,518	2,480	3,913	5,588	56%
Belgium	683	1,094	1,555	1,929	2,197	2,351	28%
Others	9,169	12,041	16,470	21,190	25,723	29,784	27%
Total	32,225	42,208	56,387	71,047	85,512	98,855	25%

Exhibit 6.5 Digital TV household growth forecast in Europe

In 1994, Pierre Lescure took over as CEO having been Rousselet's blue-eyed boy for the previous ten years. Lescure knew the company well. It had an increasing number of subscribers, was the undisputed market leader with no visible signs of competition, had a constant and positive EBIT and a high level of stock market confidence.

Being the hand-picked protégé of André Rousselet, Lescure's vision was to maintain the leadership position of Canal Plus in France and continue expansion in Europe. He modified his strategy of growth through acquisition. In September 1996, Canal Plus announced its decision to expand its presence in Europe by acquiring the NetHold company. According to CEO Pierre Lescure:

> The acquisition of NetHold gives Canal Plus a unique opportunity to become the leader in pay TV in Europe and particularly to build a strong south European arc of influence with countries such as Spain, France and Italy. The acquisition of NetHold also open doors to the new markets of Scandinavia, the Netherlands and Belgium.

Soon after the NetHold acquisition, Canal Plus realized that transforming markets and channels was not easy. The south crescent (Spain, France and Italy) had the potential to become the first pay TV market in Europe, but the cost of achieving this objective had sky-rocketed, particularly because of the investment required in the Italian peninsula, both in terms of programme rights and marketing budgets.

The beginning of the Messier era

As Canal Plus continued with its strategy of expansion in Europe, there were new developments in the holding company of Canal Plus. In January 1996, Jean-Marie Messier became CEO of Générale des Eaux, a conglomerate group with a large number of activities (its historical business was water distribution in France). In 1997, Messier launched a public offering of Havas Media. Générale des Eaux assumed a 30 per cent stake in Havas Media and Canal Plus became directly linked to Générale des Eaux.

In July 1999, Messier was able to increase his share in the TV channel as part of a three-way merger between Canada's Seagram and Canal Plus. This was possible due to an exchange of shares with the Richemont group, which led Vivendi to control 49 per cent of the company's capital. The French authorities wanted the company's French channel to remain independent, so Vivendi Universal struck a deal in which it owned 49 per cent of Canal Plus SA, a publicly traded entity that owned the French Canal Plus television operations. Other operations included the film production house StudioCanal and the 66 per cent owned Canal Satellite digital pay TV service. Continuing with its restructuring efforts, Messier changed the name of Générale des Eaux to Vivendi Group. In June 2000, Messier transferred the water and waste management business to Vivendi Environment and celebrated the birth of a new media and telecommunications conglomerate, Vivendi Universal, which boasted business units in music, publishing, TV and film (Canal Plus, Universal Pictures, Universal Studios), entertainment parks, telecoms (Cegetel and SFR – two major mobile operators in France) and the internet. Messier, within a span of less than eight years, built a conglomerate with his vision of convergence. He believed that media content and communication (home phone, mobile telephone and internet) would merge and he wanted to create a worldwide player that would be able to provide a full range of services in this field.

Based in Paris, the new Vivendi Universal executive committee was chaired by Jean-Marie Messier. The committee also comprised Vice-President Edgar Bronfman Jr (previously Head of Universal) and Pierre Lescure, Chief Operating Officer (COO). The main focus of Vivendi Universal was to boost efficiency and profitability from its operations by creating and producing content (Universal Studios, Studio Canal), developing attractive television programming (13th Street, Canal Plus, Planète, etc.) and increasing the number of subscribers in the global media industry (TV, mobile phone, internet). In a joint speech, in December 2000, Messier, Bronfman and Lescure declared:

> Together, we are going to create a new world where the consumer – the citizen of the new century – will be able to receive any information, entertainment, or service on any of the media screens that we use in our daily life, be it mobile telephone, TV, movies or internet. Together we are going to create a company out of a common border: multicultural, generously open to the world and its diversity.

This project was a visionary one. But this idealistic vision confronted harsh reality. By 2001, the internet bubble had burst, the telecoms market had crashed and the ensuing economic slowdown in the USA and Europe was demonstrated by about

▶ 10 per cent unemployment in France and a mounting debt due to acquisitions made by Vivendi. The company was stuck with a total debt of 13 billion euros and its market share value had decreased 80 per cent by 2002. This marked the turning point in the group's history. Under ever increasing pressure, Pierre Lescure, CEO of Canal Plus, faced a very difficult situation. The countdown for Jean-Marie Messier's downfall had begun. Vivendi Universal group looked extremely vulnerable and so was Canal Plus. Jean-Marie Messier fired Pierre Lescure on 16 April 2002. But, three months later, Jean-Marie Messier himself was ousted by the board of Vivendi Universal and Jean-René Fourtou, who was recognized as one of the brightest captains of French industry, was ushered in as the new CEO. In his first speech, he stressed:

> In the coming weeks, every possible action which will have a positive impact on cash flow, will be taken. I am confident that we will be able to find a solution to our cash flow situation. We should be able to save Vivendi Universal from bankruptcy.

At this stage every possible scenario was detailed in the press, including the fact that Vivendi Universal would sell its main assets, such as Canal Plus, to Lagardere Group, and SFR (the mobile division) to Vodafone (which owns 46.5 per cent of SFR), and that its US activities (mainly Universal Music, Universal Studios and US networks) would be re-bought by the Bronfman family (the initial shareholders of Universal Studios). Most media analysts speculated on a possible split in the Vivendi group. Fourtou was in a critical position.

Fourtou's first step was to appoint new top management in which he had complete confidence. To do this in the most transparent and comprehensible way, key people were nominated to major group activities. Between June 2002 and January 2003, Xavier Couture (nominated by Jean-Marie Messier) acted as CEO of Canal Plus. Fourtou nominated Bertrand Méheut as COO of the group in September 2002. Méheut brought in Eric Pradon as Executive VP, Finance, acting as Chief Financial Officer (CFO), and Christian Sanchez as Executive VP, HR, and Support Functions (both from Vivendi Publishing) to assist him in restructuring Canal Plus *fast* and saving the company from bankruptcy.

The restructuring of Canal Plus

In February 2003, Bertrand Méheut, became the new CEO of Canal Plus. His first objective was to restructure the group as fast as he could (see Exhibits 6.6(a) and 6.6(b)). A detailed presentation was made to investors in November 2003, which gave a comprehensive understanding of Méheut's strategy. In his presentation, Méheut detailed the situation of 2002 – when despite a turnover of 4.8 billion euros, the company lost 325 million euros and had net debt of 5.1 billion euros (see Exhibit 6.7). Four reasons were outlined for the situation: a lack of strategy; a lack of a rigorous cost control culture; a financial structure without any control and which was totally dependent on Vivendi

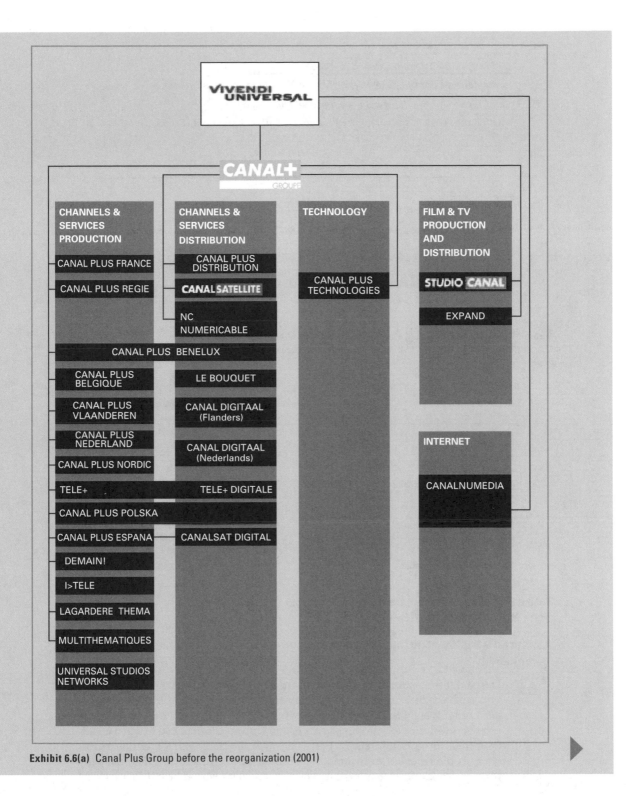

Exhibit 6.6(a) Canal Plus Group before the reorganization (2001)

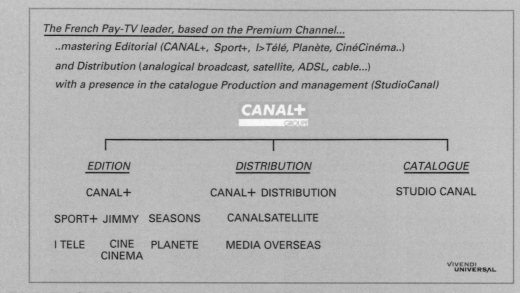

Exhibit 6.6(b) Canal Plus Group after the reorganization (2003)
Source: 'Présentation Investisseurs Groupe Canal Plus', November 2003

Result of operations	1998	1999 (pro format)	1999 (reported)	2000	2001	2002	2003
Net revenues	1.501	1.465	1.613	1.589	1.530	1.520	1.477
Operating income	258	22	−23	66	83	26	70
Income tax	15	−11	−22	−22	−27	−12	−21
Net income	75	19	−336	26	36	39	33
Net cash flow from activities	348		−14	350	289	182	133
Net cash flow	−612		949	186	16	29	23
Net debt		577	4775	1027	468	406	344
Total dividend	101	101	101	19	23	25	23
Average nb of employee	1610	1890	1890	1767	767	752	762
Total payroll	97	110	110	63	54	53	48
Net dividends (€ per share)	0.80	0.80	0.80	0.15	0.18	0.20	0.21

Exhibit 6.7 Canal plus financial summary (in million euros)
Source: annual reports, 1998, 1999, 2000, 2001, 2002, 2003

Universal's backing; and an inadequate management team. Looking back, Eric Pradon commented:

> I arrived three years before, just after Pierre Lescure was fired in June 2002. Canal Plus was in a dire crisis and so was Vivendi Universal. Jean-Marie Messier had been fired. When Jean-René Fourtou arrived as CEO of Vivendi Universal; it was a very critical time for the company. Vivendi Universal's debt had reached an all-time high of 40 billion euros. For Canal Plus the debt was 5.1 billion euros, whereas the revenues were around 4.4 billion euros. At this time, the company was in a bankruptcy situation but nobody had really realized how difficult Canal

Plus's situation was. There was no possibility to pay the debt. Canal Plus survived because of Vivendi Universal's support. Vivendi Universal acted as the banker of Canal Plus Group. With Fourtou at the helm of Vivendi, a new management team arrived at Canal Plus. I was brought in along with Christian Sanchez from Vivendi Publishing, Christian became VP for HR and I became the CFO. There was a need for new thinking at the management level. Changes occurred at both the top and middle management levels. And now we think that we have reached a new beginning, and are proud to be part of this new adventure.

In his speech to the financial community, Bertrand Méheut outlined five objectives for 2003 that could lead to success in the restructuring programme. First, a new management team would take charge; second, divestiture; third, cost reductions; fourth, new editorial guidelines; and, fifth, a new corporate culture (see Exhibit 6.8 for more details). According to Eric Pradon, the CFO of the group:

> Two aspects needed to be understood at the beginning of the restructuring programme, both at the Vivendi Universal level and at Canal Plus level. First for Vivendi Universal, the group decided to sell what could be sold in order to rapidly decrease the debt level. One possibility was to list Canal Plus on the stock market but the financial situation was too critical to convince potential investors. The only option was to go for a total organizational restructuring of the group.

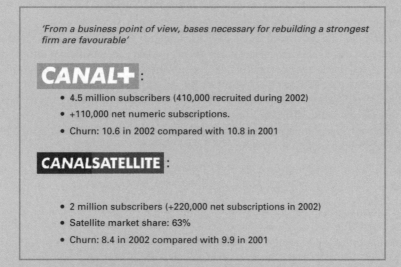

Exhibit 6.8 Strong foundation to rebuild

At the beginning of his term, a new board was set up by Bertrand Méheut. New talent came on board with the nomination of Guillaume de Vergès as VP in charge of the editing division, and Rodolphe Belmer as VP Marketing & Strategy. This team was responsible for implementing the new strategy. In December 2003, Rodolphe Belmer became COO of Canal Plus Group.

In the divestiture plan, one of the first measures taken was to reduce and sell unprofitable assets. This plan included both foreign (Scandinavia and Italy) as well as French assets (Canal Plus technologies). The group expected to gain 1.3 billion euros from the sales. Eric Pradon reflected thus:

> The strategy was to focus on our core business, pay TV in France. For every other non-profitable business, either we had to reorganize or restructure the portfolio. We decided to sell assets outside France. Channels like Tele+ (Italy), Canal Plus Scandinavia and Canal Plus Belgium were sold. We hesitated about Poland. Though Poland was losing money, we decided to merge it with its competitor and to put in a new management team. These changes brought positive results and now Canal Plus Poland is profitable. We sold companies such as Canal Plus Technologies (a subsidiary that produced decoders for the channel), SportFive (a marketing company that looked after sports rights) and Expand (a TV production company). At the end of 2003, Vivendi Universal recapitalized Canal Plus Group and this helped the group decrease its debt by 3 billion euros. Additionally, the sale of assets brought in a further amount of 1.5 billion euros. The positive results in the last two years have enabled Canal Plus to realize a positive cash flow of 0.6 billion euros. We have now completely dealt with the entire debt situation.

On the organizational restructuring of the Canal Plus group, Eric Pardon commented:

> Together with portfolio restructuring, we concentrated on our organizational restructuring at Studio Canal, the movie production arm of the group. We changed the focus of the company as production of movies is a very risky business. In one year, you have one blockbuster, two movies with medium results and six to seven very bad surprises. An American studio can afford that because its market is worldwide. So we decided to close down all internal productions and shifted to a co-production model. Additionally, we balanced the risks of Studio Canal by selling off its catalogue (the third largest catalogue in the world). With all these concerted efforts, today Studio Canal has turned around and has shown positive for the second successive year, with an EBIT reaching 10 per cent of revenues.

During the cost -cutting phase, both Eric Pradon and Christian Sanchez worked together. According to Christian Sanchez:

> Eric and myself rapidly found a way to improve the situation. We had to say 'no' to most of the requests we received. One of the first measures taken was the cancellation of the Formula One contract. We had the rights for both pay TV and video on demand. The bottom line was very simple: on one side revenue of 1 million euros and, on the other side, costs of around 20 million euros. Another measure was related to 'exotic assets'. In its golden years Canal Plus had acquired two submarines from James Cameron for shooting documentaries in the Mediterranean Sea. We sold them immediately. Our key decision was to focus on our strong assets and sell all non-profitable activities, and our Italian activities were at the top of that list; Poland was not in such a critical situation. That's why we decided to keep it.

Second, we identified all the back-up services (Controlling, HR, Sales administration) that, were no longer playing their roles and had no control on the expenses that Canal Plus was incurring. The buying department was also uncontrolled and was not effectively undertaking its mission. We implemented a set of basic rules for any investment above 10 k euros – a bidding system would be carried out. The total amount of the buying is around 700 m euros per year in the group; therefore it was worth setting up a system to optimize this spending. This department is not in charge of editorial content and rights acquisitions (sport, movies, TV series) but, for example, the technical resources dedicated to broadcasting football matches follow the new buying procedures.

We found that there were too many administrative people and not enough resources on the ground (sales, marketing, etc.). For example in HR, when I arrived in May 2002, the number of new recruitments since January was around 200. Most of them were administrative people. Astonishingly this happened when the Group was at its worst: the HR department had even decided to recruit two new people in charge of this recruitment plan! I decided to stop all new recruitment.

Cost reduction was carried out in two main areas, a 50 per cent reduction in programme costs (mainly sports, Club Europe, Champions League, Formula One) and the rest in overhead (holding overhead). The new management wanted to save 200 million euros on a yearly basis through cost cutting. According to Christian Sanchez:

The SAP experience was interesting in this perspective. SAP was implemented before the new management team took charge. The previous management had realized that lack of control has had negative effects on the company. Two solutions could have been implemented at that stage: try to change the people and their habits, which was impossible at that time, or implement a 'Stalinian process'. They chose the second solution: SAP. But in fact, the negative habits were stronger than the processes that the new system could inculcate; SAP did not succeed in structuring the company. It was both very time and money consuming. Additionally, SAP didn't correspond to our job specificities and did not match the invoicing norms we followed here. Lastly, we decided to outsource IT and G&A management.

Canal Plus rationalized its HR practices together with cost-cutting mechanisms. Summarizing the cost-cutting process at Canal Plus, Eric Pradon felt that: 'The key point of the restructuring, was to balance costs and revenues. Cost cutting is easy; in the first year this is usually what you do; but this is not for long term. A long-term strategy is to work on the revenues. And this is what we have done from the second year onwards.'

Christian Sanchez worked on the HR processes in areas of task management, payroll and rightsizing. According to him:

We created an HR book for managers in order to standardize information. We wrote an HR Legal Guide in order to ensure that every team manager behaved in and applied appropriate ways at all occasions. This was a necessity as the Legal Department didn't focus on key issues and there was no coordination between use of external advisers and lawyers. This had led to significant external charges. Today, functions are closer to the 'ground battlefield'.

We hesitated to restructure payroll policies, but finally we preferred to retain them internally because of the diverse employees' contracts. A major issue we had to cope with was to make managers responsible for the wages policy. We have three categories of wages at Canal and for each we have set up a coherent and fair system. For lower management, compensation is a mix of individual and collective wage increase; for middle management individual increase; and for senior and top management, a bonus on achieving the objectives. Earlier the yearly wage increase was around 7 per cent and we decided to cut it down to 2 per cent, a normal figure for a group that needs to make savings. But this decision has not been accepted by a large majority of managers because they think in individual terms and rarely in collective terms for the Group.

Concerning the bonus we have changed rules as in the previous system. Every year most of the managers got their full bonuses. A new system called BSO (bonus on objectives) is now in place. Out of 3,000 people in the group, only 400 benefit from this system. This has to be communicated clearly to the subordinates.

I have had several arguments over this. One of the most common was 'My job is very specific, nobody in the group is doing exactly the same, you cannot compare my job in any other service or division.' But if you want to set up and run a consistent human resources strategy you need to establish a system that permits job comparisons in the group. We have created a CFT (classification des fonctions types – a standardized jobs classification) in order to harmonize salaries and other advantages (like car, mobile phone, BlackBerry, etc.) for every position. This CFT covers 600 people ('cadres' – managers) in the group, and enables us to be consistent.

Additionally, we set up means to associate employees with company results; thus in 2005 a profit-sharing system (called 'intéressement') has been credited to all employees. But for most employees, this effort to motivate them seems normal as the company earlier allocated this bonus even in 2002 when the Group had reached a debt level of 5 billion euros! This is a legacy that dates back to 1997, much before the arrival of Vivendi Universal.

A rightsizing plan was implemented that included the announcement of around 330 layoffs and the outsourcing of 138 jobs. Eric Pradon and Christian Sanchez explained, 'Cost cutting was also part of implementing a huge social plan for the company. Officially we had about 330 layoffs but it is actually much more in real terms.'

The focus was on Canal Plus premium. Cornerstone programmes – movies, sport, news, documentaries and entertainment – were clearly identified. Specific efforts were dedicated to unencrypted programmes, particularly during prime time (6 pm to 9 pm), with strong signatures and anchormen interviewed for these positions. In September 2003, major French production companies and individual French producers were asked to pitch for the new programme grid for channels like Canal Satellite and NBA+. Management decided to retain investment in programmes at the earlier level of 1 billion euros for 2003–04.

Together with the above steps, Canal Plus decided to renew the company culture. The first step was to create shared management principles centred on results and clients.

The process of editorial renewal was initiated in order to develop innovation and deliver attractive programmes. Christian Sanchez commented:

> Every division within Canal Plus was acting independently without any coordination. This had led to a position where Canal Plus Group was spread over 25 sites and with more than 70 leases. The top management had no accurate idea of the diverse decisions that ensued from these offices. For example, the PR department felt that the lack of clear objectives decreased the effectiveness of communication. My analysis holds to this day. In the group, the most favoured business unit was the editing part – the 'channel' – it was considered superior to the subscription and sales departments.

Office relocation was a necessity as it enabled a mix of new culture and services to be established. The renewal of a company culture went hand in hand with the relocation of the historic headquarters of Canal Plus to new offices in the Boulogne-Billancourt area. This move, in September 2004, made it possible for the Group to have two major sites, whereas in 2003, employees were dispersed around 30 different sites. Eric Pradon commented:

> One of the first priorities was to change the culture of the company. We needed to move from a certain image of Canal Plus to a new image of a vibrant group. A major step in this direction was the change of headquarters. This enabled the company to go from 27 sites to 2 major sites, plus 5 secondary sites. Canal Plus Distribution (Sales & Subscription Department) was based in the HQ, whereas the editing department was in the second site.
>
> During the final years of the previous management, the company was no longer run and led effectively, a feeling that was widespread in the company. Today employees know that the company has a leader and that he knows how to manage the company in difficult times. A second task was to implement procedures; the group had no procedures in most fields until the restructuring. Many decisions were ad hoc and the culture of management control was lacking in the Group. We created one Communication Department which is in charge of press relations, editing and publishing, festivals, fairs, partnerships, etc. Most of these changes we witness today were carried out by the top management and not with the help of consulting companies. It was the decision of a small group of top executives.

Bertrand Méheut had successfully achieved the two objectives that Jean-René Fourtou had bestowed on him. He managed the portfolio restructuring of this 'global French television' division and raised cash by selling activities (primarily international ones) to buyers at the best possible prices. In the financial report published at the end of the first quarter of 2003, he said:

> Today, Canal Plus is at the centre of a restructuring programme covering all of Canal Plus Group's operations in Europe. The goal was to create a stronger, more aligned organization that can generate sustainable profitability in a difficult and increasingly competitive environment. An organization built primarily on our French operations, resting squarely on our core competencies of production and distribution of pay TV channels.

▶ During a year shaped by numerous upheavals inside and outside the company, Canal Plus consistently demonstrated its vitality and inventiveness. Our teams had always been closely attuned to subscribers' desire and interests. In 2002, this focused commitment resulted in an excellent satisfaction rate among subscribers. For the first time in four years, the churn rate actually improved, beating all forecasts. ,,

In an internal note in March 2003, Bertrand Méheut was asked to comment on the debt of 5 billion euros owed to the company's major shareholder Vivendi. Bertrand Méheut commented:

"" The priority was to sell assets like Canal Plus Technologies or TELE+ (the Italian subsidiary) but this will not be enough to reduce our total debt. We should be instrumental in setting up a new organization which has to go through rightsizing (251 direct layoffs and 138 positions externalized). The French premium channel is at the heart of these changes. It is a cornerstone of the new structure that is currently being assembled, with the deployment of a simplified organizational structure that will foster skills sharing and synergy. ,,

Bertrand Méheut described 2003 as a year of recovery that restored confidence. He detailed that:

"" The implementation of a broad-based restructuring, asset disposal and cost-cutting plan enabled us to end the year with a consolidated operating profit for the first time since 1996. The Canal Plus channel is our core business. Innovative programming, a first-rate line-up and exclusive content make it an exception among the premium channels of France. In 2003, we set out to rebuild a strong, aligned pay TV organization around this powerful, vibrant core, with recognized talent in premium and theme channel creation. We deployed new management with proven experience in content distribution and subscriber management. We have succeeded in this goal and, today, the Canal Plus Group far outpaces other French pay TV companies, with more than eight million subscribers. ,,

Méheut concluded: 'Our commitment was supported by our shareholder, Vivendi Universal, which recognized our accomplishments by approving our recapitalization plan in December 2003. Looking forward, 2004 will be a year of renewal for the Canal Plus Group.'

Conclusion

In mid-April 2004, Bertrand Méheut announced Canal Plus results for 2003: a positive 247 million euros (vis-à-vis a loss of 325 million in 2002) (see Exhibit 6.9). He mentioned:

"" It is the first time since 1996 that Canal Plus has generated a positive result. Current debt is under 800 million euros. We should not forget that Canal Plus group is the first TV player in France both in terms of turnover and subscribers. Additionally the churn,[1] which has been deteriorating in the last three years, has now stabilized. ,,

---

Financial situation at the end of 2002

- Turnover   €4.8 billion
- Net cash flow*   €(740) million
- Operational income   €(325) million
- Net debt   €5.1 billion

*(including variation of liquid assets)

Provisions at the end of 2003

- 8.1 million subscribers (+125,000 vs Dec 2002)
- Including 4.9 million for Canal Plus Premium
- EBITDA > €500 million
- A <u>positive</u> operational cash flow
- A recapitalization of €3 billion
- A net debt evolved from €5.1 billion to €850 million

Financial objectives at the end of 2004

- Turnover   ~ €3 billion
- EBITDA margin   ~ 10%
- Operational income   > €130 million
- Operational cash flow   > €120 million

Exhibit 6.9 Future outlook

considered perimeter CANAL+ Premium (Canal+ SA, Canal+ Distribution et Canal+ Régie),
CanalSatellite, Media Overseas, Chaînes thématiques (MultiThématiques, iTélé, Sport+), StudioCanal

Source: 'Présentation Investisseurs Groupe Canal Plus', November 2003

Eric Pradon commented on the value that this turnaround of Canal Plus created:

> Regarding the stock market value, the Vivendi Universal share price which was at
> €15 is now at €23 and most of the analysts believe that the value should be around
> €26–30 per share. Today the market capitalization of Canal Plus is evaluated at
> around 5 billion euros. We have moved slowly but steadily, step by step. Winning
> the French Football league broadcasting rights in November 2004 was a great
> accomplishment. We now have much better knowledge of our subscribers'
> expectations and they see Canal Plus as a specific channel.

Nevertheless, rumours of a takeover bid by Murdoch for Vivendi Universal and/or
Vodafone buying SFR (the second mobile operator in France) were widespread.
Lagardere could also be considered a potential raider. Some analysts pointed out that the
fast restructuring of both Vivendi Universal and Canal Plus could provide Jean-René
Fourtou and Bertrand Méheut with the eagerness to go further and build a new giant.
Eric Pradon thinks:

> The future of Canal Plus can be seen from different levels. First, our core business,
> pay TV in France. We need to outgrow our main competitor, TPS. Today the
> scenario is locked but we need to break this status quo and Canal Plus should be
> the ultimate leader in the future. Second, we have no debt, therefore we are in a
> position where we could now invest and evaluate different options. The first
> option is to invest in our core business: pay TV; potential countries could be
> eastern European countries. The Asia option is no longer on the agenda because

▶ we need to be strongly structured in terms of international management to go ahead. Another option could be to invest in media in France, like local press and radio. Several TV players are competing in the same market now; TF1 and M6 were free-to-air TV channels and are now entering the pay TV market. While Canal Plus, by submitting iTELE, is emerging as a potential new entrant on the free-to-air digital terrestrial television market. Today, all TV companies need to convince subscribers and advertisers. "

On the future of Canal Plus, Christian Sanchez reflects:

" The speed of new technologies outpaces the speed of industrial capacity and changes the game constantly. Is our business model based on pay TV still profitable? Will we be able to cope with the current trends such as movie piracy, technological changes or telecom operators who offer free-to-view channels? Additionally, the arrival of Hertzian Numerical Television in France will create a new indirect competitor for pay TV operators. The 3G is offering a new window for televisions. This multiplication in the numbers of channels, together with the development of new technologies will play a role in the future on our customer bases. Does our model have enough strength to overcome these new realities? "

In May 2004, NBC and Vivendi Universal, the entertainment arm of Vivendi, merged with NBC in the USA to create NBC Universal, a global player whose turnover was more than $15 billion in 2005. After the successful restructuring of Canal Plus and its shareholding company Vivendi, Bertrand Méheut and his top management team were wondering what would be next.

Note

[1] Churn is the resilience matrix expressed as a percentage of total subscribers that stop subscription.

? *Case questions*

Read the case carefully, then answer the following questions.

1 Analyse the historical success of Canal Plus in France.

2 What were some of the competencies that helped Canal Plus internationalize? What were the causes of its failure?

3 Assess the media industry and the strategies that Canal Plus took to compete. Comment on the role of technology in this industry.

4 Analyse the restructuring turnaround strategy of Canal Plus. Comment on its redesign and transformation process.

5 What would you think would be some of the potential scenarios the Group has to consider to continue its evolution?

PART 4
The Emerging Management Imperative

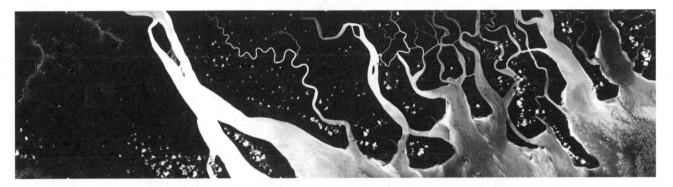

Part Contents

CHAPTER 7

Strategies for emerging markets

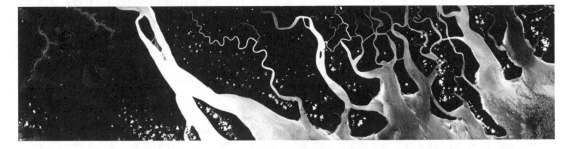

The previous chapter discussed the organizational restructuring of the global corporation. Such restructuring is mostly necessitated by major external or internal adjustments. In the recent past there has been a flurry of these adjustments in emerging markets. This chapter focuses on these emerging market, and the strategies adopted by successful and not-so-successful global companies. It discusses first entrants vs late movers in emerging markets and draws upon the specificities of emerging markets and the resultant strategies that might be favourable under these circumstances.

The often quoted *Dreaming with BRICs: The Path to 2050* report by Goldman Sachs[1] argues that, over the next 50 years, Brazil, Russia, India and China – the BRIC economies – could become a much larger force in the world economy. This report and the other follow-up reports have renewed interest in what academics and researchers have been referring to over the past decade as emerging markets (EMs). EMs are countries that usually are characterized by: *information asymmetry*, which might hinder the effective functioning of institutions, especially capital markets; *misguided regulations* that are often influenced by political goals; *inefficient judicial systems* that might lead to market failure;[2] *lack of proper intellectual property regulations* that might create a bottleneck for FDIs; and *stringent labour regulations*, which might cause scepticism for global corporations. More often than not, they also experience political volatility, regional instability teething troubles with infrastructure, and less developed institutional practices, which result in increasing corruption, bureaucratic red tape and failure to enforce contracts. Thus, in most of these

---

[1] http://www2.goldmansachs.com/insight/research/reports/99.pdf.

[2] Khanna, T. and Palepu, K. (1997) 'Why focused strategies may be wrong for emerging markets', *Harvard Business Review*, July–August, 3–10.

emerging economies,[3] state-owned public-sector enterprises or diversified business groups have remained the dominant form of corporations, which, with their experience, have built parallel institutions within their corporate structures that allow them to transact business relatively more efficiently than their foreign counterparts. With the increasing globalization of markets, the liberalization and deregulation of these emerging markets have picked up speed. With these changes in the external environment, many of these public-sector enterprises are being privatized. Business groups are being redesigned and reorganized in order to ready themselves for competition not only in their home markets but also in the global market. The Boston Consulting Group (BCG) published a report in 2006 on the 100 largest multinationals from emerging economies (a category that excludes Singapore). Within this list, there were 44 MNCs from China, 21 from India, 12 from Brazil, 7 from Russia, 6 from Mexico and 10 others from Egypt, Indonesia, Malaysia, Thailand and Turkey. In 2007, the combined output of emerging economies accounted for more than half of total world GDP (measured at purchasing power parity). This means that the rich countries no longer dominated the global economy. The developing countries also have a far greater influence on the performance of the rich economies than is generally realized. Emerging economies are driving global growth and having a big impact on developed countries' inflation, interest rates, wages and profits. As these newcomers become more integrated into the global economy and their incomes catch up with those of the rich countries, they will provide the biggest boost to the world economy since the Industrial Revolution. Thus, strategies for EMs have received considerable attention in the past decade.

Scholars have argued that focused strategies might be wrong for emerging markets and there has to be a right way to redesign the existing conglomerates in these markets. Others have gone a step further and argued that it is not only about the logic of core competence vis-à-vis diversification, but about redesigning the corporation to fit market needs. It is also about survival for these local dinosaurs. They can learn from the first movers, the western corporations, or they might follow a late-entrant strategy in the globalization game. This is coupled with the fact that FDI flows have increased more than ten times in the last decade in EMs, China has surpassed the USA in FDIs and BRIC countries hold more than 30 per cent of the world's total reserves. With extension of the BRIC countries to other emerging markets, such as Mexico, Argentina, South Africa, Egypt, Turkey, Poland, Iran, Nigeria, Indonesia, Philippines and Vietnam, the focus of the global corporations has shifted to these high-growth regions. Thus some key strategic postures for global

---

[3] With growth and prosperity in the erstwhile 'underdeveloped nations' of yesteryear, the borderline between rich and poor nation states has become more indiscernible. Economies were defined as 'developed' if they were members of the Organisation for Economic Co-operation and Development (OECD), which included 30 'rich' countries (Australia, Austria, Belgium, Canada, the Czech Republic, Denmark, Finland, France, Germany, Greece, Hungary, Iceland, Ireland, Italy, Japan, Korea, Luxembourg, Mexico, the Netherlands, New Zealand, Norway, Poland, Portugal, the Slovak Republic, Spain, Sweden, Switzerland, Turkey, the United Kingdom and the United States). But with the inclusion of relatively poor economies such as Mexico, Poland, the Czech & Slovak Republic, and the exclusion of Hong Kong, Singapore and the UAE (with GDPs per person similar to those of Italy) it is somewhat a mixed selection. To add to the disarray in definition, different organizations use different definitions. For instance, JPMorgan Chase and the United Nations count Hong Kong, Singapore, South Korea and Taiwan as emerging economies. Morgan Stanley includes South Korea and Taiwan in its emerging market index, but keeps Hong Kong and Singapore in its developed markets index. The IMF schizophrenically counts all four as 'developing' in its International Financial Statistics but as 'advanced economies' in its World Economic Outlook.

corporations in emerging markets would be to adapt and be flexible with their strategies for individual markets. For example, Carrefour's strategic posture (see Case 7) is different for different markets. Even within the Latin American markets it had different strategies for Colombia in comparison to Chile. The localization strategy succeeded in Colombia, whereas though it was profitable in Chile, it was not able to gain one of the top three positions, and decided to exit the market.

Another strategic posture would be to change the rules of the game of the market. To cite an example, when Vodafone entered a new market it tried to change the rules of business within that market. In some developed markets, like New Zealand and Portugal, Vodafone integrated its acquired companies, Bellsouth and Telecel, overnight, whereas in emerging markets like India, it played a waiting game that depended not only on the brand image of the acquired company but also on the specificities of the local market. With fast integration Vodafone aggressively pushed its systems, processes and business model, which its competitors had to match.

In today's emerging markets, global corporations have painstakingly learnt that it is difficult to sell old products at lower prices and margins, sell existing products with reduced functionality and convince customers to accept lower product quality. With the arrival of the information and internet age, it is a challenge to use old product technology to develop products for local markets. Corporations can no longer ignore major differences between and within EM countries. EMs now need a dedicated approach for global companies to succeed. It is now more or less evident that EMs are a new market space, and the challenge of corporations is to suitably align their product portfolio to these markets. For example, Philips follows a differentiated strategy for these markets. For some high-end global products (e.g. flat-screen TVs and medical instruments) it sells them without any local adaptation. For mid-segment consumer products such as domestic irons it adapts its global products to local needs. Some innovations, like decorative light bulbs, are launched in EMs such as Brazil, to be exported later on to developed nations such as Canada and the USA. Further, some products are made exclusively for the local market for total market coverage, such as mixer-grinders and music systems.

A recent study by the Boston Consulting Group identified 100 corporations from emerging markets, which it terms Rapidly Developing Economies (RDEs), which are poised to become important twenty-first century multinationals. Some of these corporations are: Embraer, Sadia & Perdigao and Natura of Brazil; America Movil and Groupo Modelo of Mexico; Ranbaxy, Infosys, Tata Tea and WIPRO of India; Galanz, Haier, Chunlan Group Corp., Lenovo and Pearl River Piano of China; and Koc Holding, Vestel and Sisecam of Turkey. The RDE attacker firms are challengers to the traditional MNCs of developed nations. They harness their strengths from large, rapidly growing markets coupled with low-cost resources. They have experience in very difficult operating environments in their home markets, which have provided them with training grounds for competing with global incumbents. They have acquired the capabilities of scaling up their businesses, negotiating with governments and grabbing market space from competitors at a fast pace. The development of these dynamic capabilities for competition means threats to more established players. For example, in China, Huawei is keen to challenge Cisco's dominance. BYD's new electric hybrid car with proprietary 20 kWh lithium-ion pack, capable of a range of 60 miles, is expected to retail at US$6,000 challenging Toyota's hybrid car models.

Recent studies have suggested that there are both pros and cons for first entrants and late entrants due to the transitional nature of the EMs. **First entrants** have an immense advantage over late entrants if they can conquer the market. Some of the pros for a successful first entrant would be harnessing economies of scale and scope, unabated growth, garnering knowledge and key learnings from the JV partner, and reaping super-normal profits. These advantages accrue over time, are required for further expansion and help corporations survive when the competitive landscape becomes tougher. Most emerging markets are undergoing deregulation and market liberalization in a phased manner, and usually there are narrow windows when first entrants can benefit from such a structural change in the local economy. In these initial years, first-entrant strategies can define the rules of the game, establish favourable positions and influence the competitive landscape for years to come. For example, as a first entrant during the late 1980s, KFC reaped considerable profits when it entered China and started with its flagship store in front of Tiananmen Square. Since profits could not be expatriated at that time from China, KFC China manufactured office uniforms for the global Pepsi Group (at that time KFC was part of Pepsi) and shipped these to the USA. With time, KFC was immensely successful in China and today has more than 1,000 restaurants, which are increasing by 200 a year. A similar case was that of Volkswagen (VW), which opened its first office in Beijing in 1985 and became the first western auto manufacturer to enter China. Its entry strategy aimed to quickly conquer the fleets of official cars and taxis in the main cities of China, a unique and interesting approach for several reasons. First, it enabled VW to sell high volumes immediately and thus harness economies of scale. Second, these taxis become a permanent 'showroom' for the brand, allowing VW to become well known instantly and acquire credibility in China. Third, with time, the taxi fleets were renewed, and through favourable exchange conditions from the old model to a new VW model, the market was kept under control within the VW brand. Strengthened by this first-mover position, a successful joint venture partnership and a near 20-year monopoly on government and taxi sales, VW was the undisputed leader of the Chinese passenger car market. It repeated its success year after year until 2005 when competition became a serious threat to its business in China.

Late entrants can also reap advantages. For example, Indian pharmaceutical giant Ranbaxy, which started its export business in 1975, was able to climb the value chain in the international arena after 1993, when its Chairman and CEO (until his death in 1999) decided that Ranbaxy should move into the high-margin businesses of selling branded generics in large markets such as China and Russia, before entering developed markets in Europe and the USA with acquisitions. In 2008, the company was bought by Daiichi Sankyo of Japan for US$4.43 billion. Motorola, a late entrant in India, was at first baffled by this huge market. It had no clue how to battle against well-known brands such as Nokia and Samsung, which were already in the market. When its sales representatives entered stores in Indian cities, they were alarmed to see their brands hidden behind a pile of shining Nokia and Samsung handsets. Their strategy of head-on competition was not working so they devised a unique approach of direct selling, borrowed from fmcg companies, which had used it to target urban and rural housewives. Sales started to pick up for Motorola as it brought the product right to the consumer. Motorola sidestepped, confronted and challenged the age-old business model for emerging markets.

Mahindra & Mahindra (farm equipment industry) of India has been grabbing market share from John Deere of the USA and Komatsu of Japan, with brands such as the Mahindra 5003, a powerful 45-horse power, high-quality, small tractor that sells for far less than competing models.

The world is yet to witness how emerging MNCs from India and China fare in the future. The TATA companies – Tata Steel and Tata Motors – should reap benefits from their acquisition of Corus of UK, the Rover and Jaguar car brands of the USA and Birla Group's Hindalco acquisition Novelis of Canada, respectively. Similarly, the 20 per cent acquisition of Standard Bank of South Africa in 2007 by Industrial and Commercial Bank of China witnessed the slow but steady growth of the Chinese presence in Africa in banking, infrastructure and natural resource projects. Pearl River Piano of China acquired Ritmuller to become the world leader in piano manufacturing, thus enabling it to acquire the capability to build such a brand, which was otherwise slow and costly.

Strategies for the 'base of the pyramid'

The term 'base of the pyramid', or BOP, as coined by C.K. Prahalad,[4] has become fashionable as global corporations realize that there are about 5 billion customers around the world who have been ignored until recently. These potential customers are different and their needs are different, too. Most of these customers are in emerging economies such as Brazil, Russia, India and China. To date, most of the global corporations have targeted only elite and upper-middle-class customers while ignoring the rest. This has created a gap in developing more innovative products and services for consumers in the mass markets who live in and represent the bottom of the pyramid – almost 80 per cent of the global population.

In spring 2003, ten teams of MBA students were selected to work on a special 'XMAP' project to document how companies across the world were working successfully to provide products and services and improve the living conditions of the poorest of the poor.[5] For example, over the last 50 years, Casas Bahia has grown from one man selling blankets and bed linen door to door to the largest retail chain in Brazil, offering electronics, appliances and furniture. With its emphasis on serving the poor customer, its low prices and credit determined by payment history rather than formal income (70 per cent of CB customers have no formal or consistent income), Casas Bahia grosses over $1 billion a year and has fostered deep loyalty in its customers. In India, ITC's eChoupal system is transforming India's agricultural supply chain by setting up rural farmer-entrepreneurs with internet access, collaborating with the government of Uttar Pradesh and using modern technology to accurately weigh farmers' crops (and paying them promptly), thereby reducing systemic corruption, and giving farmers both better prices for their crops and a sense of dignity and confidence in being connected to the rest

---

[4] Prahalad, C.K. (2004) *The Fortune at the Bottom of the Pyramid*. Wharton School Publishing.

[5] http://www.bus.umich.edu/FacultyResearch/ResearchCenters/ProgramsPartnerships/IT-Champions/default. htm#XMAP

of the world. Similarly, EID Parry provides local entrepreneurs with the technological backing to run internet kiosks in rural villages, and with a web portal to support farmers with access to fertilizers and tools, education and crop disease diagnosis, and a direct market for their crops of rice and sugarcane. Similar examples abound in Microcredit in Bangladesh and India, E+Co as a solar energy provider in Nicaragua, and inexpensive artificial prosthetic feet/lower limbs by Jaipur Foot (a non-profit organization) in India. Other examples include: Unilever and P&G selling Sunsilk and Pantene shampoos in India for less than $0.02 per mini-sachet; Narayana Hrudayalaya of India selling health insurance for less than $0.20 per person per month in India; and Amul, one of India's largest processed food cooperatives, selling a wide range of food products to millions of poor people. Many people in China and Latin America have low spending power, but still want to buy popular models with ample features, while Indian consumers prefer washing machines, mixer-grinders and music systems that offer superior output at a low price.

Other studies have shown that, while a few market opportunities do exist, like the $2,000 Nano car produced by the TATAs, the market at the BOP is generally too small to be very profitable for most global companies. For example, research at Philips showed that Indian middle-class consumers would like a high-powered mixer-grinder home appliance that does not make much noise. Its market research also showed that families would like to opt for compact music systems with multiple functionalities. This means going back to the drawing board for a new design for this market. Philips invested in the new design and benefited from the investment not only in a 300 million middle-class Indian market, but also by exporting this model to similar emerging markets. Thus, with the relationship and trust-building exercise that Philips carried out within the local market of India, its products could travel profitably to higher-income markets as adding functionalities to low-cost models is simpler that removing features from high-cost models.

Emerging markets of Asia

The most discussed emerging markets of today are China and India, but until ten years ago South East Asia was the world's fastest-developing region. After their recovery from the financial crisis of 1997–98, the emerging markets of SE Asia – Indonesia, Malaysia, Philippines, Singapore and Thailand – crossed the stage of 'emerging' and moved towards the developed stage. The area has had several years of strong growth and its governments' finances have been greatly improved. The region has 570 million people and a head-start in economic development over much of the rest of Asia, especially China and India. China and India, on the other hand, are home to more than one-third of the world's population.

China

China continued its economic reforms from the late 1970s within a communist regime. China's evolution had its peculiarities. In 1964, recently estranged from its Soviet patron, it devoted a larger share of its GDP (1.7 per cent) to R&D than it ever has since. With the deregulation and liberalization of its industries and attractive FDI policies spearheaded by the state, China has experienced explosive growth. Its GDP has quadrupled during the last

30 years, its exports have increased from $78 billion in 1993 to a staggering $974 billion in 2006, and in 2007 it became the second-largest economy in the world (after the USA in purchasing power parity terms). China's prowess today is best demonstrated by its state-sponsored 'mega-projects', such as its supercomputers and pebble-bed nuclear reactors. In terms of emerging global corporations, Huawei is one of China's leading makers of telecoms equipment. It is the sixth-biggest vendor in the world, and won a third of all new contracts for third-generation (3G) telephony. The company devoted 10 per cent of its revenues ($8.5 billion in 2006), and almost half of its manpower to R&D. Its elusive chairman, Ren Zhengfei, who still runs the company he founded almost 20 years ago, is a veteran of the People's Liberation Army, and his employees, who do boot camp-style callisthenics in the morning, subscribe to a 'wolf spirit' of winning deals and working like a dog. This surely is a company befitting a tech superpower. For example, it split its mobile phone base station into two lighter parts, which could be installed separately and more cheaply.

With such growth there are challenges to balance. China struggled to sustain job growth for tens of millions of workers laid off from state-owned enterprises, migrants from the mainland and new entrants to the workforce. Roughly 150 million rural workers drift between villages in central and west China and the huge cities in the east, many subsisting through part-time, low-paid jobs. There is still a stark discrepancy between coastal China and the interior in terms of communications and transportation, regional differences in language and autonomous local governments. Due to its membership in the WTO in 2001, China's role as a global manufacturing site expanded, triggering massive exports to Europe and the USA, which in turn triggered explosive growth and a rise in the prices of crude and commodities. China buys roughly 20 per cent of the world's aluminium, copper, washing machines, soybeans, poultry and ice cream. It consumes roughly one-third of the world's coal, cotton, fish, rice and cigarettes. The country buys one-quarter of the world's steel and one-half of its pork. It is home to 20 per cent of the world's cell phone users. Global corporations such as Wal-Mart sourced over $30 billion of merchandise from China in 2007. Airbus, Coca-Cola, General Motors, McDonald's, Motorola and Volkswagen have been first entrants to this market and reaped huge profits.

India

With its 1.1 billion population, the largest democracy, continuous GDP growth at about 9 per cent and an ever increasing ability to inspire entrepreneurs, India has generated enormous international interest. Historically, India's GDP grew at 0.8 per cent per year, the same as its population, between 1900 and 1950. GDP grew at about 3.5 per cent per year from 1950 to 1980, a growth sometimes referred to as the 'Hindu rate of growth'. Government policy until 1991 was one of 'licence–permit–quota raj', with a monopolistic public sector, overregulated private enterprise and stringent price and production controls that discouraged foreign investments. It was an inward-looking and import-substituting (rather than outward-looking and export-promoting), mixed economy. As always, the economy is vulnerable to the impact of bad weather on the key agricultural sector. Moreover, despite the constant optimism that seems to surround India, doing business in the country is complicated by bureaucracy and over-regulation, while economic reform will face entrenched political resistance. After much debate, the Indian government has lowered trade barriers and tax rates, broken state monopolies, unshackled industries, encouraged competition and become liberalized and deregulated. It took 17 years, and is still continuing. Even with these immense strides, about 25 per cent of the population remains below the poverty line, which means poor nutrition, hygiene and infant mortality, low education levels, poor skills and high under-employment. In the last decade, 1 per cent of the population has crossed the poverty line every year. In the political scenario, there is a 58-year-old feud with its neighbour, Pakistan, over Jammu and Kashmir. There is still tension with China over part of the border, but significant progress has been made recently. There is also limited insurgency in some areas, such as at the borders of Bangladesh, Myanmar and China, and in scattered pockets in central India. With this as a backdrop, India's rise is not new but unique. It is not as classic an Asian strategy as that of China, Singapore or Hong Kong, of exporting labour-intensive, low-priced manufactured goods to the West; rather it relied on its domestic market more than exports, consumption more than investment, services more than industry and high-end rather than low-end manufacturing. The Indian economy has also insulated itself from global downturns, showing a degree of stability due to its consumption-driven and people-friendly model of growth. This growth has been driven by entrepreneurs, not the government as in the case of China, with competitive private companies, a booming stock market and a modern and well-disciplined financial sector. And growth should be faster still if India is able to cash in on its 'demographic dividend'. Its young population will add 71 million people to its workforce in the next five years, or nearly a quarter of the world's extra workers. Second, India is producing world-class global corporations at a much faster rate than is China. The best known are the wizards of software and 'business process outsourcing' – Indian firms have two-thirds of the global market in offshore IT services and nearly half that in BPO. Now BPO is leading to the business models of 'knowledge process outsourcing' and 'research process outsourcing'. More than 125 *Fortune* 500 companies have R&D sites in India. General Electric's technology centre in Bangalore is working on advanced propulsion systems for jet engines. Tata Consultancy Services (TCS), from the TATA Group produces the software for Ferrari's Formula One cars. India's drugmakers offer 60,000 finished medicines; only three countries produce more volume. India's Bajaj Auto has teamed up with Renault-Nissan to produce low-cost cars in India.

Some of the challenges are in sectors such as infrastructure (roads and power), and public services (education and drinking water), which are woefully inadequate and might limit growth. Even as the economy has been booming, many public services have worsened. India's top computer scientists are feted around the world, yet most children in rural areas lack the basic education needed to find more productive work. Some of the other challenges that face the Indian business environment are overly strict labour laws, a public sector that is still largely inefficient, and reforms that have failed to create a broad-based, labour-intensive industrial revolution. Instead, the environment has created a high-tech services revolution in sectors such as information technology enabled services (ITeS), telecoms, pharma and, automotive components. For example, India has a peta-project to build its own 'petaflop' computer, which could handle $10\{+1\}\{+5\}$ floating-point operations per second, as fast as any in the world. Its emerging global corporations, such as Bharat Forge, Ranbaxy, Jet Airways, Infosys, Reliance Infocomm, Tata Motors,

Tata Steel, Hindalco, Wipro and Ranbaxy, are now on the global radar, with combined global acquisitions of about $40 billion in 2006–07. Tata Steel, which dates back to the days of the British Raj, leapt into the league of top producers when it bought Britain's Corus, which includes the steelmaking remnants of the old imperial power, and the luxury car brands Rover and Jaguar.

Case introduction: Carrefour: conquest of Latin America

Since its merger with Promodès in 1999, Carrefour has ranked as the French world challenger and European leader in the retail industry. Carrefour followed an aggressive growth strategy, going global from the early 1970s. Its first advantage in the international retail sector market were its acquisitions and adapting itself to the respective local cultures and consumer habits, especially those in emerging markets. By doing so, it became the second largest retail company worldwide. Carrefour saw moderate success in penetrating the developed markets of the United States and the UK, but was mostly successful in implementing its multi-format strategy in emerging markets such as eastern Europe, Asia and Latin America. The Latin American market marked the highest growth rate for Carrefour, especially in countries like Colombia, where the growth rate at comparable exchange rates was more than 30 per cent in 2003.

This case appears after the readings for this chapter.

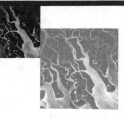

READING 13
How to win in emerging markets*

*Satish Shankar, Charles Ormiston, Nicolas Bloch,
Robert Schaus and Vijay Vishwanath*

Though competitive barriers in Asia, Latin America and Eastern Europe are many, a look at the companies that are thriving there reveals some secrets that make success more likely.

Village roads can be impassable, home cooking is still a way of life, product prices can be below the cost of production in developed markets, and local products often have generations of loyal customers. Nevertheless, emerging markets in Asia, Latin America and Eastern Europe are delivering some of the strongest revenue and profit growth for global makers of fast-moving consumer goods – everything from snacks to toothpaste – despite concerns that lower prices translate into lower profits.

Emerging-market leaders like Coca-Cola, Unilever, Colgate-Palmolive, Groupe Danone and PepsiCo earn 5% to 15% of their total revenues from the three largest emerging markets in Asia: China, India and Indonesia. The story is similar in Russia and Eastern Europe, where these companies often dominate their target categories and routinely exceed internal corporate benchmarks for profitability. And the trend is likely to continue: The gross domestic product of emerging markets equaled the gross domestic product of advanced nations for the first time in 2006, with much of the growth coming from the 'BRICET' nations – Brazil, Russia, India, China, Eastern Europe and Turkey.

Until the past few years, emerging markets were a relatively low priority to the leading consumer products companies with a few exceptions, even though these markets are home to about 85% of the world's population. The obstacles are still real – in emerging markets, multinationals compete on unfamiliar terrain dominated by local players, sell at price points below those in their home countries, and wrestle with deep-seated social and cultural customs. But with growth slowing in the mature markets of North America, Japan and Western Europe, some consumer goods companies have figured out how to tap into the purchasing power of a new and growing middle class – which has rising income, credit cards and access to personal loans – in these emerging markets. The fast-moving consumer goods market leaders have proved that, when armed with the right strategies, they can beat domestic competitors. But what separates the winners from the losers?

---

* *MIT Sloan Management Review*, Spring 2008.

Flexible thinking, to begin with. Successful companies are willing to break away from business as usual. They reconfigure global products to compete with consumers' preferences for popular local brands, both in price and taste. Or, as with Rossiya – the leading chocolate brand in Nestlé S.A.'s Russian portfolio – companies skillfully steer acquired brands with 50 years of tradition under their own umbrella. They adapt Western marketing and business management practices to local customs. And they develop the resourcefulness to overcome inevitable barriers. For example, where the transportation infrastructure is poor, they might develop workarounds to distribute their products, as Unilever Group did with its fleet of motorcycles to reach customers in remote villages in Indonesia.

For those that surmount the obstacles, the rewards can be great. In some consumer product categories, growth in emerging markets is three times that of developed markets. While each market requires different adaptations, the emerging-market winners share six common practices. (See 'Keys to Emerging-Market Success')

They enter the mass market to achieve scale in distribution, brand building and operations. Historically, multinationals in developing nations targeted niche premium segments – those that traditionally delivered the highest profit margins, Typically, these companies could not bring their costs low enough to sell to less affluent consumers, many of whom still lived in the countryside. The multinationals often were stuck with low growth, while local players were expanding rapidly in the low-end segments. And local players – making the most of their low costs, better distribution and increasing sophistication – also began launching brands in the premium segment as the middle class started to grow.

A good example is the cigarette business in Indonesia, where foreign players were limited to less than 10% of the market with brands like Marlboro, Dunhill and Lucky Strike. In 2003, one local player, PT Hanjaya Mandala Sampoerna Tbk., launched A Mild, a kretek (clove and tobacco) cigarette for the premium segment. The success of that brand propelled local players like PT Djarum to attack the premium and near-premium segments with brands like L.A. Lights.

As local companies moved into the premium and near-premium market segments, multinationals realized that the mass-market opportunity was too big and important to ignore – they needed to enter the mass market for both the opportunity and to play defense. What's more, participating in the mass segment allows multinationals to drive down the costs of their premium products by achieving economies of scale in raw materials purchasing, manufacturing, sales, distribution and brand building.

In 2005, for example, Philip Morris International Inc. purchased family-owned Sampoerna in a $5.2 billion transaction. It was the largest deal by a foreign investor in Indonesia. In addition to the many benefits that come with achieving scale, the acquisition will help Philip Morris and Sampoerna make the most of distribution synergies that can help them expand both companies' brands in Indonesia and in markets like Malaysia, Singapore, Brunei and Brazil. Said Sampoerna president director Martin King, 'In Indonesia, Sampoerna has an unparalleled distribution network, whereas Philip Morris has a very good distribution system and sales force in many other countries around the world.' Among the first offspring from the corporate marriage: In July 2007,

Philip Morris introduced Marlboro Kretek Filter, a new cigarette aimed at extending the Marlboro brand in Indonesia's market for clove-and-tobacco cigarettes.

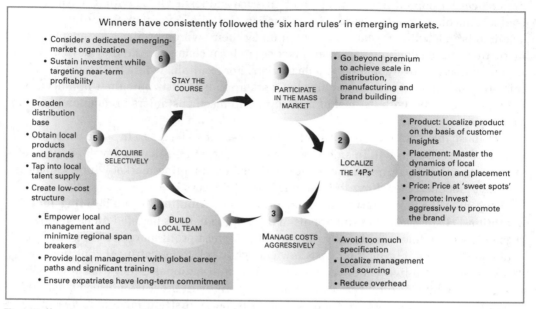

Figure 1 Keys to emerging-market success

The Philip Morris-Sampoerna acquisition has been an enormous success – the combined company's volume jumped 9.1% in the first year, and market share rose 1.5%, to more than 28%, enabling it to overtake Jakarta-based PT Gudang Garam Tbk, as market leader.

They localize at every level. Homegrown competitors have several incumbent advantages, including consumer understanding and loyalty, lower costs and home court advantages with government regulators. But by taking the time to learn and master local market complexities, multinationals can gain a competitive edge. That often requires fundamental changes to the product offering – switching to significantly smaller pack sizes, using unconventional distribution channels and developing products in local flavors, to name a few.

For its part, Procter & Gamble Co. knew that winning over Chinese toothpaste consumers meant catering to local preferences and health beliefs. After extensive research, P&G rolled out a reformulated version of Crest. Chinese consumers can find the Crest brand in fruit and tea flavors, with herbal elements, and there's even a salt version, catering to the Chinese belief that salt promotes whiter teeth. P&G's approach to localization helped boost its toothpaste sales in China from nearly zero in 1997 to 25% of the market in 2007.

The Coca-Cola Co, accelerated its growth in the Russian soft drinks market by acquiring the second-largest Russian fruit juice maker, Multon, through its Greek subsidiary, Coca-Cola Hellenic Bottling Co, S.A., in 2005. It thus positioned itself to ride the local preference for fruit juice drinks. Russia is the largest producer and consumer of fruit juice in Eastern Europe, where fruit juice sales shot up 64% between 1998 and 2003. Coca-Cola credited the acquisition, along with a marketing push, with helping deliver an above-average sales increase of 7% in 2005 across North Asia, Eurasia and the Middle East.

Unilever has used innovative distribution solutions to tap the consumer market in rural India. It trained more than 25,000 Indian village women to serve as distributors, extending its reach to 80,000 villages. The program generates about $250 million yearly from villages that otherwise would be too costly to serve.

Localizing also means taking an aggressive approach to brand building. That was the foundation for Coca-Cola's dramatic success in China, where it leads all carbonated soft-drink sales, with a 51% market share led by its Coke and Sprite brands against PepsiCo's 30% share. Coca-Cola's sales maintained a 16% to 17% annual growth rate in the latest five years, and it even hit 18% in the second quarter of 2007. By spending twice as much as PepsiCo on advertising and promotion – including sponsoring sports events in China, Chinese Olympic teams and Beijing's 2008 Olympic bid – Coca-Cola eclipsed domestic and multinational competitors alike to attain the No. 1 position, Now, China is Coca-Cola's fourth-largest market, approximately 5% of its worldwide sales.

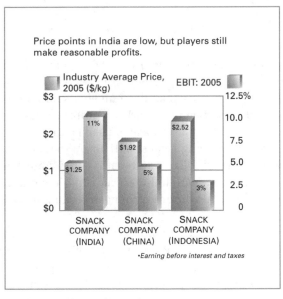

Figure 2 Can mass yield profits?
Source: ACNielsen Corp. data: Bain & Co.Inc. analysis

At the crux of all localization strategies is pricing. Global marketers cannot beat out local brands unless they find the local pricing sweet spot – a price that is competitive in the local marketplace and that also delivers a profit. (See 'Can Mass Yield Profits?') Finding that affordable price point usually requires reconfiguring existing products or creating new ones specific to a market. For example, Singapore-based Petra Foods Ltd., the world's fourth-largest chocolate maker, prices its popular chocolate treat for

Indonesian consumers at two pricing sweet spots – 500 and 1,000 rupiahs (approximately five and 10 U.S. cents). Those prices coincide with the pocket money typically given to children for treats.

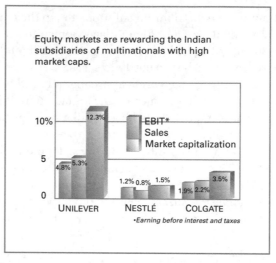

Figure 3 Subsidiaries growing

Sources: Annual reports: Bloomberg: Reuters; market cap numbers for India from last fiscal year end to match EBIT and sales data

They develop a 'good-enough' cost mentality. Between the traditional premium and low-end market segments is the large and flourishing market for what we call 'good-enough' products, with higher quality than low-end goods but affordable prices that still generate profits. Feeding the good-enough market requires aggressive management of costs. Among the techniques: taking advantage of used capital equipment or more labor-intensive production processes, using local suppliers and outsourcing. For example, a major multinational food company discovered that it could source capital equipment from India at a third of the price it paid to European suppliers without compromising its stringent quality standards. Cost discipline also means reducing overhead and localizing management.

Winners look at everything they can control to shift the competitive dynamics in their favor – from changing the specifications for packaging material to imposing greater operating efficiency to lowering overhead and using local equipment.

For multinationals catering to the premium end of the market, a strategic acquisition can help slash costs enough to make them competitive. (See 'Subsidiaries Growing.') For example, in 2000, Colgate-Palmolive Co. invested $21 million for a 40% stake in Sanxiao, a low-cost toothpaste brand in China. The domestic company had a 30% cost advantage over Colgate. By localizing manufacturing at a Sanxiao facility, Colgate was able to reduce its costs by 60%, which allowed the company to lower the price of its goods by an equal percentage and thus expand into the good-enough segment. Colgate's benefits multiplied when it started using the factory as a worldwide distribution center.

They think globally, hire locally. Too often, multinationals count on expatriates to guide their entry into emerging markets, an approach that can backfire. Expatriates can drive up costs and frequently fail to deliver the deep market understanding offered by local managers. Instead of parachuting in expert expatriates on short assignments, winning multinationals cultivate world-class local management teams that provide a competitive edge in product design, promotion and distribution. The primary role of expatriates shifts from managing to developing local talent and transferring knowledge.

Market leaders foster loyalty by empowering local teams and providing them with global opportunities. It's a talent pool they can tap when entering other emerging markets. Procter & Gamble, the most successful consumer products company in China, has staked its future on its Chinese recruits, who represent nearly all of its employees in China – with one-quarter of them holding Chinese university degrees. When companies do hire expatriates, they make sure there's a long-term commitment.

But the tight local management pools also require creativity, flexibility and commitment. Fast-moving consumer goods players risk becoming the training ground for their local competitors, which are sometimes ready to promote faster and pay better than traditional pay scales allow. A sales force turnover exceeding 50% per year can result.

They make sure local acquisitions have a strong business fit. A strategic acquisition can accelerate a multinational's entry into an emerging market by adding popular local brands to its product lineup, broadening its reach with a stronger distribution network, providing a local talent pool and lowering operating costs. In July 2007, Coca-Cola acquired the Russian beverage group Aquavision, giving itself state-of-the-art, expanded production capabilities. The move builds on Coca-Cola's previous purchase of Multon, the leading Russian fruit juke maker, strengthening the multinational's position in Eastern Europe's hotly contested soft drinks market.

In India, Frito-Lay Inc. increased its market share – and profits – when it bought the local brand Uncle Chipps in 2000. The Indian chips complemented Frito-Lay's brand portfolio, both in price and flavors. After the acquisition, Frito-Lay relaunched the Uncle Chipps brand at a lower price, positioning it as cheaper than Lay's, its flagship potato chip brand. Instead of competing against each other, Frito-Lay has two products targeted at different consumer segments. It also trimmed the number of Uncle Chipps flavors, dropping one that was similar to its saucy ketchup offering. Again, the goal was to have complementary, not competing, flavors. To reduce manufacturing costs, Lay's moved production to a local plant.

Gillette, which was acquired by P&G in 2005 and is the world's largest battery maker, scored a major coup in 2003 by acquiring the Fujian Nanping Nanfu Battery Co. Ltd., the major Chinese rival to its Duracell batteries. The acquisition gave Gillette much more than just a hot-selling Chinese battery brand. The deal had hidden assets: a state-of-the-art manufacturing plant and a distribution network with over three million retailers throughout China. With Nanfu's low-cost factory, Gillette was able to reduce production costs and use the retailing network to extend the reach of its Duracell product line. Gillette protected both Duracell's and Nanfu's brands in their respective segments. The dual branding, cost synergies, sales growth, broadened product portfolio, economies of scale and superior distribution access to more than three million retail outlets in China enabled Gillette to increase its operating margins in the country significantly.

They organize for emerging markets. The leaders maximize their investments by building dedicated emerging-market capabilities. This enables them to approach each emerging market with strategies crafted to distinguish the characteristics they find there from the established practices they pursue in developed economies. For example, British American Tobacco PLC, one of the most successful consumer goods companies in emerging markets, has long had a stable of international management talent that it deploys across Asia, Africa and Latin America.

A U.K. multinational has taken this a step further by creating a formal emerging-markets organization separate from its other international operations. By putting the emerging-markets operations under one tent, it expects to sharpen management's focus and improve managers' ability to evaluate the relative risk-return trade-offs across its emerging-markets portfolio. This will also promote cross-market learning about what works and what doesn't – crucial lessons that otherwise might be lost if emerging-market insights were blurred in a vast global operation.

Groupe Danone, the French food conglomerate, has substantial presence in major emerging markets in Asia such as India, Indonesia and China, which share several common characteristics – huge geographic area; a high proportion of mom-and-pop outlets, especially in rural areas; and low price points. The company has learned a lot from operating in these markets, such as positioning brands to appeal to local consumers, using low-cost Asian production equipment, keeping a tight lid on overhead and changing the specifications for packaging and raw materials to produce 'good-enough' products, These lessons have been effectively cross-pollinated across the various emerging markets in which Danone operates.

With consumer markets in Asia and Eastern Europe growing at double-digit rates, multinationals are moving fast to build their brands – and the expertise to manage them in emerging markets. Indeed, succeeding in emerging markets is essential if multinationals are to defend – and increase – their share of the global market. How they fare in emerging markets is a critical indicator of how they will fare in the world.

SATISH SHANKAR and *CHARLES ORMISTON* are partners with Bain & Co. Inc. in Singapore. *NICOLAS BLOCH* coleads Bain's European Consumer Products Practice and is a Bain partner in Brussels. *ROBERT SCHAUS* is a Bain partner in Moscow and Kiev. *VIJAY VISHWANATH* leads Bain's Global Consumer Products Practice and is a partner in Boston. Comment on this article or contact the authors through smrfeedback@mit.edu.

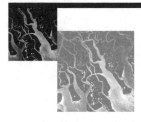

READING 14
Strategies that fit emerging markets*

Tarun Khanna, Krishna G. Palepu, and Jayant Sinha

Fast-growing economies often provide poor soil for profits. The cause? A lack of specialized intermediary firms and regulatory systems on which multinational companies depend. Successful businesses look for those institutional voids and work around them.

CEOs and top management teams of large corporations, particularly in North America, Europe, and Japan, acknowledge that globalization is the most critical challenge they face today. They are also keenly aware that it has become tougher during the past decade to identify internationalization strategies and to choose which countries to do business with. Still, most companies have stuck to the strategies they've traditionally deployed, which emphasize standardized approaches to new markets while sometimes experimenting with a few local twists. As a result, many multinational corporations are struggling to develop successful strategies in emerging markets.

Part of the problem, we believe, is that the absence of specialized intermediaries, regulatory systems, and contract-enforcing mechanisms in emerging markets – 'institutional voids,' we christened them in a 1997 HBR article – hampers the implementation of globalization strategies. Companies in developed countries usually take for granted the critical role that 'soft' infrastructure plays in the execution of their business models in their home markets. But that infrastructure is often underdeveloped or absent in emerging markets. There's no dearth of examples. Companies can't find skilled market research firms to inform them reliably about customer preferences so they can tailor products to specific needs and increase people's willingness to pay. Few end-to-end logistics providers, which allow manufacturers to reduce costs, are available to transport raw materials and finished products. Before recruiting employees, corporations have to screen large numbers of candidates themselves because there aren't many search firms that can do the job for them.

Because of all those institutional voids, many multinational companies have fared poorly in developing countries. All the anecdotal evidence we have gathered suggests

---

* *Harvard Business Review*, June 2005.

Harvard Business Review and Harvard Business School Publishing content on EBSCOhost is licensed for the individual use of authorized EBSCOhost patrons at this institution and is not intended for use as assigned course material. Harvard Business School Publishing is pleased to grant permission to make this work available through 'electronic reserves' or other means of digital access or transmission to students enrolled in a course. For rates and authorization regarding such course usage, contact permissions@hbsp.harvard.edu.

that since the 1990s, American corporations have performed better in their home environments than they have in foreign countries, especially in emerging markets. Not surprisingly, many CEOs are wary of emerging markets and prefer to invest in developed nations instead. By the end of 2002 – according to the Bureau of Economic Analysis, an agency of the U.S. Department of Commerce – American corporations and their affiliate companies had $1.6 trillion worth of assets in the United Kingdom and $514 billion in Canada but only $173 billion in Brazil, Russia, India, and China combined. That's just 2.5% of the $6.9 trillion in investments American companies held by the end of that year. In fact, although U.S. corporations' investments in China doubled between 1992 and 2002, that amount was still less than 1% of all their overseas assets.

Many companies shied away from emerging markets when they should have engaged with them more closely. Since the early 1990s, developing countries have been the fastest-growing market in the world for most products and services. Companies can lower costs by setting up manufacturing facilities and service centers in those areas, where skilled labor and trained managers are relatively inexpensive. Moreover, several developing-country transnational corporations have entered North America and Europe with low-cost strategies (China's Haier Group in household electrical appliances) and novel business models (India's Infosys in information technology services). Western companies that want to develop counter-strategies must push deeper into emerging markets, which foster a different genre of innovations than mature markets do.

If Western companies don't develop strategies for engaging across their value chains with developing countries, they are unlikely to remain competitive for long. However, despite crumbling tariff barriers, the spread of the Internet and cable television, and the rapidly improving physical infrastructure in these countries, CEOs can't assume they can do business in emerging markets the same way they do in developed nations. That's because the quality of the market infrastructure varies widely from country to country. In general, advanced economies have large pools of seasoned market intermediaries and effective contract-enforcing mechanisms, whereas less-developed economies have unskilled intermediaries and less-effective legal systems. Because the services provided by intermediaries either aren't available in emerging markets or aren't very sophisticated, corporations can't smoothly transfer the strategies they employ in their home countries to those emerging markets.

During the past ten years, we've researched and consulted with multinational corporations all over the world. One of us led a comparative research project on China and India at Harvard Business School, and we have all been involved in McKinsey & Company's Global Champions research project. We have learned that successful companies work around institutional voids. They develop strategies for doing business in emerging markets that are different from those they use at home and often find novel ways of implementing them, too. They also customize their approaches to fit each nation's institutional context. As we will show, firms that take the trouble to understand the institutional differences between countries are likely to choose the best markets to enter, select optimal strategies, and make the most out of operating in emerging markets.

Why composite indices are inadequate

Before we delve deeper into institutional voids, it's important to understand why companies often target the wrong countries or deploy inappropriate globalization strategies. Many corporations enter new lands because of senior managers' personal experiences, family ties, gut feelings, or anecdotal evidence. Others follow key customers or rivals into emerging markets; the herd instinct is strong among multinationals. Biases, too, dog companies' foreign investments. For instance, the reason U.S. companies preferred to do business with China rather than India for decades was probably because of America's romance with China, first profiled in MIT political scientist Harold Isaacs's work in the late 1950s. Isaacs pointed out that partly as a result of the work missionaries and scholars did in China in the 1800s, Americans became more familiar with China than with India.

Companies that choose new markets systematically often use tools like country portfolio analysis and political risk assessment, which chiefly focus on the potential profits from doing business in developing countries but leave out essential information about the soft infrastructures there. In December 2004, when the McKinsey Global Survey of Business Executives polled 9,750 senior managers on their priorities and concerns, 61% said that market size and growth drove their firms' decisions to enter new countries. While 17% felt that political and economic stability was the most important factor in making those decisions, only 13% said that structural conditions (in other words, institutional contexts) mattered most.

Just how do companies estimate a nation's potential? Executives usually analyze its GDP and per capita income growth rates, its population composition and growth rates, and its exchange rates and purchasing power parity indices (past, present, and projected). To complete the picture, managers consider the nation's standing on the World Economic Forum's Global Competitiveness Index, the World Bank's governance indicators, and Transparency International's corruption ratings; its weight in emerging market funds investments; and, perhaps, forecasts of its next political transition.

Such composite indices are no doubt useful, but companies should use them as the basis for drawing up strategies only when their home bases and target countries have comparable institutional contexts. For example, the United States and the United Kingdom have similar product, capital, and labor markets, with networks of skilled intermediaries and strong regulatory systems. The two nations share an Anglo-Saxon legal system as well. American companies can enter Britain comfortable in the knowledge that they will find competent market research firms, that they can count on English law to enforce agreements they sign with potential partners, and that retailers will be able to distribute products ail over the country. Those are dangerous assumptions to make in an emerging market, where skilled intermediaries or contract-enforcing mechanisms are unlikely to be found. However, composite indices don't flash warning signals to would-be entrants about the presence of institutional voids in emerging markets.

In fact, composite index-based analyses of developing countries conceal more than they reveal. (See the exhibit 'The Trouble with Composite Indices.') In 2003, Brazil, Russia, India, and China appeared similar on several Indices. Yet despite the four countries' comparable standings, the key success factors in each of those markets have turned out to be very different. For instance, in China and Russia, multinational retail chains and local retailers have expanded into the urban and semi-urban areas, whereas in Brazil, only a few global chains have set up shop in key urban centers. And in India, the government prohibited foreign direct investment in the retailing and real estate industries until February 2005, so mom-and-pop retailers dominate. Brazil, Russia, India, and China may all be big markets for multinational consumer product makers, but executives have to design unique distribution strategies for each market. That process must start with a thorough understanding of the differences between the countries' market infrastructures. Those differences may make it more attractive for some businesses to enter, say, Brazil than India.

Companies often base their globalization strategies on country rankings, but on most lists, it is impossible to tell developing countries apart. According to the six indices below, Brazil, India, and China share similar markets while Russia, though an outlier on many parameters, is comparable to the other nations. Contrary to what these rankings suggest, however, the market infrastructure in each of these countries varies widely, and companies need to deploy very different strategies to succeed.

	Brazil	Russia	India	China
Growth Competitiveness Index ranking* (out of 104 countries; for 2003)	57	70	55	46
Business Competitiveness Index ranking* (out of 103 countries; for 2003)	38	61	30	47
Governance Indicators (percentile rankings)** (out of 199 countries; for 2002)				
Voice and accountability	58.I	33.8	60.2	10.1
Political stability	48.1	33.0	22.2	51.4
Government effectiveness	50.0	44.3	54.1	63.4
Regulatory quality	63.4	44.3	43.8	40.2
Rule of law	50.0	25.3	57.2	51.5
Control of corruption	56.7	21.1	49.5	42.3
Corruption Perceptions Index ranking*** (out of 145 countries; for 2004)	59	90	90	71
Composite Country Risk Points**** (for January 2005; the larger the number, the less risky the country)	70	78	72	76
Weight in Emerging Markets Index (%)***** (for February 2004; out of 26 emerging markets)	6.96%	5.16%	5.02%	4.76%

The trouble with composite indices

Sources: * World Economic Forum, 'Global Competitiveness Report,' 2004–2005

** World Bank Governance Research Indicator Country Snapshot, 2002

*** Transparency International, Corruption Perceptions Index, 2004

**** The PRS Group, *International Country Risk Guide*, January 2005

***** Barclays Global Investors, iShares '2004 Semi-Annual Report to Shareholders'

How to map institutional contexts

As we helped companies think through their globalization strategies, we came up with a simple conceptual device – the five contexts framework – that lets executives map the institutional contexts of any country. Economics 101 tells us that companies buy inputs in the product, labor, and capital markets and sell their outputs in the products (raw materials and finished goods) or services market. When choosing strategies, therefore, executives need to figure out how the product, labor, and capital markets work – and don't work – in their target countries. This will help them understand the differences between home markets and those in developing countries. In addition, each country's social and political milieu – as well as the manner in which it has opened up to the outside world – shapes those markets, and companies must consider those factors, too.

The five contexts framework places a superstructure of key markets on a base of sociopolitical choices. Many multinational corporations look at either the macro factors (the degree of openness and the sociopolitical atmosphere) or some of the market factors, but few pay attention to both. We have developed sets of questions that companies can ask to create a map of each country's context and to gauge the extent to which businesses must adapt their strategies to each one. (See the exhibit 'Spotting Institutional Voids.') Before we apply the framework to some developing countries, let's briefly touch on the five contexts.

Political and social systems

As we've discussed, every country's political system affects its product, labor, and capital markets. In socialist societies like China, for instance, workers cannot form independent trade unions in the labor market, which affects wage levels. A country's social environment is also important. In South Africa, for example, the government's support for the transfer of assets to the historically disenfranchised native African community – a laudable social objective – has affected the development of the capital market. Such transfers usually price assets in an arbitrary fashion, which makes it hard for multinationals to figure out the value of South African companies and affects their assessments of potential partners.

The thorny relationships between ethnic, regional, and linguistic groups in emerging markets also affects foreign investors. In Malaysia, for instance, foreign companies should enter into joint ventures only after checking if their potential partners belong to the majority Malay community or the economically dominant Chinese community, so as not to conflict with the government's longstanding policy of transferring some assets from Chinese to Malays. This policy arose because of a perception that the race riots of 1969 were caused by the tension between the Chinese haves and the Malay have-nots. Although the rhetoric has changed somewhat in the past few years, the pro-Malay policy remains in place.

Executives would do well to identify a country's power centers, such as its bureaucracy, media, and civil society, and figure out if there are checks and balances in place. Managers must also determine how decentralized the political system is, if the government is subject to oversight, and whether bureaucrats and politicians are independent from one another. Companies should gauge the level of actual trust among the populace as opposed to enforced trust. For instance, if people believe companies won't vanish with their savings, firms may be able to raise money locally sooner rather than later.

Openness

CEOs often talk about the need for economies to be open because they believe it's best to enter countries that welcome direct investment by multinational corporations – although companies can get into countries that don't allow foreign investment by entering into joint ventures or by licensing local partners. Still, they must remember that the concept of 'open' can be deceptive. For example, executives believe that China is an open economy because the government welcomes foreign investment but that India is a relatively closed economy because of the lukewarm reception the Indian government gives multinationals. However, India has been open to ideas from the West, and people have always been able to travel freely in and out of the country, whereas for decades, the Chinese government didn't allow its citizens to travel abroad freely, and it still doesn't allow many ideas to cross its borders. Consequently, while it may be true that multinational companies can invest in China more easily than they can in India, managers in India are more inclined to be market oriented and globally aware than managers are in China.

The more open a country's economy, the more likely it is that global intermediaries will be allowed to operate there. Multinationals, therefore, will find it easier to function in markets that are more open because they can use the services of both the global and local intermediaries. However, openness can be a double-edged sword: A government that allows local companies to access the global capital market neutralizes one of foreign companies' key advantages.

The two macro contexts we have just described – political and social systems and openness – shape the market contexts. For instance, in Chile, a military coup in the early 1970s led to the establishment of a right-wing government, and that government's liberal economic policies led to a vibrant capital market in the country. But Chile's labor market remained underdeveloped because the government did not allow trade unions to operate freely. Similarly, openness affects the development of markets. If a country's capital markets are open to foreign investors, financial intermediaries will become more sophisticated. That has happened in India, for example, where capital markets are more open than they are in China. Likewise, in the product market, if multinationals can invest in the retail industry, logistics providers will develop rapidly. This has been the case in China, where providers have taken hold more quickly than they have in India, which has only recently allowed multinationals to invest in retailing.

Product markets

Developing countries have opened up their markets and grown rapidly during the past decade, but companies still struggle to get reliable information about consumers, especially those with low incomes. Developing a consumer finance business is tough, for example, because the data sources and credit histories that firms draw on in the West don't exist in emerging markets. Market research and advertising are in their infancy in developing countries, and it's difficult to find the deep databases on consumption patterns that allow companies to segment consumers in more-developed markets. There are few government bodies or independent publications, like *Consumer Reports* in the United States, that provide expert advice on the features and quality of products. Because of a lack of consumer courts and advocacy groups in developing nations, many people feel they are at the mercy of big companies.

Labor markets

In spite of emerging markets' large populations, multinationals have trouble recruiting managers and other skilled workers because the quality of talent is hard to ascertain. There are relatively few search firms and recruiting agencies in low-income countries. The high-quality firms that do exist focus on top-level searches, so companies must scramble to identify middle-level managers, engineers, or floor supervisors. Engineering colleges, business schools, and training institutions have proliferated, but apart from an elite few, there's no way for companies to tell which schools produce skilled managers. For instance, several Indian companies have sprung up to train people for jobs in the call center business, but no organization rates the quality of the training it provides.

Capital markets

The capital and financial markets in developing countries are remarkable for their lack of sophistication. Apart from a few stock exchanges and government-appointed regulators, there aren't many reliable intermediaries like credit-rating agencies, investment analysts, merchant bankers, or venture capital firms. Multinationals can't count on raising debt or equity capital locally to finance their operations. Like investors, creditors don't have access to accurate information on companies. Businesses can't easily assess the creditworthiness of other firms or collect receivables after they have extended credit to customers. Corporate governance is also notoriously poor in emerging markets. Transnational companies, therefore, can't trust their partners to adhere to local laws and joint venture agreements. In fact, since crony capitalism thrives in developing countries, multinationals can't assume that the profit motive alone is what's driving local firms.

Several CEOs have asked us why we emphasize the role of institutional intermediaries and ignore industry factors. They argue that industry structure, such as the degree of competition, should also influence companies' strategies. But when Harvard Business School professor Jan Rivkin and one of the authors of this article ranked industries by profitability, they found that the correlation of industry rankings across pairs of countries was close to zero, which means that the attractiveness of an industry varied widely from country to country. So although factors like scale economies, entry barriers, and the ability to differentiate products matter in every industry, the weight of their importance varies from place to place. An attractive industry in your home market may turn out to be unattractive in another country. Companies should analyze industry structures – always a useful exercise – only after they understand a country's institutional context.

Mapping Contexts in Brazil, Russia, India, and China

The five contexts (below) can help companies spot the institutional voids in any country. An application of the framework to the four fastest-growing markets in the world reveals how different those countries are from developed nations and, more important, from one another.

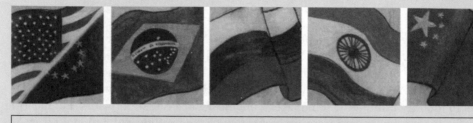

POLITICAL AND SOCIAL SYSTEM

U.S./EU	Brazil	Russia	India	China
Political Structure				
Countries have vibrant democracies with checks and balances. Companies can count on rule of law and fair enforcement of legal contracts.	The democracy is vibrant. Bureaucracy is rampant. There are pockets of corruption in federal and state governments.	A centralized government and some regional freedoms coexist. Bureaucracy is stifling. Corruption occurs at all levels of government.	The democracy is vibrant. The government is highly bureaucratic. Corruption is rampant in state and local governments.	The Communist Party maintains a monopoly on political power. Local governments make economic policy decisions. Officials may abuse power for personal gain.
Civil Society				
A dynamic media acts as a check on abuses by both companies and governments. Powerful nongovernmental organizations (NGOs) influence corporate policies on social and environmental issues.	Influential local media serves as a watchdog. The influence of local NGOs is marginal.	The media is controlled by the government. NGOs are underdeveloped and disorganized.	A dynamic press and vigilant NGOs act as checks on politicians and companies.	The media is muzzled by the government, and there are few independent NGOs. Companies don't have to worry about criticism, but they can't count on civil society to check abuses of power.

OPENNESS

U.S./EU	Brazil	Russia	India	China
Modes of Entry				
Open to all forms of foreign investment except when governments have concerns about potential monopolies or national security issues.	Both greenfield investments and acquisitions are possible but difficult entry strategies. Companies team up with local partners to gain local expertise.	Both greenfield investments and acquisitions are possible but difficult. Companies form alliances to gain access to government and local inputs.	Restrictions on greenfield investments and acquisitions in some sectors make joint ventures necessary. Red tape hinders companies in sectors where the government does allow foreign investment.	The government permits greenfield investments as well as acquisitions. Acquired companies are likely to have been state owned and may have hidden liabilities. Alliances let companies align interests with all levels of government.

LABOR MARKETS

U.S./EU	Brazil	Russia	India	China
Workers Market				
The level of unionization varies among countries. Industrial actions take place in Europe, especially in the manufacturing and public sectors, but not in the United States.	Trade unions are strong and pragmatic, which means that companies can sign agreements with them.	Trade unions are present, but their influence is declining except in certain sectors, such as mining and railways.	The trade union movement is active and volatile, although it is becoming less important. Trade unions have strong political connections.	Workers can join the government-controlled All-China Federation of Trade Unions, Historically, there were no industrial actions, but there have been recent strikes at Hong Kong- and Taiwan-owned manufacturing facilities.

CAPITAL MARKETS

U.S./EU	Brazil	Russia	India	China
Debt and Equity				
Companies can easily get bank loans. The corporate bond market is well developed. The integration of stock exchanges gives companies access to a deep pool of investors.	A good banking system exists, and there is a healthy market for initial public offerings. Wealthy individuals can invest in offshore accounts.	The banking system is strong but dominated by state-owned banks. The consumer credit market is booming, and the IPO market is growing. Firms must incorporate local subsidiaries to raise equity capital.	The local banking system is well developed. Multinationals can rely on local banks for local needs. Equity is available to local and foreign entities.	The local banking system and equity markets are underdeveloped. Foreign companies have to raise both debt and equity in home markets.
Venture Capital (VC)				
VC is generally available in urban areas or for specific industry clusters. VC is not as readily available in southern Europe.	A few private equity players are active locally.	Only companies in the most profitable businesses, such as real estate development and natural resources, can access VC.	VC is available in some cities and from the Indian diaspora.	VC availability is limited.
Accounting Standards				
Apart from off-balance-sheet items, a high level of transparency exists. In the European Union, accounting practices should become more uniform after 2005 because of new norms.	The financial-reporting system is based on a common-law system and functions well.	The modified Soviet system of financial reporting works well. Banks are shifting to international accounting standards.	Financial reporting, which is based on a common-law system functions well.	There is little corporate transparency, China's accounting standards are not strict, although the China Securities Regulatory Commission wants to tighten disclosure rules.
Financial Distress				
Efficient bankruptcy processes tend to favor certain stakeholders (creditors, labor force, or shareholders) in certain countries.	Processes allow companies to stay in business rather than go out of business. Bankruptcy processes exist but are inefficient.	Bankruptcy processes and legislation are fully developed. Corruption distorts bankruptcy enforcement.	Bankruptcy processes exist but are inefficient. Promoters find it difficult to sell off or shut down 'sick' enterprises.	Companies can use bankruptcy processes in some cases. Write-offs are common.

PRODUCT MARKETS

U.S./EU	Brazil	Russia	India	China
Product Development and Intellectual Property Rights (IPR)				
Sophisticated product-design capabilities are available. Governments enforce IPR and protect trademarks, so R&D investments yield competitive advantages.	Local design capability exists. IPR disputes with the United States exist in some sectors.	The country has a strong local design capability but exhibits an ambivalent attitude about IPR. Sufficient regulatory authority exists, but enforcement is patchy.	Some local design capability is available. IPR problems with the United States exist in some industries. Regulatory bodies monitor product quality and fraud.	Imitation and piracy abound. Punishment for IPR theft varies across provinces and by level of corruption.
Supplier Base and Logistics				
Companies use national and international suppliers. Firms outsource and move manufacturing and services offshore instead of integrating vertically. A highly developed infrastructure is in place, but urban areas are saturated.	Suppliers are available in the Mercosur region. A good network of highways, airports, and ports exists.	Companies can rely on local suppliers for simple components. The European region has decent logistics networks, but trans-Ural Russia is not well developed.	Suppliers are available, but their quality and dependability varies greatly. Roads are in poor condition. Ports and airports are under-developed.	Several suppliers have strong manufacturing capabilities, but few vendors have advanced technical abilities. The road network is well developed. Port facilities are excellent.
Brand Perceptions and Management				
Markets are mature and have strong local and global brands. The profusion of brands clutters consumer choice. Numerous ad agencies are available.	Consumers accept both local and global brands. Global as well as local ad agencies are present.	Consumers prefer global brands in automobiles and high tech. Local brands thrive in the food and beverage businesses. Some local and global ad agencies are available.	Consumers buy both local and global brands. Global ad agencies are present, but they have been less successful than local ad agencies.	Consumers prefer to buy products from American, European, and Japanese companies. Multinational ad agencies dominate the business.

LABOR MARKETS

U.S./EU	Brazil	Russia	India	China
Market for Managers				
A large and varied pool of well-trained management talent exists.	The large pool of management talent has varying degrees of proficiency in English. Both local and expatriate managers hold senior management jobs.	The large pool of management talent has varying degrees of proficiency in English, and it is supplemented by expatriate managers. Employment agencies are booming.	The country has a highly liquid pool of English-speaking management talent fueled by business and technical schools. Local hires are preferred over expatriates.	There is a relatively small and static market for managers, especially away from the eastern seaboard. Many senior and middle managers aren't fluent in English. A large number of managers are expatriates. Some members of the Chinese diaspora have returned home to work.

Source: Media reports and interviews with academics and business people.

Spotting Institutional Voids

Managers can identify the institutional voids in any country by asking a series of questions. The answers — or sometimes, the lack of them — will tell companies where they should adapt their business models to the nation's institutional context.

POLITICAL AND SOCIAL SYSTEM

1 To whom are the country's politicians accountable? Are there strong political groups that oppose the ruling party? Do elections take place regularly?

2 Are the roles of the legislative, executive, and judiciary clearly defined? What is the distribution of power between the central, state, and city governments?

3 Does the government go beyond regulating business to interfering in it or running companies?

4 Do the laws articulate and protect private property rights?

5 What is the quality of the country's bureaucrats? What are bureaucrats' incentives and career trajectories?

6 Is the judiciary independent? Do the courts adjudicate disputes and enforce contracts in a timely and impartial manner? How effective are the quasi-judicial regulatory institutions that set and enforce rules for business activities?

7 Do religious, linguistic, regional, and ethnic groups coexist peacefully, or are there tensions between them?

8 How vibrant and independent is the media? Are newspapers and magazines neutral, or do they represent sectarian interests?

9 Are nongovernmental organizations, civil rights groups, and environmental groups active in the country?

10 Do people tolerate corruption in business and government?

11 What role do family ties play in business?

12 Can strangers be trusted to honor a contract in the country?

OPENNESS

1 Are the country's government, media, and people receptive to foreign investment? Do citizens trust companies and individuals from some parts of the world more than others?

2 What restrictions does the government place on foreign investment? Are those restrictions in place to facilitate the growth of domestic companies, to protect state monopolies, or because people are suspicious of multinationals?

3 Can a company make greenfield investments and acquire local companies, or can it only break into the market by entering into joint ventures? Will

that company be free to choose partners based purely on economic considerations?

4 Does the country allow the presence of foreign intermediaries such as market research and advertising firms, retailers, media companies, banks, insurance companies, venture capital firms, auditing firms, management consulting firms, and educational institutions?

5 How long does it take to start a new venture in the country? How cumbersome are the government's procedures for permitting the launch of a wholly foreign-owned business?

6 Are there restrictions on portfolio investments by overseas companies or on dividend repatriation by multinationals?

7 Does the market drive exchange rates, or does the government control them? If it's the latter, does the government try to maintain a stable exchange rate, or does it try to favor domestic products over imports by propping up the local currency?

8 What would be the impact of tariffs on a company's capital goods and raw materials imports? How would import duties affect that company's ability to manufacture its products locally versus exporting them from home?

9 Can a company set up its business anywhere in the country? If the government restricts the company's location choices, are its motives political, or is it inspired by a logical regional development strategy?

10 Has the country signed free-trade agreements with other nations? If so, do those agreements favor investments by companies from some parts of the world over others?

11 Does the government allow foreign executives to enter and leave the country freely? How difficult is it to get work permits for managers and engineers?

12 Does the country allow its citizens to travel abroad freely? Can ideas flow into the country unrestricted? Are people permitted to debate and accept those ideas?

PRODUCT MARKETS

1 Can companies easily obtain reliable data on customer tastes and purchase behaviors? Are there cultural barriers to market research? Do world-class market research firms operate in the country?

2 Can consumers easily obtain unbiased information on the quality of the goods and services they want to buy? Are there independent consumer organizations and publications that provide such information?

3 Can companies access raw materials and components of good quality? Is there a deep network of suppliers? Are there firms that assess suppliers' quality and reliability? Can companies enforce contracts with suppliers?

4 How strong are the logistics and transportation infrastructures? Have global logistics companies set up local operations?

5 Do large retail chains exist in the country? If so, do they cover the entire country or only the major cities? Do they reach all consumers or only wealthy ones?

6 Are there other types of distribution channels, such as direct-to-consumer channels and discount retail channels, that deliver products to customers?

7 Is it difficult for multinationals to collect receivables from local retailers?

8 Do consumers use credit cards, or does cash dominate transactions? Can consumers get credit to make purchases? Are data on customer creditworthiness available?

9 What recourse do consumers have against false claims by companies or defective products and services?

10 How do companies deliver after-sales service to consumers? Is it possible to set up a nationwide service network? Are third-party service providers reliable?

11 Are consumers willing to try new products and services? Do they trust goods from local companies? How about from foreign companies?

12 What kind of product-related environmental and safety regulations are in place? How do the authorities enforce those regulations?

LABOR MARKETS

1 How strong is the country's education infrastructure, especially for technical and management training? Does it have a good elementary and secondary education system as well?

2 Do people study and do business in English or in another international language, or do they mainly speak a local language?

3 Are data available to help sort out the quality of the country's educational institutions?

4 Can employees move easily from one company to another? Does the local culture support that movement? Do recruitment agencies facilitate executive mobility?

5 What are the major postrecruitment-training needs of the people that multinationals hire locally?

6 Is pay for performance a standard practice? How much weight do executives give seniority, as opposed to merit, in making promotion decisions?

7 Would a company be able to enforce employment contracts with senior executives? Could it protect itself against executives who leave the firm and then compete against it? Could it stop employees from stealing trade secrets and intellectual property?

8 Does the local culture accept foreign managers? Do the laws allow a firm to transfer locally hired people to another country? Do managers want to stay or leave the nation?

9 How are the rights of workers protected? How strong are the country's trade unions? Do they defend workers' interests or only advance a political agenda?

10 Can companies use stock options and stock-based compensation schemes to motivate employees?

11 Do the laws and regulations limit a firm's ability to restructure, downsize, or shut down?

12 If a company were to adopt its local rivals' or suppliers' business practices, such as the use of child labor, would that tarnish its image overseas?

CAPITAL MARKETS

1 How effective are the country's banks, insurance companies, and mutual funds at collecting savings and channeling them into investments?

2 Are financial institutions managed well? Is their decision making transparent? Do noneconomic considerations, such as family ties, influence their investment decisions?

3 Can companies raise large amounts of equity capital in the stock market? Is there a market for corporate debt?

4 Does a venture capital industry exist? If so, does it allow individuals with good ideas to raise funds?

5 How reliable are sources of information on company performance? Do the accounting standards and disclosure regulations permit investors and creditors to monitor company management?

6 Do independent financial analysts, rating agencies, and the media offer unbiased information on companies?

7 How effective are corporate governance norms and standards at protecting shareholder interests?

8 Are corporate boards independent and empowered, and do they have independent directors?

9 Are regulators effective at monitoring the banking industry and stock markets?

10 How well do the courts deal with fraud?

11 Do the laws permit companies to engage in hostile takeovers? Can shareholders organize themselves to remove entrenched managers through proxy fights?

12 Is there an orderly bankruptcy process that balances the interests of owners, creditors, and other stakeholders?

Applying the framework

When we applied the five contexts framework to emerging markets in four countries – Brazil, Russia, India, and China – the differences between them became apparent. (See the exhibit 'Mapping Contexts in Brazil, Russia, India, and China.') Multinationals face different kinds of competition in each of those nations. In China, state-owned enterprises control nearly half the economy, members of the Chinese diaspora control many of the foreign corporations that operate there, and the private sector brings up the rear because entrepreneurs find it almost impossible to access capital. India is the mirror image of China. Public sector corporations, though important, occupy nowhere near as prominent a place as they do in China. Unlike China, India is wary of foreign investment, even by members of the Indian diaspora. However, the country has spawned many private sector organizations, some of which are globally competitive. It's difficult to imagine a successful business in China that hasn't had something to do with the government; in India, most companies have succeeded in spite of the state.

Brazil mixes and matches features of both China and India. Like China, Brazil has floated many state-owned enterprises. At the same time, it has kept its doors open to multinationals, and European corporations such as Unilever, Volkswagen, and Nestlé have been able to build big businesses there. Volkswagen has six plants in Brazil, dominates the local market, and exports its Gol model to Argentina and Russia. Brazil also boasts private sector companies that, like Indian firms, go head-to-head in the local market with global firms. Some Brazilian companies, such as basic materials company Votorantim and aircraft maker Embraer, have become globally competitive.

Russia is also a cross between China and India, but most of its companies are less competitive than those in Brazil. A few multinationals such as McDonald's have done well, but most foreign firms have failed to make headway there. There are only a few strong private sector companies in the market, such as dairy products maker Wimm-Bill-Dann and cellular services provider VimpelCom. The Russian government is involved, formally and informally, in several industries. For instance, the government's equity stake in Gazprom allows it to influence the country's energy sector. Moreover, administrators at all levels can exercise near veto power over business deals that involve local or foreign companies, and getting permits and approvals is a complicated chore in Russia.

One level deeper, the financial markets in Brazil, Russia, India, and China vary, too. In Brazil and India, indigenous entrepreneurs, who are multinationals' main rivals, rely on the local capital markets for resources. In China, foreign companies compete with state-owned enterprises, which public sector banks usually fund. The difference is important because neither the Chinese companies nor the banks are under pressure to show profits. Moreover, financial reporting in China isn't transparent even if companies have listed themselves on stock exchanges. State-owned companies can for years pursue strategies that increase their market share at the expense of profits. Corporate governance standards in Brazil and India also mimic those of the West more closely than do those in Russia and China. Thus, in Russia and China, multinationals can't count on local partners' internal systems to protect their interests and assets – especially their intellectual property.

The three strategy choices

When companies tailor strategies to each country's contexts, they can capitalize on the strengths of particular locations. Before adapting their approaches, however, firms must compare the benefits of doing so with the additional coordination costs they'll incur. When they complete this exercise, companies will find that they have three distinct choices: They can adapt their business model to countries while keeping their core value propositions constant, they can try to change the contexts, or they can stay out of countries where adapting strategies may be uneconomical or impractical. Can companies sustain strategies that presume the existence of institutional voids? They can. It took decades to fill institutional voids in the West.

Adapt your strategies

To succeed, multinationals must modify their business models for each nation. They may have to adapt to the voids in a country's product markets, its input markets, or both. But companies must retain their core business propositions even as they adapt their business models, if they make shifts that are too radical, these firms will lose their advantages of global scale and global branding.

Compare Dell's business models in the United States and China. In the United States, the hardware maker offers consumers a wide variety of configurations and makes most computers to order. Dell doesn't use distributors or resellers, shipping most machines directly to buyers. In 2003, nearly 50% of the company's revenues in North America came from orders placed through the Internet.

The cornerstone of Dell's business model is that it carries little or no inventory. But Dell realized that its direct-sales approach wouldn't work in China, because individuals weren't accustomed to buying PCs through the Internet. Chinese companies used paper-based order processing, so Dell had to rely on faxes and phones rather than online sales. And several Chinese government departments and state-owned enterprises insisted that hardware vendors make their bids through systems integrators. The upshot is that Dell relies heavily on distributors and systems integrators in China. When it first entered the market there, the company offered a smaller product range than it did in the United States to keep inventory levels low. Later, as its supply chain became more efficient, it offered customers in China a full range of products.

Smart companies like Dell modify their business model without destroying the parts of it that give them a competitive advantage over rivals. These firms start by identifying the value propositions that they will not modify, whatever the context. That's what McDonald's did even as it comprehensively adapted its business model to Russia's factor markets. In the United States, McDonald's has outsourced most of its supply chain operations. But when it tried to move into Russia in 1990, the company was unable to find local suppliers. The fast-food chain asked several of its European vendors to step up, but they weren't interested. Instead of giving up, McDonald's decided to go it alone. With the help of its joint venture partner, the Moscow City Administration, the company identified some Russian farmers and bakers it could work with. It imported cattle from Holland and russet potatoes from America, brought in agricultural specialists from Canada and Europe to improve the farmers' management practices, and advanced the farmers money so that they could invest in better seeds and equipment.

Then the company built a 100,000 square-foot McComplex in Moscow to produce beef; bakery, potato, and dairy products; ketchup; mustard; and Big Mac sauce. It set up a trucking fleet to move supplies to restaurants and financed its suppliers so that they would have enough working capital to buy modem equipment. The company also brought in about 50 expatriate managers to teach Russian employees about its service standards, quality measurements, and operating procedures and sent a 23-person team of Russian managers to Canada for a four-month training program. McDonald's created a vertically integrated operation in Russia, but the company clung to one principle: It would sell only hamburgers, fries, and Coke to Russians in a clean environment – fast. Fifteen years after serving its first Big Mac in Moscow's Pushkin Square, McDonald's has invested $250 million in the country and controls 80% of the Russian fast-food market.

Change the contexts

Many multinationals are powerful enough to alter the contexts in which they operate. The products or services these companies offer can force dramatic changes in local markets. When Asia's first satellite TV channel. Hong Kong-based STAR, launched in 1991, for example, it transformed the Indian marketplace in many ways. Not only did the company cause the Indian government to lose its monopoly on television broadcasts overnight, but it also led to a booming TV-manufacturing industry and the launch of several other satellite-based channels aimed at Indian audiences. By the mid-1990s, satellite-based TV channels had become a vibrant advertising medium, and many organizations used them to launch products and services targeted at India's new TV-watching consumer class.

The entry of foreign companies transforms quality standards in local product markets, which can have far-reaching consequences. Japan's Suzuki triggered a quality revolution after it entered India in 1981. The automaker's need for large volumes of high-quality components roused local suppliers. They teamed up with Suzuki's vendors in Japan, formed quality clusters, and worked with Japanese experts to produce better products. During the next two decades, the total quality management movement spread to other industries in India. By 2004, Indian companies had bagged more Deming prizes than firms in any country other than Japan. More important, India's automotive suppliers had succeeded in breaking into the global market, and several of them, such as Sundram Fasteners, had become preferred suppliers to international automakers like GM.

Companies can change contexts in factor markets, too. Consider the capital market in Brazil. As multinationals set up subsidiaries in those countries, they needed global-quality audit services. Few Brazilian accounting firms could provide those services, so the Big Four audit firms – Deloitte Touche Tohmatsu, Ernst & Young, KPMG, and Price-waterhouseCoopers – decided to set up branches there. The presence of those companies quickly raised financial-reporting and auditing standards in Brazil.

In a similar vein, Knauf, one of Europe's leading manufacturers of building materials, is trying to grow Russia's talent market. During the past decade, the German giant has built 20 factories in Russia and invested more than $400 million there. Knauf operates in a people-intensive industry; the company and its subsidiaries have roughly 7,000 employees in Russia. To boost standards in the country's construction industry, Knauf opened an education center in St. Petersburg in 2003 that works closely with the

State Architectural and Construction University. The school acts both as a mechanism that supplies talent to Knauf and as an institution that contributes to the much-needed development of Russian architecture.

Indeed, as firms change contexts, they must help countries fully develop their potential. That creates a win-win situation for the country and the company. Metro Cash & Carry, a division of German trading company Metro Group, has changed contexts in a socially beneficial way in several European and Asian countries. The Düsseldorf-based company – which sells everything to restaurants from meats and vegetables to napkins and toothpicks – entered China in 1996, Russia in 2001, and India in 2003. Metro has pioneered business links between farmers and small-scale manufacturers in rural areas that sell their products to small and midsize urban companies.

For instance, Metro invested in a cold chain in China so that it could deliver goods like fish and meats from rural regions to urban locations. That changed local conditions in several important ways. First, Metro's investment induced farmers in China to invest more in their agricultural operations. Metro also lobbied with governments for quality standards to prevent companies from selling shoddy produce to hapless consumers. By shifting transactions from roadside markets to computerized warehouses, the company's operations brought primary products into the tax net. Governments, which need the money to invest in local services, have remained on the company's side. That's a good thing for Metro since, in developing markets, the jury is always out on foreign companies.

Stay away

It may be impractical or uneconomical for some firms to adapt their business models to emerging markets. Home Depot, the successful do-it-yourself U.S. retailer, has been cautious about entering developing countries. The company offers a specific value proposition to customers: low prices, great service, and good quality. To pull that off, it relies on a variety of U.S.-specific institutions. It depends on the U.S. highways and logistical management systems to minimize the amount of inventory it has to carry in its large, warehouse-style stores. It relies on employee stock ownership to motivate shop-level workers to render top-notch service. And its value proposition takes advantage of the fact that high labor costs in the United States encourage home owners to engage in do-it-yourself projects.

Home Depot made a tentative foray into emerging markets by setting up two stores in Chile in 1998 and another in Argentina in 2000. In 2001, however. the company sold those operations for a net loss of $14 million. At the time, CEO Robert Nardelli emphasized that most of Home Depot's future growth was likely to come from North America. Despite that initial setback, the company hasn't entirely abandoned emerging markets. Rather, it has switched from a greenfield strategy to an acquisition-led approach. In 2001, Home Depot entered Mexico by buying a home improvement retailer, Total Home, and the next year, it acquired Del Norte, another small chain. By 2004, the company had 42 stores in Mexico. Although Home Depot has recently said that it is exploring the possibility of entering China, perhaps by making an acquisition, it doesn't have retail operations in any other developing countries.

Home Depot must consider whether it can modify its U.S. business model to suit the institutional contexts of emerging markets. In a country with a poorly developed capital market, for example, the company may not be able to use employee stock ownership as a compensation tool. Similarly, in a country with a poorly developed physical infrastructure, Home Depot may have difficulty using its inventory management systems, a scenario that would alter the economics of the business. In markets where labor costs are relatively low, the target customer may not be the home owner but rather contractors who serve as intermediaries between the store and the home owner. That change in customer focus may warrant an entirely different marketing and merchandising strategy – one that Home Depot isn't convinced it should deploy yet.

• • •

While companies can't use the same strategies in all developing countries, they can generate synergies by treating different markets as part of a system. For instance, GE Healthcare (formerly GE Medical Systems) makes parts for its diagnostic machines in China, Hungary, and Mexico and develops the software for those machines in India. The company created this system when it realized that the market for diagnostic machines was small in most low-income countries. GE Healthcare then decided to use the facility it had set up in India in 1990 as a global sourcing base. After several years, and on the back of borrowed expertise from GE Japan, the India operation's products finally met GE Healthcare's exacting standards. In the late 1990s, when GE Healthcare wanted to move a plant from Belgium to cut costs, the Indian subsidiary beat its Mexican counterpart by delivering the highest quality at the lowest cost. Under its then-CEO, Jeff Immelt, GE Healthcare learned to use all its operations in low-income countries – China, Hungary, Mexico, and India – as parts of a system that allowed the company to produce equipment cheaply for the world market.

Parent company GE has also tapped into the talent pool in emerging markets by setting up technology centers in Shanghai and Bangalore, for instance. In those centers, the company conducts research on everything from materials design to molecular modeling to power electronics. GE doesn't treat China and India just as markets but also as sources of talent and innovation that can transform its value chain. And that's how multinational companies should engage with emerging markets if they wish to secure their future.

ANDY KLUMP, *NIRAJ KAJI*, *LUIS SANCHEZ*, and *MAX YACOUB* provided research assistance for the Dell and McDonald's examples in this article.

TARUN KHANNA (tkhanna@hbs.edu) is the Jorge Paulo Lemann Professor and *KRISHNA G. PALEPU* (kpalepu@hbs.edu) is the Ross Graham Walker Professor of Business Administration at Harvard Business School in Boston. They are the coauthors of 'Why Focused Strategies May be Wrong for Emerging Markets' (HBR July–August 1997) and 'The Right Way to Restructure Conglomerates in Emerging Markets' (HBR July–August 1999). *JAYANT SINHA* (jayant_sinha@mckinsey.com) is a partner at McKinsey & Company in New Delhi.

CASE 7: CARREFOUR: CONQUEST OF LATIN AMERICA

José Luis Duran, CEO of Carrefour, sat quietly in his office reviewing his strategy of fine-tuning the portfolio of the second largest food retailer in the world. He had deep respect for his predecessor Daniel Bernard, ex-CEO of Carrefour, as the former finance director of his management team. He looked intently at some of the 30 countries in which Carrefour operated and thought about the accomplishment over the past 19 years and the achievement of raising Carrefour to the number two position in the world market and the most international of supermarket chains. He reflected upon the recent past when Daniel Bernard was eased out of his position by Carrefour's controlling shareholders and he was brought in as the financial wizard to achieve the overall profitability of the group, especially in the French market. His main concern was whether the company would be able to maintain and improve on the growth rate it had achieved up to this point.

The post-merger integration issues with Promodès, like changes in the assortment, back office problems and stock-out situations, were beginning to ease. During this integration phase, the group witnessed depressed financial results, but, with time, the group was slowly producing important synergies, allowing it to achieve better earnings. On the other hand, in mature markets like France, growth was stagnating and Carrefour reported a modest sales increase of 2.1 per cent in 2003. In the first quarter of 2004, sales declined 1.8 per cent on a like-for-like basis.

Overall growth seemed more and more difficult to achieve and maintain. Results were increasingly becoming uncertain and the company moved away from its home market as global and regional competition increased. Even in the domestic market, the simple strategy of increasing purchasing power was not sustainable. The strategy for the large-scale retail and distribution industry needed to be rethought in order to respond better to the needs of more demanding consumers and to gain new customers in countries not yet saturated in the retail business and that offered higher growth potential.

Carrefour was a French company with its European operations accounting for more than three-quarters of its annual sales of €90.6 billion in 2004. In 2003, France accounted for 50.6 per cent of the sales, the rest of the Europe accounted for 36.2 per cent, and Latin America and Asia accounted for 6.6 per cent each. José Luis Duran wondered if higher investment in emerging markets could be the answer to the slow growth in mature markets, or would it be better to focus more on mature markets? He wondered whether Carrefour would be as successful in emerging markets as it had been at home and in near-home markets, or if the risk of venturing further into emerging markets was worth the investment Carrefour had already made.

Iana Torres, while on her MBA in International Agri-Food management programme, prepared this case under the supervision of Ashok Som. The case was developed from generalized experience and published sources as a basis for class discussion rather than to illustrate either effective or ineffective handling of an administrative situation.

History of Carrefour

In 1959, the Fournier and Defforey families created the company Carrefour. The first Carrefour supermarket opened in 1960. Three years later, a large self-service store, known as a hypermarket was opened in a Paris suburb. The store was defined as a self-service store for food items and sundries, spanning more than 2,500 square metres of floor space. This hypermarket opened in Sainte-Geneviève-des-bois with 12 checkouts and 400 parking spaces. Carrefour went public in 1970 on the Paris Stock Exchange and began its international expansion.

Foreseeing restrictions on large-sized stores because of France's Royer Law[1] and saturation in the domestic market, Carrefour's strategy had been to grow by means of foreign direct investments. In 1969, for the first time, the French retailer broke out of its home country with the opening of a store in Belgium.

In the 1970s, similar advances were made into Switzerland, Britain, Italy and Spain. However, Carrefour soon withdrew from the Belgian and British markets as it could not achieve a leadership position there. The company's overseas development continued with stores in South America, a market that was first penetrated via Brazil. In the late 1970s, it opened a hard-discount line of stores under the name Ed in France.

In the 1980s, new stores were opened in Argentina and Taiwan. In the late 1980s, Carrefour opened its first subsidiary in North America, but sales fell far short of expectations and it withdrew three years later. At the same time, the company continued to make advances into the Asian market.

In the early 1990s, Carrefour took over the French hypermarket chains of Euromarché and Montlaur. It opened the first hypermarket, named Continent, in Greece and simultaneously launched Carrefour Vacances (travel services). The mid-1990s brought more international expansion, with new stores in Italy, Turkey, Mexico, Malaysia, Thailand, Korea, Hong Kong, Singapore and Poland. Carrefour also took a controlling stake in Comptoirs Modernes, which had 16 Mammouth hypermarkets that became partners of the group and switched to the name Carrefour. It entered the supermarket arena with Stoc and launched convenience store activity with Marché Plus. In the late 1990s Carrefour opened its first hypermarkets in Chile, Colombia and Indonesia. 1999 was a significant year in the history of Carrefour, as it merged with Promodès to create the largest European food retailing group and the second largest in the world (see Exhibit 7.1). During this period it added 85 supermarkets in Brazil through the acquisition of regional chains Lojas Americanas, Planaltao, Roncetti, Mineirao, Rainha, Dallas and Continente.

In 2000, Carrefour strengthened Promodès's ties with its partners by increasing its equity ownership in the retail chains Norte in Argentina, Gruppo GS in Italy, Marinopoulos in Greece and GB in Belgium. The Carrefour and Maus groups teamed up to form a niche in the hypermarket business in Switzerland. Pryca and Continente merged in Spain to become Carrefour and, in France, a merger with Continent led to all its hypermarkets on the continent adopting the Carrefour banner and its supermarkets adopting the Champion name in France. In addition, the online supermarket Ooshop was launched, Carrefour, Sears and Oracle created the first worldwide electronic marketplace for retailers named GlobalNetXchange, and the company opened its first hypermarket in Japan.

Company	Home country	Sales ($US million)
Wal-Mart Stores, Inc.	USA	229,617.0
Carrefour Group	**France**	**64,762.3**
The Home Depot, Inc.	USA	58,247.0
The Kroger Co.	USA	51,760.0
Metro AG	Germany	48,124.4
Royal Ahold	Netherlands	47,114.3
Target Corporation	USA	42,722.0
Tesco plc	United Kingdom	39,517.2
Costco Companies	USA	37,993.1
ITM Enterprises	France	36,183.7

Exhibit 7.1 Top ten retailers worldwide (2003)
Source: www.retailindustry.about.com

In 2001, the group went through a restructuring phase and sold off some of its non-core businesses, such as Picard Surgelés. A 42 per cent stake in Cora was sold to Deutsche Bank. It inaugurated 17 Carrefour service stations on France's motorway networks, and Carrefour Argentina took over the management of Norte, the largest food retailer in Argentina. The company also acquired the Espirito Santo group's interest in Carrefour Portugal, and Carrefour and Metro AG disposed of their cross-holdings in France and Italy (see Exhibit 7.2).

Year	Events
1959	The Carrefour company is created.
1960	Carrefour opens its first supermarket in Annecy, Haute-Savoie.
1961	The LLC Promodis, the forerunner of Promodès, is created. The company was formed through a merger of two wholesaler families from Normandy, managed by Paul-Auguste Halley and Leonor Duval-Lemonnier.
1962	Promodès opens its first supermarket in Mantes-la-Ville (Yvelines).
1963	Carrefour invents a new store concept: the hypermarket. The first Carrefour hypermarket opens in Sainte-Geneviève-des-bois, with a floor area of 2,500 sq.m, 12 checkouts and 400 parking spaces.
1969	The Promodès supermarkets adopt the Champion store name. Carrefour opens its first hypermarket outside of France, in Belgium.
1970	Carrefour shares are listed on the Paris stock exchange.
1972	Promodès hypermarkets adopt the Continent store name. Convenience stores will operate under the name Shopi.
1973	Carrefour opens its first hypermarket in Spain, under the store name Pryca.
1975	Carrefour opens its first hypermarket in Brazil.
1976	Carrefour introduces 'produits libres', which are products without a brand name but 'just as good, and cheaper'.
1977	Promodès creates the convenience store chain 8 à Huit.
1979	Development of the hard discount: Carrefour creates the Ed chain, and Promodès the Dia banner in Spain.

1981   Carrefour introduces its own payment card: the Pass Card.
        Promodès branches out into franchising with Champion supermarkets.

1982   The first Carrefour hypermarket opens in Argentina.

1984   Carrefour launches Carrefour Insurance Services.

1985   Carrefour brand name products are introduced.

1988   Promodès acquires the 128 supermarkets of the Primistères group. Introduction of the slogan 'With
        Carrefour, I get the best of everything.'

1989   The first Carrefour hypermarket opens in Asia, in Taiwan.

1991   Carrefour takes over the French hypermarket chains Euromarché and Montlaur.
        Opening of the first Continent hypermarkets in Greece.
        Vacances launches Carrefour Vacations Services.

1992   Carrefour creates its first quality systems, which guarantee product origin and traceability.

1993   Carrefour opens its first stores in Italy and Turkey.

1994   Carrefour opens its first hypermarkets in Mexico and Malaysia.

1995   Carrefour opens its first hypermarkets in China.
        Promodès launches the brand name Reflets de France, created to preserve the traditions of French
        cuisine.

1996   Carrefour continues to grow in Asia, adding Thailand, Korea and Hong Kong to its list. Promodès
        acquires the convenience store chain Félix Potin.

1997   Carrefour opens its first hypermarkets in Singapore and Poland.
        Promodès acquires the supermarket chain Catteau.
        Carrefour introduces the brand names Escapades Gourmandes, specializing in rare or little-known
        traditional products, and Carrefour Bio, a certified organic line of food products.

1998   Carrefour takes a controlling interest in Comptoirs Modernes: 16 Mammouth hypermarkets become
        partners of the group and switch to the Carrefour store name, while Carrefour incorporates
        supermarket activity with Stoc and convenience activity with Marché Plus.
        Promodès acquires minority stakes in foreign food retailing groups: GB in Belgium, Norte in Argentina
        and GS in Italy.
        Carrefour opens its first hypermarkets in Chile, Colombia and Indonesia.
        Promodès introduces the brand name Destination Saveurs, a line celebrating exotic products.

1999   Carrefour and Promodès merge to create the top European food retailing group (second largest worldwide).
        Carrefour acquires 85 supermarkets in Brazil, through the regional chains Lojas Americanas, Planaltao,
        Roncetti, Mineirao, Rainha, Dallas and Continente.

2000   Carrefour strengthens Promodès's ties with its partners by increasing its ownership equity in Norte in
        Argentina, Marinopoulos in Greece and taking control of GB in Belgium and Gruppo GS in Italy.
        The Carrefour and Maus groups team up in the hypermarket niche in Switzerland.
        Carrefour, Sears and Oracle create the first worldwide market for online retailing:
        GlobalNetXchange.
        After the two groups merge, all Continent hypermarkets become Carrefour stores and supermarkets
        adopt the Champion name in France. Pryca and Continente merge in Spain to become Carrefour stores.
        Launch of the online supermarket Ooshop.
        Carrefour opens its first hypermarket in Japan.
        Launch of the global shareholding plan reserved for Carrefour employees. Over 200,000 of them
        (60 per cent of the workforce) subscribe to this plan.

2001   Carrefour sells its interest in Picard Surgelés.
        Carrefour inaugurates 17 Carrefour service stations on France's motorway networks
        Carrefour Argentina takes over management of Norte, the leader in food retail in Argentina.
        Carrefour acquires the Espirito Santo group's interest in Carrefour Portugal.
        Carrefour and Metro AG dispose of their cross-stakes in France and Italy.
        Carrefour sells its 42 per cent stake in Cora to Deutsche Bank.

Exhibit 7.2 Evolution of Carrefour
Source: www.carrefour.com

▶ In 2002, 660 new stores were opened, with Asia accounting for 42 per cent of the new stores. Carrefour used 18 different banner names for its stores, depending on the type of store and its geographical location. It was market leader in 9 out of the 30 different countries in which it operated, with sales worth €76.7 billion[2] ($98 billion) and about 400,000 employees (see Exhibit 7.3).

Exhibit 7.3 Breakdown of the Carrefour workforce
Source: www.carrefour.com

In 2003, the firm opened another 969 stores under the group banners and acquired hard discount stores such as El Arbol in Spain and Edeka/Treff in France, supermarkets Laurus in Belgium and 12 hypermarkets belonging to Ahold in Poland. In 2004, it had a total of 10,378 stores and total sales[3] of €78.9 billion ($102 billion) up 6 per cent from the previous year. Hypermarkets contributed 57.7 per cent of total sales, supermarkets accounted for 25.5 per cent, hard discounters for 7.5 per cent and others the remaining 9.3 per cent (see Exhibit 7.4). In 2005, it has annual sales of €90.6 billion with 11,000 stores.

Country	Hypermarkets	Supermarkets	Hard discount	Cash & carry	Proxy	Total
Argentina	24	141	299			464
Brazil	85	113	133			331
Colombia	11					11
Mexico*	*27*					*27**
AMERICAS	**147**	**254**	**432**	**0**	**0**	**833**
China	41		55			96
Korea	27					27
Japan*	*7**					*7**
Taiwan	31					31
Indonesia	11					11

Malaysia	7					7
Singapore	2					2
Thailand	19					19
ASIA	**145**	**0**	**55**	**0**	**0**	**200**
FRANCE	**216**	**1005**	**588**	**155**	**1611**	**3575**
Spain	124	200	2566	32		2922
Belgium	56	271			156	483
Switzerland	11					11
Greece	13	101	278		51	443
Italy	40	379		13	645	1077
Poland	(14+)15	(3+)67				82
Portugal*	7*		355*			362*
Czech Rep.	13					13
Turkey	11	5	182			198
Romania	2					2
Other	23	98			56	177
EUROPE	**315**	**1121**	**3381**	**45**	**908**	**5770**
TOTAL GROUP	**823**	**2380**	**4456**	**200**	**2519**	**10378**

Exhibit 7.4 Total stores world wide 2003
*Sold in 2005; (+) Addition in Poland in 2005
Source: Carrefour annual report 2003.

The retail sector in France

Retail shops in a country can generally be divided into five types. **Hypermarkets** have a floor area between 2,500 and 25,000 square metres. They corresponded to the concept of 'everything under the same roof', with an important segment of non-food products. The main French players in this sector are Carrefour, Leclerc, Auchan, Géant Casino, Intermarché, Cora and Super U (more than 1,100 hypermarkets in total). *Supermarkets* have a floor area of between 400 and 2,500 square metres. They sell various products, mainly food (more than 5,900 supermarkets in total). *Hard discount shops* are smaller size shops with a floor area of between 200 and 800 square metres, and are often situated in the centre of towns. They sell a limited range of products at very low prices (more than 2,533 shops in total). *Convenience stores* are very small shops with a floor area of less than 200 square metres. They are present both in towns and rural areas, and are often managed by franchisee managers (more than 2,500 shops in total). *Cash & carry and food service outlets* were designed to meet the needs of restaurant and food industry professionals (more than 3,000 shops in total).

Historically, competition existed between the stores that sold a large variety of product lines and the 'specialized' shops that focused on particular products such as clothing, furniture, toys, etc.

▶   The trend in the retail food sector had been consolidation and integration. In order to remain competitive, companies sought economies of scale and scope. Mergers led to a very concentrated and competitive environment. Small players are considered potential targets for buy-outs. Overall, the food retail industry is dominated by a few big leaders globally, with numerous small to medium-sized retailers at the local level.

Saturated French market

After 40 years of continuous growth driven by the excellent performance of its hypermarkets, the late 1990s seemed more complex for Carrefour. From 1990, increasing its market share in the French market had become more and more difficult. Having created a revolution in the consumption habits of French society and become 'temples of consumption', the hypermarket model had begun to slow down.

From the marketing point of view, the hypermarket's concept suffers from two main issues. First, the sociological evolution of French society – the general ageing of the population, working women and single households, which have eroded the traditional model of a family going to the suburbs at the weekend for their weekly shopping. People are also seeking more welcoming and personalized settings, and are opting for stores that privilege the 'buying experience', which the giant hypermarkets do not offer. Second, there was the rise of a new form of competition with the opening of convenience stores. These stores appeared because customers wanted more time for leisure and to have to spend less time shopping, thus preferring to shop closer to their homes. Hard discount and smaller-sized shops had become more attractive as the social structure of countries had evolved. They have also benefited from municipal policies in favour of the revitalization of town centres. Specialized shops for furniture, sports equipment and clothing have made a dent in the non-food sales of hypermarkets, resulting in their offering the strict minimum in this segment: 'In France, hypermarkets had two major growth drivers – opening new stores and selling at low costs. But to stop them from becoming too powerful, government had cut these two growth drivers with the Raffarin and Galland laws'.

The Raffarin law, promulgated in 1996, aimed to protect smaller retail shops by forbidding the siting of new hypermarkets in town centres. In 1998, the Galland law forbade sales at a loss, which narrowed the price difference between hypermarkets and the smaller shop formats. These laws restricted Carrefour's opening new space in France to foster its growth; due to these regulatory constraints, during 1998–2002 the company could add only 40,000 square metres of new space. During the same period, its competitors opened 300,000 square metres of hypermarket space, while hard discounters opened more than 600,000 square metres of new space. Carrefour had to be content with extensions of its existing stores. In 2003 no new hypermarket space was opened, but around 40,000 square metres were added through extensions, and around 70,000 square metres of space for supermarkets from both new openings and extensions. In spite of these efforts, Carrefour had been slowly losing its market share in France, from 24.5 per cent in 1999 to 22.9 per cent in 2003.

In general, the hypermarkets of all retail companies had been witnessing a reduction in their market shares. The main beneficiaries of this trend had been the hard discount shops. Though Carrefour still dominated the French market with about 52 per cent of the total retail market share in 2002, it had been slowly losing its market share.

The international strategy of Carrefour

With operations in about 30 countries, Carrefour is the most international of the supermarket chains. Daniel Bernard, former Chairman and CEO of Carrefour used to say, 'There is a race and a lot of people are qualified for the race. But to go global, you need to be early enough. Generally in new countries you need to be the first in for the first win. When you arrive as number three or four, it is too late'.

Carrefour's strategic intent has been based on the belief that it 'will quit any overseas market in which it cannot become one of the top-three retailers', which was reiterated by José Luis Duran, CEO of Carrefour, in April 2005.

Carrefour had been globalizing since the very early stages of its development. The globalization of Carrefour had been based on the gamble that hypermarkets, a western consumption model, could be adapted well to emerging countries through the different retailing concepts of supermarkets, hard discounters and convenience stores. This belief evolved into a growth strategy that consisted of building group market share best suited to the local market in each country with these types of stores.

Carrefour's strategy was based on a decentralized structure that empowered local managers to manage their multiple-format stores. Local managers were empowered to make decisions on segmentation, renovation and product assortment strategies that would appeal to the needs and demands of the local customers. This strategy of 'clusterization' segmented stores into categories of A, B and C according to the local demography and spending power of local consumers. This clusterization was supported by significant capital expenditure to reconfigure the stores according to the needs of the local market. Investment decisions were made to improve back office processes, to integrate the logistics system, to use working capital more efficiently and to achieve organic growth through commercial dynamics. This clusterization strategy, leading to the multiple-format set-up of hypermarkets, supermarkets, hard discounters and convenience stores, resulted in significant economies of scale (see Exhibit 7.5).

With experience, reorganizing the sales area and product staging became the group's areas of expertise. It allowed Carrefour to continue modernizing its networks. For example, in Argentina, using this clusterization strategy, 80 supermarkets were reconfigured and renovated to bear the Norte banner. This strategy resulted in an increase in like-for-like sales of 18.5 per cent in the last quarter of 2003. In Asia, many stores adopted new logistics concepts for fresh food, thereby gaining a competitive advantage over their main rivals, the street markets. In Thailand, 60 per cent of their store network was remodelled. According to a senior manager at the Carrefour HQ: 'Carrefour chose its new target countries on the basis of two factors: (a) high demographical growth potential (important urban population and high birth rate); and (b) low competitive intensity – the country must not already be the realm of an MNC'.

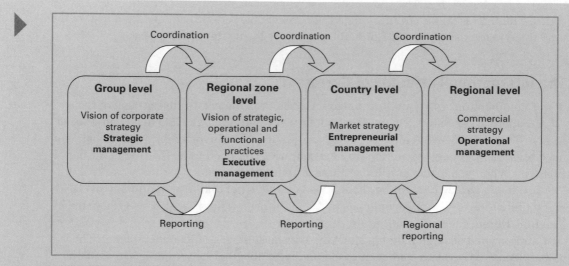

Exhibit 7.5 Decentralized structure
Source: www.carrefour.com

Legal considerations played an important part in Carrefour's growth. Latin American countries, for example, were characterized by a welcoming policy towards foreign direct investments and relaxed laws restricting the surface areas of hypermarkets. This was often seen as one of the reasons this region was considered an area for the organic growth of Carrefour after Europe. On the other hand, tighter legislation in Asia, notably in China, delayed Carrefour's expansion.

Carrefour's main goal for each of its stores was to set a benchmark in retailing among its competitors and highlight cost advantage. Its stores aimed to provide the benefits of convenience, broad selection and quality at especially low prices. Carrefour stores emphasized the company's market positioning towards the discount end through a policy of low prices and large-scale promotions that were hard to match. This positioning became a competitive advantage against local retailers with less developed economies of scale that did not allow them to provide the same value to the customer as Carrefour did. Commenting on Carrefour's expansion, Daniel Bernard, CEO of the Group, said:

> During 2002, our Group continued to win market share based on strong sales momentum and many new store openings in the 30 countries where we have our operations. We enhanced the appeal of our banners and built customer loyalty with our strong discount positioning as well as our focus on innovation and quality. The pace of the expansion picked up with the addition of 963,000 square metres of sales space in 2002 under the Group's banners, compared to 150,000 square metres in 2001.

Multi-format strategy: a strong worldwide positioning in discount

The optimization of resources through synergies like centralizing purchases, and worldwide efforts to pool knowhow and logistical tools had borne results. The gains obtained through economies of scale permitted Carrefour to opt for aggressive discounting and promotional campaigns to support its low price positioning.

In Europe, the synergies achieved in France, Italy, Spain and Belgium bolstered sales in Carrefour stores, which managed to maintain a very aggressive price positioning compared to the average in the market. These synergies also benefited from the international deployment of product ranges. Spain witnessed an introduction of 444 new products and Italy 280. Meanwhile, 1,400 retailer brands took the Carrefour name in Belgium. The Dia brand was introduced in France and the Ed brand in Spain. Commenting on this, Daniel Bernard, CEO of the Carrefour Group, said:

> Carrefour also enjoyed the first fruits of its multiple-format strategy in western Europe and Latin America, passing on the gains derived from pricing synergies to the greater benefit of consumers. Because we put the customer first, we have systematized the implementation of a programme for long-term growth that encompasses the safety and quality of our products, environmental protection, and a commitment to ethics and our employees.

The Group was able to grow its market share through an aggressive pricing policy, and a revamped marketing programme combined with quality products and a successful customer loyalty programme. Carrefour's rationale behind its price positioning was to make consumer products accessible to a greater number of people by tailoring products and concepts to consumers' needs and expectations. Consumers appreciated the benefits of buying quality products at low prices, giving Carrefour the loyalty of its clientele.

Private labels

Carrefour's private-label lines also played an important role in gaining the commercial dynamics the company aimed for. The goal was to provide customers with the products that best suited their expectations about price, safety, quality, availability and size. The Group reinforced innovation in its private-label product lines by introducing new product concepts in all its retail formats.

Its efforts to tailor products to different consumers led to the launch of numerous private-label lines. The Carrefour Group had 13 excellent value-for-money store brands, which were often updated in both food and non-food products, four of which, the Reflets de France, N°1, J'aime and Bio lines, had an international scope. Store brands represented a significant share of sales, ranging from an average of 25 per cent to 80 per cent for some product groups in France. Other important and well-recognized private-label brands that had a similar appeal were: Destinations Saveurs, Escapades Gourmandes and Grand Jury, and other brands tailored for specific geographical regions, such as Tierra Nuestra (Spain), Terra d'Italia (Italy) and Souvenir du Terroir (Belgium).

In 2002, Carrefour's Champion and Dia brands continued to increase their market share in various product lines. Dia introduced between 300 and 450 new listed items in its various sales outlets. In Italy in particular, the network's growth was supported by the

▶ introduction of more than 1,600 new listed items. Of these, 420 were sold under the newly created Di per Di brand, 920 were *GS* products and 280 were new Carrefour products.

The group's global strategy to strengthen its commercial dynamics was highly leveraged in 2003 by powerful sales in the private-label lines N°1 and Produits Carrefour International, especially in those countries most affected by economic crises. N°1 was introduced in Argentina into Norte's product range and other stores of Latin America, Poland and Belgium; and Produits Carrefour International had a common range across France, Belgium, Italy and Spain, which was about 15 per cent to 20 per cent cheaper than the traditional Carrefour label. Sales of the high-quality Bio lines continued to rise in all countries in which they were introduced, advancing strongly in western Europe and Latin America.

The conquering of Latin America

The Carrefour Group had been experiencing a continuous increase in sales globally, even after taking into account the impact of the exchange rates that had adversely affected sales in emerging markets such as Asia and Latin America. These two emerging regions represented the highest growth for the company in like-for-like business, showing that the concept was well accepted and economies of scale had been effective. But the currencies of these markets had devalued, masking excellent results in sales growth. Despite the short-term difficulties in these regions, the company was aware of the high business potential these countries represented and had made a strong commitment to conquer them.

The move to Latin America started in 1975 with the opening of the first hypermarket in Brazil. In 1982, Carrefour entered the Argentinean market. In 1994 it opened its first store in Mexico and, four years later, in Colombia and Chile. During 2002–03, the group witnessed high like-for-like growth and continuous change in strategy for better adaptation in each of the Latin markets. For a breakdown of sales in the Latin market see Exhibit 7.6.

	Population in 2002 (in '000)	Average annual growth 2002–07	Growth in GDP 2002	GDP/capita (in USD ppa) 2002	2002 inflation	Sales under banners (in € million)
Argentina	37,811	1.1%	−16.0%	12,064	29.0%	1,519.7
Brazil	172,174	0.8%	1.5%	7,689	6.5%	3,666.0
Chile	15,504	1.0%	2.2%	9,616	2.1%	135.2
Colombia	43,597	1.6%	1.2%	6,090	5.7%	295.2
Mexico	101,751	1.4%	1.5%	8,927	4.8%	729.9
TOTAL						6,347.0

Exhibit 7.6 Sales information for Carrefour in Latin America
Source: Carrefour annual report 2003

The management expectations for the region's development and growth potential were well expressed by Philippe Jarry, Director of the America Region, thus:

> 66 Despite the general devaluation of currencies in the region, in 2002 the Group recorded a good performance in all the Latin American countries. Hypermarkets in Brazil and Colombia held particularly firm and the recovery of supermarkets in these two countries bore fruit in the second half. In Argentina, we gained market share as a result of our policy of low prices and our commitment to our customers. We also relaunched our policy of expansion in the other countries. We had successful store openings in Brazil, Colombia and Mexico. In 2002, with over 700 stores, Latin America recorded sales of €6,347 million, representing 7 per cent of Group sales. This performance, achieved in a difficult economic [constant revaluation of the euro] and political climate, is proof of the relevance of our strategy, which consists of adapting our business model [consistent low price positioning, major promotional campaign; the multi-format organization together with clusterization] to the specific characteristics of each country. We are now ready to take advantage of the slightest rebound in the region. 99

In 2003, Carrefour's total sales in the region were €5,588 million, 11.9 per cent lower than the previous year, supposedly due to weak currencies in Brazil and Argentina. But these numbers masked an increase of 11.1 per cent at constant exchange rates, expansion gains of 6.2 per cent, and net sales worth €4619 million representing a constant forex, an increase of 8 per cent. Latin America represented 6.6 per cent of the total Group sales (see Exhibit 7.7).

Region	Sales incl. VAT (€m)	Like for like (%)	Expansion (%)	Total ctt ex rates (%)	Currencies (%)	Total (%)
France	39959	1.4	0.7	2.1	0.0	2.1
Europe ex France	28410	3.9	4.5	8.4	−0.2	8.2
Latin America	5588	4.9	6.2	11.1	−23.1	−11.9
Asia	5037	−0.8	17.9	17.1	−16.7	0.4
Total	78994	2.5	3.5	6.0	−3.1	2.9

Exhibit 7.7 Full-year sales (2003)
Source: Carrefour annual report 2003

Brazil

Carrefour had developed a regional approach through a partial decentralization of responsibilities in the purchasing arm of its business. It established 12 regional negotiating units that worked together with hypermarkets and supermarkets, adapting purchases and prices to each specific market requirement, including national brands. This integrative and tailored purchasing system permitted Carrefour to optimize the stores' sales by designing brochures with products better adapted to the needs of each local market and that were, therefore, more attractive and effective.

The price positioning in the country was supported by many promotional campaigns that helped boost the stores' financial performance. These promotions, which helped Carrefour win back market share, were a combination of several short promotional campaigns per week and major campaign themes of high interest to the population, such as the football World Cup, which increased the sales of TV sets by about 20 per cent.

A combination of a low price policy, promotional campaigns and a specific multi-format organization (hypermarkets with the Carrefour brand, supermarkets with the *Champion* banner and hard discounters with the *Dia* banner) helped Carrefour grow by 12 per cent in its like-for-like sales in 2003, worth €3174 million despite the ongoing recession. But at current currency exchange levels, sales dropped 13.4 per cent. In 2003, Carrefour Brazil had 85 hypermarkets and 113 supermarkets. After its recent entry in the Sao Paulo market, the Dia hard discount format almost doubled its number of stores from 69 to 133 stores. The future goal in Brazil as reflected by one of the managers was 'to continue with this performance by emphasizing our price positioning and accelerating hypermarket expansion through acquisitions'.

Argentina

Carrefour entered the Argentinean market in 1982. It took over the management of Norte in 2001, the largest food retailer in Argentina, and became the biggest retailer in the country. In 2002, Argentina experienced a profound financial crisis that led to a 270 per cent devaluation of the Argentinean peso, a general decline in the economic conditions of the population and an inflation rate close to 80 per cent. In this context, the strategy of Carrefour, Norte and Dia was to expand their 'price leader' products, adapting them to consumer patterns that increasingly focused on food items. The Group continued the consolidation of the Norte network and completed its repositioning with 80 remodelled supermarkets and 47 supermarkets that switched to the Norte banner. Synergies were achieved by consolidating and moving the logistics of hypermarkets and supermarkets, and the two brands Carrefour and Norte, to a single headquarters. Dia, which was perfectly adapted to local conditions, continued to expand through 23 new stores.

The Carrefour and *Norte* networks confirmed their price positioning in Argentina. They promised to 'pay back ten times the difference' if a product could be found anywhere else at a lower price, and introduced the 'price leader' line in Norte stores with a new slogan: 'the best price is here'. In order to ensure the availability of 'price leader' products on the shelves, Carrefour supported small local producers by sharply reducing payment times.

The growth in Argentina continued despite the adverse economic situation. Carrefour expanded in strategic regions in Argentina, such as the city of Mendoza where it purchased 12 supermarkets and placed them under the Norte banner. It also organized supply for these supermarkets by creating a production centre that delivered to the bakery, pastry, deli and cheese departments of local stores.

Argentina showcased a leading example of Carrefour's clusterization strategy in Latin America. The strategy resulted in an excellent recovery of like-for-like sales in hypermarkets. Towards the last quarter of 2003, hypermarkets posted an increase of 18.5 per cent compared to the beginning of the year when sales had dropped by more than 30 per cent. At the end of 2003, Carrefour had 24 hypermarkets, 141 supermarkets and 299 hard discount stores. Sales at €1336 million represented growth of 4.3 per cent at constant exchange rates and −12.1 per cent at current exchange rates.

Mexico

In Mexico, Carrefour was one of the top five retailers in a fragmented market, where 80 per cent of business is concentrated in Mexico City. In 2002, it initiated a new development model that included leasing stores and a smaller size of hypermarket, a new 6,000 square metre store concept that met customer expectations and was easier to establish in dense urban areas such as Mexico City. The group completed the reorganization of its product lines in order to increase the visibility of its products and accelerate sales growth.

Carrefour Mexico took advantage of the experience acquired in Brazil to implement a new marketing policy. Tested in July 2002 in Guadalajara, it consisted of adapting product lines and communication campaigns to local consumption patterns, which resulted in an 18 per cent increase, on average, in sales between January and August 2002. In 2003, with 27 hypermarkets, the company achieved sales worth €605 million, representing a growth of 11 per cent at constant exchange rates and −17.1 per cent at current exchange rates. In early 2005, Carrefour sold its portfolio in Mexico as part of its portfolio restructuring programme. The Mexico operation was not delivering a respectable return on capital. Being Fifth in the market, Carrefour could not achieve critical mass and its desired market share.

Chile

Chile had a fragmented and differentiated retail market that experienced intense competition. The two main retailers in the country had about 50 per cent of the total market share. Grupo D&S was the leader with 30 per cent and Cencosud (after the acquisition of stores belonging to Santa Isabel) had about 20 per cent of market share. The Chilean market was also characterized by strong competition from local retailers, which are very flexible and quick to imitate the best practices of their competitors, have high logistics efficiency, and continuously innovate with new products and services to suit local needs and tastes. These new offers contain products, such as garden instruments, camping paraphernalia and furniture, and services such as beauty salons, tourism agencies and specialized bookstores.

Carrefour entered the Chilean market in 1998 and worked closely with suppliers to develop new products to target the very demanding Chilean consumer. In 2002, Carrefour signed its first quality beef line with local producers: Carrefour Natural Calidad Hereford. The meat came from free-range animals raised on extensive farmlands. The feed for these animals was completely natural (grass for seven months and fodder in the winter) and excluded any type of transgenic foods. The launch was a success; in the stores that offered them, the products accounted for 15 per cent of total sales.

▶ The company strove to consolidate its market share by initiating large-scale sales promotions and expanding store offerings such as 'price leaders', meat 'quality lines' and store brands. These product offerings were developed according to the nature of the region as 80 per cent of sales revenues were earned on food products and only 7 per cent from consumer products. In 2002, total gross sales were worth €135.2 million and 11.1 per cent growth in sales revenue at constant exchange rates.

By the end of 2003, Carrefour had seven hypermarkets and held sixth position in the food retailing business in Chile. In general, the year brought positive results for the company, with sales worth €139.1 million, representing a total growth of 22.3 per cent at constant exchange rates and 2.9 per cent growth at current exchange rates. But Carrefour could not achieve the first two positions in the initial years of its entry into the Chilean market.

By 2004, the company announced that, as part of its ongoing drive to improve its profitability, it had signed an agreement to transfer its seven Chilean stores to the local retail group 'Distribucion y Servicios' (D&S). The final transfer of the Chilean subsidiary's capital had been effective from 7 January 2004 and the total transfer price was 100 million euros, representing a turnover of more than 60 per cent before taxes. Analysts believed that the exit of Carrefour from the Chilean market was a result of the ability of local competitors to easily imitate Carrefour's strategy of low prices, while Carrefour had a difficult time finding a suitable product range for the Chilean market. As Fernando Montino, business manager at the DKSH consultancy in Chile, said:

> ❝ No foreign retailers have been able to succeed in the Chilean market. Home Depot had to quit a couple of years ago and JC Penny and now Carrefour. There are no foreign retailers in Chile. The common factor is the lack of knowledge of the Chilean consumer. Carrefour could not grow because it was not competitive and could not add value. ❞

According to reports in the Chilean press, Carrefour decided to withdraw as a result of its failure to achieve its goal of becoming one of the leaders in the retail industry in Chile, despite its relatively good performance. Its success in other markets had been built on adapting to the demands of local consumers, but for some reason it appeared to be unable and unwilling to invest in the same strategy in Chile.

Carrefour had made a strong effort to understand the culture and needs of each market in Latin America. It had adapted a strategy of working with different retail formats and a wide range of products according to the specific requirements expected by the consumer in the region. Though it was present in different store formats, the majority of its sales came from the hypermarkets that contribute 75 per cent of sales, followed by the supermarkets with 20.7 per cent and hard discount stores with 4.2 per cent. The product range in each country particularly leans towards 'value for low price'. Carrefour's private-label product lines, carefully selected for each market, had been key to its growth throughout the region. This was more so in Colombia, the country with the highest growth in sales among Carrefour's Latin American operations, at 30.9 per cent at constant exchange rates and 12.7 per cent at current exchange rates (see Exhibit 7.8).

	2003 sales (€m)	2002 sales (€m)	Change (%)	Change on constant exchange rates (%)
France	39959.0	39147.2	2.1	2.1
Spain	12052.1	11108.1	8.5	8.5
Italy	6452.6	5900.7	9.4	9.4
Belgium	4609.3	4446.0	3.7	3.7
Greece	1808.7	1612.5	12.2	12.2
Portugal	1095.7	957.3	14.5	14.5
Poland	808.2	827.1	−2.3	11.9
Switzerland	487.0	505.0	−3.6	0.0
Turkey	664.6	497.0	33.7	15.9
Czech Rep./Slovakia	431.7	413.3	4.3	6.1
Europe	**28409.9**	**26267.0**	**8.2**	**8.4**
Brazil	3174.5	3666.0	−13.4	12.0
Argentina	1336.3	1519.7	−12.1	4.3
Mexico	605.2	729.9	−17.1	11.0
Colombia	332.9	295.2	12.7	30.9
Chile	139.1	135.2	2.9	22.3
Americas	**5588.0**	**6346.0**	**−11.9**	**11.1**
Taiwan	1183.4	1381.0	−14.3	1.9
Korea	1219.0	1242.9	−1.9	12.1
Chine	1325.1	1194.3	10.9	32.6
Thailand	406.4	416.4	−2.4	12.7
Malaysia	202.4	225.9	−10.4	7.1
Indonesia	378.9	313.2	21.0	33.6
Japan	235.9	156.9	50.4	64.8
Singapore	86.4	86.0	0.5	17.1
Asia	**5037.5**	**5016.6**	**0.4**	**17.1**
Group	**78994.4**	**76776.8**	**2.9**	**6.0**

Exhibit 7.8 Breakdown of country sales, 2003 (including VAT)
Source: www.carrefour.com

Colombia *Chévere*[4]

Colombia's economy, having been stable for many years, went through a very difficult time from 1999 to 2001, with weak domestic and foreign demand, austere government budgets and serious internal armed conflict. But, after 2002, the new government of President Alvaro Uribe introduced several financial reforms and a programme of 'democratic security', the country had strongly reduced guerrilla and illicit drug problems, and had re-established trust in its people and in foreign investors. Colombia's economy consolidated in 2003, presenting total economic growth of 3.7 per cent and an

▶ important appreciation of the Colombian peso. Household consumption, private investment and internal demand also saw significant improvements (see Exhibits 7.9, 7.10, and 7.11). In 2004, IMD Switzerland, one of the two most recognized entities that measures global competitiveness, reclassified Colombia in 32nd position, next to important economies such as those of India, Israel, Korea, Portugal and Hungary. In addition, the international qualifier firm Fitch improved Colombia's competitiveness grade from 'negative' to 'stable', which helped Colombia stabilize its foreign exchange reserves and provided opportunities for greater economic growth of 4 per cent in 2004.

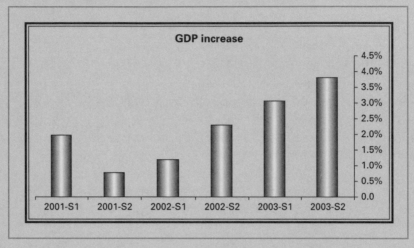

Exhibit 7.9 Colombia's GDP and exchange rate towards the US dollar to 30 April 2004
Source: Carrefour annual report

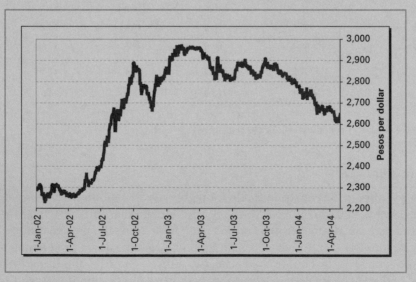

Exhibit 7.10 Colombia's peso exchange rate towards the US dollar to 30 April 2004
Source: Banco de la Republica de Colombia

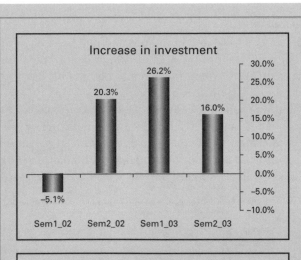

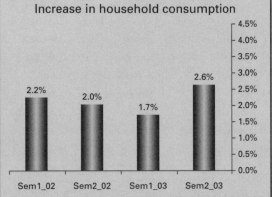

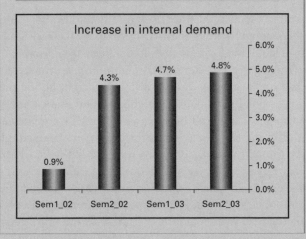

Exhibit 7.11 Colombia's general economic indicators
Source: Banco de la Republica de Colombia

> ### The Colombian retail market

The Colombian retail market had been immature and had been developing over the past few years. In 2002, the retail sector represented 1.5 per cent of the country's GDP. It still had low penetration of the world retail players and had mainly been composed of both formal and informal retail distribution channels.

The formal distribution channels were composed of mini-markets, supermarkets and hypermarkets. It was headed by national organizations with strong positioning for the national consumer. The leaders in the retail business were Almacenes Exito, followed by Carulla-Vivero and Olimpica. Carrefour occupied the 4th position (5th in food retailing) and La 14, Cafam, Colsubsidio, Comfandi and Surtimax occupied the following positions respectively (see Exhibit 7.12).

Rank	Argentina	Brazil	Chile	Colombia	Mexico
1	Disco (Ahold)	Carrefour	Grupo D&S	Alm Ecenes/Exito (Ahold)	Wal-Mex
2	Grupo Norte Carrefour	P. Azucar (Casino)	Sta Isabel (Ahold)	Carulla/Vivero	Gigante
3		Sonae	Jumbo	Olimpica	Com.Mex
4	Coto	Bom Preco (Ahold)	Unimarc	Carrefour	Soriana
5	Jumbo	Sendas	San Francisco	LA 14	Chedraui
6	Libertad (Casino)	Sé	Montserrat	CAFAM	Casaley
7	La Anonima	Wal-Mart	Rendic	Colsubsidio	Carrefour
8	Wal-Mart	Coop. Rhodia	Montecarlo	Comfandi	Calimax
9	San Cayetano	G. Barbosa	Agas	Surtimax	HEB

Exhibit 7.12 Ranking per value of Latin American food retailers
Source: based on information taken from an ACNielsen report, 2002

The informal distribution channel was based on the traditional system of trading. The informal channels were composed of *galerias*, big street markets located in special zones consisting of groups of small food stands that do business from 5 am to 3 pm. They sell most of the supplies during the day. *Vendedores ambulantes*, street vendors, carry small amounts of food to sell on the streets, under traffic lights or in public places. *Tiendas* are 'mom-and-pop' stores or small stores in the neighbourhood that cater for the people of the respective neighbourhoods. These traditional grocery stores were normally located inside a house, run by the family, and usually a part of the house had been adapted to hold the inventory. They were normally managed by one member of the family involved in the tasks of purchasing, packaging, selling, dealing with customers and receiving payments. No cash register is used because sales are mostly small cash purchases done to cover daily needs.

The informal channel occupied an important position for many products, the total national sales in this channel were sometimes as high as the total sales in the supermarkets and the hypermarkets. These types of small distributors, though they sell small quantities, are widely spread throughout the country. There are more than 130,000 small stores that sell through these informal retail channels and compete with formal retail businesses such as Carrefour.

Strategy of Carrefour Chévere

Carrefour entered the Colombian market in 1998 through a joint venture with a 55 per cent stake. Other shareholders were Valores Bavaria, a Colombian company owning 35 per cent and Sigla, a Spanish company owning 10 per cent. By June 2003, Carrefour had acquired 100 per cent of shares, demonstrating its growing interest in Colombia. According to an executive manager of Carrefour Colombia, the attractiveness of the Colombian market, regardless of the political and social problems, had been driven by four main factors: 'It is the second largest country in terms of population in South America with more than 40 million inhabitants, the population is not concentrated in only one city, it had steady economic growth and the distribution is not mature yet – no big players have arrived'.

In 2002, the Group obtained sales worth €295 million up from €228.5 million in 2001, representing a growth in nominal terms of 29.2 per cent and sales increased 45.7 per cent at current exchange rates. It was a significant sales increase for the company after the subsidiaries in Indonesia and Czech Republic. Carrefour's *Chévere* strategy, was explained thus by an executive manager:

> The most difficult aspect we encountered here is the very short-term approach that local players have. They are focused on achieving high profitably in a short span of time – often at the expense of their consumers – rather than having a long-term strategy to build brand awareness and customer loyalty. As a result we discovered when we entered this market the considerable importance of local brands, which prevented potential brands to develop. The quality was also poor. This can be explained by a market protected from international quality standards due to high tariff barriers. But nowadays companies exporting to sophisticated countries have been encouraged to enhance their quality level and to invest in updated production equipment.

Similarly, another manager explained that, due to their Latin heritage, 'Relationships are based on mutual knowledge and personal liking. People are much more emotional, and are likely to show their emotions, which for example might be unheard of in Nordic countries. The social and economic appearance is of utmost importance in building relationships'.

Carrefour's strategy to enter the Colombian market had been culture-centric and dependent on knowledge of the consumers. Carrefour had mainly focused on a continuous expansion strategy, an aggressive pricing policy, the launching of private-label products, powerful promotional campaigns and the introduction of the multi-format concept. The expansion had been only through the hypermarket format and only under the Carrefour banner. It is now present in four main cities, with six stores in Bogotá, three in Medellin, two stores in Cali and one in Pereira.

The private label market: pricing policy and private label

The private-label market is growing in Latin America, where 50 per cent of the households buy private-label products in supermarkets. The principal motivations to purchase private-label goods were low prices, good quality and trust in the supermarket chains. The purchase of private labels had been a growing trend in Latin America, with the highest penetration in Colombia with 74 per cent of households (see Exhibit 7.13).

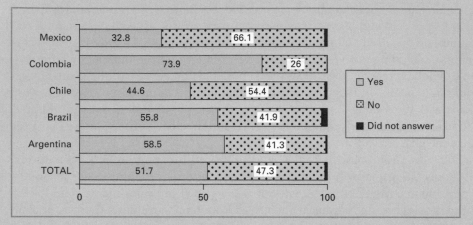

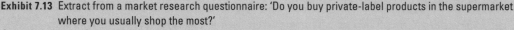

Exhibit 7.13 Extract from a market research questionnaire: 'Do you buy private-label products in the supermarket where you usually shop the most?'

Source: Latin America Survey, ACNielsen/CBPA, 2002

The aggressive pricing policy was difficult to accomplish but had been one of the key drivers of success in Colombia. As one executive manager expressed: 'On the one hand it was tough to match the high growth rate of the informal sector (more than 40 per cent per year) with Carrefour's structure, systems and capacity, while on the other to continue to be the most price aggressive to improve profitability'.

From the perspective of an average consumer, the golden rule in the local market was low price, and Carrefour promised the lowest prices in the market. But price was not the only variable affecting consumer behaviour. Other factors such as choice of products, service and special offers also played important roles. Carrefour's strategy had been that the selection in the store be suited to the needs of the consumer, and its strength lay in the good balance of an ongoing concern for quality and variety coupled with low prices. In the quest to give the consumer a broad variety at the lowest price and expand to capture other market segments attracted by differentiated products or who were more price-sensitive, Carrefour worked on a strategy with its private-label products. Commenting on this strategy, an executive manager said:

> Private labels were introduced a few years ago by competitors such as Olimpica, Carulla and Exito. The strategy they rolled out for private label was a good-quality product to position a bit lower than national brands, with the aim of counterbalancing the power of national brands not offering enough margin; their strategy had been to increase their margins. Carrefour's strategy with its private label had been different. The Carrefour brand was introduced as soon as Carrefour entered this market with imported products (olive oil, whiskies, pastas, wines, etc.) to have an extremely competitive price and thus to develop new markets with high quality and unbeatable price positioning. This strategy had been very successful while the exchange rate was reasonable. This year [2003] Carrefour

introduced the brand N°1 to propose entry-range products with normal quality standards at the lowest positioning of the market. This new brand is becoming a reference for the market and represents around 7 per cent of total sales of grocery products with only 200 SKUs.[5] In 2004 we will develop the Carrefour brand with local suppliers to launch products at an excellent quality level at the lowest price possible that will provide the 'best value for money'. 〝

Carrefour's private brand label in Colombia was N°1 and it is also in 10 out of the 30 countries in which the Group is present. It includes basic products such as grains, flours, pastas, and personal and domestic care products. According to an executive manager, N°1 was launched as an attempt to satisfy the economic needs of the consumer, especially in products of most importance to Colombians: 'Carrefour is looking to win customers' loyalty by offering a brand that will sell at an economy price throughout the year'.

The N°1 private-label line had 200 products, of which only seven were imported. This emphasizes the company's social commitment to employing national labour where 30 per cent of the product line is produced by small and medium-sized enterprises. The growth expectations for the N°1 brand in 2004 were to expand the product range to 350 products. Head of Carrefour Colombia, Jean Noel Bironneau, expressed the company's goal for the long term as: 'In the future, we hope to have 100 per cent produced in Colombia and export these products to other hypermarkets in the world'.

Local adaptation and innovative promotional campaigns

The ability to adapt to local needs allowed Carrefour to gain the acceptance of Colombian consumers. It positioned itself among the top retailers in the country in under five years. Carrefour's adaptation to the Colombian market had not only been in the variety of product choices carefully selected to match consumer preferences, but also in its innovative marketing approach. Its slogan since its entry into the Colombian market had been 'Carrefour **Chévere**'. *Chévere* is a word used to communicate with consumers in a friendly manner using their everyday language. All Carrefour stores hoist a Colombian flag at the entrance. The stores are painted yellow, blue and red (the colours of the Colombian flag) which in a subtle manner mixes with the company's colours (blue and red). This perhaps helped Colombians overcome the strong patriotic feelings they had, which could have negatively affected Carrefour, as consumers recognize it as a foreign company. But Colombians strongly accepted the French company and increasingly continued to shop every week in its stores. They witnessed that Carrefour did not impose its French culture, but rather understood local customs and tried to provide its customers with a typical Colombian environment.

The marketing strategy was adapted according to the context of the country. It continuously launched innovative promotional campaigns, such as 'Operation VAT[6] reimbursed', which was launched when the Colombian government announced an increase in VAT in mid-2002, which reduced household spending. Carrefour used this opportunity to launch an extraordinary campaign in early September 2003: 'Pay the VAT and come back for it'. Information and training sessions prepared store managers and personnel for this campaign. During a particular week, customers received a purchase

▶

voucher equivalent to the amount of VAT paid on their purchases. These vouchers could be redeemed from 1–31 October. During this period, Carrefour Colombia posted a 15 per cent increase in sales over October 2002.

Due to a high outflux of inhabitants emigrating to different countries over the past few years, one of the sources of income in Colombia has become the repatriation of foreign exchange by non-resident Colombians. These foreign exchange earnings per quarter add up to almost €615.4 million ($800 million, see Exhibit 7.14). Carrefour had been receptive to this trend and agreed with Western Union Bank to offer the service of international transfers in its stores. In addition, if someone decided to convert part of this transfer into a Carrefour bonus to be used for purchases at a later date in its stores, Carrefour gave the customer an additional 3 per cent of the net value of the bonus.

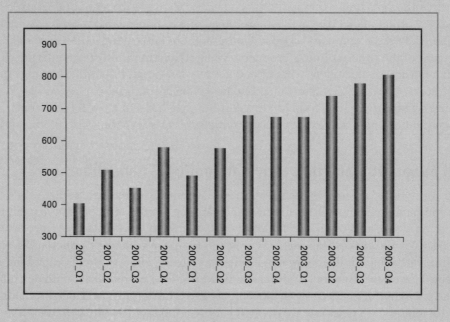

Exhibit 7.14 Foreign money transfers sent to Colombian families (US $ million)
Source: Banco de la República

Future outlook

Carrefour demonstrated a strong commitment to the Latin America markets and made significant investments in local life through its fair trade lines and humanitarian projects. In the future, the expansion could continue to new cities with the promise to consumers of 'the best value for money'. It will continue to strengthen the private-label market and launch creative promotions that will help the Carrefour brand build strong ties with its consumers.

Carrefour's expansion in international markets catapulted it to the number two position in the global food retail business. A key coordinated effort in this area had been its commitment to develop and adapt its shared values in international markets.

Carrefour traced the full life cycle of being historically successful in the home market, expanding in foreign markets like Asia (China, Indonesia, Thailand, Malaysia, Korea), western and eastern Europe (Italy, Turkey, Poland, the Czech Republic) and succeeding in other foreign markets, like Latin America (Brazil, Argentina and Colombia, where Carrefour had sizeable operations spanning 20 years).

Now it was José Luis Duran's turn, being in the hot seat, to replicate the international success of Carrefour in its home market and woo back French customers. It was a dilemma he needed to solve very soon.

Notes

[1] The Royer Law in France requires special approval for any proposed new retail store bigger than 300 square metres.

[2] For the whole case, the exchange rate is taken as €1 = US$1.3.

[3] Carrefour 2003 annual report, delivered 4 March 2004. Sales on constant exchange rates including VAT.

[4] The word *chévere* is Colombian jargon meaning 'cool!'.

[5] Stock keeping units: a common term for a unique numeric identifier, typically used in the retail sector to identify a product in the stores.

[6] Value added tax.

? Case questions

Read the case carefully and then answer the following questions.

1 Comment on the exponential growth Carrefour had in the last decade. In this context what does globalization mean for the retail sector in general and Carrefour in particular?

2 What is the rationale for expansion in emerging markets vis-à-vis consolidating in mature markets? Do you think that Carrefour's current strategy of rapid expansion by acquisition is the most preferred one? How is value created in this process?

3 Why do you think Carrefour has become so successful in Latin America, and in Colombia especially? Comment on its multi-format and pricing strategy, and private label business.

4 Discuss the impact of cultural issues (a French company operating in Latin America) on Carrefour's general strategy in Latin America, and particularly in Colombia?

CHAPTER 8

Ethics and corporate social responsibility challenges

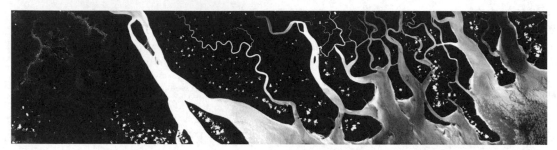

The previous chapter discussed emerging management imperatives when operating and managing a successful global company. This chapter discusses the ethical dilemmas that global companies face while conducting business in different geographic locations. The discussion focuses on corporate social responsibility when dealing with issues such as bribery and corruption, child labour, piracy, counterfeiting and governance.

Ethics has many definitions. There are complexities when attempting to define ethics as related to corporations because, as entities, corporations do not have ethics. An employee makes his or her own interpretation based on personal belief about whether a decision, behaviour or action in the context of a particular environment is correct or incorrect. With a change in context, individuals can rationalize their decisions and may deviate from their personal beliefs and interpretation. Generalizing, ethics more often than not conforms to the acceptable social norms, standards, religion or values of a particular culture. Thus ethical dilemmas and decisions are most often specific to a culture. Again, within a specific culture, employees, as individuals, may have different ideas about what constitutes ethical or unethical behaviour. These ideas depend on the individual's level of education, economic standing, status in society, religion, and exposure to different cultures and beliefs.

Christian values in the West, Shintoism in Japan, Taoism and Buddhism in China, Hinduism in India, and Islam in the Middle East and in Asia, have made the understanding of global business ethics a more complex task, but also a more interesting one. Religion affects the individual's behaviour to a great extent. For example, in the West, formal networking and getting work done through relationships and friends is sometimes viewed with raised eyebrows. In the USA, each individual prefers to be seen as a self-made person who has achieved success on his or her merits and hard work rather than through connections. However, networking and using relationships in business is the name of the game in Latin, Middle Eastern and most Asian countries. Another example in multicultural ethical behaviour is the concept of gift-giving. In Asia, gift-giving is a religious, cultural and social phenomenon that pervades personal and professional life. But this is not so in the West, especially in the USA, where gifts with a high value may in professional life be considered as bribes.

Some ethical questions that haunt global corporations are those listed below.

- Is child labour permissible? Of course not. But when close to 600 million people live below the poverty line, i.e. below $1 a day or do not have one meal a day, in China and India, how will these people feed their children?

- Can corporations lay off or fire employees? The answer is yes in the USA. But in most emerging and developing countries there are no state social or medical benefits. So the government has to protect the interests of the labour force with strict labour laws governing rationalization of the workforce. Is this ethical?

- Should pharmaceutical companies, which have spent millions of dollars on R&D, give away drugs for AIDS, tuberculosis and other diseases to impoverished nations in Africa? On one hand for the benefit of mankind they should, while on the other they also need to maximize profits and serve their stakeholders.

- Should tobacco companies be allowed to market harmful products around the globe, especially to younger generations?

- Is giving gifts to build networks and relationships acceptable in business?

Corporations manage ethical challenges in many ways. Some explicitly lay down an ethical code of conduct, whereas others train their personnel by example. In some corporations there could be an explicit, laid-down code of conduct. While, in others, top management acts as a role model and builds a tacit code of conduct within the organization.

The concepts of ethical and socially responsible behaviour are closely related.

Corporate social responsibility (CSR) is now a core part of any global strategy. As corporations globalize, they are faced with the challenge of being responsible citizens. There are many definitions available for CSR and they are usually found on company websites in order to reinforce their commitment to stakeholders. Key features of the definitions can be summarized as follows.

- It is the decision making and implementation process that guides company activities in the protection and promotion of, and investment in international human rights, labour and environmental standards. It influences the workplace, the marketplace, the supply chain, the community and the public policy realm.

- It involves a commitment to contribute to the economic, environmental and social sustainability of communities through the ongoing engagement of stakeholders.

- It has to comply with legal requirements within its operations and in its relations with the societies and communities where it operates.

It is now well documented that global corporations overwhelmingly embrace the idea that firms have societal and environmental obligations in addition to ensuring corporate profitability. The term CSR is often used interchangeably with concepts such as corporate responsibility, corporate citizenship, corporate philanthropy, social enterprise, sustainability, sustainable development, triple bottom line, corporate ethics and, in some cases, corporate governance. Though these terms are different, they all point in the same direction as corporations are facing new demands to engage in public–private partnerships. There is growing pressure to be accountable not only to shareholders, but also to employees, consumers, suppliers, local communities, policy makers and society at large.

The concept of CSR is promoted by the idea that corporations can no longer act as isolated economic entities operating in detachment from broader society. Some of the issues that promote CSR are those listed below.

- *The role of government:* in the past, governments have relied on legislation and regulations to deliver social and environmental objectives to both the public and the private sector. With liberalization, deregulation and globalization, this scenario is changing fast. Shrinking government resources have led to the exploration of voluntary and non-regulatory initiatives.

- *Demands for greater disclosure:* there is growing demand for corporate disclosure from stakeholders, including customers, suppliers, employees, communities, investors and activist organizations. Corporations are introducing codes of conduct for their suppliers and other stakeholders to ensure that other company policies or practices are in line with their own CSR code, and practices followed by others do not tarnish their reputation.

- *Customer interest and investor pressure:* there is evidence that the ethical conduct of corporations exerts a growing influence on the purchasing decisions of customers. Investors are changing the way they assess companies' performance and are making decisions based on criteria that include ethical concerns. More and more investors are using environmental, social responsibility and ethical considerations when investing in corporations.

- *Competitive labour markets:* employees are increasingly looking beyond extrinsic rewards and seeking out employers whose philosophies, work culture and operating practices match their own principles. Thus, to recruit and retain skilled employees, corporations are adapting to international guidelines.

CSR: international guidelines

With discussions in the global arena, the concept of corporate social responsibility is now firmly planted on the global business agenda. Some of the benefits that accrue at the corporation level have been documented. Practising CSR might lead to a perceived improved financial performance through enhanced brand image and reputation, increased sales and thus customer loyalty, ability to attract and retain employees, reduced regulatory oversight, access to capital and workforce diversity. In terms of benefits to the community, there might be an increase in charitable contributions, employee volunteer programmes, corporate involvement in community education, plus development of homelessness programmes. For the environment, benefits might be in the form of renewable energy, conserving energy, greater material recyclability, better product functionality, and integration of environmental management tools into business plans such as life cycle assessment and costing, environmental management standards and eco-labelling.

At the 2002 World Economic Forum, 36 chief executives from global corporations such as Coca-Cola, Siemens and Renault signed a document supporting CSR as a central component of any business strategy. They argued that the framework to be adopted for being a responsible business must move beyond philanthropy and be integrated into core business strategy and practice. To ensure this happens, top management must remain committed through clear responsibilities, resources and leadership roles. The framework provided scope for putting the principles of CSR into practice, as follows.

- *Provide leadership:* set the strategic direction for corporate citizenship and engage in the wider debate on globalization and the role of business in development; articulate purpose, principles and values internally and externally; promote the 'business case' internally; engage the financial sector to enter the debate on globalization and the role of business in development.

- *Define what it means for the corporation:* define the key issues, stakeholders and spheres of influence that are relevant for corporate citizenship in the company and industry.

- *Make it happen:* establish and implement appropriate policies and procedures, and engage in dialogue and partnership with key stakeholders to embed corporate citizenship into the company's strategy and operations; put corporate citizenship on the board agenda; establish internal performance, communication, incentive and measurement systems; engage in dialogue and partnership; encourage innovation and creativity, and build the next generation of business leaders.

- *Be transparent:* build confidence by communicating consistently with different stakeholders about the company's principles, policies and practices in a transparent manner within the bounds of commercial confidentiality; agree on what and how to measure; develop a graduated programme for external reporting; be realistic.

The social indicators used to measure CSR were (a) community, (b) health and safety, (c) employment, (d) training and education, (e) charitable donations, (f) ethics, (g) supply chain, (h) human rights, (f) socially responsible investment, and (g) child labour.

Managing compliance

Managing across borders increasingly includes difficult ethical dilemmas that can be explained in terms of managing compliances. As discussed in Chapter 2, a global strategy might be accompanied by exportive people management and universal ethical norms, a multi-domestic strategy by adaptive people management and relativism, and a transnational strategy by integrative people management and cosmopolitan ethics.

Corporate philanthropy

Philanthropy derives its origin from the Greek language, where the word means 'love for mankind'. When corporations that are for-profit donate directly to charitable organizations or to individuals in need, with the intention of improving their quality of life it is termed corporate philanthropy. Corporations and consumers have long seen corporate philanthropy as a way for companies to benefit the communities where they are located – donating funds to local schools, hospitals and the community. In recent years, however, as society's expectations of companies have risen and as many companies have begun operating in more far-flung locations, they are expected to address a growing list of needs. Corporations that in the 1970s were held accountable only for direct, contractually specified or regulated consequences of their actions today find themselves held to account for the consequences of their actions in areas as disparate as offshoring, obesity, excessive consumer debt, environmental sustainability, and the governance of resource-rich, low-income nations. The expense of voluntary grants is typically planned as part of the corporation's annual budgeting process. Thus it is a key component of the strategic initiative of a corporation's broader goal of social responsibility, which might include cash gifts, product donations and employee volunteerism, which serves as a major link between the corporation and the communities it serves.

Corporate philanthropy can be an effective tool for corporations that are trying to meet consumers' rising expectations of the role businesses should play in society. It enables a sustainable strategy of the corporation's goals and values to be put forth to various internal and external stakeholders. But these goals and values, which need strategic investments, have to be measured by the actual outcomes achieved through the charitable returns.

For example, Sony has, since 1987, committed to improve people's lives by focusing its key businesses on several distinct areas: arts education; arts and culture; health and human services; civic and community outreach; education; the environment; and volunteerism. Orange Group's corporate philanthropy policy focuses on three global themes – disability, education and culture – where the Orange Foundation is working to help autistic people and improve quality of life for the visually or hearing impaired, help adult literacy, support the education of young girls in developing countries and promote collective vocal music. While, for the Renault Foundation, due to its global alliances, it is focusing on training foreign students from prestigious universities to be at ease in a multicultural environment.

The McKinsey Quarterly[1] conducted a survey on the state of corporate philanthropy in 2007, and received responses from 721 executives around the world – 74 per cent of them CEOs or other C-level executives – followed by interviews with 21 CEOs up to February 2008. About a fifth of the respondents said that their corporate philanthropy programmes are very or extremely effective at meeting social goals and stakeholder expectations. However a small group of respondents said that their companies are reaching beyond traditional corporate goals for philanthropy programmes – such as enhancing the

---

[1] http://www.mckinseyquarterly.com/The_state_of_corporate_philanthropy_A_McKinsey_Global_Survey_2106.

company's reputation or brand – to pursue more concrete business goals, such as gaining information on potential markets. Their approach to focusing the programmes also differs from the approach at other companies. In addition to social goals, the vast majority of corporations – nearly 90 per cent – seek business benefits from their philanthropy programmes as well. When respondents were asked what business goals they try to reach through philanthropy, they most often said that their goals include enhancing the corporate reputation or brand. And some 80 per cent of respondents said finding new business opportunities should have at least some role in determining which philanthropic programmes to fund, compared with only 14 per cent who said finding new business opportunities should have no weight. It is notable, however, that some 30 per cent of the responses to the question asking about business goals indicated that some companies are trying to reach very concrete goals, such as building knowledge about potential new markets and informing areas of innovation.

In another study[2] it was concluded that charitable actions to enhance corporations' profitability depend on the type of industry. For example, it was seen that corporate philanthropy and profits are positively related only in industries with high advertising intensity and high competition, such as beverage and retail industries, whereas in low-advertising industries, such as computer chips and business-to-business services, there might actually be a negative association between philanthropy and profits. Corporations can portray a feel-good effect by saying that they are either selling fair trade coffee, not using any 'Third World' sweatshop labour, not procuring diamonds from conflict zones, etc. It was theorized that, generally, corporate philanthropy may be good for the bottom line because it helps to convince consumers that a company and its products are trustworthy.

Bribery and corruption

The definition of bribery is as diverse as it is culture-specific. International definitions of corruption for policy purposes are much more common. One frequently used definition that covers a broad range of corrupt activities is the *abuse of public or private office for personal gain*.[3] This definition can be a useful reference for policy development and awareness raising, as well as for elabourating anticorruption strategies, action plans and corruption prevention measures. Apart from this general definition, there are as many different definitions of corruption as there are manifestations of the problem itself. These definitions vary according to cultural, legal or other factors. Even within these definitions, there is no consensus about what specific acts should be included or excluded. Some examples are listed below.

- *Transparency International:* corruption involves behaviour on the part of officials in the public sector, whether politicians or civil servants, in which they improperly and

---

[2] http://knowledge.wharton.upenn.edu/article.cfm?articleid=1638.

[3] http://www.oecd.org.

unlawfully enrich themselves, or those close to them, by the misuse of the public power entrusted to them.

■ The *Korean Independent Commission against Corruption* promotes the reporting of any public official involving an abuse of position or authority of violation of the law in connection with official duties for the purpose of seeking grants for himself or a third party.

■ The *Asian Development Bank:* corruption involves behaviour on the part of officials in the public and private sectors, in which they improperly and unlawfully enrich themselves and/or those close to them, or induce others to do so, by misusing the position in which they are placed.

Child labour

Any work done by children that harms or exploits them in some way (physically, mentally, morally or by blocking access to education) can be defined as child labour. But there are varying definitions of the term that are used by international organizations, non-governmental organizations, trades unions and other groups. Global corporations usually follow a universal approach (e.g. through a corporate code of ethics). Global corporations with a child labour code point out, however, that it cannot include everything as codes need to be adopted to host country demands. For example, host country and home country norms sometimes diverge, with different perceptions of what constitutes child labour, the age of the child, the position of children in society and the standards that must be adopted.

Global corporations such as Levi Strauss, Nike, Sara Lee, Wal-Mart and IKEA are well known for their global codes of ethics. Levi Strauss, for example, notes that:

> A code of conduct is a statement of principles, which should be supported by implementation policies in the factories from which the company sources. Therefore, not everything is detailed in a code of conduct, as often the solutions to situations are on a case-by-case basis, depending on what is the most suitable form of support.

And Nike states that 'Codes of conduct are not the only formal strategies that companies have. In case the use of child labour is detected, other formal policies come into force.' However, these policies are not visible within the publicly displayed code. IKEA has been deliberate in promoting the fact that its products must be manufactured under acceptable working conditions by its suppliers. The company works closely with UNICEF and Save the Children to prevent child labour.

Almost all multinationals that stipulate a minimum age for employment explicitly mention host-country specificity. They thus adopt a multinational ethical strategy. Only a very small percentage adhere to a minimum age requirement that applies to all locations, and is thus universal. An example is Sara Lee, which states that 'while the legal definition of "children" sometimes varies from country to country, Sara Lee will not knowingly employ individuals who are under 15 years of age.' India passed a law in 2006 banning 'child labour' by those who are under 14 years of age.

IPR, piracy, counterfeiting

Trademarks are used by producers to distinguish their products from competing products. They generally create expectations with respect to the quality and characteristics of the products concerned, and therefore serve as an important informational tool that consumers use to evaluate different products. Improper use of a trademark compromises or destroys its value to producers and consumers. Copyrights are the rights given to authors of creative works, such as movies, music, software and written work. A patent is an instrument that enables the holder to exclude unauthorized parties from making, using, offering for sale, selling or importing a protected product as well as a product obtained using a patented process. Design rights concern the ornamental or aesthetic aspect of an article. Infringements undermine the ability of rights holders to recover their investment costs and/or otherwise benefit from their innovative or creative work.

Counterfeiting and piracy are terms used to describe a range of illicit activities linked to intellectual property rights (IPR) infringement. The infringement of IPRs described in the WTO Agreement on Trade-Related Aspects of Intellectual Property Rights (TRIPS) includes trademarks, copyrights, patents and design rights, as well as a number of related rights. The intellectual property system is a basic legal system that promotes mankind's economic development, social progress, scientific and technological innovation, and cultural prosperity. As science and technology is developing rapidly worldwide, and the pace of economic globalization is accelerating, the status of the intellectual property system in economic and social life has reached a historic high. Thus, the protection of such rights both at the global and local levels is a key necessity and a challenge within the context of the international community.[4]

Counterfeiting and piracy are illicit businesses in which criminal networks thrive. International trade in counterfeit and pirated products reached $200 billion in 2005. This total does not include domestically produced and consumed counterfeit and pirated products, and the significant volume of pirated digital products being distributed via the internet. If these items were added, the total magnitude of counterfeiting and piracy worldwide could well be several hundred billion dollars more.[5]

Fake goods are being produced and consumed in most economies, with Asia emerging as the main region for such trade and China as the single largest source of production. In recent years there has been an alarming expansion of the types of products being infringed, from luxury items (such as deluxe watches and designer clothing), to items that have an impact on personal health and safety (such as pharmaceutical products, food and drink, medical equipment, personal care items, toys, tobacco and automotive parts). The nature of pirated goods varies from market to market, with the main market for counterfeit car parts, for example, being the Middle East, while consumption of counterfeit tobacco products is highest in Latin America, Africa and Asia. Counterfeit drugs are a major problem in Africa and there have been big seizures of these fake products in Europe and North America.

---

[4] http://www.oecd.org/dataoecd/13/12/38707619.pdf.

[5] *Ibid*.

Counterfeit electrical components, food and drink, and household products are appearing worldwide, with Africa, Asia and Latin America key regional markets.[6]

The market for counterfeit and pirated products can be divided into two important sub-markets. In the *primary market*, consumers purchase counterfeit and pirated products believing they have purchased genuine articles. The products are often substandard and carry health and safety risks that range from mild to life threatening. In the *secondary market*, consumers looking for what they believe to be bargains knowingly buy counterfeit and pirated products. The policies and measures to combat counterfeiting and piracy in the two markets differ, so it is important to know how much of a threat each poses when considering product-specific strategies.[7]

Counterfeiting and piracy are long-standing problems that are growing in scope and magnitude. They are of concern to governments because of (i) the negative impact that they can have on innovation, (ii) the threat they pose to the welfare of consumers, and (iii) the substantial resources that they channel to criminal networks, organized crime and other groups that disrupt and corrupt society. They are of concern to international business because of the impact that they have on (i) sales and licensing, (ii) brand value and firm reputation, and (iii) the ability of firms to benefit from the breakthroughs they make in developing new products. They are of concern to consumers because of the significant health and safety risks that substandard counterfeit and pirated products could pose to those who consume the items.[8]

Two of the principal challenges for global corporations in combating counterfeiting and piracy are to (i) find ways to enhance enforcement, such as increasing cooperation between governments and business, increase criminal penalties to deter criminals and toughen sanctions to more effectively redress the harm caused to rights holders, and (ii) raise awareness of counterfeiting and piracy issues.

Corporate governance

Corporate governance (CG) is the system and process by which corporations are directed and controlled by their owners. It addresses the division of rights and responsibilities among different stakeholders in the corporation such as the board, managers, employees, shareholders and other stakeholders. It specifies and aligns the rules and procedures for making decisions on corporate affairs. These procedures provide the structure through which the objectives of the corporations are set, and the routines of attaining those objectives and monitoring performance are achieved. With formalization of governance principles, corporations are not only concerned for the benefit of the shareholders, but broadly with financial performance, social performance and environmental performance, sometimes referred as the *triple bottom line*.

CG issues arise due to *principle-agent* problems, which, simply put, is the separation of ownership from managerial control of a corporation. Agency theory is directed at the ubiquitous agency relationship, in which the principal (owner) delegates work to the agent

---

[6] *Ibid.*

[7] *Ibid.*

[8] *Ibid.*

(manager), who performs that work. Thus agency theory is concerned with resolving two problems that can occur in this agency relationship. The first arises when (a) there is a conflict between the desires or goals of the principal and agent, and (b) it is difficult or expensive for the principal to monitor the daily operational management of the business affairs of the agent. From the principal or shareholder's perspective, the corporate resources and profits should be spent judiciously, and the agents or managers will not opt for benefits at the shareholders' expense. The shareholders also want to ensure that they receive a positive return on their investment. Under this circumstance the principal and agent may prefer different actions because they might have different attitudes towards risk.

Examples like Arthur Andersen, Worldcom, Enron, Qwest and Tyco in the USA, Parmalat in Italy, Ahold in the Netherlands, Nestlé in Switzerland and Société Générale in France show that corporate fraud and scandals can wreak havoc on the stock market and shatter investor confidence. All these cases reinforce the vital role of ethics in the conduct of business. Most of these scandals and the ensuing losses could have been avoided if proper governance principles had been structured judiciously. It is difficult to say that effective corporate governance may prevent executive fraud but it may enable the firm to recover from its consequence. New ethical laws such as the Sarbanes-Oxley (SOX) Act enforced in the USA in 2002, stipulate that the CEO and CFO of a corporation must approve and declare accurate financial statements to the SEC for publication. SOX compliance is the tedious process of managing and declaring the unstructured content related to financial controls and making that content appropriately accessible for audit and verification internally and externally such that it helps to ensure transparency of all disclosures. Global corporations have to comply not only with home country compliance measures but also with host country norms and rules. Ethical norms might be different for different countries, and global corporations have to rely on the local subsidiary to comply with the local rules. Though compliance with new guidelines can become a substantial burden for global corporations, such as ABB operating from Sweden, doing business in the USA and coordinating reporting for dispersed global subsidiaries, the risk and cost of non-compliance might outweigh the benefits. Thus, effective corporate governance may create capabilities that could be used as a source of competitive advantage for the benefit of not only shareholders but all stakeholders.

Case introduction: CSR: strategies to develop markets

Relentless public pressure on corporations to act responsibly has made the role of the corporation in society a hotly debated topic. Central to the debate are the issues of corporate social responsibility (CSR) and corporate philanthropy. At one end of the CSR spectrum are those who believe that the sole responsibility of corporations is to make profits for themselves and their shareholders. By doing so, they are best serving society by stimulating the economy, creating wealth for shareholders and jobs for employees, and constantly innovating to meet society's needs. At the other end are those who feel that it is the moral obligation of corporations to solve the world's most pressing problems, ranging from global warming to poverty to HIV/AIDS.

This case appears after the readings for this chapter.

READING 15

Corporate social responsibility: whether or how?*

N. Craig Smith

While corporate social responsibility (CSR) was widely discussed in the last forty years of the twentieth century, the idea that business has societal obligations was evident at least as early as the nineteenth century. In Britain, visionary business leaders in the aftermath of the Industrial Revolution built factory towns – such as Bourneville (founded by George Cadbury in 1879) and Port Sunlight (founded by William Lever in 1888 and named after the brand of soap made there) – that were intended to provide workers and their families with housing and other amenities when many parts of the newly industrialized cities were slums. A similar pattern also emerged in the United States – George Pullman's town built on the outskirts of Chicago was described as 'the most perfect city in the world.'[1]

Consider Saltaire, founded in 1851 by Sir Titus Salt (1803–1876) just outside Bradford, then the world's wool textile capital. In the mid-nineteenth century, Bradford was also known as the most polluted town in England, with factory chimneys churning out black, sulphurous smoke and factory effluent and sewage being dumped into the local river that also provided the town's drinking water, leading to cholera and typhoid. Average life expectancy in Bradford was only 20 years. Daniel Salt and Sons was one of the most important textile companies in Bradford and the largest employer. In response to conditions in the city and needing a suitable site for a new factory, Titus Salt moved from Bradford and built a new industrial community called Saltaire. By the time of his death in 1876, this included 850 houses for his workers, each served with fresh water from Saltaire's own reservoir, as well as a park, church, school, hospital, and a library.

Unfortunately, Saltaire was the exception rather than the rule and the 'dark Satanic mills' described by William Blake (1757–1827) were more the norm. Moreover, this was a form of paternalistic capitalism; like Lever and Cadbury, Salt also wished to promote moral virtue among his workers. As an account of the founding of Saltaire observes, 'Bradford was polluted, unhealthy and immoral; at Saltaire the physical, material, and moral improvement of the workers was to be promoted by a good employer.[2] Nonetheless, while Salt would not have been familiar with the term, he clearly supported

California Management Review, Vol. 45, No. 4, Summer 2003.

Financial assistance provided by London Business School is gratefully acknowledged.

the fundamental idea embedded in corporate social responsibility, 'that business corporations have an obligation to work for social betterment.'[3]

Salt and other philanthropic industrialists of the Victorian period were motivated by a desire to do good, but they were also motivated by enlightened self-interest. Salt recognized that his mill workers would be more productive if he offered an improved work environment and better living conditions. He also realized that Saltaire would be less vulnerable to the political unrest and militancy evident at that time among some sections of the population in Bradford, and strikes and other disputes were rare in Saltaire. Indeed, historian Styles asked 'Was Salt's paternalism (consciously or not) ultimately a device for securing a compliant, captive workforce which could be indoctrinated into disciplined behavior that ensured continued profits?'[4] While acknowledging that the realization of Salt's vision secured the continuing profitability of his business, Styles rejects these pejorative interpretations of Salt and Saltaire: 'It fulfilled the obligations he believed he owed his workers.'[5]

Key characteristics of CSR

CSR refers to the obligations of the firm to society or, more specifically, the firm's stakeholders – those affected by corporate policies and practices. Saltaire and other early examples of paternalistic capitalism reveal three important characteristics of CSR. First, it is not a new idea, the hype surrounding it today notwithstanding.[6] Second, although there is a clear difference between CSR stemming from a desire to do good (the 'normative case') and CSR that reflects an enlightened self-interest (the 'business case'), a firm's reasons for engaging in CSR might reflect a mixture of these motivations. Third, while there is substantial agreement that CSR is concerned with the societal obligations of business, there is much less certainty about the nature and scope of these obligations. Salt's ideas for social betterment did not meet with universal approval and he opposed legislation to prohibit child labor. Even corporate champions of CSR today, such as Starbucks meet with criticism from NGOs (non-governmental organizations) and others.[7] As Sethi observed nearly 30 years ago, the operational meaning of CSR is supremely vague.[8]

Prominence of CSR

Historical origins notwithstanding, CSR has never been more prominent on the corporate agenda. It has been one of the leading topics at recent World Economic Forum (WEF) meetings. A report from the WEF observes that the three key pressures of 'corporate competitiveness, corporate governance, and corporate citizenship, and the linkages between them, will play a crucial role in shaping the agenda for business leaders in the coming decade.'[9] It continues:

> In the face of high levels of insecurity and poverty, the backlash against globalization, and mistrust of big business, there is growing pressure on business leaders and their companies to deliver wider societal value. This calls for effective management of the company's wider impacts on and contributions to society, making appropriate use of stakeholder engagement.[10]

Similarly, the World Business Council for Sustainable Development (WBCSD), a coalition of 120 international companies, refers to the increasing calls for business to assume wider responsibilities in the social arena and claims that CSR 'is firmly on the global policy agenda.'[11] Among the many other organizations that are advocating greater attention to CSR are the International Business Leaders Forum (IBLF), Business for Social Responsibility (BSR), and Business in the Community (BITC).[12]

Governmental organizations also are involved. In the U.K., the government has appointed a minister for CSR and in its second report on CSR, published in 2002, the Department of Trade and Industry (DTI) states: 'The Government has an ambitious vision for corporate social responsibility: to see private, voluntary, and public sector organizations in the U.K. take account of their economic, social, and environmental impacts, and take complementary action to address key challenges based on their core competences – locally, regionally, nationally, and internationally.'[13] The European Commission adopted a new strategy on CSR in July 2002. Announcing the policy paper, Anna Diamantopoulou, Commissioner for Employment and Social Affairs commented: 'Many businesses have already recognized that CSR can be profitable and CSR schemes have mushroomed. However, the EU can add value in at least two key ways: by helping stakeholders to make CSR more transparent and more credible, and by showing that CSR is not just for multinationals – it can benefit smaller businesses too.'[14]

A shift in the debate on CSR?

Historically, there have been periods of heightened interest in CSR in the past, such as the late 1960s and early 1970s.[15] At that time, business organizations such as The Conference Board in the U.S. and the Confederation of British Industry in the U.K. issued calls for business to give greater attention to CSR. What is different today is that these calls are more broadly expressed, more specific, and more urgent. The calls are coming from business associations with the express purpose of promoting CSR (e.g., WBCSD, BSR, IBLF) as well as the general business associations and they are also coming from governmental organizations (e.g., U.K.'s DTI). Often, these calls include concrete recommendations for action, such as CSR audits and stakeholder engagement (e.g., WEF, WBCSD).

The urgency stems from a realization that the criticism of business is more far-reaching than ever before. This is in part because, with globalization, business itself is more pervasive and more powerful. The extent of this criticism is evidenced, for example, by protests at global meetings of the World Trade Organization since Seattle in 1999 as well as actions targeting individual firms.[16] Moreover, the demands for greater social responsibility are coming from mainstream quarters of society, as well as protesters at global meetings.[17] In 2002, the accounting and governance scandals associated with Enron, WorldCom, and other major corporations have further damaged the public standing of business.

However, criticism of business is also more far-reaching because more is expected of business today, with the growing recognition of the failure of governments to solve many social problems and, for this and other reasons, the diminished scope of government (at least in the U.S. and Europe). The private sector is increasingly called upon to address social problems and, accordingly, shoulder greater social responsibilities in addition to righting the wrongs for which it is more directly responsible, such as pollution or inadequate product safety.[18]

The terrorist attacks in the U.S. on September 11, 2001 have also added to the urgency of the calls for greater attention to CSR, with businesspeople seemingly now more attuned to global inequities. A survey of 264 *Fortune* 1000 CEOs found that 52% believed that corporations acting responsibly to communities around the world can reduce support for terrorist groups.[19]

The CSR responses of individual firms appear to be more widespread and more substantive than we have seen in the past. Most large corporations now at least espouse a commitment to CSR and in some cases their initiatives appear to go substantially beyond corporate philanthropy and corporate communications that attempt to defend the firm's societal impacts.[20] Certainly, CSR is no longer the preserve of Public Affairs or restricted to smaller firms that champion CSR in line with social enterprise goals, such as the Body Shop or Ben and Jerry's. Even corporate critic Naomi Klein talks of a 'massive shift' in a more socially responsible direction by many multinationals, though she views the response as haphazard and inadequate.[21] The impression created overall is that the debate about CSR has shifted: it is no longer about whether to make substantial commitments to CSR, but how?

This article examines the pressures for greater attention to CSR. Should firms be making a substantial commitment to CSR? More specifically, is there a requirement for some firms to make a greater commitment to CSR, but not others? Does an increased requirement for some firms also indicate the form that CSR should take? What other challenges need to be overcome in the development and execution of CSR initiatives? It suggests that is the answer to *whether* to make a substantial commitment to CSR lies the clues as to *how* such a commitment should be made. Of critical consideration is the extent to which arguments in general for greater attention to CSR have specific application to individual firms. CSR strategy for any given firm may be best formulated through an understanding of where these arguments do or do not apply to that organization.

Some firms may find that there is a compelling business case for making a substantial commitment to CSR. For these firms, greater attention to CSR may even be inescapable and the challenge is developing CSR initiatives consistent with a strategic purpose, deciding on their form and scope, and overcoming major potential obstacles to their implementation. For other firms, the business case may be less evident and the case for greater attention to CSR must be made on normative grounds.

Developing country access to essential medicines

A detailed example drawn from the pharmaceutical industry more clearly differentiates between the normative and the business case for CSR. It also illustrates the extent to which CSR can have profound implications and how, for some multinational corporations, it may even assume a strategic significance. Pharmaceutical companies are well known for their philanthropic activities. These activities extend beyond support for charities and include giving away large quantities of their products. Often cited is the example of Merck's development of a treatment for onchocerciasis ('river blindness'), a tropical disease that afflicts people in some of the world's poorest regions. In 1978, the World Health Organization (WHO) estimated that 340,000 people were blind as a result of the disease, a further one million had some visual impairment, and around 18 million were infected. Merck discovered a treatment and although there was no commercial market for the drug, invested tens of millions of dollars in its development. In 1987, Merck set up the Mectizan Donation Program to organize the free distribution of the drug in collaboration with WHO, the World Bank, and other partners. Around 25 million people a year are treated under the program and avoid the risk of premature blindness.[22] Other pharmaceutical companies have since developed similar initiatives. GlaxoSmithKline (and Merck) donate large quantities of medicines as part of a program in conjunction with WHO to eliminate Lymphatic Filariasis ('elephantiasis'), Novartis donates drugs as part of a program to eliminate leprosy, and Pfizer makes azithromycin available for the treatment of trachoma.[23] Although large numbers of people have been treated under such programs and undoubtedly have an improved quality of life as a result, this did not prevent the industry's vilification over its response to the HIV/AIDS crisis, particularly in the context of South Africa.[24]

More than 4 million people in South Africa are HIV infected. In 1997, the South African government announced plans to permit the distribution of generic versions of patented HIV/AIDS drugs that were estimated to be 1/50th of the cost of the patented versions (that were averaging $12,500 per patient per year). However, this plan was accused of violating the government's obligations under the TRIPS (Trade-Related Aspects of Property Rights) agreement, to which it was a party as a member of the World Trade Organization. The following year, a consortium of drug companies brought suit against the South African government and named individuals as defendants, including Nelson Mandela. Accused of putting profits before people, the industry stated that 'the case is nothing to do with blocking access to medicines, or price fixing. It's about patents. Patents do not block medicines. They stimulate research and development.'[25] Nonetheless, in a humiliating back down in April 2001, the pharmaceutical companies dropped the case. As the Boston Globe commented, 'With their boardrooms raided and their executives being hounded in the streets, 39 of the world's largest drug makers caved to public pressure. ... It was hailed as a stunning triumph for the developing world: A $360 billion industry was brought down by a country that represents just half of one percent of the pharmaceutical market.'[26]

GlaxoSmithKline (GSK) was a major target of protesters. It is the second-largest pharmaceutical company with sales of $27.5 billion in financial year 2000 and 108 manufacturing sites in 41 countries. It serves 140 global markets and has an annual R&D budget in excess of $4 billion. It is the market (and R&D) leader in the HIV/AIDS category and the company that (as Burroughs Wellcome) had first introduced drugs for the treatment of HIV/AIDS. According to WHO, AIDS is the second biggest killer of all infectious diseases worldwide and 95% of HIV/AIDS sufferers live in the least developed countries that represent only 10% of the world's population. It was estimated that more than 53 million men, women, and children had been infected worldwide as of 2001 and in that year alone five million people became infected with HIV, three million died of AIDS, and forty million were living with the AIDS virus on a daily basis. Two-thirds of those infected live in Sub-Saharan Africa.

Following the South African court case, GSK and other pharmaceutical companies heavily discounted their HIV/AIDS medicines to developing countries. The industry fear, however, was that this move threatened the central tenets of its business model. Investments in R&D and profits – consistently among the highest of any industry – depended upon the monopolistic pricing of patent-protected drugs. Moreover, discounting in developing country markets raised the possibility of downward pressure on prices in the lucrative developed country markets, particularly as HIV/AIDS was not restricted to developing countries (unlike most tropical diseases) and information on price differentials and drug profit margins would become widespread. There was also the prospect of parallel imports – discounted drugs distributed in developing country markets finding their way back to developed country markets. Some industry leaders spoke of firms focusing their efforts on lifestyle drugs such as Prozac or Viagra rather than killer diseases such as HIV/AIDS and they could see little incentive for continued R&D on tropical diseases.

The South African court case and the access problem reveal an industry in crisis over the scope and meaning of social responsibility. Sophia Tickell, Senior Policy Advisor at the NGO, Oxfam observed that the industry's critics were able to argue convincingly that 'a business model is unacceptable if it makes the defense of industrialized country markets a greater priority than the health of poor people in developing countries.'[27] The access issue is now a strategic consideration for every major pharmaceutical company. In the last two years, the industry has moved, albeit reluctantly, from having well-regarded programs of philanthropy, such as donating medicines for tropical diseases, to having to rethink its business model to incorporate CSR at the core.

In the specific case of GSK, CEO Jean-Pierre Garnier stated that the protection of intellectual property was not an obstacle to access to drugs. In June 2001, GSK rolled out a detailed access strategy. It made commitments in three areas: to continue investment in R&D on diseases that affect the developing world; to offer sustainable preferential (not-for-profit) pricing arrangements in least developed countries (LDCs) and Sub-Saharan Africa for currently available medicines that are needed most (for HIV/AIDS and other diseases, such as malaria); and, to take a leading role in community activities that promote effective healthcare.[28] Several NGOs welcomed the new policy. Tickell commented: 'This is really positive. It is better than all the other initiatives the industry suggested.' Nonetheless, others remained concerned and even some investors have questioned whether GSK has done enough.[29]

Pressures for greater attention to CSR

Normative or business case?

Business leaders can be expected to say that CSR is important, especially in today's social and political climate.[30] Garnier, however, appears to have done much more than this. At GSK's annual meeting in May 2001, campaigners from Oxfam, dressed in lab coats, had called for GSK to do more for LDCs by donating a percentage of drug revenues to a global health fund established by Kofi Annan, the United Nations Secretary General. Garnier's response was unprecedented. He defended GSK's actions on the access issue and then suggested that the company's priority was public health, not simply shareholder value:

> Some months ago, when the newly merged GlaxoSmithKline was formed, I said that I did not want to be head of a company that caters only to the rich. I made access to medicines in poorer countries a priority and I take this opportunity to renew that pledge. We have 110,000 people who go to work every morning because they are pro-public health. We have to make a profit for our shareholders but the primary objective of any policy put forward in the industry is public health.[31]

The quote suggests a normative, moral basis for GSK's response to the access issue. Simply put, 'it is the right thing to do.' In this respect, it is consistent with the motives earlier attributed to Salt and long-standing ideas about business as a good citizen. More formally, a normative basis for CSR may be found in theories of moral philosophy. Thomas Donaldson, for example, draws on social contract theory. His social contract for business is founded on consent – that corporations exist only through the cooperation and commitment of society. This suggests an implicit agreement between the corporation and society. He asks: 'If General Motors holds society responsible for providing the condition of its existence, then for what does society hold General Motors responsible? What are the terms of the social contract?'[32] The simplest form of the contract is to specify what business needs from society and what, in turn, are its obligations to society. This approach can be used to ground the 'license to operate' argument that the WEF and others advance in support of CSR.[33] With the access issue, it might be used to develop a normative basis for justifying actions by the pharmaceutical industry to assist HIV/AIDS victims in LDCs.

However, as with Salt and other examples of paternalistic capitalism, there are quite possibly mixed motives underlying GSK's response to the access issue. Garnier acknowledged a requirement to make a profit for shareholders. Conceivably, this requirement might be met through its actions on access or, perhaps more likely, these actions reduce the risk of eroding shareholder value. Clearly, for example, shareholders' economic interests would be served if GSK's access policy motivates employees and these effects more than outweigh the costs associated with increasing access (including the possibility of reduced profit margins on HIV/AIDS drugs in developed country markets). More important, perhaps, is avoiding the potential scenario where the industry's business model is fundamentally changed and government regulation dictates its every action.

It might be suggested that the pharmaceutical industry example is a special situation. GSK does, after all, produce life-saving products (though firms in other industries are also under pressure to give away their products in LDC markets). Further, HIV/AIDS is a pandemic that, if infection continues on its current trajectory, is projected to affect more than half the world's population. This view bolsters the normative case for action on access, but it also helps explain why external forces such as NGOs have pressured the industry and strengthened the business case as a result.[34] Some might even argue that action on access was unavoidable. However, while this example might be considered extreme in certain respects, it does illustrate the increased pressures for attention to CSR that many firms face today.

Traditional arguments for CSR

Arguments advanced in support of CSR have long recognized enlightened self-interest as well as beliefs about corporate good citizenship and a beneficial social role of business.[35] CSR can be in the enlightened self-interest of business in many ways (though not necessarily in the same way for any given firm). Paternalistic capitalism benefited from the improved living conditions employees found in its factory towns. The modern corporation has benefited from CSR as a result of avoiding or pre-empting legal or regulatory sanctions, such as DuPont's profitable exploitation of more environmentally friendly chlorofluorocarbon (CFC) alternatives.[36] CSR also has benefited firms through direct or indirect economic efficiencies. For example, Starbucks' employee turnover is said to be less than a third that of the average for the retail food industry. This is attributed to Starbucks' socially responsible practices (including a full benefits package for part-time employees) and provides economic efficiencies due to lower costs of staff recruitment and training.[37]

Added pressures

Along with heightened societal expectations and demands of business, the globalization of large corporations has led to firms increasingly operating in countries with very different and generally much lower standards of living than found in their domestic base. More extensive media reach coupled with advances in information technology (e.g., NGO use of web sites) has allowed rapid and widespread exposure of alleged corporate abuses in even the most remote corners of the world, as both Shell (oil spills in Nigeria exposed on television documentaries) and Nike (exposure of sweatshop labor conditions in its subcontractor operations in Asian LDCs) have learnt to their cost.

Democracy is now more widespread. In part, and more obviously, this came with the collapse of communism. However, there is also a sense that people now 'matter' in places where – to those in power – they didn't matter before. Hitherto, their rights were few, politically and in actuality. While there are still many countries where democracy is largely absent in the formal sense, some elements of democracy are possible when NGO and media attention is given to corporate complicity in human rights abuses. For example, the U.S. firm Unocal has been judged legally liable for the abuse of Myanmar villagers by military security guards when they were forced to build an oil pipeline.[38]

Thus, while the traditional arguments for CSR remain important, there are additional pressures for attention to CSR today. A critical consideration for many firms is reputational risk, heightened by the greater visibility and criticism of corporate practices, particularly by NGOs.[39] As a result, the business case for CSR is much stronger.

Consider the approach of Starbucks. While acknowledging a normative case, Starbucks emphasizes a business case for CSR as follows:

> 66 Consumers are demanding more than 'product' from their favorite brands. Employees are choosing to work for companies with strong values. Shareholders are more inclined to invest in businesses with outstanding corporate reputations. Quite simply, being socially responsible is not only the right thing to do; it can distinguish a company from its industry peers.[40] 99

Safeguarding the corporate reputation and brand image have become ever more important as markets have become more competitive and reputations and image have become more vulnerable. Simply put, firms may be penalized by consumers – and others – for actions that are not considered socially responsible.

Reputational risk in consumer markets

Boycotts are one manifestation of this pressure. In the 1990s, the business press reported both that consumer boycotts work and that they were increasing in number. *The Economist*, for example, observed: 'Pressure groups are besieging American companies, politicizing business, and often presenting executives with impossible choices. Consumer boycotts are becoming an epidemic for one simple reason: they work.'[41] Research has found that product boycott announcements are associated with significant negative stock market reactions.[42] Stock market reactions reflect investor beliefs about boycotts having an effect on sales, both directly and indirectly, through harm to the firm's and brand's reputation.

Recent prominent consumer boycotts include the European boycott of Royal Dutch/Shell in 1995 over its plan to dump the Brent Spar oil platform at sea. As a result of the boycott, Shell suffered widespread adverse publicity, as well as up to a 50% decline in sales in some markets.[43] It agreed to the demand by Greenpeace that it abandon sea disposal. However, Shell's decision to dismantle the oil platform on land was almost certainly less socially responsible than the planned disposal at sea, and Greenpeace later admitted that it had overestimated the pollution risk of the platform.[44] Shell's problems were compounded by public reactions to reports of environmental harm as a result of its operations in Ogoniland, Nigeria, and the company's apparent failure to use its influence to prevent the execution by Nigerian authorities of Ken Saro-Wiwa and eight other Ogonis, who had been protesting Shell's presence in Ogoniland as well as on a broader array of social and political issues. Criticism of Shell by environmentalists and human rights activists and the associated boycotts were said to be key contributors to a fundamental transformation in the company efforts to meet its social and ethical responsibilities.[45]

Another example is the ongoing multi-country boycott of Nike over alleged sweatshop conditions at Asian suppliers. Nike is a market leader in the footwear and apparel industry with sales of $9 billion. Ten years ago, Nike asserted that because it did not own its overseas contractors, workplace standards inside their factories were not its responsibility. However, a campaign by NGOs led to the admission by Phil Knight, Nike's CEO, that 'Nike has become synonymous with slave wages, forced overtime, and arbitrary abuse.' In 1997, in a remarkable reversal, Knight announced that three Indonesian suppliers were to be terminated over workplace conditions and stated: 'Good shoes come from good factories and good factories have good labor relations.' Today, while the extent to which Nike sales have suffered is unclear, it continues to fight attacks on its image. It has over 90 people employed in CSR positions and invests heavily in independent third-party audits of its suppliers, the results of which it agrees to publish even though they might be unfavourable.[46]

Boycotts may be only the most manifest example of a broader phenomenon of consumer behavior influenced by perceived CSR lapses.[47] Surveys of consumers report that many claim to be influenced in their purchasing decisions by the CSR reputation of firms. For example, a 1999 survey of 25,000 consumers in 23 countries found that 40% had at least thought about punishing a specific company over the past year they viewed as not behaving responsibly.[48] Academic research by Brown and Dacin found that 'negative CSR associations ultimately can have a detrimental effect on overall product evaluations, whereas positive CSR associations can enhance the product evaluations.'[49] According to Sen and Bhattacharya, key moderators of consumer responses to CSR are individual consumer-specific factors (such as consumers' personal support for CSR issues and their general beliefs about CSR) and company-specific factors (such as the CSR issues a company chooses to focus on and the quality of its products).[50] Their findings highlight the likelihood of differences across consumers in their response to CSR and differences in the type of CSR practices that might serve to generate favorable consumer sentiment. This heterogeneity in responses to CSR points to the likelihood that firms differ in their exposure to reputational risk in consumer markets.

Firms may be rewarded by increased patronage if they have a reputation for being socially responsible. No longer is this the preserve of a handful of companies serving a small segment of consumers, such as Ben and Jerry's, Stonyfield Farms, and the Body Shop. There is also evidence to suggest that some consumers will pay a premium for CSR. One of the more noteworthy successes of the ethical shopping movement is the growth in sales of free-range eggs, now accounting for 35% of sales in the U.K. although they are 25% more expensive than eggs laid by battery hens. However, at least some of the preference for free-range eggs is attributed to salmonella fears, with free-range eggs seen as safer. Fair trade coffee is another example, accounting for retail sales of $64 million in the U.S. and Canada in 2002, with imports up 50% over 2001. In the U.K., fair trade coffee is 12% of the roast and ground coffee market. Cafedirect, the leading U.K. supplier, attributes its success to product quality and offering a premium product as well as adherence to fair trade principles.[51]

Overall, however, evidence to suggest that a significant proportion of consumers will pay more for CSR is scant. According to the Co-operative Bank's Ethical Purchasing Index, the combined U.K. market share of 'ethical products' (e.g., fair trade products) over seven food and non-food segments is approximately 1.5%, equating to £7 billion in sales in 2001. Research by the Bank suggests that while around 30% of consumers might claim to be ethical consumers, few products that make ethical claims (e.g., to protect the environment or animals) have a market share greater than 3%.[52]

It is possible that the potential for CSR to provide competitive advantage may be more diffuse and more widespread than these figures suggest. CSR might make a big difference at the margin for many firms given the increased competitiveness of consumer markets.

Frank Walker of Walker Information has observed: 'As more and more organizations meet the quality requirements of the marketplace ... the consumer will want to know what the company behind the product or service stands for in today's society, and to make certain that they are not contributing to any corporation that is harming society, its resources, or its people.'[53] In highly competitive markets, CSR might provide a valuable basis for differentiation. Hence, a broad array of firms now include environmental claims within their advertising (e.g., automobile manufacturers).

Reputational risk would appear to be largely but not solely a concern for consumer goods companies. Many B2B firms face similar pressures indirectly because of the reputational concerns of their customers, be they retailers or further removed from the consumer in the supply chain. Retailers such as Home Depot in the U.S. and B&Q in the U.K. have pressured suppliers on environmental impacts. For example, 22% of B&Q's sales are of timber and timber-related products, over 99% of which are independently certified as coming from well-managed (sustainable) forests.[54] There is also some evidence of social criteria in B2B purchasing independent of supply chain considerations, and public sector procurement is also increasingly subject to social criteria.[55]

Reputational risk in labor and equity markets

Product markets are not the only source of pressure, employees and investors have concerns about company CSR practices as well as consumers.[56] In the labor market, some employees express a preference for working for more socially responsible companies.[57] It has long been known that tobacco companies have difficulties recruiting the best talent. This effect has become more widespread, particularly in tight labor markets, as potential and current employees consider the corporate social performance of their employer. For example, Edward Jones was the number one company in *Fortune* magazine's 2002 list of best U.S. companies to work for. Its employees praise the company's ethics, with 97% citing its management's honesty. Moreover, employees who are aware of a firm's CSR activities have been found to be more likely to speak highly of it.[58] Belief in the potential value placed by employees on CSR is clearly evident in the GSK example.

Reputation is also important in equity markets. According to the Social Investment Forum, $2.32 trillion or nearly one out of every eight dollars under professional management in the United States was involved in socially responsible investing in 2001.[59] The Dow Jones Sustainability Index (introduced in 1999) and FTSE4Good (2001), list companies that meet socially responsible investing criteria. However, critics have questioned their inclusiveness: 76% of the FTSE 100 stocks qualify for the U.K. FTSE4Good index.[60] Nonetheless, the growth in investing and listing of companies according to social responsibility criteria has led to a substantial increase in social and environmental reporting by firms. Around 80% of FTSE-100 companies now provide information on their social or environmental policies. In France, legislation introduced in 2002 makes such reporting mandatory. Increasingly, companies are setting up elaborate reporting mechanisms to measure their social and environmental performance. Advising business on its ethical and social responsibilities is a multi-million pound business in the U.K. alone, with most of the consulting operations formerly associated with leading accounting practices offering services in the area as well as more specialist consultancies.

Thus, a powerful set of external forces and changes have contributed to the recent rise in prominence of CSR: increased societal expectations of business voiced, in part, by powerful NGOs; a diminution of the power and scope of government; globalization; heightened media reach, assisted by advances in information technology; and the greater spread of democracy. Prior peaks of interest in CSR have generally coincided with economic prosperity and interest has diminished at times of recession.[61] However, the depth of current societal concern about corporate practices seems unprecedented and some important developments, such as globalization, are likely to be long lasting and their influence on CSR sustained. Many companies appear to be doing more in response to the pressures for increased attention to CSR, especially in light of their apparent importance within ever more competitive product, employment, and equity markets and the potential for reputational risk. However, there are those who question greater corporate attention to CSR.

Dangers of do-gooding executives

Consider Garnier's statement of aspirations for GSK: 'The pharmaceutical industry today sells 80% of its products to 20% of the world's population. I don't want to be a CEO of a company that caters only to the rich. ... I want those medicines in the hands of many more people who need them.[62] The forthright expression of such a vision was uncharacteristic for a pharmaceutical industry executive. It is also the sort of statement that deeply troubles CSR critics such as David Henderson and Ethan Kapstein.[63] They suspect that 'do-gooding' executives are pursuing personal visions of a better world using shareholders' money and often with insufficient regard for the likely effectiveness or possible ill-consequences of their initiatives. Kapstein acknowledges that it is hard to argue against making drugs available to patients who desperately need them, but is concerned about what this means for the industry: 'the possible adverse consequences of this decision need to be considered. If the giveaway means lower profits for manufacturers – and thus less incentive for innovation – this victory will prove a hollow one for future patients with deadly and debilitating diseases.'[64]

Forty years ago in *Capitalism and Freedom*, Friedman claimed that 'there is one and only one social responsibility of business – to use its resources and engage in activities designed to increase its profits so long as it stays within the rules of the game, which is to say, engages in open and free competition, without deception or fraud.'[65] Friedman's famous dictum on corporate social responsibility was part of an attack on much broader conceptions of the social role of business, which Friedman viewed as fundamentally subversive.

There is more to commend Friedman's arguments than his critics generally allow.[66] First, he was not opposed to the idea that firms have societal obligations that must be fulfilled. He was only opposed to activities that went beyond a narrowly defined role for the corporation. In this way, the uncertainty about the societal obligations of the firm, discussed at the outset of this article, is substantially diminished. Friedman believed that business satisfied its social responsibilities through conventional business activities, primarily producing needed goods and services at prices that people could afford. In this respect, his argument can be traced back to Adam Smith, who recognized that in the pursuit of self-interest the businessperson is 'led by an invisible hand to promote an end which was no part of his intention.'[67]

Second, Friedman reasoned that a more expansive role for the corporation was a worrisome departure from the competitive model of capitalism. More specifically, he argued that CSR amounted to spending someone else's money (notably shareholders' or customers') and muddied decision making by diluting the focus on profit and placing the firm at a competitive disadvantage as a result. He also questioned whether managers were competent to engage in social issues, whether the imposition of their values in the social arena was desirable and whether they were potentially usurping the role of government. However, it is now widely accepted that Friedman's position was founded on an inaccurate economic model and was unrealistic in its attempt to isolate business from society when the two are so interdependent. As Mintzberg wrote: 'the strategic decisions of large organizations inevitably involve social as well as economic consequences, inextricably intertwined ... there is no such thing as a purely economic strategic decision.'[68]

Nonetheless, there are grounds for concern about some CSR initiatives. On the one hand, there is so often little real substance to what some firms claim to do.[69] The amount spent touting a firm's CSR achievements is sometimes more than the amount spent on the CSR activity itself.[70] On the other hand, there is the issue of the legitimacy of substantive corporate involvement in social issues – 'Do we want corporations playing God?' This is perhaps today the most potentially valid of Friedman's original criticisms of CSR, though it can be argued that corporate power is increasingly held in check by NGOs, whose legitimacy, in turn, relies on public support.

CSR in the shareholders' interest

Friedman's most powerful argument against CSR was always that it was not in the shareholders' interest and many managers still find this idea appealing. However, the business case for CSR – if supported – makes this argument largely moot. Roger Martin has observed that firms often engage in CSR 'precisely because it enhances shareholder value' and, more specifically, that some CSR activities 'create goodwill among consumers in excess of their price tag.'[71] Margolis and Walsh found that nearly 100 studies have examined the relationship between corporate social performance (CSP) and corporate financial performance (CFP) over the last 30 years.[72] Most studies point to a positive relationship between CSP and CFP. Of the 80 studies that examined whether CSP predicts CFP, 42 found a positive relationship, 19 found no relationship, 15 studies reported mixed results, and only 4 studies found a negative relationship. Not surprisingly, it is generally inferred that CSR does produce financial dividends for firms, but this conclusion needs to be treated with caution because there are major methodological problems associated with such studies.

Formulating a response

How any individual firm formulates a CSR strategy should reflect an understanding of whether (and why) greater attention to CSR is warranted by that particular organization. The WBCSD advises that a 'one-size-fits-all' approach to CSR strategy (e.g., universal codes) may not provide the right answer.[73] Equally, however, the generally asserted reasons for greater attention to CSR also may not have universal application. Consider the following examples:

- Du Pont's leadership in the development of CFC alternatives might not have been enlightened self-interest were it not also the market (and R&D) leader in the category; similarly, GSK's leadership on the access issue might make less (business) sense if it were not also the leading provider of drugs for the treatment of HIV/AIDS, tuberculosis, and malaria (three of the top five killer diseases overall and especially prevalent in LDCs).

- While reputational risk is particularly relevant to global brands in consumer markets, firms with smaller, local brands might be less vulnerable, especially if the corporate name differs from the brand name familiar to consumers; equally, firms in B2B markets far removed from consumers as end users have much less reputational risk, especially if their products are marketed as commodities;

- Employees typically do prefer to work for socially responsible firms, but tobacco companies have been able to attract people by paying more, despite the pariah status of the industry; similarly, many investors stick with tobacco stocks because of their generally high levels of return.

- A mining company has every reason to be concerned about environmental impacts threatening its 'license to operate,' but this is far less of a concern for a financial services company.

The purpose here is not to identify the many criteria by which we might assess a firm's vulnerability to criticism for CSR failings (there are consultancy organizations dedicated to providing this service). However, if a business case is to be advanced for CSR initiatives, the organizational fit with any given rationale requires close scrutiny. This applies equally to elements of a CSR strategy intended to enhance the firm's reputation and exploit an upside potential of CSR.[74] Consider some of the questions that should be asked by a firm planning to develop a more socially responsible version of an existing product:

- How likely is it that these improvements would be in advance of a regulatory requirement to be instituted in this industry? (There might be advantages from developing and launching the product ahead of a change in regulations.)

- How responsive is the firm's customer base to CSR? Research would be required to ascertain whether a more socially responsible version of an existing product would appeal to the intended market segment – there is likely to be considerable variation in the extent to which a firm's served market responds to various possible CSR initiatives (e.g., not tested on animals, more environmentally benign, manufactured with materials from fair trade sources).

- Would customers be willing to pay more for the new product? (Generally, few consumers will pay a premium for CSR.)

■ If the firm's customer base is CSR-responsive, but unwilling to pay more, would the improvement provide a sustainable advantage relative to competitors? Could it be easily copied?

Similar questions would need to be formulated with CSR initiatives intended to satisfy investors, employees, or other stakeholders. The decision on increased attention to CSR is thus likely to be highly idiosyncratic, a function of both the characteristics of the individual firm and its fit with the elements of potential CSR initiatives.

Developing the right CSR strategy

Clearly, a firm's social responsibility strategy, if genuinely and carefully conceived, should be unique, despite the sameness of the growing number of corporate reports on CSR.[75] As well as a fit with industry characteristics, it should reflect the individual company's mission and values – what it stands for – and thus be different from the CSR strategy of even its closest competitors.[76] Many company CSR statements do not seem to be reflective of a deep commitment to CSR or, at least, they suffer from a failure to identify the issues that matter most for measurement, management, and reporting.[77] Phil Watts, Group Managing Director of Royal Dutch/Shell Group, has observed that 'CSR is not a cosmetic; it must be rooted in our values. It must make a difference to the way we do our business.'[78] Shell's CSR report, published annually since 1998, is a good example of a company that provides quantified evidence of its social and environmental performance.[79]

While there is not a generic CSR strategy, there are common elements. There will be substantial overlap among the stakeholders identified by any firm – all will at minimum identify obligations to customers, employees, suppliers, and the community. However, the characteristics of these stakeholders and the form of the obligations of any specific firm to that stakeholder group are likely to vary considerably. For example, at the core of British Telecom's CSR strategy is a belief in a 'better world' where everyone has access to the benefits of information and communications technology (ICT), a belief that is said to shape BT's obligations to its stakeholders. This is reflected not only in a commitment to improved levels of customer satisfaction for all its customers, but also to services for elderly, disabled, and low income customers that increase their access to ICT in excess of regulatory requirements.[80] The first CSR report from Westpac, an Australian bank, also identifies obligations to customers but is markedly different.[81] It includes a newly introduced Personal Customer Charter, with commitments to transparency of fees and services and to privacy. It also reports on the bank's performance in areas such as accessibility and availability of banking services (e.g., banking services in rural areas, new ATM technology for vision impaired consumers), complaint resolution rates, and responsible lending (e.g., data on accounts overdue).

Developing the right CSR strategy requires an understanding of what differentiates an organization – its mission, values, and core business activities. At British Telecom, a 'hot topic' is the digital divide and CSR initiatives address digital inclusion, with attention to capability (people having the skills to use digital technology) as well as connectivity (physical access).[82] Contribution to the community finds a different guise at Starbucks. All proceeds (and a minimum of $75,000) from the Georgetown Starbucks in Washington, D.C., are donated to The Starbucks Memorial Fund. Established following an armed robbery of the store in 1997 that left three employees dead, the Fund contributes to violence prevention and victim assistance programs in the D.C. area. More recently, attention has been focused on coffee sourcing and particularly the plight of poorer small farmers, who are now being supported through a commitment to buying fair trade coffee (one million pounds in 2002–2003).[83] Not surprisingly, the CSR initiatives of Shell and other firms in resource extraction industries (e.g., BP, Rio Tinto) reflect the profound impact these firms can have upon the natural environment coupled with the human rights issues often directly or indirectly associated with their activities.[84]

Stakeholder engagement

In figuring out a CSR strategy, stakeholder engagement must be at the core.[85] As noted earlier, there can be considerable uncertainty about a firm's obligations to its stakeholders. However, if CSR is fundamentally about obligations to stakeholders, their engagement is more likely to lead to informed management thinking and decision making. The form this engagement should take can be subject to much debate. Some might view stakeholders as having a substantial input on decision making, while others see stakeholders as more of an information resource, with it being 'management's job to manage.' Either way, engagement is critical. As WBCSD put it:

> The essence of corporate social responsibility is to recognize the value of external stakeholder dialogue. Because of this, we place stakeholder engagement at the center of CSR activity. CSR means more than promulgating a company's own values and principles. It also depends on understanding the values and principles of those who have a stake in its operations.[86]

However, this assumes a skill set and openness on the part of management that may not exist. The values of NGO members, for example, are often dramatically different from those of corporate executives. Their objectives as well as perspectives on issues are also likely to differ. In many cases, at least with hot issues, management and representatives of stakeholder groups talk past each other. There is also the assumption of a willingness on the part of the stakeholder groups to participate in such a dialogue. It is not unusual for some groups to refuse to engage with management. There is little prospect of many animal rights activists, for example, getting involved with firms they describe as 'evil,' such as drug testing laboratories.

One response to this problem has been for firms to recruit talent from the non-profit sector, though this is still unlikely to work in the case of extreme issues. Shell provides a good example of a firm promoting openness. Shell explains that it is committed to open and transparent debate with its stakeholders. 'Tell Shell' provides a global discussion forum with e-mail postings on topics and issues related to Shell. Postings are both critical and supportive of Shell, with occasional postings by the firm in response or to raise issues.[87]

Given the right people, the firm must still identify which representatives of stakeholder groups it should engage with. Here the problem is, in part, one of the 'squeaky wheel gets the grease.' WBCSD suggests that firms need to consider the legitimacy, the contribution, and influence of the group and the likely outcome, including whether engagement is likely to result in a productive relationship.[88] Appropriate mechanisms for engagement also need to be determined.

Measurement of social performance

Formulating CSR strategy also requires an understanding of the firm's current CSP. This includes developing appropriate metrics for measuring social and environmental performance and goal setting. Shell refers to 'key performance indicators' (KPIs), which are 'benchmarks used to drive improvements whilst independently measuring progress against clearly defined goals.'[89] As well as providing metrics, the use of KPIs gives substance to Shell claims of a commitment to CSR. As these KPIs are often developed in collaboration with stakeholders, such as NGOs, reports of how the firm is delivering on that commitment have credibility. However, there are major challenges to be overcome. Clearly firms can report on readily quantifiable performance measures, such as greenhouse gas emissions or hours worked by employees. It is more difficult to develop KPI's where more qualitative data is all that is available, as, for example, with many aspects of support for human rights or company impacts on other species (e.g., biodiversity, treatment of animals).

Implementation of CSR programs

Having formulated CSR strategy, CSR programs need to be determined. This is where potentially abstract visions of CSR must become concrete. Many challenges are likely in the execution of those programs. To return to the pharmaceutical industry example, after GSK determined that it would do something about access, management had to develop appropriate programs to make medicines available to those without. Yet even with this decision made, its societal obligations were uncertain. Where to begin? Many tricky decisions must be made, for example, with respect to beneficiaries (assessments of needs, treatment/disease categories), scope of the program (where? what scale?), and form of distribution (which channels? free or at cost?).

GSK has made its drugs more widely available in LDCs. However, in the HIV/AIDS category, take-up is pitifully low: only 30,000 of the estimated 28.5 million people with the disease in sub-Saharan Africa receive the anti-retroviral drugs that have made it treatable in developed countries. It is unlikely that take-up would be much higher if they were given away. A far bigger obstacle to access is the limited health care infrastructure in LDCs and, for HIV/AIDS medications, their strict monitoring and compliance regimen.[90] Further, GSK is already facing a problem of parallel imports. Drugs destined for Africa at prices close to marginal cost have been illegally re-exported and resold in the Netherlands and Germany.[91] While there are remedies, such as stricter enforcement of laws on illegal re-importing and dual-branding strategies, this problem represents a substantial challenge to GSK's implementation of a two-tiered pricing structure.

How much is enough?

Consider the example of Nike and its commitment to monitoring workplace conditions of its suppliers. The scale of this monitoring task is huge; Nike has over 800 contract suppliers, employing over 600,000 people in 50 countries. For companies making a substantial commitment to CSR, a key strategic and implementation question is: How much is enough? For Nike, this extends to more specific issues such as: What level of resources should it devote to monitoring? How frequently should sites be audited?

How should it respond to the dilemmas that often arise in this context, such as the use of child labor? If children above a set age are to [be] employed by its suppliers, should it provide funding for their schooling?

Similarly, how far should GSK assist in drug distribution and administration, given infrastructure shortcomings in many LDC markets? Should GSK be involved in healthcare problems that are unrelated to drug therapy, such as the availability of clean water? How much should be invested in R&D to develop medicines for tropical diseases, when only losses are foreseeable for these potential products?

No good deed goes unpunished

Despite careful attention to whether a CSR strategy fits a given organization and situation, it still has the potential to backfire. Sometimes, this can be due to the firm having drawn attention to itself as a result of taking a stand on CSR, such as the recent protests at Starbucks. At other times, it might result from poor implementation. Consider companies that identify an opportunity to contribute to education. On the face of it, this would be a welcome or at least innocuous activity and highly appropriate for some firms in light of their core business activities. Yet CSR initiatives in this area have been viewed as highly controversial. For example, both Coca-Cola and Pepsi bottlers have signed contracts with public school districts in the U.S. that provide millions of dollars of much-needed support for educational purposes in exchange for exclusive distribution rights. Following protests from parents concerned about children's sugar-laden diets and the commercialism of schools, Coca-Cola announced plans to discourage its bottlers from such deals.[92] CSR initiatives can make worthwhile contributions to social problems. However, as this example indicates, and consistent with the concerns expressed by Friedman, the indirect cost of such initiatives may be an imposition of corporate values. Critics of the factory towns of paternalistic capitalism had similar concerns. Failings of the public school system notwithstanding, many might argue that it is the role of government to provide adequate funding for schools and to provide a commercial-free learning environment.

Another example is Microsoft, a company that has various CSR initiatives addressing the 'digital divide.' It has offered to give away its software to schools in developing countries. In South Africa, for example, the offer to give its software to all 32,000 public schools would entail the loss of most of the $2 million of annual revenues from this sector. However, such programs have been criticized as an attempt to foster and retain captive markets for its products.[93] Microsoft's motives have been impugned; as one critic observed: 'Businesses are opportunistic and driven by shareholder interests. … There is a fine line between charity and exploitation.' If this reaction is typical, then there is a problem for advocates of the business case for CSR. If a business case exists for a CSR initiative, then there is always the prospect of it being attacked as cynically self-serving (and, if there is not a business case, shareholders might question why the firm is engaged in it).

Perhaps, in these cases, there are solutions that would permit corporate involvement in funding public schools and to help bridge the digital divide. Greater social acceptance might be forthcoming through more appropriate implementation. For example, one measure proposed by Coca-Cola was to reduce the amount of advertising on vending machines.

Conclusions

Few firms adopt the normative case for CSR and assert a moral basis for obligations beyond those to stockholders, at least without also claiming a business case (those that do are mostly privately held). It has been claimed by U.K. business leaders, for example, that a company should 'balance and trade off the competing claims of customers, suppliers, employees, investors and the communities in which it operates.'[94] The implication of this view of the firm balancing stakeholder interests – a fiduciary duty to shareholders notwithstanding – is that the interests of shareholders might in some instances be considered secondary to those of other claimants, not an argument that sits easily with many managers of public corporations. Nonetheless, some managers might well choose to exercise their discretion consistent with beliefs about management action on social issues.[95] Ultimately, if such action is grounded in an accurate assessment of society's best interests, then the normative case may well also be consistent with the long-term interests of the firm, though there is no guarantee of this.

Many firms have found the business case for greater attention to CSR to be compelling, particularly given reputational risk and other pressures of the contemporary business environment. For some corporations (e.g., in the mining and pharmaceutical industries) CSR may be unavoidable and it appears to have assumed strategic significance. However, it is unclear whether this is peculiar to these industries or an early warning of pressures likely to be faced more broadly. This article has argued that the widely touted *general* rationale for making a more substantial commitment to CSR must be assessed relative to the *specific* vulnerabilities and opportunities of a particular organization. This assessment, in turn, should help clarify societal obligations and thereby (if the business case is persuasive) inform the formulation of a CSR strategy and decisions about specific CSR programs. Nonetheless, there remain major challenges in developing and implementing CSR strategy, especially the measurement of corporate social performance and engaging with stakeholders. There are also possible questions about the legitimacy of CSR initiatives. Concerns might be voiced about the appropriateness of management action on social issues and there may be a backlash against a well-intentioned CSR initiative; concerns that become all the more important if CSR assumes a more central role in corporate strategy. These challenges might well undercut an otherwise convincing business case.

While a business case might be identified for many CSR initiatives, what of those that do not appear to offer any return to shareholders? Martin has proposed that, absent an economic incentive, collective action is required that would involve other firms as well as governments and NGOs.[96] For GSK and the access issue, this suggests a requirement for involvement of other parties because of the limited economic incentives for action by the pharmaceutical industry alone (the problem also demands the collaboration of multiple participants, such as health care organizations and governments, because of the specialized skills or resources they can bring). However, it is unclear as yet whether these other parties will come to the table; the response from governments to requests for contributions to Kofi Annan's global fund is modest, to date.

Notes

[1] Margaret Crawford, *Building the Workingman's Paradise: The Design of American Company Towns* (New York, NY: Verso, 1995); 'The Strange Death of Corporationville,' *The Economist,* December 23, 1995, p. 73.

[2] John Styles, *Titus Salt and Saltaire: Industry and Virtue* (Shipley, England: Salts Estates Ltd., 1994), pp. 12–13.

[3] William C. Frederick, 'From CSR$_1$ to CSR$_2$: The Maturing of Business-and-Society Thought,' *Business and Society*, 33/2 (1994): 151.

[4] Styles, op. cit., p. 38. Crawford [op. cit.] suggests that this motivation was evident in the founding of a number of American company towns.

[5] Styles, op. cit., p. 39.

[6] As Frederick [loc. cit.] writes: 'By the mid-1920s, business representatives and executives were beginning to speak of the need for corporate directors to act as trustees for the interests, not just of stockholders, but other social claimants as well . . . Corporate philanthropy, the history of which stretched back into the 19th century, was accompanied by a growing belief that business and society were linked together in organic, if not yet well understood, ways.'

[7] Since March 2001, thousands of activists are said to have taken part in protests outside Starbucks's cafes in over 300 cities in the U.S., Canada, New Zealand, and England over the poverty of third world coffee farmers and other issues. See, for example, <www.obgo.org/starbucks.htm>.

[8] S. Prakash Sethi, 'Dimensions of Corporate Social Performance: An Analytical Framework,' *California Management Review*, 17/3 (Spring 1975): 58–64. See note 9 on the meaning and terminology of CSR.

[9] World Economic Forum's Global Corporate Citizenship Initiative in partnership with The Prince of Wales International Business Leaders Forum (WEF), 'Responding to the Challenge: Findings of a CEO Survey on Global Corporate Citizenship,' <www.weforum.org/corporatecitizenship>, January 2003, p. 2. Also see 'Global Corporate Citizenship: The Leadership Challenge for CEOs and Boards,' <www.weforum.org/corporatecitizenship>, January 2002. In the latter document, the WEF acknowledges the use of different terminology for what it refers to as 'corporate citizenship,' including 'corporate responsibility,' 'sustainable development,' and the 'triple-bottom-line.' Each can have nuances of meaning (e.g., the term sustainable development often is used to emphasize environmental impacts). In this article, the term corporate social responsibility is used to be consistent with the established academic literature of the field.

[10] WEF (2003), op. cit., p. 2.

[11] WBCSD, 'Corporate Social Responsibility: Meeting Changing Expectations,' report from World Business Council for Sustainable Development, March 1999, <www.wbcsd.ch>, p. 2.

[12] The sheer volume of publications emanating from organizations advocating CSR in itself speaks to the increased prominence of the topic.

[13] UK Government Department of Trade and Industry, 'Business and Society: Corporate Social Responsibility Report 2002,' <www.dti.gov.uk>, p. 4.

[14] Institute for Global Ethics, 'Europe Tackles Corporate Social Responsibility,' <www.globalethics.org/newsline>, July 30, 2002.

[15] See, for example, David Vogel, *Lobbying the Corporation: Citizen Challenges to Business Authority* (New York, NY: Basic Books, 1978); S. Prakash Sethi, *Up Against the Corporate Wall: Modern Corporations and Social Issues of the Seventies* (Englewood Cliffs: Prentice Hall, 1974).

[16] Naomi Klein, *No Logo* (London: Flamingo, 2000); Noreena Hertz, *The Silent Takeover* (London: Random House, 2001).

[17] Roger L. Martin, 'The Virtue Matrix: Calculating the Return on Corporate Responsibility,' *Harvard Business Review*, 80/3 (March 2002): 68–75; Steve Hilton and Giles Gibbons, *Good Business* (New York, NY: Texere, 2002).

[18] Many U.S. and global firms are responding by devoting significant time and resources in support of community involvement projects. See David Hess, Nikolai Rogovsky, and Thomas W. Dunfee, 'The Next Wave of Corporate Community Involvement: Corporate Social Initiatives,' *California Management Review*, 44/2 (Winter 2002): 110–125.

[19] Survey by Jericho Communications in 2002, <www.jerichopr.com/releases/jericho3>.

[20] SustainAbility, *Trust Us: The Global Reporters 2002 Survey of Corporate Sustainability Reporting* (London: SustainAbility and the United Nations Environment Program, 2002); Hess et al., op. cit.

[21] Klein, op. cit., p. 434.

[22] <www.merck.com/about/philanthropy/9.htm>.

[23] Sophia Tickell, 'Why Philanthropy Is Not Enough: Lessons from the Pharmaceutical Industry,' in Roger Cowe, ed., *No Scruples: Managing to be Responsible in a Turbulent World* (London: Spiro Press, 2002).

[24] Much of the following discussion of this example is based on N. Craig Smith and Anne Duncan, 'GlaxoSmithKline and Access to Essential Medicines,' London Business School case study, January 2003.

[25] 'Drug Price Wars: Helping the Poor will Help the Industry,' *The Guardian*, April 18, 2001.

[26] Kurt Shillinger, 'AIDS Drug Victory Sours in South Africa: Government Still Refusing to Supply AZT,' *Boston Globe,* April 23, 2001, p. A8.

[27] Tickell, op. cit., pp. 65–66.

[28] 'Facing the Challenge: Our Contribution to Improving Healthcare in the Developing World,' GlaxoSmithKline, Brentford, United Kingdom, 2001.

[29] CalPERS, America's largest pension fund, has asked GSK to evaluate its 'humanitarian efforts' and report whether it is offering the 'lowest possible prices for its (HIV/AIDS) drugs (in developing countries), including licensing generics, without hurting its long-term business.' See Chris Gaither, 'Investing With an Agenda: CalPERS Social, Corporate Activism Drawing Attention in Bear Market as Some Fear Its Aggressive Tactics May Cost Governments, Firms Money,' *Boston Globe*, April 20, 2003, p. E1.

[30] One noteworthy exception is Lee Raymond, CEO of Exxon, who has taken a markedly different and public position on the environmental impacts of the oil industry than Exxon's 'greener' competitors, Shell and BP. *The Economist* writes: 'Judged by his financial record alone, Mr. Raymond could claim to be the most successful oil boss since Rockefeller of Standard Oil . . . what happens to Mr. Raymond's reputation in the years to come will be a barometer of the relative strengths of red-blooded capitalism and of the kinder, gentler, greener, more socially responsible – and perhaps less profitable – version.' See 'The Unrepentant Oilman,' *The Economist*, March 13, 2003.

[31] Smith and Duncan, op. cit.

[32] Thomas Donaldson, *Corporations and Morality* (Englewood Cliffs, NJ: Prentice Hall, 1982), p. 42.

[33] WEF (2003), op. cit.

[34] For an alternative viewpoint, see Ian Maitland, 'Priceless Goods: How Should Life-Saving Drugs Be Priced?' *Business Ethics Quarterly*, 12 (October 2002): 451–480. Maitland argues against restraints on drug pricing and profits, suggesting it is precisely because life-saving drugs are priceless that firms should be free to charge market prices for them.

[35] See, for example, Robert D. Hay, Edmund R. Gray, and James E. Gates, *Business and Society* (Cincinnati: South-Western Publishing, 1976).

[36] Thomas Hoffman, 'Say Goodbye to Ozone-Wrecking Chemicals,' *Computerworld*, June 5, 1995, p. 105.

[37] John Leming, 'Workers Benefit from Tight Market; Service Industries Offer Employees Health Cover to Lure Them on Board,' *Journal of Commerce*, June 15, 1998, p. 5A; <www.starbucks.com/aboutus/CSR_FY01_AR. pdf>. This is not intended to suggest that caring for employees always pays, there are many examples to the contrary. See Aaron Feuerstein and Malden Mills example in Martin, op. cit.

[38] Pui-Wing Tam, 'Myanmar Human Rights Suit Is Reinstated,' *The Wall Street Journal*, September 19, 2002.

[39] John Elkington, *Cannibals with Forks* (Oxford: Capstone Publishing, 1999). Debora L. Spar and Lane T. La Mure, 'The Power of Activism: Assessing the Impact of NGOs on Global Business,' *California Management Review*, 45/3 (Spring 2003): 78–101.

[40] <www.starbucks.com/aboutus/CSR_FY01_AR.pdf>.

[41] 'Boycotting Corporate America,' *The Economist*, May 26, 1990, p. 69.

[42] Wallace N. Davidson, III, Abuzar El-Jelly, and Dan L. Worrell, 'Influencing Managers to Change Unpopular Corporate Behavior Through Boycotts and Divestitures: A Stock Market Test,' *Business and Society*, 34/2 (1995): 171–196.

[43] Lynn Sharp Paine and Mihnea Moldoveanu, 'Royal Dutch/Shell in Nigeria,' case study 9-399-126, Harvard Business School, Boston, MA, 1999.

[44] Nicholas Schoon, 'Greenpeace's Brent Spar Apology,' *The Independent*, September 6, 1995, p. 3.

[45] Roger Cowe, 'Boardrooms Discover Corporate Ethics,' *Guardian Weekly*, March 28, 1999, p. 27; Shell, *Profits and Principles – Does There Have To Be a Choice?* (London: Shell International, 1998).

[46] Tom McCawley, 'Racing to Improve Its Reputation: Nike Has Fought to Shed Its Image as an Exploiter of Third-World Labor Yet It Is Still a Target of Activists,' *Financial Times,* December 21, 2000, p. 14; Philip Rosenzweig, 'How Should Multinationals Set Global Workplace Standards?' *Financial Times*, March 27, 1998, p. 11 (surveys); <www.nikebiz.com/labor>. See Klein [op. cit.] for a more skeptical view of Nike's response to the sweatshop issue.

[47] N. Craig Smith, *Morality and the Market: Consumer Pressure for Corporate Accountability* (London: Routledge, 1990).

[48] <www.mori.com/polls/1999/millpoll>.

[49] Tom J. Brown and Peter A. Dacin, 'The Company and the Product: Corporate Associations and Consumer Product Responses,' *Journal of Marketing*, 61 (January 1997): 69.

[50] Sankar Sen and C.B. Bhattacharya, 'Does Doing Good Always Lead to Doing Better? Consumer Reactions to Corporate Social Responsibility,' *Journal of Marketing Research*, 38 (May 2001): 225–243.

[51] Michael Skapinker, 'The Problem with Ethical Shoppers,' *Financial Times*, November 30, 2002, p. 10; Simon Caulkin, 'Once a Minority Cause, Fairtrade Is Now Becoming Mainstream,' *The Observer*, February 2, 2003, p. 6.

[52] Ibid.

[53] Quoted in Robert L. Gildea, 'Consumer Survey Confirms Corporate Social Action Affects Buying Decisions,' *Public Relations Quarterly* 39 (Winter 1994–1995): 21.

[54] See <www.homedepot.com> and <www.diy.com/aboutbandq/sustainability/history/Timber>.

[55] Minette E. Drumwright, 'Socially Responsible Organizational Buying: Environmental Concern as a Noneconomic Buying Criterion,' *Journal of Marketing*, 58/3 (July 1994): 1–19.

[56] Sandra A. Waddock, Charles Bodwell, and Samuel B. Graves, 'Responsibility: The New Business Imperative,' *The Academy of Management Executive*, 16/2 (May 2002): 132–148.

[57] WEF (2003), op. cit.

[58] UK DTI, op. cit.

[59] Assets in professionally managed, socially screened investment portfolios rose to $2.01 trillion in 2001, an increase of 35% on 1999. Altogether, over $2.3 trillion was in professionally managed portfolios utilizing one or more of the three dynamic strategies that together define socially responsible investing in the U.S. – screening ($1,421 billion), shareholder advocacy ($305 billion), and/or community investing ($7.6 billion) (a further $592 billion is in both screening and shareholder advocacy). See Social Investment Forum, *2001 Report on Socially Responsible Investing Trends in the United States* (Washington, D.C.: Social Investment Forum, 2001).

[60] Steve Johnson, 'The FTSE4Good Index: 'Lite' Index Is Accused over Quality Standards,' *Financial Times*, May 11, 2002, p. 9 (Money section).

[61] There is some survey evidence to suggest a reduction in expenditure on CSR in 2002 [see Jericho Communications, op. cit.]. John Elkington has also observed some belt-tightening, including closures of CSR departments, but he sees this as a potentially useful removal of 'camouflage' rather than a diminution of substantive CSR activity [source: private communication].

[62] Jean-Pierre Garnier's speech to GSK employees shortly after the merger of Glaxo Wellcome and SmithKline Beecham. Smith and Duncan, op. cit., p. 1.

[63] David Henderson, *Misguided Virtue: False Notions of Corporate Social Responsibility* (Wellington, New Zealand: New Zealand Business Roundtable, 2001); Ethan B. Kapstein, 'The Corporate Ethics Crusade,' *Foreign Affairs*, 80/5 (2001): 105–119.

[64] Kapstein, op. cit.

[65] Milton Friedman, *Capitalism and Freedom* (Chicago, IL: University of Chicago Press, 1962), pp. 60–6

[66] Smith, op. cit., pp. 69–75.

[67] Adam Smith, *The Wealth of Nations* (London: Everyman, 1971 [1776]), Vol. 1, p. 400.

[68] Henry Mintzberg, 'The Case for Corporate Social Responsibility,' *The Journal of Business Strategy*, 4/2 (Fall 1983): 12.

[69] SustainAbility, op. cit.

[70] Philip Morris spent $100 million touting its $75 million in charitable donations in 1999. It spent $250 million in 2000. See Ronald Alsop, 'Perils of Corporate Philanthropy,' *Wall Street Journal*, January 16, 2002, p. B1.

[71] Martin, op. cit., p. 70.

[72] Joshua D. Margolis and James P. Walsh, *People and Profits* (Mahwah, NJ: Lawrence Erlbaum, 2001).

[73] WBCSD, 'Corporate Social Responsibility: Making Good Business Sense,' report from World Business Council for Sustainable Development, January 2000, p. 22, <www.wbcsd.ch>.

[74] See Hess et al. [op. cit.] for some excellent examples of corporate community involvement.

[75] SustainAbility, op. cit.

[76] This is consistent with the approach recommended by Hess et al. [op. cit.] in the more specific case of CSR in the form of 'corporate social initiatives.'

[77] Described as 'materiality' by SustainAbility, op. cit., p. 2.

[78] WBCSD (2000), op. cit., p. 7.

[79] <www.shell.com>. It is one of the 'Magnificent Seven' top reports in 'Trust Us' [Sustain-Ability, op. cit.]. In 2000, for example, Shell reported that 60 people (55 contractors and 5 Shell employees) died in work activity, up from 47 in 1999, and described this as 'unacceptable.' Most of the deaths were in road accidents in developing countries and Shell said it was responding to the problem with road safety awareness and training programs.

[80] <www.btplc.com/Betterworld>. BT is also in SustainAbility's 'Magnificent Seven.'

[81] Westpac, *A Fresh Perspective: Our First Social Impact Report* (Sydney: Westpac Banking Corporation, 2002).

[82] <www.btplc.com/Betterworld>.

[83] <www.starbucks.com/aboutus/CSR_FY01_AR.pdf>.

[84] <www.shell.com>; <www.bp.com>; <www.riotinto.com>.

[85] WEF (2003), op. cit.; WBCSD (2000), op. cit.

[86] WBCSD (2000), op. cit., p. 15.

[87] <www.shell.com>.

[88] WBCSD (2000), op. cit.

[89] <www.shell.com>.

[90] This industry perspective is questioned by WHO and UNAIDS (the Joint United Nations Programme on HIV/AIDS): 'While far greater investments in health and social services infrastructure are needed to expand access to treatment on a massive scale, many countries have underutilized health system capacity that, but for the lack of financing and affordability, could be used to expand treatment today.' See WHO and UNAIDS, 'Accelerating Access Initiative: Widening Access to Care and Support for People Living with HIV/AIDS. Progress Report June 2002,' (Geneva: WHO), p. 2.

[91] Geoff Dyer, 'Netherlands Acts Against Re-Sold AIDS Drugs,' *Financial Times*, October 3, 2002, p. 8.

[92] 'U.S. Schools Reject Coke's Plan to Teach the World,' *Australian Financial Review*, July 6, 2001, p. 27.

[93] Duncan McLeod, 'Suspicion over Microsoft Gift to Poor Schools,' *Financial Times*, October 8, 2002, p. 12.

[94] Royal Society for the Encouragement of Arts, Manufactures and Commerce (RSA), *Tomorrow's Company: The Role of Business in a Changing World* (London: RSA, 1995).

[95] For discussion of the potential role of managers' personal preferences, see Spar and La Mure, op. cit.

[96] Martin, op. cit. He refers to these projects as 'structural CSR' and cites the promulgation of regulations requiring air bags in automobiles as one example.

N. CRAIG SMITH is an Associate Professor of Marketing and Business Ethics at London Business School. <ncsmith@london.edu>

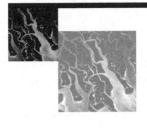

Managing to be ethical: debunking five business ethics myths*

Linda Klebe Treviño and Michael E. Brown

In the aftermath of recent corporate scandals, managers and researchers have turned their attention to questions of ethics management. We identify five common myths about business ethics and provide responses that are grounded in theory, research, and business examples. Although the scientific study of business ethics is relatively new, theory and research exist that can guide executives who are trying to better manage their employees' and their own ethical behavior. We recommend that ethical conduct be managed proactively via explicit ethical leadership and conscious management of the organization's ethical culture.

The twenty-first century has brought corporate ethics scandals that have harmed millions of employees and investors, and sent shock waves throughout the business world. The scandals have produced 'perp walks' and regulatory backlash, and business ethics is once again a hot topic. Academics and managers are asking: What caused the recent rash of corporate wrongdoing, and what can we do, if anything, to prevent similar transgressions in the future? Perhaps because everyone has opinions about ethics and personal reactions to the scandals, a number of pat answers have circulated that perpetuate a mythology of business ethics management. In this article, we identify several of these myths and respond to them based upon knowledge grounded in research and practice.

Myth 1: it's easy to be ethical

A 2002 newspaper article was entitled, 'Corporate ethics is simple: If something stinks, don't do it.' The article went on to suggest 'the smell test' or 'If you don't want to tell your mom what you're really doing ... or read about it in the press, don't do it.'[1] The obvious suggestion is that being ethical in business is easy if one wants to be ethical. A further implication is that if it's easy, it doesn't need to be managed. But that suggestion disregards the complexity surrounding ethical decision-making, especially in the context of business organizations.

Academy of Management Executive, 2004, Vol. 18, No. 2.

Ethical decisions are complex

First, ethical decisions aren't simple. They're complex by definition. As they have for centuries, philosophers argue about the best approaches to making the right ethical decision. Students of business ethics are taught to apply multiple normative frameworks to tough dilemmas where values conflict. These include consequentialist frameworks that consider the benefits and harms to society of a potential decision or action, deontological frameworks that emphasize the application of ethical principles such as justice and rights, and virtue ethics with its emphasis on the integrity of the moral actor, among other approaches.[2] But, in the most challenging ethical dilemma situations, the solutions provided by these approaches conflict with each other, and the decision-maker is left with little clear guidance. For example, multinational businesses with manufacturing facilities in developing countries struggle with employment practice issues. Most Americans believe that it is harmful and contrary to their rights to employ children. But children routinely contribute to family income in many cultures. If corporations simply refuse to hire them or fire those who are working, these children may resort to begging or even more dangerous employment such as prostitution. Or they and their families may risk starvation. What if respecting the rights of children in such situations produces the greater harm? Such business decisions are more complex than most media reports suggest, and deciding on the most ethical action is far from simple.

Moral awareness is required

Second, the notion that 'it's easy to be ethical' assumes that individuals automatically know that they are facing an ethical dilemma and that they should simply choose to do the right thing. But decision makers may not always recognize that they are facing a moral issue. Rarely do decisions come with waving red flags that say, 'Hey, I'm an ethical issue. Think about me in moral terms!'[3] Dennis Gioia was recall coordinator at Ford Motor Company in the early 1970s when the company decided not to recall the Pinto despite dangerous fires that were killing the occupants of vehicles involved in low-impact rear-end collisions. In his information-overloaded recall coordinator role, Gioia saw thousands of accident reports, and he followed a cognitive 'script' that helped him decide which situations represented strong recall candidates and which did not. The incoming information about the Pinto fires did not penetrate a script designed to surface other issues, and it did not initially raise ethical concerns. He and his colleagues in the recall office didn't recognize the recall issue as an ethical issue. In other examples, students who download their favorite music from the Internet may not think about the ethical implications of 'stealing' someone else's copyrighted work. Or, a worker asked to sign a document for her boss may not recognize this as a request to 'forge' legal documents.

Researchers have begun to study this phenomenon, and they refer to it as moral awareness, ethical recognition, or ethical sensitivity. The idea is that moral judgment processes are not initiated unless the decision-maker recognizes the ethical nature of an issue. So, recognition of an issue as an 'ethical' issue triggers the moral judgment process, and understanding this initial step is key to understanding ethical decision-making more generally.

T. M. Jones proposed that the moral intensity of an issue influences moral issue recognition,[4] and this relationship has been supported in research. Two dimensions of moral intensity – magnitude of consequences and social consensus – have been found in multiple studies to influence moral awareness.[5] An individual is more likely to identify an issue as an ethical issue to the extent that a particular decision or action is expected to produce harmful consequences and to the extent that relevant others in the social context view the issue as ethically problematic. Further, the use of moral language has been found to influence moral awareness.[6] For example, in the above cases, if the words 'stealing' music (rather than downloading) or 'forging' documents (rather than signing) were used, the individual would be more likely to think about these issues in ethical terms.

Ethical decision-making is a complex, multi-stage process

Moral awareness represents just the first stage in a complex, multiple-stage decision-making process[7] that moves from moral awareness to moral judgment (deciding that a specific action is morally justifiable), to moral motivation (the commitment or intention to take the moral action), and finally to moral character (persistence or follow-through to take the action despite challenges).

The second stage, moral judgment, has been studied within and outside the management literature.[8] Lawrence Kohlberg's well-known theory of cognitive moral development has guided most of the empirical research in this area for the past thirty years.[9] Kohlberg found that people develop from childhood to adulthood through a sequential and hierarchical series of cognitive stages that characterize the way they think about ethical dilemmas. Moral reasoning processes become more complex and sophisticated with development. Higher stages rely upon cognitive operations that are not available to individuals at lower stages, and higher stages are thought to be 'morally better' because they are consistent with philosophical theories of justice and rights.

At the lowest levels, termed 'preconventional,' individuals decide what is right based upon punishment avoidance (at stage 1) and getting a fair deal for oneself in exchange relationships (at stage 2). Next, the conventional level of cognitive moral development includes stages 3 and 4. At stage 3, the individual is concerned with conforming to the expectations of significant others, and at stage 4 the perspective broadens to include society's rules and laws as a key influence in deciding what's right. Finally, at the highest 'principled' level, stage 5, individuals' ethical decisions are guided by principles of justice and rights.

Perhaps most important for our purposes is the fact that most adults in industrialized societies are at the 'conventional' level of cognitive moral development, and less than twenty per cent of adults ever reach the 'principled' level where thinking is more autonomous and principle-based. In practical terms, this means that most adults are looking outside themselves for guidance in ethical dilemma situations, either to significant others in the relevant environment (e.g., peers, leaders) or to society's rules and laws. It also means that most people need to be led when it comes to ethics.

The organizational context creates additional pressures and complexity

Moral judgment focuses on deciding what's right – not necessarily doing what is right. Even when people make the right decision, they may find it difficult to follow through and do what is right because of pressures from the work environment. Research has found that principled individuals are more likely to behave in a manner consistent with their moral judgments, and they are more likely to resist pressures to behave unethically.[10] However, most people never reach the principled level. So, the notion that being ethical is simple also ignores the pressures of the organizational context that influence the relationship between moral judgment and action.

Consider the following ethical-dilemma situation. You find yourself in the parking lot, having just dented the car next to you. The ethical decision is relatively simple. It's about you and your behavior. No one else is really involved. You have harmed someone else's property, you're responsible, and you or your insurance company should pay for the repairs. It's pretty clear that you should leave a note identifying yourself and your insurance company. Certainly, there may be negative consequences if you leave that note. Your insurance rates may go up. But doing the right thing in this situation is fairly straightforward.

Contrast that to business-context situations. It is much harder to 'just say no' to a boss who demands making the numbers at all costs. Or to go above the boss's head to someone in senior management with suspicions that 'managing earnings' has somehow morphed into 'cooking the books.' Or to walk away from millions of dollars in business because of concerns about crossing an ethical line. Or to tell colleagues that the way they do business seems to have crossed that line. In these situations, the individual is operating within the context of the organization's authority structure and culture – and would likely be concerned about the consequences of disobeying a boss's order, walking away from millions of dollars in business, or blowing the whistle on a peer or superior. What would peers think? How would the leadership react? Would management retaliate? Is one's job at risk?

It may seem curious that people often worry about whether others will think of them as too ethical. But all of us recognize that 'snitches' rarely fit in, on the playground or in life, and whistleblowers are frequently ostracized or worse.[11] The reasons for their ostracism are not fully understood, but they may have to do with humans' social nature and the importance of social group maintenance. Research suggests that people who take principled stands, such as those who are willing to report a peer for unethical behavior, are seen as highly ethical while, at the same time, they are thought to be highly unlikable.[12] Nearly a third of respondents to the 2003 National Business Ethics Survey[13] said 'their coworkers condone questionable ethics practices by showing respect for those who achieve success using them.' Further, about forty per cent of respondents said that they would not report misconduct they observed because of fear of retaliation from management. Almost a third said they would not report misconduct because they feared retaliation from coworkers.

If you think this applies only to the playground or the factory floor, ask yourself why we haven't seen more CEOs proclaiming how appalled they are at the behavior of some of their peers after recent ethics scandals. Yes, we heard from a few retired CEOs. But very few active senior executives have spoken up. Why not? They're probably uncomfortable passing moral judgment on others or holding themselves up as somehow ethically better than their peers. So, social context is important because people, including senior executives, look to others for approval of their thinking and behavior.

In sum, being ethical is not simple. Ethical decisions are ambiguous, and the ethical decision-making process involves multiple stages that are fraught with complications and contextual pressures. Individuals may not have the cognitive sophistication to make the right decision. And most people will be influenced by peers' and leaders' words and actions, and by concerns about the consequences of their behavior in the work environment.

Myth 2: unethical behavior in business is simply the result of 'bad apples'

A recent headline was 'How to Spot Bad Apples in the Corporate Bushel.'[14] The bad-apple theory is pervasive in the media and has been around a long time. In the 1980s, during a segment of the McNeil Lehrer Report on PBS television, the host was interviewing guests about insider trading scandals. The CEO of a major investment firm and a business school dean agreed that the problems with insider trading resulted from bad apples. They said that educational institutions and businesses could do little except to find and discard those bad apples after the fact. So, the first reaction to ethical problems in organizations is generally to look for a culprit who can be punished and removed. The idea is that if we rid the organization of one or more bad apples, all will be well because the organization will have been cleansed of the perpetrator.

Certainly there are bad actors who will hurt others or feather their own nests at others' expense – and they do need to be identified and removed. But, as suggested above, most people are the product of the context they find themselves in. They tend to 'look up and look around,' and they do what others around them do or expect them to do.[15] They look outside themselves for guidance when thinking about what is right. What that means is that most unethical behavior in business is supported by the context in which it occurs – either through direct reinforcement of unethical behavior or through benign neglect.

An example of how much people are influenced by those around them was in the newspaper in November, 2002. Police in New Britain, Connecticut confiscated a 50-ft. long pile of stolen items, the result of a scavenger hunt held by the 'Canettes,' New Britain high school's all-girl drill team. According to the Hartford Courant, police, parents, and school personnel were astonished that 42 normally law-abiding girls could steal so many items in a single evening. But the girls had a hard time believing that they had done anything wrong. One girl said: 'I just thought it was a custom ... kind of like a camaraderie thing, [and] if the seniors said it was OK and they were in charge, then it was OK!' In another incident in May 2003, suburban Chicago high school girls engaged in an aggressive and brutal 'hazing ritual' that landed five girls in the hospital.[16] We might say that these are teenagers, and that adults are different. But many of these teenagers are about to start jobs, and there are only a few years between these high school students and young people graduating from college. Most adults are more like these teens than most of us think or would prefer. The influence of peers is powerful in both cases.

When asked why they engaged in unethical conduct, employees will often say, 'I had no choice,' or 'My boss told me to do it.' Stanley Milgram's obedience-to-authority experiments, probably the most famous social psychology experiments ever conducted, support the notion that people obey authority figures even if that means harming another person.[17] Milgram, a Yale psychologist, conducted his obedience-to-authority experiments in the Hartford community on normal adults. These experiments demonstrated that nearly two-thirds of normal adults will harm another human being (give them alleged electric shocks of increasing intensity) if asked to do so by an authority figure as part of what was billed as a learning experiment. Were these people bad apples? We don't think so. Most of them were not at all comfortable doing what they were being asked to do, and they expressed sincere concern for the victim's fate. But in the end most of them continued to harm the learner because the authority figure in a lab coat told them to do so.

How does this apply to work settings? Consider the junior member of an audit team who discovers something problematic when sampling a firm's financials and asks the senior person on the audit team for advice. When the leader suggests putting the problematic example back and picking another one, the young auditor is likely to do just that. The leader may add words such as the following: 'You don't understand the big picture' or 'Don't worry, this is my responsibility.' In this auditing example, the harm being done is much less obvious than in the learning experiment and the junior auditor's responsibility even less clear, so the unethical conduct is probably easier to carry out and more likely to occur.

The bottom line here is that most people, including most adults, are followers when it comes to ethics. When asked or told to do something unethical, most will do so. This means that they must be led toward ethical behavior or be left to flounder. Bad behavior doesn't always result from flawed individuals. Instead, it may result from a system that encourages or supports flawed behavior.

A corollary of the bad-apples argument is that ethics can't be taught or even influenced in adults because adults are autonomous moral agents whose ethics are fully formed by the time they join work organizations, and they can't be changed. This is simply not true. We know from many empirical studies[18] that the large majority of adults are *not* fully formed when it comes to ethics, and they are *not* autonomous moral agents. They look outside themselves for guidance in ethical dilemma situations, and they behave based to a large extent upon what those around them – leaders and peers – expect of them. So, we have to look at the very powerful signals that are being sent about what is expected. We also know that the development of moral reasoning continues into adulthood. Those who are challenged to wrestle with ethical dilemmas in their work will develop more sophisticated ways of thinking about such issues, and their behavior will change as a result.

Myth 3: ethics can be managed through formal ethics codes and programs

If people in organizations need ethical guidance and structural support, how can organizations best provide it? Most large organizations now have formal ethics or legal compliance programs. In 1991 the U.S. Sentencing Commission created sentencing guidelines for organizations convicted of federal crimes (see *www.ussc.gov* for information). The guidelines removed judicial discretion and required convicted organizations to pay restitution and substantial fines depending upon whether the organization turns itself in, cooperates with authorities, and whether it has established a legal compliance program that meets seven requirements for due diligence and effectiveness. These formal programs generally include the following key elements: written standards of conduct that are communicated and disseminated to all employees, ethics training, ethics advice lines and offices, and systems for anonymous reporting of misconduct. The Sarbanes-Oxley law, passed during the summer of 2002, requires corporations to set up an anonymous system for employees to report fraud and other unethical activities. Therefore, companies that did not previously have such reporting systems are busy establishing them.

Research suggests that formal ethics and legal compliance programs can have a positive impact. For example, the Ethics Resource Center's National Business Ethics Survey[19] revealed that in organizations with all four program elements (standards, training, advice lines, and reporting systems) there was a greater likelihood (78 per cent) that employees would report observed misconduct to management. The likelihood of reporting declined with fewer program elements. Only half as many people in organizations with no formal program said that they would report misconduct to management.

Yet, creating a formal program, by itself, does not guarantee effective ethics management. Recall that Enron had an ethics code, and the board voted to bypass its conflict-of-interest policy.[20] Not surprisingly, research suggests that actions speak louder than words. Employees must perceive that formal policies go beyond mere window dressing to represent the real ethical culture of the organization. For example, the National Business Ethics Survey reports that when executives and supervisors emphasize ethics, keep promises, and model ethical conduct, misconduct is much lower than when employees perceive that the 'ethics walk' is not consistent with the 'ethics talk.'[21] In another study[22] formal program characteristics were found to be relatively unimportant compared with more informal cultural characteristics such as messages from leadership at both the executive and supervisory levels. In addition, perceived ethics program follow-through was found to be essential. Organizations demonstrate follow-through by working hard to detect rule violators, by following up on ethical concerns raised by employees, and by demonstrating consistency between ethics and compliance policies and actual organizational practices. Further, the perception that ethics is actually talked about in day-to-day organizational activities and incorporated into decision-making was found to be important.

So, for formal systems to influence behavior, they must be part of a larger, coordinated cultural system that supports ethical conduct every day. Ethical culture provides informal systems, along with formal systems, to support ethical conduct.[23] For example, the research cited above found that ethics-related outcomes (e.g., employee awareness of ethical issues, amount of observed misconduct, willingness to report misconduct) were much more positive to the extent that employees perceived that ethical conduct was rewarded and unethical conduct was punished in the organization. Further, a culture that demands unquestioning obedience to authority was found to be particularly harmful while a culture in which employees feel fairly treated was especially helpful.

The fall of Arthur Andersen

Barbara Toffler's book *Final Accounting: Ambition, Greed, and the Fall of Arthur Andersen* (2003)[24] can help us understand this notion of ethical (or unethical) organizational culture. Andersen transformed over a number of years from having a solid ethical culture to having a strong unethical culture. The company's complete demise is a rather dramatic example of the potential results of such a transformation.

In the mid-1990s, Arthur Andersen did not have a formal ethics office, but it did have formal ethical standards and ethics training. Ironically, it also established a consulting group whose practice was aimed at helping other businesses manage their ethics. Barbara Toffler was hired to run that practice in 1995 after spending time on the Harvard Business School faculty and in her own ethics consulting business. After joining Andersen, Toffler learned quickly that the firm's own ethical culture was slipping badly, and she chronicles that slippage in her book.

The book opens with the following statement 'The day Arthur Andersen loses the public's trust is the day we are out of business.' Steve Samek, country managing partner, made that statement on a CD-ROM concerning the firm's Independence and Ethical Standards in 1999. It was reminiscent of the old Arthur Andersen. Andersen's traditional management approach had been a top-down, 'one firm' concept. Arthur Andersen had built a strong ethical culture over the years where all of the pieces fit together into a seamless whole that supported ethical conduct. No matter where they were in the world, if customers were dealing with Andersen employees, they knew that they could count on the same high-quality work and the same integrity. Employees were trained in the 'Andersen Way,' and that way included strong ethics. Training at their St. Charles, Illinois training facility was sacred. It created a cadre of professionals who spoke the same language and shared the same 'Android' values.

Founders create culture and Arthur Andersen was no exception. Toffler says that in the firm's early days, the messages from the top about ethical conduct were strong and clear. Andersen himself said, 'My own mother told me, "Think straight – talk straight." ... This challenge will never fail anyone in a time of trial and temptation.' 'Think straight, talk straight' became a mantra for decades at Arthur Andersen. Partners said with pride that integrity mattered more than fees. And stories about the founder's ethics became part of the firm's lore. At the young age of 28, Andersen faced down a railway executive who demanded that his books be approved – or else. Andersen said, 'There's not enough money in the city of Chicago to induce me to change that report.' Andersen lost the business, but later the railway company filed for bankruptcy, and Arthur Andersen became known as a firm one could trust. In the 1930s Andersen talked about the special responsibility of accountants to the public and the importance of their independence of judgment and action. Arthur Andersen died in 1947 but was followed by leaders with similar convictions who ran the firm in the 1950s and 1960s, and the ethical culture continued for many years. Pretty much through the 1980s, Andersen was considered a stable and prestigious place to work. People didn't expect to get rich – rather they wanted 'a good career at a firm with a good reputation.'

But, the ethical culture eventually began to unravel, and Toffler attributes much of this to the fact that the firm's profits increasingly came from management consulting rather than auditing. The leadership's earlier commitment to ethics came to be drowned out by the firm's increasing laser-like focus on revenues. Auditing and consulting are very different, and the cultural standards that worked so well in auditing didn't fit the needs of the consulting side of the business. But this mismatch was never addressed, and the resulting mixed signals helped precipitate a downward spiral into unethical practices. Serving the client began to be defined as keeping the client happy and getting return business. And tradition became translated into unquestioning obedience to the partner, no matter what one was asked to do. For example, managers and partners were expected to pad their prices. Reasonable estimates for consulting work were simply doubled or more as consultants were told to back into the numbers.

The training also began falling apart when it came to hiring experienced people from outside the firm – something that happened more and more as consulting took over. New employees had always been required to attend a three-day session designed to indoctrinate them into the culture of the firm, but new consultants were told not to forego lucrative client work to attend. So, Toffler never made it to the training, and many other consultants didn't either.

By the time Toffler arrived at Andersen, the firm still had a huge maroon ethics binder, but no one bothered to refer to it. Ethics was never talked about. And, she says, 'when I brought up the subject of internal ethics, I was looked at as if I had teleported in from another world.' The assumption, left over from the old days in auditing, was that 'we're ethical people; we recruit people who are screened for good judgment and values. We don't need to worry about this stuff.' But, as we all learned, their failure to worry about ethics led to the demise of the firm.

Could a formal ethics office have helped Arthur Andersen? Probably not, unless that office addressed the shift toward consulting, identified the unique ethical issues faced in the consulting side of the business, developed ethical guidelines for consulting, and so on. It is easy for formal ethics offices and their programs to be marginalized if they don't have the complete support of the organization's leadership and if they are inconsistent with the broader culture. In fact, Andersen still had ethics policies and they still talked about ethics in formal documents. But the business had changed along with the culture that guided employee actions every day, while the approach to ethics management had not kept pace.

Myth 4: ethical leadership is mostly about leader integrity

In our discussion of Arthur Andersen, we suggested the importance of leadership. But what is executive ethical leadership? The mythology of ethical leadership focuses attention narrowly on individual character and qualities such as integrity, honesty, and fairness. The *Wall Street Journal* recently ran a story on its website entitled 'Plain Talk: CEOs Need to Restore Character in Companies.' It said, 'The chief problem affecting corporate American right now is not the regulatory environment or snoozing board directors. It's character.'[25] But as Arthur Andersen demonstrated, leaders must be more than individuals of high character. They must 'lead' others to behave ethically.

Recent research has found that certain individual characteristics are necessary but not sufficient for effective ethical leadership. Such leadership at the executive level is a reputational phenomenon. In most large organizations, employees have few face-to-face interactions with senior executives. So, most of what they know about a leader is gleaned from afar. In order to develop a reputation for ethical leadership, an executive must be perceived as both a 'moral person' and a 'moral manager.'[26]

Being perceived as a 'moral person' is related to good character. It depends upon employee perceptions of the leader's traits, behaviors, and decision-making processes. Ethical leaders are thought to be honest and trustworthy. They show concern for people and are open to employee input. Ethical leaders build relationships that are characterized by trust, respect and support for their employees. In terms of decision-making, ethical leaders are seen as fair. They take into account the ethical impact of their decisions, both short term and long term, on multiple stakeholders. They also make decisions based upon ethical values and decision rules, such as the golden rule.

But being perceived as a 'moral person' is not enough. Being a 'moral person' tells followers what the leader will do. It doesn't tell them what the leader expects *them* to do. Therefore, a reputation for ethical leadership also depends upon being perceived as a 'moral manager,' one who leads others on the ethical dimension, lets them know what is expected, and holds them accountable. Moral managers set ethical standards, communicate ethics messages, role model ethical conduct, and use rewards and punishments to guide ethical behavior in the organization.

Combining the 'moral person' and 'moral manager' dimensions creates a two-by-two matrix (see Figure 1). A leader who is strong on both dimensions is perceived to be an *ethical leader*. We can point to Arthur Andersen as an exemplar of ethical leadership. He was known as a strong ethical person who also clearly led his organization on ethics and values. People knew what they could expect of him, and they knew what he expected of them from an ethics perspective. Another example of ethical leadership is James Burke, CEO of Johnson & Johnson during the early 1980s Tylenol crisis (when Tylenol was laced with cyanide in the Chicago area). Burke handled that crisis masterfully, recalling all Tylenol at a huge financial cost to the firm. But his ethical leadership had begun much earlier when he first took the CEO helm. He focused the organization's attention on the company's longstanding credo and its values. He demanded that senior executives either subscribe to the credo or remove it from the wall. He didn't want to run a hypocritical organization. He also launched the credo survey, an annual survey that asks employees how the company is doing relative to each of the credo values. Bill George, recently retired CEO of Medtronic, is a more current example of an ethical leader. In his book *Authentic Leadership*, George calls for responsible ethical leadership in corporate America while recounting his own struggles to stay true to the company's mission and to himself.[27]

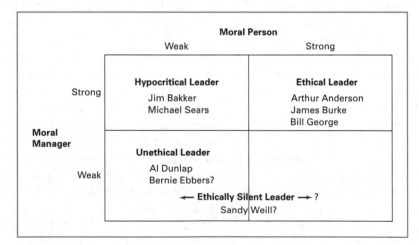

Figure 1 Executive ethical leadership reputation matrix
Figure adapted with permission from Treviño, L. K., Hartman, L. P., Brown, M. 2000. Moral person and moral manager: How executives develop a reputation for ethical leadership. *California Management Review*, 42(4): 128–142.

A leader who is neither a moral person nor a moral manager is an *unethical leader*. In our research, Al Dunlap was frequently identified as an unethical leader. Subject of a book entitled *Chainsaw*,[28] Dunlap was known as an expert turnaround manager. But while at Sunbeam, he also became known for 'emotional abuse' of employees. As a result of his demands to make the numbers at all costs, employees felt pressure to use questionable accounting and sales techniques, and they did. Dunlap also lied to Wall Street, assuring them that the firm would reach its financial projections. In the end, Dunlap could no longer cover up the sorry state of affairs, and he left a crippled company when the board fired him in 1998. In 2002, he paid a $500,000 fine for financial fraud and agreed never to serve as an officer or director of a public corporation. Unfortunately, there are many candidates for a more current example of unethical leadership: Dennis Kozlowski from Tyco, Bernie Ebbers from WorldCom, and Richard Scrushy from Health-South are just a few executive names attached to recent business scandals.

Leaders who communicate a strong ethics/values message (who are moral managers), but who are not perceived to be ethical themselves (they are not moral persons) can be thought of as *hypocritical leaders*. Nothing makes people more cynical than a leader who talks incessantly about integrity, but then engages in unethical conduct himself and encourages others to do so, either explicitly or implicitly. Hypocritical leadership is all about ethical pretense. The problem is that by spotlighting integrity, the leader raises expectations and awareness of ethical issues. At the same time, employees realize that they can't trust the leader.

Jim Bakker, the founder of PTL Ministries, is our favorite example of a hypocritical leader. At its peak, his television ministry had 2000 employees and reached more than ten million homes. Bakker preached about doing the Lord's work while raising funds for his Heritage USA Christian theme park. The problem was that he sold more memberships than could ever be honored. He tapped millions of dollars donated by his followers to support PTL operating expenses including huge salaries and bonuses for his family and high ranking PTL officials. PTL filed for bankruptcy in 1987, and Bakker spent eight years in prison.[29]

Michael Sears, recently fired from Boeing for offering a job to an Air Force procurement specialist while she was overseeing negotiations with Boeing, represents a more recent example of a hypocritical leader. Sears had played a significant role at the Boeing Leadership Center which is known for its programs related to ethics. Also, shortly before his firing. Sears released advance copies of his book *Soaring Through Turbulence* which included a section on maintaining high ethical standards.[30]

We call the final combination *ethically silent leadership*. It applies to executives who are neither strong ethical nor strong unethical leaders. They fall into what employees perceive to be an ethically neutral leadership zone. They may be ethical persons, but they don't provide leadership in the crucial area of ethics, and employees aren't sure where the leaders stand on ethics or if they care. The ethically silent leader is not perceived to be unethical but is seen as focusing intently on the bottom line without setting complementary ethical goals. There is little or no ethics message coming from the top. But silence represents an important message. In the context of all the other messages being sent in a highly competitive business environment, employees are likely to interpret silence to mean that the top executive really doesn't care how business goals are met, only that they are met, so employees act on that message. Business leaders don't like to think that their employees perceive them as ethically silent. But given the current climate of cynicism, unless leaders make an effort to stand out and lead on ethics, they are likely to be viewed that way.

Sandy Weill, CEO of Citigroup, may fit the ethically silent leader category. The company has been playing defense with the media, responding to ugly headlines about ethics scandals, especially at its Smith Barney unit where stock analysts were accused of essentially 'selling' their stock recommendations for banking business. Weill's management style is to hire competent people to run Citigroup's units and to let them do their jobs. That may work well for other aspects of the business, but ethics must be managed from the top and center of the organization. According to *Fortune* magazine, Weill has now 'gotten religion,' if a bit late. Weill has 'told his board that he feels his most important job from now on is to be sure that Citigroup operates at the highest level of ethics and with the utmost integrity.' New procedures and business standards are being developed at corporate headquarters, and a new CEO was appointed at Smith Barney. However, *Fortune* also cites cynicism about this recent turnabout, noting that Weill is often 'tone deaf' on ethical issues.[31]

So, developing a reputation for ethical leadership requires more than strong personal character. Employees must be 'led' from the top on ethics just as they must be led on quality, competitiveness, and a host of other expected behaviors. In order to be effective ethical leaders, executives must demonstrate that they are ethical themselves, they must make their expectations of others' ethical conduct explicit, and they must hold all of their followers accountable for ethical conduct every day.

Myth 5: people are less ethical than they used to be

In the opening to this article, we said that business ethics has once again become a hot topic. The media have bombarded us with information about ethics scandals, feeding the perception that morals are declining in business and in society more generally.

According to a poll released by the PR Newswire in summer 2002, sixty-eight per cent of those surveyed believe that senior corporate executives are less honest and trustworthy today than they were a decade ago.[32] But unethical conduct has been with us as long as human beings have been on the earth, and business ethics scandals are as old as business itself. The Talmud, a 1500-year-old text, includes about 2 million words and 613 direct commandments designed to guide Jewish conduct and culture. More than one hundred of these concern business and economics. Why? Because 'transacting business, more than any other human activity, tests our moral mettle and reveals our character' and because 'working, money, and commerce offer … the best opportunities to do good deeds such as … providing employment and building prosperity for our communities and the world.'[33]

So, unethical behavior is nothing new. It's difficult to find solid empirical evidence of changes over time. But studies of student cheating have found that the percentage of college students who admit to cheating has not changed much during the last thirty years.[34] Some types of cheating have increased (e.g., test cheating, collaboration on individual assignments). Other types of cheating have declined (e.g., plagiarism, turning in another student's work). Certainly, given new technologies and learning approaches, students have discovered some clever new ways to cheat, and professors have their work cut out for them keeping up with the new methods. But the amount of overall cheating hasn't increased that much. Further, when employees were asked about their own work organizations, the 2003 National Business Ethics Survey found that employee perceptions of ethics are generally quite positive. Interestingly, key indicators have actually improved since the last survey conducted in 2000.[35]

Alan Greenspan said it well on July 16, 2002: 'It is not that humans have become any more greedy than in generations past. It is that the avenues to express greed [have] grown so enormously.' So, unethical behavior is nothing new, and people are probably not less ethical than they used to be. But the environment has become quite complex and is rapidly changing, providing all sorts of ethical challenges and opportunities to express greed.

If ethical misconduct is an ongoing concern, then organizations must respond with lasting solutions that embed support for ethics into their cultures rather than short-term solutions that can easily be undone or dismissed as fads. The risk is that the current media focus on unethical conduct will result in 'faddish' responses that offer overly simplistic solutions and that result inevitably in disillusionment and abandonment. Faddish solutions often result from external pressures to 'do something' or at least look like you're doing something. The current focus on scandal certainly includes such pressures.[36] But the recognition that unethical conduct is a continuing organizational problem may help to convince managers that solutions should be designed that will outlast the current intense media focus.

What executives can do: guidelines for effective ethics management

Building upon what we have learned, we offer guidelines for effective ethics management. The overarching goal should be to create a strong ethical culture supported by strong ethical leadership. Why culture? Because we've seen that being ethical is not simple, and that people in organizations need ethical guidance and support for doing the right thing. Executive leaders must provide that structure and ethical guidance, and they can do that best by harnessing multiple formal and informal cultural systems.[37] People should respond positively to the kind of structure that aims to help them do the right thing. If management says, 'We want you to do the right thing, the ethical thing, and we're going to try to create a culture that helps you to do that,' employee response should be quite positive so long as employees believe that management is sincere and they observe consistency between words and actions.

First: understand the existing ethical culture

Leaders are responsible for transmitting culture in their organizations, and the ethical dimension of organizational culture is no exception. According to Schein, the most powerful mechanisms for embedding and reinforcing culture are: (1) what leaders pay attention to, measure, and control; (2) leader reactions to critical incidents and organizational crises; deliberate role modeling, teaching, and coaching by leaders; (3) criteria for allocation of rewards and status; and (4) criteria for recruitment, selection, promotion, retirement, and excommunication.[38]

If leaders wish to create a strong ethical culture, the first step is to understand the current state: What are the key cultural messages being sent about ethics? It's a rare executive who really understands the ethical culture in an organization. And the higher you go in the organization, the rosier the perception of the ethical culture is likely to be.[39] Why? Because information often gets stuck at lower organizational levels, and executives are often insulated from 'bad news,' especially if employees perceive that the organization 'shoots the messenger.' Executives need anonymous surveys, focus groups, and reporting lines, and people need to believe that the senior leaders really want to know, if they are to report honestly on the current state of the ethical culture.

In surveys, ask for employee perceptions of supervisory and executive leadership and the messages they send by their communications and behavior. And listen to what employees say. Ask employees whether they perceive that they are treated fairly, and whether the company acts as if it cares about them, its customers, and other stakeholders. Find out what messages the reward system is sending. Do employees believe that ethical 'good guys' are rewarded and unethical 'bad guys' are punished in the organization? What do employees think is required in order to succeed or to be fired? Follow the kinds of calls coming in to ethics telephone lines. Learn whether employees are asking questions and reporting problems. Use this information to identify needs for training and other interventions. In focus groups, find out who the organizational heroes are (is it the sales representative who steps on peers in order to get ahead or a manager who is known for the highest integrity?). Ask what stories veterans would tell a new hire about ethics in your organization.

Second: communicate the importance of ethical standards

Employees need clear and consistent messages that ethics is essential to the business model, not just a poster or a website. Most businesses send countless messages about competition and financial performance, and these easily drown out other messages. In order to compete with this constant drumbeat about the short-term bottom line, the messages about ethical conduct must be just as strong or stronger and as frequent. Simply telling people to do the right thing, is not enough. They must be prepared for the types of issues that arise in their particular business and position, and they must know what to do when ethics and the bottom line appear to be in conflict. Executives should tie ethics to the long-term success of the business by providing examples from their own experience or the experiences of other successful employees.

Make sure that messages coming from executive and supervisory leaders are clear and consistent. Train employees to recognize the kinds of ethical issues that are likely to arise in their work. Demand discussion of ethics and values as part of routine business decision-making. When making important decisions, ask, 'Are we doing the "right" (i.e., ethical) thing? Who could be hurt by this decision? How could this affect our relationships with stakeholders and our long-term reputation?' Share those deliberations with employees. Finally, be sure to let employees know about exemplary ethical conduct. For example, the famous story about Arthur Andersen losing the railway business because he refused to alter the books was recounted over and over again in the firm and made it absolutely clear that 'think straight, talk straight' actually meant something in the firm.

Third: focus on the reward system

The reward system may be the single most important way to deliver a message about what behaviors are expected. B.F. Skinner knew what he was talking about. People do what's rewarded, and they avoid doing what's punished.[40] Let's look at the positive side first – can we really reward ethical behavior? In the short term, we probably cannot. For the most part, ethical behavior is simply expected, and people don't expect or want to be rewarded for doing their jobs the right way.[41] But in the longer term, ethical behavior can be rewarded by promoting and compensating people who are not only good at what they do, but who have also developed a reputation with customers, peers, subordinates, and managers as being of the highest integrity. The best way to hold employees accountable for ethical conduct is to incorporate evaluation of it into 360 degree performance management systems and to make this evaluation an explicit part of compensation and promotion decisions. The idea is that the bottom line and ethical performance both count; unless individuals have both, they should not advance in the organization.

Also, exemplary behavior can be rewarded. At Lockheed Martin, at the annual Chairman's meeting, a 'Chairman's Award' goes to an employee who exhibited exemplary ethical conduct in the previous year. All senior corporate leaders are expected to expend effort each year to find examples of exemplary ethical conduct in their own business units and make nominations. The award ceremony, attended by all 250 senior executives, is exactly the kind of 'ritual' that helps to create an ethical culture. Stories are shared, they become part of the organization's lore, the potential impact growing as the stories accumulate over time.[42]

Perhaps even more important than rewarding ethical conduct is taking care not to reward unethical conduct. That's what began to happen at Arthur Andersen as generating revenue became the only rewarded behavior, and it didn't matter how you did it. For example, consultants were rewarded for making a project last by finding reasons (legitimate or not) to stay on. Toffler says, 'Like the famous Roach Motel, consultants were taught to check in, but never check out.'[43] So, clients were overcharged, consulting jobs were dragged out, and colleagues were 'screwed' along the way because the rewards supported such unethical conduct.

And what about discipline? Unethical conduct should be disciplined swiftly and fairly when it occurs at any level in the organization. The higher the level of the person disciplined, the stronger the message that management takes ethics seriously. That's what is behind the 'perp walks' we have observed in the media. The public wants to see that fraudulent conduct among America's executives will not be tolerated. Similarly, inside organizations, employees want to see misconduct disciplined, and disciplined harshly.[44] Overall, employees must perceive that good guys get ahead and bad guys don't – they get punished. But, remember, it's often not enough to punish or remove a bad guy or a bad apple. The system should be checked to see if the existing reward system or other messages contributed to the bad behavior.

Fourth: promote ethical leadership throughout the firm

Recall that being a 'moral person' who is characterized by integrity and fairness, treats people well, and makes ethical decisions is important. But those elements deal only with the 'ethical' part of ethical leadership. To be ethical leaders, executives have to think about the 'leadership' part of the term. Providing ethical 'leadership' means making ethical values visible – communicating about not just the bottom-line goals (the ends) but also the acceptable and unacceptable means of getting there (the means). Being an ethical leader also means asking very publicly how important decisions will affect multiple stakeholders – shareholders, employees, customers, society – and making transparent the struggles about how to balance competing interests. It means using the reward system to clearly communicate what is expected and what is accepted. That means rewarding ethical conduct and disciplining unethical conduct, even if the rule violator is a senior person or a top producer. Find a way to let employees know that the unethical conduct was taken seriously and the employee disciplined.

Ethical cultures and ethical leaders go hand in hand. Building an ethical culture can't be delegated. The CEO must be the Chief Ethics Officer of his or her organization.[45] Many CEOs may feel that they would rather pass on this challenge – that they don't really know how to do it – or they may prefer to believe that everyone in their organization is already ethical. But ethics is being 'managed' in their organizations with or without their attention to it. Benign neglect of the ethical culture simply leads to employees reaching the conclusion, rightly or wrongly, that leaders don't care as much about ethics as they do about other things. Leaders develop a reputation in this arena. Chances are that if the leader hasn't thought much about this reputation or hasn't been very proactive about it, people in the organization will likely label him or her as an ethically neutral leader. That doesn't mean that the leader is ethically neutral or doesn't take ethics into account in decision-making. It does mean that people aren't sure where the leader stands on the frequent conflicts between ethics and the bottom line. Without explicit guidance, they assume that the bottom-line messages are the most important.

As we've said, senior executives are extremely important. They set the tone at the top and oversee the ethical culture. But from an everyday implementation perspective, front-line supervisors are equally important because of their daily interactions with their direct reports. An ethical culture ultimately depends upon how supervisors treat employees, customers, and other stakeholders, and how they make decisions. Do they treat everyone honestly, fairly and with care? Do supervisors point out when their group is facing a decision with ethical overtones? Do they consider multiple stakeholder interests and the long-term reputation of the organization in decision-making? Do they hold themselves and their people accountable for ethical conduct? Or, do they focus only on short-term bottom-line results?

Ethics isn't easy

Unethical conduct in business has been with us as long as business transactions have occurred. People are not necessarily more unethical today, but gray areas abound along with many opportunities to cross into unethical territory. Much unethical conduct is the result not just of bad apples but of neglectful leadership and organizational cultures that send mixed messages about what is important and what is expected. It isn't easy to be ethical. Employees must recognize ethical issues in their work, develop the cognitive tools to make the right choices, and then be supported in those choices by the organizational environment. Executives must manage the ethical conduct of their employees as proactively as they manage any important behavior. And the complexity of the management system should match the complexity of the behavior being managed.

The best way to manage ethical conduct is by aligning the multiple formal and informal cultural systems in support of doing the right thing. Cultural messages about the importance of trust and long-term relationships with multiple stakeholders must get at least as much attention as messages about the short-term bottom line, and employees must be held accountable for ethical conduct through performance management and reward systems.

Notes

[1] St. Anthony, N. Corporate ethics is simple: If something stinks, don't do it. *Star Tribune (Minneapolis-Saint Paul) Newspaper of the Twin Cities.* 28 June 2002.

[2] For a simple overview of these theories, see Treviño, L. K., & Nelson, K. 2003. *Managing business ethics; Straight talk about how to do it right.* 3d ed. New York: Wiley.

[3] Gioia, D. 1992. Pinto fires and personal ethics: A script analysis of missed opportunities. *Journal of Business Ethics,* 11(5,6): 379–389; Gioia, D. A. 2003. Personal reflections on the Pinto Fires case. In Treviño & Nelson.

[4] Jones, T. M. 1991. Ethical decision making by individuals in organizations: An issue-contingent model. *Academy of Management Review,* 16: 366–395.

[5] May, D. R., & Pauli, K. P. 2000. The role of moral intensity in ethical decision making: A review and investigation of moral recognition, evaluation, and intention. Manuscript presented at the meeting of the National Academy of Management, Toronto, August, 2000.

[6] Butterfield, K., Treviño, L. K., & Weaver, G. 2000. Moral awareness in business organizations: Influences of issue related and social context factors. *Human Relations,* 53(7): 981–1018.

[7] Rest, M. 1986. *Moral development: Advances in research and theory.* New Jersey: Praeger.

[8] Weber, J. 1990. Managers' moral reasoning: Assessing their responses to three moral dilemmas. *Human Relations,* 43: 687–702; Weber, J., & Wasieleski, 2001. Investigating influences on managers' moral reasoning: The impact of context, personal, and organizational factors. *Business and Society,* 40(1): 79–111; Treviño, L. K. 1986. Ethical decision making in organizations: A person-situation interactionist model. *Academy of Management Review,* 11(3): 601–617; Treviño, L. K. 1992. Moral reasoning and business ethics. *Journal of Business Ethics,* 11: 445–459.

[9] Kohlberg, L. 1969. Stage and sequence: The cognitive developmental approach to socialization. In *Handbook of socialization theory and research.* D. A. Goslin, ed. Rand McNally, 347–380.

[10] Thoma, S. J. 1994. Moral judgment and moral action. In J. Rest & D. Narvaez (ed.). *Moral development in the professions: Psychology and applied ethics.* Hillsdale, NJ: Eribaum: 199–211.

[11] Miceli, M., & Near, J. 1992. *Blowing the whistle.* New York: Lexington Books.

[12] Treviño, L. K., & Victor, B. 2004. Peer reporting of unethical behavior: A social context perspective. *Academy of Management Journal,* 353: 38–64.

[13] Ethics Resource Center. 2003. *National Business Ethics Survey; How employees view ethics in their organizations.* Washington, DC.

[14] PR Newswire. How to spot bad apples in the corporate bushel. 13 January 2003. Ithaca, NY.

[15] Treviño & Nelson; Jackall, R. 1988. *Moral mazes: The world of corporate managers.* New York: Oxford University Press.

[16] Drill team benched after scavenger incident, Sleepover busted. *Hartford Couranf,* 15 November 2002; Paulson, A. Hazing case highlights girl violence. *Christian Science Monitor,* 9 May 2003.

[17] Milgram, S. 1974. Obedience to *authority; An experimental view.* New York: Harper & Row.

[18] Rest, J. S. (Ed.). 1986. *Moral development: Advances in research and theory.* New York: Praeger. Rest, J. S., et al. 1999. *Postconventional moral thinking: A neo-Kohlbergian approach.* Mahwah, NJ: Eribaum.

[19] Ethics Resource Center, 2003. op. cit.

[20] Schmitt, R. B. Companies add ethics training: Will it work? *Wall Street Journal* (Eastern edition), 4 November 2002: Bl.

[21] Ethics Resource Center, 2003. op. cit.

[22] Treviño, L. K. et al: 1999. Managing ethics and legal compliance: What works and what hurts. *California Management Review*, 41(2): 131–151.

[23] Treviño & Nelson.

[24] Toffler, B. L., with J. Reingold. 2003. *Final accounting: Ambition, greed, and the fall of Arthur Andersen.* New York: Broadway Books. All of the following material on Toffler's experience at Arthur Andersen is from this source.

[25] Kansas, D. Plain talk; CEOs need to restore character in companies. *WSJ.COM.* Dow Jones & Company, Inc., 7 July 2002.

[26] Treviño, L. K., Hartman, L. P., & Brown, M. 2000. Moral person and moral manager; How executives develop a reputation for ethical leadership. *California Management Review*, 42(4): 128–142; Treviño, L. K., Brown, M., & Pincus-Hartman. 2003. A qualitative investigation of perceived executive ethical leadership; Perceptions from inside and outside the executive suite. *Human Relations*, 56(1): 5–37.

[27] George, B. 2003. Authentic *leadership: Rediscovering the secrets to creating lasting value.* San Francisco: Jossey-Bass.

[28] Byrne, J. 1999. *Chainsaw: The notorious career of Al Dunlap in the era of profit-at-any-price.* New York: HarperBusiness.

[29] Tidwell, G. 1993. Accounting for the PTL scandal. *Today's CPA.* July/August: 29–32.

[30] Frieswick, K. Boing. *CFO Magazine,* 1 January 2004) *www.cfo.com.*

[31] Treviño & Nelson; Loomis, C. Whatever it takes. *Fortune,* 25 November 2002: 76.

[32] PR Newswire. Big majority believes tough new laws needed to address corporate fraud; modest majority at least somewhat confident that Bush will support such laws. 27 July 2002.

[33] Kahaner, L. 2003. *Values, prosperity and the Talmud. Business lessons from the ancient rabbis.* New York: Wiley.

[34] McCabe, D., & Treviño, L. K. 1996. What we know about cheating in college. *Change: The Magazine of Higher Learning.* January/February: 28–33; McCabe, D. L., Treviño, L. K., & Butterfield, K. 2001. Cheating in academic institutions: A decade of research. *Ethics and Behavior,* 11(3): 219–232.

[35] Ethics Resource Center, 2003. op cit.

[36] Abrahamson, E. 1991. Managerial fads and fashions. *Academy of Management Review,* 16: 586–612; Carson, 1999; Gibson, J. W., & Tesone, D. V. 2001. Management fads; Emergence, evolution, and implications for managers. *The Academy of Management Executive,* 15: 122–133.

[37] Treviño & Nelson, K.

[38] Schein, E. H. 1985. *Organizational culture and leadership.* San Francisco, CA; Jossey-Bass.

[39] Treviño, L. K., Weaver, G. A., & Brown, M. 2000. Lovely at the top. Paper presented at the Academy of Management meeting, Toronto, August.

[40] Skinner, B. F. 1972. *Beyond freedom and dignity.* New York: Bantam Books.

[41] Treviño, L. K., & Youngblood, S. A. 1990. Bad apples in bad barrels: A causal analysis of ethical decision-making behavior. *Journal of Applied Psychology,* 75: 376–385.

[42] Treviño & Nelson.

[43] Toffler, p. 123.

[44] Treviño, L. K. 1992. The social implications of punishment in organizations; A justice perspective. *Academy of Management Review,* 17: 647–676; Treviño, L. K., & Ball, G. A. 1992. The social implications of punishing unethical behavior; Observers' cognitive and affective reactions. *Journal of Management,* 18: 751–768.

[45] Treviño, Hartman, & Brown.

LINDA K. TREVIÑO is professor of organizational behavior and Franklin H. Cook Fellow in Business Ethics in the Smeal College of Business Administration at The Pennsylvania State University. She received her Ph.D. in management from Texas A&M University. Her research interests focus primarily on the management of ethics in organizations. She has co-authored two books and numerous articles on this topic. Contact: *L.Trevino@psu.edu.*

MICHAEL E. BROWN is an assistant professor of management in the Sam and Irene Black School of Business at Penn State-Erie. He received his Ph.D. in management from The Pennsylvania State University. His main research interests are in the areas of ethics and leadership. Contact: *mbrown@psu.edu.*

This case details the strategies of three corporations that raise questions on the role of the corporation in society. Central to the debate are the issues of corporate social responsibility (CSR), ethical behaviour and corporate philanthropy. At one end of the spectrum are those who fall in line with Milton Friedman's view that the sole responsibility of corporations is to act in their own self-interest – that is, making profits for themselves and their shareholders. By doing so, they are best serving society by stimulating the economy, creating wealth for shareholders and jobs for employees, and constantly innovating to meet society's needs. At the other end are those who feel that it is the moral obligation of corporations to solve the world's most pressing problems, ranging from global warming to poverty to HIV/AIDS. The three short case studies presented here look at the CSR programmes of the Bill and Melinda Gates Foundation, GlaxoSmithKline and Philip Morris/Altria Group Inc., and try to give a perspective on the different approaches towards corporate responsibility adopted by these companies to serve society.

Bill & Melinda Gates Foundation: torch bearers for corporate philanthropy

Introduction

> We believe that from those to whom much is given, much is expected. We benefited from great schools, great health care, and a vibrant economic system. That is why we feel a tremendous responsibility to give back to society.[1] (Bill and Melinda Gates)

> At the end of the day, those of us in philanthropy won't be judged by how smart we were, how much we cared, or how much money we gave away. We're going to be judged by the impact we had.
>
> Impact isn't simply paying out as much money as the government requires us to each year. It's not even helping to open new schools, develop new vaccines, create hardier varieties of crops, or build new housing.
>
> Bill and Melinda created this foundation because they believe that all people, wherever they live, deserve the chance to live healthy and productive lives.[2] (Ex-CEO Patty Stonesifer)

These words form the core of the principles that guide the working of the largest charity foundation in the world,[3] the Bill & Melinda Gates Foundation. The foundation

---

Ruchir Chaturvedi, while on his ESSEC MBA programme, prepared this case under the supervision of Professor Ashok Som. The case was developed from generalized experience and published sources as a basis for class discussion rather than to illustrate either effective or ineffective handling of an administrative situation.

supports grantees in all 50 states of the USA and has worked in 100 countries all over the world. With total grants committed since its inception in 1994 amounting to $16.5 billion (see Exhibit 8.1 for details) and an asset trust endowment of about $35.9 billion,[4] the Bill & Melinda Gates Foundation has shown the corporate world many ways to give back to society.

On 26 July 2006, Warren Buffet announced his pledge to the Bill & Melinda Gates Foundation by allocating 10 million B shares of Berkshire Hathaway to be given to the foundation in a phased manner every year,[5] which resulted in the foundation receiving an endowment of $1.6 billion on 24 August 2006, $1.76 billion on 11 July 2007 and $1.8 billion on 1 July 2008.

The Gates' philanthropy focuses on four areas – education, world public health and population, non-profit, and civic and arts organizations.

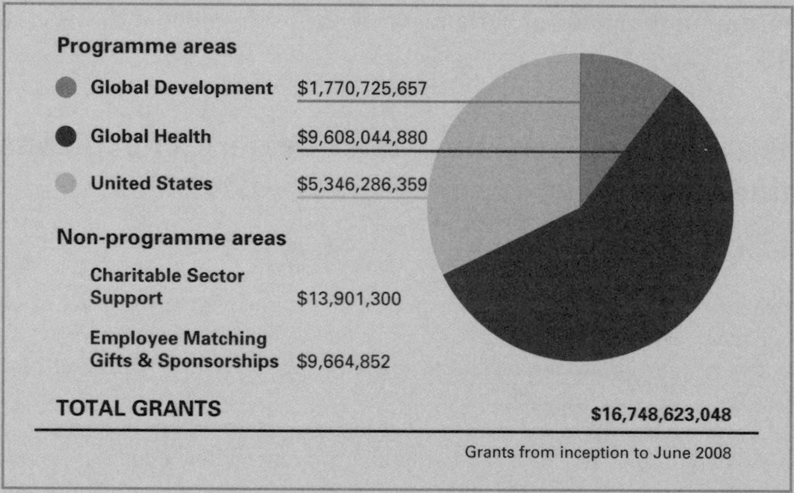

Programme areas	
● Global Development	$1,770,725,657
● Global Health	$9,608,044,880
● United States	$5,346,286,359
Non-programme areas	
Charitable Sector Support	$13,901,300
Employee Matching Gifts & Sponsorships	$9,664,852
TOTAL GRANTS	**$16,748,623,048**

Grants from inception to June 2008

Exhibit 8.1 Total grants by Bill & Melinda Gates Foundation since its inception

The story so far

Bill Gates took to philanthropy at the peak of his career. His mother, Mary Gates, was a school teacher and a prominent local philanthropist. She was also the chairwoman of the United Way International. His father, William H. Gates II, a lawyer, was also active in development activities and worked for community bodies like the International Planned Parenthood Federation, a family-planning organization.

The report of the 1994 International Conference on Population and Development, held in Cairo, Egypt, laid the foundations for much of the Gates Foundation's subsequent activities in supporting 'Third World' countries' efforts on population control, immunization and health care. In 1994, Bill and Melinda Gates consolidated their contributions to address two main initiatives: global health and community needs in the Pacific Northwest. William H. Gates Sr agreed to manage the new

William H. Gates Foundation, formed in December 1994 with an initial stock gift of about $94 million.

On 23 July 1997, Bill and Melinda Gates announced the launch of the Gates Library Foundation with a donation of $200 million, to bring computers and internet access to public libraries in low-income communities in the United States and Canada. Former Microsoft executive Patty Stonesifer took on the foundation's leadership. In December 1998, Bill and Melinda Gates made a contribution of $20 million to the Seattle 'Libraries for All' programme and launched its Libraries Online initiative in partnership with the American Library Programme. By 2000, Microsoft had donated software and $17 million to 200 libraries in the USA.[6]

In January 1999, Bill and Melinda donated $4.2 billion to the W.H. Gates Foundation.[7] In 2000, Bill Gates, facing antitrust suit filed by the US government, realized the importance of philanthropy inspired by the words of Andrew Carnegie, who said 'He who dies rich, dies disgraced.'[8] After his visit to Soweto, a poverty-stricken community in Africa, and reading about problems of global poverty and disease, Gates created the Bill & Melinda Gates Foundation. On 24 January 2000, the W.H. Gates Foundation and the Gates Learning Foundation were merged with the Bill & Melinda Gates Foundation with a further $5 billion donation by Melinda Gates. A total endowment of $17 billion was also donated in the form of Microsoft stock, which was later converted into other assets by the foundation staff to insulate the organization from Microsoft. (Exhibit 8.2 shows the foundation endowment timeline.)

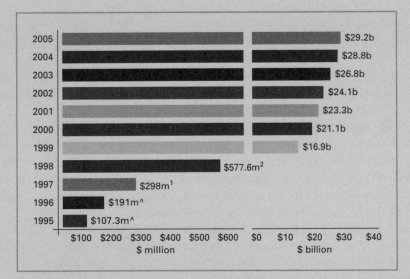

Exhibit 8.2 Bill & Melinda Gates Foundation endowment timeline

Figures include total assets as of 31 Dec, of respective year, except where noted.

^ As of 3/31 of respective year

[1] Includes $296.6m (as of 3/31/97) to William H. Gates Foundation; $1.4m (as of 7/31/97) to Gates Learning Foundation

[2] Includes $312.4m (as of 3/31/98) to William H. Gates Foundation; $265.2m (as of 7/31/98) to Gates Learning Foundation

▶   From its inception, the three primary themes of the foundation have been 'Third World' health care, library and information technology and education. These led to the organizational strategies of the foundation. In 2006, the foundation reorganized into three programmes: Global Development, Global Health and United States. As of 2008, the three programme presidents are Allan C. Golston, US programme; Dr Tadataka 'Tachi' Yamada, Global Health programme; and Sylvia Mathews Burwell, Global Development programme.[9]

A professional approach

'I think of philanthropy in two ways. From a purely rational perspective, if we can save lives, that's great. But if you can meet people, you can take the statistics and map it to the individuals. It's uplifting; I encourage you to do it. Drawing people in is what this is all about.'[10] These words by Bill Gates summarize his perspective on philanthropy. To increase the effectiveness of its activities, the foundation has worked with a diverse mix of partners like governments, other foundations, the private sector and non-profit organizations.

Under the US programme, the foundation focuses on imparting education to the underprivileged and aims to significantly increase the number of students who graduate from high school with the skills needed to succeed in college and work, improving the lives of at-risk children and youth, and expanding access to information through technology in public libraries serving disadvantaged communities.[11] The foundation has partnered with districts in the USA to start new schools, and now supports over 1,500 innovative high schools across the nation. The foundation has also been awarding various scholarships to promising students who don't have the financial means to attend college.[12]

In 2005, the foundation's single biggest grant of $1 billion was awarded to the United Negro College Fund, America's largest minority higher education assistance organization.[13] The foundation's Library programme aims to provide internet access to libraries in rural areas of the USA. With partners at city, state and national levels, in January 2007, the foundation launched a new five-year grant-making strategy to help libraries maintain high-quality computer and internet access by supporting hardware and connectivity upgrades in communities where 10 per cent or more of people live in poverty. The foundation gave $8.3 million in matching grants to help libraries in ten states add or replace public computers for their patrons.[14]

The foundation's Global Health programme focuses on diseases and health conditions that cause the most illness and death, and receive the least attention and resources – diseases such as tuberculosis and malaria, which barely exist in rich countries but still kill millions in the developing world, and AIDS, which infects 5 million new people every year, the vast majority of them in poor countries.[15] The programme's priorities are addressing the health issues of the underprivileged in underdeveloped countries.

In November 1999, the foundation granted $26 million to UNICEF for eliminating maternal neonatal tetanus (MNT). The foundation also raised $100 million by collaborating with Becton Dickinson, the world's largest manufacturer of injections. This partnership also included UNICEF, the US committee for UNICEF, the WHO, PATH (Programme for Appropriate Technology in Health) and UNPF (United Nations Population Fund). In March 2001, the foundation awarded $10 million to the UNDP/ World Bank/WHO special programme for R&D in tropical diseases to facilitate the development of new tests for the diagnosis of TB. The foundation is also a major supporter of the Global Alliance for Vaccines and Immunization (GAVI), which comprises of government representatives, drug companies and charities. The foundation has made significant grants for programmes concerning prevention of HIV/ AIDS virus transmission[16] (see Exhibit 8.3 for estimates of HIV-infected population), development of malaria vaccines[17] and development of drugs used for treating TB infections.[18]

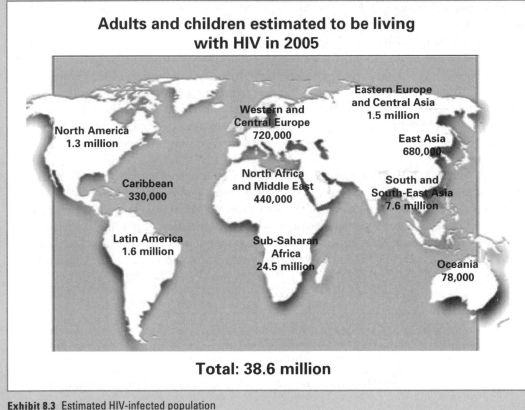

Exhibit 8.3 Estimated HIV-infected population
Source: UNAIDS

Strategic management

However, unlike many other charities, Gates brought a managerial approach to his initiatives by regularly monitoring the investments made by the foundation and discontinuing funding to projects that failed to be accountable. As advice to the new

CEO, Jeff Raikes, the outgoing CEO, Patty Stonesifer, says 'The danger isn't in what people do tell you – it's in what they don't. It's amazing what people won't tell you when you have billions of dollars to give away.'[19] Mark Kane, former director of PATH's child vaccine programme was witness to how Gates stopped funding a project when he saw that the members of the board did not take the issue seriously.

While providing vital funding for the development of vaccines and other therapies, Bill and Melinda Gates also recognize that medicines alone are not the entire solution, and support partnerships with organizations that deliver and sustain the advances that their foundation makes possible. A hallmark of the foundation's grant-making has been its ability to leverage resources through strategic collaboration with partners across a variety of sectors. Patty Stonesifer summarized the foundation's philosophy by paraphrasing an old saying: 'If you want to go fast, go alone. If you want to go far, go together.'

Assessing the impact of the Bill & Melinda Gates Foundation's strategic approach to giving in the area of global health, Mark R. Kramer, the managing director of the Foundation Strategy Group (FSG) and founder of the Center for Effective Philanthropy said, 'Their focus on public–private partnerships has broken down many of the artificial barriers between nonprofits, for-profits and governments that impede effective multi-sector solutions. Medicines for Malaria Ventures, the International AIDS Vaccine Initiative and Malaria Vaccine Initiative, all combine philanthropic dollars, government, NGOs and for-profit pharmaceutical companies in a coordinated search for solutions. Working across sectors can be far more impactful than staying within the nonprofit sector alone.'[20]

On 27 June 2008, Bill Gates gave up his day-to-day role at Microsoft to dedicate more time to the foundation. His aim now is to focus on raising global awareness of the foundation's issues, building partnerships worldwide and helping shape the foundation's strategies.[21] Through strategic partnerships, a strong foundation of guiding principles and a vision to serve humanity in the best way possible, the leaders of the Bill & Melinda Gates Foundation are poised to take philanthropy to a new dimension. (See Exhibit 8.4 for the fact sheet.)

Guided by the belief that every life has equal value, the Bill & Melinda Gates Foundation works to help all people lead healthy, productive lives. In developing countries, it focuses on improving people's health and giving them the chance to lift themselves out of hunger and extreme poverty. In the United States, it seeks to ensure that all people – especially those with the fewest resources – have access to the opportunities they need to succeed in school and life. Based in Seattle, the foundation is led by CEO Jeff Raikes and co-chair William H. Gates Sr, under the direction of trustees Bill and Melinda Gates and Warren Buffett.

Grantmaking areas

- Global Development programme
- Global Health programme
- United States programme

We also have a small Charitable Sector Support initiative.

Locations

- Seattle, Wash.
- Washington, DC
- Beijing, China
- Avahan Initiative – Delhi, India

Leadership

- Bill Gates, Co-chair
- Melinda French Gates, Co-chair
- William H. Gates Sr, Co-chair
- Jeff Raikes, Chief Executive Officer
- Allan C. Golston, President, US programme
- Dr Tadataka 'Tachi' Yamada, President, Global Health programme
- Sylvia Mathews Burwell, President, Global Development programme
- Alex Friedman, Chief Financial Officer
- Connie Collingsworth, General Counsel
- Martha Choe, Chief Administrative Officer
- Heidi Sinclair, Chief Communications Officer
- Geoff Lamb, Managing Director of Public Policy

Statistics*

Number of employees: approximately 626
Asset trust endowment: $35.9 billion***
Total grant commitments since inception: $16.5 billion
Total 2007 grant payments: $2.007 billion

Geographic reach

The foundation supports grantees in all 50 states and the District of Columbia. Internationally, we support work in more than 100 countries.

Illustrative Grant Commitments

- The GAVI Alliance – $1.5 billion
- United Negro College Fund, Gates Millennium Scholars programme – $1.37 billion
- Malaria Vaccine Initiative – $287 million
- Alliance for a Green Revolution in Africa – $264.5 million
- Save the Children, Saving Newborn Lives – $110 million
- United Way of King County, Seattle, Wash. – $85 million
- Mexico, National Council on Culture and the Arts, Global Libraries programme – $30 million
- Consultative Group to Assist the Poor, microfinance technology – $24 million
- Chicago Public Schools, curriculum support – $21 million
- Opportunity Online programme, multiple library systems – $16.4 million

Exhibit 8.4 Bill & Melinda Gates Foundation fact sheet*

* http://www.gatesfoundation.org/MediaCenter/FactSheet/

** As of 1 July 2008

*** Endowment includes $1.6 billion from the first instalment of the gift from Warren Buffett recorded 24 August 2006, the second instalment of $1.76 billion recorded on 11 July 2007, and the third instalment of $1.8 billion recorded on 1 July 2008

▶ ## GlaxoSmithKline: healing the world

Introduction

> " Our company mission is to make people feel better and live longer – the connections
> to CR are very obvious and fundamental. I don't see a need for a separate CR
> strategy because CR is so integrated into the purpose of our business and the way
> we do business. For example, the issue of access to medicines is one of the four
> cornerstones of our business strategy.[22]
>
> (Sir Christopher Gent, Chairman, Corporate Responsibility Committee, GSK) "

GlaxoSmithKline was formed in 2000 with the merger of Glaxo Wellcome and
SmithKlineBeecham, two of Europe's largest pharmaceutical companies. Today, with a
market capitalization of £114 billion and annual sales of £22.7 billion, it is one of the
world's largest drug manufacturers, employing 100,000 people in over 100 countries
across the world.

Since the merger, the company has been a forerunner in corporate responsibility
initiatives under the leadership of CEO Jean-Pierre Garnier, whose words, 'I don't want to
be the CEO of a company that caters only to the rich. … I want those medicines in the
hands of many more people who need them', embody the spirit of even the employees of
GSK, a company committed to improving the health of all of the world's people.

HIV/AIDS in South Africa

The emergence of the South African HIV/AIDS crisis was the most significant
catalyst in the shift of global public opinion about the role of pharmaceutical companies
in the advancement of human health and welfare. Every single day 13,000 people are
infected with HIV/AIDS and 8,000 die as a result of it. Estimates vary, but nearly
40 million people are infected with the disease (see Exhibit 8.5), equivalent to the
population of Spain. A further five million were infected in 2005 alone. A 2004 UN
report warned that the epidemic has cut to less than 40 years the average life expectancy
of people in seven countries in sub-Saharan Africa: Central African Republic, Lesotho,
Malawi, Mozambique, Swaziland, Zimbabwe and Zambia.[23] In 2000, the South African
Medical Research Council projected that approximately six million South Africans
would die of AIDS by 2010. An International Labor Organization report released for the
UN Conference on HIV/AIDS held in Durban, South Africa, in June 2000, predicted that
by 2020 the economic growth rate in certain sub-Saharan countries would decrease by
25 per cent as a result of death due to AIDS.

In the mid-1980s millions of dollars were poured into developing drugs to treat and
eliminate HIV and AIDS. In March 1987, Wellcome (prior to its merger with Glaxo)
introduced the antiretroviral (ARV) treatment drug, zidovudine (AZT), under the brand
name Retrovir. Between 1995 and 1997, Roche, Merck and Abbott Laboratories released
new drugs along with data proving that drug combinations delayed the onset of AIDS for
those with HIV and reduced the symptoms for those with full-blown AIDS. By 2001,
23 HIV/AIDS drugs had received FDA approval. However, the drugs alone cost $10,000

to $15,000 per patient per year, which was totally out of reach to the population of least developed countries (LDCs). According to the UN, more than 1.2 billion people, with 290 million in sub-Saharan Africa alone, were living on less than $1 a day.[24]

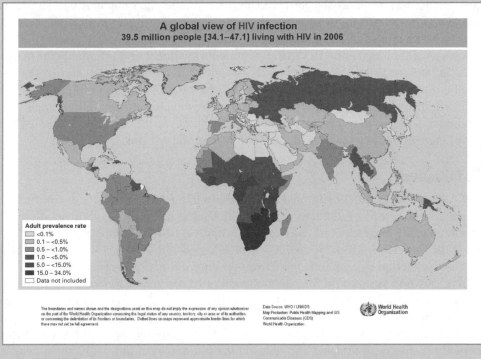

Exhibit 8.5 HIV/AIDS across the world
Source: © WHO 2007. All rights reserved

The challenges

In 1998, GSK and 41 other pharmaceutical companies, including Boehringer-Ingelheim, Bristol-Meyers Squibb, Merck, Roche and Eli Lilly, filed a lawsuit against the South African government. The lawsuit was centred on the Medicines and Related Substances Control Amendment Act of 1997, which was introduced to the South African Parliament by then President Nelson Mandela. The amendment allowed the government to import generic drugs or give out compulsory licences in case of national emergency. The government argued that the measure was necessary in order for the country to get access to drugs that people could afford.

However, the industry consortium argued that the South African government would be acting in violation of the WTO's Trade-Related Aspects of Intellectual Property Rights (TRIPS) agreement. The industry consortium believed that any action that might weaken the wider establishment and enforcement of IP protection would threaten the industry's business model by cutting the financial incentives necessary to ensure pharmaceutical innovation. By 2000, AIDS activists and public opinion viewed the

▶ dispute as primarily involving a conflict between intellectual property rights and access to essential drugs.

Right from the beginning, GSK has been the target of activists who claim that it is a social responsibility of the pharmaceutical industry to help ensure universal access to essential medicines. In February 2001, Oxfam International, a confederation of 12 NGOs formed in an effort 'to find lasting solutions to poverty, suffering and injustice', launched its 'Cut the Cost' campaign against the pharmaceutical companies, particularly GSK, demanding that they make the HIV/AIDS treatments available and affordable for people in LDCs. In January 2001, Oxfam provided GSK with a document which argued that enforcement of global patent rules had the effect of keeping drug prices high in LDCs and that GSK should take steps to resolve the situation by developing and delivering a comprehensive access to essential medicines policy that would assist in addressing the inequity between treatment in developed and developing nations.

GSK's initiatives

In 1997, WHO and SmithKline formed a partnership to target their efforts to eliminate lymphatic filariasis (LF) by 2020. By 2001, the LF Global Alliance, involving GSK, the WHO and 28 other organizations, was a major initiative. GSK's Global Community Partnerships function built upon the LF Global Alliance and worked towards expanding GSK's Positive Action programme, which was an international programme of HIV education, care and support. In May 2000, GlaxoWellcome joined five other companies in a partnership with WHO and UNAIDS to create the Accelerating Access Initiative. The aim was to enhance access to HIV/AIDS drugs in LDCs through a three-pronged approach of establishing national and local-level HIV/AIDS treatment plans and delivery systems, to improve access to essential drugs and to lower the ultimate cost of treating more people.

In March 2001 GSK cut prices by as much as 90 per cent in Africa.[25] Garnier said that the prices of three AIDS drugs (Trizivir, Ziagen and Agenerase) would be reduced to sell at cost in 63 of the world's poorest countries including sub-Saharan Africa. In addition, GSK said it would continue offering preferential prices on its drug Combivir (a mix of AZT and 3TC) to governments, charities and NGOs in developing countries. In March 2001, Garnier contacted his counterparts at Roche, Boehringer Ingelheim and Merck to explore the possible withdrawal of the case against the South African government. On 5 April 2001, UN Secretary General Kofi Annan hosted a meeting of seven pharmaceutical company CEOs along with the heads of WHO and UNAIDS, with the intention of establishing a new constructive partnership with research-based industry and trying to focus UN member governments. Two weeks later the drug manufacturers dropped their case; Kofi Annan responded by emphasizing the need for shared responsibility, and called for governments, intergovernmental agencies, NGOs and businesses to work in partnership to address the HIV/AIDS crisis, rather than focus on just the price.

In October 2001, GSK granted a voluntary licence to Aspen Pharmacare, South Africa's largest producer of generic medicines, to allow it to manufacture GSK's antiretrovirals, Retrovir, Epivir and Combivir, in South Africa and to sell them to the South Africa government and others in the non-profit sector. GSK waived its royalty fee and instead required a 30 per cent fee on net sales to be paid as a donation to NGOs managing HIV/AIDS programmes in South Africa. In July 2002, GSK released the results of the one-year-old access policy, which showed a tenfold increase in the shipments of preferentially priced Combivir to LDCs. GSK also reported securing 95 agreements to supply preferentially priced HIV/AIDS medicines to 31 countries, including the some of the world's poorest.[26] On 5 September 2002, GSK announced a further reduction of its non-profit preferential prices for its HIV/AIDS drugs by 33 per cent and its antimalarial medicines by 38 per cent. It further announced securing 115 agreements to supply preferentially priced HIV/AIDS drugs in 41 countries.

The future

In 2007 GSK marked 15 years of its Positive Action programme, which helps communities living with HIV/AIDS. January 2008 marked the tenth anniversary of GSK's programme to help eliminate lymphatic filariasis. During those ten years GSK has donated 750 million albendazole tablets, reaching over 130 million people.[27] GSK has negotiated eight licensing agreements for its ARVs in Africa. Some of its voluntary licences cover individual countries or trade blocs while others cover all of sub-Saharan Africa. In August 2007 GSK gave consent to enable a Canadian company, Apotex, to manufacture a generic fixed-dose combination ARV, containing two molecules over which GSK has patent rights, for the treatment of HIV/AIDS in Rwanda.[28]

In March 2008, GlaxoSmithKline announced a new strategy to expand markets and increase access to medicines in low- and middle-income countries. Through an internal policy known as 'tearing down the barriers', the company has established differential pricing schemes within and between India, South Africa and other developing countries, in hopes of shifting to a new low-price, high-volume business model. While similar initiatives have existed for AIDS antiretrovirals, the GSK strategy notably moves beyond the 'big three' infectious diseases to tackle the growing challenge of diabetes and other non-communicable diseases, with a dual market among rich and poor.

The policy is under test in nations including India, South Africa and Morocco, which have a significant and growing middle class as well as many people with far lower incomes and little access to subsidized health care, and is designed to generate a premium to recover development costs on new medicines from wealthier people in emerging economies without excluding those who cannot afford to pay. GSK hopes that a greater volume of sales to a larger share of the population will offset lower prices, as well as freeing up governments' scarce health resources in developing countries to focus on treating their most impoverished.[29]

While on one hand, GSK along with NGOs, non-profit organizations, various governments and other companies, continues to make essential medicines accessible to the world's population, the industry will always be under constant surveillance and will come under attack from organizations like Oxfam, who will keep pushing the companies to contribute more towards the health care of people of LDCs. GSK is clearly committed to forming stronger ties with governments and associations, and developing more programmes to show the world that it is indeed a company that employs 110,000 people who go to work every morning because they are pro-public health and that the primary objective of any policy put forth by the company is public health.

▶ ## Altria Group/Philip Morris: inherently evil?

Introduction

Altria Group is the parent company of Philip Morris USA, John Middleton and Philip Morris Capital Corporation. Altria Group owns 100 per cent of the outstanding stock of Philip Morris USA, John Middleton and Philip Morris Capital Corporation. Philip Morris USA is the largest tobacco company in the United States, with approximately half the US cigarette market. John Middleton is a leading manufacturer of machine-made large cigars. In addition, Altria Group has a 28.5 per cent economic and voting interest in SABMiller plc, one of the world's largest brewers.

The company's biggest seller, Malboro, is the world's most popular and widely recognized cigarette brand. With a market capitalization of $43.58 billion and net revenues of $73.8 billion[30] in 2007, up 10.1 per cent from 2006, the company is one of the largest cigarette manufacturers in the world.

Although the company supports programmes and initiatives that take a positive youth development approach to reducing underage tobacco use, and its website and annual reports are full of mentions of various corporate responsibility programmes, it still is a company whose very existence depends on attracting new customers to its deadly products. No matter how much money it donates to various causes, it is still the leader of an industry that is going to be responsible for 9 million deaths by 2020, more than three-quarters of them in the developing world.

Dr Jekyll and Mr Hyde

Philip Morris is well aware of the importance of CSR, especially for a corporation whose products literally *kill* its customers, making the corporation dependent on a steady stream of new customers for its survival. When corporate goals are not aligned with society's interests, as is the case with Philip Morris, 'corporate social responsibility needs to be an important part of corporate strategy,' says economist and business scholar Geoffrey M. Heal. 'Indeed, it can be a matter of survival, as societies penalize companies perceived to be in conflict with underlying values.'[31]

In 1998, the Master Settlement Agreement ended a four-year legal battle between the US states and the tobacco industry leaders, including Philip Morris. The Tobacco Settlement addressed public health and youth access issues by prohibiting youth targeting in advertising, marketing and promotions. This settlement thus forced Philip Morris and the other large tobacco companies to drastically change their corporate culture, as well as their marketing and advertising strategies. Philip Morris's CSR initiatives regarding the health dangers of smoking go directly against business goals: increasing profits through market expansion – that is, selling more cigarettes. However, these CSR programmes might still make business sense by improving the company's image and complying with the requirements of the settlement.

In 1995, Philip Morris USA announced the 'Action Against Access' programme, and became a founding member and major sponsor of the Coalition for Responsible Tobacco Retailing and its *We Card* programme. In 1998, the company voluntarily established a

Youth Smoking Prevention (YSP) department. The YSP department has applied significant resources to grant-making to youth-development organizations, producing tools and resources to help parents talk to their kids about not smoking, supporting youth access prevention initiatives to help keep cigarettes and other tobacco products out of kids' hands, and youth smoking prevention advertising. The Youth Smoking Prevention department was created with the objective of helping to prevent kids from smoking cigarettes. The department focuses its efforts in three areas: parents' communication, grant programmes and youth access prevention.[32] The grants given out by the company through its various initiatives total more than $125 million and have reached about a million kids. However, critics maintain that these anti-smoking initiatives are nothing more than acts of compliance with the Tobacco Settlement and preventive measures for future lawsuits.

Philip Morris has shifted its corporate growth strategy to focus on international markets, particularly countries in the developing world, where 930 million of the world's 1.3 billion smokers reside.[33] Philip Morris already exports more than 60 per cent of its total sales, and children in overseas markets could be of interest for expanding its customer base.[34] Philip Morris regularly engages in lobbying governments to pass regulation favourable to its cause. In 2000, Philip Morris gave the government of the Czech Republic a detailed financial report suggesting that smoking was beneficial to the Czech Republic because of the huge cost savings in social services *due to early mortality caused by smoking*.[35]

In 'The competitive advantage of strategic philanthropy', Michael Porter and Mark R. Kramer argue that strategic philanthropy not only increases the effectiveness of philanthropic efforts, it enhances the context in which the corporation operates and can actually improve business performance.[36] What makes the philanthropic efforts of Altria/ Philip Morris so unique and interesting is that many of them – particularly their health-related giving – directly contradict the primary objective of the corporation: to sell more cigarettes. In the case of Philip Morris, perhaps the most strategic philanthropy is an indirect approach. It supports the arts and HIV/AIDS research, both popular causes among the gay and lesbian community, a demographic group with a smoking rate that is twice the national average for all adults.[37] Altria/Philip Morris is well aware of the fact that smoking rates are highest in the south, among the poor, and among African-Americans.[38] It is no surprise, then, that much of its philanthropic effort focuses on the south, the poorest region of the country and the region with the highest African-American population. Aside from potentially attracting new customers, these efforts could pay large dividends in smoothing out, or at least minimizing, potential future conflicts.

Critics observe that the Youth Smoking Prevention programmes of companies like Philip Morris stress several common themes: (1) smoking is an 'adult choice'; (2) children start smoking because of peer pressure and a lack of proper role modelling and guidance from their parents; and (3) an emphasis on 'the law' as the reason not to smoke. None discusses the fact that nicotine is addictive, that smoking or passive smoking causes disease, or that tobacco marketing has a role in promoting smoking. In designing its youth campaigns, the company takes care not to contradict or interfere with tobacco advertising. Presenting smoking as an 'adult choice', a 'forbidden fruit' and an act of rebellion are common industry marketing themes.[39]

In January 2001, Philip Morris launched the 'Think. Don't Smoke' campaign to reach out to school kids about the ill effects of smoking; 26 million book covers were sent to 43,000 schools across the US by Philip Morris showing children on snowboards and skis, and warning them: 'Don't Wipe Out. Think. Don't Smoke' (see Exhibit 8.6). The free covers sparked protests from education and health advocates across the country, who called the brightly coloured fold-over covers a smoke screen that violates a 1998 ban on tobacco advertising to children. The critics charged the covers' attempt to link Philip Morris's name more to fun in the snow than to the 'don't smoke' message and considered that the covers contained subliminal smoking messages.

'The need isn't for Philip Morris to do anti-smoking campaigns,' said Matt Myers, the top lawyer for the advocacy group Campaign for Tobacco-Free Kids.[40] 'The need is for Philip Morris to stop doing advertising that makes its products more popular among children than any other brands.' Some smoking opponents, wary of any help from tobacco companies, say their ads avoid mention of the realities of smoking, like lung cancer. Critics claim that such prevention programmes consistently fail to address the health consequences of tobacco use and never mention that nicotine is addictive.[41] In fact 'Think. Don't Smoke' advertisements have also been associated with an increase in intention to smoke in the following years.[42]

Exhibit 8.6 Philip Morris 'Think. Don't Smoke' campaign

Harsh reality

Anti-smoking proponents say that citizens and policy makers should reject any 'educational' programmes by the tobacco industry. If the tobacco industry were sincere in its stated desire to contribute to reducing youth smoking, it would stop opposing policies and programmes that have been demonstrated to be effective. Policy makers who believe that the industry would do anything that would negatively affect the recruitment of new smokers are ignoring history and fooling themselves.

Notes

1 Letter from Bill and Melinda Gates, http://www.gatesfoundation.org/AboutUs/OurValues/GatesLetter/.
2 Message from Patty Stonesifer, Annual Report 2007, Bill & Melinda Gates Foundation.
3 *Guinness Book of World Records*, 2000.
4 http://www.gatesfoundation.org/MediaCenter/FactSheet/.
5 Letter from Warren Buffet to Bill and Melinda Gates, http://www.berkshirehathaway.com/donate/bmgfltr.pdf.
6 *Ibid.*
7 *Ibid.*
8 'Rory Carroll on Bill Gates' Philanthropy', op. cit.
9 http://www.gatesfoundation.org/AboutUs/QuickFacts/Timeline/.
10 'Bill Grows Up', op. cit.
11 United States Programme Fact Sheet, http://www.gatesfoundation.org/UnitedStates/.
12 http://www.gatesfoundation.org/UnitedStates/Education/Scholarships/default.htm.
13 Cronin, Jon, 'Bill Gates: billionaire philanthropist', http://news.bbc.co.uk/2/hi/business/3913581.stm.
14 http://www.gatesfoundation.org/UnitedStates/USLibraryProgram/Backgrounder/default.htm.
15 Letter from Bill and Melinda Gates, http://www.gatesfoundation.org/AboutUs/OurValues/GatesLetter/.
16 http://www.gatesfoundation.org/GlobalHealth/Pri_Diseases/HIVAIDS/HIVBackgrounder.htm.
17 http://www.gatesfoundation.org/GlobalHealth/Pri_Diseases/Malaria/Malaria_Backgrounder.htm.
18 http://www.gatesfoundation.org/GlobalHealth/Pri_Diseases/Tuberculosis/TB_Backgrounder.htm.
19 Message from Patty Stonesifer, Annual Report 2007, Bill & Melinda Gates Foundation.
20 Crafting partnerships for vaccinations and healthcare, Bill & Melinda Gates Foundation, http://www.synergos.org/globalgivingmatters/features/0401gates.htm.
21 http://br.thenewsmarket.com/GatesFoundation/br/Story/StoryDetails.aspx?hidStoryGUID=24bff066-def9-4794-bcfd-fddf2dee552f&hidListingPage=LatestNews.aspx&hidFromStory=1.
22 GlaxoSmithKline Corporate Responsibility Report 2007.
23 http://www.gsk.com/infocus/pandemic.htm.
24 United Nations Basic Facts, December 2000.
25 'Glaxo to widen access to cheap AIDS drugs', Reuters News, 21 February 2001.
26 *Facing the Challenge – One Year On*, published by GSK in July 2002.
27 http://www.gsk.com/about/ataglance.htm.
28 GlaxoSmithKline Corporate Responsibility Report 2007.
29 Jack, Andrew, 'GSK varies prices to raise sales', 16 March 2008, www.ft.com.
30 Altria Group Inc., 2007 annual report.
31 *Hermes* magazine, http://www2.gsb.columbia.edu/hermes/fall2004/article_endpaper.cfm.
32 http://philipmorrisusa.com/en/cms/Responsibility/Helping_Reduce_Underage_Tobacco_Use/Our_Focus_Areas/default.aspx.
33 http://www.news.harvard.edu/gazette/2003/09.18/26-tobacco.html.
34 http://www.nytimes.com/2001/08/24/business/24smok.html.
35 Public Finance Balance of Smoking in the Czech Republic, 28 November 2000.
36 Porter, Michael E. and Mark R. Kramer, 'The competitive advantage of strategic philanthropy', *Harvard Business Review*, December 2002.
37 http://www.tobacco.org/news/211439.html.

▶ 38 http://www.cdc.govmmwr/preview/mmwrhtml/mm5444a3.htm.

39 Kwechansky Marketing Research I. Report for Imperial Tobacco Limited – subject project plus/minus [Minnesota selected document]. Imperial Tobacco, 7 May 1982. Bates No. 566627751/7824. Younger adult smokers lifestyles and attitudes [Minnesota selected document]. Brown and Williamson Tobacco Company. Undated. Bates No. 170052241/2255.

40 http://tobaccofreekids.org.

41 DiFranza, J.R. and McAfee, T. (1992) 'The Tobacco Institute: helping youth say "yes" to tobacco' (Editorial), *Journal of Fam. Pract*, 34, 694–96.

42 Farrelly, M.C., Healton, C.G., Davis, K.C., Messeri, P., Hersey, J.C. and Haviland., M.L. (2002) 'Getting to the truth: evaluating national tobacco countermarketing campaigns', *Am J Public Health*, 92, 901–7.

? *Case questions*

Read the case carefully, then answer the following questions.

1 Analyse the different approaches of the CSR efforts of the three companies to develop their markets.

2 Classify the programmes into pure corporate philanthropy, risk management or strategic CSR. Which one do you think is the more effective strategy, in what conditions and in which markets?

3 Discuss the need for CSR programmes in industries like tobacco and health care.

CHAPTER 9

Preparing for the future: leadership challenges

The previous chapter focused on corporate social responsibility, dealing with issues such as piracy, counterfeiting, governance and the social obligations of global companies. This final chapter discusses future leadership challenges and focuses on the roles, responsibilities and people skills that are required to catapult global companies to their next objective. Rather than be predictive at this stage this concluding section acts as a point of departure for proactive discussions on the tortuous future evolution of the global company.

The introductory discussions in the previous chapters, the readings and the vivid descriptions in earlier cases have shown that the global corporations of today are starkly different from earlier-generation corporations. Most of the global corporations are still mainly located in the top-five industrialized nations but soon might become more prevalent in emerging markets. For example, as illustrated earlier, the Boston Consulting Group study of 100 global corporations of rapidly developing economies shows that the growth of these corporations is expanding very quickly in industries such as pharmaceuticals, automobiles and white goods. This has occurred mostly due to the deregulation and liberalization of industries in these markets. In turn, this has resulted in increased cross-border mergers and acquisitions, a redefining of the strategic nature of industries and the corporations' roles in nation states, global competition and the obsolesence of technology. All this together has created complex, multiple and often diverse, conflicting demands.

The transnational model of Bartlett and Ghoshal propounded that the ability to compete in today's changing environment has given rise to multiple strategic capabilities of global scale efficiency, national responsiveness, and worldwide innovation and learning capabilities. This hypothesis of changed demands has a bearing on management systems and processes, and the organizational structures that link them. To align the change in structure with the new management systems and processes the transnational corporation had been characterized by an integrated network of assets and resources, high responsiveness and flexibility, together with highly coordinated processes.

539

To make this change process work efficiently, the role of managers as leaders is critical. Without skilled, knowledgeable managers, making decisions on interpreting new markets, turbulence in industries, integration from different markets and coordination of actions across markets won't be easy. For this to be orchestrated seamlessly, new forms of organization need to be developed in order to deliver results on a global basis. This is a substantial challenge for top management.

This brings us to the leadership challenges that global corporations face in the twenty-first century. Most of the leaders are grappling with issues regarding the appropriate response of business to new realities. Their strategic thinking is neither final nor the perfect solution to the dilemmas they face in an ever changing business landscape. What may be the best decision today might turn out to be one of the most difficult decisions after a couple of years. History has repeated itself regarding this, as can be enumerated from the mergers of Daimler and Chrysler, HP and Compaq, the acquisition of Blue Circle by Lafarge, and Vivendi's acquisition of Universal Studios and others. Most leaders seek to match their idealism with a keen eye to the bottom line. Their rhetoric in external and internal public relations can best be understood if one separates the simple vision-mission-goal statement of the corporation and can follow it through to the strategy of the corporation. Usually this is very difficult to do as most vision statements are not relevant, clear or simple. They are just replicas of too many promises. To be able to provide continuity and communicate effectively are the foundational characteristics of a true leader. Those managers who possess these characteristics have the potential to be the leaders of tomorrow. For example, Matsushita had a 150-year mission plan, while Komatsu could 'encircle' and become a close second to Caterpillar within ten years. Aligning resources to create competencies, some of which are core competencies, and to use these core competencies to create capabilities for competitive advantage to provide strategy is the objective of the leader and the top management team. As markets globalize, leaders of corporations will be effective and efficient if they can leverage managing capital (resources), goods (products), labour (workforce) and information (communication). To coordinate these four portfolios of processes requires leadership but might just fall short of achieving superior performance, as was hypothesized in the last decade.

Going one step further, research has shown that some of the most important areas that the leaders of the next generation of global corporations will need to bear in mind are to *enhance social equity, enhance corporate social responsibility, create and distribute value, enhance innovation and human creativity,* and *enhance ethical standards while trying to transform personally and collectively to align with the needs of the environment.*

Enhancing social equity is a grave concern for the leaders of today as the divide between rich and poor within and among developed, developing and emerging states is a critical challenge. For example, the production of the cheapest car, the Nano, by the TATA Group of India raised eyebrows as it also raised eyebrows when the Group acquired Rover and Jaguar. On one hand, the Nano is meant to serve the masses at the bottom of the pyramid, while on the other hand, the luxury brand Jaguar is meant to serve the affluent. Chapter 8 discussed issues regarding enhancing corporate social responsibility and how global corporations are enabling greater business accountability. The creation and distribution of value has been less discussed by academicians and practitioners as a leadership challenge since it seems to be at the heart of governance principles. However, the Chairman and Chief Mentor of Infosys, one of the leading software corporations from

India, sees it as a major challenge for the future. This is because value is more often created by an organization in terms of shareholder wealth, employee retention and other measures; however, when the leadership changes, how one can ensure that the values are transferred? The question is how employees and others within a corporation are enabled, regardless of sex, race and/or position in the hierarchy, to participate in all aspects of the organization. This might be an essential driver for the future benefit of the corporation and its people. It might lead to a better understanding of the business environment, the ability to sense new opportunities and challenges, and foster human resource development and satisfaction among employees, thus generating retention and a trusted workforce.

Today's business context is continuously challenging global corporations' trustworthiness, their identity, their conduct, their social impact and their uncompromising level of ethics. Business is becoming the most influential institution in the world today. Many leaders, especially leaders who have created their global corporations from scratch, like Bill Gates of Microsoft, Michael Dell of Dell, Narayana Murthy of Infosys, Bernard Arnault of LVMH and others, tend to believe that the emerging era of global interdependence and connectedness through technology will create far more new opportunities than during the previous decade. To manage such a change process requires revising one's thoughts on what is the reality, sound reasoning and a reframing of intuition, as well as a firm grasp of ever evolving scientific knowledge. Thus, to transform the corporation, leaders need to change themselves along with the corporation.

In the twenty-first century, as global competition intensifies, convergence of technologies is no longer a distant reality. As the world become flatter, opportunities from consolidation increase and emerging nations develop faster and faster to catch up with their rich, developed counterparts. In some cases corporations are redesigning their global organizational structure for better control, and for local adaptability and flexibility. In other instances they are trying to integrate seamlessly their global acquisitions in order to benefit from the synergies they have promised their shareholders. Thus, next-generation leaders are juggling performance and growth, while trying to find the best design for their corporation – an ever illusive leadership challenge for the next-generation global corporation.

Case introduction: LVMH: managing the multi-brand conglomerate

LVMH Moët Hennessy Louis Vuitton, based in France, is one of the world's leading luxury goods companies. It operates in wines, spirits, fashion goods, leather goods, perfumes, cosmetics, watches, jewellery and retailing. The company employs approximately 56,000 people. Its global distribution network grew from 828 stores in 1998 to 1,592 in 2004. The majority of sales are derived from the fashion and leather goods division, with Europe (including France) being the biggest regional contributor. The company is the largest and most widely spread luxury goods company, with a strong brand portfolio and distribution skills. LVMH's 'star brands' are a key foundation of the group's strategy and, over time, the company has built one of the strongest brand portfolios in the sector, with 60 top brands among its five divisions and other operations. At the core of the fashion and leather business is the Louis Vuitton brand itself. This 'star of star brands' is estimated to generate more than 80 per cent of earnings in the segment.

This case appears after the readings for this chapter.

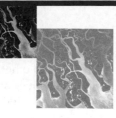

READING 17
Leadership in the 21st century*

Kathleen E. Allen, Juana Bordas, Gill Robinson Hickman, Larraine R. Matusak, Georgia J. Sorenson and Kathryn J. Whitmire

For years scholars have been trying to define or describe the nature of leadership. Today, driving forces exist that suggest that the purpose of leadership in the 21st century, rather than the definition, must be the focal point of our leadership studies.

Therefore, recognizing the context of these changing times. we propose that the *purpose of leadership* in the 21st century is

- To create a supportive environment where people can thrive, grow, and live in peace with one another;
- To promote harmony with nature and thereby provide sustainability for future generations; and
- To create communities of reciprocal care and shared responsibility – one where every person matters and each person's welfare and dignity is respected and supported.

Upon reflection it is easy to recognize that this approach to leadership will be confronted with many challenges. Among these challenges are some prominent trends that appear to be shaping thought and action for the future. A few of these challenges can be presented as dynamic trends. These are

1 Globalization;
2 Increasing stress on the environment;
3 Increasing speed and dissemination of information technology; and
4 Scientific and social change.

Our human consciousness and capacities mutually shape these trends. They illustrate the point that leadership in the future will need to be anchored in a purposeful set of assumptions that are intended to advance human capacity and consciousness. The following narrative is intended to provide a framework for understanding the implications for leadership; it is obviously not all-inclusive.

Source: reprinted with permission of the authors.

*In Hickman G. R. (ed.) (1998) *Leading Organizations – Perspectives of a New Era*. Sage Publications.

Prominent trends

Globalization. There is an increasing global consciousness in all sectors and societies of the world. This shift in thought and action has affected all sectors of society. Instead of focusing merely on the United States, the marketing of U.S. consumer goods, manufacturing, and even entertainment has drastically expanded to worldwide status.

This globalization of manufacturing, marketing, and competition has created multinational organizations designed to compete in the broader economic playing field. The economy itself has become global. The economic challenges of Mexico, Great Britain, or any country affect the global economy. The stock markets are interdependent.

Increasing stress on the environment. Issues related to the environment and its ability to support the world's populations in the future are becoming increasingly challenging. While the United States may lead the world in pollution control, environmental problems do not stay within the boundaries of any one nation. Struggles between economic interests and environmental interests continue all over the world. We see this exhibited in the debate over the use of old growth forests, wetland preservation, fishing rights, and legislation on chemicals that effect the atmosphere. Concerns about our fresh-water table will probably increase as industrial runoff and other such violations challenge us. Landfills continue to be overloaded with waste, triggering increased pressure for recycling. Toxic waste, land development, and complex environmental phenomena all contribute to issues of health education and human and animal welfare.

Increasing speed and dissemination of information technology. Mass communication has connected the world in ways that were unheard of fifty years ago. While the Pentium chip may be the latest addition to computers this year, just around the comer is the advent of nano-technology. Nano-technology will allow the application of techniques in every discipline from microbiology to political science that will drastically decrease the size of equipment and increase the capacity of processing and disseminating information. Today, electronic bits of information are transferred almost instantaneously. Information is rapidly disseminated throughout the world via the Internet, CNN, and major news networks. The result is that we know what has happened halfway around the world almost instantaneously. It is nearly impossible to keep information private.

Information technology is made up of 'bits,' and 'bits' do not behave like consumer goods. Consumer goods can be stopped at country borders and their worth can be declared. 'Bits' travel electronically across borders with little possibility of control. This may explain why we now have permeable boundaries among our organizations, communities, and individuals. For example, when the Chinese students were protesting in Tiananmen Square, they were also communicating by fax and other media to the rest of the world. The immediate information was very difficult, if not impossible, for the Chinese government to control. There are numerous similar examples.

Scientific and social change. The recent announcement of the cloning of a sheep heralds the shape of things to come from genetic engineering. Genetic engineering is just one of the scientific changes that will reshape our lives. Biomedical technology will not just continue to reveal the secrets of the gene code, but it will radically change the way we cure diseases and produce and grow our food. Social change will require new political, social, educational, and organizational structures. The perceptions of gender roles will also be reshaped and communicated widely. All of these changes will mingle with one another with little time delay.

These four trends are mutually shaped by, and interact with, the ethical and spiritual dimension of human beings. The challenge and questions for leadership then become, Can humans develop the self-discipline to choose how they currently interact with each other and the environment? Can we develop the ability to live in peace with each other? Can we learn to live in harmony with nature? Can we increase the speed at which we learn about complex, dynamic challenges and problems? Will the human race develop and support the required diversity to match and surpass the complexity of the dynamic system of the future? How far does our current consciousness extend? What is the effect of our current human capacity on the challenges of today and of the future?

While any one of these four dynamic trends would be more than enough to deal with, they cannot be treated as separate issues. They are highly interdependent and because of this it is difficult to discuss them as discrete identities. As they interact, they create an interesting set of implications that will have a powerful effect on how we practice leadership in the future.

Implications for leadership

1 *Increasing diversity in our daily lives.* Globalization has not only affected our traveling, markets, and perspective, it has also stimulated immigration and along with it population growth. This phenomenon creates a significant increase in diversity in our communities and in the workforce. Increased diversity in our lives will continue to challenge the assumptions many organizations have used to shape standards of practice. Leadership practices that recognize diversity as a positive asset of organizations and communities will need to be employed. New systems thinking will be required to design processes that increase inclusiveness and diversity in decision making.

2 *Increasing change.* The magnitude and speed of change will continue (Conner, 1992, *Managing at the Speed of Change*). The discomfort of having a decreasing amount of time to respond to change will be experienced. The complexity of change events will increase. Because the total system will be more interconnected, the number of facets that need to be considered will also increase. This will require leadership to design, support, and nurture flexible, durable organizations and groups. It will also require a systemic understanding in order to respond positively to the change events.

3 *Complexity.* As stated above our world is composed of a wide variety of infrastructures that are becoming increasingly complex and interwoven. Each one of the dynamic trends mentioned above is a complex system in and of itself. However, they all interact with one another creating a large, dynamic nonlinear system with smaller nonlinear dynamic systems nested within them. In these systems, sequential cause and effect are much more difficult to track and predict. Leadership will need to pace and intuit the changing complexity of the system. Complexity challenges every individual's capacity to fully understand or intuit the many interrelated systems. For this reason, complexity requires shared leadership and multiple perspectives.

4 *Interdependence.* This complex, changing system is also interdependent. Interdependence shapes complexity and complexity shapes interdependence. The dynamic trends of ecological stress, information technology, globalization, and scientific and social change all demonstrate the impact of interdependence and demand a total systems approach. The challenge and implication for leadership will be to initiate and practice a systems perspective.

5 *Increasing tensions around value differences.* There will be more tensions between individual rights and the common good of the larger community. We will be faced with the ethical ramifications of our organizations decisions as they influence not just the individual organization or corporation but also the community and the world. This will require that leadership be practiced with a significant ethical dimension that focuses on sustainable principles.

6 *Increasing gap between the rich and poor.* There will be continuing tension between the rich and the poor. This will affect both individuals and nations. This tension will include both economics and natural resources. This widening gap will require a leadership that recognizes justice and equity issues as well as economic and ecological concerns.

7 *Increasing requirement for continuous learning.* As stated repeatedly, these dynamic trends are continuously changing and interacting. The implication for leadership is the responsibility to encourage the speed at which individuals learn and to provide opportunities for these individuals to grow in understanding how this learning can be brought into the changing relationship with the community or organization.

Recognizing the trends that have been articulated here as powerful forces that demand a new form of leadership, and focusing on the purpose rather than the definition of leadership, leads us to assert that a shared, collaborative form of leadership will be the most successful approach in the next century.

Shared/collaborative leadership

This new leadership paradigm has been called by a number of different names: shared, participatory, collective, collaborative, cooperative, democratic, fluid, inclusive, roving, distributed, relational, and post-heroic. While consensus on the name of this 'new leadership' has not been reached, there is a growing understanding that the patterns of hierarchical leadership that served us in the past are not well suited to the global complexity, rapid change, interdependency, and multifaceted challenges described above.

In the information age, the primary challenge will be to encourage the new, better-educated work force to be committed, self-managing, and lifelong learners. This 'people focused' leadership has its roots in democratic traditions. It is founded on the belief that in the complex future 'answers are to be found in community' (Wheatley) in group-centered organizations where 'everyone can learn continually' (Senge). Followers are being transformed into partners, coleaders, lifelong learners, and collaborators.

As the demand for this new leadership grows, the command and control leaders at the top of the pyramid are being challenged to change. They are expected to become leaders who are facilitators, stewards, coaches, designers, and teachers (Senge). They are being challenged to become leaders who 'walk their talk' and model the way, inspiring others, delegating and serving. Effective leaders are recognizing that every person has leadership qualities that can and must be recognized and used.

The new leadership paradigm, therefore, is restructuring our conceptual framework of what the practice of leadership is and our understanding of what effective leaders do. It is transforming the role of 'followers' and revolutionizing the design of organizations for the 21st century.

A recent brochure from the Robert Greenleaf Center on Servant-Leadership captures this spirit: 'The old organizational pyramids of the nineteenth century are crumbling, being replace by up side down pyramids and circles and connections.'

The term collaborative and reciprocal leadership is used here to describe the process that is at the heart of this change. Since collaborative leadership is more adaptable and fluid, focusing on relationships and the needs of people, so too, our intention is not to fixate on a definition or a set concept that describes the 'new leadership.' What is more important is to assist people to acquire the understanding and skills of the purpose of the new leadership and to describe for them how collaborative leadership principles can work for them in the context in which they choose to lead.

Evolution or progress requires the integration of past, present, and future. In the midst of unceasing change in an interdependent world, this recognition provides the solid ground from which to move into the uncertainty of tomorrow with an assurance that collaborative structures have served people well in the past and can show the way to collectively shape the future.

Principles of collaborative/reciprocal leadership

A basic premise of collaborative leadership is recognition that no one person has the solutions to the multifaceted problems that a group or organization must address. Leadership in this context requires a set of principles that empower all members to act, and employ a process that allows the collective wisdom to surface. These principles must be based on an understanding that people have the knowledge and creativity to respond to the problems they face. They encourage the development of organizations that support collective action based on shared vision, ownership, and mutual values.

The evolution of collaborative leadership has been deeply influenced by the natural sciences as well as history. The Newtonian concept of a mechanistic world where people followed directions and where repetitive, learned responses were sufficient has given way to an organic, systems-oriented, and dynamic understanding of how people, groups, and organizations operate. This systems perspective requires nonlinear, holistic and multifaceted approaches to leadership that stress interactive participation, open communication, continuous learning, and attention to relationships.

The function of leadership then becomes the creation of systems, structures, and environment where this interaction and learning can occur. As Wheatley has stated, 'Leadership is making sure you have the right patterns in place.' Senge refers to this as fashioning an environment 'where everyone takes on the responsibility for learning.'

While change and adaptability are key aspects of a systems approach, there are core principles that nurture the interaction and learning that are essential to collaborative leadership. Following are seven of these principles:

1 *Promoting a collective leadership process.* 'Post-heroic' leadership moves away from the theory that the 'great man' has the answers to a shared, distributed, and fluid concept of leadership. This is based on the belief that depending on the need, situation, and requirements, different people assume the leadership role and that everyone has leadership potential. Collaborative leaders create supportive and open environments that encourage initiation, facilitate the sharing of information, and value each person's contribution. At the same time, individuals are encouraged to learn and stretch their leadership potential. Leadership, therefore, is assisting people to grow and learn.

   In Scott Peck's work on building community, for example, the 'leader' is a facilitator whose role is to create and hold the 'safe space' where people can discover themselves and learn to relate to one another authentically. The focus is shifted from the individual leader to the group, community, or organization. In fact, at times, the nominal leader may not even be visible.

2 *Structuring a learning environment.* An organization or group that is learner focused supports continuous self-development and reflection. Practices such as listening, promoting open-mindedness, seeking constructive feedback, sharing ideas, and viewing conflict as an opportunity for growth are embedded in the culture. People closest to the problem or opportunity are encouraged to interact and find solutions or innovative approaches. To do this, Senge believes the group must function 'in a mode of inquiry, knowing that nobody knows and everybody can learn continually.'

   As the group or organization practices learning together, open communication, mutual trust, shared meaning, and a sense of collective ownership emerge. Senge refers to this as 'communities of commitment where people are continually learning how to learn together.' Thus, people can venture out of their comfort zones and take the risks inherent in managing change.

3 *Supporting relationships and interconnectedness.* In collaborative leadership, the relationships and interconnectedness of people become a primary dynamic. Values such as respect, honesty, expecting the best from others, and the ability to exercise personal choice lay the foundation for covenant relationships to emerge. These relationships are based on trust and mutual responsibility. Collaborative leadership focuses attention on building the individual's and group's capacity to live these values, to benefit from their interdependence, and to recognize that conflict and differences can foster growth and creativity.

   Relationships are also strengthened through the development of a shared vision that allows people to set common directions, have mutual goals, and rise above self-interest. Shared vision and values function as a governing force where people can organize and manage themselves thereby getting the job done without the need for control or rigid policies and procedures.

4 *Fostering shared power.* For leadership to be collaborative or shared, power and ownership must be distributed throughout the organization. Shared power implies

that everyone has responsibility for leading, decision making, and learning. Groups and teams are often used to make decisions sometimes with a consensus format. Accountability and responsibility are based on individual integrity and peer agreements.

As people collaborate around common goals, partnerships and coalitions evolve resulting in lateral networks of mutual influence (Rost and Nirenberg). Kil Janow in *The Inventive Organization* describes this process as multiple relationships acting in a flexible, flattened structure based on partnerships, self-regulation, and interdependence.

In *Re-Inventing the Corporation,* Naisbitt and Aburdene refer to this as a lattice or grid where power is found in the center not at the top. Hierarchical structures are thus replaced by criss-crossing networks, overlapping, changing, and fluid boundaries. This web-like structure supports optimum participation, interaction, and empowerment.

5 *Practicing stewardship and service.* Stewardship is the cornerstone of reciprocal or shared leadership because it turns hierarchical leadership upside down. Stewardship focuses on ensuring that other people's needs are being served and not on exercising privilege, power, and control. According to Block, stewardship chooses partnership over patriarchy or hierarchy; empowerment over dependency; and service over self-interest. Thus, the leader is 'in service, rather than in control.'

In his landmark work, *The Servant as Leader,* Robert Greenleaf describes this commitment as 'wanting to serve first. Then conscious choice brings one to aspire to lead.' The litmus test of collaborative leadership is based on whether people's needs are being served. As people feel respected and valued as partners they can create a community of shared responsibility.

6 *Valuing diversity and inclusiveness.* For people to respect each other, build trust, and communicate openly, they must learn to accept and value individual differences. Valuing diversity is the rich soil that nurtures relationships, partnerships, and collaborative networks. This is reflected in the Scott Peck statement, 'Perhaps the most necessary key to the achievement of community is the appreciation of differences.'

Respecting each person's perspective and personal style frees them to contribute their ideas and talents so that people can learn together. Furthermore, this inclusiveness is a key aspect of transforming followers into stakeholders and nurturing collective ownership. It is an understanding that creativity and excellence are enhanced through diversity. Fostering authentic diversity can be accomplished by respecting different perspectives, fostering open-mindedness, practicing dialogue, and listening with attention and empathy.

7 *Committing to self-development.* The movement to collaborative or shared leadership is at its heart a personal transformation that is fueled by 'a commitment to work on yourself first.' Greenleaf believed that the motivation to serve was based on the desire for one's 'own healing.'

The understanding that one's inner life reflects positively or negatively on one's leadership can serve to bring authenticity and humility to the leadership process. By working on personal learning and growth, leaders model the way for others to focus on their own personal mastery and proficiency.

This authenticity and the ability to actually 'live' the principles of collaborative leadership is reflected in Wheatley's statement, 'We must be what we want to become, we must in every step of the way, embody the future toward which we are aiming.' This resonates with the words of Mahatma Gandhi, who recognized that personal transformation was the heartbeat of leadership: 'We must be the change we wish to see in the world.' With the proper understanding, education, and training, every individual can begin to use the leadership gifts that they possess.

So, if these are the principles of collaborative leadership, then what are the practices or functions that collaborative leaders must practice? Based upon the premises we have stated in this document, namely,

- that as we approach the 21st century we must focus on the purpose rather than the definition of leadership,
- that the new leadership paradigm is collective and reciprocal, and
- that there are powerful trends moving us in this direction

we make the following recommendations for leadership practices for the 21st century.

Collective leadership practices in the 21st century

Practices are activities, customs, and ways of operating used by an individual, group, organization, or community. We view practices as an integral component of organic or natural living systems and the means by which collective leadership is exercised. Embedded and articulated in the statement of purpose and leadership practices are our values and beliefs. We think that successful leadership will model the following collective leadership in the 21st century.

Purpose of leadership in the 21st century

To create a supportive environment where people can thrive and grow and live in peace with one another.

Collective leadership practices

1 *Develop structures and processes to support collective leadership by*

- holding shared vision and core values in trust and operationalizing them;
- generating and supporting interdependent and interdisciplinary group processes;
- establishing and sustaining inclusiveness of stakeholders;
- creating and maintaining a free flow of information;
- facilitating fluidity and flexibility in group processes and structures;
- sharing and distributing power and authority among all group members;
- building a system of peer responsibility and accountability;
- demonstrating equity; and
- cultivating ritual and celebration.

2 *Foster human growth and development through*

- engaging in continuous self-development and reflection;
- enhancing and using intuition;
- strengthening and sustaining spirituality:
- coaching and nurturing the development of others;
- creating opportunities for people to experience success (efficacy);
- promoting group and community capacity building and progress;
- expecting the best from people; and
- celebrating individual and group success.

3 *Facilitate learning by*

- creating learning communities;
- including diverse individuals and perspectives;
- fostering and demonstrating open-mindedness;
- developing meaning and insight through individual and collective reflection;
- seeking feedback and critique to enhance development;
- developing creative and intuitive abilities;
- sharing ideas through engaging in dialogue;
- practicing deep listening;
- using creative tension to foster change and new ideas; and
- acknowledging and using 'mistakes' as opportunities to learn, reflect, and forgive.

To promote harmony with nature and thereby provide sustainability for future generations.

4 *Enhance the quality of life and preservation of nature by*

- understanding the interdependent relationship between human and natural systems and working to enhance their viability;
- practicing 'enoughness' (bigger or more is not always better);
- achieving balance in emotional, spiritual, and physical aspects of life;
- using a long-term perspective thereby creating viability for current and future generations;
- generating and supporting systems thinking (wholistic thinking) as a basis for action;
- facilitating self-organizing, self-regulating, and self-renewing systems;
- using natural conflict to foster growth and change;
- recognizing and promoting the spiritual connectedness of all life; and
- generating and sustaining peace among ourselves and aiding peace efforts globally.

To create a community of reciprocal care and shared responsibility – one where every person matters and each person's welfare and dignity is the concern of us all.

5 *Create caring communities of leaders and participants through*

■ developing trusting relationships;

■ attending to the well-being (basic needs and human rights) of others and providing opportunities for them to sustain themselves;

■ supporting basic freedom for others and providing opportunities for them to maintain freedom for themselves; and

■ maintaining opportunities for people to make choices for themselves that are not harmful to others, and honoring the choices they make.

6 *Demonstrate courage by*

■ taking risks;

■ tackling the difficult issues;

■ serving others;

■ challenging others when they depart from core values held in trust; and

■ initiating change, transforming self, groups, and institutions,

7 *Model integrity and authenticity by*

■ showing mutual respect;

■ carrying out responsibilities;

■ being accountable for one's actions;

■ modeling integrity and authenticity (walk the talk);

■ being honest with self and others;

■ demonstrating equity; and

■ practicing inclusiveness.

Transition from positional to collective leadership

Creating an environment where collective leadership is practiced starts with a *shared vision* supported by a set of specific values or beliefs which are integrated into the person's behavior (Wheatley & Kellner-Rogers, 1996). Some 'inner work' is required for a person who wants to practice this form of leadership. Without this inner work, the practice of authentic collective or shared leadership does not occur. This inner work starts with values and beliefs. People who practice shared leadership believe that all people have the capacity to lead themselves. Further, they believe that the gifts and resources needed to accomplish a task can be found in the members of the group, not in a single leader. Therefore, the goal of positional leaders is not to direct or tell but to provide a structure that allows people to lead themselves.

This means that positional leaders distribute or *share the 'power'* of their position. In this way, they enable groups to assume the responsibility and discover their own capacity to work together, decide, plan, and act. They are willing and able to share the power of their position to the maximum degree possible under the given circumstances. Their personal power remains evident, but they share their positional power. They may substitute or transmute the need for positional power into the joy of seeing the group evolve as a learning organization or community.

Another major element, after weaving the shared vision, is *modeling*. There is integrity in their vision of shared leadership that is reflected in the way they structure and respond to the development of the group. This integration of practice, vision, and modeling gives group members confidence that leaders 'walk their talk' as reflected in their belief in each individual and their collective action.

Collective/Reciprocal leaders spend time *structuring the environment* as a learning environment. This may include establishing the expectation of success. Then, the group is encouraged to take risks and challenge the way things have always been done. Group members are even encouraged to challenge their own beliefs about what they can or cannot accomplish without specific direction from a positional authority.

Risk taking is supported by the creation of a safety net. The safety net creates an environment where group members believe that it is safe to challenge and exercise personal choice in achieving the mutually stated goals. Peter Block once said that people trade sovereignty or freedom of choice for safety. A step in the critical passage to the new paradigm of shared leadership requires the members of the group to practice the freedom of choice that comes with being responsible and accountable to themselves and each other (Chaleff, 1995; Kelley, 1992).

Information is shared with all group members so that they have adequate knowledge and understanding about the task to make an enlightened decision (Wheatley & Kellner-Rogers, 1996). Positional leaders need not be the primary source of the information. In most cases, the members need to rely on each other and on their ability to gather accurate information rather than on a positional authority. This shift in the source of information triggers greater self-sufficiency and greater interdependence. By receiving power, choice, and information, members begin to believe that they can influence the situation and the outcome. This belief is reinforced by the subsequent accumulation of actual successes.

The interdependent structures and relationships help to ensure an understanding of the distribution of different talents among group members. This facilitates the acceptance by the group of different points of readiness to practice this combination of individual responsibility and shared leadership and accountability. It also helps members discover that they can both learn with, and depend upon, each other.

These interdependent structures support group members as they work together to successfully accomplish the specified task. As groups learn this new behavior, they need the assurance that the ambiguity or the anxiety they may be experiencing due to this different way of operating is normal and that their feelings are a part of group transformation. A group often experiences ambiguity, frustration, disorientation, fear, insecurity, and a frantic desire for the positional leaders to rescue them. All this shifts the role of leaders to that of facilitators, supporters, consultants, and sometimes teachers. For group members, the result of this experience is excitement, ownership of the process and product, confidence and competence, and better ideas and learning.

All these practices, and perhaps others of which we are not aware, are needed to meet the challenges of the future as we practice collaborative leadership.

References

Block, P. (1993). *Stewardship: Choosing Service Over Self-Interest*. San Francisco: Berrett-Koehler.

Chaleff, I. (1995). *The courageous follower: Standing up to and for our leaders*. San Francisco: Berrett-Koehler.

Conner, D. (1995). *Managing at the speed of change: How resilient managers succeed and prosper where others fail*. New York: Villard.

Goldstein, J. (1993). Revisioning the Organization: Chaos, Quantum Physicals and OD – An Interview With Margaret Wheatley. *Organizational Development Journal*, 2(2).

Greenleaf, R. K. (1991). *The Servant as Leader*. Indianapolis: The Robert K. Greenleaf Center.

Janov, J. (1994). *The Inventive Organization: Hope and Daring at Work*. San Francisco: Jossey-Bass.

Kelley, R. E. (1992). *The power of followership: How to create leaders people want to follow, and followers who lead themselves*. New York: Doubleday/Currency.

Naisbitt, J. & Aburdene, P. (1986). *Re-Inventing the Corporation*. New York: Warner Books.

Palmer, P. (1994). 'Leading From Within: Out of the Shadows and Into the Light.' In J. Conger (Ed.), *Spirit at Work*. San Francisco: Jossey, Bass.

Peck, M. S. (1987). *The Different Drum: Community Making and Peace*. New York: Simon & Schuster.

Rost, J. C. (1994). 'Leadership Development in the New Millennium.' *The Journal of Leadership Studies*, 1(1), 91–110.

Senge, P. M. (1990). *The Fifth Discipline: The Art and Practice of a Learning Organization*. New York: Doubleday.

Wheatley, M. J. (1992). *Leadership and the New Science: Learning About Organizations From an Orderly Universe*. San Francisco: Berrett-Koehler.

Wheatley, M. J. & Kellner-Rogers, M. (1996). *A simpler way*. San Francisco: Berrett-Koehler.

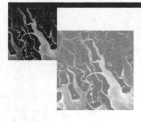

READING 18
Achieving and maintaining strategic competitiveness in the 21st century: the role of strategic leadership*

R. Duane Ireland and Michael A. Hitt

Competition in the 21st century's global economy will be complex, challenging, and filled with competitive opportunities and threats. Effective strategic leadership practices can help firms enhance performance while competing in turbulent and unpredictable environments. The purpose of this paper is to describe six components of effective strategic leadership. When the activities called for by these components are completed successfully, the firm's strategic leadership practices can become a source of competitive advantage. In turn, use of this advantage can contribute significantly to achieving strategic competitiveness and earning above-average returns in the next century.

> It is possible – and fruitful – to identify major events that have already happened, irrevocably, and that will have predictable effects in the next decade or two. It is possible, in other words, to identify and prepare for the future that has already happened.
>
> Peter Drucker, 1997.

Grounded in the insights and understanding that experience provides, conventional wisdom holds that it is very difficult to predict the future with high degrees of accuracy. In fact, Peter Drucker goes so far as to suggest that 'In human affairs – political, social, economic, or business – it is pointless to try to predict the future, let alone attempt to look ahead 75 years.'[1] Notwithstanding this difficulty, the capability implied by Drucker's comment above is encouraging. It is both possible and productive for firms to identify and prepare for a future that has already happened. Thus, although it is difficult for organizations to predict their future accurately, examining events that have already taken place allows them to know how to prepare for a future whose state has been influenced.

Based on this approach, we present a description of the strategic leadership practices that will contribute to corporate success during the 21st century. More precisely, our

*Academy of Management Executive, 1999, Vol. 13, No. 1.

position is that the global economy is a major irrevocable event whose existence has already had a major influence on today's strategic leadership practices and offers insights about practices that should be used in the future. By examining appropriate and often innovative strategic leadership practices currently being used successfully by visionary organizations, it is possible to identify and understand practices that will be effective in the next century. This analysis is important, because strategic leadership may prove to be one of the most critical issues facing organizations. Without effective strategic leadership, the probability that a firm can achieve superior or even satisfactory performance when confronting the challenges of the global economy will be greatly reduced.[2]

Strategic leadership is defined as a person's ability to anticipate, envision, maintain flexibility, think strategically, and work with others to initiate changes that will create a viable future for the organization.[3] When strategic leadership processes are difficult for competitors to understand and, hence, to imitate, the firm has created a competitive advantage.[4] Because the creation of sustainable competitive advantage is the universal objective of all companies,[5] being able to exercise strategic leadership in a competitively superior manner facilitates the firm's efforts to earn superior returns on its investments.

The global economy

There is virtually uniform agreement that the complexity, turbulence, and extraordinary changes during the 1980s and 1990s are contributing to the rapid development of an ultracompetitive global economy. Joseph Gorman, TRW's CEO, suggests that a transformational change is occurring, from regional economies and industries to global ones.[6] A key reality of our time, the commercial interactions that are taking place in the global economy are becoming the dominant force shaping relationships among nations. The fact that '… the proportion of trade among nations as a share of global income has increased from 7 percent to 21 percent since the end of World War II demonstrates why the globalization of commercial markets has an important effect on individual countries.'[7] Thus, in the global economy, products are shipped anywhere in the world in a matter of days; communications are instant; and new product introductions and their life cycles have never been shorter, with six months the norm in some high-tech industries.[8]

The incredible breadth and depth of the global economy's effects are shown by the suggestion that in the 21st century, nation-states will lose their sovereignty, technology may replace labor, and corporations may come to resemble amoebas – collections of workers that are subdivided into dynamic, ever-changing teams to competitively exploit the firm's unique resources, capabilities, and core competencies. Thus, some analysts argue with conviction that the large number of structural changes occurring simultaneously in the international system are resulting in economies and communication systems that are more integrated. For example, it has been predicted that by 2150, all or most of the global economy will be part of a '… single market, perhaps complete with a single currency and monetary authority.'[9] However, others believe that the political structures supporting various economies and their communication systems will remain somewhat fragmented and may even be reduced to ethnic units during the 21st century.[10] Changes such as these may culminate in corporations that would be unrecognizable to many employees and world citizens today.[11] The global economy may create a need for individual citizens to maintain separate loyalties – one to their own unique traditions and institutions, the other to the characteristics of a rapidly evolving international culture.

The new competitive landscape

The global economy has created a new competitive landscape – one in which events change constantly and unpredictably.[12] For the most part, these changes are revolutionary, not evolutionary in nature. Revolutionary changes happen swiftly, are constant, even relentless in their frequency, and affect virtually all parts of an organization simultaneously.[13] The uncertainty, ambiguity, and discontinuity resulting from revolutionary changes challenge firms and their strategic leadership to increase the speed of the decision-making processes through which strategies are formulated and implemented.[14] In the global economy, knowledge work and knowledge workers are the primary sources of economic growth – for individual firms and for nations. Thus, in the 21st century, the ability to build, share and leverage knowledge will replace the ownership and/or control of assets as a primary source of competitive advantage.[15]

However, certain conditions of the new competitive landscape, including the expectation that the world's economy will grow substantially during the first 20 years of the next century, also create opportunities for companies to improve their financial performance.[16] Organizations in which strategic leaders adopt a new competitive mindset – one in which mental agility, firm flexibility, speed, innovation, and globalized strategic thinking are valued highly – will be able to identify and competitively exploit opportunities that emerge in the new competitive landscape. These opportunities surface primarily because of the disequilibrium that is created by continuous changes (especially technological changes) in the states of knowledge that are a part of a competitive environment. More specifically, although uncertainty and disequilibrium often result in seemingly hostile and intensely rivalrous conditions, these conditions may simultaneously yield significant product-driven growth opportunities.[17] Through effective strategic leadership, an organization can be mobilized so that it can adapt its behaviors and exploit different growth opportunities.[18]

Strategic leadership

In the 1960s and early 1970s, situations facing the firm were thought to be the primary determinant of managerial behaviors and organizational outcomes. Compared with the influence of conditions in the firm's external environment, managers were believed to have little ability to make decisions that would affect the firm's performance.

The great leader view of strategic leadership

In 1972, John Child, a prominent organization theorist, argued persuasively that an organization's top-level managers had the discretion or latitude to make choices that would, indeed, affect their firm's outcomes.[19] In particular, because top managers have the responsibility for the overall performance of their firms, these individuals have the strongest effect on the firm's strategic management process. In Child's view, strategic leaders, armed with substantial decision-making responsibilities, had the ability to influence significantly the direction of the firm and how it was to be managed in that pursuit. Strategic leadership theory holds that companies are reflections of their top managers, and, in particular, of the chief executive officers, and that '... the specific knowledge, experience, values, and preferences of top managers are reflected not only in their decisions, but in their assessments of decision situations.'[20]

Substantial numbers of CEOs have adopted the notion that strategic leadership responsibilities are theirs alone. One of their primary tasks is to choose a vision for the firm and create the conditions to achieve that vision. Thus, as a result of the significant choice options available to the CEO as the firm's key strategic leader, this individual often worked as a Lone Ranger when shaping the firm. Isolated from those being led, the firm's key strategic leader commanded his/her organization primarily through use of top-down directives.[21] Particularly when these choices resulted in financial success for the company, the key strategic leader was recognized widely as the 'corporate Hercules.'[22]

Appropriate for its time, the theory of strategic leadership contributed to organizational success. But the environmental conditions in which this theory was used have changed dramatically because of the global economy. In the past few decades, environmental conditions were relatively stable and predictable compared with the current and predicted states of these conditions in the 21st century.

The relative stability and predictability of the past few decades resulted in manageable amounts of uncertainty and ambiguity. Change was often treated as linear in many industries; major competitors were largely domestic, not global companies; organizations were structured in hierarchical configurations that were supported by selection and promotion practices. However, conditions associated with the global economy's new competitive landscape – shorter product life cycles, ever-accelerating rates and types of change, the explosion of data and the need to convert it to useable information – prevent single individuals from having all of the insights necessary to chart a firm's direction. Moreover, some believe that having strategic leadership centered on a single person or a few people at the top of a hierarchical pyramid is increasingly counterproductive.[23] Constrained by their abilities to deal with rapidly increasing amounts of data and the general complexity of the global economy, top managers are now challenged to discharge their strategic leadership responsibilities differently.[24] Insightful top managers recognize that it is impossible for them to have all of the answers, are willing to learn along with others, and understand that the uncertainty created by the global economy affects people at the top as well as those lower down in the organization.[25]

The great groups view of strategic leadership

In the 21st century, the nature of the organization in which effective strategic leadership practices occur will be different. In the view of noted business thinker Charles Handy, a public corporation should and will be regarded not as a piece of property owned by the current holders of its shares, but as a community. More properly thought of as citizens than as employees, people involved with an organizational community remain together to pursue a common purpose. A community is something to which a person belongs and that belongs to no one individual. The community's citizens have both responsibilities to pursue the common good and rights to receive benefits earned through its attainment.

In an organizational community, strategic leadership is distributed among diverse individuals who share the responsibility to create a viable future for their firm. Handy argues that many citizens will need to serve their communities as leaders and will need to be dispersed throughout the firm.[26] When allowed to flourish as involved leaders, people spark greatness in each other. As Italian author Luciano De Crescenzo noted, 'We are all angels with only one wing, we can only fly while embracing each other.'[27]

Combinations or collaborations of organizational citizens functioning successfully have been labeled great groups. These collaborations usually feature managers with significant profit and loss responsibilities, internal networkers 'who move about the organization spreading and fostering commitment to new ideas and practices,' and community citizens with intellectual capital that stimulates the development and/or leveraging of knowledge.[28] Members of great groups rely on one another to create an environment in which innovations occur regularly and knowledge is generated and dispersed constantly. Consistent leadership between and among all of the firm's great groups results in innovative strategic thinking and rapid acceptance of organizational changes that, even when difficult, are required to enhance firm performance. Top managers who facilitate the development of great groups – groups in which strategic leadership takes place among a range or people with different talents – have shifted the locus of responsibility to form adaptive solutions to issues from themselves to the organization's full citizenry.[29]

As knowledge sharing and developing entities, great groups have several characteristics.[30] First, members of great groups have accepted their responsibility for firm outcomes. Involved and committed, these people understand the significance of their work and their responsibility to each other.[31] Second, great groups seek to learn from multiple parties, including contractors, suppliers, partners, and customers. Group members are committed to the position that 'No matter where knowledge comes from, the key to reaping a big return is (for the group) to leverage that knowledge by replicating it throughout the company so that each unit is not learning in isolation and reinventing the wheel again and again.'[32]

The third great group characteristic concerns information and knowledge. Increasingly, the information great groups gather to form knowledge and to understand how to use knowledge already possessed must come from events and conditions outside the organization. In Peter Drucker's view, it is primarily information from outside that allows a business to decide '... how to allocate its knowledge resources in order to produce the highest yield. Only with such information can a business also prepare for new changes and challenges arising from sudden shifts in the world economy and in the nature and content of knowledge. The development of rigorous methods for gathering and analyzing outside information will increasingly become a major challenge for businesses and for information experts.'[33] Great groups respond positively to Drucker's challenge and are learning how to interpret external information in competitively relevant terms. In the 21st century, it will be increasingly vital for the firm's strategic leadership processes to adopt this perspective regarding the acquisition and use of information flows.

Another characteristic of great groups is their maintenance of records of individuals' knowledge stocks. With these records, people can quickly find others who possess the knowledge required to solve problems as they arise. Maintaining and using these records demonstrates these groups' ability to work smarter through their collective insights and the skills resulting from them.[34] Finally, great groups understand that the firm's method of strategic leadership results in a constantly changing configuration of responsibilities. Across tasks, every member of a great group serves, at different times, as a leader, peer, or subordinate. The operationalization of this understanding results in mutual influence relationships among the firm's top managers and all organizational citizens, including those with formal managerial responsibilities.[35]

Perhaps the most important 'great group' in an organization is the top management team (TMT) formed by the CEO. The top management team is a relatively small group of executives, usually between three and ten people. These individuals are at the apex of the organization and provide strategic leadership.[36]

Because of the complexity of the new competitive landscape, both in its structure and dynamism, the collective intellect generated by a top management team is necessary for effective strategic leadership to occur in the firm. A philosopher's view demonstrates this point: 'None of us is as smart as all of us.'[37] The large number of organizational stakeholders alone makes it necessary to depend on a team of top executives for strategic leadership. The global economy, more than any other factor, has created the need for the top management team to effectively exercise strategic leadership in organizations. The knowledge needed to understand and operate in many global markets is substantial, thereby requiring a team effort. In fact, global firms such as Asea Brown Boveri (ABB) believe that it is necessary to have a culturally diverse TMT to successfully operate in such markets. This is particularly important because of the emphasis on gaining the external knowledge necessary to develop a collective vision for the organization and to gain the multiple constituencies' commitment to pursuit of the vision.

Because of multiple stakeholders with competing interests, there is need for a heterogeneous TMT, one with members having different knowledge sets and skills.[38] The CEO remains the top leader, but must use these different knowledge sets and skills to successfully manage the organization. Viewing the other members of the TMT as partners allows the CEO to do this effectively. Beyond this, top managers should treat all employees as partners, especially in flatter, matrix type organizations – an organizational form that will be used increasingly in 21st century firms. In such organizations, top managers manage across traditional boundaries (e.g., functions), building the horizontal organization in the process.[39]

Even though the operational details of effective strategic leadership are continuing to change as the global economy evolves, the CEO remains accountable for the entire firm's performance. The board of directors will hold the CEO accountable for guiding the firm in ways that best serve the interests of owners (e.g., shareholders) and other stakeholders. Tomorrow's organizations will still require a great leader to be successful. Great leaders are able to share responsibility for leading and managing business units, sharing information and ideas widely with others and seeking mutual influence among all who have accepted the responsibility to contribute to the formation and achievement of the firm's direction.

Six components of strategic leadership

What will be different in 21st century companies is how top mangers discharge their strategic leadership responsibilities. They will no longer view their leadership position as one with rank and title, but rather as a position of significant responsibility to a range of stakeholders. Instead of seeking to provide all the right answers, they will strive to ask the right questions of community citizens they have empowered to work as partners with them. They can choose to form a community of colleagues rather than a company of employees constrained by traditional hierarchical configurations.

The top managers must affect the behaviors of many stakeholders, especially those of organizational citizens, working often as a coach. The organizational community is one in which citizens' creative energy is released, and their self-confidence enhanced, when they are inspired to assume responsibility for leading themselves through the work of great groups.[40] Sharing among inspired and committed citizens facilitates the emergence of the collective magic that creates intellectual capital and knowledge. An effective strategic leader 'finds glory in the whole team reaching the summit together.'[41]

John Browne, CEO of British Petroleum Company, believes that the top manager must stimulate the organization rather than control it. The top manager provides strategic directives, encourages learning that results in the formation of intellectual capital, and verifies that mechanisms exist to transfer intellectual capital across all of the firm's parts. Browne believes that 'the role of leaders at all levels is to demonstrate to people that they are capable of achieving more than they think they can achieve and that they should never be satisfied with where they are now.'[42] Heinrch von Pierer, president and CEO of Siemens AG, says that 'As we move into what will be a century of unprecedented challenges, successful leaders will rely even more intensely on strengths that have become crucial in recent years – speed of decisions, flexibility, capable delegation, teamwork, the ability to build for the long term while meeting short-term needs – and vision. Increasingly, networked and globalized thinking will be essential for coping with the accelerating pace of change.'[43]

Based on the evidence discussed above, we believe that 21st century strategic leadership should be executed through interactions that are based on a sharing of insights, knowledge, and responsibilities for achieved outcomes. These interactions should occur between the firm's great leaders – the top managers – and its citizens. These interactions take place as the firm satisfies the requirements associated with six key effective strategic leadership practices. Although considered individually, it is through the configuration of all six activities that strategic leadership can be effective in the 21st century organization.

Determining the firm's purpose or vision

The task of determining the direction of the firm rests squarely on the CEO's shoulders. Joe Gorman, TRW's CEO, believes that the top manager, often working in concert with the TMT, must provide general guidelines as to where the firm intends to go and the key steps to be taken to reach that end.[44] J. Tracy O'Rourke, CEO of Varian Associates, Inc., endorses Gorman's view: 'Clearly, if you're going to do well over time, you have to have some ability – yourself or in combination with others – to come up with a vision ... and then follow it up with believable and implementable action plans. In most corporate structures, the only person who can do that is the CEO.'[45] A recent survey of 1,450 executives from 12 global corporations found that the ability to 'articulate a tangible vision, values, and strategy' for their firm was the most important of 21 competencies considered to be crucial skills for global leaders to possess in the future.[46]

Various definitions of purpose or vision have been offered. However, the one advanced recently by John Browne, British Petroleum's CEO, captures the attributes of an effective organizational purpose for 21st century firms. Browne argues that as a description of who the firm is and what makes it distinctive, purpose indicates what a company exists to achieve and what it is willing and not willing to do to achieve it. Browne also believes that a clear purpose '… allows a company to focus its learning efforts in order to increase its competitive advantage.'[47] Visions that facilitate development of this type of focus make sense to all organizational citizens, stretch citizens' imaginations but are still within the bounds of possibility, are understood easily, and create a cultural glue that allows units to share knowledge sets.[48]

Once the CEO and the TMT have set the general organizational purpose, all other citizens, including the TMT, will be empowered to design and execute strategies and courses of action to accomplish that end.[49] Empowered organizational citizens working individually or as members of great groups in pursuit of the firm's purpose will be able to provide valuable feedback to the CEO and the TMT. This feedback will help the top executives develop the type of insights required to revisit the purpose regularly to verify its authenticity.

Rockwell International's new vision is for the company to become 'the world's best diversified high-technology company.' The CEO and TMT believe that the actions necessary for this vision to be reached are the aggressive pursuit of global growth, the execution of leading-edge business practices, and the manufacture and distribution of products that will allow the firm's customers to be the most successful in the world in their business operations.

Critical to efforts to achieve the firm's vision is the active involvement of Rockwell employees (organizational citizens). At locations throughout the world, employees are to be challenged to take determined actions that will help the firm achieve its purpose. To select appropriate actions, employees/citizens are formed into 23 implementation teams (or great groups) that are asked to identify strengths and weaknesses. Each unit is to develop recommendations that when accomplished will allow it to become the best in the world at completing a particular task or set of activities.[50] This pattern – wherein organizational citizens work as members of a community that is seeking to serve the common good – will be linked with effective strategic leadership practices in the 21st century.

The blurring of industry boundaries stimulates the emergence of new and sometimes aggressive competitors with significant resource bases and creates interesting challenges for firms' strategic leadership processes.

The announced entrance in early 1998 of the Korean giant, Samsung Group, into the world's automobile manufacturing industry demonstrates this challenge. Although as of mid-1997 Samsung had never built and delivered to a customer a passenger car, it was in the midst of a $13 billion investment to manufacture 1.5 million cars annually. The vision driving these commitments and actions was for Samsung to rank among the world's top ten automakers by 2010. A demonstration of this vision is the billboard outside Samsung's new automobile manufacturing facility in Pusan: 'Our dream and Korea's future.'

Samsung Group's ambitious auto manufacturing goal surprised at least some industry analysts who noted that the global auto industry was awash in excess production capacity – a problem not expected to abate in the foreseeable future. One noted industry observer said 'the world is not waiting breathlessly for a Samsung car ... There's no logical opening in the marketplace where Samsung can step in and fill a vacuum. Its sales will have to come out of someone else's hide.[51] Evidence was also emerging in mid-1997 that at least some of South Korea's conglomerates were encountering difficult performance challenges because of too much diversification at too rapid a pace. Although Samsung's future competitive intentions could be affected by these general problems,[52] some believe it would be a serious mistake to underestimate Samsung's ability to make its vision a reality. In the words of Richard Pyo of Credit Suisse First Boston in Seoul, 'Many people say that Samsung's plans are crazy and too risky, but the Korean economy has developed on gambles.'[53]

As this example suggests, every automobile manufacturing company's strategic leadership is challenged to analyze carefully Samsung Group's ability to achieve its vision in the world's auto marketplace. To respond successfully to this challenge, both the top managers (strategic leaders) and organizational citizens (through their work in great groups) in companies competing against Samsung Group's auto unit should use significant amounts of external information to select appropriate competitive responses.

Exploiting and maintaining core competencies

Core competencies are the resources and capabilities that give a firm a competitive advantage over its rivals. The relatively unstable market conditions resulting from innovations, diversity of competitors, and the array of revolutionary technological changes occurring in the new competitive landscape have caused core competencies rather than served markets to become '... the basis upon which firms establish their long-term strategies.[54] In the 21st century, an ability to develop and exploit core competencies will be linked even more positively and significantly with the firm's success.

Only the combinations of a firm's resources and capabilities that are valuable, rare, costly to imitate, and for which there are no equivalent strategic substitutes can be rightly identified as core competencies.[55] Only when uniform agreement exists within the organizational community about which resources and capabilities are indeed core competencies can appropriate actions be designed to exploit them in the marketplace.[56] The large retailer Nordstrom Inc., for example, is thought to have core competencies in its customer service and ability to package merchandise in ways that provide unique value to customers. Dell Computer Corporation's distribution system is a key competitive advantage. Competencies in the general area of marketing and specific applications of special skills in advertising campaigns and its global brand name are recognized as core competencies for Philip Morris. In each of these cases, following agreement about their identification as core competencies, strategic leaders work tirelessly to apply the competencies in ways that will improve company performance.

The sharing of knowledge or intellectual capital that is unique to a particular organization will influence significantly the choices strategic leaders make when seeking to use core competencies in novel, yet competitive ways. Through the reciprocal sharing of knowledge and the learning that results from it are a firm's core competencies nurtured effectively.

Knowledge is shared and learning occurs through superior execution of the human tasks of sensing, judging, creating, and building relationships.[57] The importance of knowledge for firms seeking competitive advantage in the global economy is shown by the following comment about Owens Corning's positive financial performance. 'In the past year a series of moves in sales and marketing, information systems, and manufacturing and distribution have come together in a coherent strategy that is transforming this Midwestern maker of humdrum materials into a global competitor whose real business is knowledge.'[58] Indeed, with rare exceptions, in the 21st century, a firm's productivity will lie more in its collective intellect – that is, in its collective capacity to gain and use knowledge – rather than in its hard assets such as land, plant, and equipment.[59]

The competitive value of core competencies increases through their use and continuing development.[60] A firm's privately held knowledge is the foundation of its competitively valuable core competencies and is increasing in importance as a driver of strategic decisions and actions. The most effective strategic leadership practices in the 21st century will be ones through which strategic leaders find ways for knowledge to breed still more knowledge. While physical assets such as land, machinery, and capital may be relatively scarce on a global basis, ideas and knowledge 'are abundant, they build on each other, and they can be reproduced cheaply or at no cost at all. In other words, ideas don't obey the law of diminishing returns, where adding more labor, machinery or money eventually delivers less and less additional output.'[61]

Johnson & Johnson's CEO is a strategic leader who believes in developing and nurturing his firm's knowledge base. Asked to describe factors that account for his company's success, he suggested that his company is 'not in the product business. (It) is in the knowledge business.'[62] However, knowledge cannot breed knowledge and core competencies cannot be emphasized and exploited effectively in the global marketplace without appropriate human capital.

Developing human capital

Human capital is the knowledge and skills of a firm's entire workforce or citizenry. Strategic leaders are those who view organizational citizens as a critical resource on which many core competencies are built and through which competitive advantages are exploited successfully. In the global economy, significant investments will be required for the firm to derive full competitive benefit from its human capital. Some economists argue that these investments are 'essential to robust longterm growth in modern economies that depend on knowledge, skills, and information.'[63] Continual, systematic work on the productivity of knowledge and knowledge workers enhances the firm's ability to perform successfully. Citizens appreciate the opportunity to learn continuously and feel greater involvement with their community when encouraged to expand their knowledge base. Ongoing investments in organizational citizens result in a creative, well-educated workforce – the type of workforce capable of forming highly effective great groups.

The importance of educational investments in citizens is being supported in a growing number of corporations. Andersen Consulting, for example, allocates six percent of its annual revenue to education and requires each professional employee to complete a minimum of 130 hours of training annually. Intel Corp. spends $3,500 per year per person on education. General Motors Corp. and General Electric have appointed chief knowledge officers. Warren Bennis suggests that 'this institutionalization of education is not some fringe, feelgood benefit. It is tangible recognition that education gives the biggest bang for the corporate buck.' A recent study showed that companies that invest 10 percent more in education receive an 8.5 percent increase in productivity. In contrast, companies boosted their productivity by only three percent as a result of a 10 percent increase in capital expenditures.[64]

The global economy allows firms to earn a financial premium by using competitively superior practices in the location, selection, and subsequent development of human capital. One key reason is that skilled labor is expected to be in short supply during the first part of the 21st century. For example, a million new jobs in high technology will be created over the next decade with almost no increase in the supply of human resources to fill these jobs.[65]

A survey of human resource managers conducted by the American Management Association revealed that 47 percent of the respondents worked in firms that faced skilled labor shortages. Interestingly, 54.7 percent of the same group of respondents also believe that the shortages in skilled personnel will be worse in 2000 and beyond. As of mid-1997, at least 190,000 information technology jobs were vacant in U.S. companies. A 43 percent decline in the number of college graduates earning undergraduate degrees in computer science between 1988 and 1997 suggests more serious labor shortages ahead.[66]

Skilled labor shortages have unintended negative consequences. Talented, dedicated, and motivated employees often become frustrated and dissatisfied when asked to work continuously with those without equivalent skills and commitments. As a successful financial analyst explained: 'I could not fathom, let alone accept, the extreme variations in work ethic, attention to detail, and commitment to job and company. All my prior work and school experience had been with creative, energized self-starters. It took me months, if not years, to value the diverse work styles and varying motivators of the work force I encountered.'[67] Thus, a challenge for tomorrow's strategic leaders is to find ways to encourage each employee to fulfill her or his potential. Especially when faced with labor shortages, the organizational community's common good can be reached only when each member of the great group is committed to full participation.

Greater workforce diversity is another issue that will confront 21st century strategic leaders. Organizational communities will comprise individuals from multiple countries and cultures that may have unique and idiosyncratic value structures. CEOs and TMTs should learn to appreciate the beliefs, values, behaviors, and business practices of companies competing in a variety of regions and cultures. Organizational citizens can then better understand the realities and preferences that are a part of the region and culture in which they are working.

Peter Brabeck-Letmathe, CEO of Nestle SA, believes that it is increasingly important for top managers to speak at least two to three languages.[68] Cross-border and culture transfers among organizational citizens will be used prominently in the 21st century, as will experts who help people understand the nuances of other cultures. As at ABB today, many firms' TMTs will be culturally diverse. Success will depend on the ability of a firm's top managers to form a community of citizens rather than a band of employees working for a firm.

Sustaining an effective organizational culture

Organizational culture refers to the complex set of ideologies, symbols, and core values shared throughout the firm. Several business writers believe that the challenges to firms in the 21st century will be not so much technical or rational as cultural – 'how to lead the organizations that create and nurture knowledge; how to know when to set our machines aside and rely on instinct and judgment; how to live in a world in which companies have ever increasing visibility; and how to maintain, as individuals and organizations, our ability to learn.'[69]

Culture provides the context within which strategies are formulated and implemented. Organizational culture is concerned with decisions, actions, communication patterns, and communication networks. Formed over the life of a company, culture reflects what the firm has learned across time through its responses to the continuous challenges of survival and growth. Culture is rooted in history, held collectively, and is of sufficient complexity to resist many attempts at direct manipulation. Because it influences how the firm conducts its business, as well as the methods used to regulate and control the behavior of organizational citizens, culture can be a competitive advantage.

In the global economy, strategic leaders capable of learning how to shape a firm's culture in competitively relevant ways will become a valued source of competitive advantage. Chrysler's CEO Robert Eaton and President Robert Lutz are strategic leaders thought to be sources of competitive advantage for their firm. The secret to his company's recognition as 'Detroit's profitability champion,' Eaton suggested, is the 'Chrysler difference; a corporate culture that rejects Motown's hidebound bureaucratic traditions.' Some analysts support this suggestion, noting that 'no group of managers has stirred up Detroit more since Ford's fabled Whiz Kids of the 1950s.' In one writer's view, the firm's tone 'is set by Eaton, whose low-key demeanor belies a fierce competitive streak, and Lutz, the swashbuckling ex-Marine with a flair for product creation. But behind Eaton and Lutz, Chrysler boasts a little-known cast of managers who've become the envy of the industry.'[70] Integrating this culture with Daimler-Benz's may prove to be challenging. One the other hand, a successful integration of these cultures could result in a competitive advantage for the new firm.

The social energy that drives Southwest Airlines is largely a product of CEO Herb Kelleher and the managers who surround him. The firm's culture is responsible for the company's steady growth, above-average profitability, and the avoidance of employee layoffs for more than 25 years. Actions that exemplify Southwest's culture include: 'Pilots hold barbecues to thank mechanics; flight attendants sing safety instructions on board; agents hang mirrors on their computers to make sure they're smiling when taking reservations; Kelleher is generous with hugs and kisses.' Employees are committed to treating coworkers and customers with respect and dignity, having fun, and working hard. An indication of the culture's desirability is that 137,000 people applied in 1996 for only 5,000 Southwest Airlines' job openings.[71]

Effective cultures are ones in which organizational citizens understand that competitive advantages do not last forever and that the firm must move forward continuously. When citizens are comfortable with the reality of constant change and the need for a never-ending stream of innovations, patterns and practices are in place that can enhance global competitiveness.

Emphasizing ethical practices

Ethical practices serve as a moral filter through which potential courses of action are evaluated.[72] The influence of top managers on the firm's ethical practices and outcomes is accepted by business practitioners, academics, and society. In the 21st century, effective strategic leaders will use honesty, trust, and integrity as the foundations for their decisions. Strategic leaders displaying these qualities are capable of inspiring their employees and developing an organizational culture in which ethical practices are the behavioral norm. Acer CEO Stan Shih notes that for his employees there is simply no alternative to dealing honestly with all of the firm's stakeholders. Shih's belief that human nature is basically positive and good could be the force driving his forthright and ethical business practices.[73]

The challenge for strategic leaders is how to instill normative values that guide corporate action and individuals' behaviors.[74] In the final analysis, ethical decision-making processes result in the use of organizational resources to obtain benefits desired by legitimate stakeholders. A strategic leader's commitment to pursuits in which legal, ethical, and social concerns have been taken into account is thought to be both morally right and economically efficient.

Establishing ethical practices will be difficult for strategic leaders in the 21st century's global economy because of the significant diversity of the cultures and economic structures within which firms will compete. An understanding of the interests of all legitimate stakeholders will come only through analysis of and sensitivity to cultural diversity. A strategic leader's commitment to serve stakeholders' legitimate claims will contribute to the establishment and continuation of an ethical organizational culture. Employee practices that take place in such a culture become the set of accepted and expected commitments, decisions, and actions that should be taken when dealing with the firm's stakeholders.

Establishing balanced organizational controls

Organizational controls are the formal, information-based procedures that strategic leaders and managers use to frame, maintain, and alter patterns of organizational activities.[75] The new competitive landscape makes it difficult to establish such controls, which, by their nature, limit employees' behaviors. Controls influence and guide work in ways necessary to achieve performance objectives. The new competitive landscape is replete with opportunities that are addressed most effectively through innovation and creativity. Strategic leaders able to establish controls that facilitate flexible, innovative employee behaviors will earn a competitive premium for their firm.

Top managers are responsible for the development and effective use of two types of internal controls – strategic controls and financial controls.[76] Strategic controls require information-based exchanges among the CEO, top management team members, and organizational citizens. To exercise effective strategic control, top managers must acquire deep understandings of the competitive conditions and dynamics of each of the units or divisions for which they are responsible. Exchanges of information occur through both informal, unplanned meetings and interactions scheduled on a routine, formal basis. The effectiveness of strategic controls is increased substantially when strategic leaders are able to integrate disparate sets of information to yield competitively relevant insights. Because their emphasis is on actions rather than outcomes, strategic controls encourage lower-level managers to make decisions that incorporate moderate and acceptable levels of risk. Moreover, a focus on the content of strategic actions provides the flexibility managers and other great group members require to take advantage of competitive opportunities that develop rapidly in the new competitive landscape.

Financial controls entail objective criteria (e.g., various accounting-based measures) that strategic leaders use to evaluate returns earned by company units and those responsible for their performance. By focusing on performance-induced outcomes, financial controls encourage the accomplishment of short-term performance goals. An emphasis on financial rather than strategic controls makes managerial rewards contingent on achievement of financial outcomes. Therefore, an emphasis on short-term financial performance goals encourages risk-adverse managerial decisions and behaviors.

Effective top managers seek to develop and use a balanced set of strategic and financial controls. Typically, this outcome is achieved by using strategic controls to focus on positive long-term results while pursuing simultaneously the requirement to execute corporate actions in a financially prudent and appropriate manner. In this fashion, strategic leaders are able to use strategic controls to increase the probability that their firm will gain the benefits of carefully formulated strategies, but not at the expense of the type of financial performance that is critical to successful strategy implementation processes and to the firm's ability to satisfy selected stakeholders. Nonetheless, the diversity of the global economy, coupled with the dynamic challenges embedded within the new competitive landscape, highlight the increasing importance of strategic controls. Providing the leadership required for the firm to compete successfully in multiple countries and cultures demands strategic leadership practices that are oriented largely to the integration of disparate competitive information and the use of broad-based strategic controls.

Recommendations for effective strategic leadership practices

Competition in the 21st century's global economy will occur in postindustrial societies that differ dramatically from the industrial societies they are replacing.

Industrial societies and the commercial enterprises operating within them have been focused primarily on activities intended to create wealth. Technological and scientific advances were the principal means through which wealth was created in such sectors as medicine, agriculture, communications, energy, transportation, and electronics. In the postindustrial era, information-based technology and internationalization are the primary wealth-creation activities. In this era, '(1) much of the economic production occurs in service and high-technology sectors; (2) there is increasing globalization of finance, production, labor, and product markets, (3) economic growth is confronted with ecological limits, and (4) there is a movement toward democratization of markets and politics' in many of the world's countries.[77]

The attributes of the postindustrial era create more risk for firms that attempt to create wealth by competing in multiple marketplaces. Strategic leaders face challenges that may become pervasive as more market democratization processes occur throughout the world. These leaders are offered the following recommendations.

A growth orientation

The realities of competition in the global economy demand a corporate focus on growth rather than on downsizing and cost reductions. A variety of strategic approaches can be used in the pursuit of growth, including acquisition, innovation and product development, extreme decentralization, and concentration on product line extensions to provide customers with additional value. The means are less critical than the desired outcome. The most effective strategic leaders will be capable of working with all organizational citizens to find ways to match the firm's resources, capabilities, and core competencies with relevant growth-oriented opportunities.

Knowledge management

Strategic leaders must enable their organizations to develop, exploit, and protect the intellectual capital contained in their citizens' knowledge bases. They are challenged to develop pathways through which knowledge can be transferred to people and units where it can be further developed and used to pursue strategic competitiveness. Managing knowledge in this manner challenges conventional thinking and increases the likelihood that the firm will be able to create new competitive space in its markets. In the words of Warren Bennis, 'the key to competitive advantage in the 1990s and beyond will be the capacity of leadership to create the social architecture that generates intellectual capital. Success will belong to those who unfetter greatness within their organizations and find ways to keep it there.'[78]

Through voluntary arrangements such as strategic alliances, joint ventures, technology exchanges, and licensing agreements, firms pool their resources to create goods and services with economic value. They create knowledge that, in turn, facilitates the development of competitively valuable goods or services.[79] Strategic leaders who learn how to manage such collaborations will become a source of competitive advantage for their organizations. The most effective strategic leaders will develop the skills required to engage simultaneously in competitive and cooperative behaviors.[80] Companies that both effectively cooperate and compete with other enterprises will earn above-average financial returns. The creativity of great groups will be instrumental in isolating cooperative projects from those for which competitive behaviors are more appropriate.

Mobilization of human capital

Implied throughout is the need for companies to adapt to the significant changes in the global economy. To cope with changes in the world's societies, technologies, and markets, 21st century strategic leaders will be challenged to mobilize citizens in ways that increase their adaptive abilities. Leaders should refrain from providing answers; instead, their focus should be on asking challenging questions. They should request that citizens working as members of great groups consider relevant information to determine how the firm can use its knowledge base to achieve strategic competitiveness. Asking citizens to accept their roles as leaders and colleagues while working in great groups can be expected to mobilize their efforts around key strategic issues. Facilitating citizens' efforts to challenge the historical conduct of business in the firm also can galvanize them as they seek to accomplish relevant goals. The development and mobilization of human capital is vital if the firm is to achieve the strategic flexibility that is linked with success in the new competitive landscape.[81]

Developing an effective organizational culture

As the social energy that drives the firm, culture exerts a vital influence on performance. To facilitate the development of values oriented to growth and success, 21st century strategic leaders should commit to being open, honest, and forthright in their interactions with all stakeholders, including organizational citizens.

Such a commitment supported James Bonini's work as the manager of Chrysler Corp.'s big-van plant in Windsor, Ontario. At the young age of 33 and with limited manufacturing experience, Bonini needed the support of the plant's [84] managers, 1,800 workers, and officials of the local Canadian autoworkers' union. In a display of candor and honesty, Bonini acknowledged his youth and inexperience to those he was to lead and solicited help from everyone involved with the plant. He scheduled town hall meetings to hear workers' ideas and complaints, met with union officials, and made certain that each employee knew him. He made frequent visits to the plant floor to verify that work was proceeding as intended and to request workers' insights regarding improvements. Employees responded positively to Bonini's candor, honesty, and integrity.[82]

Remaining focused on the future

The significant differences between effective strategic leadership practices in the 20th and the 21st centuries are presented in Table 1. CEOs who apply practices associated with 21st century strategic leadership can create sources of competitive advantage for their organizations. The competitive advantages resulting from the work of CEOs as chief leaders and the contributions of great groups as members of organizational communities will allow firms to improve their global competitiveness.

Strategic leaders must use some of their time and energies to predict future competitive conditions and challenges. Companies in the United States, Europe, and Japan have intensified their competitive actions in the world's emerging markets. This emphasis is understandable, given that emerging markets constitute a new and important competitive frontier. However, high levels of risk are associated with these significant opportunities. Major reversals in the trend toward democratization of countries' markets and their accompanying political structures could have significant implications for strategic leaders and their firms.[83] Effective strategies leaders should

20th Century Practices	21st Century Practices
Outcome focused	Outcome and process focused
Stoic and confident	Confident, but without hubris
Sought to acquire knowledge	Seeks to acquire and leverage knowledge
Guided people's creativity	Seeks to release and nurture people's creativity
Work flows determined by hierarchy	Work flows influenced by relationships
Articulated the importance of integrity	Demonstrates the importance of integrity by actions
Demanded respect	Willing to earn respect
Tolerated diversity	Seeks diversity
Reacted to environmental change	Acts to anticipate environmental change
Served as the great leader	Serves as the leader and as a great group member
Views employees as a resource	Views organizational citizens as a critical resource
Operated primarily through a domestic mindset	Operates primarily through a global mindset
Invested in employees' development	Invests significantly in citizens' continuous development

Table 9.1 Strategic leadership practices

seek information that will allow them to predict accurately changes in various global markets. Strategic collaborations, with host governments and other companies, are a valuable means of dealing with changing conditions in emerging economic structures. By aligning their strategies with an emerging country's best interests, firms increase their chance of competitive success in volatile situations. Failure to develop these understandings will inhibit strategic leaders' efforts to lead their firms effectively in the 21st century.

Notes

[1] Five business thinkers, Peter F. Drucker, Esther Dyson, Charles Handy, Paul Saffo, and Peter M. Senge were asked recently by *Harvard Business Review* to describe the challenges they see already taking shape for executives as they move into the next century. See P. F. Drucker, E. Dyson, C. Handy, P. Saffo and P. M. Senge, Looking Ahead: Implications of the Present, *Harvard Business Review*, 75(5), 1997, 18–32.

[2] The importance of strategic leadership for 21st century firms is described in: M. Davids, Where Style Meets Substance, *Journal of Business Strategy*, 16(1), 1995, 48–60; R. P. White, P. Hodgson, and S. Crainer. *The Future of Leadership* (London: Pitman Publishing, 1997).

[3] Additional definitional information about strategic leadership can be found in: C. M. Christensen, Making Strategy: Learning by Doing, *Harvard Business Review*, 75(6), 1997, 141–156; M. A. Hitt, R. D. Ireland, and R. E. Hoskisson, *Strategic Management: Competitiveness and Globalization*, Third Edition (Cincinnati: South-Western College Publishing Company, 1999).

[4] John Browne, CEO of British Petroleum, describes a wide range of competitive approaches being used at BP. See S. E. Prokesch, Unleashing the Power of Learning: An Interview with British Petroleum's John Browne, *Harvard Business Review*, 75(5), 1997, 147–168.

[5] The universal need for each firm to develop a competitive advantage serves as a foundation for two authors' analysis of how strategic management can be improved. For additional information on this subject, see: A. Campbell and M. Alexander, What's Wrong with Strategy? *Harvard Business Review*, 75(6), 1997, 42–51.

[6] Mr. Gorman's viewpoint is included in an article in which potential reasons for the recent success of U.S. firms in the global economy are examined. For further information see: G. P. Zachary, Behind Stocks' Surge is an Economy in Which Big U.S. Firms Thrive, *Wall Street Journal*, November 22, 1995, A1,A3.

[7] Based on an argument that globalization is a reality of our time, one business writer offers intriguing perspectives regarding the level and degree of economic interdependence of the world's nations. To explore his views further, see: R. Ruggiero, The High Stakes of World Trade, *Wall Street Journal*, April 28, 1997, A18.

[8] In light of the global economy, an interesting set of predictions about the nature of business firms and their leaders in the 21st century can be found in: S. Makridakis, Management in the 21st Century, *Long Range Planning*, 22, April, 1989, 37–53.

[9] The director of the Institute for International Economics offers his optimistic perspective about the characteristics of a global economy in: C. F. Bergsten, The Rationale For a Rosy View, *The Economist*, September 11, 1993, 57–58.

[10] Peter Drucker made these observations in an address to the Knowledge Advantage Conference sponsored by the Ernst & Young Center for Business Innovation. See Peter Drucker on The Next 20 Years, *Executive Upside*, March, 1997, 3.

[11] To better understand the possible nature of the global marketplace in the future, a senior writer reviewed several books. His reviews can be found in: F. R. Bleakley, The Future of the Global Marketplace, *Wall Street Journal*, March 15, 1996, A13.

[12] Unpredictable events affect firms of all sizes. An analysis of the effects of the new competitive landscape on high-growth entrepreneurial firms, is presented in: R. D. Ireland and M. A. Hitt, Performance Strategies for High-Growth Entrepreneurial Firms, *Frontiers of Entrepreneurship Research*, 1997, 90–104.

[13] In a recent article, two prominent researchers argue convincingly that 'the complexity of political, regulatory, and technological changes confronting most organizations has made radical organizational change and adaptation a central research issue.' To further explore this central issue see: R. Greenwood and C. R. Hinings, Understanding Radical Organizational Change: Bringing Together the Old and the New Institutionalism, *Academy of Management Review*, 21, 1996, 1022–1054.

[14] Rapidly changing business conditions result in a premium being placed on the firm's ability to speed up its operations. Recent research suggests that this ability is especially important to develop a competitive advantage in firms in industries with shortened product life cycles. Arguments supporting this position are presented in: E. H. Kessler and A. K. Chakrabarti, Innovation Speed: A Conceptual Model of Context, Antecedents, and Outcomes, *Academy of Management Review*, 21,1996,1143–1191.

[15] Both Drucker and Senge emphasize this point in their descriptions of events that have already happened that are shaping the future for 21st century firms. For more information, see: Drucker, Dyson, Handy, Saffo, and Senge, 'Looking Ahead: Implications of the Present,' 18–32.

[16] This positive projection of growth for at least the beginning part of the 21st century is presented in: *Dallas Morning News*, Futurists See Bright 21st Century, June 11, 1997, D2.

[17] An insightful treatment of the link between corporate entrepreneurship and the pursuit of organizational growth in firms facing challenging competitive environments is presented in: S. A. Zahra, Environment, Corporate entrepreneurship, and Financial Performance: A Taxonomic Approach, *Journal of Business Venturing*, 8, 1993, 319–340.

[18] For additional information about how firms can mobilize to adapt their behaviors for competitive reasons, see: R. A. Heifetz and D. L. Laurie, The Work of Leadership, *Harvard Business Review*, 75(1), 1997, 124–134.

[19] Further arguments regarding the choices firms can make through the work of their strategic leaders and other key decision makers can be found in the following classic: J. Child, Organizational Structure, Environment and Performance: The Role of Strategic Choice, *Sociology* 6, 1972, 1–22.

[20] In a recent article, two researchers present a detailed analysis of different perspectives of strategic leadership that appear in the academic literature. This work is intended to present what the authors consider to be a 'more realistic view of top managers' work.' To examine the researchers' perspectives, see: A. A. Cannella, Jr. and M. J. Monroe, Contrasting Perspectives on Strategic Leaders: Toward a More Realistic View of Top Managers, *Journal of Management*, 23, 1997, 213–237 (the quote in our article appears on page 213 of the Cannella and Monroe publication).

[21] The historical isolation between strategic leaders and those they led is described in: P. M. Senge, Communities of Leaders and Learners, *Harvard Business Review*, 75(5), 1997, 30–32.

[22] W. Bennis, Cultivating Creative Genius, *Industry Week*, August 18, 1997, 84–88.

[23] This point is described in greater detail in Bennis, Cultivating Creative Genius.

[24] Some believe that understanding how to gather and interpret data is the organizational challenge of the next century. To evaluate this possibility, see: J. Teresko, Too Much Data, Too Little Information, *Industry Week*, August 19, 1996, 66–70.

[25] For a discussion of how uncertainty affects people at both upper and lower organizational levels, see: R. P. White, Seekers and Scalers: The Future Leaders, *Training & Development*, January, 1997, 21–24.

[26] Known widely as a preeminent business thinker, Charles Handy explains his thoughts about organizational communities in: C. Handy, *The Age of Unreason* (Boston: Harvard Business School Press, 1989).

[27] This quotation appears in: Bennis, Cultivating Creative Genius, 88.

[28] To explore the concept of great groups further, see W. Bennis, *Organizing Genius: The Secrets of Creative Collaboration* (Reading, MA.: Addison-Wesley Publishing Company, 1997).

[29] To learn how effective leaders allow all organizational employees to play an active role in helping firms become adaptive, see: Heifetz and Laurie, The Work of Leadership.

[30] To learn the views of British Petroleum's CEO about the value and nature of teams (or great groups) in the global economy, see: Prokesch, Unleashing the Power of Learning: An Interview With British Petroleum's John Browne.

[31] The importance of group members accepting the responsibility to support one another in their work is discussed in another one of Charles Handy's books: C. Handy, *The Age of Paradox* (Boston: Harvard Business School Press, 1994).

[32] Among many points discussed by John Browne, the importance of learning how to leverage knowledge is given the most attention. See Prokesch, op. cit.

[33] The criticality of external information for firms seeking high performance in the global economy is described in: P. F. Drucker, The Future That Has Already Happened, *Harvard Business Review*, 75(5), 1997, 20–24.

[34] The importance of collective work, and how such work can be stimulated, is discussed in: P. B. Vaill, *Managing As a Performing Art: New Ideas for a World of Chaotic Change* (San Francisco: Jossey-Bass, 1989).

[35] The inclusive roles of organizational leaders is noted in: G. Dutton, Leadership In a Post-Heroic Age, *Management Review*, October, 1996, 7.

[36] An excellent, comprehensive analysis of strategic leadership and the role of the top management team as part of strategic leadership, appears in: S. Finkelstein and D. C. Hambrick, *Strategic Leadership: Top Executives and Their Effects on Organizations* (St. Paul: West Publishing, 1996).

[37] This quote is taken from: Bennis, Cultivating Creative Organizations.

[38] Research results regarding the value of heterogeneous top management teams is explored carefully and in a detailed manner in: Finkelstein and Hambrick, *Strategic Leadership*.

[39] D. F. Abell, Mastering Management – Part 16, *Financial Times*, February 23, 1996, 13.

[40] The important link between self-confidence and the successful completion of significant types of organizational work is discussed in: R. D. Ireland, M. A. Hitt, and J. C. Williams, Self-Confidence and Decisiveness: Prerequisites for Effective Management in the 1990s, *Business Horizons*, 35(1), 1992, 36–43.

[41] B. A. Nagle, Wanted: A Leader for the 21st Century, *Industry Week*, November 20, 1995, 29.

[42] This quote, and the importance of letting organizational citizens know that their strategic leaders want them to try different methods to satisfy the demands of new challenges, appears on page 158 of Prokesch, op. cit.

[43] Viewpoints of other leaders, in addition to von Pierer, can be found in: W. H. Miller, Leadership at a Crossroads, *Industry Week*, August 19, 1996, 43–57.

[44] Other aspects of Mr. Gorman's perspectives about the value of a corporate purpose are included in: Miller, Leadership at a Crossroads.

[45] Mr. O'Rourke offered this viewpoint as part of his description of what a leader must do to lead effectively. His perspectives can be studied fully by reading: W. H. Miller, Leadership's Common Denominator, *Industry Week*, August 19, 1997, 97–100.

[46] A full list of the 21 competencies identified by the survey's 1,450 participants can be viewed by reading: Davids, Where Style Meets Substance.

[47] This view is explained more fully in Prokesch, op. cit.

[48] Charles Handy considers these points in two books: *The Age of Paradox* and *The Age of Unreason*.

[49] This point is articulated in: *The Economist*, The Changing Nature of Leadership, June 10, 1995, 57.

[50] Full details regarding actions framed by Rockwell's strategic leaders to achieve the firm's vision can be found in: Its Time to Change Your Perception of Rockwell, Rockwell International Corporation Annual Report, 1995.

[51] An intriguing analysis of decisions made by Samsung Group's strategic leaders regarding the firm's entry into the world's automobile manufacturing industry is featured in: L. Kraar, Behind Samsung's High-Stakes Push Into Cars, *Fortune*, May 12, 1997, 119–120.

[52] Large conglomerates, called chaebols, have played important roles in the growth of South Korea's economy. However, some evidence suggests that these huge firms may encounter additional competitive challenges in the future. Details of these challenges, and some of the chaebols' responses to them, are presented in: M. Schuman and N. Cho, Troubles of Korean Conglomerates Intensify, Signaling End of an Era, *Wall Street Journal*, April 25, 1997, All.

[53] Kraar, Behind Samsung's High-Stakes Push Into Cars, 119.

[54] Some research proposes that knowledge is the most strategically significant source of core competence and thus, of competitive advantage for firms competing in the complex global economy. In a recent publication, this issue is explored through the development of a knowledge-based theory of organizational capability. To examine this theory see: R. M. Grant, Prospering in Dynamically-Competitive Environments: Organizational Capability as Knowledge Integration, *Organization Science*, 7, 1996, 375–387.

[55] Jay Barney's work informs our understanding of the criteria of sustainability. Two publications in which Barney's arguments are detailed are: J. B. Barney, Looking Inside for Competitive Advantage, *Academy of Management Executive*. IX(4), 1995, 49–61; J. B. Barney, Firm Resources and Sustained Competitive Advantage, *Journal of Management*, 17, 1991, 99–120.

[56] The value of understanding the nature of a firm's core competencies is accepted widely. However, one researcher suggests that little guidance is available to help strategic leaders and their co-workers to define carefully their firm's capabilities and core competencies. The experiences of three top-level management teams are described in: K. E. Marino, Developing Consensus on Firm Competencies and Capabilities, *Academy of Management Executive*, X(3), 1996, 40–51.

[57] T. A. Stewart, *Intellectual Capital* (New York: Doubleday/ Currency, 1997).

[58] T. A. Stewart, Owens Back From the Dead, *Fortune*, May 26, 1997, 118–126.

[59] Three researchers have identified actions effective strategic leaders and their firms take to maximize the value of this critical organizational resource. These guidelines are offered in: J. B. Quinn, P. Anderson, and S. Finkelstein, Leveraging Intellect, *Academy of Management Executive*, X(3), 1996, 7–27.

[60] Based on organizational meta-learning processes, firms are able to continue gaining competitive advantages by exploiting dynamic core competencies. How this is accomplished is described in: D. Lei, M. A. Hitt, and R. Bettis, Dynamic Core Competences Through Meta-Learning and Strategic Context, *Journal of Management*, 22, 1996, 549–569.

[61] Economist Paul M. Romer's work is thought by some to be controversial. Romer's analyses suggest that ideas and technological discovery are the main drivers of a nation's economic growth. An introduction of these arguments is offered in: B. Wysocki, Jr., For This Economist, Long-Term Prosperity Hangs on Good Ideas, *Wall Street Journal*, January 21, 1997, Al, A8.

[62] H. Rudnitsky, One Hundred Sixty Companies For the Price of One, *Forbes*, February 26, 1996, 56–62.

[63] The potential value of additional national expenditures being allocated to education and training initiatives is explored by a prominent economist in: G. S. Becker, Why the Dole Plan Will Work, *Business Week*, August 26, 1996, 16.

[64] These points are discussed in Bennis, Cultivating Organizational Genius.

[65] J. Katkin, Close the Talent Gap, *Houston Chronicle*, November 9, 1997, C1, C5.

[66] These statistics are drawn from the following two sources: S. Baker, A. Barrett, and L. Himelstein, Calling All Nerds, *Business Week*, March 10, 1997, 38–37; D. Kunke, In Search of Expertise, *Dallas Morning News*. April 16, 1997, D1, D10.

[67] A business practitioner who participated in a debate expressed this view. The focus of the debate was the extent to which the traditional model of the MBA degree is outdated. The full text of this debate appears in: MBA: Is the Traditional Model Doomed? *Harvard Business Review*, 70(6), 1992, 128–140.

[68] For more information about Mr. Brabeck-Letmathe's views, see: Miller, Leadership's Common Denominator.

[69] These questions appear at the beginning of the interviews with Drucker, et al., op. cit.

[70] B. Vlasic, Can Chrysler keep it Up? *Business Week*, November 25, 1996, 108–120.

[71] Southwest Airlines' culture has been cited frequently as a competitive advantage for the firm. Interestingly, everyone (except consultants and U.S. competitors) is welcome to attend the sessions in which the company's culture is discussed. Additional details about the firm's culture sessions are offered in: W. Zellner, Southwest's Love Fest at Love Field, *Business Week*, April 28, 1997, 124.

[72] To explore in greater detail how ethical practices can be used as decision filters, see: J. M. Lozano, Ethics and Management: A Controversial Issue, *Journal of Business Ethics*, 15, 1996, 227–236; J. Milton-Smith, Ethics as Excellence: A Strategic Management Perspective, *Journal of Business Ethics*, 14, 1995, 683–693.

[73] L. Kraar, Acer's Edge: PCs to Go, *Fortune*, October 30, 1995, 187–204.

[74] The developing relationship between corporate social responsibility and society's expectations of corporations was considered through a special issue of *Academy of Management Review*. To examine the special issue's topics, consult the introductory comments included in: S. P. Sethi, Introduction to AMR's Special Topic Forum on Shifting Paradigms: Societal Expectations and Corporate Performance, *Academy of Management Review*, 20, 1995, 18–21.

[75] R. Simons, How New Top Managers Use Control Systems As Levers of Strategic Renewal, *Strategic Management Journal,* 15, 1994, 169–189.

[76] Extensive considerations of the differences between strategic controls and financial controls are presented in several publications including: M. A. Hitt, R. E. Hoskisson, R. A. Johnson, and D. D. Moesel, The Market for Corporate Control and Firm Innovation, *Academy of Management Journal*, 39, 1996, 1084–1119; M. A. Hitt, R. E. Hoskisson, and R. D. Ireland, Mergers and Acquisitions and Managerial Commitment to Innovation in M-form Firms, Strategic *Management Journal*, 11 (Special Issue), 1990, 29–47.

[77] P. Shrivastava, Ecocentric Management for a Risk Society, *Academy of Management Review*, 20, 1995, 119.

[78] Bennis, Cultivating Creative Genius, 87.

[79] Three researchers explain theoretically the value firms can derive through implementation of cooperative strategies formed through interfirm collaborations: A. A. Lado, N. G. Boyd, and S. C. Hanlon, Competition, Cooperation, and the Search for Economic Rents: A Syncretic Model, *Academy of Management Review*, 22, 1997, 110–141. See also K. M. Eisenhardt and C. B. Schoonhoven, Resource-based View of Strategic Alliance Formation: Strategic and Social Effects in Entrepreneurial Firms, *Organization Science*, 7, 1996, 136–150.

[80] Lado, Boyd, and Hanlon argue that 'Success in today's business world often requires that firms pursue both competitive and cooperative strategies simultaneously.' They define syncretic rent-seeking behavior as actions firms can take to earn economic rents while engaging jointly in competitive and cooperative behaviors.

[81] This point is discussed in some detail in: M. A. Hitt, B. W. Keats and S. DeMarie, Navigating in the New Competitive Landscape: Building Strategic Flexibility and Competitive Advantage in the 21st Century. *Academy of Management Executive*, 12(4), 22–42.

[82] A comprehensive description of James Bonini's experiences as a young, inexperienced manager at a Chrysler Corp. plant is offered in: G. Stern, How a Young Manager Shook Up the Culture At Old Chrysler Plant, *Wall Street Journal*, April 21, 1997, A1, A6.

[83] These possibilities, and their accompanying competitive implications for firms committed to achieving success in the global marketplace are examined in: J. E. Garten, Troubles Ahead in Emerging Markets, *Harvard Business Review*, 1997, 75(3), 38–49.

R. DUANE IRELAND holds the Curtis Hankamer Chair in Entrepreneurship at Baylor University and is the director of the Entrepreneurship Studies Program at Baylor's Hankamer School of Business. He received his PhD from Texas Tech University. He has been an associate editor of the *Academy of Management Executive* and a consulting editor for *Entrepreneurship: Theory and Practice*. He is now serving as a member of the editorial review boards for *Academy of Management Review* and *Journal of Management*. His research examines questions related to corporate-level strategy, innovation, and core competencies. Currently, he is studying issues related to the intersection between the entrepreneurship and strategic management literatures and factors that differentiate success from failure in mergers and acquisitions. He is the coauthor of *Strategic Management: Competitiveness and Globalization* and is working on three books. He has been selected as Baylor University's outstanding researcher (1998) and as the distinguished professor in the Hankamer School of Business (1986).

MICHAEL A. HITT holds the Paul M. and Rosalie Robertson Chair in Business Administration at Texas A&M University. He received his PhD from the University of Colorado and has been selected to receive an honorary doctorate from the Universidad Carlos III de Madrid for his contributions to the field. He is a former editor of the *Academy of Management Journal* and a past president of the Academy of Management. A frequent contributor to the literature, he focuses on international strategy, corporate governance, innovation, importance of intangible resources and the new competitive landscape. He is the coauthor or coeditor of several recent books, including *Down-scoping: How to Tame the Diversified Firm; Strategic Management: Competitiveness and Globalization; Managing Strategically in an Interconnected World;* and *New Managerial Mindsets*. He is a fellow of the Academy of Management and received the 1996 Award for Outstanding Academic Contributions to Competitiveness from the American Society for Competitiveness.

CASE 9: LVMH: MANAGING THE MULTI-BRAND CONGLOMERATE

Introduction

On 4 March 2004, 54-year-old Bernard Arnault stood under his Picasso painting at the LVMH headquarters in Paris and pondered the future of his fashion empire. He had just announced a 30 per cent rise in net income for 2003, with improved profits in all sectors of the business except watches and jewellery. Margins for the flagship leather goods brand Louis Vuitton topped 45 per cent due to increased publicity spending featuring the actress Jennifer Lopez in its latest global ad campaign.

As the chief shareholder in LVMH Moët Hennessy Louis Vuitton, plus ownership stakes in the high-profile labels Christian Dior, Givenchy, Christian Lacroix, Kenzo, Céline, Emilio Pucci, Fendi, Loewe, Donna Karan, and a substantial investment in Marc Jacobs, Arnault held much of the future of world fashion in his hands. His properties also include Tag Heuer watches, Moët and Chandon champagne and a chain of duty-free shops in many international airports. The fashion conglomerate's leadership in the luxury sector has been sustained by new product launches, store openings and an increased investment in communications. The group continued new launches and initiatives in 2004, including the new Damier Geant leather goods line, Théda bags, an entire new jewellery line at Louis Vuitton, a new perfume for women at Dior, a new fragrance for men at Guerlain, an array of watch and jewellery creations, and the new Ellipse Cognac from Hennessy.

LVMH also continued to develop its worldwide distribution network. The Louis Vuitton brand, celebrating its 150th anniversary, opened its largest store in the world in New York. Advancements in markets with significant potential for luxury products, such as Asia, also bolstered the group's performance. Future focus would likely be on new growth markets and regions such as China, a market with considerable potential for cognac, fashion and perfumes; Russia with Sephora, which had already shown promise in several central and eastern European countries; and India, where Louis Vuitton opened its first store in 2003.

However, the $12 billion fashion and liquor conglomerate controlled by Bernard Arnault was not without worries. Wall Street continued to question whether the company's multi-brand strategy could be sustained. Arnault had to consider the increasing importance of succession as he approached the legal retirement age and would soon need to plan for the successor who could replace him at the helm of his group.

Ashok Som wrote this case. The author gratefully acknowledges Lilly Liu, Deepak Yachamaneni, ESSEC MBA exchange students, and Boris Gbahoué, ESSEC MBA student, for their research help. The case was developed from generalized experience and published sources as a basis for class discussion rather than to illustrate either effective or ineffective handling of an administrative situation.

▶ ## History of LVMH

Established in 1987, LVMH was created by the fusion of two fashion houses: Louis Vuitton, a leather goods specialist founded in 1834, and Moët-Hennessy, a wine and spirits group created in 1971. The luxury group grew through key acquisitions and the development of new products. Under the leadership of Bernard Arnault, the 1990s saw a period of great expansion with the purchase of large stakes in the company's subsidiaries. In recent years, the luxury group had begun to shed some of its portfolio, with the strategy of focusing on its 'star' brands, defined by Arnault as 'timeless, modern, fast-growing, and highly profitable' brands (see Exhibit 9.1 for a list of the recent acquisitions and divestitures). Observers commented that, 'This collection of global brands was the stepping stone for realizing lucrative synergies in the fashion business, which would add to the bottom line'.

Wines & spirits	Watches & jewellery	Fashion & leather	Selective retailing	Perfumes & cosmetics
Moët & Chandon*	TAG Heuer*	Louis Vuitton*	DFS*	Parfums Christian Dior*
Dom Pérignon		Loewe*	Miami Cruiseline Services*	Guerlain*
Veuve Clicquot*	Zenith*	Céline*	Sephora*	Parfums Givenchy*
Krug	Christian Dior Watches*	Berluti*	Le Bon Marché*	Kenzo Parfums*
Mercier	Fred*	Kenzo*	La Samaritaine*	Laflachère*
Ruinart	Chaumet*	Givenchy*		Bliss*
Château d'Yquem*	OMAS*	Christian Lacroix*		BeneFit Cosmetics*
Chandon Estates*		Marc Jacobs*		Fresh*
Hennessy*		Fendi*		Make Up For Ever*
Cloudy Bay		StefanoBi		Acqua di Parma*
Cape Mentelle		Emilio Pucci*		Perfumes Loewe*
Newton		Thomas Pink*		
MountAdam		Donna Karan*		

*Indicates company status

Acquisitions

1987	Fashion house Céline
1988	Fashion house Givenchy
1991	Champagne brand Pommery
1993	Fashion house Kenzo
1994	Perfume company Kenzo, cosmetics company Guerlain
1995	Jeweller Fred
1996	Leather goods specialist Loewe
1997	DFS, the luxury goods distribution network
1998	Sephora, the fragrance and cosmetics retail chain
1999	Champagne producer Krug and the watch manufacturer TAG Heuer; a 34 per cent minority stake in the Italian luxury goods maker, Gucci
2000	LVMH purchased US start-up, Urban Decay and the Donna Karan apparel line
2001	La Samaritaine department store, Acqua di Parma perfumes, a stake in Fendi
2002	Millennium & Company, prestige wines and alcohol

New business creations

1987	Christian Lacroix
2001	Newton and MountAdam vineyards; marketing De Beers diamond jewellery in a 50–50 joint venture

Divestitures

2001	Sale of stake in Gucci to Pinault Printemps Redoute
2002	Pommery champagne brand, Hard Candy and Urban Decay
2003	Canard-Duchene to the Alain Thienot Group
	Final stake of 27.5 per cent in Phillips, de Pury and Luxembourg, an auction house
	Minority stake in Michael Kors, including cosmetics and fragrance licences
	Marc Jacobs and Kenneth Cole fragrance divisions
	Bliss spa line and Ebel watches

Exhibit 9.1 LVMH conglomerates at a glance

With over 56,000 employees and approximately €12 billion in revenue during the fiscal year 2003, the LVMH group operated in five primary sectors: wines and spirits, fashion and leather goods, perfumes and cosmetics, watches and jewellery, and selective retailing. LVMH today controls more than 60 luxury brands across its product lines. The acquisition strategy at LVMH focused on brands that had strong brand power, resulting in the company achieving leadership positions in almost every segment it served. Each division functioned as a strategic business unit with its own general manager and a top management team. These divisions also managed overseas sales of their respective lines.

Wines and spirits

Wines and spirits contributed 18 per cent of sales and 36 per cent of operating profit in 2003. LVMH, through Hennessy, holds 40 per cent of the cognac market and between 20 per cent–25 per cent of the overall champagne market. In the premium champagne segment, LVMH has a dominant 50 per cent share built around exclusive brands such as Moët Chandon and Veuve Clicquot. It also ventured outside the traditional wine belts in France and Italy to acquire high-end wine producers in California and Australia. Given the rising prominence of both California and Australia in the wine business, these moves allowed the company to market a truly global selection of wines and champagnes. However, considering the total liquor market, LVMH was not in the top ten due to the absence of its drinks in the 'popular segment', like beer, whisky and vodka. However this is in line with LVMH's strategy to focus only on high-margin activities. Analysts have suggested spinning off the wines and spirits businesses as a separate unit as they consider it to be non-core to LVMH's fashion image. For example, the sale of Pommery, a profitable champagne brand in 2001, was a strategic move by LVMH. The brand was bought for the vast lands it owned in the champagne region, as high-quality land is limited in this region, LVMH wanted more land to produce more grapes for its Moët and Veuve brands of champagne. When Pommery was purchased, its land was also acquired but, when it was sold, the land was retained and only the brand was sold.

Fashion and leather goods

Fashion and leather goods contributed 35 per cent of sales and 60 per cent of operating profit in 2003, and had an operating margin of 32 per cent. Much of the sales of this division were concentrated in the Asia-Pacific region, particularly Japan, which accounts for 33 per cent of sales, which in this segment are directly attributable to the Louis Vuitton brand. This label grew by leaps and bounds under the leadership of its legendary designer, Marc Jacobs. Demand for Louis Vuitton products often exceeded supply, requiring customers to go on a waiting list that often took several months to clear. The Louis Vuitton label, combined with the strength of the LVMH group, provided opportunities for expanding into new brands and products. Using this as a launching pad, the company engaged in significant brand expansion efforts to reach a wider audience. These efforts were well supported by fashion buyers.

The company leveraged synergies across its fashion brands. For example, its Kenzo production facility was transformed into a logistics platform for men's ready-to-wear products serving other brands such as Givenchy and Christian Lacroix. Given the historically lower profit margins in the ready-to-wear market, synergies resulting in cost savings boosted profitability. As Muriel Zingraff, Harrods fashion and beauty director, observed, 'What I will say is that we may have more patience with smaller brands if they are owned by a parent company such as LVMH or the Gucci Group'.

Perfumes and cosmetics

The perfumes and cosmetics (P&C) unit contributed 18 per cent of sales and 8 per cent of operating profit in 2003. This division had an enviable collection of brands such as Christian Dior, Guerlain, Kenzo and Givenchy. The company recently acquired popular US brands such as Bliss, Hard Candy, Urban Decay and Fresh, geared towards a younger clientele. These acquisitions were an integral part of the drive to internationalize LVMH's perfumes and cosmetics offerings. Europe is the largest market for perfumes, perhaps due to the heritage of the brands the company offered. The P&C division was able to leverage R&D synergies across brands, while its R&D expenditure remained in line with industry norms, LVMH was able to generate twice the average growth rate in the industry. It is believed that the R&D skills would help boost sales of the acquired companies. As part of a larger drive to consolidate margins in this division, the company integrated R&D, production, distribution, sourcing and other back-office operations across brands, moves that proved beneficial. For example, integrating the purchasing function across brands resulted in cost savings in raw materials of 20 per cent. Analysts believed the division was well positioned to reap the spillover benefits arising from the co-branding strategy under which many of the brands were linked directly to ready-to-wear apparel brands, a unique avenue of differentiation at LVMH.

Watches and jewellery

The latest portfolio addition at LVMH, watches and jewellery, contributed 4 per cent of sales and –2 per cent of operating profit in 2003. In the watches section, the company owned prestigious brands that included Tag Heuer, Ebel and Zenith. In jewellery, the company's brands included Fred Joallier and Chaumet. The purchase of the Zenith brand was crucial to LVMH's strategy to expand its watches operations. Most watches have an identical manufacturing process, and brands reflect minor differences in quality.

According to industry sources, there are only three manufacturers in the world from whom all the luxury watchmakers source their products. It is noteworthy that Zenith is the only manufacturer in the world of a certain component used in every watch. LVMH wanted a platform to sell more watches by utilizing its design experience and the production knowhow of Zenith. Watches could be one of the most lucrative segments at LVMH, with margins as high as 80 per cent.

Unlike its constellation of brands in other divisions, many think that the company does not have the same star power in watches and jewellery. Competitors such as Richemont, Hermès and Bulgari seem to have more recognizable brands and more upscale products in this category. However, tangible synergies appear to be a definite possibility because the division could centralize the manufacturing and utilize Tag Heuer's expertise in retail distribution across all brands. The jewellery business is also extremely competitive due to the presence of leading brands such as Cartier and Van Cleef & Arpels. Despite the Place Vendôme heritage of both Chaumet and Fred Joallier, neither of them are currently profitable.

Selective retailing

Selective retailing contributed 25 per cent of sales and 5 per cent of operating profit in 2003. The vertical integration strategy of LVMH came to fruition when the selective retailing arm was established. The division manages LVMH investments in Sephora, DFS Galleria and Miami Cruiseline Services. While this division contributed 26 per cent of company sales in 2002, it had not made a profit in the previous three years. DFS Galleria, with 150 duty-free and general merchandise stores, is the world's largest travel retailer. Acquired in 1996, the business was a victim of poor timing since the Asian financial crisis hit soon thereafter. LVMH has since instituted several good management practices, including the execution of a strategy that would reduce DFS's reliance on Asian airports, selective closing of underperforming stores and the creation of DFS Galleria stores in large metropolitan areas. Despite these changes, Japanese travellers remained the company's most important and loyal customers, and any economic development that hurt Japanese travel would invariably find its way to DFS's bottom line.

Miami Cruiseline Services (MCS) was acquired in January 2000. It offers retail services on cruise ships and accounts for 76 per cent of the world's major cruise lines (over 100 ships) as its customers. Conceived as an extension of the DFS concept, Miami Cruiseline focused primarily (90 per cent) on North American passengers, thus counterbalancing the overreliance on Japanese tourists. It also managed duty-free operations at the Miami International Airport, the gateway to Latin America, opening up the possibility of strengthening LVMH's brands in a region of the world where they have been underrepresented.

In addition to these distribution-based assets, LVMH acquired La Samaritaine, the prestigious Paris department store. The company also entered the retailing end of the made-to-order tailoring business with the acquisition of Thomas Pink, the legendary Mayfair tailoring house, which has a worldwide reputation for excellence in shirts.

▶ Thomas Pink has retail outlets in the United States as well. LVMH also took a minority stake in the 200-year-old UK fashion retailer, Asprey & Garrard, which has global aspirations of its own.

The functioning of the group

LVMH's five product groups are decentralized into production and distribution subsidiaries. Some of the major brands have their own national subsidiaries. Overlaying this, there is a regional structure with corporate headquarters in Paris, New York, Tokyo and Amsterdam. The wine and spirits division of Moët Hennessy has its own headquarters, with main offices in France and regional headquarters in Singapore.

Depending on the geographic region, LVMH has different organizational set-ups. In France, the hub of LVMH has individual headquarters for every brand, with an LVMH headquarters handling some centralized activities. In contrast, in New York, the central LVMH office houses the LVMH and Givenchy brands, while Dior and Fendi have their own US offices. Tokyo centralizes the human resources function and each brand operates independently on all aspects of business.

The group's decentralized organizational structure helps the company foster efficiency, productivity and creativity. LVMH strives to create a highly motivating and dynamic atmosphere for its employees, emphasizing individual initiative and offering real responsibility, often early in one's career. LVMH gives each brand almost complete freedom to pursue its creative vision. However, it does realize synergies through almost 20 per cent discount in advertising by negotiating in bulk for all its brands.

The challenge of this structure is that it requires highly entrepreneurial executive teams in each company within the group. This entrepreneurial spirit requires a healthy dose of common sense from managers, as well as hard work, pragmatism, efficiency and the ability to motivate people in the pursuit of ambitious goals.

Bernard Arnault: 'the pope of fashion'

Dubbed 'the pope of fashion', Bernard Arnault has spent the past 15 years building LVMH from a small clothing manufacturer to a conglomerate comprising approximately 50 of the world's most powerful brands. Trained as an engineer at the Ecole Polytechnique in France, Arnault joined his family's construction business, where he worked for 13 years, before becoming president of the company in 1978. In 1984, he left his family business to reorganize a French state-owned holding company, Boussac, which owned Christian Dior. In the late 1980s, Bernard Arnault took control of LVMH. With growing success in his business, Arnault acquired Givenchy (1988) and Kenzo (1993). Today, through a complex web of partnerships, he owns at least 33 per cent of the company's stock.

Bernard Arnault is deeply involved in the creative process, far more than his peers. He believes that in the creative and highly seasonal fashion business, the ability to match effective CEOs with temperamental designers can make the difference between a star and a failure. He believes that, 'to have the right DNA in a team is very rare. It's almost like a miracle'. Deemed the 'billionaire matchmaker', in the past 15 years he has formed close creative bonds with designer John Galliano, whose collections for Christian Dior have been hailed by fashion critics. His selection of Hedi Slimane did wonders for Dior Homme, and his pairing of Marc Jacobs with Louis Vuitton was a critical and financial success. His vision of the luxury and fashion industry as is, he says:

> This link to creativity, it's not far from art, and I like it very much. You must like to be with designers and creators. You have to like an image. That's also a key to success. And at the same time, you must be able to organize a business worldwide.

Industry background

> Luxury is not the contrary to poverty, but a contrary to vulgarity. (Gianni Versace)

> We are in the business of selling dreams. The strength of a brand depends on how many dreams it inspires. (Chanel)

The luxury products industry has been estimated to be worth $58 billion, excluding automobiles and travel. The breakdown by sector is shown in Exhibit 9.2.

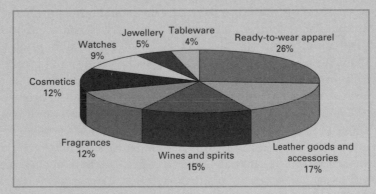

Exhibit 9.2 Breakdown of the luxury goods industry
Source: Merrill Lynch Research

Major players in the global luxury goods market include LVMH Moët Hennessey Louis Vuitton, Richemont, Christian Dior, Gucci, Tiffany, Hermés, Swatch and Bulgari. Traditionally, the luxury sector has been highly fragmented, characterized by a large number of family-owned and medium-sized enterprises. In the past two decades, it has been increasingly dominated by multi-brand luxury conglomerates. Although smaller companies still thrive in this environment by serving niche markets, larger luxury goods companies have acquired or overtaken many of their smaller competitors (see Exhibit 9.3 for luxury market growth, by sector).

Sectors of the luxury products industry	Annual sales growth, 1998–2002
Home fashions	>10%
Ready to wear	10
Accessories	10
Leather goods	<10
Watches and jewellery	8
Perfume and cosmetics	6
Crystal and silverware	5
Shoes	4

Exhibit 9.3 Luxury market growth, by sector
Source: Eurostat

Survival of the multi-brand strategy

LVMH and France's biggest retail-to-luxury group Pinault-Printemps-Redoute (PPR), which controls Gucci, led the consolidation spree in the luxury industry in the late 1990s. More luxury conglomerates have emerged through acquisitions, and many separate brands have united under a holding company structure intended to spread best practices and impose commercial and financial discipline. The goal is to allow firms to grow strongly without over-exploiting a particular brand and killing exclusivity.

However, Michael Zaoui, Morgan Stanley's head of mergers and acquisitions in Europe, doubts the viability of the multi-brand model, citing the slump in luxury M&A activity since 1999: 'It's a hotly debated issue ... but is the multi-brand model holding up?' asks Zaoui, whose investment bank has been involved in every Gucci acquisition since 1999, as well as the initial public offerings of Bulgari SpA and Burberry plc.

According to Zaoui, M&A in luxury goods slumped to $800 million in 2002 from $10 billion in 1999, and the rate of return on capital employed in the sector dropped to 20 per cent in 2001 from 32 per cent in 1997. As companies seek to stretch their brands to target new customers, some 1,400 new luxury goods stores have opened since 1999, the equivalent of strategic investments worth $4.5 billion. Large advertising budgets are required to attract people to the new stores. According to Zaoui, the ten leading luxury companies spent $1.1 billion on advertising in 2001, which is equivalent to 8 per cent of sales, compared with 6 per cent of revenue in 1995: 'This expansion trend increases the inflexibility of the cost base ... it can reduce margins if the growth's not there'.

'Luxury for the masses'

There has been a systemic change in the luxury products market. In the past decade, Gucci sunglasses, Prada handbags and Louis Vuitton suitcases have become must-have items for many thousands of middle-class buyers. According to Boston Consulting

Group's newly released book, *Trading Up: The Transforming Power of New Luxury*, the trend in the market is towards mass elitism. While traditional luxury brands such as Louis Vuitton, Rolls-Royce and Hermés remain items for the elite, luxury has been democratized for all. According to BCG, 'new luxury' ranges from a Starbucks frappuccino to a Porsche, and can be extended across categories like personal care, homewares and appliances, oral care, toys, restaurants and wines.

Consumers are in a 'state of heightened emotionalism' and often address feelings of being overworked, isolated, lonely, worried and unhappy by shopping for premium-priced products. 'New' luxury is the idea that middle-class consumers trade up to premium products because of emotional needs, to give them a sense of indulgence and personal fulfilment. They spend a disproportionate amount of their income on such goods, and trade down in other categories perceived to be less important. For example, a consumer might visit a Dior boutique to spend several hundred euros on a Gucci handbag, then go to Wal-Mart or Carrefour to buy cotton socks.

This new middle-class market for luxury products creates a wide range of challenges for luxury conglomerates like Gucci and Louis Vuitton, as they have to understand and cater to a different target consumer.

Market trends

In 2003, the luxury retail market segment was adversely affected by SARS (Severe Acute Respiratory Syndrome) in Asia, the United States led a war against Iraq, the euro was strengthening and a weak 'feel-good factor' was spreading worldwide. SARS in Asia – which represents 30 per cent of sales in the luxury retail market segment – led to a general decline in travel and spending. Consumers in the United States spent less in 2003 due to the war in Iraq and a weak economy. According to a study by Cotton Inc., published by *Women's Wear Daily*, consumers put 39 per cent of their disposable income into savings and 14 per cent to pay down debt in 2003. The strengthening of the euro led to a drop in tourism, which translated into lower sales in the luxury retail segment since a significant portion of luxury retail sales is generated by Japanese tourists. A strong euro also means equal sales in foreign currencies appear as less euro revenues. All these events contributed to the weak 'feel-good factor' in 2003.

The luxury sector is cyclical and correlates partially to economic conditions. The luxury retail market segment appeared to be rebounding in 2004 after two years of lacklustre performance. Mr Arnault predicted that the coming years would be 'very good for luxury because the world economy is doing well. The US is booming, interest rates are very low and there is a lot of optimism, Japan is recovering, and China and the Far East are growing fast'. Consumers dug into their pockets during the 2003/2004 holiday season to purchase more of the finer things in life. This turnaround in the luxury retail market segment ended the slump that had plagued the market since the 11 September 2001 terrorist attacks.

However, signs of a turnaround in the luxury retail market were surfacing as consumer confidence improved and spending increased. In addition, performance in the luxury retail market segment was expected to improve throughout 2004. According to

▶ Mike Niemira, Chief Economist for the New York-based International Council of Shopping Centers, '2004 will be a year of transition. Luxury items are strong and I think they are going to continue to be strong'. Consumer spending in the United States was propelled by the rebounding stock markets, President Bush's $350 billion tax-cut plan and improving employment rates. Consumer spending in Asia also recovered after the SARS epidemic.

In the long term, growth opportunities for the luxury retail market remained positive. The market was driven by Japan, Europe and the United States, however it would go on to include other parts of Asia such as China and eastern Europe as the regions became richer.

Competition

Traditionally, the luxury goods sector has been very fragmented and dominated by small and medium-sized companies, which have over the years developed an expertise in a particular product. But since the late 1990s, the boom years, the sector had been governed by multi-product and multi-brand conglomerates. Growth by acquisition was an important strategy for all major players in the industry. Conglomerates tried to pre-empt each other in acquiring brands that had managed to survive successfully. The race changed the dynamics of the industry from 'creativity focused' to more 'financially focused'. The years since 2000 seriously dampened spirits as sales stagnated and the conglomerates paid a heavy price for their acquisition spree.

Produt sector	LVMH businesses	Primary competitors
Fashion and leather goods	Louis Vuitton, Loewe, Céline, Berluti, Kenzo, Christian Lacroix, Givenchy, Marc Jacobs, Fendi, StefanoBi, Emilio Pucci, Thomas Pink, Donna Karan	Prada, Versace, Armani, Saint-Laurent, Chanel, Ralph Lauren, MaxMara, Burberry, Ferragamo, Hugo Boss, Gucci, Hermès, Bulgari, Lancel, etc.
Jewellery and watches	TAG Heuer, Zenith, Dior Watches, FRED, Chaumet, OMAS*	Oméga, Breitling, Vendôme-Cartier, Cartier, Van Cleef & Arpels, Rolex, Baume et Mercier
Perfume and cosmetics	Parfums Christian Dior, Guerlain, Parfums Givenchy, Kenzo Parfums, Laflachère, BeneFit Cosmetics, Fresh, Make Up For Ever, Acqua di Parma, Perfumes Loewe *	Many brands, including Lancôme, Lanvin et Armani, all brands under L'Oréal, Chanel, Yves Saint-Laurent, Gautier, Calvin Klein, Ralph Lauren, Estée Lauder, Shiseido, Hard Candy*, Bliss*, specialty perfumeries, etc.
Wines and spirits	Moët & Chandon, Dom Pérignon, Veuve Clicquot, Krug, Mercier, Ruinart, Château d'Yquem, Chandon Estates, Hennessy, Cloudy Bay, Cape Mentelle, Newton, MountAdam	Pommery*, Marne et Champagne, Laurent Perrier, Seagram, Johnny Walker, Smirnoff, Rémy Cointreau, Rémy Martin, Courvoisier, etc.
Distribution	DFS, Le Bon Marché, La Samaritaine, Sephora, sephora.com, Miami Cruiseline Services	Many stores and retailing franchises

Exhibit 9.4 Representative primary competitors, by business unit
* Indicates former LVMH businesses

As the luxury goods industry looked to move beyond the three turbulent years, the independent and family-controlled companies that yielded the spotlight to sprawling conglomerates during the boom years were claiming a measure of vindication. Leaders of several of the world's leading fashion houses said their strategy of resisting corporate advances had worked. It gave them better control over product direction at a time when consumers were showing signs of weariness with the glitz and hype of some of fashion's biggest names. 'Never be exploited; don't give up control of design,' says Giorgio Armani, head of the company he owns.

While keeping it in the family made sense from a brand-development standpoint, it had limitations. During the past three years, a weak global economy tested the financial resources of a number of family-owned luxury goods houses. There was also the question of what would happen to companies that became associated with the name, charisma and creativity of a larger-than-life founder. While Armani himself steadfastly resisted the idea of offering shares to the public, he refused to rule out the option of bringing in a big strategic investor, expressing willingness to partner with LVMH or PPR.

Selling to a bigger holding company does not always mean that a former privately controlled designer has to compromise on identity. When Phillips-Van Heusen bought Calvin Klein to help the biggest US shirt maker compete against department stores, industry insiders were sceptical that Klein would be able to retain complete design control over his empire. Finances at one of the world's most recognizable brands were dismal. The designer had reportedly been losing up to $25 million a year on its couture collection and millions more on retail operations. Rather than clamping down on Klein's creativity, Phillips spun the label into two new mid-range sportswear lines and pledged to cut costs while keeping Klein's 100 designers. Klein continues to play an important role in the image-making of the company. This example shows how designers can funnel their creative energies and co-exist with large conglomerates that offer substantial financial support – as both parties have adopted a middle path in the quest for control.

Gucci–PPR: after Tom Ford, what?

Originally a reseller of luggage imported from Germany, Gucci took advantage of economic expansion following the First World War. Since then, the company has displayed an innovative streak, improvising leather alternatives. After the Second World War, Gucci began its global expansion strategy with a store in New York in 1953. The company suffered setbacks in the 1970s and 1980s after scandals and murder plots. There was intense fighting within the Gucci family, which resulted in poor strategy and dilution of valuable brand equity. In the late 1980s, Investcorp bought 50 per cent of the company. The revival of Gucci commenced with the appointment of Domenico De Sole as CEO, who hired Tom Ford, a highly acclaimed designer who revamped Gucci's product designs. The company took firmer control of the brand, its products and the distribution. Investcorp sold its holdings through an IPO in 1996, making a fivefold return on its original investment. This was followed by a bitter battle for control of Gucci by LVMH and PPR. Finally, after poison pill measures taken by Gucci management failed to deter LVMH, PPR raised its offer and took control of the group. The move was

▶

▶ welcomed by Domenico De Sole and Tom Ford, who preferred PPR to LVMH for fear of losing their 'creative licence' if LVMH took over Gucci.

Gucci started a multi-brand model later than LVMH. It acquired Yves Saint Laurent's fragrance and ready-to-wear apparel lines and added the renowned shoemaker, Sergio Rossi, to its umbrella of brands. The multi-brand strategy was expected to deliver important synergies. Unfortunately, the benefits were never realized and YSL pulled down the group's earnings year after year. In the meantime Gucci continued its aggressive ascent, choreographed by De Sole and Ford. The brand is strong in North America today and its strategy of portraying Gucci as a youthful and sensuous brand has appealed immensely to Americans.

After the PPR group acquired majority control of Gucci, it started infringing on the independence enjoyed by the creative duo of De Sole and Ford. It is ironic that the very same group that was supposedly chosen to protect creative freedom was curtailing it. Tensions with the chairman of PPR group, Pinault, led to both De Sole and Ford refusing to renew their contracts after 2004.

According to analysts, 'The decade-old revival of Gucci from almost a dead brand to one of the most promising ones today made Tom Ford a bigger name than Gucci, and PPR would have immense trouble replacing him'. Adding to PPR's woes, in September 2003 a US court started investigations against Pinault for fraud in an unrelated acquisition in the 1990s. These drawbacks have indeed put a question mark over whether Gucci and PPR can continue their growth in future after Ford exits.

A nagging concern for the PPR group is whether Ford is going to be hired by rival LVMH group. Bernard Arnault was openly critical of Pinault and De Sole but refrained from saying anything against Ford, since the Gucci episode in 2000. He was quoted as crediting Ford as 'one of the best designers of his time'. This could reflect Arnault's intention to hire Ford after his exit from Gucci, which would significantly affect the dynamics at LVMH. Sources familiar with the situation feel that Ford is more likely to join a smaller company or launch his own label than join LVMH. The reason for his quitting is the constraint over his freedom and, given the temperament of Mr Arnault, Ford might not want an association with LVMH.

This has created a buzz in the industry as to where Ford is headed and also whom PPR would recruit to replace him. It seems particularly interesting as the new job profile for position of head of Gucci seems to all for a person from outside the luxury industry. It remains to be seen if it proves a good option to recruit a person from outside the industry for this top position, and how a key figure in this industry can make, break or manage a conglomerate.

Managing a multi-brand conglomerate

Creativity and innovation are synonymous with success in the fashion business. As analysts recently observed, 'Luxury brands must foster an appreciation for and tolerance of creativity that is unconstrained by commercial or production constraints.' In almost all its acquisitions, LVMH has maintained the creative talent as an independent pool without attempting to generate synergies across product lines or brands. Lately, though, the sourcing has slowly been centralized to gain synergies and cost savings with a centralized purchasing mechanism.

Bernard Arnault believes that, 'If you think and act like a typical manager around creative people – with rules, policies, data on customer preference and so forth – you will quickly kill their talent'. The company has been decentralized by design and has a very small cadre of managers.

However, industry insiders cite that all is not well with a financial man like Bernard Arnault at the helm. His management style is described as providing 'constrained freedom'. For example, a manager for Céline could recruit a person himself, independent of the central LVMH human resources department, but he must send a copy of the CV of the person he has hired so that head office is aware of the new development. Though his managers are given autonomy, they know they are being watched and who has the final word in case of any conflict.

Another concern is the ruthless pursuit of the bottom line. LVMH believes in running businesses profitably. Managers are supported as long as they make money over the stipulated minimum: 'You have freedom as long as you exceed your targets. Once you do not … there is no freedom any more'. The emphasis is on profit, and if any division or company did not deliver, it would promptly be sold off. This approach contrasts with the traditional and creative view of haute couture, which though it loses money on different sets of collections, waits for the market to accept its designs over a period of time.

Managing 'star brands'

The core pillar of LVMH's current business strategy is 'star brands,' coupled with innovation and quality. More specifically, Bernard Arnault describes the group's stellar financial performance in 2003 as 'a consequence of the priority placed on internal growth and profitability, the development of brands around the dual goals of innovation and quality, and the conquest of new markets' (see Exhibit 9.5 for key financials). According to Bernard Arnault, a star brand is:

> Timeless, modern, fast-growing, and highly profitable … There are fewer than ten star brands in the luxury world, because it is very hard to balance all four characteristics at once – after all, fast growth is often at odds with high profitability – but that is what makes them stars. If you have a star brand, then basically you can be sure you have mastered a paradox.

According to him, star brands are born only when a company manages to make products that 'speak to the ages' but the feel is intensely modern. Such products are designed to sell fast, raking in profits for the fashion empire. This is a paradox and he confides that 'mastering the paradox of star brands is very difficult and rare'.

Bernard Arnault has never specified what those ten 'star brands' are, but using his criteria, the following luxury labels could be considered star brands: Christian Dior, Louis Vuitton, Hermés, Cartier, Giorgio Armani, Gucci, Chanel and Prada. Of these, LVMH controls just two – Dior and Vuitton, of which he says: 'If you take Vuitton, which has existed for more than 150 years, I think, today, it is also modern. Dior has been there for 50 years, but also I think it is the most hip fashion brand today'.

	2002	2001	2000	1999	1998	5yr. growth
Total current assets	7 168	8 260	8 280	6 887	5 414	32,40%
Total current liabilities	6 890	8 017	9 829	8 615	6 328	8,88%
Total assets	20 658	22 540	21 124	19 671	16 008	29,05%
Total liabilities	12 864	15 122	14 947	13 194	9 408	36,73%
Total common equity	6 022	5 618	4 696	5 400	5 736	4,99%
Income statement	**2002**	**2001**	**2000**	**1999**	**1998**	**5yr. growth**
Sales	12 693	12 229	11 581	8 547	6 936	83,00%
Cost of goods sold	3 806	3 466	3 821	2 698	2 197	73,25%
Net income	556	10	705	636	429	29,65%

Exhibit 9.5 Consolidated group performance (€ million)
Source: Thomson Analytics Financial Database

Innovation

Bernard Arnault believes that innovation *is* 'the ultimate driver of growth and profitability. Our whole business is based on giving our artists and designers complete freedom to invent without limits'. He has acknowledged past mistakes, including the rapid expansion of the Sephora beauty and fragrance supermarkets, for which he said LVMH paid too much. After expanding too quickly in the United States, the company had to close stores and reposition the unit. In a business based on giving artists and designers the freedom to create without limits, LVHM allows each brand to run itself, headed by a creative director. Only 250 out of the 56,000 employees are based in the Paris headquarters, the essence of the business is to identify the right creative people to stimulate new and cutting-edge ideas, and trust their instincts.

Quality

In the luxury products business, quality is essential in production as well as in product development. This is also an essential element in LVMH's success strategy. For example, to exercise the utmost control over the quality of its Louis Vuitton 'star brand', the company owns manufacturing facilities employing more than 4,000 people in France, Spain and the United States, among other countries. While LVMH produces its Louis Vuitton brand in-house, the firm outsources part of the production of its other fashion labels, such as Céline and Fendi. 'For all of our brands, we manufacture part of the overall production within our facilities to be sure that there is a consistency between what is done by external subcontractors and what we do,' explained Jean-Paul Vivier, Executive Vice President of the LVMH Fashion Group.

Managing people

Human resources and the management of talent are critical for the luxury conglomerate. When Arnault first began his consolidation, the group was full of problems and only a few of the companies were profitable. HR Director Concetta Lanciaux confided that his primary concern was to 'have the best managers'. Lanciaux's challenge was particularly difficult because there was a scarcity of executives in luxury goods at the time. Most firms were small, family-owned companies, without graduates or succession planning. LVMH had to recruit and develop talent from different fields. Regarding the mobilization of LVMH's resources Bernard Arnault said:

> In a global context, the progress of LVMH in 2003 will be based above all on the excellence of the fundamentals and its capacity to mobilize its internal resources. We can rely on our traditional strengths, namely the talent of our managers and employees, and their determination to make the difference, the appeal of our major brands, the certain values – more than ever in a difficult period, the creativity and excellence of our products and the power of our distribution networks.
>
> We are continuing to deploy the organic growth strategy … while still carrying out the sale of non-strategic assets, we will maintain strict management focus, enabling us to reinvest the cost savings achieved in the driving forces of our growth.

LVMH encouraged and passed on the knowhow, skills, the spirit of excellence and the ethic that conveys, through its creations and products, an exceptional art of living, which is appreciated worldwide. The awakening and education of young people to these values has always constituted an essential part of the group's goal. LVMH carried out various original initiatives for young people in France and abroad. It is through these initiatives that primary school children, high school students, art students, young artists and designers, as well as those closer to the group's new work opportunities such as college and higher education students, can benefit. In 1991, for example, LVMH partnered with Paris-based business school ESSEC to launch the luxury brand marketing LVMH ESSEC chair, funded with FF10 million. Further partnerships have since been launched in Asia as well.

The company had to hire people with experience in other industries, such as consumer goods, and select people with 'good taste'. Lanciaux cited engineering and business schools as specific sources of talent. LVMH also instituted a strong company-wide induction and training programme, as well as on-the-job training to introduce the world of luxury to its capable, bright novices to the industry. As Lanciaux explained:

> With some 40 brands potentially competing against each other in the group, recruitment and everyday business becomes complex. In the case of our group, what builds value and profits is the ability to act in an autonomous way and create new products. The business is built on the number of innovative products that come out every year – 20 per cent to 30 per cent of the turnover is based on new products. Therefore our companies senior executives have to have a large dose of autonomy and creative capacity. People use these as aspirational products, so we need people who manage and dream – and make others dream.

▶ Despite the group's aggressive growth through acquisition, LVMH tried to treat such moves sensitively, with a vision of integration. Lanciaux commented:

> ❝ First of all, it was about respecting, identifying and then preserving all the assets of the company – not changing everything at once. One of the mistakes that companies in this situation make is that they want to change everything and bring in their own culture. When we buy these brands, we buy them to develop them. To develop the brand, the first thing you need to know is what makes that brand. Very often it's a number of people who are behind it, often invisible ... You have to find them, make them visible. This means that we have been able to preserve the integrity of these brands. Our style is not to go in there and replace everybody – never. ❞

Jean-Paul Vivier, Executive Vice President of LVMH, agrees that the group seeks to foster creativity not just among its design teams but also with professionals throughout the business. He compares the process to mixing the perfect cocktail – LVMH tries to build a work environment that promotes creativity and at the same time adheres to strict business disciplines.

Integration, training and top management seminars designed to support business strategies have played an essential role in the professional development of the LVMH group. Since 2001, it has steadily increased the number of training days for all personnel categories within the group and in centres located in Paris, New York, Hong Kong and Tokyo. The total number of training days in 2001 was 103,585 worldwide. Each of the companies developed a specific training programme that reflects its own vision of excellence and strategic objectives. At Louis Vuitton, which operates in 44 countries, vendors from all over the world participate in 'brand immersion' seminars organized in Asnières, the company's birthplace and communications centre. They tour the workshops built in 1859 and the Louis Vuitton travel museum. These sites are filled with the spirit of the company, which has remained constant even as it adapts to changing fashions and trends – a spirit embodied in the skills of the craftsmen, the details, and a unique talent for anticipating, analysing and meeting the requirements of the contemporary world. In 1999, Hennessy developed a teaching game called 'Strateco' that takes place over two days. It is designed to make all non-managerial employees more aware of economic influences affecting the companies and their operating realities. Another programme, Decompartmentalizing People and their Jobs, presents the mission, organization and business of each department to the company's managers and brings together participants from the various departments. Finally, the inter-company seminars offered to all the group's managers focus on topics of mutual interest, and are primarily designed to develop or perfect management, communication and leadership skills.

American designer Michael Kors joined LVMH and successfully revived Céline, a dusty brand. However, it didn't seem that anyone at LVMH noticed. During Kors' six and a half year tenure at Céline, the position of CEO turned five times, from Nan Legeai, to Bernard Divisia, to Yves Carcelle, to Thierry Andretta and, finally, to Jean-Marc Loubier. At the same time, Bernard Arnault attended only two of Kors' fashion shows for Céline. In total, Kors estimated that he spent a total of three hours in Bernard Arnault's company, including the two shows and two 'hellos' when he ran into Arnault at the Dior store in Paris. Kors said:

> Was I mistreated? No. Was I neglected? Yes. I never felt as though there was a strategy at LVMH as far as pitting the designers against each other or the brands against each other. It's just that I never felt anyone was watching the smaller companies at all, but everybody was spending their time on the two first-born children – Louis Vuitton and Christian Dior. In a way, if you're a nice kid, no one pays attention to you. If you are a bad kid, you get spoiled.

Also interesting is the case of Marc Jacobs. In 1997, Marc Jacobs was struggling to keep his namesake brand afloat. Bernard Arnault approached him with an irresistible offer to lend his creative flair to the venerable but stodgy Louis Vuitton label in return for LVMH underwriting his beleaguered design firm.

Jacobs' designs helped boost sales and buzz around the $3.8 billion Louis Vuitton brand, which accounts for 60 per cent of LVMH's operating profit. His multicoloured Murakami handbag alone drove more than $300 million in sales. The 41-year-old designer also developed his own Marc Jacobs label, which soared to about $75 million in sales in 2003, helped by a $50 million investment from LVMH.

However, tensions arose between the designer and the company. Jacobs believes his ambitions to develop his own brand were hindered by LVMH. He complained that the French conglomerate hadn't invested enough in the Marc Jacobs business and had locked him out of critical decisions about operations at his own line. For example, in May 2003, LVMH, while closing its US fragrance division, sold the Marc Jacobs perfume too, to Coty Inc., without informing or consulting the designer. None of the proceeds went to Jacobs, and instead went directly to LVMH.

Due to its heavy dependence on creative and modern designs, the departure of key creative personnel would be devastating to Vuitton. There had been speculation that Jacobs might leave unless LVMH gave more backing to his clothing line. As seen in the example of Tom Ford and Domenico De Sole's departures from luxury rival Gucci, losing its young star designer could spell trouble for the Louis Vuitton brand.

However, in May 2004, a spokesman in Paris confirmed that Moët Hennessy Louis Vuitton SA had resolved a year-long dispute with the New York designer Marc Jacobs, the artistic director of Louis Vuitton, and his business partner Robert Duffy, president of Marc Jacobs, by signing them to ten-year employment contracts and committing to invest in the partners' Marc Jacobs International fashion house. Under the new agreement Marc Jacobs and Robert Duffy received salary raises – and for the first time – stock options. According to Robert Duffy, 'Now, Marc and I can achieve our dream of turning Marc Jacobs into a global powerhouse'.

The future

While the Louis Vuitton brand remains enormously profitable, none of the other labels has rivalled its level of commercial success. With its current dependence on star designers such as John Galliano and Marc Jacobs, the group's success is highly correlated to the whim of the creative. Given the current internal politics and recent

▶

▶ departure of Michael Kors, will consumers remain loyal to the brand or the designer? The bigger question is, can LVMH oversee so many luxury brands, make them all profitable and maintain the highest standards of creativity? How will this 'loose' conglomerate that Bernard Arnault created in the last decade be integrated and managed effectively?

(€ million)	2001	(1)	2002	(1)	2003	(1)
Wines & spirits	2,232	18%	2,266	18%	2,116	18%
Fashion & leather goods	3,612	30%	4,207	33%	4,149	35%
Perfumes & cosmetics	2,231	18%	2,336	18%	2,181	18%
Watches & jewellery	548	4%	552	4%	503	4%
Selective retailing	3,493	29%	3,337	26%	3,039	25%
Other businesses and eliminations	113	1%	− 5	0%	− 25	0%
Total	**12,229**		**12,693**		**11,963**	

Exhibit 9.6a Net sales by business group
(1) As a per cent of total sales
Source: LVMH annual report, 2003

(€ million)	2001	(1)	(2)	2002	(1)	(2)	2003	(1)	(2)
Wines & spirits	676	43%	30%	750	37%	33%	796	36%	38%
Fashion & leather goods	1,274	82%	35%	1,280	64%	30%	1,311	60%	32%
Perfumes & cosmetics	149	10%	7%	161	8%	7%	178	8%	8%
Watches & jewellery	27	2%	5%	− 13	−1%	N/S	− 48	−2%	N/S
Selective retailing	− 213	−14%	N/S	20	1%	1%	106	5%	3%
Other businesses and eliminations	− 353	−23%	N/S	− 190	−9%	N/S	− 161	−7%	N/S
Total	**1,560**			**2,008**			**2,182**		

Exhibit 9.6b Income from operations by business group
(1) As a per cent of total sales
(2) Operating margin
Source: LVMH annual report, 2003

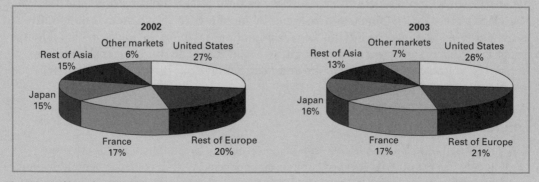

Exhibit 9.7 Net sales by geographic region
Source: LVMH annual report, 2003

North America	344
Latin America	16
France	277
Europe	401
Africa & Middle East	6
Asia	287
Japan	232
Pacific Region	29

Exhibit 9.8 LVMH global reach (number of stores in 2003)
Source: LVMH annual report, 2003

Brand	2003 sales (billions)	Per cent change*	Operating margin
Louis Vuitton	$3.80b	16%	45.0%
Prada	$1.95b	0.0%	13.0%
Gucci**	$1.85b	−1.0%	27.0%
Hermés	$1.57b	+7.7%	25.4%
Coach	$1.20b	+34.0%	29.9%

Exhibit 9.9 Benchmarking Louis Vuitton vs other luxury brands
 *At constant rate of exchange
**Gucci division of Gucci Group

Source: company reports; *BusinessWeek*

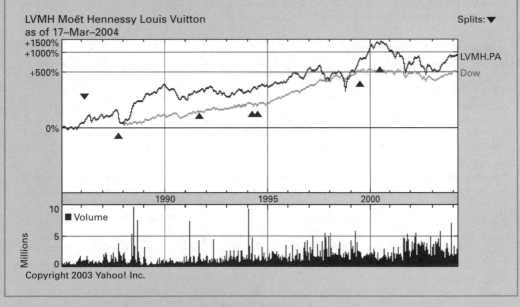

Exhibit 9.10 LVMH Stock Performance, 1985 to March 2004
Source: http://uk.finance.yahoo.com

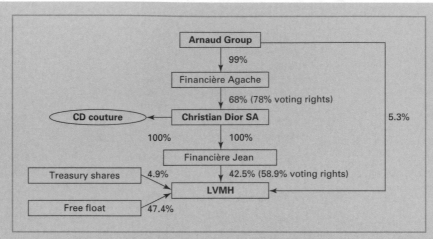

Exhibit 9.11 LVMH group shareholder structure
Source: company data; UBS Warburg

Creativity
Comes up with a lot of new and unique ideas; easily makes connections among previously unrelated notions; tends to be seen as original and value-added in brainstorming sessions.

Strategic Agility
Sees ahead clearly; can anticipate future consequences and trends accurately; has broad knowledge and perspective; is future oriented; can articulately paint credible pictures and visions of possibilities and likelihood; can create competitive and breakthrough strategies and plans

Innovation Management
Is good at bringing the creative ideas of others to market; has good judgment about which creative process of others; can facilitate effective brainstorming; can project how potential ideas may play out in the market place.

Managing Vision & Purpose
Communicates a compelling and inspired vision or sense of core purpose; talks beyond today; talks about possibilities; is optimistic; creates mileposts and symbols to rally support behind the vision; makes the vision sharable by everyone; can inspire and motivate entire units or organizations.

Customer Focus
Is dedicated to meeting the expectations and requirements of internal and external customers; gets first-hand customer information and uses it for improvements in products and services; acts with customers in mind; establishes and maintains effective relationships with customers and gains their trust and respect.

Priority Setting
Spends his/her time and the time of others on what's important; quickly zeros in on the critical few and puts the trivial many aside; can quickly sense what will help or hinder accomplishing a goal; eliminates roadblocks; creates focus.

Building Effective Teams
Blends people into teams when needed; creates strong morale and spirit in his/her team; shares wins and successes; fosters open dialogue; lets people finish and be responsible for their work; defines success in terms of the whole team; creates a feeling of belonging in the team.

Action Oriented
Enjoys working hard; is action oriented and full of energy for the things he/she sees as challenging; not fearful of acting with a minimum of planning; seizes more opportunities than others.

Drive for Results

Can be counted on to exceed goals successfully; is constantly and consistently one of the top performers; very bottom-line oriented; steadfastly pushes self and others for results.

Hiring and Staffing

Has a nose for talent; hires the best people available from inside or outside; is not afraid of selecting strong people; assembles talented staffs.

Motivating Others

Creates a climate in which people want to do their best; can motivate many kinds of direct reports and team or project members; can assess each person's hot button and use it to get the best out of him/her; pushes tasks and decisions down; empowers others; invites input from each person and shares ownership and visibility; makes each individual feel his/her work is important; is someone people like working for and with.

Business Acumen

Knows how businesses work; knowledgeable in current and possible future policies, practices, trends, and information affecting his/her business and organization; knows the competition; is aware of how strategies and tactics work in the market place.

Integrity and Trust

Is widely trusted; is seen as a direct, truthful individual; can present the unvarnished truth in an appropriate and helpful manner; keeps confidences; admit mistakes; doesn't misrepresent him/herself for personal gain.

Learning on the Fly

Learns quickly when facing new problems; a relentless and versatile learner; open to change; analyzes both successes and failures for clues to improvement; experiments and will try anything to find solutions; enjoys the challenge of unfamiliar tasks; quickly grasps the essence and the underlying structure of anything.

Delegation

Clearly and comfortably delegates both routine and important tasks and decisions; broadly shares both responsibility and accountability; tends to trust people to perform; lets direct reports finish their own work.

Exhibit 9.12 The 16 leadership factors
Identified by 450 LVMH Group senior executives during LVMH House sessions (October 2001)
Source: LVMH

? *Case questions*

Read the case carefully then answer the following questions.

1 What does globalization mean to the luxury industry? Within the luxury industry what is the international strategy of LVMH? How does this differ from the strategy its competitors? Can this strategy be sustained?

2 What is your assessment of LVMH's diversification? Does it make sense for the company to compete with a scope that includes champagne, jewellery, fashion, cosmetics and retailing? How does it add value to its different businesses? Is LVMH missing opportunities for synergy between its many businesses?

3 What is LVMH's core competence? How well has it exploited its core competence in its various diversification moves and strategic acquisitions?

4 How well does LVMH manage its diversified empire? Does LVMH's structure support its strategy? Does LVMH do enough to realize possible synergies between divisions? What possible synergies can you identify that LVMH could exploit?

5 What are the factors influencing companies that seek growth through acquisitions in this industry? How are they managing and integrating these acquisitions? Is that growth sustainable?

6 How does LVMH manage its creative assets? How does it differ from its competitors in this? How is LVMH 'cultivating' leaders for tomorrow?

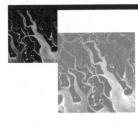

Index

M